Becoming an Effective Policy Advocate

From Policy Practice to Social Justice

Becoming an
Effective
Policy
Advocate

Seventh Edition

From Policy Practice to Social Justice

Brooks/Cole Empowerment Series

BRUCE S. JANSSON

University of Southern California

BROOKS/COLE
CENGAGE Learning·

Australia • Brazil • Japan • Korea • Mexico • Singapore • Spain • United Kingdom • United States

BROOKS/COLE
CENGAGE Learning·

Becoming an Effective Policy Advocate:
From Policy Practice to Social Justice,
Seventh Edition
Bruce S. Jansson

Executive Editor: Mark Kerr

Senior Acquisitions Editor: Seth Dobrin

Assistant Editor: Suzanna Kincaid

Editorial Assistant: Coco Bator

Managing Media Editor: Elizabeth Momb

Senior Brand Manager: Elisabeth Rhoden

Market Development Manager:
Kara Kindstrom

Manufacturing Planner: Judy Inouye

Rights Acquisitions Specialist:
Roberta Broyer

Art and Cover Direction, Production
Management and Composition:
PreMediaGlobal

Text Researcher: Pablo D'Stair

Cover Image: © Denis Jr. Tangney/
iStockphoto

For product information and technology assistance, contact us at
Cengage Learning Customer & Sales Support, 1-800-354-9706.

For permission to use material from this text or product,
submit all requests online at **www.cengage.com/permissions**.
Further permissions questions can be e-mailed to
permissionrequest@cengage.com.

Library of Congress Control Number: 2012954255

Student Edition:

ISBN-13: 978-1-285-06407-9

ISBN-10: 1-285-06407-0

Loose-leaf Edition:

ISBN-13: 978-1-285-17707-6

ISBN-10: 1-285-17707-X

Brooks/Cole

20 Davis Drive
Belmont, CA 94002-3098
USA

Cengage Learning is a leading provider of customized learning solutions with office locations around the globe, including Singapore, the United Kingdom, Australia, Mexico, Brazil, and Japan. Locate your local office at **www.cengage.com/global**.

Cengage Learning products are represented in Canada by Nelson Education, Ltd.

To learn more about Brooks/Cole, visit **academic.cengage.com/ brooks/cole**

Purchase any of our products at your local college store or at our preferred online store **www.cengagebrain.com.**

Printed in the United States of America
1 2 3 4 5 6 7 16 15 14 13 12

Brief Contents

Contents

Special Features

Policy Advocacy Challenges

Preface

I invented the concept, "policy practice," in a book that was published in 1984 when I discovered that policy texts and curriculum hardly discussed how social workers might actually work to reform policies. I greatly expanded my discussion of policy practice in the first six editions of this book in 1990, 1994, 1999, 2003, 2008, and 2011—and in this seventh edition. Beginning in 1999, I used the term "policy advocacy" to describe policy practice that aims to help vulnerable populations obtain needed rights, opportunities, services, and benefits.

Some faculty may wonder whether policy practice and policy advocacy require sufficient space in the curriculum of their schools to merit a textbook devoted entirely to them. They should consider several rationales for giving policy practice and policy advocacy a strong presence in foundation policy courses. Policy practice and policy advocacy provide a means of covering many of the ten core competencies and the 41 recommended practice behaviors of the Educational Policy and Accreditation Standards (EPAS). The column on the right in the following EPAS table informs the reader in which chapter icons appear that identify where these competencies and practice behaviors are discussed in this seventh edition of *Becoming an Effective Policy Advocate.* (EPAS tables appear at the ends of each chapter to inform readers where the competencies and practice behaviors are discussed in each of them.)

Becoming an Effective Policy Advocate, 7E now includes explicit references to the Educational Policy and Accreditation Standards' (EPAS) ten core competencies and 41 recommended practice behaviors. The column on the right informs the reader in which chapters the icons appear.

The 10 Competencies and 41 Recommended Practice Behaviors (EPAS 2008):	Chapter(s) Where Referenced:
EP 2.1.1 Identify as a professional social worker and conduct oneself accordingly:	
a. Advocate for client access to the services of social work	12
b. Practice personal reflection and self-correction to assure continual professional development	3, 4
c. Attend to professional roles and boundaries	
d. Demonstrate professional demeanor in behavior, appearance, and communication	
e. Engage in career-long learning	1
f. Use supervision and consultation	
EP 2.1.2 Apply social work ethical principles to guide professional practice:	
a. Recognize and manage personal values in a way that allows professional values to guide practice	1, 2, 8, 10, 14
b. Make ethical decisions by applying standards of the National Association of Social Workers Code of Ethics and, as applicable, of the International Federation of Social Workers/International Association of Schools of Social Work Ethics in Social Work, Statement of Principles	1, 2, 13

c. Tolerate ambiguity in resolving ethical conflicts	2, 8, 13
d. Apply strategies of ethical reasoning to arrive at principled decisions	2, 8
EP 2.1.3 Apply critical thinking to inform and communicate professional judgments:	
a. Distinguish, appraise, and integrate multiple sources of knowledge, including research-based knowledge and practice wisdom	2, 6, 7, 8, 10, 14
b. Analyze models of assessment, prevention, intervention, and evaluation	6, 11
c. Demonstrate effective oral and written communication in working with individuals, families, groups, organizations, communities, and colleagues	6, 9-11
EP 2.1.4 Engage diversity and difference in practice:	
a. Recognize the extent to which a culture's structures and values may oppress, marginalize, alienate, or create or enhance privilege and power	1, 2, 7
b. Gain sufficient self-awareness to eliminate the influence of personal biases and values in working with diverse groups	7
c. Recognize and communicate their understanding of the importance of difference in shaping life experiences	
d. View themselves as learners and engage those with whom they work as informants	
EP 2.1.5 Advance human rights and social and economic justice:	
a. Understand forms and mechanisms of oppression and discrimination	1, 2, 4, 5, 10
b. Advocate for human rights and social and economic justice	1–7
c. Engage in practices that advance social and economic justice	1, 3–5
EP 2.1.6 Engage in research-informed practice and practice-informed research:	
a. Use practice experience to inform scientific inquiry	2
b. Use research evidence to inform practice	2, 3, 5, 7, 9, 14
EP 2.1.7 Apply knowledge of human behavior and the social environment:	
a. Utilize conceptual frameworks to guide the process of assessment, intervention, and evaluation	6–11, 13
b. Critique and apply knowledge to understand person and environment	2, 3, 14
EP 2.1.8 Engage in policy practice to advance social and economic well-being and to deliver effective social work services:	
a. Analyze, formulate, and advocate for policies that advance social well-being	1–3, 7–11, 13, 14
b. Collaborate with colleagues and clients for effective policy action	1–3, 6, 8, 10, 11, 13
EP 2.1.9 Respond to contexts that shape practice:	
a. Continuously discover, appraise, and attend to changing locales, populations, scientific and technological developments, and emerging societal trends to provide relevant services	3–6, 9, 11–13
b. Provide leadership in promoting sustainable changes in service delivery and practice to improve the quality of social services	1, 4, 8, 10, 13
EP 2.1.10 Engage, assess, intervene, and evaluate with individuals, families, groups, organizations, and communities:	
a. Substantively and affectively prepare for action with individuals, families, groups, organizations, and communities	3, 6, 10, 11, 13
b. Use empathy and other interpersonal skills	6, 10
c. Develop a mutually agreed-on focus of work and desired outcomes	13

d. Collect, organize, and interpret client data	6, 7, 13
e. Assess client strengths and limitations	6
f. Develop mutually agreed-on intervention goals and objectives	9, 11
g. Select appropriate intervention strategies	
h. Initiate actions to achieve organizational goals	8, 13
i. Implement prevention interventions that enhance client capacities	1, 7
j. Help clients resolve problems	
k. Negotiate, mediate, and advocate for clients	3, 9, 10, 13
l. Facilitate transitions and endings	
m. Critically analyze, monitor, and evaluate interventions	

Faculty should consider three additional rationales for prioritizing policy practice and policy advocacy in policy foundation courses. First, the Code of Ethics of the National Association of Social Workers (NASW) requires social workers to engage "in social and political action that seeks to ensure that all people have equal access to the resources, employment, services, opportunities they require to meet their basic human needs and to develop fully." They cannot fulfill this ethical obligation if they do not possess knowledge and competencies to be policy practitioners and policy advocates since these resources, employment, services, and opportunities require supportive social policies in organizational, community, and legislative settings. Second, many social work students are not familiar with policy practice and policy advocacy—and are unlikely to engage them if they receive only superficial coverage of them, such as from a single chapter in a textbook. Third, students need sufficient time to understand policy practice and policy advocacy because they are multi-faceted interventions that include analysis, politics, values, and interactional skills—skills that are used singly and in tandem.

This book makes policy advocacy accessible to students in many ways. It provides a policy practice framework with eight tasks and four skills to enable students to view policy practice as a practice intervention. This framework is presented in Chapter Three in a new format to make it more accessible to students. Policy tasks include deciding what is right and wrong in order to determine whether and when to initiate policy advocacy (**Task 1**); navigating policy and advocacy systems in agency, community, governmental, or legislative settings (**Task 2**); engaging the agenda-setting task (**Task 3**); analyzing problems (**Task 4**); writing proposals (**Task 5**); enacting policies (**Task 6**); implementing policies (**Task 7**); and assessing policies (**Task 8**). The framework also describes analytic, political, value-clarifying, and interactional skills to implement these eight tasks.

This book contains many case illustrations and brief video clips that portray the work of policy advocates to bring policy advocacy to life. The three-minute video clips feature policy advocates as they discuss the policy tasks and skills in specific situations. *Note for instructors: To access the videos featured in this textbook, log into **http://login.cengage.com** and view materials in the Social Work CourseMate for Becoming an Effective Policy Advocate, 7th Edition.* Other strategies aim to make policy advocacy accessible to students. Each chapter begins with a "Policy Predicament" that students address at the end of each chapter with policy practice concepts provided in that chapter. Examples include the Occupy Movement in Chapter One, strategies to decrease inequality in the United States in Chapter Six, implementation of the Affordable Care Act of 2010 in Chapter Thirteen, and movement of juvenile offenders from incarceration to community diversion projects in Chapter Fourteen.

I've also updated many Policy Advocacy Challenges (PACs) that ask students to discuss and analyze specific advocacy situations or problems. New ones include a PAC on challenges in rebuilding Haiti and Japan respectively after the monumental earthquake of 2010 and the tsunami of 2011 in Chapter Five, developing legislation to reduce economic inequality in Chapter Six, contesting ideological objections to distributing sterilized needles to drug users to prevent the spread of HIV in Chapter Fourteen, and using mixed methods in evaluating policies in Chapter Fourteen.

I've illustrated many policy advocacy concepts, moreover, from developments during the presidency of Barack Obama, as well as the presidential and Congressional elections of 2012. These include controversies over immigration, budget battles to reduce the deficit, the Affordable Care Act, the spring uprising in North Africa in 2011 and 2012, and tactics used by presidential candidates. I've included more materials on use of social media in policy practice and policy advocacy as illustrated, for example, during the presidential election of 2012.

I've re-written Chapter Fourteen on policy assessment to make policy evaluation more accessible to students. I've added fresh content to discussion of global and immigration issues in Chapter Five.

The following strategy is used to organize the chapters in this edition:

- Chapters One and Two discuss Task 1 by defining policy practice and policy advocacy, discussing why social workers have an ethical duty to engage in them, identifying challenges in providing advocacy, urging students to join the reform tradition of the social work profession, and discussing ethical reasoning.
- Chapter Three presents a dynamic model of policy practice and policy advocacy that features eight tasks and four skills, and is illustrated by an extended case example.
- Chapters Four and Five discuss Task 2 by analyzing respectively the "playing field" of policy practice in the United States and in global arenas.
- Chapter Six discusses Task 3 by analyzing how policy practitioners and policy advocates place issues on policy agendas.
- Chapters Seven, Eight, and Nine discuss Tasks 4 and 5 by presenting and using a six-step model of policy analysis that analyzes how policy practitioners and policy advocates engage in policy analysis, develop proposals, engage in debates, and make effective presentations.
- Chapters Ten, Eleven, and Twelve discuss Task 6 by analyzing how policy practitioners and policy advocates develop and use power resources, develop political strategy, and engage in ballot-based advocacy.
- Chapter Thirteen discusses Task 7 by analyzing how policy practitioners and advocates impact policy implementation.
- Chapter Fourteen discusses Task 8 by analyzing how policy practitioners and advocates assess policies.

Acknowledgments

Elaine Sanchez Wilson, M.P.P., has made invaluable additions to this revision. She has contributed some Policy Advocacy Challenges under her byline, adding new substantive topics to the book in these challenges. She has updated Internet sites.

Twenty-nine people, including myself, have contributed video materials and written materials to this book, including written Policy Advocacy Challenges and video clips. I thank Russell Henderson, Rebecca Kendig, and Ron McClain for their still-relevant video clips, as well as Bob Erlenbusch's superb video clips drawn from his extensive advocacy for homeless persons in Los Angeles, California, and Washington, DC.

Reviewers of the manuscript that led to this edition including the following: Crystal Collins-Camargo, University of Louisville; John Conahan, Kutztown University; Elizabeth Danto, Hunter College; Lorraine Marais, Hawaii Pacific University; Kelly Patterson, University at Buffalo; and Solveig Spjeldnes, Ohio University.

Thanks to my wife, Betty Ann, for her support during this revision process.

An Invitation to Students Using This Text

As the nation slowly emerges from its worst economic downturn since the Great Depression, the Great Recession of 2007 to 2009, you will need to engage in policy practice and policy advocacy to help persons devastated by this economic disaster as well as to help members of many vulnerable populations who do not receive needed services, benefits, rights, and opportunities. View this course as an opportunity to expand your horizons and to gain skills in policy practice and policy advocacy in agency, community, governmental, and legislative settings. This course, too, will allow you to fulfill the requirement in NASW's Code of Ethics that social workers engage in advocacy.

This book contains many materials designed to make this topic user-friendly and practice-oriented including:

- a dynamic model of policy practice and policy advocacy
- three-minute video clips spread throughout the book that explain concepts relevant to policy practice and policy advocacy by experienced policy practitioners. These are accessible through Cengage Learning's Social Work CourseMate. The website brings course concepts to life with interactive learning, study, and exam preparation tools that support the printed textbook. Access an integrated eBook, learning tools including glossaries, flashcards, quizzes, videos, and more. Go to CengageBrain.com to register or purchase access.
- Policy Advocacy Challenges spread throughout the book that give real-life examples of specific policy issues and policy-practice strategies
- Many Internet sites relevant to policy practice and policy advocacy throughout the book, as well as ways to use social media

Consider this text to have a policy faculty of 30 people including myself. They are:

1. Gail Abarbanel, MSW and LCSW, the founder and Executive Director of the Rape Treatment Center in the Santa Monica-UCLA Medical Center.
2. Mimi Abramovitz, DSW and Professor in the School of Social Work and Director of the Social Welfare Program of the Graduate Center of the City University of New York, who has written extensively on social policy issues in such areas as welfare and policy discrimination against women.
3. Michele Baggett, a documentary filmmaker with extensive experience in the mass media. She is a native of New Orleans who filmed most of the video clips in this book at sites in New Orleans and Los Angeles. She recently obtained her MSW at the School of Social Work of the University of Southern California.
4. Alicia Case, MSW, who contributed a policy presentation she made while a student at the USC School of Social Work.
5. Laura Chick, MSW, the former Controller of the City of Los Angeles and the first woman to win an election for a citywide office in Los Angeles. She was appointed Inspector General of the California Office by Governor Arnold Schwarzenegger in April 2009 to oversee $50 billion of stimulus funds given to California by the stimulus program enacted by Congress in early 2009.
6. Stephanie Davis, MA, the Research Librarian at the University of California at Irvine.

7. Anneka Scranton, MSW, DPA, a policy advocate for many decades, who volunteers with the Global Fund for Women and organizes members of churches in the central coastal regions of California to become policy advocates.

8. Ron Dear, DSW, Emeritus Associate Profession, who was a lobbyist for the University of Washington for many years in Olympia where he was a faculty member at the School of Social Work of the University of Washington.

9. Sarah-Jane Dodd, MSW, Ph.D., an Associate Professor at the School of Social Work at Hunter College, who has written extensively on ethics and who helped with the development of a prior edition of this book.

10. Bob Erlenbusch, Ph.D., formerly Executive Director of the Los Angeles Coalition to End Hunger and Homelessness and President of the Board of the National Coalition for the Homeless in Washington, DC. He is currently the Executive Director of the Sacramento Housing Alliance.

11. Ralph Fertig, JD and MA, Clinical Professor at the School of Social Work of the University of Southern California. He was a freedom rider in the civil rights movement, Executive Director of the Metropolitan Washing Planning and Housing Association, and Executive Director of the War on Poverty in City of Los Angeles, as well as a federal administrative judge.

12. Emanuel Gale, Ph.D., Professor Emeritus of Social Work and Gerontology at the School of Social Work at the California State University at Sacramento.

13. Rachel Gardner, MSW Candidate at the USC School of Social Work, who contributed a Policy Advocacy Challenge that describes an array of policy practice actions by members of her class.

14. Gretchen Heidemann, MSW, a doctoral student at the USC School of Social Work and contributor of Policy Advocacy Challenges to this book, Internet sites, on-line teaching and learning aides, and a revised teaching manual.

15. Russell Henderson, MSW and LCSW, the organizer of the Rebuilding Louisiana Coalition, a lobbyist with the Louisiana legislature for 25 years, and teacher of social policy and community organization at Dillard University in New Orleans.

16. Robert Hernandez, MSW, who contributed a policy presentation on homelessness when he was in the MSW program at the USC School of Social Work.

17. Rachel Katz, MPP, a program analyst in the Finance Department of the City of Long Beach, California and contributor of some Policy Advocacy Challenges to this book.

18. Dennis Kao, MSW and Ph.D., an Assistant Professor at the School of Social Work at the University of Houston. He served as an advocate for many years with the Asian Pacific American Legal Center focusing on immigrant rights.

19. Rebecca Kendig, MSW and LCSW, the Executive Director of Case Services Management of the Youth Empowerment Project in New Orleans.

20. Patsy Lane, MSW, the former Director of the Department of Human Services of the City of Pasadena.

21. Ron McClain, MSW, LCSW, and JD, the President and CEO of Family Service of Greater New Orleans.

22. Victor Manola, MSW, Ph.D., Associate Professor in the Department of Social Work at California State University at Los Angeles who has been reelected to the City Council of the City of Artesia in Los Angeles County and has been mayor of the City of Artesia.

23. Carolyn Ryan, MSW, who contributed a policy presentation she made while a student in the USC School of Social Work.

24. Ramon Salcido, DSW, an Associate Professor at the School of Social Work at the University of Southern California who has consulted extensively with political

candidates and headed the macro concentration at USC's School of Social Work for many years.

25. Bob Schneider, Ph.D. and Emeritus Professor at the School of Social Work of Virginia Commonwealth University, who founded Influencing State Policy and has written extensively on advocacy.

26. Sam Taylor, DSW and Emeritus Associate Professor from the USC School of Social Work, who has been a community organizer and policy activist for many years.

27. Jessica Van Tuyl, MSW, who has a special interest in the mental health needs of lesbian, gay, bisexual, transgendered, queer, questioning youth.

28. Ali Wagner, MSW, who contributed a policy presentation made while she was an MSW student at the USC School of Social Work.

29. Elaine Sanchez Wilson, MPP, former journalist who helped revise this book into its seventh edition.

I am the Margaret W. Driscoll/Louise M. Clevenger Professor of Social Policy and Social Administration at the School of Social Work at the University of Southern California. I invented the term *policy practice* to help social workers gain skills to become policy practitioners and advocates. I truly hope that this interactive text with a faculty of 29 people will broaden your social work practice so that you can engage in policy practice and policy advocacy to make our society a more humane place for vulnerable populations.

Becoming an
Effective
Policy
Advocate

From Policy Practice to Social Justice

PART 1

Becoming Motivated to Become a Policy Advocate and a Leader

Policy Practice and Policy Advocacy as the Fourth Dimension of Social Work Practice

Many social problems that require the determined work of social reformers beg creative solutions in the United States and in the world. Social workers should engage in policy advocacy to become leaders to create a more humane society.

This book discusses an intervention that has emerged relatively recently in the social work profession: policy practice and policy advocacy. We define *policy practice* as efforts to change policies in legislative, agency, and community settings by establishing new policies, improving existing ones, or defeating the policy initiatives of other people. By this definition, people of all ideological persuasions, including liberals, radicals, and conservatives, engage in policy practice. People who are skilled in policy practice increase the odds that their policy preferences will be advanced. By *policy advocacy,* we mean policy practice that aims to help relatively powerless groups, such as women, children, poor people, African Americans, Asian Americans, Latinos, Native Americans, gay men and lesbians, and people with disabilities, improve their resources and opportunities. Thus, policy practice generally refers to efforts to change policies, whereas policy advocacy refers to efforts to help powerless groups improve their lot.

Chapter One argues that policy practice and policy advocacy are as important to social workers as their other three intervention disciplines: direct service, community, and administrative practice. Social workers must be conversant with social policies and able to seek changes in these policies to advance such values as social justice and fairness and the well-being of citizens and specific groups. They also need to work to change the composition of government to increase the likelihood that decision makers will seek policies that truly help citizens. We argue that policy advocates often encounter barriers, such as opposition from persons and groups with different values, entrenched interests, and mistaken beliefs about the causes and nature of specific social problems and issues. Since policy changing work is often associated with controversy and conflict, policy advocates must obtain perspectives and skills that enable them to be effective change agents. By becoming policy advocates, we join social reform traditions not only in American society but also in the social work profession; we work for policy reforms in communities, in social agencies, in local governments, in state governments, in the federal government, or through the courts. We discuss how electoral politics is pivotal to policy advocacy and the key attributes that policy advocates need, such as a vision, persistence, and the ability to tolerate uncertainty.

Chapter Two discusses moral reasons, as well as political and ethical imperatives, for policy practice and policy advocacy. Using the moral principles of beneficence, justice, and fairness, we argue that ethical professionals should supplement their one-on-one counseling by changing policies in agencies, communities, and legislatures.

Joining a Tradition of Social Reform

Policy Predicament	Occupy Movement and Inequality

"We are the 99 percent. We are getting kicked out of our homes. We are forced to choose between groceries and rent. We are denied quality medical care. We are suffering from environmental pollution. We are working long hours for little pay and no rights, if we're working at all. We are getting nothing while the other 1 percent is getting everything."—quoted text from the We Are the 99 Percent Campaign, part of the Occupy Wall Street Movement

In September 2011, a group of protestors joined a battle cry to "Occupy Wall Street" and gathered in Zuccotti Park, located in Lower Manhattan's Financial District. Decrying social and economic inequality, high unemployment rates, corporate corruption, and a host of other issues, the protestors set up sleeping bags and blankets, and later tents, in the plaza. They vowed to remain there until society was made more equitable. Although in a couple months the encampment was forcefully dissolved, the group nevertheless sparked a flurry of mass demonstrations in cities across the country. With the world watching, these Americans, tired of the status quo, were inspired to voice their discontent and demand social justice. See Policy Practice Challenge 1.6 to analyze how economic inequality is linked to health disparities.

LEARNING OUTCOMES

We discuss in this chapter a tradition of social work advocacy that long has existed within both American society and the social work profession. In particular, students will be prepared to discuss how policy advocates do the following:

1. Seek changes in policies to improve the well-being of members of vulnerable populations
2. Seek policy reforms that are in the general interest
3. Work from an ecological or systems perspective

4. Change many kinds of policies, including informal ones
5. Prioritize policy changes that assist oppressed populations
6. Encounter and surmount barriers to reform
7. Join a tradition of social reform in American society and in the social work profession
8. Develop attributes that support policy advocacy
9. Try to change the composition of government by participating in electoral politics

Focus of This Book: A Hands-On Framework for Reforming Policies

The National Association of Social Workers requires social workers to engage in "Political and Social Action," as outlined in the society's Code of Ethics.

It states that:

1. "Social workers should engage in social and political action that seeks to ensure that all people have equal access to the resources, employment, services, and opportunities they require to meet their basic human needs and to develop fully. Social workers should be aware of the impact of the political arena on practice and should advocate for changes in policy and legislation to improve social conditions in order to meet basic human needs and promote social justice.
2. Social workers should act to expand choice and opportunity for all people, with special regard for vulnerable, disadvantaged, oppressed, and exploited people and groups.
3. Social workers should promote conditions that encourage respect for cultural and social diversity within the United States and globally. Social workers should promote policies and practices that demonstrate respect for difference, support the expansion of cultural knowledge and resources, advocate for programs and institutions that demonstrate cultural competence, and promote policies that safeguard the rights of and confirm equity and social justice for all people.
4. Social workers should act to prevent and eliminate domination of, exploitation of, and discrimination against any person, group, or class on the basis of race, ethnicity, national origin, color, sex, sexual orientation, age, marital status, political belief, religion, or mental or physical disability."

EP 2.1.2b

This book provides a hands-on framework to be used to reform policies in agency, community, and legislative settings. It identifies eight specific tasks that policy practitioners and policy advocates undertake to change policies in a framework discussed at the outset of Chapter Three. The first two chapters of this book are devoted to defining such terms as policy practice and policy advocacy as well as discussing why social workers should engage in policy practice and policy advocacy in the first place. All remaining chapters in the book are devoted to each of these eight tasks. Consider this book, then, as a road map to fulfilling social workers' ethical commitment to promoting social justice.

Diversity and Policy Advocacy

When discussing diversity, most people focus on the unique cultures and perspectives of specific groups, such as women, African Americans, Asian Americans, Native Americans, gay men and lesbians, persons with physical and mental disabilities, older Americans, and children. Indeed, clinicians need extensive knowledge of different cultures and perspectives when working with members of various groups, lest they be insensitive to their needs and preferences.

But social workers risk ignoring many of the social and economic needs of these groups if they limit themselves to the knowledge of their cultures and perspectives. Members of each group have experienced various kinds of discrimination and prejudice in American history, both in distant times and in recent history; discrimination and prejudice remain active in contemporary society, even though civil rights and other protections have been enacted. Moreover, each of these groups experiences structural discrimination—a series of obstacles that, singly and together, interfere with the advancement of their members into the social and economic mainstream of American society.

American society has a variety of *vulnerable populations,* who have experienced discrimination and prejudice over an extended period and whose members' well-being (as measured by economic and other criteria) often reflects the structural barriers they have encountered. These vulnerable populations include *racial groups, sociological groups, dependent groups, nonconformist groups, model groups,* and *economic groups.* Racial groups, such as African Americans, Latinos, and Native Americans, have been subjected not only to overt racism in personal interactions with employers, teachers, physicians, the police, and people in other professions, but also to policy discrimination as reflected in schools, training programs, housing, community amenities, and correctional and law enforcement programs that give poorer services or fewer resources to them than they give to Caucasian populations. Sociological groups include women, older persons, and people with disabilities, who are often expected to assume relatively dependent roles in society, either in places of employment or in the broader society. They are often denied access to certain kinds of jobs, to promotions, and to roles within decision-making bodies because of widespread beliefs that they are incapable of moving beyond residual or lower-level roles within society. Disabled persons are often encouraged by the medical system to be dependent. Dependent groups, such as children, must often rely upon society for basic amenities, such as financial assistance, health care, dental care, and adequate housing, but are often given inadequate governmental support because they lack political clout. Nonconformist groups are subjected to discrimination because they are widely viewed as violating important social norms, such as sexual norms (gay men and lesbians), social norms (criminal offenders and juvenile delinquents), or social expectations (persons with mental illnesses). Model groups, such as Jewish Americans, Asian Americans, and some white ethnic Americans, are denied resources and services because many Americans believe they have no social problems. Economic groups include persons in low- and moderate-income groups who often lack sufficient resources, well-paying employment, or stable employment. Lack of resources, in turn, precludes them from some life options that are available to more affluent persons, such as safe neighborhoods, adequate housing, and economic security.

EP 2.1.2b

Discrimination against members of vulnerable populations, either expressed in personal encounters with others or through policy discrimination, often shows up in statistical measures of the economic and social well-being of members of specific vulnerable populations. Members of racial groups tend to have, for example, fewer resources, lower life expectancies, and poorer educational achievement than Caucasian populations. Women are more likely to be poorer than men, particularly when they are single heads of households. Persons with physical and mental disabilities are far more likely to be poor than other members of society. Gay youth are more likely than nongay youth to commit suicide. Children are more likely than adults to live in poverty.

A critic might ask, "But don't these differences in economic, health, and other measures of well-being stem from the intrinsic problems of members of these vulnerable populations (such as medical problems in the case of the disabled) or from the culture or work ethic of members of impoverished groups?" It is true; members of these groups do sometimes contribute to their own problems. For example, a disabled person may simply choose not to seek employment because he or she has accepted the norms of dependency widely ascribed to disabled persons or because he or she possesses a mental problem such as depression. Similarly, low-income persons of color sometimes exacerbate the problems of other persons in their communities by resorting to violent behavior or abusing drugs.

Yet efforts to generalize actions of specific persons to entire populations are doomed to failure. When entire groups have economic, education, health, and other indicators of well-being that are sharply divergent from the dominant population, we can rightly surmise that external forces and policies impact them adversely and contribute to these outcomes. When a disproportionate percentage of single female heads of households is immersed in poverty, we can rightly ask what factors, singly and in tandem, affect or influence the economic outcomes of this population so that, as a group, its members suffer disproportionate poverty when compared to double-headed families or single females with no children.

When examining structural discrimination, we identify policies; familial, cultural, community, and economic factors; and life experiences that *systematically* shape the lives of specific groups, so they fall behind other groups that are not subject to structural discrimination. We can understand why such groups as low-income African Americans or single heads of households lag behind white males with college degrees in income only by examining a constellation of factors that systematically impinge on them. In the case of low-income, inner-city African Americans, such factors include the following:

- Overt discrimination on the basis of race
- Subtle discrimination that relegates African Americans to poorly paid positions and education tracks that steer them away from college preparation
- Segregated communities that are distant from places of employment
- Lack of family and community role models who have secured higher levels of education
- Overcrowded schools
- Low expectations from school personnel, including excessive tracking
- Childhood poverty exacerbated by governmental policies such as the absence of family allowances
- Family and personal stress stemming from poverty
- Lack of recreational programs
- Exposure to violence, such as from gangs
- High rates of mortality among adolescent males
- Lack of user-friendly health systems that provide preventive services
- Lack of well-paying, accessible, and stable employment
- Lack of access to the old-boy networks that give some people an inside track to jobs and educational opportunities

EP 2.1.4a
and EP 2.1.5a

If we compare suburban white children, whose parents have college educations, with African American inner-city residents, the harsh workings of structural discrimination immediately become evident. These suburban children rarely confront these barriers, and if they do encounter specific ones, they rarely encounter a constellation of barriers. It is not surprising that suburban white residents are often unsympathetic to inner-city African Americans. Assuming from their own experiences that a level playing field does exist, many of them believe that the inner-city residents lack personal characteristics, such as the work ethic, that would bring them out of poverty.

Consider single women with children who have high school diplomas or less. Regardless of their ethnicity, these women are likely to secure only relatively low-paying work because they cannot compete for the higher-paying jobs usually filled by persons with higher levels of education. As single parents, moreover, they must frequently support their children without financial assistance from another parent, even though governmental authorities have placed more emphasis in recent years on collecting funds from absent parents. Because the United States does not fund day care for many women for sustained periods, their meager paychecks are often depleted by day-care costs. Because employers are not required by law to provide fringe benefits, many low-wage-earning women do not have health insurance, so they must obtain health care for themselves or their children in crowded, difficult-to-access public clinics. Some of these women cannot afford cars, so they must use a time-consuming public transportation system that sometimes does not even have routes convenient to their workplaces. It is small wonder, then, that millions of poorly educated single mothers and their children remain mired in poverty for extended periods, no matter how hard they work to achieve a better economic standard. As with inner-city African Americans, poverty brings additional stresses to individuals and families who must struggle to make ends meet, who cannot afford amenities that others take for granted, and who often must live in blighted communities where rents are relatively low (see Policy Advocacy Challenge 1.1).

We should not merely take a short-term perspective when we examine the effects of external forces and policies. Most African Americans, for example, were deprived of land, civil liberties, and education in the 19th century and well into the 20th century—often

EP 2.1.5c

Policy Advocacy Challenge 1.1

Mapping Structural Discrimination

Note for instructors: To listen to this audio clip, or any videos featured in this textbook, log into **http://login .cengage.com** and view online materials at your Instructor Companion Site for *Becoming an Effective Policy Advocate*, 7th Edition. Under "Book Resources" on the left-hand side of your screen, click the tab for "Videos."

Take any vulnerable population that lags behind the general population on specific social or economic indicators; for example, single mothers, released prisoners, or unemployed persons. Identify a constellation of factors that lead to structural discrimination against this group by contrasting it with another group in the population that is not as subject to structural discrimination.

Identify specific kinds of policy reforms that have been enacted to ameliorate such structural discrimination. What additional reforms would help the subgroup's members improve their economic and social status?

Why are social workers' clinical skills not sufficient to redress structural discrimination?

Listen to the audio clip and discuss how the economic recession of 2007–2009 impacted families. Specifically, discuss the circumstances that forced the Greens into a homeless shelter and the barriers to their ability to acquire their own housing again. How did such factors as the availability of jobs, minimum wage policies, and the costs of housing and child care impact this family? What are some of the differences between single mothers with children and intact couples with children in situations of homelessness? What policies could assist these two subpopulations in transitioning out of homelessness? Do you agree with the shelter director that the root cause of homelessness is poverty and that the government has a responsibility to help the poor? If so, what policies would you recommend to combat poverty as the root cause of homelessness?

EP 2.1.4a
and EP 2.1.5a

relegated to rural areas of the South where they lived in appalling poverty. Unlike white immigrants from Italy, Ireland, and eastern Europe, they were not allowed to participate in the emerging industrial order of northern cities in the 19th century. African Americans began moving to the North in large numbers only well into the 20th century. They were consigned to play catch up under equally appalling conditions in northern cities, such as segregated communities, exclusion from trade unions, hiring and promotion prejudice in the workplace that consigned them to unskilled and uncertain jobs, poor health care, and poor schools—not to mention police brutality. It is hardly surprising that gangs and substance abuse festered in low-income African American areas, which further impeded upward mobility. Policy developments of preceding eras, then, impeded the ability of contemporary African Americans to achieve parity with Caucasian Americans, whose upward economic assent was built upon generations of their children obtaining education, the accumulation of assets (such as savings and houses), and heightened expectations.

Policy advocates are sometimes not content merely with equalizing policies of vulnerable populations and the dominant population. Because of the effects of long-term oppression on members of these populations, we should sometimes favor *compensatory* strategies, such as extra tutoring or smaller classes in schools, outreach health services to encourage persons who do not usually use the health care system services to do so, or providing community-based services in areas where persons are particularly impoverished. Similarly, affirmative action is sometimes needed to move members of vulnerable populations more rapidly into employment and education—particularly when we conclude that their members would not otherwise achieve parity with the dominant population in the foreseeable future.

When identifying a variety of factors that lead certain vulnerable populations to lag behind the dominant population with respect to specific indicators of well-being, we must beware of several dangers. These include excessively stigmatizing groups, viewing them as excessively dependent, or relying on panaceas. Many individuals do make it up and out despite structural discrimination, such as African Americans who enter professions, single heads of households who successfully juggle raising children and careers, and persons with paraplegia who use technology to care for themselves and enter the workforce. Nor should we view members of vulnerable populations as passive victims of fate. American history is replete with advocates' determined efforts from these groups to mobilize resources, self-help projects, networks, alliances, and policy advocacy to better their condition. Our challenge is to empower them to develop creative solutions for overcoming barriers they encounter and provide them with social policies that allow them to obtain resources, housing, and services from different levels of government and the private sector. We should not succumb to the belief that specific policies will have a magical effect. To help single mothers improve their economic condition, for example, we need multiple, interacting policies that help them improve their lot, such as greater funding for child care, increases in the minimum wage, expansion of the earned income tax credit (EITC, which gives low-income workers a tax rebate), increases in housing subsidies, more training and remedial education, and expansion of food stamp subsidies and health insurance for children and families.

In policy practice and policy advocacy, then, social workers must consider diversity at more than just the cultural level. This allows social workers to address environmental factors that stack the deck against a subgroup's members and that powerfully shape their collective destinies. Social workers can use policy advocacy to remedy or address problems such as the following:

- The feminization of poverty, with roughly one-fourth of American children living in impoverished households

- Inner-city poverty concentrations of African Americans, Latinos, Asian Americans, and Native Americans
- Extraordinary differences in educational attainment between white people and many people of color
- Large disparities between men and women in earnings and high-level positions in employment
- Disproportionate poverty among persons with physical and mental disabilities
- Discrimination against gay men and lesbians
- A dearth of services for people who abuse substances
- Problems of frail older people who need various kinds of tangible assistance but who are impoverished
- Inadequate safety net programs to allow low-income persons to overcome excessive economic problems
- Violence against women (see Policy Advocacy Challenge 1.2)
- Affordable housing for low-income Americans

EP 2.1.5b

Policy Advocacy Challenge 1.2

Enhancing the Rights of Children Who Are Sexually Assaulted in School

Gail Abarbanel, MSW, LCSW, Executive Director, Rape Treatment Center, Santa Monica–UCLA Medical Center

As a social worker, I view social policy reforms as a way to give meaning to the experiences of my clients, as well as a means to serve them better. The following case example illustrates these two functions. Jennifer, a 12-year-old girl attending a Los Angeles middle school, was raped by another student, during the school day, on the school campus. After she reported the crime, she was re-victimized by her eighth-grade classmates, who ridiculed and harassed her. Jennifer was also ostracized by some of her friends, who informed her that their parents had told them that they could no longer associate with her.

When the school district scheduled a disciplinary hearing, Jennifer received very little notice and no information about the procedures. When Jennifer and her parents arrived at the hearing, they were told that this 12-year-old child would have to go into the hearing room alone. No one was allowed to accompany her—no parent, no counsel, no support person—while she was subjected to cross-examination by the accused student's representative. The accused student, however, was allowed to have his parents and a legal representative present to support him during the entire proceeding.

Jennifer had been profoundly traumatized by the rape. She was too fragile psychologically, as most other 12-year-old children would be, to testify under the conditions set by the school district. However, she was informed by school officials that, without her testimony, there would be no disciplinary action. The hearing was postponed.

As a result of the Rape Treatment Center's (RTC's) efforts on the victim's behalf, when the hearing was finally held, Jennifer was allowed to be accompanied by an American Civil Liberties Union attorney.

However, the attorney was required to remain silent. The school district officials seated Jennifer very close to, and directly opposite, the father of the boy who had raped her. The accused student's representative who questioned Jennifer insulted and taunted her. She also asked Jennifer to demonstrate some of the degrading things that had been done to her during the assault, an abusive practice called "reenactment" that would not be permitted in most legal proceedings involving either child or adult victims.

The hearing process was devastating for Jennifer. She was powerless, just as she had been during the rape. Again, she was re-victimized—this time by the school district's disciplinary system.

(continued)

As the founder and director of the RTC at Santa Monica–UCLA Medical Center and a longtime advocate for victims of sexual assault, I intervened to protect this child, *and* I sought a remedy that would provide legal protection for other child victims and would prevent this kind of discriminatory treatment in the future. I turned to Assemblywoman Sheila Kuehl (D-Santa Monica), our representative in the state legislature. Together, we drafted legislation to establish rights for children who are sexually assaulted in their schools.

Under the new law, which became effective January 1, 1997, child victims are given many of the same rights afforded to accused students in school disciplinary hearings, such as the right to have a support person accompany them during their testimony and to request a closed hearing. In addition, the victim's irrelevant sexual history is protected from disclosure. Sexual assault victims have had these rights in the criminal and civil justice systems for many years. However, in most states, the education codes recognize only the rights of accused students while overlooking the needs of victims. The new law corrects this inequity.

Passage of this legislation is only a first step. Students must be informed about the new rights and protections available to them if they are victimized. Schools must change their policies and procedures to implement the reforms required by the new law. The RTC has an established, school-based, sexual abuse prevention program that reaches thousands of students each year, as well as administrative personnel in schools throughout the community we serve. This program has enabled us to educate school personnel and students about the new law. Fifteen years later, in 2012, it educates new student cohorts and teachers.

Advancing the Public Interest at Home and Abroad

EP 2.1.8a

While policy advocates often focus on problems and issues affecting vulnerable populations, they also tackle problems of citizens in general, which we call the public interest. They want child-care services, for example, that improve the developmental and cognitive well-being of *any* children who use them. They want schools that provide first-rate counseling services to children so that any children who develop mental health or substance abuse problems can obtain quality services. They want preventive services that diminish the incidence of major social problems that afflict citizens whether or not they are members of a vulnerable population. For example, policy advocates might seek laws that disallow smoking in public places and require health-risk notifications on cigarette packages, seek antipollution measures, fight for better public transportation systems, or seek a living-wage policy for all workers.

As we discuss in Chapter Five, policy advocates do not limit their activity to the United States. With the reduction of trade barriers, for example, many American corporations have relocated their operations abroad to escape high wages, antipollution regulations, and corporate taxes they confront in the United States. To the extent that they impose inhumane practices on other nations in a quest to expand their profits, policy advocates battle for international standards that govern wages and pollution and seek to protect wages of American workers who are often given an ultimatum to accept lower wages to forestall their company from replacing their jobs with lower-wage workers abroad. Issues of immigration across national borders are germane, as well, to policy advocates who grapple with such issues as when immigrants should receive citizenship and how immigrants' rights should be protected in the United States. Since policy advocates are interested in the well-being of persons no matter their location, some of them pursue issues of global social justice, such as how wealthy nations such as the United States can assist third-world nations with poverty and such illnesses as AIDS.

Using an Ecological Perspective

An ecological or systems perspective is highly useful in policy advocacy. As our discussion of vulnerable populations suggests, citizens' lives are impacted by multiple factors, including economic, cultural, social, community, and physiological factors, as well as discrimination or prejudice. Existing policies are part of their ecology: They not only limit resources, services, and opportunities that they receive but also provide them. When developing policy proposals, advocates often examine the problems and populations that will be impacted by these proposals from an ecological perspective. They ask, for example, what forces and factors in the lives of welfare recipients influence whether they can secure and retain employment; then they seek policies that address these ecological factors. (We discuss an ecological perspective at greater length in Chapter Seven.)

What Policy Practitioners and Policy Advocates Seek to Change

Policy advocates aim to change social policies. This book uses a simple, problem-solving definition of *social policy* as "a collective strategy that *prevents* and *addresses* social problems." Our definition is similar to that of the late Richard Titmuss, an English social policy theorist.[1]

Defining social policy as goal-driven problem solving has several advantages. First, it makes clear that policies are established to prevent and address social problems that include the following:

Victimization of persons by landlords, corporations, businesses, realtors, restaurant owners, and others by providing them with unsafe rentals, providing them unsafe products, not providing consumers with sanitary food, and not paying employees sufficient resources to allow them to survive. These kinds of problems are often addressed by *regulations* such as the federal minimum wage, housing codes, U.S. Food and Drug Administration, and local living wage.

Inability of citizens to meet their survival needs, thus imperiling their nutritional, housing, health, and other basic needs. These kinds of problems lead to *needs-meeting policies* that provide to citizens basic health and economic benefits, such as food stamps, Medicaid and Medicare health benefits, Supplemental Security Income (SSI), and rent-supplement programs.

Inability of citizens to find employment or obtain skills and knowledge to find employment that can meet their basic needs. These kinds of *opportunity-enhancing policies* include public education, job-training programs, and vocational education.

Inability of citizens to cope with mental health, marital, substance abuse, and familial problems. These *social service policies* include a wide range of mental health, child welfare, and substance abuse programs.

Inability of citizens to navigate complex service-delivery systems. *Referral and linkage policies* establish case management, ombudsman, and outreach programs.

Discriminatory treatment of members of specific vulnerable populations by employers, schools, public facilities, transportation companies, landlords, and others. *Civil rights policies* prohibit specific infringements of the civil rights of vulnerable populations' members, including the Civil Rights Acts of 1964 and 1965, local antihate laws prohibiting attacks on members of vulnerable populations and defiling places of worship, and the Americans with Disabilities Act of 1990.

Violations of human rights such as opposing infringements of civil liberties and legal rights of persons from the Middle East in the wake of the 9/11 attacks.

Excessive inequality between low- and high-income persons. *Equality-enhancing policies* have targeted resources to low-income populations, such as the federal EITC; progressive features of federal, state, and local tax codes that tax affluent citizens more heavily than low-income citizens; and a host of programs that target to low-income populations services or resources, such as Medicaid, SSI, and food stamps.

Inability of low-income Americans to accumulate such assets as savings accounts and real estate. *Asset accumulation policies,* such as federal legislation stimulating individual investment accounts, give citizens tax incentives and resources to initiate savings accounts and purchase houses.

Lack of public amenities necessary for recreation and commerce for citizens. Federal, state, and local governments enact *infrastructure development policies* that promote construction of roads, parks, bridges, and public transportation.

Lack of sufficient jobs in certain portions of cities to support their citizens. Various levels of government offer *economic development policies* such as tax incentives and loans to businesses that locate themselves in low-income areas.

Low rates of participation in the political process by low-income persons that increase the disinclination of government to adequately fund programs to help them. Policies geared toward *facilitating political participation and increasing the political power of oppressed populations* include state and federal policies that prohibit excessive campaign contributions by special interests and that reapportion political districts so that they do not discriminate against persons of color.

Insufficient resources devoted to specific problems or issues by governments or even specific agencies or organizations, which require *budget-changing policies.*

EP 2.1.8a

Protective policies that help persons who are subject to abusive or violent behaviors and actions of others, such as protective services programs for children and policies that protect women from battering.

EP 2.1.10i

We include *prevention* in our definition of social policy because policy advocates want not only to address existing social problems but also to prevent them when possible. Much like public health advocates have succeeded in obtaining many antismoking, gun-control, and auto-safety measures that have saved many lives and averted injuries, social work advocates have put in place early detection programs for such mental health problems as depression, programs to prevent youth from leaving school prematurely, programs that help isolated elderly persons join day-treatment programs, and day-care and job-training programs to help persons improve their economic condition.

We should note, as well, that many policies are geared toward improving defects in the operations of agencies that implement specific social policies. Imagine, for example, that a legislator succeeds in enacting legislation that provides prenatal services meant to decrease premature births and birth defects. Imagine, as well, that the person who sponsored the legislation finds, several years later, that it has had little impact on the rates of premature births or birth defects in an inner-city Latino area. Assume that the legislator also discovers that neither bilingual nor outreach staff have been hired, that clinic hours are limited to daytime hours, and that programs are located at inconvenient sites for Latinas, such as at a distant public hospital. The following are problems in the human services systems that are often the targets of policy reform in specific agencies, specific service networks, or legislation establishing new programs.

- *Fragmentation.* Barriers make it difficult for clients or consumers to obtain services from multiple programs.
- *Discontinuity.* Clients cannot obtain consistent, accessible services over a period of time.
- *Lack of access.* Barriers make services hard to use at specific sites.
- *Discrimination.* Service providers are hostile or indifferent to specific kinds of clients.
- *Creaming.* Providers deliberately seek clients with less serious problems.
- *Wastage.* Different providers serve the same population for the same problem, or services are not provided efficiently.
- *Lack of outreach.* Providers make little effort to seek persons who do not currently use services.
- *Incompetent staff.* Staff are asked to perform tasks for which they have little training.
- *Lack of cultural sensitivity.* Providers make little effort to match their services to the cultural perspectives of the clients they serve such as by having bilingual staff or staff versed in specific cultures.
- *Inadequate funding.* Services are funded at such low levels that important activities are compromised or deleted.

EP 2.1.9b

Our definition of social policy as collective strategy to prevent and address social problems makes clear that policies are developed in many places, as the example of commitment procedures for people with mental illness illustrates. Policies may come down from the highest levels, including state mental health officials, county mental health departments, various courts, and even federal authorities. Although these *high-level policies* influence their work, staff in county mental health units may implement them in strikingly different ways. The staff at one county hospital may commit many more persons than the staff at another hospital, because each defines *imminent threat* differently.

Social welfare policies are often divided into mental health, health, child and family, income maintenance, school, industrial, corrections, housing, gerontology, and other sectors. This division of policies into sectors partly reflects specializations among professionals, providers, and funders, as well as specific legislative committees that write legislation in these areas. While the division of policies into these sectors allows us to identify policies that are directed to specific kinds of needs and issues, it can also contribute to excessive fragmentation between the sectors. Many consumers of health services, for example, need mental health services, but they must often go to different agencies to get them and may find their mental health needs, such as depression, not recognized or treated by health professionals. Rather than coordinating their services, specialized agencies sometimes erect turf barriers.

Social policy is a kind of ladder extending from different levels of government to persons in the population who use services or programs. Policy advocates can intervene at any point in this policy ladder or at several points. They may seek to establish outreach programs so that consumers know about and use specific programs. They sometimes seek to change the policies of individual agencies, such as specific not-for-profit, for-profit, or public agencies. They may seek to change the policies or regulations of higher-level agencies in counties, municipalities, or townships. They may seek redress in state or federal venues. Or they may seek court rulings that place restrictions on how local mental health agencies commit mental patients involuntarily to mental institutions.

Our definition of social policy eliminates the problem of establishing rigid boundaries between social policy and other kinds of policies. Most commentators agree that public welfare, child welfare, medical, and job-training policies are social policies, but they are less certain about income tax, environmental, economic, transportation, and other policies. Our definition suggests that specific policies *become* social policies whenever they influence social problems. For example, income tax proposals that increase or decrease the resources of poor persons become social policies when they affect poverty and unemployment. By the same token, tax policies that regulate how corporations depreciate their equipment are not social policies unless they can be shown to be relevant to such problems as poverty and unemployment.

Thus far, we have emphasized the content or substance of policies by focusing on the kind of social problems that specific policies address. Now we turn our attention to the different forms of policies and where they are located. *Statutes* containing policies are established when local, state, and federal governments approve legislation. *Policy objectives* (or mission statements) are a kind of policy because they shape the actions and choices of officials, executives, and staff. When a state mental health agency decides to drastically reduce the populations of mental institutions, its officials and staff are committed to this objective and programs consonant with it. Imagine how services might change if, instead, top officials wanted to increase long-term institutional services for a range of mental conditions.

By the same token, *rules and regulations* are a kind of policy because many social policies constrain the activities of officials, staff, and consumers. For example, rules and regulations place many restrictions on mental health personnel when they wish to commit someone involuntarily to a mental hospital. They must base their commitment on evidence that the person will harm themselves or others if not committed, and they must go through specific procedures, including holding hearings and providing legal counsel to the person being committed. The operations of every publicly funded program are shaped by administrative regulations issued by government agencies, including who is eligible, what kinds of staff are hired, how records are kept, and the content of services. (Some of these operating policies are also defined in statutes.)

Budgets are a kind of policy because they determine what resources are devoted to specific, enacted policies—resources that determine whether a policy will be effective and who will receive it. Budgets also determine priorities, such as what programs are emphasized. During the Great Recession from 2007 to 2009, and its aftermath, advocates fought hard in Washington, DC, to obtain payroll tax relief for 160 million workers.

Court rulings are another important kind of policy. Courts have made many rulings, for example, that require social workers to protect the confidentiality of information given to them by clients, patients, or consumers. They sometimes rescind cutbacks in services and benefits. They are sometimes controversial, such as the *Roe v. Wade* ruling by the U.S. Supreme Court in 1973 that overruled state laws that made abortions during the first trimester illegal.

Formal or *written policies* can certainly be considered social policy, whether they are issued by legislation or they are court rulings, administrative guidelines, or budget documents. It is less immediately clear whether *informal* or *nonwritten policies* qualify as social policy. The issue requires some examination. When written policy contains relatively vague and ill-defined terms, officials must often develop informal policies to fill in the gaps. For example, some laws restrict involuntary commitment to persons who pose an imminent danger to themselves or others. Staff who require a strict standard may resist committing someone who has not actually attempted suicide but threatened to commit it, whereas other staff may believe that merely threatening suicide falls within this restriction. Though such standards have not been recorded in official policy, they are policies because they have the same effect as written policy. They are collectively defined rules that profoundly shape the actions of direct-service staff and their administrators.

Informal policies are absolutely critical to social policy because they cover a wide range of issues. For example, in a child welfare department, informal policies shape how staff conceptualizes child welfare. Do they see their job exclusively as helping children who have been seriously abused or neglected, or do they also want to construct preventive programs to educate at-risk parents about parenting? Do they believe it is their job to link their services with schools, medical services, and job-training programs for parents, or do they see their work as isolated from other programs? Do they want to work with troubled families over an extended period, or do they see their responsibility primarily to remove children from such families?

Our definition of social policy, then, emphasizes both *formal* and *informal* policies. If the former includes rules, procedures, court rulings, and budgets that bind specific persons to specific courses of action, then the latter comprises subjective views of persons and groups. We cannot understand the workings of social agencies, legislators, or heads of governments without understanding both dimensions of social policy.

Without suggesting that any of them is more or less important than the others, we might distinguish four categories: (1) official, written policies; (2) informal, unwritten policies; (3) personal orientations toward policy, such as an aversion to specific rules or a strong support of a specific policy; and (4) personal policy actions, such as obeying or disobeying a policy in a specific work setting. Bisno calls the fourth type "policy-in-action," whereas I have named it *actualized policy*.[2] All of these policy-related categories are important in social policy.

Many kinds of policies cause or help to resolve specific social problems (see Policy Advocacy Challenge 1.3).

Policy Advocacy Challenge 1.3

Multiple Policies Impacting Single Motherhood

EP 2.1.4a

Based on your own knowledge, discuss how single motherhood may be caused or sustained by the following kinds of policies. You might consider policies regarding housing, police, shelters, substance abuse, mental health, schools, child welfare agencies, or any other organization.

- Formal policies at federal, state, and local levels
- Policy objectives
- Rules and regulations
- Budgetary issues
- Court rulings
- Statutes
- Informal policies

Also consider what kinds of policies different groups in your community might favor, including business groups, activists, social service agencies, hospitals, elected officials from districts of different levels of income, realtors, and various kinds of civic groups.

Policy Advocacy as a Developmental Process

Policies seldom emerge suddenly, but always during a developmental process. Policy advocates need to both understand this process and be able to work skillfully within it. We identify and discuss eight tasks you will employ in order to become an effective policy advocate.

1. Policy advocates begin their work by *deciding what is right and wrong.* They are willing to commit effort to policy advocacy because they believe the *status quo* is flawed for both ethical and analytic reasons.
2. They have to decide where to focus or direct their advocacy intervention *when navigating policy and advocacy systems*, such as by deciding whether to change local, state, or federal policies or to focus on public policies or policies of a specific organization.
3. When presenting problems to agency, community, and legislative decision makers, advocates engage in *agenda-setting tasks.*
4. When they use social science research that probes their causes and analyze policy options to find a solution that they prefer, practitioners perform *problem-analyzing tasks.*
5. Practitioners *develop proposals* when they create solutions to specific problems in an effort to improve agency services. Proposals may be relatively simple, such as those that change an agency's intake policies, or complex, such as those that establish major social programs.
6. Practitioners engage in *policy-enacting tasks* when they develop strategies to have a policy approved and to elect political candidates who are responsive to social workers' ethical commitments. When complex political processes are involved, strategy may consume major amounts of time and resources and demand frequent revisions. On other occasions, strategy may consist of one presentation at a critical meeting or personal discussions with highly placed decision makers.
7. *Policy implementation* involves identifying why a policy has not been adequately implemented and developing corrective strategies.
8. *Policy-assessing tasks* require evaluating a policy and deciding what changes to make if the evaluation is negative.

Additionally, policy practitioners (and therefore policy advocates) use four basic skills as they engage in each of the stages of the policy development process:

1. *Analytic skills* are useful in obtaining data, identifying policy alternatives, comparing their relative merits, and developing recommendations.
2. *Political skills* help practitioners assess the policies' feasibility, identify power resources, and develop and implement political strategy.
3. *Interactional skills* help practitioners make contacts, develop networks, build personal relationships, identify old-boy networks, communicate effectively, and facilitate coalitions and committees.
4. Policy practitioners often need *value clarification* or *ethical reasoning skills.* They have to decide what objectives they favor when analyzing problems and developing policy proposals.

We discuss these tasks and skills in more detail in Chapter Three.

EP 2.1.8a

Challenges Encountered by Policy Advocates

Policy advocacy is important and challenging work. By changing laws, rules, regulations, budgets, and objectives, policy advocates can positively impact the lives not just of specific individuals or families (as in direct-practice social work), but of large numbers of individuals and families. For example, prior to the enactment of the food stamp program, millions of low-income families lacked the resources to provide proper nutrition to their members.

If policy advocacy is often rewarding, it is also challenging for several reasons. Indeed, policy advocates often encounter opposition or controversy when they try to change specific policies. Controversy or opposition likely arises for several reasons, including a crowded field, divergent interests, divergent values and ideology, and different beliefs about whether a specific policy is, or will be, effective in addressing a specific social problem.

A Crowded Field

Unlike direct-service work, for example, policy advocates rarely have the field to themselves. This is because social policies, and policies generally, commit or bind large groups of persons and organizations to specific courses of action by establishing ground rules that guide or direct their activity. Therefore, many groups, persons, and interests take an interest in specific policies, especially when someone wants to initiate a new one or change an existing one.

Influencing Tangible Interests of Persons, Groups, and Corporations

When examining interests, policy advocates often ask, "Who benefits from the status quo, and who believes their practical interests would better be met by some or major reforms?" Since specific persons, interest groups, and corporations often benefit from specific policies, they often oppose changes in them or want only changes that advance their own needs. As persons who have sought to reform American medical care have frequently discovered, pharmaceutical companies, insurance companies, health plans, and the American Medical Association, for example, have often blocked needed reforms. Indeed, consumers are often the least represented in policy deliberations that can be dominated by persons and groups with resources to hire lobbyists and give funds to politicians and political parties.

Divergent Values and Ideologies

People often support or oppose policies because they believe the policies impinge on their fundamental values. As developments in the United States during the past three decades suggest, conservatives and liberals often battle over policies. Indeed, *ideology* is a shorthand way of summarizing persons' values, as can be seen in Table 2.1. The conflict between conservatives and liberals was highly evident in the presidential campaign of 2012, as an opposing Republican and an incumbent liberal president battled over many policy issues.

Policy Advocates Stand on the Shoulders of Many Preceding Reformers

An overview of recent American history shows that policy advocates have improved considerably the well-being of millions of Americans. Assume, for example, that Medicaid had not been created in the mid-1960s. Without Medicaid, the health care needs of low-income populations, already seriously underserved by public clinics, would have reached catastrophic proportions because local and state governments lack the resources to address them. Older citizens who have exhausted their Medicare benefits would be unable to rely on the Medicaid program, and hundreds of thousands of them would be forced into nursing homes even worse than those they would have encountered in

Policy Advocacy Challenge 1.4

Using the Web as a Policy Advocate

Gretchen Heidemann, MSW, Ph.D. Candidate

As a social work student, you have a wide range of resources you can use to learn more about policy issues and to stay informed about the issues relevant to your studies and clients.

LIBRARIES

Libraries are the best source of information because their mission is to serve the people in their community by providing access to information. Your local public library or your university or college library is not only a place to find books on your topics, but it is the place to find librarians, who can help you form your research strategies and navigate the library system. Most libraries subscribe to electronic databases and catalogs that allow you to find citations and full text to articles, news, legislative information, political information, statistics, funding sources, and more. Before you start your research, visit your college or university library and talk to a librarian to get an overview of the databases your library subscribes to and how to access those tools.

GOVERNMENT DEPOSITORIES

Some university and college libraries are government depositories. This is a federal program that provides thousands of government documents for research and community purposes. If you're looking for any kind of federal government information, a government documents library is the place to start. Check with a librarian at your institution to see if there is a library in your area that collects government documents. The federal government is also publishing many documents on the Web. In the following chapters, you'll learn more about how to find that information.

THE INTERNET

The Web is, in general, a great tool for finding information. Searching the Web is easy, and the quality of search engines has improved greatly since the Internet became part of the public consciousness.

The following are a few recommendations for information related to policy advocacy:

USA.gov. The federal government's search engine, connecting you to government agencies, reports, statistics, and much more. **www.usa.gov**

Thomas. Search congressional legislation, including bill summaries and status, congressional records, schedules and calendars, and what issues are on the congressional floor right now. **http://thomas.loc.gov/**

National Association of Social Workers (NASW). Find out about our professional organization's grassroots advocacy efforts, legislative advocacy network, political action committee, and government relations. **www.socialworkers.org/advocacy/default.asp**

Influencing State Policy (ISP). ISP assists social work faculty and students in learning to effectively influence the formation, implementation, and evaluation of state-level policy and legislation. Explore the site to learn more about ISP and use the resources provided. **http://statepolicy.org/**

Political Blogs. Weblogs, or *blogs*, can be a great source of information on current events and political issues and often include posts by both professional political pundits and average citizens. There are countless blogs from all ends of the political spectrum. For a list of blogs, visit **http://directory.etalkinghead.com/** or **http://bloggerschoiceawards.com**

Social networking sites. The latest craze on the Internet, social networking sites, such as Facebook (**www.facebook.com/**), Twitter (**http://twitter.com/**), and Tumblr

EP 2.1.1e

(**www.tumblr.com**), can be a great way to follow and support electoral candidates, join social and political causes, and connect with others who share similar political interests and concerns.

Local, state, and federal government sites: Many cities, states, and the federal government have mandates to make information accessible to citizens on the Web. A good place to start looking for information on policy issues relevant to your community is your city or state website (e.g., City of Chicago, Cook County, Illinois State website).

IssueLab: More than 400 nonprofit organizations contribute their research to this site, which hosts a searchable directory of topics ranging from children and youth to homelessness, human rights, immigration, and prison reform. **www.issuelab.org/home**

the 1970s. Many persons with AIDS, often financially devastated by the expense of medical procedures, would receive no services unless physicians and hospitals donated them.

Indeed, we can proceed through each of the major enactments of the 1960s and the succeeding decades and render a similar prognosis. Assume, for example, that Medicaid, SSI, and the food stamp program did not exist. Would that not have led to a homeless population many times the size of that existing in the 1980s and 1990s? Would economic inequality in the United States, already far greater than in European nations and Canada, not have become even worse? Considerable progress has also been made in addressing poverty among older persons; challenges to the civil rights of vulnerable populations; unemployment and lack of services for persons with disabilities; malnutrition; the health needs of certain groups in the population, such as persons with kidney failure; the preschool needs of low-income children; and psychological conditions such as depression. Many persons of color markedly improved their economic and social situation in the decades following the 1960s, and many African Americans and Latinos entered the middle and upper-middle classes, partly as a result of affirmative action and civil rights laws that prohibited job-related discrimination.

Nor do we have to look to the distant past to find policy enactments that have greatly improved the lives of many Americans. If the Congress enacts some version of national health insurance during the presidency of Barack Obama, for example, as many as 43,000 preventable deaths of medically uninsured persons might be averted each year.

We should not ignore the short-term humanitarian function of social programs. Even when they do not solve social problems, they provide resources and support to people who are experiencing such problems as unemployment, catastrophic health conditions, and mental trauma. Whether we are guided by specific religious teachings or by ethics, we realize that persons who experience hardship or trauma need assistance to diminish their suffering. This simple maxim guided the giving of alms to impoverished people in the Middle Ages, the providing of economic resources to impoverished people during recessions and the Great Depression in the United States, and the development of shelters for homeless people in contemporary society.

In many cases, problems that had seldom been recognized in prior eras were publicized and addressed by new policies because of the determined work of policy advocates. Rape, child abuse, Alzheimer's disease, spousal abuse, reading and learning disorders, discrimination against gay men and lesbians, and the needs of people with disabilities have existed throughout American history, but they have come to be widely recognized as important problems only recently. Victims of rape, for example, were subjected to punitive treatment, such as imputations of blame by judges and doctors, until many jurisdictions enacted laws that protected their rights. People with developmental disabilities were often placed in institutions in the 1950s instead of being mainstreamed in schools, communities, and employment. Children with reading difficulties were routinely dropped from school rolls in the 1950s, whereas now they often receive special services. Policy reforms emanated from a heightened public awareness of these problems and contributed to the public's knowledge of them, as individuals saw social programs' benefits to themselves, their relatives, and their friends. Moreover, social programs have often raised public expectations about the rights and needs of specific groups in the population. In 1950, Americans commonly assumed, for example, that people with paraplegia would be bedridden and institutionalized. By the 1990s, many Americans were aware of these individuals' rights and capabilities, including access to mechanized wheelchairs, independent living arrangements, occupational therapy, and employment. We can reasonably argue that the nation would have suffered harm in the absence of reforms enacted in the Progressive Era, the New Deal, and the Great Society; expansions of civil rights and entitlements in the 1970s; the Child Care and Development Block Grant of 1990; the expansion of the EITC in the 1990s; and the stimulus programs of 2009 geared to restarting a faltering economy.

Reformers have also prevented the enactment of many reforms that would have harmed many Americans. Some conservatives have wanted to, for example, bar gay men and lesbians from teaching in public schools, retain antisodomy laws of states that would allow gay men to be imprisoned for engaging in consensual sex with other men, bar immigration of gay men and deny them citizenship, exclude gay men and lesbians from civil rights legislation prohibiting discrimination by employers, and ban gay men and lesbians from the military. Only by assertive action through legislative and legal channels were advocates able to overturn these policies or their enactment.

While specific policies have failed or have had mixed results, the combined effects of social reforms have transformed the lives of tens of millions of Americans in positive ways. Most contemporary Americans cannot remember and can barely comprehend the institution of slavery, imprisonment for indebtedness, capital punishment for relatively minor crimes, poorhouses, 14-hour workdays, unsafe working conditions, child labor, routine denial of civil rights, lynching of African Americans, flagrant violations of the legal rights of radicals, the incarceration of people who publicly discussed birth control, the routine firing of gay men and lesbians, widespread malnutrition, and the denial of education to persons with disabilities.

EP 2.1.5a

Yet much remains to be done with respect to homelessness, huge inequalities, specific kinds of discrimination, eradication of such diseases as AIDS, poor education, and underfunded services. Effective policy advocacy is needed to address these and many other problems and to prevent serious problems from arising in the first place among specific populations.

Policy Devolution, Technology, Globalization, and Policy Advocacy

As the nation moves further into the 21st century, policy advocacy should become an even more vital component of social work practice. In a sweeping departure from the growth of policy powers of the federal government in the Great Society of the 1960s, many federal policies were devolved to state and local governments in the 1980s and 1990s. In the case of so-called block grants, the federal government provides funds to the states for social policy purposes and allows them to decide how to use these resources with minimal federal guidelines.[3] (In Chapters Seven and Eight, we discuss how the federal government supplanted the Aid to Families with Dependent Children [AFDC] program in 1996 with a block grant.)

This devolution of authority has meant that many policies influencing the lives of clients, consumers, and citizens are shaped by state legislatures, county boards of supervisors, and municipal governments. The social work profession used to be able to focus much of its reforming energies on the federal government; now it must *also* establish a reforming presence in hundreds of locations around the nation.

In short, devolution has accentuated the need for policy-reforming work by dispersing key decisions to smaller units of government and disseminating many policies that used to be decided at the national level. If social workers do not actively lobby for policies that will help their clientele in numerous jurisdictions, other groups will dictate these policies, often with scant interest in the well-being of stigmatized or impoverished populations. Indeed, through policy practice and policy advocacy, the profession works to shape devolution so that it will help rather than harm clients, consumers, and citizens.

Policy advocacy is also needed to help equalize conditions and opportunities for tens of millions of Americans whose economic and social well-being have deteriorated in the wake of the technological revolution that has transformed the American economy as well as the impact of globalization. As recently as the 1960s, huge numbers of Americans earned good wages in union jobs in automobile, steel, and other manufacturing industries. As these basic industries relocated to other nations and were replaced by low-paying service industries, such as fast-food establishments, the wages of many Americans plummeted. An economic chasm has widened between persons with limited education and work experience and those with college degrees and advanced skills.[4]

EP 2.1.5b

The social work profession has an ethical obligation to work to diminish this inequality. It needs to support social and economic opportunities that enable less affluent persons to better their lot through such programs as job training, remedial education, substance abuse counseling, preschool education, and family services. The profession should also work for redistributive programs that will provide resources and services to less affluent persons by such vehicles as an expanded EITC, housing subsidies, preventive medical care, and health insurance. It needs to support the goal established by President Barack Obama to have the United States graduate more students from institutions of higher education than any other nation by 2020.

As we discuss in more detail in Chapter Five, policy advocacy must span international boundaries due to the accelerating movement of capital and labor between nations and due to global warming. Large numbers of immigrants now exist, for example, in virtually every state—immigrants who are subject to considerable prejudice, poor working conditions, and low pay. The movement of jobs across national boundaries often adversely impacts domestic workers and undermines their ability to get wage concessions from employers. Global warming could endanger vast numbers of persons in coastal areas in the United States and elsewhere.

But social workers can work for these kinds of reforms only if they develop intervention skills that allow them to be effective policy advocates. This book's aim is to foster social reform work by discussing eight specific tasks and four skills that social workers must master to become effective policy advocates.

Becoming an Effective Policy Advocate

Just as in direct-service, administrative, or community-organizing practice, we become *effective* policy advocates only as we learn key concepts and develop pivotal skills. Moreover, we need certain perspectives to deal with the uncertainties of changing policies.

Let us discuss some concepts, skills, and perspectives as a prelude to examining them in greater detail in succeeding chapters.

Developing a Vision

Policy advocates need a vision of a preferred state of affairs in specific agencies, communities, regions, states, or the nation. If we cannot envision an ideal state of affairs, we are unlikely to find fault with existing policies. This vision derives from our values, beliefs, and ideology as well as from a desire to help vulnerable or oppressed people who receive inferior or negligible assistance. We do not attempt to define the vision in narrowly ideological terms because policy advocacy benefits from a variety of perspectives. The vision is nonetheless promoted and fueled by discontent with how existing policies and institutions measure up to an ideal.

Indeed, not only is a vision a driving force, but it can also enhance a practitioner's political interests and build his or her credibility. A person has succeeded in communicating that vision when others describe him or her as someone who "has principles and really cares" or "is committed to changing things." By contrast, we tend to mistrust people who we feel are "only in it for themselves" or who "bend with the wind." Of course, inflexibility and dogmatism detract from policy practice, so people have to compromise between pragmatism and the beliefs or values that constitute their vision.

Social workers can create a vision by learning how policies have evolved in specific agencies and communities. They should also understand the policy implications of broad theoretical frameworks, such as an environmental approach. The vision may derive from identifying with the needs and aspirations of powerless or oppressed populations.

Assuming that we have some empathy for the downtrodden, historical perspectives sensitize us to the discrimination, racism, inequality, and suffering that have prompted various policy reforms. We have inherited the missions of the reformers before us, including some of the profession's founders, such as Jane Addams, who devoted remarkable energy to policy practice in a society that lacked the policies that we now take for granted. In a compelling argument, Jerome Wakefield contends that "distributional justice" provides a central mission for the social work profession, distinguishing it from other professions and traditional psychotherapy.[5]

EP 2.1.2b

Seeking Opportunities for Policy Advocacy

Social workers of all stripes can assertively seek opportunities for policy advocacy, either as part of their employment or outside their work. To be effective advocates, social workers must ask: "What systemic or environmental factors cause or exacerbate specific kinds of problems that my clients experience?" (See Policy Advocacy Challenge 1.6.) We can try to change policies in the community or our agencies, for instance, on task forces or committees. Within our agencies, as part of our employment, we can modify policies that we view as deficient or develop new programs. In each case, we take a broader perspective that allows us to see more factors that adversely affect our clients and need to be remedied.

Social workers can engage in policy advocacy outside their working hours by helping advocacy groups, working with their professional association, or participating in political campaigns. They can work to educate the public about important issues in their communities by participating in forums, writing letters to the editor or op-ed pieces, or working with the mass media to disseminate information.

Policy advocacy sometimes aims at ambitious changes such as the enactment of legislation. Other kinds of policy advocacy, such as changing a specific policy in an agency or even initiating an idea in a staff meeting, are more modest.

EP 2.1.8a

Taking Sensible Risks

Policy advocates have to be sensible risk takers. It is unwise to squander finite amounts of time and energy on trivial or hopeless causes, even though ethical considerations sometimes prompt us to participate in difficult battles. However, we also need to be willing to take risks. As we discuss in Chapter Ten, some of us refrain from seeking policy changes because we underrate our own power (or that of our allies) or exaggerate the power of our opponents. Indeed, failures of omission are as important as errors of commission. In some cases, it is better to commit errors in trying to correct flawed policies than to avoid participating at all.

Balancing Flexibility with Planning

Policy advocates must develop plans to guide their work, but they must also be able to improvise during unexpected events. Planning helps organize their work into a purposeful, coherent pattern and clarifies which tasks to accomplish. Improvising allows them to seize unexpected opportunities, counter their opponents' arguments, and adopt new strategies that they did not anticipate in an earlier game plan. A policy practitioner makes plans by asking: "In light of the time and risk that I wish to take, what actions and arguments will help me obtain my objectives?" The advocate considers various strategies, either simple or more complex. The resultant plan then represents a decision that certain actions and arguments, rather than others, will yield an acceptable outcome. In light of the uncertainties of many situations, however, these hypotheses must often be guarded and subject to modification when circumstances dictate. Policy practice plans are made to be altered, because they reflect our best initial guesses.

Policy advocates need to be flexible enough to alter their style or approach situationally; like administrators, community workers, and direct-service practitioners, they need to improvise strategies as events unfold.

Being Appropriately Assertive

Policy advocates must be appropriately assertive if they wish to change policies in agencies, communities, and legislatures. They have to initiate discussions with key decision makers or locate intermediaries who can assume this role. They must learn not to be intimidated by powerful persons such as authority figures, legislators, and government officials. Yet they need to carry themselves in ways that do not unnecessarily antagonize possible allies or persons who might prove helpful in making specific policy changes. Just as direct-service practitioners develop their clinical skills, so must policy advocates learn to be appropriately assertive in specific situations. Such a noteworthy person as Eleanor Roosevelt, who was shy and withdrawn as a younger woman, gradually developed skills that made her a highly successful policy advocate.

Developing Multiple Skills

Advocates who believe they can reduce policy practice to a simple set of recommended rules or a single style are likely to be disappointed when they discover that those rules or that style are not useful in some situations. Policy advocates need an array of analytic, political, interactional, and value clarification skills to use, singly or together, in specific situations and during extended policy deliberations. Because external realities require a combination of skills, a one-dimensional policy advocate is likely to be frustrated.

Policy advocates, just like direct-service, community, and administrative practitioners, need several skills. Some skills are analytic; we need good ideas about the reforms we want in order to be effective advocates. Other skills are process and people oriented, as our discussion of political and interactional skills throughout this book suggests. Still others involve ethical reasoning, particularly when we confront moral dilemmas.

To develop these skills into competencies, we need to work at them in the same way that we hone direct-service, administrative, or community work skills.

Being Persistent

Policy advocates often need persistence, as the inspirational lives of such social reformers as Jane Addams and Martin Luther King, Jr., suggest. These people had an ability to persevere even in the face of repeated defeats and formidable obstacles. Unlike some of their colleagues who left reform causes after early battles, Addams and King maintained their devotion to social reform. Indeed, Jane Addams, who founded the pioneer social settlement Hull House in 1889, persevered not only during the Progressive Era, but also during the 1920s to support innumerable social reforms. If Martin Luther King, Jr., had not been assassinated, no doubt he would have been active in social reforms for decades more. He demonstrated that he was not inclined to rest on his laurels after any of his victories in the civil rights movement of the 1960s.

Of course, few of us have the persistence or the energy of these heroic figures. However, every community has particularly dedicated social workers who participate in many policy frays in their agencies and communities, and in broader arenas, even while they perform heavy direct-service, administrative, or community work functions. We do not know why some people persevere while others cannot, but we can learn from people who have this ability, and we can seek to emulate them. Perhaps their persistence stems, in part, from a combination of their vision or moral purpose and an ability not to be deterred by personal attacks or policy defeats. A vision provides a rationale for policy practice, independent of the vagaries of particular moments or the defeats and recriminations that any policy advocate experiences.

Policy advocates need perspective to avoid pessimism and self-recrimination in the wake of defeats or partial successes. No single person or group is likely to prevail on the complex playing field of policy deliberations. Advocates must realize that defeats are more likely when people champion the needs of stigmatized and relatively powerless groups, which lack the clout of more powerful interests.

Tolerating Uncertainty

Policy advocates must be able to tolerate uncertainty, because policy practice often lacks structure and boundaries. While relatively few people participate in specific direct-service transactions, an open field often exists in policy practice, which continually draws new people into issues. Policy advocates often do not know what to expect when they initiate a proposal. Will it be associated with conflict, consensus, or apathy? And often, they cannot predict how much time and energy an issue will require.

Becoming a Policy Advocate

EP 2.1.5c

Policy practice can serve many purposes. In some cases, we want to advance our own interests or those of the profession, perhaps by seeking new licensing laws or better reimbursement from insurance companies. Using policy practice to advance personal or professional interests is not unethical if they have ethical merit. If professional social workers give persons counseling that elevates their well-being, then policy advocacy that seeks licensing and reimbursement for professional social workers is ethically sound.

At the same time, social workers should include policy advocacy in their policy practice, which means helping relatively powerless and oppressed populations. Ethical principles, such as social justice, fairness, and beneficence, which we discuss in Chapter Two, dictate that practitioners should engage in this work even if it brings no tangible return to them or to the profession.

When evaluating the outcome of policy advocacy, we should take into account the degree of difficulty encountered. People who undertake difficult tasks or encounter formidable opposition will lose relatively frequently, no matter how skilled they are. Conversely, people who work only on simple issues will probably emerge victorious on numerous occasions. If we were to evaluate policy practitioners solely on the basis of their policy victories, we would risk giving high marks to excessively cautious people.

Indeed, defeats do not necessarily suggest that policy practitioners have been unsuccessful. When people take the initiative to propose policies, they sensitize or educate other people who may not have been aware of specific issues. While this result brings no immediate successes, the defeated policy practitioner can reintroduce another proposal at a more propitious moment and hope that people who are now aware of the issue will change their position.

Combining Pragmatism with Principles

Policy advocates must often compromise for political reasons. With respect to controversial issues in organizational, community, and legislative settings, people rarely realize all of their goals. Yet there is a danger of making premature or excessive compromises that unnecessarily dilute a policy practitioner's goals. There is no simple way to resolve the tension between a pragmatic desire to achieve policy gains and a desire to retain provisions that a policy practitioner values. Indeed, policy advocates often encounter ethical dilemmas that they can resolve only by considering the merits of alternative courses of action and making difficult choices among them. This tension was evident during the debates over national health insurance in the Congress in 2009. Liberals, who favored provisions that would expand Medicare and create a "public option" that would allow the government to establish and implement a public insurance program to compete with private insurance companies, encountered strong opposition from fellow Democrats. They had to decide whether to push for their policy goals or to compromise in hopes of obtaining votes needed for passage of health reforms from moderate and conservative Democrats.

The Rewards of Policy Advocacy

Social workers who surmount barriers to policy practice are often richly rewarded for their tenacity. Sometimes they attain notable successes when new programs are established, funding is enhanced for a program, or deficient policies are ended or modified. In such cases, social workers help entire populations and communities.

However, policy advocates who take on difficult challenges realize that they may not prevail in specific battles. Entrenched or conservative interests sometimes have the resources and power to circumvent or defeat policy advocates. Or when new policies have been enacted, they may receive inadequate resources or may be sabotaged by opponents during implementation. In such cases, advocates are still amply rewarded by the realization that they gave policy reform their best effort and that they have joined legions of prior reformers who fearlessly tackled difficult issues. Some of these failures led to tangible victories farther down the road, educating citizens to the need for policy reforms and inspiring other reformers at some future point to resume the reforming effort.

Changing the Composition of Decision Makers

No matter how skilled policy advocates are, they cannot obtain needed reforms in social policy unless they attract support from decision makers—whether legislators, mayors, members of county boards of supervisors, governors, presidents, or top appointees in government agencies. Even in agency settings, the composition of boards of directors, as well as persons in key administrative positions, powerfully shape what kinds of reforms are possible.

Policy advocates cannot, of course, easily change the composition of decision makers, but they are ethically derelict if they do not try. One vehicle is electoral politics, which is the nation's institutionalized method of selecting decision makers. It is true that electoral politics is often a corrupted process. Special interests often gain disproportionate power by contributing heavily to those candidates who represent their interests. Moreover, many poor people and members of some vulnerable populations tend to vote less frequently than persons in the middle, upper-middle, and upper classes—an unfortunate tendency that tilts policy making away from those who would make the United States a more just society.

Yet policy advocates have had striking successes both in American history and in recent years. The Democratic Party, which has been somewhat more reformist than the Republican Party during and since the New Deal, has often controlled one or both chambers of Congress as well as the presidency. Progressive governors and mayors have often been elected in state and local jurisdictions and are frequently members of state assemblies and senates, city councils, and boards of supervisors. Had this *not* been true, the many policy reforms of the last 80 years would not have been enacted.

In Chapter Twelve, we discuss many ways that policy advocates can participate in the electoral process, such as volunteering during campaigns, serving as official campaign aides, registering voters, initiating or working on propositions that are placed on the ballot, and donating (or raising) funds to and for specific candidates or parties. We also discuss how policy advocates can actually build public service careers by running for elective office themselves and taking civil service or appointive positions in government agencies. A recent survey found that 416 social workers have run for political office in recent decades at local, state, and federal levels—and eight persons with MSW degrees held office in the U.S. Congress in 2009.[6]

Policy advocates can also seek administrative positions in social agencies, since these positions give them an inside track in shaping agency policies and implementing them.

EP 2.1.5c

Getting Started

Some readers of this book may think, "It is fine for others to participate in policy advocacy, but it isn't something I can do." For persons who envision careers limited to counseling or administration, for example, the world of policy advocacy can sound daunting. It is more complex. Its outcomes are sometimes uncertain. It requires time commitments and knowledge of new subjects such as policy analysis and politics.

Do remember two things, however: Policy advocates seldom act alone; they usually work in tandem with existing advocacy groups or with persons who have experience in policy advocacy. Many of you will select an issue or policy that interests you while you are reading this book. You will soon discover that some persons and groups have already done policy advocacy work with respect to it. In some cases, lobbyists for NASW or other professional organizations closely linked to social workers will be quite familiar with your issue or policy. So you may be volunteering for them or working in concert

Policy Advocacy Challenge 1.5

Social Work Students Fight Cuts in Mental Health Spending

Rachel Gardner, MSW Candidate at USC School of Social Work

EP 2.1.5b

Our policy class was divided up into groups for an advocacy project. My group was assigned to focus on mental health. We really had no idea where to begin. I suggested we look into how the economy is affecting services rendered to mental health clientele. A group member found an article about how the governor was proposing to cut funding for Prop 63, the Mental Health Services Act of 2004, in order to solve the California budget crisis. The proposition, which was placed on a special election ballot in May 2009, would have taken $460 million away from mental health services. We made the following efforts to stop passage of the proposition and preserve funding for mental health services: (1) lobbied at the state capitol, (2) had two articles printed in the media (*Long Beach Press Telegram* and *Orange County Register*), (3) attended a meeting with the governor hosted by the *LA Times* in which a group member's question was chosen and addressed by the governor, (4) attended and addressed the Costa Mesa mayor and city councilperson, which was broadcast on Channel 24, (5) interviewed mental health clients about how the budget cuts would affect them, (6) cosponsored a public forum about the special election propositions, (7) networked with Prop 63 coauthor about what actions we could take locally, (8) made presentations in classes for students in the Mental Health concentration on how budget cuts would affect future employment opportunities in the mental health field, (9) cosponsored a "brown-bag" event for all University of Southern California students to attend during their lunch break with a guest speaker, (10) created an online petition to go to the governor, (11) created a special group on MySpace, (12) created a special group on Facebook, (13) created a blog, (14) created and distributed a flyer on how the proposition would affect the community, (15) attended and participated in the Great American Write In, and (16) networked with NASW.

EP 2.1.8b

with them or, at the very least, learning about specific issues from them. In succeeding chapters, we discuss how you can forge linkages with persons and groups familiar with your issue.

Remember, as well, that many social work students have not only read about policy advocacy, but have also actually made a strong beginning, even during their professional training, in critically analyzing existing policies and seeking changes in them, either in their field placements or in policy advocacy projects. (See Policy Advocacy Challenge 1.5 for a social work student's description of the efforts she and her classmates took to stop the passage of a California proposition that would have cut funding for mental health services in spring 2009.)

Becoming Leaders

Policy advocacy provides a route toward leadership in the profession and society. By seeking to change social policies that impact vulnerable populations, policy advocates aspire to change existing rules, policies, and budgets. As they assume these broader functions, they become leaders who are recognized by their peers and others as trying to make a difference in the lives of citizens. The need for leaders who take the initiative in addressing social issues is illustrated by issues such as homelessness that are sustained by inadequate social policies, economic forces, and social problems.

<table>
<tr>
<td>

Policy Advocacy Challenge 1.6

Unnatural Causes, a PBS Documentary

</td>
<td>

A PBS documentary, titled "Unnatural Causes," discusses how our health is powerfully shaped by social and economic determinants, such as our social class and our level of education. View a four-minute segment of this documentary by going to www.pbs.org/unnaturalcauses/video_player.htm?hourone. For more information about how the social environment and existing policies affect health care, go to www.pbs.org/unnaturalcauses/explore_learn.htm and click on Overcoming Obstacles to Health: Report from the Robert Wood Johnson Foundation to the Commission to Build a Healthier America. Then click on "Overcoming Obstacles to Health" and review that charts and text on pp. 1 to 30. Then discuss the following questions.

1. What evidence suggests that social-economic factors are often more important than genes in shaping differences in the health of low income persons and persons of color as compared to relatively affluent persons of Caucasian background?
2. What kinds of social and economic factors shape health outcomes and why?
3. Will expansion of health coverage, such as in national health insurance, end these "health disparities"?

Why are low income persons of color often less likely to follow healthy lifestyles, such as through diet and exercise, as compared to more affluent persons of Caucasian background?

</td>
</tr>
</table>

Joining the Reform Tradition Within Social Work

Most professions are relatively conservative and are concerned mostly with licensure, training, and the enhancement of the remuneration of their members. Like public health, which also has had a strong activist tradition, social work has had a social reform tradition extending back to the formation of the social work profession. Such founders of social work as Jane Addams militantly supported an array of social reforms in the Progressive Era at the beginning of the 20th century, including housing codes to protect tenants, governmental inspection of food to avert illness, factory regulations to protect workers, and pensions for single mothers with children to avert dire poverty.[7]

In succeeding eras, many social workers joined this reform tradition by working for policy reforms in local, state, and federal jurisdictions. Their work was bolstered by numerous theorists who developed a systems or environmental perspective on human behavior, arguing that social inequality, blighted neighborhoods, inadequate resources, unemployment, environmental pollution, discrimination, and economic uncertainty cause human suffering and contribute to such clinical conditions as depression and poor health.[8]

But narrower perspectives about social work coexisted with the reformist vision of Addams. Even at the profession's outset, such persons believed the profession should focus on casework, with scant involvement in social reform.[9] Myriad other theorists in succeeding decades adhered to this narrower view of the profession as they developed numerous clinical strategies that gave scant importance to environmental factors, discrimination, or poverty.

Narrower perspectives are deficient on at least three grounds, however, as is discussed at more length in Chapter Two. By failing to address the societal factors that contribute to inequality, they neglect such values as social justice and fairness. With attention riveted exclusively on the problems of individuals, they do nothing to reform the human services delivery system so that it will provide services that are congruent with recent medical and social science findings. By abandoning the political arena, they allow other groups, with values and perspectives in opposition to the needs of clients, consumers, and citizens, to dominate public policy.

Honest differences of opinion often do exist among social workers. They may disagree about the merits of specific policies. They may support different political candidates. They may draw upon conflicting research findings to support their preferred policies. Yet we are linked by shared commitment to social justice even as we may differ about how best to advance it.

EP 2.1.2a
and EP 2.1.5c

What You Can Now Do

Chapter Summary

You are now equipped with an orienting perspective that will start you on the road to being a policy advocate. You can do the following:

- Articulate an ethical rationale for becoming a policy advocate from a social justice perspective.
- Identify an array of policies, formal and informal, that shape human services and the well-being of specific vulnerable populations as well as the public interest.
- Distinguish between policy practice and policy advocacy.
- Identify specific barriers to policy advocacy.
- Discuss different ideologies.
- Identify social reform traditions in the nation and the profession.
- Identify some attributes of effective policy advocates.
- State why policy advocates often try to change the composition of government.
- Understand how homelessness provides a context for policy advocacy, and demonstrate why it is needed to help vulnerable populations.

Chapter Two discusses ethical, political, and analytic rationales for participating in policy advocacy.

Competency Notes

EP 2.1.1e Engage in career-long learning (p. 19): Social workers use websites to enhance their learning.

EP 2.1.2a Recognize and manage personal values in a way that allows professional values to guide practice (p. 29): Social workers develop a vision of a better society.

EP 2.1.2b Make ethical decisions by applying standards of NASW's Code of Ethics (pp. 4, 5, 22): Social workers become advocates for vulnerable populations.

EP 2.1.4a Recognize the extent to which a culture's structures and values may oppress, marginalize, alienate, or create or enhance privilege and power (pp. 6, 8, 15): Social workers empower vulnerable populations.

EP 2.1.5a Understand forms and mechanisms of oppression and discrimination (pp. 6, 8, 20): Social workers understand barriers confronting vulnerable populations.

EP 2.1.5b Advocate for human rights and social and economic justice (pp. 9, 27): Social workers obtain and implement laws that protect members of vulnerable populations.

EP 2.1.5c Engage in practices that advance social and economic justice (pp. 7, 24, 26, 29).

> **EP 2.1.8a   Analyze, formulate, and advocate for policies that advance social well-being** (pp. 10, 12, 16, 22): Social workers use multiple skills to engage in policy practice.
>
> **EP 2.1.8b   Collaborate with colleagues and clients for effective policy action** (p. 27): Social workers collaborate with advocacy groups when engaging in policy practice.
>
> **EP 2.1.9b   Provide leadership in promoting sustainable changes in service delivery and practice to improve the quality of social services** (p. 13): Social workers work to improve the organizations where they work.
>
> **EP 2.1.10i   Implement prevention interventions that enhance client capacities** (p. 12): Social workers work for policies that prevent social problems.

Endnotes

1. Richard Titmuss, *Commitment to Welfare* (New York: Pantheon Press, 1968), p. 156.
2. Conversation with Wilbur Finch, who attributed this phrase to Herb Bisno.
3. Bruce Jansson and Susan Smith, "Articulating a 'New Nationalism' in Social Policy," *Social Work* 41 (September 1996): 441–451.
4. For discussion of inequality in American society, see Claude Fischer et al., *Inequality by Design: Cracking the Bell Curve Myth* (Princeton, NJ: Princeton University Press, 1997).
5. Jerome Wakefield, "Psychotherapy, Distributive Justice, and Social Work, Parts 1 and 2," *Social Service Review* 62 (June & September 1988): 187–210, 353–384.
6. Shannon Lane and Nancy Humphreys, "Social Workers in Politics: A National Survey of Social Work Candidates and Elected Officials," *Journal of Policy Practice* 10, no. 3 (2011): 225–244.
7. For example, see Carol Meyer, *Social Work Practice: A Response to the Urban Crisis* (New York: Free Press, 1970), and Carel Germain and Alex Gitterman, *The Life Model of Social Work Practice* (New York: Columbia University Press, 1980).
8. Mary Richmond, *Social Diagnosis* (New York: Russell Sage Foundation, 1917).
9. Harry Specht, "Social Work and the Popular Psychotherapies," *Social Service Review* 64 (September 1990): 345–347.

Suggested Readings

Definitions of Policy and Social Welfare Policy

Brian Hogwood and Lewis Gunn, *Policy Analysis for the Real World* (London: Oxford University Press, 1994), pp. 12–31.

Martin Rein, *Social Policy: Issues of Choice and Change* (New York: Random House, 1970), pp. 5–8.

Richard Titmuss, *Commitment to Welfare* (New York: Pantheon Press, 1968), p. 156.

Materials That Link Policy to Direct-Service Practice

Chauncey Alexander, "Professional Social Workers and Political Responsibility," in Maryann Mahaffey and John Hanks, eds., *Practical Politics: Social Work and Political Response* (Washington, DC: National Association of Social Workers, 1982), pp. 22–25.

Robert Goodin, *Reasons for Welfare: The Political Theory of the Welfare State* (Princeton, NJ: Princeton University Press, 1988), pp. 123–228.

Seymour Halleck, *Politics of Therapy* (New York: Science House, 1971), pp. 11–38.

Yeheskel Hasenfeld, "Power in Social Work Practice," *Social Service Review* 61 (September 1987).

Alvin Schorr, "Practice as Policy," *Social Service Review* 59 (June 1985): 178–196.

Michael Sosin and Sharon Caulum, "Advocacy: A Conceptualization for Social Work Practice," *Social Work* 28 (January–February 1983): 12–17.

Harold Weissman and Andrea Savage, *Agency-Based Social Work: Neglected Aspects of Clinical Practice* (Philadelphia, PA: Temple University Press, 1983).

Overviews of Policy Deliberations
James Anderson, *Public Policy-Making* (New York: Praeger, 1975).

Bruce Jansson, *Theory and Practice of Social Welfare Policy: Analysis, Processes, and Current Issues* (Belmont, CA: Wadsworth, 1984), pp. 49–55.

Policy Practice and Policy Advocacy
Mimi Abramovitz, "Should All Social Work Students Be Educated for Social Change?" *Journal of Social Work Education* 29 (Winter 1993): 6–11, 17–18.

Josefina Figueira-McDonough, "Policy Practice: The Neglected Side of Social Work Intervention," *Social Work* 38: 179–188.

Norman Wyers, "Policy Practice in Social Work: Models and Issues," *Journal of Social Work Education* 27 (Fall 1991): 241–250.

Policy Practice and Policy Advocacy in Specific Settings
Ron Dear and Rino Patti, "Legislative Advocacy," *Encyclopedia of Social Work,* 18th ed., vol. 2 (Washington, DC: National Association of Social Workers, 1987).

Karen Haynes and James Mickelson, *Affecting Change: Social Workers in the Political Arena* (New York: Longman, 1999).

Maryann Mahaffey and John Hanks, eds., *Practical Politics: Social Work and Political Response* (Silver Spring, MD: National Association of Social Workers, 1982).

Herman Resnick and Rino Patti, *Change from Within: Humanizing Social Welfare Organizations* (Philadelphia, PA: Temple University Press, 1980).

Ramon Salcido and Essie Seck, "Political Participation among Social Work Chapters," *Social Work* 37 (November 1992): 563–564.

2 Articulating Four Rationales for Participating in Policy Advocacy

Policy Predicament

In our practice of social work, we see much inequality. Many of our clients have poor health. They may be dependent on welfare relief. They may have received an inadequate education. They may work long hours for little pay—that is, if they have a job at all. They may have been ushered from home to home, as foster children. They may have lost their homes during the recent housing bubble debacle. We discuss four rationales for engaging in policy advocacy to eliminate homelessness in the United States in Policy Advocacy Challenge 2.10 at the end of this chapter.

By the end of this chapter, you will have learned four rationales for engaging in policy advocacy to comply with our profession's Code of Ethics, including its call for greater social justice.

LEARNING OUTCOMES

1. To promote the values that lie at the heart of social work and that are included in the profession's code of ethics, such as social justice, fairness, self-determination, and confidentiality
2. To promote the well-being of clients, consumers, and citizens by shaping the human services system to conform to the latest findings of social science and medical research
3. To create effective opposition to groups and citizens that run counter to the National Association of Social Workers code of ethics and the well-being of clients, consumers, and citizens, and to put pressure on decision makers to approve and retain policies that advance citizens' well-being
4. To change the composition of government so that legislators and decision makers are more likely to advance such values as fairness and social justice and promote the well-being of citizens

The Ethical Rationale for Policy Advocacy

We discuss the first of the eight policy tasks in this chapter, that is, deciding whether an existing policy is meritorious or whether we should try to modify it or change it. We often evaluate the ethical merit of specific policies through a process known as ethical reasoning.

Beneficence and Professional Practice

We discuss three levels of practice in this section: policy-sensitive practice, policy-related practice, and policy advocacy. Professionals of all kinds are bound by codes of ethics to place their clients' needs first. We describe this moral imperative to enhance clients' well-being as beneficence because it is a term widely used in moral philosophy.[1] Professionals, including social workers, act unethically when they knowingly harm clients, such as by providing them with unnecessary or inferior services. Professionals are also morally obligated to select interventions, diagnostic tests, and treatments that will most enhance their clients' well-being.

However, clients' well-being extends beyond a narrow definition of professional practice. For example, a lawyer is morally irresponsible if he or she helps a client obtain a divorce but has no interest in the client's economic fate after the divorce is final. (In fact, so many women have become mired in poverty when they must raise children single-handed that some experts use the phrase "the feminization of poverty.") This lawyer should expand his or her professional work beyond mere technical responsibility. Similarly, social workers need to expand their professional practice beyond counseling to helping clients deal with broader economic and social factors. They have two moral obligations: to make their professional recommendations with sensitivity to their clients' economic, social, and policy realities and to engage in brokerage, liaison, and advocacy work for specific clients to improve these realities.[2] We call the first moral obligation *policy-sensitive practice* because it requires professionals to take into account their clients' economic and social realities, many of which derive from societal policies. Professionals giving technical advice are aware that the client or patient may also confront negative policy-related consequences. They also need to teach clients skills to help them confront barriers, find resources, and manage their own cases. The social worker seeks to equip clients with the ability to take charge of their personal destinies in the future. The term *empowerment* is commonly used to describe these survival skills.[3]

EP 2.1.7b

Professionals should also use brokerage, liaison, and case advocacy services for specific clients. We call these services *policy-related services* because they involve such skills as mediation and conflict management, which resemble the skills used in policy practice. Brokerage is the negotiation of services for specific clients with other institutions and persons. A teacher, for example, may broker an agreement with a welfare office to obtain resources for a child with dyslexia. They engage in case (or micro) advocacy when they "go to bat" for specific clients, such as by helping them obtain second opinions in the medical system or by questioning poor quality or ill-advised services.

They engage in policy advocacy when they move beyond direct service, policy sensitive practice, and policy-related practice to change policies in agency, community, legislative, and government-settings. Possible activities include developing and working in coalitions, using power, developing tactics, lobbying, engaging in political campaigns, conducting policy-related research, drafting policy proposals, and reforming the implementation of specific programs.

Let's summarize what social workers must do when they provide policy-sensitive, policy-related, and policy-advocacy interventions. When social workers perform *policy-sensitive activities*, they should recognize the following:

- Some problems or pathologies reflect situational and environmental pressures rather than deep-seated characteristics.
- Some apparent problems or pathologies are functional adaptations to oppressive realities.
- Survival skills are often as important to people (particularly persons who have been excluded from mainstream institutions) as purely intrapsychic interventions.
- Some persons need help to overcome feelings of inferiority that stem from exposure to oppressive ideology and institutions and to become more assertive.
- Empowerment, or learning skills that will counter oppressive realities, is often as important as purely intrapsychic interventions.

When social workers perform *policy-related activities*, they should realize the following actions are often necessary:

- They will need to negotiate service arrangements between clients and family members or institutions such as schools, welfare departments, child welfare departments, and clinics.
- They will need to connect persons to other persons, networks, or institutions.
- They must be case advocates for clients or must empower clients to become their own advocates.

When social workers engage in *policy advocacy*, they realize:

They must identify policies in organizational, community, government, and legislative settings that cause or exacerbate social problems of their clientele, such as providing them with inadequate income, shelter, and mental health services, They must attempt to modify dysfunctional policies usually in liaison with others (see Policy Advocacy Challenge 2.1).

Social workers can initiate social reform projects or work through chapters of the National Association of Social Workers (NASW) or other professional organizations, or they can help existing advocacy and community groups. Indeed, empowerment, or helping individuals assert their needs, extends to helping oppressed groups assert their rights collectively, either through community-based organizations or broader advocacy groups.[4] Social workers can volunteer their services to these advocacy groups, serve as consultants to them, help them find resources, and conduct research for them. Policy advocacy can realize fully the environmental approach to social work practice.

Policy Advocacy, Powerless Groups, and Social Justice

We often engage in policy advocacy to obtain benefits, services, rights, and opportunities for specific populations, such as helping persons with disabilities to obtain benefits, services, access to job training and jobs, transportation, homemaker aides, and other forms of assistance that derive from high-level policies.

But we can also justify policy advocacy from the vantage point of social justice because we find inequalities in society morally objectionable, whether they exist among social classes or between mainstream society and a specific population, such as persons with disabilities. But should we be concerned about inequality in society? Let us discuss varieties of inequality, some reasons why inequalities violate ethical standards, and the ways in which policy practitioners use policy practice to decrease inequality.

<table>
<tr>
<td>

</td>
<td>

Bob Erlenbusch, board member of the National Coalition for the Homeless in Washington, DC, authored this plan and implemented it when he was the director of a shelter for homeless persons. All staff, including security staff, cooks, and social service staff, engaged in policy advocacy as a part of their work.

ADVOCACY FITNESS PLAN: AEROBICS FOR ADVOCATES

Becoming politically fit is a lot like becoming physically fit—just as your muscles need regular exercise and increased activity over time, so do your political muscles. Stop using them and you'll quickly become politically flabby; use them and your advocacy fitness will soar.

So what follows is a quick and easy *10 Step Advocacy Fitness Plan,* a kind of Aerobics for Advocates—low, medium, and high impact:

LEVEL 1. LOW IMPACT This level is like the exercises in which your feet do not leave the floor and your movements are quite gentle. Even if you do not get further than Level 1, by the end of the year, you will be better informed and will have gotten a few more people thinking about the issue.

Low Impact: Every MONTH do at least one of the following:

1. *Get on the mailing list*. Get on a mailing list of an advocacy organization that focuses on an issue your organization cares about.
2. *Join a coalition.* Join a coalition that embraces the issue your organization cares about.
3. *Invite a speaker.* Invite a speaker to educate your organization about an advocacy issue ... (from) the coalition that you have just joined. This will give your agency's board of directors, staff, volunteers, and clients an opportunity to be educated about issues that are directly affecting them.
4. *Know your nonprofit advocacy rights.* Educate yourself, agency staff, and board of directors about your agency nonprofit advocacy rights. For example ... you can educate all you want (on an advocacy issue) ... but are limited to how much of your budget can be applied to lobbying. You can register clients to vote on site. You cannot ... take positions on candidates running for public office, (but) you ... can take positions on local state initiatives and/or referendums.

LEVEL 2. MEDIUM IMPACT This level is comparable to exercises in which body movements are more energetic, the pace is faster ... but the impact is far more dramatic.

Medium Impact: Every WEEK do at least one of the following:

1. *Write a policy maker (local, state, or federal) on an issue you care about.* Practice what you already know, and exercise your political muscles. Once you've done it a few times, it will get easier. As with most things in life, the first time is the hardest. The more you do it, the better advocacy aerobic shape you will be in.
2. *Call a policy maker (local, state, or federal).* Ditto. Especially at the federal level, it is good to know that all U.S. senators and representatives have local telephone numbers, and some have toll-free numbers. Always ask to speak to the person who handles the issue that you are calling about.
3. *Visit a policy maker (local, state, or federal).* Ditto again. It is not enough to read about making a visit; sooner or later you need to use what you have learned. Try it; you may like it. Always remember that you are the expert and that policy makers are relying on input on issues from community-based organizations like yours.

(continued)

</td>
</tr>
</table>

**Policy
Advocacy
Challenge 2.1**
(continued)

LEVEL 3: HIGH IMPACT This level is like the exercise routine in which you jump up and down, fling your arms and legs, and quickly work up a sweat. At this point, you will be a true citizen activist, with advocacy muscles taut and working at their peak. Go for it!

1. *Involve your clients in writing, calling, visiting policy makers.* In an exercise program, no one knows how your body feels, where it hurts, where it is tired, better than you. So too in advocacy aerobics. No one knows the issue better than those affected by the issue, whether it is experiencing homelessness or being on welfare. Unfortunately, this voice is often left out in policy debates, but it is the most moving one when policy makers hear it. Your role as an employee in a nonprofit agency can be to facilitate this voice.

2. *Bring your clients to testify at hearings.* Nothing is more moving than to hear the impact of policy makers in real human terms. As agency staff, we can describe an issue, but our clients bring that issue to life—they put a face on it for policy makers. Remember, usually policy makers will be moved by this kind of testimony and want to "fix" it for that client. Your job is to make sure that the systemic issue that person symbolizes is addressed.

BONUS POINT

1. *Five percent of all your staff job descriptions are devoted to advocacy.* Direct service is a difficult work. But it is often made more difficult because your staff are working on the symptoms of larger systemic problems (lack of housing and health care) with no way to affect the issues. By taking advocacy into their job description, they now have a way to address the larger issues, through joining a coalition, calling, writing, visiting policy makers, testifying, or attending or organizing a rally. Your nonprofit agency can move beyond case advocacy to systemic advocacy with your vision to do so.

EP 2.1.8a

POINTS TO DISCUSS ABOUT THE ADVOCACY FITNESS PLAN

Discuss this Advocacy Fitness Plan with respect to the following points:

1. Is it feasible to implement this plan in most not-for-profit agencies?
2. Should policy advocacy be conceptualized not only as an activity that occurs "off the job" but also as integral to professional work?
3. Can employees of public agencies engage in policy advocacy?

Varieties of Inequality If we were to analyze the current status of groups of American citizens on an array of dimensions, such as housing, income, neighborhood amenities, and health, we would find vast disparities among them. Social class provides a shorthand method of summarizing many of these disparities because persons in the upper classes tend to possess more income (and therefore better housing, better neighborhood amenities, and better health) than those in the lower classes. We can also analyze disparities in current status between specific populations and the mainstream population. If we define white adult males as the mainstream population, for example, we can compare their average income with that of a specific other population, such as women, Latinos, African Americans, or children.[5]

We could also analyze the disparities among citizens not by current income and related indicators, but by access to opportunities, such as education, health services, assets (e.g., houses), networks (e.g., acquaintances with clout), and rights (e.g., freedom from discrimination in jobs or promotions). Opportunity is, to some extent, the flip side of current status, since having opportunities allows us to obtain or improve our current status, such as income. The feminists' complaint that women are often excluded from old-boy networks, for example, recognizes that promotions and jobs (current status) often depend on contacts that give persons an inside track; excluded from these networks, women often lose jobs and promotions to males. Indeed, current status and access to opportunities are reciprocal; people whose income increases, for example, can afford expensive housing, which tends to be near better schools and jobs and gives them access to opportunities, which, in turn, allows their income to increase again.

When Inequalities Violate Ethical Standards   Inequalities of status and opportunity are inevitable in any society. Short of a fiat by someone with complete control over the economy who wants full equality, certain persons, classes, and populations will have greater current status and access to opportunities than others. Such inequalities exist even in noncapitalist societies, as illustrated by differences in wealth and status within Native American tribes or between nobles and serfs in feudal society. But inequalities emerge in a particularly striking fashion in capitalistic societies, where those who control corporations or work in highly paid occupations such as law and medicine secure vastly greater income, assets, and access to opportunities than other people. Moreover, patterns of inheritance perpetuate these differences and discrepancies. The descendants of wealthy persons not only inherit wealth but also obtain access to opportunities by virtue of contacts, schooling, and other advantages.[6]

EP 2.1.5a

We confront formidable intellectual challenges when we ask, "What degrees and kinds of inequalities are morally objectionable?" We have to be clear, for example, whether we are questioning inequalities in status or access to opportunities. We need to discuss issues of threshold: At what threshold, or degree, is inequality morally objectionable? We also have to decide why inequality is objectionable, if at all. To the extent that we dislike inequalities, we must decide what kinds of policies should be used to reduce them.

We do not have the ethical field to ourselves. Many philosophers have wrestled with issues of equality. To summarize and analyze their different conclusions and arguments

---

Policy Advocacy Challenge 2.2

Empowering Clients or Citizens to Seek Social Justice

Rebecca Kendig, MSW, LCSW
Go to
www.cengage.com
to watch this video clip.

View the Policy Advocacy Challenge Video 2.2 in which Rebecca Kendig, executive director of Case Services Management for the Youth Empowerment Project in New Orleans, discusses how she links African American youth to an advocacy organization that seeks to decrease police brutality and unfair treatment of young African American adults. What information did the youth provide to the advocacy group to facilitate their work?

is beyond the scope of this book, but to introduce the topic, we will briefly analyze some tenets of a leading contemporary philosopher, John Rawls. In his seminal work, *A Theory of Justice*, Rawls argues that we can best construct our moral vision of a good society by trying to imagine its internal arrangements from behind a "veil of ignorance," which obscures our own current status (such as income) or personal access to opportunities.[7] Rawls says that if we are aware of our current status and are, for example, relatively well-off, we are likely to want a society that will perpetuate our economic well-being, even if others do not share in it. Therefore, we should retreat behind this veil, where our personal income and opportunities are not known to us. When conceptualizing the ideal society from this vantage point, we are likely to conclude that society should allow only those inequalities that will preserve or further the common good of society. We will reach this conclusion because we would not want to take a chance on being stuck in the lower reaches of a relatively inegalitarian society. We realize most people are in those lower reaches, whereas in egalitarian societies, people have similar statuses and opportunities. The rational person would, Rawls concludes, opt for an egalitarian society but would accept some inequalities. Occupations that require particular skills and training, such as brain surgery, would carry relatively high salaries to attract the most skilled and dedicated persons.

We can express Rawls's argument in simpler form by asking, "If you had the choice at the start of your existence—not yet favoring any specific society, and not knowing what social position you would hold—would you choose to live in the United States (with its relatively inegalitarian arrangements) or in a more egalitarian society such as Sweden, where discrepancies between the affluent and the less affluent classes are less marked, particularly when relatively equal access to health care and education are factored into the equation?" Rawls asserts that you would be likely to select Sweden because, on balance, you would not want to risk ending up in the American lower classes, many of whom live in blighted inner-city neighborhoods and lack health insurance.

EP 2.1.5b

Rawls's argument can be restated as the Golden Rule: Do unto others as you would have them do unto you. If you are not willing to experience the inequalities of the inner city, for example, you should not support policies that perpetuate such inequalities. This argument suggests that failure to engage in any social reform, either as a private citizen or as part of one's professional role, is tantamount to violation of the Golden Rule. If we do not want to live in inner-city areas without adequate health care and other amenities, we have a moral duty to try to improve the lot of inner-city residents and other persons who experience inequality.

We can also support efforts to reduce inequalities with economic arguments. Extreme inequalities produce undesirable economic effects on the nation.[8] At a time when Americans are competing with foreign nations, for example, they can ill afford vast reservoirs of relatively uneducated, unhealthy, and nonproductive citizens in the inner cities. But Americans have decreased the productivity of many inner-city residents by failing to invest sufficiently in people, jobs, and infrastructure.

Similarly, vast disparities in status and opportunities produce undesirable social consequences. Persons in the lower reaches of relatively inegalitarian societies often despair of their chances to improve their lot. Such alienation often induces them to improve their lot through crime and drug dealing, which harms their neighborhoods and the broader society. If they despair of being able to work through the political system, they may also participate in violent collective uprisings at enormous cost to themselves, their neighborhoods, and the nation, as the domestic disturbances of the 1960s and the 1992 Los Angeles uprising suggest.[9]

We can also advocate reducing inequality in the name of the common good (see Policy Advocacy Challenge 2.3). In recent decades, it has been fashionable to argue

Policy Advocacy Challenge 2.3

Imagining a Better Society

Anneka Scranton, MSW, DPA, Community Activist and formerly Clinical Adjunct Professor, School of Social Work, University of Southern California

All of us need to develop a vision of a better society as we aim to be policy advocates. (Policy advocacy is, after all, geared to improving society in some respect.) We can do this by a "dream exercise," in which, singly or in groups, we try to imagine a better American society in 10 or more years.

- What is your dream of a more just society?
- What is the most important change that would take place?
- How might policy advocates begin working on this agenda?

Alternatively, we can develop a vision by discussing the impact that specific policies have had upon members of our families, ourselves, or a specific client. (Select one of these persons as your point of reference.)

- How have existing policies proven inadequate to redress some specific problems or issues of your family member, yourself, or a client?
- What is the most important change that needs to take place?
- How might policy advocates begin working on this agenda?

2.1.2a

that self-interested and individualistic behavior constitutes the highest or best activity. Society benefits, conservatives have often said, when persons work hard, take risks, and build businesses to improve their incomes. Carried to an extreme, however, self-serving behavior can yield unfortunate consequences. If society fails to fund quality schools and infrastructure, for example, it jeopardizes economic growth and alienates persons who believe they cannot improve their lot.[10] Conservatives' contention that "confiscatory taxes" will jeopardize economic growth is belied by satisfactory rates of economic growth in many European nations, whose level of taxation is often far higher than the United States.[11]

One thing is certain: The United States currently has extraordinary rates of economic inequality. Millions of Americans live from paycheck to paycheck, possess no savings, have scant retirement accounts (save for Social Security), and do not have such assets as houses. A recent study of economic inequality in Los Angeles County, one of the most populous metropolitan areas of the United States, discovered that one in four workers was poor, including such diverse workers as janitors, maids, teachers, health practitioners, sewing machine operators, actors, parks and recreation workers, and parking lot attendants.[12] (The study defined poverty for the working poor as an annual income of $33,098 for a family of four based on the actual cost of living or a higher threshold than federal poverty standards of $16,700 since the federal standard does not accurately measure survival needs of citizens in L.A. County.) They discovered that inequality between the top 20 percent and the middle 20 percent of earners in Los Angeles grew significantly in the 1990s, and nationally the net worth of the top 1 percent grew by 17 percent when adjusted for inflation, while the bottom 40 percent lost an amazing 80 percent of their net worth. In the late 1990s, the top 1 percent of U.S. households owned 40 percent of the nation's wealth. Other findings included the following:

- The vast majority of the working poor, 77 percent, work full time.
- Of persons in two-adult households with children in which at least one adult reported income in the prior year, 45 percent were poor.
- Nearly 7 of 10 people in Los Angeles with no high school education were working poor.
- While Latinos make up 40 percent of the workforce, they account for 73 percent of the working poor.
- In manufacturing, 33 percent of persons, and in the personal service sector, 51 percent of workers were poor.
- Of the working poor, 59 percent lack health insurance, and half of these persons have children.
- Economic inequality widened yet further during the Great Recession of 2007 into 2009 and beyond. It became a major issue in the presidential campaign of 2012 as President Barack Obama charged that Mitt Romney, his Republican opponent, cared more about enriching the top 1 percent of the population rather than decreasing economic inequality by a combination of tax increases on affluent persons and spending on schools and other opportunity-creating programs for low- and middle-income persons.

Policy Advocacy for Vulnerable Populations

Rawls's approach to moral reasoning has considerable merit because his arguments force us to ponder ideal, or preferred, social and economic arrangements. But some readers may find Rawls's arguments relatively abstract. Why not proceed to social justice more directly by discussing specific groups who are clearly unequal to the dominant population (see Policy Advocacy Challenge 2.4)?

Consider the case of expanding the Head Start program to serve all low-income African American children. We support the program because it enhances fairness by giving low-income African American children the educational, health, and child development services many white, middle-class families have long taken for granted. White, middle-class families send their children to nursery schools, have easy access to medical care, and purchase computers and other educational aides for their children. While expanding Head Start hardly reduces societal inequality on a grand scale, as implied by Rawls's framework, it reduces some of the inequalities of low-income African American children. Take any of the vulnerable populations identified in Chapter One, and identify specific services, resources, and benefits a policy advocate might attempt to expand that members of the mainstream population can purchase with their own resources, using the doctrine of fairness to justify your policy advocacy.

Social workers can often liaise with advocacy groups in local, state, and national jurisdictions to assist specific vulnerable populations, as a volunteer, member, staff person, or board person. They can initiate their own projects. They can work through NASW. To find an advocacy group, do an Internet search, such as "advocacy for SNAP

Policy Advocacy Challenge 2.4

Thinking Critically When Using the Web

Stephanie Davis, Research Librarian, University of California, Irvine

Many websites have been developed by groups that favor particular causes or populations. Many of these websites provide invaluable information, but others provide less reliable information. If you have experience in doing research, you know that society is facing information overload. In the course of your research, you will access many different types of information using the following resources: websites, books, journal articles, magazine articles, think tank reports, agency reports, case studies, government documents, electronic journals, electronic books, and more. (We discuss websites that cover global issues in Chapter Five.)

So how do you know if information is credible or not? What is "good" information?

Throughout the research process, you will need to develop criteria for yourself to help you identify and best use the information you find. For starters, be aware that the purpose of every piece of information you find will be trying to convince you of something; they may be trying to sell you a product, persuade you to believe a certain idea or issue, influence you to vote a certain way, etc. Be a critical consumer whenever you are doing research, whether you're looking at websites or journal articles.

EXERCISE

On the Internet, assess the following two sites for their accuracy.

- **Human Rights Campaign**
    www.hrc.org
- **National Organization for Marriage**
    www.nationformarriage.org

It is important to note that part of the evaluation is whether you agree with the ideas presented on each site. However, when doing research, especially if your ultimate goal is to persuade a group to agree with you, you need to be aware of what your opposition is saying so that you can respond intelligently.

Many websites present information about vulnerable populations and the advocacy groups that represent them. The following sites relate to many of the topics we discuss in this book, including homelessness and its contributing factors:

Homelessness

- **National Alliance to End Homelessness:** www.endhomelessness.org/
- **National Coalition for the Homeless:** www.nationalhomeless.org/

Poverty

- **National Law Center on Homelessness and Poverty:** www.nlchp.org/
- **Children's Defense Fund:** www.childrensdefense.org/
- **Urban Institute:** www.urban.org/
- **Institute for Children, Poverty & Homelessness:** www.icphusa.org/

Safety Net

- **Center for Law and Social Policy:** www.clasp.org/
- **Center on Budget and Policy Priorities:** www.cbpp.org/
- **MDRC:** www.mdrc.org/

(continued)

Housing

- **National Low Income Housing Coalition:** www.nlihc.org/
- **National Housing Institute:** www.nhi.org/
- **National Housing Conference:** www.nhc.org/

Living Wage

- **Economic Policy Institute:** www.epi.org/
- **Employment Policies Institute:** www.epionline.org/

Domestic Violence

- **National Coalition Against Domestic Violence:** www.ncadv.org/
- **National Organization for Women:** www.now.org/
- **National Network to End Domestic Violence:** www.nnedv.org/

Health Care

- **American Public Health Association:** www.apha.org
- **National Coalition on Health Care:** www.nchc.org/
- **National Health Care for the Homeless Council:** www.nhchc.org/

Substance Abuse

- **National Institute on Drug Abuse:** www.drugabuse.gov/
- **Association for Addiction Professionals:** www.naadac.org/

Mental Illness

- **National Mental Health Association:** www.nmha.org
- **National Alliance on Mental Illness:** www.nami.org/

Foster Care and Juvenile Justice

- **Annie E. Casey Foundation:** www.aecf.org/
- **National Juvenile Justice Network:** www.njjn.org/
- **National Council on Crime and Delinquency:** www.nccdglobal.org/

Criminal Justice

- **ACLU:** http://aclu.org/
- **Justice Policy Institute:** www.justicepolicy.org/

Veterans' Concerns

- **National Coalition for Homeless Veterans:** www.nchv.org/index.cfm

in Madison, Wisconsin" (the Supplemental Nutritional Assistance Program). See Policy Advocacy Challenge 2.5.

The doctrine of social justice sometimes leads to painful predicaments, as with affirmative action. To decrease a specific vulnerable population's inequalities, we must sometimes take away opportunities from a privileged group, such as white males. Say we have

Listen to the Policy Advocacy Challenge Video 2.5 in which Bob Erlenbusch, board member of the National Coalition for the Homeless in Washington, DC, discusses how social workers can link themselves to advocacy groups.

Discuss the following:

1. Why individual policy advocates, operating by themselves, can rarely influence major policies single-handedly.
2. How you can find out about specific advocacy groups, either through tapping key informants or using the Web.
3. How you can learn more about a specific advocacy group.
4. How you can work with a specific advocacy group.

a limited number of positions in an organization and want to increase the number of women in those positions. We believe that women are underrepresented because of past discrimination. We can increase the number of female employees, at least in the short term, only by reducing the proportion of male employees. Does favoring female applicants (which our doctrine of social justice supports) deny social justice to male applicants? The answer depends partly on our time frame and our ultimate objectives. The doctrine of social justice dictates a random distribution of problems, such as unemployment or lower-paying jobs. Thus, positive discrimination for female applicants is justifiable because it makes men and women more equal (hence, it is fairer) with respect to jobs and higher positions, even if only within a particular organization. Were we to consider hiring women only when female applicants were better qualified than males, it would take decades to achieve parity. Affirmative discrimination for women was developed to move the clock ahead. From this perspective, to find an ethical alternative to affirmative action is hard because any other policy would fail to redress historic patterns of inequality, at least until resources and opportunities are more randomly distributed in our population.[13]

Other Ethical Principles in Policy Advocacy

We have emphasized the ethical principles of beneficence, social justice, and fairness as rationales for policy advocacy. We have argued that these principles require ethical social workers to engage in policy practice. But what about other ethical principles, such as honesty, self-determination (or autonomy), confidentiality, and preservation of life, namely, the other ethical principles discussed widely in religious and philosophical literature?[14] When ethicists discuss various principles, they commonly refer to the following:

- *Autonomy.* The right to make critical decisions about one's own destiny
- *Freedom.* The right to hold and express personal opinions and take personal actions
- *Preservation of life.* The right to continued existence

EP 2.1.2d

- *Honesty.* The right to correct and accurate information
- *Confidentiality.* The right to privacy
- *Equality.* The right of individuals to receive the same services, resources, or opportunities as other people
- *Due process.* The right to procedural safeguards when accused of crimes or when benefits or rights are withdrawn
- *Societal or collective rights.* The right of society to maintain and improve itself by safeguarding the public health and safety

Many philosophers have declared that right-living persons should adhere to these principles as well as to those of beneficence and social justice we have already discussed. These principles often arise, of course, in professionals' interpersonal work, whether they are physicians, attorneys, teachers, or social workers. Professionals are urged by their codes of ethics to share information with their clients and not to deceive them (honesty), to let their clients make the important decisions that arise during their interaction with professionals (self-determination), to preserve clients' privacy by not divulging information about them to other people (confidentiality), and to act to advance clients' well-being (beneficence).[15] These ethical principles apply, as well, to policy advocacy, which often seeks to advance them.

Other Types of Ethical Reasoning

We have just discussed moral reasoning that relies on various ethical principles such as honesty, an approach philosophers call *deontology.* Another approach to ethical reasoning, known as *utilitarianism,* uses a different method of reasoning to formulate ethical recommendations. Utilitarians criticize reliance on ethical principles on the grounds that people often differ on the definitions or weighting of principles or because the principles sometimes conflict. When terminal patients want assistance in dying, for example, the principles of autonomy (or self-determination) and not-killing conflict, so ethical resolution is difficult.

Preferring to use empirical data to make ethical choices, utilitarians analyze the likely outcomes or consequences of specific choices and choose the option that has the best outcomes.[16] When comparing two treatment options for people with depression, for example, they would select the option that was more effective as demonstrated by empirical data. Their approach is similar to persons in direct practice who support evidence-based practice that aims to provide interventions that have been shown to be effective by empirical outcomes research. For example, policies opposing smoking in public places might be supported by utilitarians who cited evidence showing that secondhand smoke often causes such adverse health outcomes as lung cancer.

Utilitarians examine not only the outcomes associated with specific options, but also their relative cost. They might oppose a medical treatment that costs $2 million per patient even if it helped some patients recover, on grounds that the ratio of cost ($2 million per patient) to benefit (the numbers of patients cured) was too high. They might prefer a policy or treatment option with a relatively low cost-to-benefit ratio, such as prenatal care that is relatively inexpensive to provide but that averts serious health problems.

Utilitarians, in turn, are criticized by first-principle ethicists. Good data about the effects of specific proposed policies are often lacking or conflicting. In the case of obesity, for example, experts differ in their appraisal of its effects on health outcomes—even if they could agree on a definition of it. We sometimes support policies that do not have low cost-to-benefit ratios, such as providing expensive medical interventions to persons with relatively poor prospects of survival on grounds that they would otherwise die or be severely harmed as in the case of drug cocktails for persons with AIDS that can often cost $60,000 per year. In some cases, preoccupation with advancing the nation's well-being can lead us to flawed positions. In the infamous Tuskegee experiment, for example, African American men with syphilis were not treated deliberately so that researchers could study the unchecked course of the disease and increase their knowledge of the disease. While the researchers supported their work on grounds that it might reveal useful information about syphilis, they were correctly criticized by many persons for violating norms of honesty and putting the men's lives and well-being at risk.

Both utilitarians and first-principle ethicists are, in turn, criticized by *relativists* (sometimes called *intuitivists*), who contend that most people make ethical choices not through an extended process of reasoning, but through norms they derive from their culture.[17] When people in our colonial period placed wrongdoers on public display, they accepted a widely held norm that this punishment was morally acceptable. Some relativists also contend that ethical choices are often shaped by self-interest. When Congress debates health policy, for example, such groups as the American Medical Association, the American Hospital Association, and the American Association of Retired Persons often support policy options that will benefit the members of their associations. It seems at first glance that choices based on self-interest must be morally flawed. In fact, however, moral people often couple their personal interests with ethical choices. Take the case of social workers who support expanded funding for mental health programs. While they take this position partly to advance the well-being of persons with mental conditions, they also realize that enhanced funding would provide employment for more social workers. Likewise, advocates for specific populations, such as women, African Americans, or Latinos, try to advance the collective interests of these groups. If we contend that all self-interested choices are immoral, we wrongly call into question an array of meritorious policies.[18]

Yet relativists also draw criticism from other ethicists. Without any first-order principles or any consideration of consequences, ethical choices would have no basis. We could even use relativism to justify the rampant discrimination against African Americans in the South in the 1950s on the grounds that it was consonant with the culture of the region—a conclusion that would clearly be ethically erroneous.

We cannot also ignore practical matters when making ethical choices. Some choices may be ethically meritorious, but impossible to get approved by legislatures or other decision makers. In the case of health care reform in the United States, for example, a universal single-payer approach, such as that used in Canada, has considerable ethical merit on grounds of fairness and beneficence and on utilitarian grounds to the extent it improved patients' well-being, but American politicians are unlikely to enact such a plan in the near future based on their opposition to it in the past.

Toward an Eclectic Approach to Ethical Reasoning

In light of the criticisms of each of the preceding approaches to ethical reasoning, a good case can be made that we should ask a variety of questions that reflect all the philosophical stances considered here. We should consider first the principles that have a wide following in Western societies, whether derived from a reasoning process, as in the case of Rawls, or from religious sources. We should examine the likely consequences of specific choices, as suggested by utilitarians. We should realize that cultural norms as well as self-interest shape ethical choices, as argued by relativists. And we should not ignore practical considerations, such as the political feasibility of specific options.

EP 2.1.2c

Policy Advocacy Challenge 2.6

Ethical Reasoning by Frontline Social Workers

Gretchen Heidemann and Bruce Jansson, Ph.D.

Take the example of hospitals in Los Angeles "dumping" patients with no address onto the streets of Skid Row. In March 2007, 62-year-old Carol Ann Reyes was dropped off by a taxicab on the curb in the heart of downtown Los Angeles' Skid Row wearing nothing but a hospital gown. A video camera outside a rescue mission caught Ms. Reyes wandering confusedly up and down the sidewalk for several minutes before someone helped her. She had been discharged from an area hospital where she had been for three days after taking a fall. Her medical records showed that she suffered from dementia, extremely high blood pressure, and a persistent cough and fever. What she did not have was an address. Carol Ann had been sleeping in a park more than 16 miles away from the crime-ridden streets of Skid Row before she was hospitalized. Despite a California Health Code that requires all hospitals to make "appropriate arrangements for post-hospital care" and for "continuing health-care requirements" before discharging any patient, the hospital discharged Ms. Reyes without any medication or instructions for follow-up care to an area of the city with which she was completely unfamiliar. City officials alleged that as many as 150 patients were similarly "dumped" over a two-year period. More than 50 of those cases were investigated by the Los Angeles City Attorney, including that of a man who was dropped off on the streets of Skid Row barefoot, with face bandaged, and could hardly walk. One of the hospitals involved agreed to a $1 million settlement for dumping a paraplegic man. Another made a $1.5 million settlement for dumping a 32-year-old man suffering from paranoid delusions. Two other hospitals were given stiff fines and required to develop protocols for discharging homeless patients to ensure their dignity and continuum of care. Attorneys representing the hospital repeatedly denied guilt and asserted that the actions did not amount to "dumping."

Had you seen these practices, which clearly reflected informal and formal policies of Los Angeles area hospitals, and alerted local authorities, you would have engaged in policy advocacy, since you would have sought not merely to redress the conditions for specific patients, but to change the formal and informal policies of the hospitals themselves.

What ethical principles did these hospitals violate? What ethical rationale might the hospital administrators have been using to justify their actions? Discuss why many frontline hospital staff did not report ethical violations to external authorities. What would you have done?

As Box 2.1 shows, ethical reasoning forces us to consider many kinds of information when making ethical choices.[19] It requires us to integrate or synthesize this information in a process of ethical reasoning. In this process, we look for points of convergence and divergence. If deontological and utilitarian perspectives converge to suggest that a specific course of action or a specific policy choice is more meritorious than others, we can be fairly certain of our resulting decision. If these different perspectives lead us in diverging paths, that is, suggest different actions or choices, we have to devote more time and thought to seeking some resolution.

We may face an ethical dilemma when we have two or more options, each with some ethical merit.[20] We must then engage in a protracted process of ethical reasoning to decide which option, on balance, is preferable when principles, outcomes, self-interest, and practical considerations are entered into the balance. Reasonable people often come to different conclusions in such cases.

BOX **2.1**

BOX **2.1**   An Eclectic Approach to Ethical Reasoning

Some Considerations Drawn from Deontologists

- Identify ethical principles that are relevant to an ethical dilemma and decide, on balance, which choices or actions best satisfy them.
- When ethical principles conflict, that is, point to different choices, seek a compromise solution that satisfies each to some degree.

Some Considerations Drawn from Utilitarians

- Conduct research to identify the likely consequences of specific options or actions, or when data are lacking, use knowledge about human behavior to infer the likely effects of specific policies.
- Select the option or choice that will maximize the positive consequences for society or one (or more) of its subunits.

Some Considerations Drawn from Relativists

- Analyze cultural factors that shape the ethical choices of people in specific historical periods, while considering other factors, such as institutional and fiscal realities.
- Analyze how the interests of people, including ourselves, shape policy choices.

Practical Considerations

- Consider the practical implications of specific policies, such as their political feasibility and their cost, as well as administrative aspects.

Returning to Divergent Values and Ideologies

EP 2.1.2a

Many persons bring clusters of values to their policy practice that powerfully shape how they view problems and the kinds of solutions that they seek. As can be seen in Table 2.1, conservatives, libertarians, liberals, and radicals have different ethical perspectives on multiple issues. Conservatives prioritize such values as freedom (or liberty), localism in social policy, and individualism. Because conservatives also tend to believe that the private markets are relatively effective and humane in distributing societal resources, they are less inclined than liberals to favor regulations of corporations. They favor relatively low taxes, believing that citizens' resources belong to themselves. They favor diminution of federal power, preferring to transfer many federal policy roles to state and local governments. They want to increase the role of private charity in American society while reducing public expenditures. They often oppose regulations that constrain corporations, such as antipollution laws; increases in the minimum wage; work-safety regulations; and proposals to allow consumers to sue health maintenance organizations. Of course, not all conservatives are alike in their views. For example, during the presidential primaries of 2012, Newt Gingrich and Rick Santorum accused Mitt Romney of supporting many moderate policies, while Ron Paul supported libertarian policies. So-called moderate Republicans often want relatively more public spending, more government regulations, and less military spending than more conservative

TABLE 2.1   Comparison of Different Ideologies

	CONSERVATIVES	LIBERTARIANS	LIBERALS	RADICALS
Views of federal government	Negative, except in military and international policy and as source of subsidies for business	Negative	Relatively positive	Positive, unless it is under control of moneyed interests
Views of state and local government	Relatively positive	Negative	Divided, but federal government is often preferred	Less positive than views of federal government
Views of causes of social problems	Emphasis on personal and cultural factors	Unclear	More emphasis than conservatives on environmental factors	Environmental factors generated by moneyed interests
Views of capitalism	Positive	Positive	Positive, but regulations are favored	Negative, unless workers are empowered
Views of human nature	Relatively optimistic about affluent people, less optimistic about poor people	Favor policies that maximize the liberty of all people	Relatively optimistic about poor people but less optimistic about rich people	Pessimistic about moneyed interests but optimistic about other people
Views of safety net	Want relatively meager safety net	Unclear	Want relatively generous safety net	Favor generous safety net
Attitudes toward abortion and other moral issues	Divided, but a significant faction favors government controls	Dislike government regulation of social matters	Usually oppose restrictions on abortion but favor restrictions on drugs	Often oppose restriction of social matters
Core value	Liberty, though some government incentives and regulations are favored	Liberty	Liberty, but social justice is also important	Social justice
Views of non-governmental and govern-mental programs	Favor nongovernmental initiatives	Favor nongovernmental initiatives	Favor a mixture of both	Favor governmental programs, but often recom-mend worker or citizen inclusion in government decisions
Views of sub-groups that lag behind others in economic status or that experience discrimination	Tend to deny their existence or minimize discrimination	Unclear	Favor some redistribution and strong civil rights	Emphasize oppression of vulnerable populations and seek major corrective action

Republicans. Those drawn from fundamentalist churches often take positions on so-called social issues (such as abortion and regulations regarding pornographic literature) that differ from other Republicans.

One need only contrast the positions of Ronald Reagan, Newt Gingrich, and George W. Bush with those of Bill Clinton, Jesse Jackson, and Barack Obama to see that significant ideological differences exist between conservatives and liberals (see Table 2.1). Liberals place somewhat greater emphasis on social justice than conservatives, favoring slightly more redistribution of resources to low-income persons. They have traditionally been in the forefront of efforts to secure social reforms that require greater expenditure of government resources or expansion of government regulations, even when these efforts require higher taxes. They are somewhat more critical of private markets in distributing resources or advancing other goals, making them more likely than conservatives to favor a minimum or living wage, work-safety regulations, antipollution measures, and proposals that would allow consumers to sue health maintenance organizations. Liberals have traditionally been somewhat less suspicious of the government than conservatives, often turning to the federal government to implement and fund an array of social programs. Even in state and local jurisdictions, liberals are more likely than conservatives to propose and support government programs. While many conservatives have favored civil rights legislation, liberals have often been even more supportive of efforts to assist persons of color, women, the disabled, and gay men and lesbians with regulations that curtail discrimination in employment and elsewhere.

Libertarians like Congressman Ron Paul emphasize liberty or freedom. They oppose, for example, the so-called War on Drugs on grounds that citizens should be able to make their own lifestyle choices. They do not favor heavy taxation of personal income, believing citizens should be able to keep most of their resources. They oppose restrictions on abortion, censorship of pornographic literature, and most other policies that restrict individuals' liberty to make basic choices for themselves.

Defining radicalism with precision is difficult in an American society that lacks a strong socialist tradition (see Table 2.1). Yet we can find many persons in American history, such as the social work leader Bertha Reynolds, who have been more insistent on equalizing wealth and power in the United States than liberals. Members of the Occupy Wall Street movement believe that capitalism, even when somewhat regulated by government, distributes wealth in an unfair manner. This, they contend, leads to disproportionate wealth by the top 1 percent of the population. Radicals favor far higher taxation of private wealth than conservatives or liberals. They want government to redistribute resources aggressively to diminish economic inequality. They sometimes favor proposals to allow workers to acquire partial or complete ownership of corporations.

Persons with different ideologies often view the world so differently that they cannot agree what causes specific social problems or how to address them.

It should be clear when discussing ideology that none of us can be wholly "objective" when discussing many policy issues. Policy solutions to complex social problems often require us to draw upon our values and ideologies. Even centrists or moderates have values that induce them to select middle points or compromise positions as compared to radicals and conservatives.

Yet social workers' policy choices should be shaped by values as defined in the NASW code of ethics. They must prevent and eliminate discrimination against any person or group and act to ensure that all persons have access to the resources, services, and opportunities they require. They must act to expand choice and opportunity for all persons with special regard for disadvantaged or oppressed persons or groups. They must advocate changes in policy and legislation to improve social conditions and promote social justice. In other words, policy advocacy is defined by the code of ethics as integral to the professional role and in ways that will assist vulnerable populations as discussed in Policy Advocacy Challenge 2.7.

We should not forget that both conservatives and liberals often do not act on their ethical maxims. They can be bought off by corporate contributions. They sometimes succumb to public opinion even when it runs counter to deeply held beliefs. As one example, members of both political parties rely heavily on campaign contributions from an array of special interests, including banks, corporations, pharmaceutical companies, and unions.

Policy Advocacy Challenge 2.7

Using Different Ideologies to Frame Issues and Taking a Position

Bruce Jansson, Ph.D.

EP 2.1.2d

EP 2.1.2b

Take any important social issue facing the United States, such as growing economic inequality, homelessness, or substance abuse. Frame conservative, libertarian, liberal, and radical approaches to it, using the differences among these ideologies found in Table 2.1.

Defend *one* of these approaches, using ethical arguments germane to social justice, and discuss in ethical terms why another approach is less preferable from a social justice point of view.

Ponder these questions.

1. Can any of us be wholly "objective" when we confront social issues that are linked to such values as social justice or fairness? Are we "unscientific" if we allow values to shape our policy positions?
2. Can we use *both* values and empirical research to develop and defend specific policy positions? How might we do this, for example, when advocating that a specific state make the pharmaceutical "cocktail" available to Medicaid enrollees for the treatment of AIDS just as more affluent persons' cocktails are often funded by the private medical insurance they receive through their employers?
3. Can you think of an important social issue in which definitive empirical evidence may be lacking, so that we must develop and defend our policy position primarily with respect to values?
4. How would you respond to someone who said, "Why study policy advocacy, much less engage in it, if we cannot be wholly 'objective'?"
5. If we *did* withdraw from policy advocacy on grounds that it is not wholly "objective," would persons with an ideology different from that of ours *also* withdraw? If they did not, what kinds of policies would be enacted by local, state, and federal governments?
6. Can we develop rules of respectful discourse where persons with different ideologies discuss issues in ways that allows them to consider different points of view?
7. Can we engage in "respectful discourse" with persons with divergent ideologies while not ceding principles embodied in NASW's Code of Ethics that was presented in Chapter One? Consider principles such as:
   a. redistributing some resources to less affluent persons through the tax code, such as by lowering tax rates of the working poor or expanding the size of the earned income tax credit
   b. enhancing opportunities for low-income persons through job-training programs and enhanced education programs
   c. giving low-income persons in-kind goods such as food stamps, medical benefits, subsidized child care, and subsidized transportation
   d. raising the minimum wage or requiring a living wage
   e. honoring the human rights of specific groups such as legalizing gay and lesbian marriages

Many liberals, fearful of alienating voters, supported President George W. Bush's $1.3 trillion tax cut in 2001 as well as other tax cuts that he proposed, even though the tax cuts depleted the Treasury excessively, causing the nation to be burdened with large debt payments for decades to come and lacking resources for important domestic and international programs.

Radicals encounter a major dilemma in the United States, as was illustrated by Ralph Nader's run for the presidency as the Green Party's candidate in 2000. The Green Party subscribed to such ethical principles as social justice more completely than the Democrats or the Republicans, wanting major new expenditures on domestic needs and favoring many measures to address poverty and disease in third-world nations. The Green Party alone wanted to cut military spending to free up additional resources for the domestic agenda. But the Green Party confronted an ethical dilemma: If its presidential candidate drew more votes from the Democratic candidate (Al Gore) than from the Republican candidate (George W. Bush), it might give the election to Bush, a self-announced conservative. Nader's decision to run for office, then, pitted his own ethical philosophy against the risk that his candidacy might inadvertently cause many policy decisions after the election that would run strongly counter to his stated values. This risk came to fruition when Bush was narrowly elected president when he probably would have lost to Gore, had Nader withdrawn or asked voters in key states to vote for Gore.

The Analytic Rationale for Policy Advocacy

EP 2.1.6b

We have already discussed how utilitarians emphasize the role of research in shaping policy choices. We can now amplify this argument by presenting an analytic rationale for policy advocacy. In this view, advocates should support the policies that are supported by social science and medical research as well as research by economists (see Policy Advocacy Challenge 2.8). We often use the words "evidence-based practices" or "evidence-based policies" to describe policies buttressed by scientific findings.

Take the case of schizophrenia and the remarkable transformation that has occurred during the past 40 years in its treatment and in other mental health policies. It was widely believed in the 1950s that schizophrenia was caused by the controlling or coercive behaviors of the mothers of people with schizophrenia and that the well-being of people with schizophrenia required them to be institutionalized for long periods, sometimes even for life, because they could not deal with the stresses of society. These two beliefs, held by legions of competent social workers, psychologists, and psychiatrists, led to treatments and policies that are hardly comprehensible to contemporary clinicians. Clinicians not only verbally chastised the mothers of people with schizophrenia for their controlling behavior but also often advocated severing all ties between children and their mothers. Tens of thousands of people with schizophrenia were kept in the "chronic wards" of state mental institutions for decades, carefully segregated from the patients on "acute wards."[21]

A plethora of research after the 1960s suggested that these policies were misdirected and harmful to people with schizophrenia. Considerable research suggested that schizophrenia is a complex phenomenon that is not caused primarily (or, in some cases, at all) by mothers' behavior. If the mothers' behavior was its primary cause, why did many people with schizophrenia have siblings with no evidence of the malady? Considerable research implicated biological causes, suggesting that schizophrenia is a disease with genetic and physiological causes. Other research called into question the assumption that people with schizophrenia require institutionalization.[22]

Policy Advocacy Challenge 2.8

Using Evidence-Based Policies in Policy Advocacy

Bruce Jansson, Ph.D.

The quest for evidence-based policies, as well as practice, is nowhere more pronounced than in medicine. It has, in fact, become a "bandwagon" as many persons have sought to ground practice and policy in scientific evidence.[1]

Take the example of asthma, which has become an epidemic among low-income African American and Latino children in urban communities. Considerable research has identified best practices for treating this disease and for identifying some community factors that contribute to its incidence.

At the practice level, advocates want physicians to use new techniques for treating asthmatic children based on scientific research. At the policy level, advocates want major efforts to clean up the air in low-income areas, to get schools to do early case finding and hire nurses, and to develop outreach programs to teach parents how best to care for asthmatic children. They want early detection services for these children to lower rates of hospitalization.

Yet even in the case of asthma, only about 68 percent of physicians follow evidence-based practice guidelines, and this rate is even higher than an adherence rate of only 54.5 percent for practice guidelines for some other diseases. Many low-income urban populations continue to live, moreover, in relatively polluted areas, leading to higher rates of asthma among them, and many of them do not receive adequate assistance from schools or outreach projects.

Evidence suggests, moreover, that the United States continues not to enact many other policies in health care that would save lives and money. By not providing health insurance to about 46 million Americans, for example, the United States discourages many persons from seeking services early in the development of illnesses and only moved toward expanding coverage massively when President Barack Obama and his allies enacted the Patient Protection and Affordable Care Act of 2010 as amended by Congress.

Resistance to evidence-based medicine stems from many sources at both practice and policy levels. At the practice level, opponents fear that it will make providers treat all patients the same rather than using best clinical judgments. Practitioners are often victims to inertia and tradition. At the policy level, opponents oppose evidence-based policies because they are expensive, challenge corporate interests, or conflict with their ideological beliefs. Many conservatives opposed a proposed policy that the federal government distributes sterilized needles to drug addicts, for example, even though extensive research demonstrated that this policy would greatly reduce the transmission of AIDS and other diseases particularly among low-income African American and Latino populations.

Yet many evidence-based guidelines for practice and policy have been enacted. Many states require riders of motorcycles and drivers of automobiles to use helmets or seat belts, policies that have saved thousands of lives and countless injuries. Policies requiring food labeling have allowed consumers to improve their diets, and those that prohibit smoking in public places have reduced rates of lung cancer from secondary smoke. The government now allows distribution of sterilized needles to drug users. All these policies were obtained by the determined efforts of policy advocates who often had to battle corporations as well as opponents of government regulations.

See if you can identify an evidence-based policy that the United States, or specific states or localities, has not enacted? Why was it not enacted? Now identify an evidence-based policy that has been enacted. Why was it enacted? How do you account for the difference?

---

[1]For discussion of evidence-based medicine, see Stefan Timmermans and Aaron Mauck, "The Promises and Pitfalls of Evidence-Based Medicine," *Health Affairs* 24 (2005): 18–28; and A. Geligins et al., "Evidence, Pitfalls, and Technological Change," *Health Affairs* 24 (2005): 29–40.

While research strongly suggested that the long-term incarceration of people with schizophrenia was unnecessary, harmful, and wasteful, it did not demonstrate the kinds of care and supports they should receive in the community. Did they need intensive care or merely occasional contacts with clinicians? What kinds of therapy and medication would be most useful? In light of the reluctance of politicians to fund outpatient services, many people with schizophrenia also lacked access to any supportive services. Some of them became homeless, living on the streets, in shelters, or in low-cost housing—often in unsafe neighborhoods where they were exposed to crime and violence. Some moved in with relatives or spouses in community settings.[23] In the coming years, research findings should reveal the kinds of services and living arrangements that are helpful to schizophrenic persons, but even these will come to naught if policies and funding do not allow or implement them. Research needs, then, to be coupled with policy advocacy to make a difference in the lives of vulnerable populations.

Choosing Sides: Controversy and Research

We should remember, too, that researchers often disagree about specific issues. In such cases, policy advocates must decide which researcher's data and conclusions are most meritorious and must become advocates for those policies that rest on them rather than on nonmeritorious research.

The available research on social inequality provides an excellent example of conflicting research. Take the conflicting findings of two sets of researchers: Richard Herrnstein and Charles Murray's research was reported in *The Bell Curve: Intelligence and Class Structure in American Life*; and the findings of Claude Fischer, Michael Hout, et al. were reported in *Inequality by Design: Cracking the Bell Curve Myth*.[24] Both sets of researchers agree that American society is unequal and that African Americans are found disproportionately in the poorest classes, but they reach different conclusions about the reasons why African Americans are disproportionately poorer than whites.

Publishing *The Bell Curve* in 1994, Herrnstein and Murray began their analysis by contending that scores on intelligence tests form a bell-shaped curve with a few people at the lower and upper ends, and most people falling in the middle. Drawing on data from a large national survey of 10,000 Americans who were followed from 1980 onward, they asserted that intelligence scores (as measured by the Armed Forces Qualifying Test [AFQT]) are strongly associated with life outcomes. Examining white non-Latinos, they contended that people with low IQ scores are more likely than those with high scores to be poor, high school dropouts, unemployed, unmarried, unwed mothers, or welfare recipients; neglectful mothers; and criminals. When comparing the effects of social class and intelligence, they concluded that intelligence scores were better predictors of life outcomes. Herrnstein and Murray then turned to their controversial assertions about connections among race, intelligence, and life outcomes. African Americans, they asserted, score, on average, 15 points lower than whites on intelligence tests, and they attributed African Americans' higher rates of poverty, school dropouts, unemployment, single parent–headed families, use of welfare, and criminality to these lower intelligence scores.

The Bell Curve caused an immediate sensation, not just because it alleged that race and intelligence are associated, but because the authors contended that government can have little influence on social problems. If social problems are caused by personal factors such as intelligence, and if intelligence is both unchanging and caused by genetic factors, then society cannot assume a major role in reducing poverty, curtailing school dropouts, or decreasing the use of welfare. Nor should society use affirmative action, since it contributes to the problem by stereotyping African Americans and reducing their self-esteem as well as placing people in jobs for which they lack the needed skills and intelligence. These authors ended their book with the pessimistic conclusion that vast inequalities are inevitable, since they are caused primarily by differences in intelligence that cannot be influenced substantially by social remedies.

Claude Fischer and many of his sociology colleagues at the University of California at Berkeley (hereafter called the *Berkeley sociologists*) reexamined Herrnstein and Murray's data. The Berkeley sociologists had been perturbed by rising inequality in the United States, such as the marked increases in per capita income for the top 20 percent of the population compared with both the middle 60 percent and the bottom 20 percent from 1959 to 1989. They doubted that inequality is inevitable, pointing to smaller rates of inequality in other industrialized nations. And they doubted that inequality is caused primarily by personal characteristics such as intelligence, believing that persons' "social milieux" (family, neighborhood, school, and community) powerfully shape their economic destinies. These sociologists, then, suspected that inequality, rather than stemming from innate characteristics, is primarily a "social construction" that stems from specific policy choices of American society compared with those of societies with lower levels of inequality. Why otherwise, they argue, would societies with the same or similar "genetic stocks," such as the United States, Canada, England, and Sweden, vary so much in their levels of inequality? And why would levels of inequality shift over time within a single country if individual characteristics such as intelligence remain relatively constant?

The Berkeley sociologists used two major strategies: They analyzed the statistical procedures used by Herrnstein and Murray, and they asked fundamental questions about Herrnstein and Murray's assumptions, such as those concerning intelligence tests and the relative effects of individual talent and social environment on life outcomes. The Berkeley sociologists began their analysis by noting that even Herrnstein and Murray had conceded that only 5 to 10 percent of the differences in life outcomes among their survey members had been caused by their intelligence scores, meaning that 90 to 95 percent of these differences had been caused by other factors. Put differently, even if all adults had identical intelligence scores, the inequality of household incomes would decrease only by 10 percent. Intelligence scores assume only a modest role in shaping life outcomes—hardly the huge role suggested by Herrnstein and Murray.

The Berkeley sociologists contended that the effects of intelligence scores on life outcomes are even more modest, if intelligence is scrutinized more carefully, and scores on the AFQT are powerfully shaped by people's social environment, such as what they have been taught in high school, as well as by their response to the test itself (how seriously they take it and how hard they try). Moreover, people's success in employment is determined by many factors that have no relation to intelligence scores, such as creativity, persistence, and social skills. Indeed, when the Berkeley sociologists reanalyzed the data from the survey used by Herrnstein and Murray, they found that AFQT scores in 1980 did not accurately predict how the subjects had fared 10 years later in employment markets.

EP 2.1.6a

The Berkeley sociologists also concluded that African Americans' lower scores on the AFQT did not suggest genetic causation. "Subordinate ethnic minorities" have often done more poorly in schools and on tests than dominant groups, "whether ... Eastern European Jews in 1910 in New York, the Irish in England, Koreans in Japan, or Afrikaaners in South Africa."[25] This historical perspective strongly suggests, they contended, that "it is not low intelligence that leads to inferior status; it is that inferior status leads to low intelligence test scores."[26]

If intelligence scores do not have a great effect on inequality—or on other life outcomes, such as criminality and welfare use—what factors do? The Berkeley sociologists discovered that a host of factors totally ignored by Herrnstein and Murray had significantly affected the life outcomes of the survey members, such as being female, unmarried, and a parent. Other factors associated with poverty included the attributes of persons' communities (such as the region of the country and the extent to which their communities were impoverished and had high dropout rates from high school), the number of years of schooling, and the academic track in high school. When these factors were included in the statistical analysis, and the technical errors made by Herrnstein and Murray were corrected, the Berkeley sociologists discovered that the AFQT scores had been eclipsed in explaining life outcomes by the combined effects of other community, economic, and social factors, including the survey members' likelihood of having out-of-wedlock births and of being incarcerated, on welfare, and divorced. They concluded that if all adults had the same family origins and environments (but still had different AFQT scores), inequality of household incomes would decrease by a whopping 37 percent. In short, the combined effects of familial and environmental factors, not AFQT scores, powerfully shape life outcomes. Moreover, AFQT scores are themselves profoundly shaped by community and familial factors, a fact suggesting that they are not intrinsic in one's nature but are artifacts of the social environment.

But the Berkeley sociologists were not merely content to criticize the statistical analysis of *The Bell Curve*. Moving beyond the survey findings of Herrnstein and Murray, they examined an array of social policies that influence income distribution. Some economic factors, such as the replacement of unionized and well-paying positions by service jobs in fast-food restaurants and other settings, had caused an economic deterioration in the wages of persons with high school or less education at the same time that the income of college graduates had increased.

These background economic factors, moreover, were supplemented by an array of American social policies that had also increased economic inequality during the previous 25 years. The Berkeley sociologists identified a system of inequality in the United States through "rules and rewards of the game" that had favored affluent persons, including the following: corporate decisions to pay well-educated and higher-level workers far more than less-educated and lower-level workers, reductions in the income tax rates for affluent Americans, while the tax rates for less affluent Americans were raised or stayed the same, lack of public funding for child care (whose cost seriously depleted the incomes of less affluent Americans), affluent Americans' mortgage-interest tax deductions, linking health insurance to employment rather than providing national health insurance available to all Americans, and heavy subsidies to higher-education institutions that were used primarily by affluent Americans' children. Although Americans had progressed extraordinarily in reducing poverty among elderly citizens by expanding Social Security and Medicare, they had constructed policies that had kept 20 percent of American children in poverty, compared with 9 percent of Canadian and Australian children; 7 percent of British children; and even smaller percentages of French, West German, and Swedish children. Americans had also exacerbated inequality by educational policies in secondary schools, such as having shorter school years than many other nations and tracking children from less affluent families away from college preparatory classes.

The Berkeley sociologists reexamination of the data used in *The Bell Curve*, as well as their use of findings from other social science research, suggests a causal framework radically different from that used by Herrnstein and Murray. In Herrnstein and Murray's model (see Figure 2.1), intelligence is strongly associated both with economic inequality (poverty and unemployment) and with such social problems as out-of-wedlock births, incarceration, divorce, injury, and idleness.[27] In the Berkeley sociologists' model (see Figure 2.2), "cognitive skills" (they used this term rather than intelligence) are

FIGURE 2.1 Herrnstein and Murray's Model

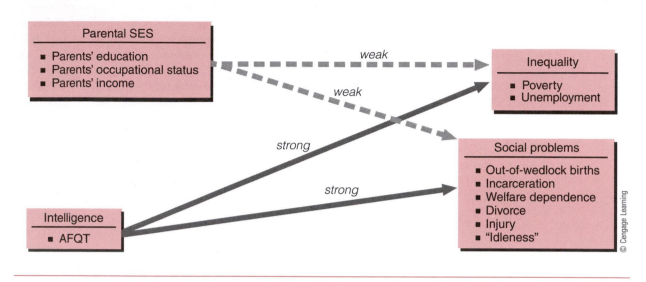

FIGURE 2.2 The Berkeley Sociologists' Model

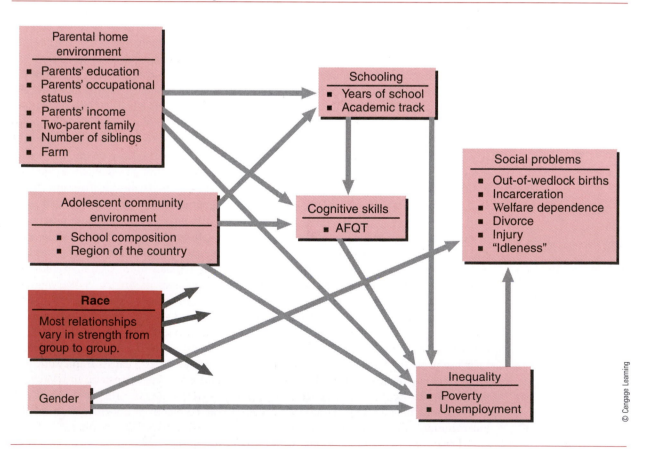

caused by an array of environmental factors, such as the parental home environment and the adolescent community environment.[28] Although cognitive skills are associated with inequality, they share this distinction with many other factors, so their effects on inequality are diminished. Indeed, their association with inequality stems partly from their association with other variables that are also associated with inequality, such as the parental home environment and the adolescent community environment. But cognitive skills are not associated with social problems, as alleged by Herrnstein and Murray, and race bears no significant relationship to cognitive skills, inequality, or social problems.

Our discussion of these two research studies suggests that policy advocates must proceed carefully when basing their actions on empirical findings. Research can be misleading, simplistic, or erroneous for a variety of reasons and, as this example suggests, must be used with caution. Researchers may make technical errors in their collection and analysis of data, they may overestimate the effects of certain variables because they have excluded other factors they ought to have considered, or they may misinterpret their data. Researchers' ideology may shape not only their research, but also their policy conclusions.

When research findings conflict or when they believe research is faulty, policy advocates should engage in policy debates about them. They should take sides, stating why they believe certain research and research findings are preferable to other research and research findings.

The Political Rationale for Policy Advocacy

Policy choices that advance fairness and social justice in American society do not frequently receive a fair hearing because the political system is rigged against poor, oppressed, and powerless groups. Powerful interest groups, whether liquor interests, the National Rifle Association, pharmaceutical companies, or the U.S. Chamber of Commerce, often wish to sustain the status quo or even to roll back social reforms. Politicians who are pledged to restrict the role of government in American affairs, even when social programs and regulations are needed to redistribute wealth and to protect oppressed groups, often control pivotal offices or possess a majority in legislative chambers. Special interests and wealthy individuals usually provide the bulk of campaign funds for the legislators of both political parties and often receive policy concessions in return for their contributions. The Supreme Court opened the door to unrestricted financing of the political campaigns with ruling in *Citizens United v. Federal Election Commission* in 2010 that allowed corporations, rich persons, and unions to create super political action committees (PACs) that would give relatively unrestricted funds to the campaigns of specific politicians. These "Super PACs" provided massive resources to specific Republican presidential candidates in primaries in 2012, as well as the campaigns of the presidential nominees of both parties.

EP 2.1.4a

American politics often favor monied interests, moreover, because many low income persons do not vote—a group so large that it could aptly be called the party of nonvoters.

If Americans who favor social justice or fairness fail to participate in the political process, they risk increasing the extent to which the political process is skewed against social reforms. One thing is certain: Persons opposed to social justice, such as some conservatives, love the political vacuum created when other people do not participate in the political process. Such defections merely allow them to realize their policy preferences more easily. Indeed, nonparticipation is a vote for the values of those who do participate, including more affluent members of society who vote at far higher rates than low-income persons or persons with relatively progressive viewpoints such as many youth.

Some critics of a political rationale for policy advocacy contend that self-interested activity is unethical, but this is not necessarily true. When social workers seek licensing laws, which now exist in all states, for example, they want (among other things) access to reimbursements from insurance companies and Medicare. When they try to make certain positions in public agencies classified (i.e., reserved for people with social work degrees), they seek to exclude other persons from these positions because they believe that social work education enhances the help available to vulnerable populations. To gauge the ethical merits of self-interested activity, we have to ask why people are seeking resources or power and how they plan to use their gains.

As Salcido and Seck argue, however, those who act only out of self-interest are morally derelict.[29] Legendary activists, such as Martin Luther King, Jr., risked their lives and ultimately lost them to advance social justice and fairness. Despite probable bad publicity, professionals should take positions on unpopular issues, such as the economic and social needs of women on welfare; the plight of prisoners on death row; the economic needs of persons in poverty; and the human rights of women, gays, lesbians, and children. Disturbingly, Salcido and Seck found evidence that some chapters of NASW engaged only in licensing issues and ignored broader issues.

Social workers need to engage in policy practice precisely because they often bring distinctive viewpoints into the policy-making process. An example is found in the comments (made during a personal conversation with the author) of Maurice Bisheff, who ran simulation games in the professional schools of the University of Southern California. He compared the tactics of business school and social work students in a simulation game known as End of the Line, in which the participants assume the role of elderly people with limited resources, such as money and food, symbolized by paper clips; players "die" when they lose their stock of paper clips. Students in the business school usually created a win-lose situation that led to a few winners and many losers. Social workers, by contrast, often invited destitute players to join supportive groups that shared their dwindling supplies of paper clips. The social workers defined the game in win-win terms that emphasized cooperative rather than competitive strategies.

Bisheff's observations may suggest that social workers are somewhat more likely to identify with the underdogs, the downtrodden, and the oppressed.

The Electoral Rationale for Policy Advocacy

We have discussed the need for participation in the political process to obtain specific reforms on grounds that, if we do not, other groups will dominate policy making. This is not sufficient, however, because we will not gain support for measures that we favor if sympathetic legislators are not included in legislative bodies. The political party that obtains a majority of the members of a legislative chamber gets an extraordinary advantage in shaping the legislation that is enacted by that chamber. It not only gets the majority of votes in that chamber, but also controls the chairs of all of its legislative committees, which allows it to determine what bills are given serious attention by the committees and when they are scheduled for votes. The political party that wins head-of-government positions such as mayoralties, governorships, and presidencies also gets a huge advantage over other parties. These heads of government appoint the heads and top staff of key government agencies, allowing them to shape how specific programs are implemented. In addition, they can use the media more easily than other politicians to publicize policies that they favor and to attack opponents' policies.

Presidents and governors appoint many of the nation's judges, which allows them to have major influence over controversial court decisions on such topics as abortion and affirmative action. Majority parties in legislatures control how boundaries of political districts are established (so-called apportionment), allowing them to gain seats for themselves by drawing lines in ways that give them an advantage in certain districts.

The ethical stakes are also high when propositions or initiatives are placed on the ballot in local and state jurisdictions. Originally intended to allow voters to bypass corrupt politicians by placing legislative proposals directly on the ballot, the proposition process has often been used by special interests and conservatives to get their policies enacted. Here, too, social workers need to participate in political campaigns to gain passage of propositions that further social justice, while working to defeat ones that do not.

Some social workers believe that electoral politics is antithetical to professionalism, viewing the development and the use of power as unethical. This view is shortsighted, however, as Jane Addams realized in the early part of this century. If persons who are committed to social justice and fairness do not engage in electoral politics, they concede electoral power to persons and parties that are not committed to these values.

Linking the Four Rationales for Policy Advocacy to Homelessness

We have discussed four reasons why social workers should become policy practitioners and policy advocates. Let us first reanalyze the many causes as well as the incidence of homelessness (see Policy Advocacy Challenge 2.9). Then let us analyze why the issue of homelessness will not be seriously remedied in the United States if many persons, including social workers, do not seek better policies through policy advocacy (see Policy Advocacy Challenge 2.10).

Policy Advocacy Challenge 2.9

Understanding the Causes of Homelessness

Gretchen Heidemann, MSW and Ph.D Candidate, USC School of Social Work

Why do more than 3 million people in one of the richest countries in the world experience homelessness each year? A common misconception is that people become homeless because of their poor personal choices or character flaws. You can probably recount having heard an average citizen step over a homeless person on the sidewalk and ask, "Why doesn't he just get a job?" or make the comment, "I'm not going to give him my money; he's just going to buy booze with it." These misconceptions about homeless persons—that they do not want to work or that they are alcohol or drug addicts—are based on little scientific evidence but are reinforced by notions put forth by the "Herrnsteins and Murrays" of this world. There is no simple explanation for why homelessness exists on such a widespread scale. However, Figure 2.3 attempts to capture the predominant causes of homelessness. Based on the best available social science research, the four main contributing factors to homelessness are poverty, an inadequate safety net, lack of affordable housing, and rising unemployment and declining wages. These factors create an overarching structure of vulnerabilities in which the poorest members of society find increasingly difficult to consistently meet the rising costs of housing. The remaining six categories address special circumstances, such as domestic violence, disasters, mental health concerns, substance abuse, lack of health care coverage, emancipation from foster care, reentry from prison, and veterans' issues, that also contribute to the problem of homelessness and create subpopulations of homeless individuals and families with unique needs and concerns.

(continued)

FIGURE 2.3 Understanding the Causes of Homelessness

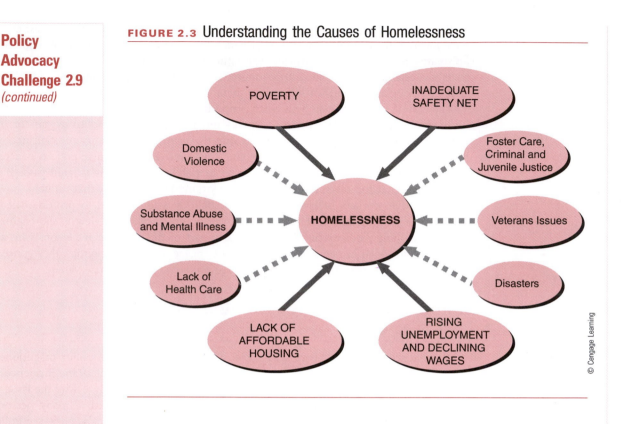

© Cengage Learning

EP 2.1.3a

POVERTY

Poverty is often cited as the leading contributor to homelessness. In 2007, 12.5 percent of the U.S. population, more than 37.3 million people, lived in poverty. Both the poverty rate and the number of poor people have increased in recent years. Since 2000, an average of about 1 million people have been added to the ranks of the poor every year.[1] Families and individuals who live in poverty are often unable to pay for basic necessities, such as housing, food, child care, health care, and education. Since housing is usually the largest of these expenses, it is often the first to be lost.

INADEQUATE SAFETY NET

Contrary to popular opinion, welfare does not provide relief from poverty. Current welfare benefits through the Temporary Assistance for Needy Families (TANF) program, even when combined with food stamps, are below the poverty level in all 50 states.[2] Proponents of the welfare reform legislation of 1996 cite the sharp decline in welfare caseloads since that time as a success. However, much of the caseload decline can be attributed to "welfare to work" programs that force recipients into temporary or part-time employment with below-poverty wages and few supports such as health insurance or child care. In addition, subsidized housing programs are so inadequate that fewer than one in four TANF families nationwide lives in public housing or receives a housing voucher.[3] Likewise, individuals

---

[1]Average annual increase in homelessness calculated utilizing statistics retrieved from the U.S. Census Bureau: www.census.gov/hhes/www/poverty/pubs-natlpov.html
[2]National Coalition for the Homeless (2008), *Why Are People Homeless?* Retrieved May 24, 2009, from www.nationalhomeless.org/factsheets/why.html
[3]National Coalition for the Homeless (2008), *Why Are People Homeless?* Retrieved May 24, 2009, from www.nationalhomeless.org/factsheets/why.html

receiving general relief (GR) and persons with disabilities receiving Supplemental Security income (SSI) frequently find that their income is far insufficient to cover their basic necessities, especially the cost of fair-market housing. Federal support for low-income housing for these struggling populations fell 49 percent from 1980 to 2003.[4] Thus the shrinking safety net, rather than lifting individuals and families out of poverty and homelessness, is actually keeping the poorest members of our national community in these vulnerable situations and contributing to the problem of homelessness.

LACK OF AFFORDABLE HOUSING

The lack of affordable housing in cities across the country, in conjunction with limited subsidized and housing assistance programs, directly contributes to homelessness. Since the 1980s, incomes have not kept pace with fair-market rent amounts, leading to a severe shortfall in available housing for the poor. The gap between the number of low-income renters and that of affordable housing units continues to grow as previously affordable units are converted to condominiums or upscale apartments. The number of single room occupancy (SRO) housing units has decreased, with a loss of over 1 million in recent decades, while the wait for a Section 8 housing voucher has increased to more than 35 months, on average, nationwide.[5] What is more, the current economic recession has seen the foreclosure of more than 1.3 million homes and rental properties, forcing many homeowners, families, and renters of foreclosed units into homelessness for the first time. Indeed, nearly two-thirds of local and state homeless coalitions say that they've seen a rise in homelessness since the foreclosure crisis began in 2007.[6]

RISING UNEMPLOYMENT AND DECLINING WAGES

The rapidly increasing unemployment rate since 2007 and stagnant or falling wages are major contributors to homelessness. More heads of households than ever before are seeking second and third jobs just to make ends meet. Even when both parents of intact families work full-time at minimum wage, their net income is often insufficient to provide for the family's basic needs. This is partially attributable to the declining real value of minimum wage (i.e., the value after adjusting for inflation). According to the Employment Policies Institute, the current real value of minimum wage ($5.85) has fallen 35 percent from what it was 40 years ago (at that time, the real minimum wage value was $8.97).[7] In addition to declining wages, the current economic recession has led to a skyrocketing unemployment rate, above 10 percent nationwide during the fall of 2009, and as high as 11 percent in California, 12 percent in Oregon, and 13 percent in Michigan.[8] When a primary wage earner loses his or her job, or is unable to meet the rising costs of housing, individuals and families often find themselves in precarious living situations, such as doubled up with extended family, in hotels or vehicles, or in shelters. Indeed, a growing segment of the homeless population, the "working homeless," includes those individuals and heads of households who are employed, but whose wages are insufficient to sustain their housing costs.

---

[4]National Low Income Housing Coalition (2001), *The Crisis in America's Housing: Confronting Myths and Promoting a Balanced Housing Policy*. Retrieved May 30, 2009, from www.nlihc.org/template/index.cfm

[5]United States Conference of Mayors, *Hunger and Homelessness Survey 2004: A Status Report on Hunger and Homelessness in America's Cities* (Washington, DC: The United States Conference of Mayors, 2004).

[6]National Coalition for the Homeless (2009), *How Many People Experience Homelessness?* Retrieved June 2, 2009, from www.nationalhomeless.org/factsheets/How_Many.html

[7]Employment Policies Institute (2009), *Minimum Wage Statistics*. Retrieved June 1, 2009, from www.epionline.org/mw_statistics_annual.cfm

[8]United States Department of Labor, Bureau of Labor Statistics (2009), *Regional and State Employment and Unemployment Summary*. Retrieved June 2, 2009, from www.bls.gov/news.release/laus.nr0.htm

(continued)

Policy Advocacy Challenge 2.9 *(continued)*

DOMESTIC VIOLENCE

Domestic violence is the immediate cause of homelessness for many women and children. Persons experiencing domestic violence, especially those who live in poverty, are often forced to choose between the abusive relationships and homelessness. According to the National Coalition Against Domestic Violence, approximately one-third of all women and children experiencing homelessness nationwide are fleeing domestic violence, and an astounding 92 percent of homeless women have experienced severe physical or sexual assault at some point in their lifetime.[9]

LACK OF HEALTH CARE

It is often said that those living in poverty are one paycheck or one illness away becoming homeless. The number of uninsured people in the United States has risen to an all-time high of 47 million or 15.8 percent of the population.[10] Fewer and fewer employers are offering health insurance plans to their workers, forcing individuals and families into a downward spiral in the event of an illness or injury. Lack of health coverage forces many to rely on care of last resort, such as in emergency rooms and free clinics. Lack of coverage also means diminished access to mental health care, substance abuse treatment, and specialized services for persons with disabilities, all of which can exert a tremendous strain on the family budget and contribute to an inability to cover housing expenses.

SUBSTANCE ABUSE AND MENTAL ILLNESS

Although addiction disorders and mental health concerns are not necessarily direct contributors to homelessness, when combined with poverty and lack of safe or supportive housing, an addiction or mental illness puts one at great risk for becoming homeless. The deinstitutionalization that occurred in the 1960s, followed by huge cuts to federal spending for substance abuse and mental health services during the Reagan era of the early 1980s, led tens of thousands of persons with severe and persistent mental illness to seek care in hospital emergency rooms and clinics that were unprepared to cope with their numbers. This created a "revolving door" phenomenon whereby patients found themselves cycling between jails and prisons, the streets, and hospital psychiatric clinics, unable to find stable, long-term care or housing.

THE FOSTER CARE, CRIMINAL JUSTICE, AND JUVENILE JUSTICE SYSTEMS

Increasingly, emancipated foster youth and former prisoners are joining the ranks of the homeless due to poor discharge planning procedures and policies that hinder their reintegration into the community. Every year more than 25,000 youth age out of the foster care system. Without a home, and often lacking family support, supervision, and other resources, these young people are at great risk for incarceration and homelessness. Indeed, 25 percent of former foster youth nationwide report having been homeless at least one night within the four years of their exit from foster care.[11] Youth and adults who are released from detention centers, jails, and prison are also at great risk for homelessness due to limited employment opportunities, difficulty obtaining housing, and the social stigma of having a criminal record. Those with drug-related charges are further denied access to public housing, welfare benefits, and financial aid for school, making reintegration virtually impossible and putting this vulnerable population at great risk for returning to the previous lifestyle and/or spiraling into homelessness.

---

[9]National Coalition Against Domestic Violence (2009), *Domestic Violence and Housing*. Retrieved May 26, 2009, from www.ncadv.org/files/Housing_.pdf
[10]Carmen DeNavas-Walt, Bernadette D. Proctor, and Cheryl Hill Lee, *Income, Poverty, and Health Insurance Coverage in the United States: 2007.* (Washington, DC: U.S. Census Bureau, 2008).
[11]Annie E. Casey Foundation, *2004 Kids Count Data Book.* (Washington, DC: Annie E. Casey Foundation, 2004).

VETERANS' ISSUES

The U.S. Department of Veterans Affairs reports that about 154,000 veterans on any given night are homeless, and an estimated one-third of all homeless adults are veterans.[12] Although homeless veterans represent service in all major combat operations from World War II to the present war in Iraq, nearly half of homeless veterans (47 percent) served in Vietnam, and one-third (33 percent) were stationed in a war zone.[13] The reasons for the high rate of homelessness among veterans are largely unknown; many cite high rates of post traumatic stress disorder and other mental health and substance abuse problems as the main contributors to homelessness among this population, while others cite a lack of family support and other social support networks. Still others maintain that veterans become homeless for the same reasons as the general homeless population; that is, due to lack of affordable housing, a living wage, health care coverage, and access to treatment for drug and alcohol abuse and mental health concerns.

NATURAL AND HUMAN-MADE DISASTERS

Hurricanes, earthquakes, fires, terrorism, and wars create immediate and large-scale human suffering. Many persons are killed or injured during disasters. Others become ill or die in their wake from exposure, lack of water, or inability to obtain medical care for injuries or illness caused by the disaster or because they cannot get health care either for injuries sustained during the disaster or for preexisting conditions. Disasters also create mid- and long-term human suffering by devastating local economies, family and social networks, housing, and local communities. Many evacuees are subjected to the trauma of long-term relocation, with its psychological stressors as well as uncertain assistance from health, mental health, housing, and other programs in their new locations. Evacuees also experience economic, health, housing, and other problems when they return to their communities in the wake of disasters. The extent of relocation and homelessness faced by residents of New Orleans in the wake of Hurricane Katrina is a case in point. The *New York Times* recently reported that the number of homeless people in New Orleans has more than doubled since Hurricane Katrina struck in 2005, while the number of shelter beds available has decreased by a third.[14] An astounding 12,000 people, or 1 in 25 residents, are homeless in New Orleans, a rate more than four times that of most U.S. cities.[15]

---

[12]United States Department of Veterans Affairs (2009), *Overview of Homelessness*. Retrieved June 2, 2009, from www1.va.gov/homeless/page.cfm?pg=1

[13]National Coalition for Homeless Veterans (2009), *Background and Statistics: Who Are Homeless Veterans?* Retrieved June 2, 2009, from www.nchv.org/background.cfm

[14]Shaila Dewan, "Resources Scarce, Homelessness Persists in New Orleans," *New York Times* (May 28, 2006).

[15]Rick Jervis, "New Orleans' Homeless Rate Swells to 1 in 25." *USA Today* (March 17, 2008).

Interlocking Rationales for Policy Advocacy

As we learned from Policy Advocacy Challenge 2.9, then, homelessness cannot be reduced in a major way if policy advocates do not secure changes along many fronts. They have to improve the safety net, secure funds for more affordable and subsidized housing, develop better mental health and substance abuse programs, help veterans transition back to civilian society and provide them with more ongoing assistance, provide more housing and services for abused women, and improve health coverage and services (see Figure 2.4).

Each of the four rationales for becoming a policy advocate is illustrated, then, by the issue of homelessness (see Policy Advocacy Challenge 2.10).

FIGURE 2.4 Four Interlocking Rationales

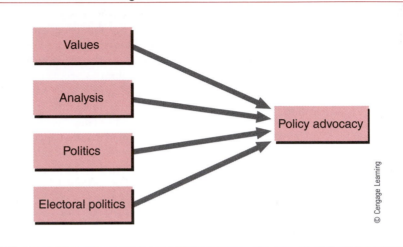

© Cengage Learning

<table>
<tr><td>

Policy Advocacy Challenge 2.10

Why We Cannot Curtail Homelessness Without Policy Advocacy

Bruce Jansson, Ph.D.

</td><td>

Develop four rationales for engaging in policy advocacy on behalf of homeless individuals in your city, region, or state. Focus on the members of a specific subpopulation of the homeless, such as women and children fleeing domestic violence, veterans, or victims of a natural disaster. Imagine what might happen if *no* policy advocacy takes place on behalf of this group.

- *Ethical rationale.* Identify specific ethical principles that suggest that policy advocates are strongly needed to address the needs of the target homeless subpopulation and to prevent future individuals from becoming homeless for the same reasons.
- *Research rationale.* Identify specific kinds of data that policy advocates might collect or obtain to make a case for improvements in housing, education and training, living wage, mental health services, addiction recovery services, or other services that would benefit the target population.
- *Political rationale.* Identify some groups that would "fill the political vacuum" if no policy advocates emerged. Select one of them and conjecture what kinds of specific policies and resource allocations they might favor as compared to policy advocates. How might their proposed policies harm the specific homeless population?
- *Electoral rationale.* Assume that *all* elected officials in Washington, DC, your state legislature, and your city council possessed conservative perspectives. Absent any opposition, what policies would they likely have sought? Does your discussion suggest the need to balance conservative legislators with legislators with different perspectives while acknowledging that moderate and liberal legislators can also develop ill-advised policies? To the extent that you believe that a mixture of legislators are needed, or that greater numbers of relatively progressive ones are needed to assist vulnerable populations, what role should policy advocates assume during specific elections?

</td></tr>
</table>

What You Can Now Do

Chapter Summary

You are now equipped with skills in ethical reasoning that are needed for policy advocacy. You can do the following:

- Discuss differences between policy-sensitive and policy-related practices and how they differ from policy practice and policy advocacy.
- Discuss Rawls's theory of social justice as it provides a rationale for working to help vulnerable populations.
- Develop an ethical position that draws together various kinds of ethical arguments.
- Present an analytic rationale for policy advocacy.
- Present a political rationale for policy advocacy.
- Discuss why policy advocates often seek to change the composition of governments and dangers that exist if they abandon the political arena and interests to others.
- Understand how to use the Web intelligently to obtain information from specific advocacy groups.

In Chapter Three, we develop a framework for policy practice that sets the stage for discussing the skills, tasks, and competencies needed by policy advocates.

Competency Notes

EP 2.1.2a   Recognize and manage personal values in a way that allows professional values to guide practice (pp. 39, 47): Social workers develop a vision of a better society.

EP 2.1.2b   Make ethical decisions by applying standards of NASW's Code of Ethics (p. 50): Social workers do not cede principles in the Code of Ethics in policy debates.

EP 2.1.2c   Tolerate ambiguity in resolving ethical conflicts (p. 45): Social workers use and combine different methods of ethical reasoning.

EP 2.1.2d   Apply strategies of ethical reasoning to arrive at principled decisions (pp. 44, 50): Social workers use ethical principles to reach ethical decisions.

EP 2.1.3a   Distinguish, appraise, and integrate multiple sources of knowledge, including research-based knowledge and practice wisdom (p. 60): Social workers use multiple sources of information and data to understand social problems.

EP 2.1.4a   Recognize the extent to which a culture's structures and values may oppress, marginalize, alienate, or create or enhance privilege and power (p. 57): Social workers understand how power differentials often lead to policies geared to the interests of powerful groups.

EP 2.1.5a   Understand forms and mechanisms of oppression and discrimination (p. 37): Social workers understand varieties of inequality.

EP 2.1.5b   Advocate for human rights and social and economic justice (p. 38): Social workers obtain and implement laws that protect members of vulnerable populations.

EP 2.1.6a   Use practice experience to inform scientific inquiry (p. 54): Social workers use their practice experience to critically analyze research findings.

EP 2.1.6b   **Use research evidence to inform practice** (p. 51): Social workers use evidence-based policies when possible.

EP 2.1.7b   **Critique and apply knowledge to understand person and environment** (p. 33): Social workers place vulnerable populations in their socio-economic environment.

EP 2.1.8a   **Analyze, formulate, and advocate for policies that advance social well-being** (p. 36): Social workers engage in policy practice in their work in their agencies.

EP 2.1.8b   **Collaborate with colleagues and clients for effective policy action** (p. 43): Social workers collaborate with advocacy groups when engaging in policy practice.

Endnotes

1. Robert Veatch, *A Theory of Medical Ethics* (New York: Basic Books, 1981).

2. For example, physicians are often implored to break down the barriers that patients encounter when seeking medical care; see Elizabeth Rosenthal, "Despite an Infusion of Public Funds, Women Find Barriers to Prenatal Care," *New York Times* (January 6, 1993), p. 6.

3. Barbara Solomon, *Black Empowerment* (New York: Columbia University Press, 1976).

4. For a discussion of how policy practitioners can help advocacy and community groups, see Kim Bobo, Jackie Kendall, and Steve Max, *Organizing for Social Change: A Manual for Activists in the 1990s* (Washington, DC: Seven Locks Press, 1991).

5. Lester Thurow, *The Zero-Sum Society* (New York: Basic Books, 1980), pp. 155–190.

6. John Rawls, *A Theory of Justice* (Cambridge: Harvard University Press, 1971), pp. 83–90, 96–100.

7. Ibid.

8. Robert Reich, *Work of Nations: Preparing Ourselves for Twenty-First Century Capitalism* (New York: Knopf, 1991), pp. 171–261.

9. Ibid.

10. Robert Bellah et al., *Habits of the Heart* (Berkeley and Los Angeles, CA: University of California Press, 1985), pp. 275–296.

11. Thurow, *The Zero-Sum Society*, pp. 155–190.

12. Paul Moore et al., *The Other Los Angeles: The Working Poor in the City in the 21st Century* (Los Angeles, CA: Los Angeles Alliance for a New Economy, 2000).

13. A defense of affirmative action is provided by John Baker, *Arguing for Equality* (London: Verso, 1987), pp. 44–51.

14. Veatch, *Medical Ethics*.

15. Various authors discuss first-order ethical principles that are applicable to social work. See Frank Loewenberg and Ralph Dolgoff, *Ethical Decisions for Social Work Practice* (Itasca, IL: Peacock, 1988); Frederic Reamer, *Ethical Dilemmas in Social Service,* 2nd ed. (New York: Columbia University Press, 1990); Frederic Reamer, *The Philosophical Foundations of Social Work* (New York: Columbia University Press, 1993); and Margaret Rhodes, *Ethical Dilemmas in Social Work Practice* (Boston, MA: Routledge & Kegan Paul, 1986).

16. The classic statement of utilitarianism is found in Jeremy Bentham, *An Introduction to the Principles of Morals and Legislation* (London: Athlone Press, 1970). For a critique of this approach, see Mackie, *Ethics,* pp. 126–134.

17. Ibid.

18. Ibid.

19. Bruce S. Jansson, *The Reluctant Welfare State,* 3rd ed. (Pacific Grove, CA: Brooks/Cole, 1997), pp. 22–23.

20. For a discussion of ethical dilemmas, see Tom Beauchamp and James Childress, *Principles of Biomedical Ethics,* 4th ed. (New York: Oxford University Press, 1994).

21. Bernard Bloom, *Community Mental Health* (Pacific Grove, CA: Brooks/Cole, 1977).

22. Erving Goffman, *Asylums: Essays on the Social Situation of Mental Patients and Other Inmates* (New York: Anchor Books, 1961).

23. Madeleine Stoner, *The Civil Rights of Homeless People* (New York: Aldine de Gruyter, 1995), pp. 79–97.

24. Claude Fischer et al., *Inequality by Design: Cracking the Bell Curve Myth* (Princeton, NJ: Princeton University Press, 1997) and Richard Herrnstein and Charles Murray, *The Bell Curve: Intelligence and Class Structure in American Life* (New York: Free Press, 1994).

25. Fischer et al., *Inequality by Design*, p. 177.

26. Ibid., p. 172.

27. Ibid., p. 73.

28. Ibid., p. 74.

29. See Ramon Salcido and Essie Seck, "Political Participation Among Social Work Chapters," *Social Work* 37 (November 1992): 563–564, for a critique of NASW chapters that focus their political activities only on issues of licensure and reimbursement.

Suggested Readings

Understanding Moral Reasoning: Utilitarian Approaches

Jeremy Bentham, *An Introduction to the Principles of Morals and Legislation* (London: Athlone Press, 1970).

Understanding Moral Reasoning: Deontological Approaches

Tom Beauchamp and James Childress, *Principles of Biomedical Ethics,* 4th ed. (New York: Oxford University Press, 1994).

Understanding Moral Reasoning: Intuitionist Approaches

Ann Fleck-Henderson, "Moral Reasoning in Social Work Practice," *Social Service Review* (June 1991): 185–202.

J. L. Mackie, *Ethics: Inventing Right and Wrong* (London: Penguin Books, 1977).

Exploring Ethical Issues That Confront Social Workers

Frank Loewenberg and Ralph Dolgoff, *Ethical Decisions for Social Work Practice,* 3rd ed. (Itasca, IL: Peacock, 1988).

Frederic Reamer, *Ethical Dilemmas in Social Service,* 2nd ed. (New York: Columbia University Press, 1990).

Margaret Rhodes, *Ethical Dilemmas in Social Work Practice* (Boston, MA: Routledge & Kegan Paul, 1986).

Exploring Ethical Issues About the Nature of the "Good Society"

John Baker, *Arguing for Equality* (London: Verso, 1987).

Robert Goodin, *Reasons for Welfare: The Political Theory of the Welfare State* (Princeton, NJ: Princeton University Press, 1988), pp. 227–359.

John Rawls, *A Theory of Justice* (Cambridge: Harvard University Press, 1971).

Frederic Reamer, *The Philosophical Foundations of Social Work* (New York: Columbia University Press, 1993).

PART

2

Surmounting Cynicism by Developing Policy-Advocacy Skills

It is easy to succumb to cynicism when we view important social problems that have festered for decades or when we understand that legislators, presidents, and other leaders are often captive to special interests or have ideologies that make them disinterested in social justice. We can surmount cynicism, however, by gaining skills, knowledge, and perspectives that allow any of us to participate effectively in policy changing work.

Chapter Three provides a framework for policy practice and policy advocacy within a political and economic context. It identifies eight policy practice tasks *and*

four policy practice skills. It provides case examples and videotaped interviews with policy advocates to demonstrate how policy can be an intervention discipline. It discusses how the development and use of power is important to policy advocacy and how analytic, interaction, and value-clarification skills are also important. By reading this chapter, you will gain a better understanding of how social workers can make policy advocacy not just as a theory-building and policy-descriptive discipline, but a practice discipline that you can use in your professional careers no matter where you work.

Obtaining Skills and Competencies for Policy Advocacy

Two Policy Predicaments

It is worth asking how policy advocacy prior to Hurricane Katrina might have better prepared New Orleans for this catastrophe. In this chapter, we provide case examples of policy advocacy in New Orleans before and after Hurricane Katrina hit the city. We also discuss how students enrolled in a master degree program in social work (MSW) in Los Angeles engaged in policy advocacy with respect to the city's huge homeless population.

LEARNING OUTCOMES

This chapter provides a general framework for policy practice in any setting—legislative, organizational, or community.

Students will explore how this framework:

1. Differentiates policy practice/advocacy from direct practice and from micro policy advocacy
2. Places policy advocacy in its contextual setting, because it never occurs in a vacuum
3. Identifies the values, ideology, interests, and goals of stakeholders in specific policy situations, including those of the policy advocates and their allies
4. Discusses patterns of participation, because an array of participants usually shape choices and outcomes
5. Identifies eight tasks that policy advocates undertake in their work
6. Identifies four skills that policy advocates should possess

Such a framework is presented in Figure 3.1, which we will now discuss and illustrate with a case example later in the chapter.

A Policy Practice Framework

The Policy Context

The framework in Figure 3.1 describes the context and tasks of policy practice and advocacy as they take place in specific agencies, communities, and legislative settings. It encourages us to ask important questions about how policy making works, both in general

FIGURE 3.1 A Systems Approach to Policy Making

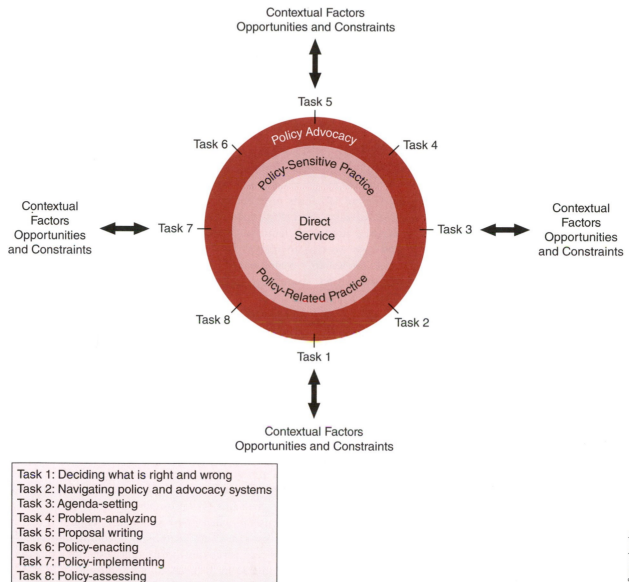

Task 1: Deciding what is right and wrong
Task 2: Navigating policy and advocacy systems
Task 3: Agenda-setting
Task 4: Problem-analyzing
Task 5: Proposal writing
Task 6: Policy-enacting
Task 7: Policy-implementing
Task 8: Policy-assessing

and in specific situations. We can ask, for example, whether political and economic forces determine the outcome of policy deliberations. In some cases, powerful interests have such clout that they can single-handedly shape the course of deliberations. Interest groups with large constituencies and many economic resources have developed extraordinary power through mass mailing, marketing, campaign underwriting, and vote-counting technology. This has been true of corporate groups such as the American Association of Automobile Dealers or those with mass membership such as the American Association of Retired

EP 2.1.9a

Persons.[1] Concerning other issues, however, powerful external interests do not exist or are locked in opposition with one another, giving policy advocates more latitude. Even when powerful interests exist, policy advocates have won noteworthy victories, such as getting national legislation that required automobile companies to install seat belts or getting states to control smoking in public places.

Contextual factors help us understand the response of public and nongovernmental officials to Hurricane Katrina's destruction after its landfall on August 29, 2005. Many factors contributed to a *positive response* in its immediate aftermath. The nation was shocked by the extent of its devastation as it viewed hours of graphic coverage on television—coverage that included floating corpses, persons shouting for assistance from rooftops, and stranded persons at the Superdome who lacked basic amenities. Stung by the negative coverage of the Federal Emergency Management Agency's (FEMA's) immediate failure to respond to the needs of citizens during and after the storm, as well as by his ill-advised and premature televised praise for the work of FEMA Director Michael Brown, President George W. Bush promised a massive reconstruction of the region with unprecedented federal resources by mid-September. (His low position in political polls, as well as partisan attacks by Democrats, also spurred him into action.) Concerned about the city and also wanting to obtain partisan advantage, Democrats lashed out at the administration for its tardy response, at FEMA for its bumbling response, and at Bush for his early inattention, stimulating Bush and fellow Republicans to propose a massive reconstruction.

Yet other contextual factors led to a marked pullback by President Bush and his party by late September in a pattern that continued through the rest of fall 2005 and into 2006. Conservatives became leery of huge expenditures and a substantial federal role in redressing Katrina's destruction. Press coverage in the week following Katrina had often emphasized looting in the storm's wake, which decreased sympathy for its victims among some segments of the population. Perhaps not fully realizing that many low-income and elderly persons lacked transportation to leave the area, some persons blamed them for some of the problems they encountered when the city flooded. When many members of the Republican Party heard the president pledge massive reconstruction at unprecedented cost and heard reports that he was considering placing it under the control of a federal agency, they influenced him to take a more cautious approach when they rebelled against him. Bush retreated from his proposal to spend as much as $250 billion on the reconstruction of New Orleans when this promise renewed attacks on the huge deficits that he had incurred as president and when many politicians demanded that he offset these expenditures with tax increases and cuts in military spending and popular programs. If Democrats had prioritized reconstruction in early fall 2005, they put more emphasis on criticizing Bush's policies in Iraq in the succeeding months.

This curious mixture of positive and negative contextual factors continued through the first term of Barack Obama's presidency, even if the balance tilted considerably toward positive factors. New Orleans became a high priority for Obama and Democrats for several reasons. More than 90 percent of African Americans voted for Obama in the presidential election of 2008—and Democrats wanted this level of support from them in the presidential election of 2012. New Orleans was a beachhead for Democrats in the South: if they could demonstrate marked successes in New Orleans, they might extend their ability to gain votes in the South in 2012 and beyond in such states as Louisiana and Georgia. Federal assistance to New Orleans markedly increased during Obama's first term, including housing programs, social service programs, and resources for community development. (The administration moved rapidly, as well, to pressure British Petroleum to fund a massive clean-up of pollution caused by the explosion at its off-shore oil rig on April 20, 2010, as well as to set aside $41 billion for costs of the spill, including payments to residents of Louisiana, Mississippi, Texas, Alabama, Georgia, and Florida who had suffered economic losses.) Progress was buoyed by the election of Democrat Mitch Landrieu as Mayor of New Orleans who replaced the prior inept Mayor, Ray Nagin, just 13 days after the BP oil spill.

Yet negative contextual factors persisted into Obama's presidency. The attention and resources of Democrats, the Congress, and the president was often diverted from New Orleans to wars in Afghanistan and Iraq. Gridlock followed the Congressional elections of 2010, which gave Republicans a majority in the House of Representatives. Bobby Jindal, a Republican governor, opposed large state commitments to New Orleans—and faced a huge state budget deficit. Landrieu had to work to correct the budget deficit of the City of New Orleans and reform a corrupt police department. Huge federal deficits, partly caused by a huge decline in federal tax revenues caused by the Great Recession that began in 2007, led to deep budget cuts of many domestic programs. Rebuilding was slowed, as well, by the many logistical challenges faced by local, state, and federal officials in a city with a depleted population, closed businesses, and high rates of crime.

This curious mixture of positive and negative contextual factors allows us to understand the *vacillating* response to Katrina evolved during the 12 months after its landfall, as well as during subsequent years. When positive factors prevailed, Congress and the president responded more affirmatively than when negative factors gained strength. Bush's resolve to develop a strong federal response to Katrina diminished as negative factors gained strength. Obama's commitment was substantial, but diminished by wars, deficits, and the gridlocked Congress. Only time would tell whether, when, and how the crisis in New Orleans would eventually be resolved.

EP 2.1.9a

Perspectives of Stakeholders and Policy Advocates

Policies are ultimately initiated, changed, or rejected by people, not by abstract forces. We can distinguish between stakeholders and policy initiators. *Stakeholders* are persons, such as the following, with a vested interest in a specific policy or issue being contested.

- Leaders and members of interest groups
- Advocacy groups that have been active in seeking policy reforms in a progressive way
- Administrators and staff of existing programs
- Legislators (and their aides) who are members, or chairs, of committees that have been active with respect to the issue or policy under consideration
- Heads of government interested in a specific policy or issue, whether they consider it politically important or they are charged with overseeing it
- Government agencies and funders who fund programs related to the policy or who monitor or regulate them
- Consumers or beneficiaries of a specific policy or issue
- Regulatory bodies or courts associated with a policy or issue, such as state departments that inspect nursing homes and child-care centers
- Professional groups associated with a program or issue, such as the National Association of Social Workers regarding licensing issues related to social work
- Associations of agencies that focus on specific issues, such as the directors of child-care centers in a particular state
- Corporate interest groups such as the U.S. Chamber of Commerce or associations representing pharmaceutical companies (in the case of health legislation)
- Heads of political parties to the extent they believe a policy or issue has political ramifications for themselves

- Leaders and members of trade unions
- Community representatives and leaders
- Agency clients

We call these persons and groups stakeholders because they have a stake in a policy or issue, either political or economic, or because they are directly affected by it. Policy advocates need to discover at the outset of policy practice who these people and groups are, because they will probably become involved when advocates try to initiate, modify, or terminate a specific policy.

Not only do policy advocates need to identify these groups, but also they need to understand the likely positions and perspectives they possess (see Policy Advocacy Challenge 3.1). Of course, stakeholders do not always act consistently. Policy advocates should be careful not to assume that past actions and perspectives always predict future ones. Sometimes conservatives support major social legislation despite their opposition to "big government," such as representatives from farm states who are strong supporters of the Supplemental Nutritional Assistance Program (SNAP, formerly the federal food stamp program).

The sheer number and variety of stakeholders varies from issue to issue. In the case of minor technical issues that affect relatively few people, only few stakeholders exist. Some minor technical changes in laws that license social workers, for example, have import primarily to social workers. In contrast, any effort to reform national health care policies in major ways is relevant to scores of stakeholder groups and hundreds of politicians, not

Policy Advocacy Challenge 3.1

Conducting Research to Support Policy Advocacy

Stephanie Davis, Research Librarian, University of Southern California, Irvine

On some levels, doing research to support policy practice is the same as doing research for a term paper. You still need to write clearly, state your arguments in a lucid and succinct manner, back up your position with other work in the same area or with statistics and other data, and cite any information that is not your idea.

However, in policy practice research, you are most likely casting a wider net in terms of the kind of information you want to find to support your case. In most cases, the term *paper research* is based mostly on finding academic research articles and books, whereas in policy practice research, your end goal is to persuade a certain group that you are right. You'll need to bring in other information such as legislation, new Congressional bills, and case studies or reports from agencies or organizations.

The following are a few research skills that will come in handy when starting your policy research:

- Know the extent of the resources in your community and make use of the expertise, such as other agencies, libraries, government departments, and educators.
- Search strategically: If you don't find the information you want at first, try searching with different keywords, in a different database, or on a different website.
- Inform yourself about your community, city, and state. This is as simple as reading a newspaper and watching the news.
- Remember that information that proves your point is just as important as information that disproves your point. You need to be aware of both.
- Familiarize yourself with the historical aspects of the problem you are trying to address in your work so that you can learn how others have approached the problem in the past and how people have been impacted by the problem.
- Evaluate the information that you find, check your facts, and cite your sources.

to mention the general public as illustrated by their involvement in the enactment of the Patient Protection and Affordable Care Act of 2010 (Affordable Care Act or the ACA).

We want to know not only which stakeholders are likely to be involved, but also the importance they bring to a policy initiative. Will the initiative be perceived in ideological terms; for example, will the stakeholders believe that it is connected to deep-seated beliefs about society and how it should operate? In the case of national health insurance, for example, conservatives and liberals brought to the table different perspectives that nearly stymied enactment of the ACA in 2010. Involvement of many stakeholders increases as they believe a policy initiative will affect their basic economic and political interests, such as taking resources from them, giving them major additional resources, or impinging on their political base of support. The American Medical Association and the American Hospital Association became key supporters of the ACA partly because Rahm Emanuel, President Obama's chief of staff, made key concessions to them that gave them augmented revenues from it. We can also ask if the policy initiative is likely to be perceived as costing a lot of money, which also raises the economic stakes to a range of persons since money is usually in short supply in legislatures and agencies. The ACA was crafted so that its costs were largely covered by specific tax increases and other revenue sources, allowing the Obama administration to argue that the nation could afford the ACA—but this contention was strongly questioned by Republicans who argued that the ACA's costs would be far higher than estimated by legislation's supporters.

If any or all of these three factors (ideology, key interests, money) are involved, we can predict high interest by a number of stakeholders. Such interest could, in turn, suggest possible conflict or, at the very least, considerable maneuvering by stakeholders as they seek resolutions that will be consonant with their ideology, interests, and available resources as was illustrated in 2009 and 2010 with respect to the ACA. The Obama administration only prevailed because Democrats had majorities in the Senate and the House in 2010 and developed clever strategy to prevent Republicans from filibustering the ACA in the Senate. They could not, however, prevent opponents of the ACA from challenging portions of it in federal courts and eventually the U.S. Supreme Court in 2012, where the Obama administration won a huge victory in June 2012 when the Court upheld the constitutionality of the ACA in a 5 to 4 decision.

Of course, the opposite is also true: Initiatives seen as not impinging on ideology, interests, or budgets will likely attract less interest and controversy. Many policy initiatives are enacted with little conflict in legislatures, communities, and agencies.

Policy initiators are persons or groups that initiate a change in existing policy. They may propose a new policy or modify or terminate an existing policy. Sometimes they are stakeholders themselves, such as a legislator or head of government who proposes new legislation. Sometimes they are advocacy groups. In rarer cases, policies are initiated by individual citizens, for example, persons who want to change existing policies because they have had bad experiences with these programs or policies. Policy initiators bring their own perspectives, values, and ideologies to the table as well as their own interests. We need to understand why they have initiated a policy proposal and whether they will invest major resources in it. Is this an issue in which they have a longstanding interest? To what extent are they connected to other stakeholders in a positive way? Do they possess the expertise and resources to be effective advocates, and do they intend to invest major resources in this initiative, such as staff time and money? How are they viewed by other stakeholders, and will these perceptions affect their likely success in obtaining collaborators and allies? Are they likely to make a credible case for the initiative, such as by drawing on available data and research?

Patterns of Participation

EP 2.1.8a

Policy initiators usually do not have the field to themselves because other people participate in policy deliberations. Some are *bystanders* who take no part in policy deliberations, and others are *policy responders* who seek to modify or change the policy proposals of the initiators. *Opposers* decide to block or modify proposals. These groups rarely remain fixed; people change groups as policy deliberations proceed. Initiators often want to expand their ranks by attracting people from other groups, just as opposers want to convert people to their position.

Issues spark different levels of conflict during policy deliberations. Some issues create a great deal of disagreement, and others are resolved with minimal conflict. Participants' actions and rhetoric reflect the level of conflict. In high conflict, people use emotion-laden language, make vigorous efforts to outmaneuver other participants, use extraordinary tactics (such as filibusters), publicize the issue through the mass media, and try to enlist others to support their position. Conflict may result in the polarization of factions and groups, such as political parties, conservatives, and liberals in legislatures; different factions in communities; or management and line staff in organizations. An absence of such conflict and alignments usually suggests consensual deliberations.

Policy deliberations often last a long time. A piece of legislation, for example, goes through subcommittees, committees, and floor debates before it is forwarded to elected officials, such as the president or the governor, for approval or veto. Policy initiatives sometimes take years to enact as their supporters work to educate others about the merits of their initiatives. Yet other issues are processed rapidly, as when heads of government place initiatives high on their agendas and successfully rally support for them. Proposals in agencies often proceed through sequences of deliberation in meetings and committees and with officials. Policy changes can be made quickly or slowly in agencies as well. Some initiatives languish for years until a new executive decides to push them. Other issues, however, are resolved rapidly, such as decisions made in agency staff meetings to modify internal policies.

The Eight Tasks of Policy Practitioners

Policy practitioners and policy advocates undertake eight tasks as we discussed in Chapter One. When *deciding what is right and wrong,* they use ethics and analysis to decide if specific policies are meritorious whether on ethical grounds or with respect to their relative effectiveness in redressing specific social problems (Task 1). If they believe that the policies lack merit, they may need to launch a policy advocacy intervention as we discussed in Chapter Two. When they decide how to *navigate policy and advocacy systems,* they decide where to focus and position their policy intervention, such as whether to seek changes at the local, state, or federal level; whether to seek changes in public policies or the policies of a specific organization; or whether to address specific social problems in international venues, such as by changing immigration policies (Task 2). We identify key venues in policy and advocacy systems in organizational, community, and government settings in Chapter Four—as well as ones in international settings in Chapter Five. In the *agenda-setting task*, practitioners gauge whether the context is favorable for a policy initiative, and they evolve early strategy to place it on policy makers' agendas (Task 3). We discuss the agenda-setting task in Chapter Six. In the *problem-analyzing task*, practitioners analyze the causes and nature of specific problems and gather information about their prevalence and geographic location (Task 4). In the *proposal-writing task*, practitioners develop solutions to specific problems (Task 5). Proposals may be relatively ambitious, such as a piece of legislation, or relatively modest,

EP 2.1.8a

such as incremental changes in existing policies. Their advocates must not only construct proposals, but defend them in private and public presentations. We discuss Tasks 4 and 5 in Chapters Seven, Eight, and Nine. In the *policy-enacting task*, practitioners try to have policies approved or enacted by using various influence and power resources, as well as strategy (Task 6). We discuss Task 6 in Chapters Ten and Eleven.

Advocates' success in legislative settings often depends upon whether they can identify sufficient numbers of elected officials who support their initiatives. Health advocates were able to secure the enactment of the ACA in 2010, for example, *only* because Democrats had majorities in both chambers of Congress. (Not a single Republican supported the ACA as enacted in 2010 in either chamber of Congress—and they would have blocked the legislation in 2011 when they had regained control of the House of Representatives in the Congressional elections of 2010.) Democrats controlled both Houses of Congress in 2009 and 2010, however, only because thousands of advocates, including many social workers, engaged in ballot-based advocacy in the presidential and Congressional elections of 2008, such as by working in specific campaigns or donating resources to specific candidates and political parties. Ballot-based advocacy is part of the policy-enacting task—and we discuss it in Chapter Twelve.

At some point, proposals are either enacted in their original or amended forms or rejected. When analyzing these outcomes, we often ask: Who won and who lost? Clear victors are those whose proposals are enacted with few changes. Sometimes, however, apparent victors have actually lost because their proposals are so diluted as to be meaningless, as Peter Bachrach and Morton Baratz noted in discussing "decisionless decisions."[2] An example of a decisionless decision is enacting a new program when no resources are available. Clear losers are those whose proposals are rejected.

Once a policy has been enacted, policy advocates undertake the policy-implementing task (Task 7). Considerable conflict may erupt during a policy's implementation as people and interest groups try to influence the priorities and directions of social programs. Members of unions, professionals, civil servants, legislators, and consumers, as well as heads of government, shape how specific policies are implemented. In other cases, specific policies are implemented with little controversy. We can anticipate considerable conflict when major provisions of the ACA are implemented in 2014 because of their sheer scope and cost, as well as high stakes for hospitals, physicians, pharmaceutical companies, and insurance companies—not to mention tens of thousands of nurses, social workers, and other health professionals. Its implementation will be greatly influenced, as well, by the outcome of the presidential and Congressional elections of 2012. We discuss the implementing task in Chapter Thirteen.

EP 2.1.6b

Policy practitioners evaluate programs when they undertake the *policy-assessing task* (Task 8). For example, researchers have assessed SNAP (formerly the food stamp program) to see if it has decreased malnutrition in specific segments of the population, evaluated the Head Start program to decide whether it enhances children's cognitive development, and analyzed the Adoption Assistance and Child Welfare Act to determine whether it has shortened children's stays in foster care. They will evaluate the ACA in coming years to ascertain whether it has lowered health costs for many Americans and provided roughly 32 million of them with health insurance in 2014. Policies that have been shown through evaluations to be effective are called evidence-based policies.

When we discuss these eight policy tasks as separate entities, we suggest that they are easily distinguishable and that they occur in the sequence depicted in Figure 3.1. In fact, advocates often engage in several of them at the same time. For example, legislators simultaneously engage in proposal-writing and policy-enacting tasks when they modify a proposal to enhance its prospects of enactment. They couple the problem-analyzing task with the proposal-writing task when they create a proposal that addresses the basic causes of a social problem or the needs of a specific group. Policy practitioners rarely accomplish the various tasks sequentially and predictably. Legislators may draft a proposal before devoting much time to analyzing the presenting problem. They may revise the proposal in response to a social scientist's comments at a legislative committee hearing. In this case, they begin with the proposal-writing task, revert to the problem-analyzing task, and then return to proposal writing. Similarly, a legislator may attempt to rally support for a vague and ill-defined proposal (the policy-enacting task), only to return to the problem-analyzing and proposal-writing tasks at a later time. This seemingly chaotic approach to policy making departs from the sequential process that some policy analysts describe, but events in the real world are often fluid.

With respect to complex policy initiative such as the ACA, many advocates engage in policy practice in different locations and with respect to different issues. Advocates in some major cities will work hard to secure the funding and implementation of health clinics funded by the ACA. Other advocates will work hard to secure the implementation of so-called insurance exchanges in specific states that allow uninsured persons to purchase health insurance at relatively low rates. Other advocates will work to defeat policy initiatives that they fear will dilute or subvert specific provisions of the ACA, such as its funding of prevention programs shown to be effective in delaying or preventing the onset of diseases like diabetes.

Our policy framework also poses interesting questions about the relationships among the phases of policy deliberations. The initial definition of an issue in deliberations (during the agenda-building and problem-analyzing tasks) often shapes people's perceptions and choices during the ensuing deliberations. With respect to the ACA, for example, President Obama and his top aides decided from the outset that they had to work *within* the framework of private insurance companies for political reasons and economic reasons. By relying heavily on them, they avoided their opposition to the ACA. By having employers foot the insurance costs of most Americans, they cut costs by having the government cover primarily persons on Medicaid and low income persons who could not afford private insurance. Critics lament that these early choices ruled out single-payer plans that many other industrialized nations possess.

Four Skills That Policy Practitioners Need

When undertaking their various tasks, policy practitioners need at least four basic skills. They need *analytic skills* to evaluate social problems and develop policy proposals, to analyze the severity of specific problems, to identify the barriers to policy implementation, and to develop strategies for assessing programs. They need *political skills* to gain and use power and to develop and implement political strategy. They need *interactional skills* to participate in task groups, such as committees and coalitions, and to persuade other people to support specific policies (see Policy Advocacy Challenge 3.2). They need *value-clarifying skills* to identify relevant ethical principles when engaging in policy practice.

Policy practice seems more complicated because it involves four skills, not one, but imagine if we argued that direct-service or administrative practice required only one skill! Although many policy theorists emphasize one or another of these skills, effective policy practitioners need all of them in many situations.

Policy Advocacy Challenge 3.2

Forming a Coalition to End Home-lessness in Guilford County, North Carolina

Gretchen Heidemann, MSW and Doctoral Candidate

EP 2.1.10a

EP 2.1.5b

In 2002, the United States Interagency Council on Homelessness issued a call to all juris-dictions (cities, counties, and states) to develop and implement a Ten Year Plan to End Homelessness. To date, more than 355 jurisdictions across the nation have developed and are implementing such plans. A task as daunting as ending homelessness requires the sus-tained effort of many players, and thus most jurisdictions have formed a coalition, public-private partnership, or task force comprised of persons from various sectors to oversee the implementation of the Ten Year Plan.

An example of a very effective coalition is the Partners Ending Homelessness in Guilford County, North Carolina, where between 1,200 and 5,000 persons are estimated to be homeless on any given night. According to K. Jehan Benton, MSW, the director of Partners Ending Homelessness, forming a coalition to plan, research, develop, implement, fund, and evaluate a Ten Year Plan to End Homelessness in Guilford County was a diffi-cult task. It involved bringing together three governmental agencies (two cities and one county) to work together despite some previous tensions, and it required breaking down barriers between service providers who often felt territorial and competitive.

Homeless Prevention Coalition of Guilford County, a group of service providers com-mitted to making a change in Guilford County, began the process. Their first step was to hire a paid consultant to help facilitate the development of the Ten Year Plan and establish a coalition. After six months of little progress, the United Way stepped in to help solidify the coalition. They secured the support of law enforcement, members of the business and faith communities, service providers, and consumers. They also gained the support of a "community champion," a local businessman who promotes the coalition and facilitates task force meetings. After eight months, the task force approved the Ten Year Plan and officially launched the partnership.

Visit Guilford County's Partners Ending Homelessness website at www.partnersending homelessness.org/, and answer the following questions:

- What specific steps did the Guilford County Task Force take to create their Ten Year Plan to End Homelessness? (You can locate this by pointing your cursor to the Ten Year Plan tab and clicking Planning Process.)
- What types of agencies, entities, and individuals are represented on the Guildford County Task Force? (You can find this by clicking the Partners tab.)
- What agencies, politicians, advocates, service providers, and other individuals or enti-ties would you pull together to form a coalition to tackle the problem of homelessness in *your* area? Who would you *not* want to involve in the coalition, and why?
- If you were to form a coalition to end homelessness in your area, who would take leadership? What sorts of working committees or action teams might you form? What roles would be assigned to these individuals and groups?
- Is your city one of the several hundred around the country that have developed a Ten Year Plan to end homelessness? If so, does a coalition or some other collaboration oversee the implementation of the plan? Perform an Internet search to see if a Ten Year Plan exists in your area.

Policy Competencies

Policy practitioners must use the four policy skills when taking concrete actions in organizational, community, or legislative settings. We call these skills *policy competencies.* We can develop these competencies only by practicing them in agency, community, and legislative settings, much as we develop skills in direct service, community organization, and administration.

Some examples that are discussed in this book are described in Table 3.1.

TABLE 3.1   Policy Competencies

Political Competencies

1. using the mass media
2. taking a personal position
3. advocating a position with a decision maker
4. seeking positions of power
5. empowering others
6. orchestrating pressure on decision makers
7. finding resources to fund advocacy projects
8. developing and using personal power resources
9. donating time/resources to an advocacy group
10. advocating for the needs of a client
11. participating in a demonstration
12. initiating litigation to change policies
13. participating in a political campaign
14. registering voters

Analytic Competencies

1. developing a proposal
2. calculating trade-offs
3. doing force field analysis
4. using social science
5. conducting a marketing study
6. using the Internet
7. working with budgets
8. finding funding sources
9. diagnosing audiences
10. designing a presentation
11. diagnosing barriers to implementation
12. developing strategy to improve implementation
13. developing political strategy
14. analyzing the context of policies and issues
15. designing policy assessments
16. selecting a policy practice style

Interactional Competencies

1. coalition building
2. making a presentation
3. building personal power
4. task group formation and maintenance
5. managing conflict

Value-Clarifying Competencies

1. identifying and using first ethical principles
2. engaging in utilitarian ethical reasoning
3. considering practical factors that influence ethical choices
4. integrating different ethical considerations in specific situations

Styles of Policy Practice

Just as different styles exist in direct-service (e.g., cognitive versus psychodynamic approaches) and community-organization practices (e.g., social action versus community development approaches), different approaches do exist in policy practice.[3] Let us contrast electoral, legislative advocacy, troubleshooting, and analytic models of policy advocacy (see Table 3.2). The *electoral style* is used when policy advocates want to get someone elected to office or when they want to initiate or contest a ballot initiative (also called a proposition). The goal is to change the composition of government by getting progressive candidates into office and defeat less progressive candidates or to get a ballot initiative enacted or defeated, depending on whether they advance such ideas as social justice. Policy advocates work with campaign organizations, political action committees (such as NASW's PACE), or political parties. They can expect a high conflict because elections and ballot initiatives are usually hotly contested. They need skills in talking with voters, framing issues, and working with campaign staff. Some policy advocates run for office themselves, as we discuss in more detail in Chapter Twelve.

TABLE 3.2 Four Styles of Policy Practice and Policy Advocacy

	BALLOT-BASED ADVOCACY	LEGISLATIVE ADVOCACY	ANALYTIC ADVOCACY	TROUBLE-SHOOTING ADVOCACY
Goal	To change the composition of governments or to get a ballot initiative enacted or defeated	To secure the enactment of, or the defeat of, specific legislative proposals	To make policy choices that are based on hard data and structured analysis	To increase the effectiveness of operating programs
Pivotal organizations to which advocates are linked	Campaign organizations, political action committees, political parties	Advocacy groups, interest groups, community agency-based organizations, professional associations	Think tanks, academic centers, government agencies, funders	Planning or oversight groups composed of insiders, outsiders, consumers, and/or others
Levels of conflict	High conflict between contending campaigns in win-lose contests	Variable conflict, but usually moderate to high conflict	Conflict between stakeholders about technical issues and interpretive issues	Usually low to moderate conflict, unless outsiders protest specific implementing policies and actions
Key skills of advocates	Developing strategy, interacting with likely voters, raising funds, media relations, using polls and focus groups	Policy analysis, lobbying, knowledge of the legislative process, building and sustaining coalitions	Research and analytic skills, obtaining and processing data, making technical presentations	Diagnosing operating programs, understanding organizational dynamics, collaborative problem solving, managing conflict

© Cengage Learning

Some policy advocates use a *legislative advocacy style* by which they hope to secure the enactment of meritorious legislation or defeat ill-conceived measures. They work with advocacy groups, community-based organizations, professional associations, and lobbyists as they try to convince legislators to adopt their measure or to defeat a measure that they dislike. Depending on the specific measure, the level of conflict can vary. (So-called hot button issues that polarize legislators by party or ideology are likely to be associated with high conflict, unlike more technical issues.) Policy advocates need skills in policy analysis, developing strategy, and working with coalitions, as well as knowledge of the legislative process and lobbying.

With an *analytic style,* policy advocates use data to develop policy proposals or evaluate how existing policies are working. They often work in or with think tanks, academic units, funders, or government agencies. They need skills in conducting research, using data, and making recommendations.

Policy advocates sometimes use a *troubleshooting* style to increase the effectiveness of operating programs or evaluate them with an eye to improving them. They need to work with planning groups that consist of members of the implementing team, sometimes mixing insiders with outside consultants, government officials, funders, or consumers. In still other cases, they work with outside groups of consumers or others who bring pressure on the staff of a program to change it. In most cases, troubleshooting involves relatively low conflict because policy advocates engage in problem solving with staff and administrators to improve the workings of a particular program. Troubleshooters need skills in diagnosing why specific programs have flawed operations or outcomes, in obtaining data to assess them, and in working collaboratively with staff and administrators.

Not everyone is skilled in each of the styles, and tensions often exist among persons who like different styles. Some policy advocates like political maneuvering and excel in it, whether the electoral or the legislative advocacy style. They are sometimes critical of the analytic style, believing that proposals, no matter how meritorious they are on technical grounds, will come to naught absent political advocacy. Persons who like to use the analytic style are sometimes critical of persons who they perceive to be excessively political since they often want policy choices to be made primarily through the use of data and research. Some troubleshooters, excelling at using collaborative planning approaches to overcome such organizational problems as turf rivalries and fragmentation, are less comfortable with high-conflict strategies sometimes used by political activists.

The astute reader can see that the different policy advocacy styles correspond to some of the eight tasks we have already discussed. Persons who use the analytic style are often most comfortable with the problem-defining, proposal-writing, and assessing tasks since these tasks often require the use of data and research. Those who use the legislative advocacy style are often most comfortable with the policy-enacting task, and persons who use the troubleshooting task are most comfortable with the policy-implementing task. The electoral style is unique because it focuses on campaigns, whether to elect candidates or to get ballot initiatives enacted. It neither aims to guide policy initiatives through the decision-making process nor troubleshoot existing programs, but to change the composition of government so that decision makers are more receptive to accepting humane policies and reforms in the implementation of social programs. Ballot initiatives, such as propositions, aim to change policy by getting voters to select policies—thus *circumventing* the regular legislative process.

In the real world, of course, the different styles are often combined in *hybrid styles* in which policy advocates combine or move between the four different styles. You cannot engage in legislative advocacy, for example, without doing at least some policy analysis, because your policy initiatives will not be credible if you use no data. You cannot be effective doing policy analysis if you are not looking ahead to political realities that your proposal will encounter when it comes before legislators. If you draft a policy that makes sense in terms of data but that has no chance of adoption by legislators, you risk spinning your wheels. Both policy analysts and legislative advocates need to anticipate issues and problems during policy implementation lest they frame and enact policies that are poorly implemented because they failed to anticipate them. All policy advocates, no matter their stylistic preferences, need to engage in ballot-based advocacy to enhance the chances that their proposals will receive a sympathetic hearing from elected public officials in local, state, and federal legislatures and offices.

Quite apart from policy styles, effective advocates need a combination of each of the four skills to be effective. Someone who relies only on good values, but does not develop and use power resources, and never uses analytic information, ought to ponder whether this narrow approach to policy practice is effective in specific agency, community, or legislative settings. Similarly, people who use only political or analytic skills risk not being effective in many situations. Policy practitioners who rely on a single skill are sometimes stereotyped: *Opportunists* rely on political skills, *do-gooders* rely on values, and *policy wonks* rely on analytic data.

Applications of Policy Tasks and Skills

When undertaking each of the eight tasks, policy advocates must often use a combination of the four skills to be successful. Do they want drastic reforms or merely modest changes in existing policies? Values arise as well when policy advocates define their motivations and loyalties. Do they identify with and seek to help certain powerless groups, the agency that employs them, or their particular work unit? Do they seek personal advancement through policy changes? Do they seek fundamental or incremental change? Policy practitioners must also determine what risks they will take in questioning existing policies, such as the loss of their jobs, in extreme cases. In addition, policy practitioners must wrestle with ethical issues related to procedural matters. Under what circumstances are deceptive, dishonest, or manipulative behaviors ethical? When is it ethical to undermine the credibility of another person or faction? When seeking support for a policy, is it ever ethical to make exaggerated claims about it? Ethical issues also arise about the substantive content of policies. For example, ethical principles are involved in involuntarily committing homeless persons with mental problems: Should laws protect homeless people's well-being or maximize their autonomy and self-determination?

Take, for example, placing a policy on the agenda of decision makers (Task 3). When they want to change existing policies, policy practitioners have to *analyze* the context to gauge whether it will support or oppose a specific policy initiative. If the situation is favorable, they may decide to proceed at once. If it is not favorable, they may devote time and effort to making the context more favorable, or they may decide to delay their policy changing work until a more propitious moment. Policy practitioners encounter analytic, political, interactional, and value-based challenges when they try to make the context more favorable.[4] Their analytic challenge is to provide technical information to convince others that the problem deserves serious attention. They can argue that a problem, such as alcoholism, has sufficiently serious effects on society to warrant attention. Policy practitioners often use trend data to suggest that a problem is becoming more serious with time, a tactic that suggests that inaction will increase the severity of the problem. They work to convince decision makers that they possess a policy or strategy that can more effectively address a social problem than existing ones.

Policy practitioners often use their analytic skills to create the impression that a crisis exists. When current data point to a problem's severity and trend data track the problem over time, decision makers are likely to believe that it demands immediate attention.[5] Policy practitioners use *political skills* to associate issues with political threats and opportunities in the minds of decision makers. Top officials in the administration of President Barack Obama targeted political advertisements toward Latinos in the presidential contest of 2012 that focused on immigration reforms, for example, to make them more likely to vote for Obama.

Policy practitioners have many ways of conveying the political importance of specific issues to decision makers. They can have discussions with important groups or funders who would like specific policy reforms in agency or legislative settings. They can imply to members of one party that members of another party may beat them to the punch if they fail to take interest in a specific issue.

Effective policy practitioners skillfully select propitious moments to inject issues into political deliberations. John Kingdon suggests that "windows of opportunity" exist when background factors are particularly favorable.[6] Perhaps a particularly scandalous condition has just been publicized, such as the neglect of someone with Alzheimer's disease. Maybe a recently elected city mayor, whose mother has Alzheimer's disease, supports funding a new initiative. Or perhaps a new research report documents the dearth of services to families of people with Alzheimer's. Alas, windows of opportunity often close quickly as the political situation changes. Democrats' desire to extend Medicare to cover prescription drugs was frustrated by the tragic destruction of New York City's Twin Towers by terrorists on September 11, 2001, which diverted Congress's attention to military issues and "homeland defense."

Policy practitioners use *interactional skills* to place issues on the agendas of decision makers. Perhaps a committee chairperson agrees to address a specific issue at a forthcoming meeting, or an agency executive decides to form a task force to examine a problem. Perhaps the aide to an influential legislator agrees to discuss an issue with a powerful member of a legislative committee so that a bill will receive preferential treatment in the committee's deliberations.

To secure a privileged position for issues, policy practitioners need to use persuasive and coalition-building competencies. In personal discussions, they need to convince others that an issue is relevant to their beliefs, that important political threats or opportunities exist, or that credible people take an interest in the issue.

Policy practitioners confront *value issues* when they seek a preferred position for a specific problem in policy deliberations. To increase the prominence of an issue, practitioners sometimes inflate figures, exaggerate a problem's negative impact on the broader society, or magnify political threats or opportunities. These tactics pose ethical questions that practitioners must consider. In other cases, they may display undue caution by avoiding relatively unpopular but important issues, thus ignoring the needs of oppressed populations.

Policy Advocacy Challenge 3.3 The Four Skills in Practice	We have discussed how policy advocates use four skills to get issues on agenda. Take any of the other tasks and discuss how policy advocates use the same four skills to undertake them. For example, how would policy advocates need four skills to analyze problems (Task 4), write proposals (Task 5), enact policies (Task 6), or implement policies (Task 7)? It may be helpful to look at Table 3.1 where specific policy competencies are presented.

Policy Advocacy Challenge 3.4

How Policy Advocacy Might Have Better Prepared New Orleans for Hurricane Katrina

Bruce Jansson, Ph.D.

EP 2.1.8a

After briefly discussing the history of hurricanes in the Gulf Coast region, we will analyze how a hypothetical aide to a member of Congress from New Orleans, whom we call Agnes Vermillion, might have used policy advocacy to better prepare her region for this impending disaster.

THE CONTEXT

A series of hurricanes had repeatedly struck the United States throughout its history, but they were particularly numerous in the 1960s and 1970s when Hurricanes Carla, Betsy, Camilla, and Agnes occurred. Nor had New Orleans been immune from them: Hurricane Betsy flooded one-half of New Orleans, for example, in 1965. Upset that relief work in these hurricanes' wake had been inadequate partly because it was spread among 100 federal agencies, state governors pressured President Jimmy Carter to establish FEMA in 1979 to coordinate federal disaster relief. But FEMA was relatively ineffectual under Presidents Ronald Reagan and George H. W. Bush, since both presidents filled its top positions with political cronies with scant expertise in natural disasters. Its inadequacies were masked, however, by the absence of major natural disasters in the 1980s.

FEMA was subjected to widespread criticism when it failed to provide timely assistance to Floridians in the wake of Hurricane Andrew in 1992. A geographically small but exceedingly savage storm, Andrew, mercifully side-stepped Miami but destroyed vast portions of such cities as Florida City and Homestead, destroying or damaging 125,000 homes. When little assistance was forthcoming, irate citizens flooded the White House with phone calls, and FEMA's bumbling response may even have contributed to the electoral defeat of George H. W. Bush, in 1992, when Republicans lost Florida to Bill Clinton.

Determined not to face a similar situation, President Clinton selected the first FEMA director (James Lee Witt) with substantial experience dealing with natural disasters. He not only energized FEMA, but also launched Project Impact to help an initial group of seven cities and eventually 250 cities prepare for natural disasters. (Tragically, New Orleans chose not to participate in Project Impact when it might have developed programs that could have softened the impact of major hurricanes for its residents.) FEMA performed admirably in the wakes of the Northridge Earthquake in Los Angeles and flooding of the lower Mississippi with Hurricane Floyd during the Clinton administration.

But the context swung in a more negative direction with the election of George W. Bush in 2000. Like his father, he also appointed political cronies to FEMA's top positions such as his campaign director, Joe Allbaugh, who quickly enacted deep cuts in its budget including ending Project Impact. FEMA was further marginalized in the wake of the destruction of the World Trade Center on September 11, 2001, when it was placed in a subordinate position in the Homeland Security Agency (HSA) and when the HSA emphasized counterterrorism over natural disasters. When Allbaugh left for the private sector, he was replaced by Michael Brown, another director with no disaster experience. Even more marginalized by the HSA and with an incompetent director, FEMA's staff became so demoralized that many of its best staff left the agency.

POLICY TASKS

Let us now return to the role of a hypothetical aide to a member of Congress from a hurricane-prone state—whom we call Agnes Vermillion—who astutely realized that her constituents would be placed in harm's way if a major hurricane struck her district in southern Louisiana. Worried as she observed the decline of FEMA during the first term of George W. Bush's presidency, she participated in a planning exercise (which they called "PAM") that FEMA organized in 2004 to simulate what would happen if a

(continued)

Category-5 hurricane (with winds as high as 170 mph) struck southern Louisiana. With technical modeling approaches developed by scientists at Louisiana State University (LSU), participants from parish, city, state, and federal agencies, as well as elected officials, received the grim news: A powerful hurricane would flood large portions of New Orleans and surrounding areas, destroy vast amounts of housing and thousands of businesses, and require massive evacuations of citizens before the hurricane struck. Not only should residents take measures to strengthen their homes and office buildings, the experts urged, but the Army Corps of Engineers should also proceed at once to fortify some levees, and officials from all levels of government, under FEMA's direction, should preposition water and food at key points in the community and develop evacuation plans and mobile "interoperable" communication systems so that each public agency from every level of government could easily communicate with one another if existing phone and communication systems were disrupted by a hurricane. An elaborate plan was constructed in which each agency promised to take specific steps.

But Vermillion soon realized that HSA officials cut funding for PAM's implementation. It wasn't difficult for her to *decide that this was wrong both for ethical and for analytic reasons.* If a large hurricane were to hit New Orleans, it would, she realized, kill and injure large numbers of persons. Nor was it difficult for her to decide *when navigating policy and advocacy systems* to focus her attention on public officials at all levels of government, since all of them would have to contribute to implementing PAM. Her challenge was *to place this issue on the agenda* of President Bush and Congress as well as state and city public officials to ensure that PAM's recommendations were implemented. To undertake this goal, she approached a senior Democratic senator from Louisiana with considerable interest in natural disasters as well as two Republican senators, respectively, from Mississippi and Texas. Working through these high-level intermediaries, Vermillion hoped to place PAM's funding on the HSA's and the president's agendas.

Vermillion *analyzed* what resources and leadership would be required to implement plans emanating from PAM. She decided that a lead staff person from FEMA, with the full backing of the HSA and the president, would have to be given the mandate to implement PAM's recommendations. Only with such high-level leadership, she decided, might differences among state, local, and federal officials be breeched so that each of them would contribute to the implementation plan. She identified the specific resources that would be needed to develop interoperable and mobile communication systems; preposition medicines, food, and water; and evacuate persons, including those who had no cars or who lacked funds to pay for lodging once they left New Orleans. She decided that community organization staff needed to be hired to link churches, synagogues, and temples into the evacuation plan to help inform persons, particularly persons not likely to read or listen to the mass media, about the need to evacuate the city if a catastrophic storm struck.

Working with the senators, she developed a legislative *proposal* for implementing PAM's recommendations with a specific budget allocation as well as a mandate to FEMA that it implement PAM's recommendations within one year. The proposal required FEMA to report back to Congress that it had implemented PAM's proposals.

Again working with the senators to secure the *enactment* of this proposal, she worked to broaden support for it by broadening the proposal to include resources for 15 cities, including New Orleans, in southern Louisiana and Mississippi as well as Texas from Galveston to the Louisiana border. (In policy practice, to modify a proposal to secure more support for it is common.) She increased resources for the proposal and now included the mandate that each of the 15 cities develop mobile interoperable communication systems, preposition supplies, and develop evacuation plans. She now included a website that would link churches, synagogues, and temples into the evolving plan as facilitators for evacuation plans. With these modifications in place, she and the three senators were able to approach three additional senators from the affected states as well as 10 members of the House of Representatives whose districts included the 15 cities. All of them agreed to cosponsor the legislation, along with the three senators, and these legislators persuaded the director of the HSA to support the legislation.

By dint of hard work, the legislation was enacted. Vermillion kept track of the legislation's implementation. She made certain that FEMA *did* appoint a public official to oversee its implementation and that it met specific implementation milestones. When the 15 cities and FEMA could not agree on which specific mobile interoperable communication device to purchase, she got the three senators to demand an emergency meeting that led to the eventual selection of a specific vendor.

Vermillion *assessed* how well the legislation was working to prepare the cities for catastrophic hurricanes at periodic points during the year when it was being implemented. As specific milestones or objectives were *not* met, she would seek remedial actions. As it became obvious that they had underestimated the difficulty of implementing specific facets of the legislation, she worked with the FEMA director of the project to find additional resources or develop new strategies.

Actual events were markedly different from this scenario. Because no one like Vermillion emerged to catalyze implementation of PAM's recommendations, they were not implemented. (Democratic Senator Mary Landrieu did make many efforts to prepare federal, state, and city authorities for a large hurricane, but she found her efforts rebuffed by the Bush administration, as well as many members of Congress who discounted the danger or were more committed to other projects. Indeed, FEMA and HSA *cut* the very resources needed to implement PAM's recommendations and did not put an official in charge of implementing them.) The tragic consequences became clear when Hurricane Katrina hit New Orleans on August 29, 2005, and lives were needlessly lost.

Yet policy advocates such as Vermillion often *do* emerge in such situations and do make a difference. To be effective advocates, they need familiarity with policy practice tasks, and they need to undertake these tasks skillfully. For example, Robert Greenstein and his staff from the Center on Budget and Policy Priorities also determined that urgent action was needed for *ethical reasons* and that *only the federal government had the resources to help citizens* in Katrina's aftermath. They engaged in *agenda building*, not only generating ideas about how to improve a variety of federal programs to make them relevant to Katrina victims, but also placing them on the agenda of public officials by sending the policy documents and talking with them in person. They even hoped that the nation would have a long-overdue debate about persistent poverty in the United States, since Katrina had exposed the depth and amount of poverty among African Americans and other Katrina victims in New Orleans. When they became alarmed by a dramatic turn in discussion of Katrina as congressional conservatives placed pressure on President Bush *not* to dramatically expand social spending and *not* to emphasize a federal role, they used the mass media to create a more favorable environment for progressive proposals.

Greenstein and his staff engaged in *problem analysis* by estimating the cost of expanding various programs such as the food stamp program and Medicaid so that they would meet the needs of Katrina survivors. They examined existing regulations to see how they might be relaxed not only for persons who lacked documents to get through current eligibility standards, but also for persons who would not meet existing standards but who had temporary need for assistance in light of the loss of their homes, property, and businesses. They estimated the costs of these specific expansions of existing programs. They engaged in the *proposal-writing task* by writing specific legislative proposals that they disseminated on their website, to the media, to legislators, and to policy staff in the White House.

Greenstein and his staff engaged in the *policy-enacting task* by lobbying key congressional staff and legislators to get these proposals enacted as well as by using the mass media. They looked forward to the *implementation task* when they insisted that the

EP 2.1.6b

(continued)

EP 2.1.8a

Department of Housing and Urban Development (HUD), rather than FEMA, should implement housing programs for Katrina's victims since they had more housing expertise and already implemented the major housing-subsidy programs of the federal government such as Section 8 housing vouchers. They engaged in the *policy assessment task* by using knowledge about the effectiveness of programs developed in the wake of prior natural disasters to help them fashion their proposals for Katrina's survivors.

USING POLICY SKILLS TO ACCOMPLISH POLICY TASKS

Vermillion would have had to use analytic, political, interactional, and value-clarifying skills to accomplish each of the eight policy-practice tasks. Let us take the example of her need to place the implementation of PAM's recommendations on the agendas of the president, the heads of HSA and FEMA, and the three senators. She needed *analytic* skills to persuade them that it was important to implement these recommendations, such as by enumerating the likely destruction of a Category-5 hurricane as described by hurricane scientists at the PAM Conference. As important, she had to convince them that it was feasible to implement PAM's recommendations in the specific time frame of one year. To do this, she went to other cities that *had* implemented similar recommendations and discovered what resources and person power that they had used. She had to help the three senators draft an initial legislative proposal that was sufficiently impressive that the 10 members of Congress would agree to cosponsor it.

She would have needed *political skills* to enlist the three senators and the 10 members of Congress in the project and to help them develop strategy to shepherd the legislative proposal through the Congress. She would have needed to work through intermediaries on occasion, such as getting a Republican senator or a member of Congress to elicit the support of the president for the project.

She would have needed *interactional skills* to develop links with key public officials, participate in meetings with them, make credible public presentations, and work with task groups charged with implementing PAM's recommendations. If senators, members of Congress, staff in the White House, aides of legislators, and FEMA and HSA officials did not like and trust her, she would have found it difficult to work with them effectively.

She would have needed *value-clarifying skills* to make difficult choices at specific points. When she decided to expand the project to include 14 cities in addition to New Orleans and to get the political support of more legislators for it, she might have wondered if this expansion would have had negative consequences for preparedness planning in New Orleans since it now had to share scarce resources with many other cities. Policy advocates often encounter such trade-offs and must ultimately make difficult value-based choices. Her decision to devote significant amounts of time to implementing PAM's recommendations would have been based on her values because it required her to give less time to competing projects. In light of the likely suffering of citizens of New Orleans if a catastrophic storm hit, and in particular its most vulnerable citizens, she might have prioritized PAM's recommendations because she had a strong commitment to social justice.

An excellent depiction of events that preceded and followed Hurricane Katrina was developed by the PBS FRONTLINE television show called *The Storm*. View this one-hour video at www.pbs.org/wgbh/pages/frontline/storm/, and discuss the following questions:

What persons engaged in policy advocacy as portrayed by the PBS video tape?

- What barriers did they confront?
- Could someone like Agnes Vermillion have made an appreciable difference in this case, or was the context so unfavorable to preventive actions that policy practice would have been relatively futile?
- Had PAM occurred when Barack Obama was president, might policy advocates have had more success in preparing the region for Hurricane Katrina?

Ballot-Based Advocacy

We have given an example of policy practice involving eight tasks and four skills. But policy practice also includes the electoral style. We will not discuss specific political campaigns since this topic will be discussed in Chapter Twelve. Suffice it to say that the eight tasks and four skills also apply to developing and managing a political campaign. A candidate often decides to run for office because he or she believes his or her opponent lacks ethical grounding to decide *what is right and wrong.* The candidate must select which office to seek as he or she *navigates policy and advocacy systems*—often selecting a specific office because he or she thinks that he or she can be successful in winning it. A candidate must decide when it is propitious to run for office in the context of background factors, his or her own track record, likely opponents, and likely assistance he or she will receive from funders and party officials (*agenda building*). He or she needs to decipher why his or her likely opponent is defeatable in the context of prior patterns of voting in the district and public opinion polls (*policy analysis*) and to make a case to contributors, volunteers, and party officials that his or her candidacy makes sense so that she stands a decent chance of winning (*proposal construction*). He or she needs to actually wage the campaign by making correct strategy choices, mustering volunteers, raising funds, and using the mass media to his or her advantage (*policy enacting and policy implementing*). Win or lose, he or she needs to *assess* his or her strategy and campaign organization so that he or she can decide whether to run again, if he or she loses, or develop strategy for the next campaign, if he or she wins.

Candidates need each of the four policy skills. They need political skills to devise strategy. They need value-clarifying skills to decide what tactics are ethical to use during the campaign, such as whether and how they would respond to (or initiate) hardball strategies such as attacking opponents' records and integrity. They need analytic skills to initiate and debate campaign issues and devise solutions to them. They need interactional skills to develop and maintain a campaign organization.

EP 2.1.5c

With the formation and expansion of PACE, the electoral style is becoming increasingly important to social workers. Tens of thousands of members of NASW now contribute to PACE in connection with their annual dues. PACE carefully screens candidates across the nation, both in local and national races, to decide which of them will receive financial assistance from NASW.

Hurricane Katrina illustrates how the work of policy advocates is made more difficult if elected officials do not prioritize policies that help vulnerable populations. Persons who believe that existing politicians, whether at city, state, or federal levels of government, are insensitive to the vulnerable citizens of New Orleans should engage in ballot-based advocacy. Some experts believe, for example, that Republicans lost the presidential election of 2008 partly because many voters had been critical of President George W. Bush's belated response to Hurricane Katrina. They can work in campaigns of specific candidates and urge PACE to support specific candidates. They can run for office themselves or encourage friends or colleagues to run for office.

The outcome of the presidential and Congressional elections of 2012 will powerfully shape the nation's social policy because it will be a classic confrontation between relatively liberal and conservative positions.

As an exercise, discuss how President Barack Obama engaged in policy-advocacy tasks and used policy-advocacy skills in the presidential campaign of 2012. How did his Republican opponent, still undecided at the time of the writing of this edition, use these tasks and skills? Which candidate was *most* skilled—and does that explain why he won the election—or were powerful background factors, like the state of the American economy, critical to the outcome? Mitt Romney.

The Variety of Policies

Social workers confront policy issues at virtually every turn. The services they provide are dictated by policies from different sources: legislatures, government agencies, courts, funders such as United Way, contracts and grants that governmental authorities use to purchase services from agencies, professional associations such as the NASW, licensing and accrediting bodies, boards of directors of agencies, and administrative staff. We argued in Chapter One, as well, that some policies emanate from the informal culture of the staff that implements policies.

We do not suggest that these policies are restrictive, because they often provide implementing staff with considerable discretion. However, in many ways, they do shape the lives and work of citizens, clients, and implementing staff alike.

These policies vary in their effects and importance. Trivial policies have little importance, such as some of the detailed policies in agencies and programs. Others, however, have considerable impact on citizens and professionals; reformers should give these policies attention when they believe them to be dysfunctional.

Policies also vary in their malleability. Some are relatively simple to change because of their source, nature, and context. Practitioners find it much easier to modify a relatively simple administrative agency policy than to change a controversial legislative policy that requires hundreds of legislators to concur.

Practitioners need not focus on a single kind of policy in their work; they can try to change simple or complex, agency or legislative, or controversial or noncontroversial policies. Our focus in this book, indeed, is on generic concepts that apply to any policy practice, no matter what the issue or the setting is.

It would be possible, of course, to study policy practice in a more specialized way by focusing on such specific settings as agencies or legislatures. We could also focus on a specific style of policy making such as the analytic style. Alternatively, we could gear our discussion of policy to a specific sector, such as child welfare policy, rather than using a range of policy examples.

However, a broader treatment of policy practice has many advantages. Concentration on a single kind of policy, for example, agency-based or legislative, would imply that that kind of policy should take precedence over other kinds. Concentration on policies that are relatively easy to change, such as some agency-based ones, would imply that social workers should not try to change more complex and controversial ones, such as legislative policies. Concentration on a single style of policy making, such as the analytic style, would imply that this style is effective in all or most situations.

A generic approach to policy practice underscores the need for flexibility. Because policy practice occurs in many kinds of settings, takes many forms, and varies with the issue and the context, we believe that it is better to understand concepts, skills, tasks, and frameworks that apply to a range of policy practice situations than it is to limit ourselves to a single style or situation.

The need for versatility in policy practice stems from the diversity of policy practices that social workers can undertake. Policy practice can occur inside agencies when advocates interact with other agency staff. Or it can take place primarily outside of agencies such as policy advocates who work with community groups, social movements, and lobbyists. Policy practice can occur in formally sanctioned or official projects, as when executives establish task forces to examine policy issues, or it can be informal, as when a direct-service worker decides to pursue an issue without the approval of higher officials. Policy practice can be planned or improvised, as when someone attends a meeting and decides on the spot to make a statement. Policy practitioners can assume affirming,

EP 2.1.5c

blocking, or bystander roles. Practice can involve an extended sequence of actions or only one or two episodes. Policy practitioners may use only one skill suited to a specific situation, or they may use several skills at once. Policy practitioners may be leaders or initiators or followers regarding a specific issue.

A generic approach to policy practice, then, sensitizes us to the wide variety of policy practice situations and actions. It does not limit policy practice to specific styles, settings, or issues. It invites us to become participants in many ways and at different points in our professional work.

This generic approach offers no quick fixes or panaceas, however. Some issues are difficult to address, and some policies are relatively intractable. Policy making does not occur on a level playing field; some people bring more power resources to the game, some can invest more time, and some have more skill than others. Policy advocates sometimes take some risks when they engage in practice, such as when employees try to change policies strongly favored by their employers. These cautionary notes should not, however, obscure the challenges and rewards associated with policy practice. Trying to change policies allows professionals to expand their boundaries and obtain the satisfaction that accompanies successful projects.

Overcoming Discomfort with Power

EP 2.1.10k

Although political skills are only one of four kinds of policy skills we have discussed in preceding chapters, they are essential to performing policy tasks. For example, people must use power resources, such as expertise and coalitions, to persuade highly placed officials to prioritize an agenda. Using power is crucial in the policy-enacting task, to help enact or block proposals. It is also integral to implementing and assessing policy as we have discussed. In addition to using power skillfully and assertively, effective policy practitioners must devote considerable time to developing power resources. They need to enhance their credibility by gaining access to networks of people who have information and power in specific settings.

Some social workers may believe that it is unethical to develop and use power or even to use it in specific situations. On further reflection, however, they should realize that all of us develop and use power in our daily lives, such as when we try to convince someone to do something, no matter how trivial it is.

All social workers use power, moreover, in their professional work. Yeheskel Hasenfeld suggests the following:

- Clinical social workers often use power.
- They interpret their clients' problems in ways that conform to the mission of their agencies and establish certain expectations about clients' roles during the helping process.
- They use sanctions and penalties for clients whose responses to services fall outside specific norms or expectations.
- They enforce (or choose not to enforce) agency procedures governing eligibility, referrals, and termination.
- They proffer comments and suggestions that steer clients toward certain actions or decisions.
- They take sides in family or other conflicts, sometimes in subtle ways.[7]

Indeed, if social workers did not use power in clinical transactions, clients would probably be disappointed. Clients expect their helpers, who presumably have considerable expertise, to guide them, offer informed suggestions, and establish realistic expectations.

As agency employees, moreover, most social workers are instructed to enforce specific policies, procedures, and protocols.

We need to demystify power and declare it a professional resource vital to both clinical work and policy practice. Like other professional skills, power needs to be observed, modeled, and practiced. (We discuss power in Chapters Ten, Eleven, and Twelve.)

We should also realize that powerless people sometimes enter a vicious circle: They are aware that they are powerless and avoid participating in policy practice, which makes them even more powerless. Social workers sometimes work in programs that receive little support from the broader society or the bureaucracies that they often must fight if they are to save programs. Moreover, most social workers are women. Rosabeth Kanter suggests that women are frequently excluded from the inner circles of power, which may erode the confidence they need to participate in policy practice.[8] This male-dominated society has also accorded background and supportive roles to women. When women and persons of color use power in ways that white males might, they are sometimes perceived as aggressive and become the targets of animosity. (We discuss in Chapter Ten how relatively powerless persons can increase their power resources.)

Social workers need, then, to see power as integral not only to their professional helping roles, but also to their policy advocacy. Moreover, social workers need to develop leadership skills so that they can initiate and assume important policy-making roles.[9] We define *policy leadership* as "taking the initiative to develop new policies and to change existing ones to improve the human condition." People who initiate policy deliberations expose themselves to some risk, but they may also receive recognition and the psychological rewards of assuming a constructive, problem-solving role. We need to perceive leadership not as a burden but, like power, as an integral part of the professional role. When social workers fail to exert policy leadership, they allow other people with less commitment to clients' well-being and to oppressed minorities' needs to shape the human services delivery system.

Social Policy's Role in Ecological Frameworks

EP 2.1.7b

The importance of policy practice has always been merely implied in ecological, or environmental, frameworks, which continue to receive prominence in the social work literature that discusses direct service and human behavior. Perhaps because the writers of this literature tend to come from the direct-service segments of the profession, they usually fail to devote sufficient attention to policy practice.[10] The logic of environmental frameworks is clear; social workers who wish to help their clients have a professional duty to try to reform those factors that cause or exacerbate their clients' problems.

As we discussed in Chapters One and Two, changing existing policies provides one strategy for helping citizens and clients. Members of vulnerable populations are subject to a variety of forces and policies (or the absence of policies) that make it difficult for them to improve their condition as compared to others. If social workers do not attempt to change these policies, they ignore key elements of the ecosystems of their clients.

EP 2.1.1b

Policy advocacy is, in short, a *professional* intervention because, like direct-service work, it is geared to improving the well-being of citizens and clients. Drawing on NASW's Code of Ethics, we also argued in Chapter Two that it is *unethical* not to engage in policy advocacy during one's career and not to support efforts by the profession to lobby policy makers and to attempt to get progressive candidates elected to office.

Policy Practice as a Unifying Theme

EP 2.1.1b

As Philip Popple suggests, it is a romantic idea to aspire to a profession that is wholly unified, when its members work in such different settings and undertake such different tasks. Indeed, he calls social work a "federated profession" that consists of various groups with different specializations and perspectives.[11] At the same time, however, if the profession lacks cohesion, it will fail to develop united positions and political clout on such important issues as licensing and funding. Moreover, social workers will lack the strong professional organizations that can influence decision makers.

Perhaps policy practice and policy advocacy can serve as one unifying theme, because it is something that all social workers do, no matter what their specialization is. It will allow social workers, singly and in groups, to shape the world to be more congruent with their values and change those policies that profoundly affect the well-being of oppressed populations. Furthermore, it will infuse social workers with the broader vision of the profession's founders, as when Jane Addams tried to persuade decision makers to enact humane policies.

What You Can Now Do

Chapter Summary

Social policy has traditionally emphasized historical, philosophical, and descriptive content, but policy advocacy and policy practice are gaining prominence in professional literature. *Policy practice* refers to the skills and strategies of those who seek to modify policies, whereas *policy advocacy* describes efforts to change policies to gain greater resources and opportunities for powerless and oppressed vulnerable populations (see Policy Advocacy Challenge 3.5).

Policy Advocacy Challenge 3.5

How MSW Students Engage in Policy Advocacy with Respect to Homelessness

Ralph Fertig, JD, MA

Clinical Professor Ralph Fertig, a former social worker, lawyer, retired federal administrative judge, and freedom rider in the civil rights movement, decided to engage the MSW students at the School of Social Work at the University of Southern California (USC) in a project to address the huge problem of homelessness in Los Angeles County. As a result of his efforts, since 2006, more than 1,000 students in Social Welfare Policy classes at the School of Social Work at USC have engaged in policy advocacy to end homelessness in Los Angeles County and beyond. A description of the course and how students successfully engaged in policy advocacy targeted at addressing the homeless crisis in the region and state is given next.

Throughout the winter of 2005–2006, students and faculty in USC's Social Welfare Policy classes met with city council members, directors of local advocacy organizations, and ministers and rabbis of prominent local churches and synagogues to develop plans for school-wide action on the issue of homelessness. At that time, a California state senator was in the process of drafting several pieces of legislation related to the problems of affordable housing and homelessness, one of which recognized "housing by right," and mandated all cities and counties throughout California to survey and develop plans to house homeless persons. One of those pieces of legislation, Assembly Bill (AB) 2634, became the centerpiece of the spring 2006 Social Welfare Policy course for more than 300 masters-level social work students.

(continued)

That spring, students mobilized support for AB 2634. Each of the 14 course sections chose a homeless subpopulation on which to focus (such as veterans, emancipated foster youth, or persistently mentally ill individuals). They developed an extensive profile of the target subpopulation by conducting research "in the streets," visiting local homeless service organizations, taking guided tours of areas such as Skid Row, and interviewing key informants. They also conducted research on relevant elected officials, such as state senators and assembly members, and arranged meetings with them. Individually and in groups, they worked toward the adoption of AB 2634 by generating support for the bill from social service, faith-based, and advocacy organizations; mobilizing support from the public at large by bringing attention to the media, circulating pamphlets about the issue, gathering signatures for a petition, and conducting town hall-style meetings; and generating support directly from elected officials by meeting with staffers, testifying before legislative bodies, and conducing a letter-writing campaign.

AB 2634 passed both houses of the CA State Legislature that spring, but was vetoed by the governor. The Social Welfare Policy instructors met in the fall of 2006 and committed to fighting on. They met again with the senator to procure his promise that he would introduce the bill again in the next legislative session. This time it would be introduced as Senate Bill (SB) 2. Having ample time to prepare for mobilization around SB 2, the course was revamped to include more sophisticated policy advocacy strategies. This time each of the 14 course sections would be assigned one state senatorial district and its two overlapping state assembly districts. Students would further be instructed to match the needs of a homeless subpopulation to the interests of their state senator or assembly member. For example, where a legislator's interest was on schools, students would document out-of-school homeless children, and where the legislator was a veteran or concerned with veterans' issues, the students would focus on studies of the homeless veteran population.

Students and instructors approached key elected officials to secure their endorsement of SB 2. They organized a conference on homelessness that filled a local temple, and where the mayor of Los Angeles and the incoming chairman of the Los Angeles County Board of Supervisors pledged their support for SB 2. When the sheriff of Los Angeles County visited the school on another matter, he was confronted by students and asked to sign a petition in support of SB 2. When a team of students welcomed the speaker of the California State Assembly to campus for another event, his vow to back SB 2 was also secured. Other public officials, state legislators, city council members, and the lieutenant governor were approached with similar results. Students followed up with the Los Angeles City Council, testifying before two committees to seek support for SB 2. By April, a unanimous city council resolution urged the state legislature and the governor to pass SB 2. Early efforts were made to work collaboratively with the California chapter of NASW to make SB 2 a focal point of the annual Lobby Days event in the state capitol, which meant that more than 800 social work students from around the state lobbied members of the California legislature in the spring of 2007 to support SB 2. The bill passed the CA State Assembly and Senate with even wider margins than AB 2634 had in the previous year. In October 2007, the governor of California signed SB 2 into law.

The obvious next step was to engage students in the implementation of the piece of legislation they had fought so hard to pass. Since SB 2 left implementation planning to local jurisdictions, meetings were held prior to the beginning of the spring 2008 semester with a number of experts from low-income housing agencies, homeless advocacy organizations, and the Los Angeles Mayor's Office to discuss best-practice policies for implementation. The uniform response was to secure an Inclusionary Zoning ordinance. A meeting with the chairman of the Los Angeles City Council's Planning and Land Use Management Committee provided an opportunity to discuss inclusionary zoning and the city's plans to implement SB 2.

The semester began with a congregate assembly of students in which a Los Angeles City Councilmember asked the class to join him in seeking the support of other Council members for his Mixed-Income Housing Ordinance. The ordinance provided that all housing developments of four or more units must include 10 to 15 percent affordable housing, offering incentives to developers to make it economically feasible. Students were assigned to city council districts and prepared testimony to deliver to their respective city councils. Although they secured the support of four of the fifteen city council members, they needed at least eight. To their disappointment, a key member of the city council stalled on the ordinance, and by the end of the semester (and still to this date), it still hadn't gone up for a vote.

Students and instructors together decided to shift their focus in the 2009 policy courses to the issue of homeless families and children. This time more than 350 students in 16 course sections focused on working with legislators to introduce legislation that would establish housing rights for homeless families and children. The students spent the semester interviewing homeless families on the streets and in shelters to document their situations, providing written testimony to the CA State Senate and Assembly on their findings, and developing "Children's Right to Housing." This 16-point resolution was presented to and endorsed by United States Congresswoman Maxine Waters in spring 2009. Representative Waters subsequently introduced House Resolution 582, Right of Children to Housing, into the 111th session of the United States Congress.

Thinking through the activities these students engaged in, and the skills they used to advocate and accomplish policy change, answer the following questions:

1. What ethical and analytic rationales did the students use to *decide that the extent and nature of homelessness is wrong (Task 1)*? In the complex American governmental system, how did they decide where to focus their interventions as they *navigated policy and advocacy systems (Task 2)*?
2. In what *agenda building, problem analyzing, proposal constructing, policy enacting, policy implementing*, and *policy assessing tasks* did the students engage in their efforts to advocate and enact policies to address the problem of homelessness (Tasks 3 through 8)?
3. What *analytical, political, interactional*, and *value-clarifying skills* did the students use in their efforts to enact policies to address the problem of homelessness?

You are now equipped to do the following:

- Diagram a policy-practice and policy-advocacy framework with a context and eight tasks.
- Discuss four policy-practice skills.
- Identify stakeholders in specific policy-advocacy situations.
- Identify four styles of policy advocacy.
- Use a case study of policy advocacy and identify policy tasks, skills, and competencies used by participants.
- Discuss why power is essential to policy advocacy.
- Discuss why policy advocacy is a *practice* discipline just as direct-service practice, administrative practice, and community organization are practice disciplines.
- Discuss why policy advocacy can be a unifying theme for the social work profession.

Policy advocates need not only a task- and skill-based framework, such as the one developed in this chapter, but also the knowledge about the way policies are developed in legislative, agency, community, and electoral situations, which we provide in Chapter Four as a prelude to discussing various policy-advocacy tasks in succeeding chapters.

Competency Notes

EPA 2.1.1b   Practice personal reflection and self-correction to assure continual professional development (pp. 92, 93): Social workers reflect on the role of the profession in seeking social justice.

EPA 2.1.5b   Advocate for human rights and social and economic justice (p. 79): Social workers use policy practice to advocate for human rights and social justice.

EPA 2.1.5c   Engage in practices that advance social and economic justice (pp. 89, 91): Social workers initiate policy practice to advance social and economic justice.

EPA 2.1.6b   Use research evidence to inform practice (pp. 77, 87): Social workers use research to identify effective policies.

EPA 2.1.7b   Critique and apply knowledge to understand person and environment (p. 92): Social workers use policy practice to help persons improve their environments.

EPA 2.1.8a   Analyze, formulate, and advocate for policies that advance social well-being (pp. 76, 77, 85, 88, 94): Social workers use a multifaceted framework and four skills to engage in policy practice.

EPA 2.1.8b   Collaborate with colleagues and clients for effective policy action (pp. 94): Social workers join with colleagues and clients when they engage in policy action.

EPA 2.1.9a   Continuously discover, appraise, and attend to changing locales, populations, scientific and technological developments, and emerging societal trends to provide relevant services (pp. 72, 73): Social workers often assess the context as they plan and implement policy advocacy.

EPA 2.1.10a   Substantively and affectively prepare for action with individuals, families, groups, organizations, and communities (p. 79): Social workers diagnose the context and stakeholders before and as they engage in policy practice.

EPA 2.1.10k   Negotiate, mediate, and advocate for clients (p. 91): Social workers develop and use power resources as they engage in policy practice.

Endnotes

1. See Hedrick Smith, *The Power Game: How Washington Works* (New York: Ballantine Books, 1988), pp. 215–269.

2. Peter Bachrach and Morton Baratz, *Power and Poverty* (New York: Oxford University Press, 1970), pp. 17–38.

3. Jack Rothman, "The Interweaving of Community Intervention Approaches," *Journal of Community Practice* 3 (3/4): 69–99.

4. For a discussion of building agendas, see Robert Eyestone, *From Social Issues to Public Policy* (New York: Wiley, 1978), and John Kingdon, *Agendas, Alternatives, and Public Policies* (Boston, MA: Little, Brown, 1984).

5. Kingdon, *Agendas, Alternatives, and Public Policies,* pp. 95–105.

6. Ibid., pp. 182–184.

7. Yeheskel Hasenfeld, "Power in Social Work Practice," *Social Service Review* 61 (September 1987): 475–476.

8. Rosabeth Kanter, *Men and Women of the Corporation* (New York: Basic Books, 1977).

9. Eleanor Brilliant, "Social Work Leadership: A Missing Ingredient," *Social Work* (September–October 1986): 327–328.

10. For an exception, see Carel Germain's contribution to Samuel Taylor and Robert Roberts, *Theory and Practice of Community Work* (New York: Columbia University Press, 1985), pp. 30–58.

11. Philip Popple, "The Social Work Profession: A Reconceptualization," *Social Service Review* 59 (December 1985): 560–577.

Suggested Readings

Value-Clarifying Skills

Robert Moroney, "Policy Analysis Within a Value Theoretical Framework," in Ron Haskins and James Gallagher, eds., *Models for Analysis of Social Policy* (Norwood, NJ: Ablex, 1981), pp. 78–102.

Martin Rein, "Value-Critical Policy Analysis," in Daniel Callahan and Bruce Jennings, eds., *Ethics, the Social Sciences, and Policy Analysis* (New York: Plenum Press, 1983), pp. 83–111.

Analytic Skills

Brian Hogwood and Lewis Gunn, *Policy Analysis for the Real World* (London: Oxford University Press, 1984).

Carl Patton and David Sawicki, *Basic Methods of Policy Analysis and Planning* (Englewood Cliffs, NJ: Prentice Hall, 1993).

Political Skills

Eugene Bardach, *The Skill Factor in Politics* (Berkeley and Los Angeles, CA: University of California Press, 1972).

Charles Lindblom and Edward Woodhouse, *The Policy-Making Process,* 3rd ed. (Englewood Cliffs, NJ: Prentice Hall, 1993). Hedrick Smith, *The Power Game: How Washington Works* (New York: Ballantine Books, 1988).

Building Agendas

Joel Best, ed., *Images of Issues: Typifying Contemporary Social Problems* (New York: Aldine de Gruyter, 1989).

John Kingdon, *Agendas, Alternatives, and Public Policies* (Boston, MA: Little, Brown, 1997).

Marc Ross and Roger Cobb, *The Cultural Strategy of Agenda Denial* (Lawrence, KS: University of Kansas, 1997).

Smith, *The Power Game,* pp. 331–444.

Analyzing Problems

Hogwood and Gunn, *Policy Analysis for the Real World,* pp. 67–87, 108–127.

Patton and Sawicki, *Basic Methods of Policy Analysis and Planning.*

Enacting Policy

Donald deKieffer, *The Citizen's Guide to Lobbying Congress* (Chicago, IL: Chicago Review Press, 1997).

Eric Redman, *The Dance of Legislation* (New York: Simon & Schuster, 1973).

Smith, *The Power Game.*

Implementing Policy

Yeheskel Hasenfeld, "Implementation of Social Policy Revisited," *Administration and Society* 22 (February 1991): 451–479.

Robert Montjoy and Laurence O'Toole, "Toward a Theory of Policy Implementation: An Organizational Perspective," *Public Administration Review* 39 (September–October 1979): 465–477.

Assessing Policy

Richard Nathan, *Social Science in Government: Uses and Misuses* (New York: Basic Books, 1988).

Patton and Sawicki, *Basic Methods of Policy Analysis and Planning,* pp. 300–328.

PART 3

The Ecology of Policy in the United States and in a Global World

Chapters Four and **Five** are germane to Task 2 of the policy-making framework, that is, navigating policy and advocacy systems.

Chapter Four analyzes the ecology of policy in the United States so that policy advocates can *navigate policy and advocacy systems.* It discusses key institutions, legislatures, and funding bodies that provide the ecology of policies in local, state, and national settings. It illustrates the ecology of policy with the issue of homelessness. Consider this chapter to provide a policy road map for advocates. At the end of the chapter, readers are asked to discuss how various parts of this road map are related to the issue of homelessness in their city or region.

Chapter Five discusses the global context of policy. Policy advocates have to understand how many domestic problems are caused or exacerbated by international factors, such as relocation of corporations abroad, migration of people across national boundaries, and environmental pollution created by the combined effects of industry and citizens. Because globalization looms large in the contemporary world, policy advocates have to broaden their horizons to understand many social problems and find ways to ameliorate them. Consider this chapter to be a policy road map to policy advocacy at a global level.

Understanding the Ecology of Policy in Governmental, Electoral, Community, and Agency Settings

Policy Predicament

When attempting to address the problem of homelessness in a specific community, policy advocates need to know how to navigate policy and advocacy systems. In Policy Advocacy Challenge 4.7, students are asked to identify some elements of these systems in their communities that are germane to the homeless.

This chapter provides policy advocates a road map to four arenas: legislatures, communities, agencies, and electoral politics in the United States. The road map does not tell them what route to take or how fast to drive, but it orients them to the landscape so that they can better find their direction once they have started the trip. It is germane to Task 2 of the policy framework presented in Chapter Three (see also Figure 3.1).

To be effective, policy advocates must understand how decisions are made in each of these four arenas, how a wide range of forces influence decision making, what rules or procedures are commonly used, who the key players are, and what are the mindsets of key officials.

LEARNING OUTCOMES

By the end of this chapter, you will be prepared to discuss:

1. The cast of players in governmental settings
2. The mindsets of public officials
3. The legislative process
4. Social agencies in their political and economic context
5. The players in organizational settings
6. Community-based organizations that influence policies
7. Electoral politics

The Players in Legislative and Governmental Settings

Anyone who conducts policy advocacy in the governmental sector must know who the key players are and what motivates them (see Policy Advocacy Challenge 4.1).

Policy Advocacy Challenge 4.1

Finding Information about Political Institutions on the Web

Stephanie Davis, Research Librarian, University of California, Irvine

Political institutions have an enormous impact on social policy. The importance of maintaining an awareness of the happenings in the political scene cannot be stated strongly enough. The following websites will help you to become knowledgeable about the structure of the government, how it works, and who the major players are.

- How Our Laws Are Made: A detailed description of the federal legislative process.
    http://thomas.loc.gov/home/lawsmade.toc.html
- THOMAS (Library of Congress): Search engine for federal bills and laws, links to biographical information, and links to additional congressional Internet services.
    http://thomas.loc.gov/
- United States Senate: Links to senators' websites, legislative agendas, votes, and more.
    www.senate.gov
- United States House of Representatives: Links to representatives' websites, legislative agendas, votes, and more.
    www.house.gov
- The White House.
    www.whitehouse.gov

EXERCISE

Using the search engines discussed in Chapter One and the evaluation techniques discussed in Chapter Two, visit these websites and answer the following questions:

- Who are your state senator and your U.S. senator?
- What are their top legislative agenda items?
- Is there any information about their campaign finances on their websites?
- Who is their constituency?

Vulnerable Populations and Stakeholders One of the best uses of the Web is to promote social justice. Organizations that represent vulnerable populations and stakeholders often use the Web to focus on the issues and challenges faced by a specific population. One excellent example is the National Organization for Women. Another good example that focuses on an issue rather than a population is the National Mental Health Association. Locate a website for a vulnerable population that interests you.

Using the resources mentioned in Chapter Two, find additional websites for vulnerable populations or other stakeholders that measure up to your criteria of accuracy.

Let us discuss elected officials (politicians), bureaucrats (unelected officials), lobbyists, and interest groups (see Figure 4.1).

Elected Officials

EP 2.1.9a

We can distinguish three kinds of elected public officials: heads of government, such as mayors, governors, and the U.S. president; legislators, such as city councilpersons, members of county boards of supervisors, state legislators, and federal legislators; and officials elected to specialized public entities such as school boards.

Heads of Government   The head of government (or chief executive) is the elected official charged with developing an administration. Thus, an administration is named after its leader, as in "the Obama administration."

FIGURE 4.1 A Schematic View of Government and Key Players

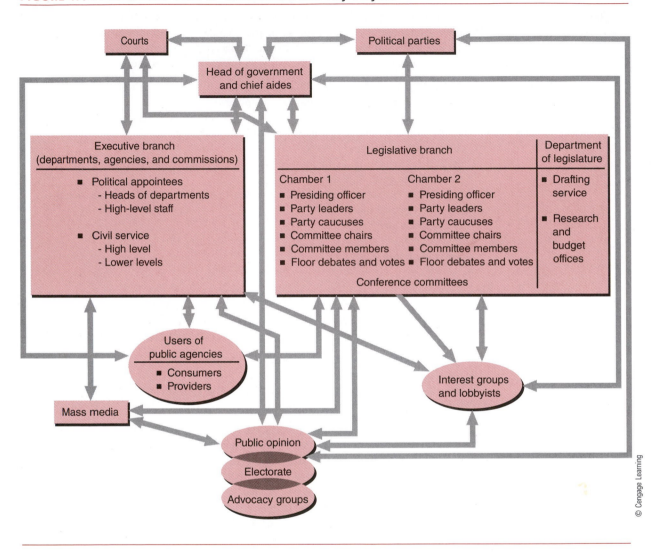

© Cengage Learning

Although some local governments have nonpartisan elections, heads of government are often the titular heads of their political party in their specific jurisdictions.[1] Once he was inaugurated, for example, Barack Obama effectively became the national head of the Democratic Party, just as many mayors and governors head their political parties in their jurisdictions.

Heads of government usually have some guiding principles that shape their approach to the central issues they confront. As the differences between George W. Bush and Barack Obama illustrate, a head of government can often be characterized as relatively liberal or conservative. Of course, ideology does not always predict how a politician will vote on specific issues.

Heads of government and other elected officials want to establish positive, popular records for their administrations that appeal to members of their own party as well as to other groups that they hope will enlarge their political base.

Their central position in government and their constitutional powers make heads of government pivotal in the unfolding of policy while they are in office. First, the U.S. president is in charge of the executive branch of government, which comprises the myriad agencies that implement federal governmental policies. These agencies are usually called *departments*, for example, the Department of Health and Human Services (DHHS). State and local governments have similar organizations, with a head and an executive branch. Heads of government appoint high-level officials in the executive branch's departments or agencies.

Second, heads of government usually initiate a budget, even though the legislators make many of the final budgetary choices. This initiating role represents an important power because it allows chief executives to influence priorities within the executive branch.[2]

Third, chief executives usually develop a legislative agenda to which they often refer in general terms in speeches, such as the president's State of the Union speech. They have vast resources to help them fashion this legislative agenda. For instance, they have personal aides in their own office, their political appointees in the executive branch, and political allies who occupy powerful positions on legislative committees or in the party in the legislature.[3] Because heads of government have a central position in government and a high profile, their legislative proposals, which members of their own party or political allies introduce into the legislature, often have an advantage over individual legislators' proposals. Even with such power, the legislative proposals of many heads of government are defeated, particularly when the opposing party holds a majority in the legislature.

Fourth, chief executives often use their central position in government as a bully pulpit.

Fifth, chief executives can issue executive orders. These are directives to specific units of government that do not require legislative approval, such as when President George W. Bush allowed many federal agencies to give grants to faith-based organizations, even though Congress had not approved the policy.

Capitalizing on the extensive coverage the mass media usually accords them, heads of government often try to gain support for legislative measures, rally opposition against legislators who may block their policies, and educate the public about specific issues.[4]

Finally, heads of government can veto legislation that the legislature has approved, an important power because legislatures often cannot muster the votes (such as the two-thirds of each chamber required in the federal government) to override a veto. Some governors have line-item vetoes over the budgets that legislatures have approved; line-item vetoes allow heads of government to unilaterally change budget figures.

Legislators and Political Parties Under the division of powers in federal, state, and local constitutions, legislatures have responsibilities and powers that often rival those of heads of government.

Foremost, legislatures can develop, approve, and reject legislation. They use this power both to respond to legislation proposed by heads of government and to introduce their own legislation.

Legislators possess extraordinary powers over budgets. When they write legislation covering particular programs, for example, they often include the amount of the funds to be used for those programs in a specific year. Heads of government cannot exceed these sums when they plan their annual budget. In a separate process, legislators decide the total appropriations for a specific year and how to divide it among various programs.

They usually begin with the budget proposed by the head of government but often make major changes in it.[5]

While not charged with actually implementing enacted legislation or writing the administrative regulations that will shape this implementation, legislatures engage in administrative oversight. Many of their standing committees hold hearings during which they ask high-level executive branch officials to discuss the operations of specific programs. Legislators also learn from their constituents about the operations of programs. When legislators believe they have found problems in programs, they have several remedial powers. First, they can amend the legislation that had established the program. Second, they can convince executive branch officials to correct problems in programs by modifying their administration. For example, if legislators find that an existing program does not serve people with disabilities, even though such service was intended to be part of the program as originally enacted, they might convince the program director to devote considerable resources to informing people with physical disabilities about the program. Third, legislators often use public hearings to expose issues, educate the public, hear feedback on proposed legislation, and put political pressure on heads of government and their appointees to correct problems. Indeed, as Hedrick Smith notes when discussing Congress, many legislators like to use the mass media to publicize specific issues, often in defiance of or without consultation with senior legislators or party officials, whose power has diminished in the decades since Watergate.[6]

Legislatures seem formidably complex, although they are structured rather similarly.

A diagram of the Wisconsin state legislature shows the essential structure of most legislatures (see Figure 4.2). Legislatures are usually divided into two houses, such as the House of Representatives and the Senate at the federal level or the Senate and the Assembly at the state level, as in Wisconsin. Usually, both houses must assent to legislation or a budget before it can become operative. Many legislatures, like the U.S. Congress, convene annually, but some state legislatures convene only every two years. Moreover, the length of legislatures' sessions varies widely: Congress meets almost nonstop, but other legislatures convene only for several months.

The members of each house or chamber of a legislature, whether local, state, or federal, are elected by districts, whose precise shape changes over time. Districts may be reapportioned as the demography of the population shifts and the courts decide that existing district lines are consequently unfair to specific groups, such as Latinos or African Americans. To understand specific legislators, then, we must analyze the characteristics of their constituents, whose preferences influence their positions on myriad issues. We might ask: Is the district relatively affluent or poor? Does it have a mix of ethnic and racial groups, or is it dominated by a single group? Is it urban, suburban, or rural? Is it dominated by a single party or evenly divided between two parties?[7] We can also ask whether specific legislators occupy relatively safe seats or whether they will face closely contested elections.

To understand how specific chambers of legislatures operate, we must first ask: Which party controls a majority of the legislature's members? The majority party appoints the chairs of all committees and has a majority of the members on each committee of that chamber. Moreover, the members of the majority party in each house elect the presiding officer of that chamber, such as the president of the U.S. Senate and the Speaker of the House. These high-level leaders have considerable power in determining when specific measures will be debated on the floor, mobilizing support for or against measures, and making important parliamentary decisions at critical junctures in floor debate. Presiding officers often have the authority to establish committees, assign members to committees, and appoint chairs of committees. In addition, they often have the

FIGURE 4.2 The Structure of the Wisconsin State Legislature

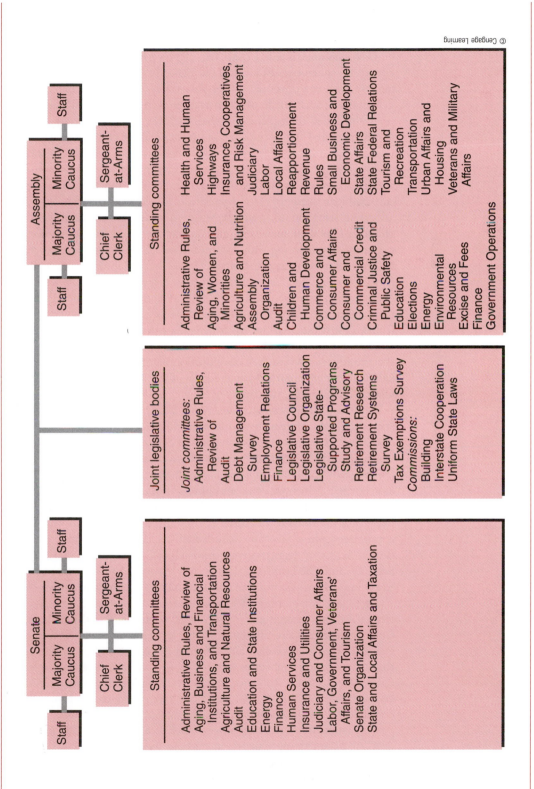

© Cengage Learning

power to decide how to route specific bills for deliberation. This power is critical because a presiding officer can often kill a bill by insisting that it go through specific committees that are known to be hostile to it.[8]

Each chamber has a second tier of powerful leaders: the floor leaders, who are also elected by caucuses and include the majority leader and the majority whip. Working in tandem with the presiding officer, these party leaders shepherd legislation through floor deliberations and decide which measures their party will support or oppose.[9]

A third tier of leaders, the chairs of the important committees of a chamber, are members of the majority party and have considerable power over the fate of legislation in their committees.[10]

Though at a disadvantage, a minority party often has considerable power in a specific chamber. It has its own leader, such as the U.S. House minority leader, who can mobilize support of or opposition to pieces of legislation. The minority party is allocated seats on all committees of a chamber in proportion to its share of the chamber's total membership, and its members sometimes obtain a majority vote on a committee by teaming with committee members of the majority party. Thus, in the era of Presidents Reagan and George H. W. Bush, Republicans could defeat congressional legislation that the Democrats strongly favored by joining with southern Democrats, even though the Democratic Party had a majority in the House of Representatives throughout the period and controlled the Senate from November 1986 onward. Republicans almost blocked the Affordable Care Act in 2010, even though Democrats had a large majority in the House, a one-vote majority at a crucial juncture, and controlled the Presidency. When they developed a majority in the House in the wake of Congressional elections of 2010 with the help of the Tea Party, they blocked most of President Obama's legislative measures.

Because of their size and the myriad issues they consider, legislatures are divided into specialized committees. In the federal House of Representatives, for example, the Ways and Means Committee processes Social Security, Medicare, and tax legislation, and the Committee on Labor and Public Welfare processes social programs such as Head Start. (See Figure 4.2, which lists the committees in each chamber of Wisconsin's legislature, and Box 4.1, which lists the committees in each chamber of the U.S. Congress.)

As we have discussed, the presiding officers of each chamber often have considerable discretion in referring measures to committees. Many pieces of legislation go to multiple committees when they pose issues that cut across committee divisions. In other cases, certain kinds of legislation are automatically referred to a specific committee. Social Security and Medicare legislation, for example, are always considered by the House Ways and Means Committee and the Senate Finance Committee in the U.S. Congress.

Each legislative committee has its own internal structure. Its chairperson may be elected by the committee's members or appointed by the chamber's presiding officer. Committee chairs are usually powerful legislators. Like presiding officers of the overall chamber, they can kill legislation by not placing it on the committee's agenda, by referring it to a hostile subcommittee, or by merely raising strong objections to it when the committee discusses it.[11] Each legislative committee has subcommittees that specialize in certain issues, within the whole committee's purview. Subcommittee chairs also have considerable power over issues that fall within their domain.

Legislation that presiding officers refer to a committee falls into two categories. Some of it is consigned, more or less at once, to the legislative junk heap because the committee, much less the full chamber, does not consider it seriously. The subcommittees and committees take other legislation seriously and mark it up in committee deliberations; that is, they amend it in various ways.

BOX **4.1** | **Standing Committees of the U.S. Congress**

Senate	House
Agriculture, Nutrition, and Forestry	Agriculture
Appropriations	Appropriations
Armed Services	Armed Services
Banking, Housing, and Urban Affairs	Ethics
Budget	Budget
Commerce, Science, and Transportation	Financial Services
Energy and Natural Resources	Education and the Workforce
Environment and Public Works	Energy and Commerce
Finance	Foreign Affairs
Foreign Relations	Government Operations
Government Affairs	Homeland Security
Judiciary	House Administration
Health, Education, Labor, and Pensions	Intelligence
Rules and Administration	Joint Economic Committee
Small Business and Entrepreneurship	Joint Select Committee on Deficit Reduction
Veterans' Affairs	Judiciary
Post Office and Civil Service	Merchant Marine and Fisheries
Public Works and Transportation	Narcotics Abuse and Control
	Natural Resources
	Oversight and Government Reform
	Rules
	Science, Space, and Technology
	Small Business
	Standards of Official Conduct
	Transportation and Infrastructure
	Veterans' Affairs
	Ways and Means

Most legislation, then, evolves over the course of deliberations that take weeks, months, or even years, and it can be amended on the floor of the chamber when the whole chamber decides whether to amend and accept or defeat a bill.

Figure 4.3 shows the usual trajectory of legislative proposals, though many variations are possible. A bill usually starts in one chamber and progresses from committees to a floor debate and then a vote. It is then referred to the other chamber, where it follows a similar course. After the second chamber enacts its own version, representatives from each chamber seek a common version, which usually requires both chambers to make concessions. If the conference committee creates a joint version, each chamber must then ratify it before it goes to the president (or governor), who then signs it into law or vetoes it. Congress can override a veto if each chamber musters a two-thirds vote. Otherwise, the legislation dies.

FIGURE 4.3 The Route that a Bill Typically follows in the U.S. Congress

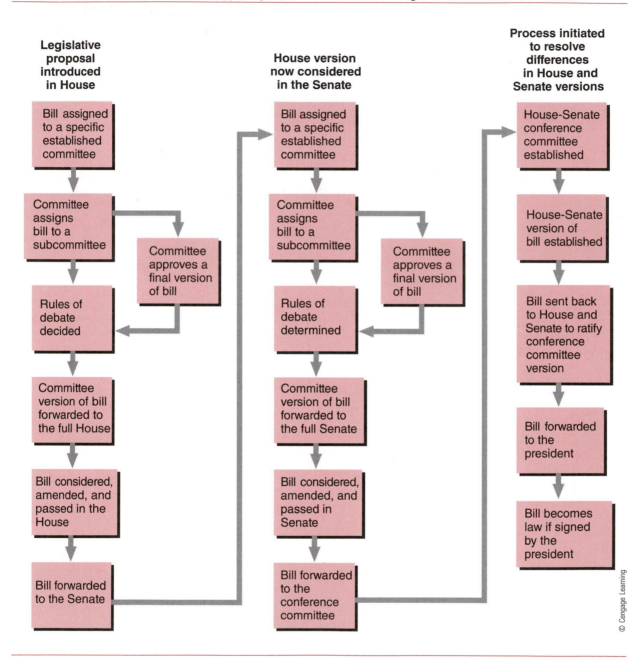

Some legislative deliberations are relatively straightforward; comparatively few amendments are offered and legislators move quickly to a decision. Other legislative deliberations, particularly those concerning controversial issues, are marked by various parliamentary maneuvers, such as the opponents' efforts to derail the legislation. In unusual cases, opponents in the Senate will even filibuster a bill by talking nonstop to prevent a concluding vote. Filibusters are not allowed in the House.[12]

Officials Elected to Special Bodies   Officials elected to some special political bodies, such as school boards, wield considerable power within their areas. Other political bodies, such as county boards of supervisors and city councils, have markedly different structures from those of the state and federal legislatures. They consist of a single chamber, and the election of their members is often nonpartisan, that is, the candidates have no party affiliations on the ballot. Many differences exist among cities; for example, some have mayors elected by the public, and others elect their mayors on a rotating basis from the city council. It is beyond the scope of this discussion to elaborate on the differences in city governments, but policy practitioners need to be versed in them to participate in local politics.[13]

Unelected Officials or Bureaucrats

Legislators are far outnumbered by unelected public officials who work in government agencies in city, county, state, and federal jurisdictions. These public officials are either political appointees or civil servants.

Political Appointees   Political appointees are high-level persons appointed to top jobs by heads of government, such as mayors, governors, or the president. They serve at the pleasure of the heads of government. They do not have long-term job security, because their mentor may dismiss them if they fall into disfavor, if they are considered to be a political liability, or when a new head of government comes into office. This new leader usually dismisses the previous staff and appoints his or her own nominees. Political appointees become spokespersons and representatives of their mentor, as when they discuss their administration's policy positions at press conferences. They are likely to have the same ideology as their mentor.[14]

Civil Servants   Unlike political appointees, civil servants obtain their jobs through competitive exams. They are hired at a specific level or grade in the civil service hierarchy and then promoted to higher grades based on annual job reviews by superiors. Those in higher grades have more power than those in lower grades, though there are many exceptions. Unlike political appointees, civil servants usually have job security, though they can be terminated as a result of funding cutbacks.[15]

Civil servants are the engines of government bureaucracies; they administer programs, draft regulations, collect data, and disburse funds to programs. Most civil servants outlast particular administrations. Indeed, civil servants are the permanent government, with real powers that equal or even exceed those of some political appointees.

Even though they receive their positions by competitive exam rather than by political appointment, some civil servants have close ties with legislators. They may have worked in the legislature as aides and developed relationships with other aides or with the staff of legislative committees.[16]

Lobbyists and Interest Groups

Lobbyists are professional advocates who represent interest groups or causes. Hired by corporations, trade associations, professional organizations, or groups representing specific populations or issues, they voice their perspectives to legislators and officials in the executive branch of governments.[17]

We can distinguish between powerful lobbyists, who represent interest groups with considerable money and clout, and shoestring lobbyists, who represent groups with relatively little money and clout. Lobbyists' power depends on several factors. Truly powerful lobbyists have funds not only to make campaign contributions to the legislators they wish to woo but also to entertain them by hosting special events, taking them out to meals, paying them to address special meetings or conferences, and funding special trips for them. Powerful lobbyists often have considerable technical resources; their affluent interest groups can hire researchers and consultants to provide legislators with proposals and technical reports. Powerful interest groups in various states and in Washington, DC, such as the American Medical Association, do not hire single lobbyists; they often hire teams of lobbyists large enough to speak to most of the people in a specific legislature during a given period. They increase their clout further by forming coalitions with other lobbyists and interest groups with similar concerns. The American Medical Association, for example, may team with other medical interest groups or some corporations to support or oppose specific pieces of legislation.[18]

By contrast, shoestring lobbyists serve smaller and poorer groups. Often acting alone, they lack the resources to make even minimal contact with many legislators, make large donations to campaign coffers, or entertain legislators. Their relative lack of funds does not imply, of course, that they are powerless: They can shape public policy on certain issues by carefully using their resources, establishing coalitions with likeminded interest groups and lobbyists, and mobilizing their constituencies to pressure public officials—for example, by writing letters to them—on important occasions.

Lobbyists' character also shapes their effectiveness. While the general public widely views lobbyists as slippery and devious, they need reputations as straight shooters to be successful with legislators. Lobbyists who are caught telling lies, such as claiming someone supports a measure when she or he does not, or deliberately giving misleading information, soon lose their credibility. Lobbyists, however, must be persistent and not let specific defeats deter them. They must engage in endless networking with legislators, civil servants, and interested citizens to form relationships that will help them achieve their goals.

Lobbyists' power hinges, of course, on the groups they represent. When we examine external pressures on legislators, then, we need to consider the power of specific interest groups. They obtain their power partly by hiring skilled lobbyists, but they also offer carrots (rewards and incentives) and sticks (implied or actual threats). The incentives include campaign contributions from political action committees (PACs) to specific politicians, volunteers to help with campaigns, and technical assistance on issues. The threats include withdrawal of these rewards, the endorsement of opponents in primaries and general elections, and the provision of funds and volunteers to opponents.[19]

Some interest groups that begin with relatively scant resources augment their power by building a reputation for the quality of the technical information they give legislators. The Children's Defense Fund and the Center for Budget and Policy Priorities in Washington have, for example, attained key positions concerning an array of issues, even though they lack the resources of, for example, the American Medical Association. By securing foundation funds, with which they have built a core of sophisticated researchers and have evolved a national constituency, these groups have developed credibility for their research and their principled positions.

Think tanks, institutions that conduct policy research and disseminate evaluations of specific policies, have also emerged to represent a range of perspectives. They issue periodic reports that carry considerable clout in Washington, as well as in the state capitals.[20]

Connections Among Interest Groups, Legislators, and Bureaucrats

Important relationships exist among lobbyists, legislators, and bureaucrats. Many lobbyists, for example, are former legislators, civil servants, or political appointees. Many civil servants are former aides to legislators, with whom they maintain important relationships, such as passing them "inside information."[21]

Iron triangles—as they are referred to—sometimes link civil servants, legislators, and lobbyists (or interest groups) when the legislature considers specific issues. For instance, if legislation about child abuse goes through a state legislature, several people who know each other and have worked together in the past may become active. Such collaboration may include lobbyists associated with children's advocacy groups; an association of the directors of public child welfare agencies around the state; professional associations, such as the state chapter of the National Association of Social Workers (NASW); a key civil servant in the state's welfare department; and an aide to a legislator with a long-standing interest in child abuse. Sharing similar points of view and past patterns of collaboration, these people may cooperate and bargain to develop a mutually acceptable policy and then may pool their resources to seek its enactment.

We do not want to imply that such relationships exist on all issues or that their power precludes important roles for other participants. But those who try to change policy in legislative settings need to be aware that these relationships exist and that they can be tapped into for technical advice or for the support of a specific measure.

Public Opinion

Politicians, bureaucrats, and lobbyists work in an environment of uncertainty. They realize that voters can end a politician's career and can bring down an administration.[22] Bureaucrats are also vulnerable to public opinion because scandals or unpopular decisions can ruin the careers of political appointees and civil servants.[23] Legislators often try to implement programs in ways that will please their constituents, as illustrated by politicians who oppose placing mental health facilities and prisons in their districts.

However, measuring public opinion is a task dogged by uncertainty. Politicians often read polls, but they realize that even accurate polls cannot predict future changes in public opinion. Politicians often gauge public opinion through mail from constituents and talking to constituents in their legislative offices and their home districts.[24]

Advocacy Groups

Advocacy groups place pressure on decision makers in city councils, boards of supervisors, and state and federal legislators. They may be community groups, coalitions, think tanks, public interest groups, groups of consumers, or professional groups like the NASW. Some advocacy groups exist for long periods, while others are relatively short-lived, such as ones developed to address a specific issue at a specific time. Advocacy groups vary in their size and staff: while some are relatively small, others have substantial resources from foundations and other sources. Policy advocates often work with advocacy groups when they seek to change policies, as we discuss in succeeding chapters.

The Electoral Process

To say the very least, the electoral process is highly competitive, because very few elections at any level of government are uncontested. The electoral process is the institutionalized guts of any democracy; it provides a nonviolent way of solving the problem of succession to office. It is competitive because it is a win–lose conflict: only one candidate can win.

The precise formats of elections are described in legal statutes and regulations that prescribe how candidates get on ballots, how votes are counted, how runoffs are held, how campaigns can be financed, and how long the terms of office are.

These precise rules vary widely not only between jurisdictions but regarding specific kinds of offices. Rules that govern school board elections, for example, are different from rules that govern federal elections.

Let us discuss the electoral process from a developmental perspective, from the early maneuvering by possible candidates through the actual elections.

Early Maneuvering

Long before most elections are held, potential candidates decide whether they want to make a run for a specific office. Potential candidates are sometimes approached by other persons, such as leaders of local, state, or national parties who want strong candidates with a good chance at winning an office. Incumbents (persons already holding office) ponder whether they wish to run for office again—or whether they want to retire from public service, move into a bureaucratic job, or seek another, often higher, office.

When deciding whether to run or rerun for a particular office, people consider various factors. Nonincumbents consider whether specific incumbents are vulnerable because of their track record in office, unpopularity in public opinion polls, access to funds, or the extent that they are backed by other opinion setters or party officials. They also consider which other nonincumbents run for a specific office because their chances diminish if other formidable candidates enter the race. Nonincumbents take into account the degree of name recognition they already possess or might develop over the course of a campaign because name recognition is crucial in many elections. They also think about whether they can develop grassroots support during a campaign, such as by eliciting support from community groups, local leaders, and volunteers. (Such successful candidates as social work Democratic Senators Debbie Stabenow and Barbara Mikulski gained early success in electoral politics by cultivating relationships with local community groups.)

Nonincumbents' motivation to run for office is often increased when their positions differ markedly from those of the incumbents. By winning, they not only gain office but substitute their positions for those maintained by specific incumbents. Candidates with a commitment to social justice often see their public service in ethical terms—not just as a way to advance their personal self-interest.

Nonincumbents face a hard reality: the overwhelming majority of incumbents win elections when they decide to rerun for office. This is so for several reasons. Incumbents tend to have relatively high name recognition because of media coverage of their prior elections and their actions while in office. They can often raise money relatively easily from special interest groups they have helped through their policy decisions while in office. They know the electoral ropes because they have already been through one or more campaigns, and they often have support from local, state, or federal party officials who do not want to lose the incumbents' seats to the opposing party.

We should not overstate the difficulties faced by nonincumbents, however. Incumbents are sometimes vulnerable. A nonincumbent can run for an empty seat when an incumbent retires or runs for another office. Nonincumbents realize, moreover, that some races are less demanding than others in terms of the resources, name recognition, and time that they require. Nonpartisan elections, such as those for school board, local planning councils, and positions on township or city councils, usually do not require the level of resources and name recognition required in partisan elections. Many nonincumbents begin their careers by not running for office at all: they get appointed to commissions in local jurisdictions or obtain jobs in government agencies or as aides to office holders. With a public-service base established, they can then scan the horizon for possible electoral races.

Laura Chick is a model example of how social workers can be elected to serve in public office. Laura Chick received her bachelor's degree in history from UCLA and her master's in social work from USC. She first entered elected office in 1993 when she defeated a 16-year incumbent for a seat on the Los Angeles City Council. She served as council-woman from 1993 to 2001, being elected to her second term with 82 percent of the vote. In 2002, she was elected as the Los Angeles city controller, a position she held from 2002 to 2008. As city controller, Ms. Chick was the first woman in the history of Los Angeles to hold citywide office. She authored the city's first blueprint to end gang violence, and released over 170 audits and reports exposing a wide range of problems throughout city government. One of those audits exposed a backlog of thousands of untested DNA rape kits at the LA Police Department, which resulted in city officials finally making the problem a priority. In 2009, Laura Chick was appointed by Governor Schwarzenegger to oversee the state's spending of $50 billion of federal stimulus funds, overusing funds "from High Speed rail to county social services programs from Redding to San Bernardino," www.laobserved.com/archive/2010/12/laura_chicks_state_post_e.php.

Laura Chick won the ProPublica Prize for Investigative Governance in 2009 for her audit exposing untested rape kits. She was named the Public Elected Official of the Year in 2008 by the NASW.

Listen to Policy Advocacy Challenge Video 4.2, where Ms. Chick discusses her decision to run for office, as well as the attributes of social workers that make them effective candidates and public officials. After you have listened to this video, ask:

1. What attributes do social workers possess that make them effective candidates?
2. What attributes do social workers possess that make them effective public officials?
3. Do you see yourself running for office at some point?

Seeking elective office is not for everybody. It takes time and effort, and it exposes persons to attacks from opposing candidates. Yet the rewards are numerous for persons who are elected to public office; they can make vitally important public-policy decisions because they are insiders whose votes count. Social workers possess characteristics that make many of them ideal candidates for public office (see Policy Advocacy Challenge 4.2).

Running Campaigns

Once nonincumbents decide to run for specific offices, they must wage successful campaigns to secure those offices. Their first challenge is to get on the final ballot by prevailing in primaries or nonpartisan races with more than two candidates. Primaries are partisan elections in which representatives of specific parties must defeat members of their own parties to get on the final ballot where they are pitted against the representatives of opposing parties. Barack Obama defeated Hillary Clinton, for example, in the Democratic presidential primaries in 2008 to become the Democratic presidential nominee en route to defeating John McCain in the presidential election of 2008. Republicans Mitt Romney, Newt Gingrich, Rick Santorum, and Ron Paul battled for the Republican presidential nomination in 2012. In nonpartisan contests with multiple entrants, the two candidates with the highest vote totals often appear on the final ballot if neither of them received more than 50 percent of the vote.

To get more votes than their opponents, candidates must find ways to persuade those who are already sympathetic to their positions to vote, and get some undecided or swing votes as well.

This requires them to engage in such tasks as the following:

- Develop positions on key issues that both speak to their natural constituency and appeal to some swing voters
- Make personal contact with many voters through campaign appearances and precinct walking
- Recruit and use volunteers to make personal contact with voters by phone and by precinct walking
- Reach voters through the mass media, such as press conferences and debates with opponents
- Reach voters through advertisements in the mass media and mailings
- Increase the pool of sympathetic voters through voter registration, particularly in areas where public opinion is supportive

EP 2.1.5c

These activities, in turn, require candidates to raise campaign funds. These funds can come from friends, political parties, PACs, and personal resources. The amount of political resources required for a specific campaign varies widely depending on the competition for a particular office. In general, partisan races, hotly contested races, and races involving positions that imbue winners with great political power (such as those for state and federal offices) are more expensive than others.

Once candidates face off, their ability to win partly depends on their skill in devising campaign strategy. They have to decide which issues to surface, what parts of the constituency to emphasize, how to respond to opponents' attacks, and how to get sufficient resources and volunteers to implement their campaigns. (We discuss campaigns in more detail in Chapter Twelve.)

Implementing Public-Service Careers   Once candidates win their first election, they begin a public-service career. Some of them will be content to serve one or more terms in that office, but others will begin a decades-long public-service career that takes them into multiple positions and offices. For example, Senator Debbie Stabenow, a social worker, became a U.S. senator only after an extended career in which she held various lower-level offices. Some persons alternate between elected offices and offices in appointive positions in the government.

The Mindsets of Elected Officials

EP 2.1.9a

Those who engage in policy practice in governmental settings need to understand the mindsets of heads of government, legislators, political appointees, and civil servants. Success in changing policy hinges on obtaining the help and support of these people. Policy practitioners can understand officials' mindsets only by examining the environment that shapes their choices.

The Environment of Public Servants: Elected Officials

Imagine that you have just spent two years planning, fund-raising, and campaigning to obtain your job. You have narrowly defeated a determined opponent who has already pledged to prevail in the next election, which is several years away. In response to this threat, you are likely to have reelection on your mind throughout your tenure. You will look at most issues with an eye to their effect on your reelection, and you will spend hours wondering about the general public's preferences. To deduce their views, you will study the following:

- Public opinion polls
- Recent outcomes of other elections in comparable districts
- The mail you receive
- The views of subgroups within your constituency, particularly those that you believe will support you in the next election
- The preferences of state or national organizations—for example, professional associations or groups such as the American Association of Retired Persons—that might contribute funds to your next campaign

Moreover, as the elected official, you will nervously eye the statements and positions of potential opponents in the next election. In some cases, you will support an issue to steal the thunder of your likely opponents, and in other cases, you will openly support issues that they oppose to publicize your differences from them. In districts divided between liberals and conservatives, relatively liberal candidates often support liberal issues to solidify their support among liberals. They realize that without committed support from this constituency, they may lose to conservative opponents.[25]

This nonstop campaigning will make you sensitive to the political ramifications of certain choices. Some issues, such as increasing funds for city parks, will cause you little or no concern. However, issues seen as more controversial by important segments of your constituency will make you hesitate before committing yourself.

If elected officials often have their ears to the ground, they are also extraordinarily busy. Assume that you are a member of several major committees and subcommittees, each of which handles many issues on which you need to brief yourself before and during policy deliberations. As you hurriedly read technical reports and briefing papers, you simultaneously try to raise funds for your reelection bid. You make weekly trips back to your district to meet with its citizens and convene regularly with lobbyists from various interest groups. Constituents also come to your offices every day to speak with you. While a caseworker (this title is used even though these persons are not usually social workers) helps you process many constituent requests, you also devote some of your energies to specific requests, for example, a request of an older woman who wants help in coping with her husband's Alzheimer's disease.[26]

You will also be concerned about your relationships with your legislative and party colleagues.

Although at times you are a relatively independent legislator who wants to make a name for yourself, you also are part of larger systems that, much as an organization controls an employee, place some limits on your actions, such as pressuring you in certain situations to go along with policies and procedures you dislike. Because you want to increase your status within these systems, you must play by their rules. As a member of legislative committees and subcommittees, you know that the chairperson holds great power and can often determine which issues will receive a serious airing in the committee and which amendments will be enacted. You belong to a political party as well, which meets regularly, agrees collectively to support or oppose certain measures, and parcels out rewards and penalties, such as committee assignments and campaign funds. If you are a complete renegade, you will suffer reprisals from high officials on your legislative committees and in your party.

Shortcuts: Aides, Lobbyists, and Priorities

With such a comprehensive agenda, you as the elected official will need to develop shortcuts. You have to rely heavily on aides to manage the bulk of your interactions with constituents, lobbyists, and others.[27] You may be compelled to delegate much of your work to these trusted aides, because without them, you cannot function. You create a division of labor by hiring specialists in legislative matters, in handling constituent demands (such as the woman who wants help with her husband's Alzheimer's disease), in fund-raising, and in public relations. In other cases, you rely heavily on lobbyists to do technical work for you, to do reconnaissance work with other legislators, to help you draft legislative proposals, and to help you write amendments to existing legislation.[28]

Early in your term, you are likely to develop priorities by taking some pieces of legislation seriously and giving only glancing attention to others. Suppose a constituent wants you to sponsor a piece of legislation (by sponsoring it, you place your name at its head with those of other sponsoring legislators), but you decide the legislation is not a priority for you. Although you agree to sponsor it as a symbolic gesture to keep your constituent's goodwill, you know you will not invest energy in promoting it. You decide, instead, to expend your political capital (your power resources) liberally on issues that may bring you large political dividends when you come up for reelection, or that appeal to you for other reasons.

The Calculus of Choice

Any policy practitioner soon discovers that several factors shape legislators' choices. Indeed, precisely because so many factors intrude, policy practitioners should refrain from discounting legislators whose voting records make them appear unpromising. We can divide the determinants of choice into eight categories. We have already discussed the *electoral considerations* that lead politicians to support or oppose measures, based on the preferences of voters, interest groups, and campaign donors.

However, electoral calculations are not always easy to make, because politicians often have poor information on which to base predictions of how the public will respond to an issue in a future election. Politicians often try to gauge what positions *existing* and *potential opponents* will take on issues. Then, they can upstage their rivals, take important issues from them, or take the opposite position.

Personal values and *life experiences* also shape politicians' positions; for example, many politicians who have had cancer show strong support for medical research.

Politicians sometimes support measures because they want to *obtain credit* for initiating a measure by going public before rival politicians take action. For this reason, politicians in the House of Representatives often vie with senators to develop legislative initiatives, and Democrats often try to develop a measure before Republicans take the initiative.

Some politicians support measures in areas where they hope to become known as *personal experts.* In the late 1980s, Senator Christopher Dodd (a Democrat) and Senator Orrin Hatch (a Republican) sought reputations as experts on day-care legislation by vigorously and publicly supporting the Act for Better Child Care.

Although they often focus on the needs of specific interest groups, politicians sometimes attend to the *public interest,* particularly when they believe voters will hold them accountable for decisions that hurt the public interest.[29] Indeed, politicians sometimes support budget cuts and corporate tax hikes, even in defiance of powerful special interests.

Politicians often base their choices on *political feasibility.* They do not want to invest effort in measures that have little or no chance of passage. In some cases, of course, politicians support measures that they believe will not be enacted. They do this to publicize their position to important parts of their constituencies.

Policy advocates must also remember that many issues have surfaced before in legislative settings. Like the rest of us, legislators often are creatures of habit; *habit* or *tradition* shapes their position on some issues. Of course, people often change their minds as they receive new information or as political realities shift.

Politicians have to decide not only how to vote but also whether to invest considerable energy in specific issues. When they want to avoid offending someone but are not really committed to a measure, as we discussed, they may give it only symbolic support. In other cases, when they personally favor an issue but fear negative consequences, they try to keep a low profile in their support. Sometimes, they openly campaign for an issue. At other times, they act as bystanders and may even absent themselves from the final voting to avoid offending either the supporters or the opponents of the legislation. In still other cases, they may openly oppose it.

Public advocates for an issue are aware, of course, that their measures are most likely to succeed if they have the support of especially powerful political leaders, such as committee chairs, the presiding officer of a chamber, and party leaders. These high-level leaders have extraordinary power, not merely in expediting measures through the legislative process but in attracting support for them from other, less powerful legislators. Policy practitioners' chances also increase as they obtain sponsors from both parties and from both relatively liberal and relatively conservative politicians. Of course, such breadth of sponsorship is not always possible.

Our discussion of the mindsets of elected officials suggests that policy advocates need to exercise caution in making premature judgments about legislators' choices. Many factors can impel them to support or oppose a measure and invest energy in it. For example, advocates of food stamp legislation were tempted to write off some conservatives who usually opposed social reforms. However, they soon found that many conservatives were becoming ardent supporters, either because they were beholden to agricultural interests (who believed the food stamp program would enhance markets for farm products) or because they were genuinely troubled by the specter of malnutrition. Moreover, some Republicans did not want Democrats to get sole credit for enacting and expanding the food stamp program, which they believed would be politically popular. Liberal advocates for enacting and expanding the food stamp program—who would have faced an uphill political battle—found these conservative allies indispensable on numerous occasions.[30] The ability of public officials to craft compromises across party lines has been greatly impeded by gridlock between the parties, such as during the Obama presidency and in many states like California, Ohio, and Wisconsin.

The Mindsets of Nonelected Officials

Policy practitioners frequently seek assistance from nonelected officials, whether political appointees or civil servants.

Political Appointees

When dealing with political appointees, remember that they were appointed by high-level political allies, such as heads of government. Appointees will not usually support, at least openly, legislation that their mentors would not approve. Therefore, one can expect political appointees to seek permission from higher authorities before they commit themselves publicly to a measure.

In the real world, however, high-level political appointees, such as the U.S. Secretary of Health and Human Services, often make choices in a relatively ambiguous context. They may like a measure (or an amended version of it) but may fail to get a definite opinion about it from higher authorities who want the measure to evolve in the legislative process before they decide whether to support or oppose it. In this situation, a high-level appointee might have some aides work on the issue and might give technical assistance to advocates of the measure. In other cases, political appointees receive word from their mentors, such as a governor or the president, that certain features of a measure are unacceptable to them and will elicit a veto, but other features are acceptable. In these cases, the head of government attempts to influence a measure by threatening to veto it if the final version contains certain provisions. In yet other cases, high-level appointees engage in a dangerous game of defiance; they quietly give background support to a proposal's advocates, even when they know that the head of government opposes the measure.[31]

Heads of government decide to support or oppose specific measures in much the same way legislators do. However, they are probably more attuned to a measure's budgetary implications than many legislators because governors, mayors, and the president initiate budgets.

The political appointees in government agencies are likely to be interested in the facets of a measure that they will be called on to implement. They will attend to details such as what resources the measure will need, what relationships will exist between different levels of government, and what rules (such as eligibility procedures) will be left vague or will be defined. Like heads of government, political appointees will be interested in a measure's budgetary implications because part of its funds may come from the department or agency.

Civil Servants

As nonelected officials who do not depend on politicians for their job tenure, civil servants often have a different perspective from that of politicians or political appointees. They commonly view themselves as professionals with specific expertise, and are not under the same compulsion to act political. Nor can they commit their bureaucracies to a specific measure, because that prerogative is reserved for political appointees who head agencies.[32]

At the same time, however, civil servants work in a political environment. They have to be sensitive to the desires of the high-level political appointees who administer their departments because they work under them, and their job promotions and job assignments are influenced by these executives. As lower-level staff in the elaborate chain of command of government, they often receive directives from high officials and may receive reprimands if they do not heed them.

Policy advocates who approach lower-level civil servants about proposed legislation should not expect them to endorse it, because departmental or agency approval can come only from the director. However, lower-level civil servants can provide indispensable technical information, such as reports, studies, and data germane to writing a proposal.[33]

The degree of cooperation that a policy advocate receives from civil servants varies widely. Some civil servants are extraordinarily helpful to those who ask for technical information, but others are relatively cloistered and appear to be irritated by external requests. Their cooperativeness is often related to their personal disposition, their values (whether they like the proposed project), and their perceptions of the advocate (whether they trust him or her). Advocates must often be persistent when seeking help from civil servants, aware that civil servants are responsible for numerous tasks.[34]

Like political appointees, civil servants sometimes give low-profile assistance to causes that they like, even without high-level departmental or agency approval. Advocacy groups sometimes find reliable contacts in government agencies who give them inside information that enhances their work.

Strategy in Legislative Settings

We have provided an overview of legislative and other governmental settings. With knowledge of the procedures used in these settings and the mindsets of the legislators and officials who inhabit them, policy advocates have to devise strategy for having legislation enacted. They need to know how to obtain assistance in developing strategy, how to find sponsors for their legislation, how to testify before committees, and how to use phone calls and letters to pressure politicians. Moreover, practitioners often try to create favorable conditions for their policies in legislatures. A practitioner might, for example, participate in a politician's campaign, attend political club meetings or parties, and contribute resources and time to a PAC (such as PACE, the political action committee of the NASW). Chapters Ten and Eleven are devoted to methods of developing and implementing political strategy.

Advocating for Resources

EP 2.1.5c

EP 2.1.5b

Policy advocates often seek legislation that establishes new programs or regulations. Such legislation is enacted by ***authorizing committees*** that write and enact legislation. Yet advocates also often want enhanced resources for a specific committee, which requires them to work through and with ***appropriations committees*** that decide what resources to allocate to specific programs and departments. Although it is important to have meritorious policies enacted into law, they are rendered ineffective if they are not given sufficient funding by legislatures. Policy advocates therefore need to pressure appropriations committees in both legislative chambers to ensure adequate funding for specific programs.

Policy advocates need to realize, as well, that resources for social policies hinge upon the kind and level of tax revenues that governments collect. Minus sufficient taxes, governments lack resources to fund meritorious policies—particularly if available resources are wasted or siphoned toward programs and policies that lack merit. In the case of the federal government, for example, Joseph Stiglitz, a Nobel-Prize-winning economist, contended that the Iraq War would ultimately cost the United States $2 trillion—resources that might otherwise have been used for social programs at home and abroad.

The Law and Social Policy

State and federal courts assume a major role in social policy, issuing many rulings that directly impact social policies. They are often guided by state and federal constitutions that establish principles for governance and civil affairs. When specific persons or groups believe that specific statutes, regulations, or practices *violate* specific constitutional provisions, they often challenge them in lower state and federal courts. The rulings of these courts are often appealed to state and federal supreme courts.

The use of legal strategies to help homeless persons is illustrated in Policy Advocacy Challenge 4.3. Policy Advocacy Challenge 4.3 illustrates, as well, how social workers can take cases to tribunals run by administrative judges, such as to appeal decisions made by federal and state programs that deny benefits for specific persons.

Policy Advocacy Challenge 4.3

The Use of the Law in Policy Advocacy

Ralph Fertig, A.M. and J.D.

Go to **www.cengage.com** to watch this video clip.

EP 2.1.5a

EP 2.1.5c

Once provision of a need has been defined as a right, then those in need may secure the protection of the law. Social welfare advocates may help define such rights through litigation or legislation, and may ensure the application of those rights through administrative tribunals.

LITIGATION

Some 12,000 to 16,000 homeless people regularly cluster in an area of downtown Los Angeles known as Skid Row. A number of social agencies provide social services and some housing. Still, there is not enough temporary shelter, transitional housing (such as single-room occupancy hotels and programs designed to help selected homeless people get through a crisis), or long-term assisted housing to meet the needs of all.

The result is that thousands of the homeless sleep on the streets of Skid Row, huddling in cardboard boxes, under highway bridges, and in dumpsters. Their 24-hour presence impacts the streets of the area. They constitute a subsociety, a magnet for other homeless people, many of those released from prison or hospitals, and for social work agencies that serve them.

But the real estate that they occupy is alongside a burgeoning commercial and high-rent residential area. Developers want to clear the seamy sights of homeless people from the neighborhood and claim their sites for luxury high-rises. Elected officials are often influenced by wealthy contributors to their campaigns and are tempted by the prospect of private developments that would generate more taxes to provide increased services for everyone.

So complaints about the homeless blocking the sidewalks, creating a sanitary problem on the public way, or intimidating shoppers and office workers in nearby buildings, together with concerns about their drawing dope dealers and prostitutes to Skid Row, led the city council to pass an ordinance (L.A., Cal. Mun. Code § 41.18(d) 2005), on the basis of which the police cleared the homeless away, tore down their cardboard shelters, and arrested those who slept on the streets.

Social workers led a protest and linked the homeless to ACLU (American Civil Liberties Union) lawyers. Two who were convicted and sentenced for violating the ordinance, along with four others who were threatened with arrest, prosecution, incarceration, and conviction for violating it, sought an injunction against the ordinance and the arrests. Under a federal civil rights statute (42 USC 1983), alleging that enforcement of the municipal code violated their constitutional rights, they filed suit in the U.S. District Court for the Central District of California (*Edward Jones v. City of Los Angeles*).

Though they lost at the trial court level, they appealed. On April 14, 2006, the Ninth Circuit reversed and remanded the case (444 F.3d 1118), ruling that because there was substantial and undisputed evidence that the number of homeless persons in the city far exceeded the number of available shelter beds at all times, the city encroached on the rights of the homeless by criminalizing the unavoidable act of sitting, lying, or sleeping at night on public sidewalks while being involuntarily homeless. The court found that the Eighth Amendment (which bars cruel and unusual punishment) prohibits the state from punishing an involuntary act or condition if it is the unavoidable consequence of one's status or being, here a consequence of being human and homeless without shelter in the city.

LEGISLATION

Thus, so long as there are not enough shelters for the homeless, the latter's right to sleep on the streets was secured in *Jones v. City of Los Angeles*. But they still need housing of all sorts, assisted with social services. That calls for private charities, public funds, and the

EP 2.1.5b

backing of local governments. Because the homeless are scattered throughout the state, and to minimize their further concentration in Skid Row pockets of vulnerability, all communities should provide their fair share of housing. But the spirit of NIMBY ("Not In My Back Yard") dominates much of local politics.

Students in USC's social welfare policy classes met with State Senator Gil Cedillo, whose district includes Skid Row. Gil Cedillo then introduced SB 1322, which required that every city or county in California identify sites, in the housing element of their general plan, where emergency homeless shelters and residential service providers would be allowed to locate, without the power of the local governing body to change the plan once it is adopted. With these anti-NIMBY provisions, the bill established "Housing by Right." The sites identified in the plan would be available for emergency shelters and assisted transitional and long-term housing within the planning period, sufficient to shelter families and individuals in need of such service. Localities are free to finance the housing, regulate developers to set aside a proportion of new housing for low income rentals, perhaps in exchange for density bonuses or other incentives, or fashion their own solutions. But they are mandated to do something to plan for and enable the housing of their homeless.

Some students went to Sacramento to lobby state senators, while others visited them in their local offices. The bill passed both houses of the California legislature, but was vetoed by the governor. USC classes then followed through to spur re-re-introduction of the bill (this time as SB 2) and to help it pass. It was signed into law in October 2007. USC students then fanned out to social agencies in the cities of Los Angeles and Orange Counties in organizing efforts to ensure its implementation at the local level.

ADMINISTRATIVE LAW Once rights are established and programs are authorized (as seen in the preceding example), programs have to be established to implement them. Generally, the enabling legislation delegates responsibility for administering such programs to a new or existing public agency, authorizing it to use rules and procedures for carrying out its work. A first draft of such regulations is submitted for a period of public review and comments are invited. Social workers frequently offer input to the proposed rules and procedures, which are considered by the agency and may be integrated into the final regulations. Once they are adopted, their implementation typically provides for an administrative tribunal to allow appeal, review, and possible modification of any actions taken with regard to any individual or group. Such tribunals are run by neutral administrative judges who can order the agency to change its practice, pay compensation, and make the client whole.

Social workers may advise their clients that they can appeal changes in their benefits from most federal and state programs such as Social Security or disability or unemployment compensation. As a policy advocate, you can link them to a lawyer (who in most cases will require a statutory fee, one set by law that will not cost your client anything). Clients can seek administrative review of discrimination on their jobs due to race, gender, religion, national origin, age (if 40 or older), or disability, drawing upon lawyers provided (without cost to the client) by the Equal Employment Opportunity Commission (EEOC) or the State Fair Employment and Housing Commission. They can appeal, for example, denial of proper compensation for overtime, and the denial or constriction of countless other benefits established in law.

As an administrative judge with the EEOC, I was able to order the hiring of a qualified man, represented by a social worker, who had applied in vain to be a mail carrier. The postal service had repeatedly passed him over because he wore a large turban and insisted on his right, as a Sikh, to wear it on the job, while delivering mail. I found the post office had violated the law against religious discrimination. He was given the job

(continued)

**Policy
Advocacy
Challenge 4.3**
(continued)

and back pay to the time when he was first denied a position, and because the government appealed my ruling to the federal court, he got more. My order was upheld, the post office had to pay him full salary for the years his case was tied up in appeal, and the post office was enjoined to never deny any work benefits to any man because he wore a turban.

Such rulings take place in administrative tribunals, but getting to them can intimidate or confuse clients. Often, the details of a client's claim are lost in the bureaucratic procedures of the agencies and overloaded intake workers through which one must begin the process. But social workers can go with their clients to the administrative agencies to ensure that their entreaties are properly understood, filed, and properly moved on to the administrative tribunal.

Social workers may also work with lawyers in preparation for and at the hearing held by the administrative judge and be witnesses on their behalf. All administrative tribunals recognize the right of social workers to fully represent their clients as advocates in place of lawyers, as in the case just described.

Furthermore, it is through the interaction among the intended beneficiaries of social programs, those who manage and distribute those benefits, and lawyers that social workers can discern needs and help transmute them into rights by helping to change the system, its policies, procedures, and regulations. Sometimes, that means going to court for injunctive relief (as in *Jones v. City of Los Angeles*); sometimes that means seeking new laws (as in SB 1322); and sometimes, it means serving as an advocate for clients, one at a time, before an administrative tribunal.

After reading Policy Advocacy Challenge 4.3, listen to the online video as Professor Fertig discusses how policy advocates can use the law to facilitate their work. Please address these questions:

1. How can the law be an ally to policy advocates?
2. Why must social work policy advocates sometimes work in tandem with, or consult, attorneys?

The Political Economy of Social Agencies

EP 2.1.9a

Just as policy advocates need to understand the structure and operations of legislatures, they must also be familiar with social agencies and their organizational processes. It is useful to analyze social agencies' political economy as a prelude to examining their policies.

To survive, social agencies require ongoing, regular resources to meet their payroll and other overhead costs. A few lucky social agencies are massively endowed by private donors, but the officials of most social agencies must frequently interact with institutions, accrediting bodies, and clients to maintain a steady flow of resources. When social agencies stop receiving support from external sources or find these sources severely constricted, they go out of existence, downsize, merge with other agencies, or renegotiate their relations with the external world by changing their mission and their fund-raising or marketing strategies.[35]

Social agencies, which have always been shaped by their political and economic context, were subjected to particularly harsh realities in the 1980s and 1990s. Traditional sources of public funds were constricted during the budget cuts and tax revolts of those decades, when many citizens sought to reduce property taxes or objected to the budget levels of local, state, and federal governments. Agencies that receive funds from campaigns such as United Way and the United Jewish Communities, which raise funds for a coalition of agencies joined in a federation, often found their allocations diminished. In the decade subsequent to the 1990s, the resources of federated campaigns have been depleted by competition from other fund-raising groups, national economic difficulties that have decreased corporations' contributions, and scandals (in the case of the national United Way, whose chief executive was accused of a misuse of funds).

The restricted flow of money from governmental agencies and federated campaigns has meant that larger numbers of social agencies have competed for the scarce resources of foundations, corporations, and private donors. Many social agencies have also found it difficult to maintain a sufficiently large proportion of paying clients. (The clients of many agencies have become poorer and beset by serious mental, economic, and other problems in an era of increasing inequality in the United States.)[36]

The revenues of social agencies come from a variety of sources, such as fees, foundations, donors, and government. Agencies need clients as well.[37] Some clients come directly to agencies through word of mouth, advertising, and outreach programs. Others come by referrals, as when one agency suggests that a client use another agency's services, or when courts or probation departments require people to obtain specific agency services. Interorganization exchanges often shape the flow of clients to an agency, as when the staffs of two organizations agree to enter a reciprocal relationship. Two organizations may negotiate an agreement whereby each agency focuses only on certain kinds of clients, while referring other clients to the other organization. Agencies may also develop joint programs funded by collaboration in writing a grant proposal or seeking a contract.

Demographic, cultural, social, and technological factors also affect agencies profoundly, as when the populations shift, public opinion changes, and new perceptions of social problems, such as family violence, evolve. These changes influence the extent to which people use agency services, the social problems they have, and the agencies they believe are relevant to their problems. While we usually think that agencies, once established, are permanent, many cease to exist when their environment changes. For example, many agencies used to provide residences for pregnant teenagers, where they stayed before giving their newborns up for adoption. With legalized, safe abortions usually available and with many young women choosing to keep their babies, many of these agencies have disappeared or markedly changed their mission.

Various pieces of legislation impose procedural requirements involving social agencies, such as the Americans with Disabilities Act of 1990, which requires agencies to accommodate people with chronic physical and mental disabilities, and the Patient Protection and Affordable Care Act of 2010, which requires clinics and hospitals to make many changes in their services such as increasing preventive services for persons at risk of diseases like diabetes. Various state laws require agencies to report certain social problems, such as child abuse; to inform patients or clients of the risks of certain procedures; to adhere to severe procedural limits when taking children from their natural parents; and to work within restrictions when committing people involuntarily to mental institutions. Federal legislation places restrictions on the use of restraints in nursing homes. Court rulings, such as those forbidding discrimination against members of specific ethnic or racial groups, also influence the procedures of many social agencies.

As we discussed earlier in this chapter, legislation that establishes and funds social programs often dictates the kinds of policies that agencies must follow in implementing them. Some program details that were left vague in the original legislation are defined later when the high-level government agency charged with implementing the program adds administrative regulations.

Some nongovernmental bodies issue regulations that agencies must follow to be accredited and inspect the agencies regularly to ensure that these regulations are being followed. Because unaccredited agencies may have difficulty hiring staff or recruiting clients, such regulations powerfully shape agencies' choices.

Community pressures on social agencies include community groups, organized groups of clients, or individual clients who may request or demand policy changes.

Citizens can place pressure on agencies, particularly governmental agencies, by complaining to government officials about specific services or policies they dislike. Pressure sometimes also emanates from the mass media, as in reports about services that clients have or have not received.

Competition within the broader community places pressure on organizations and undermines the security that agencies find in relatively stable streams of clients and resources. In the face of competition, agencies sometimes have to alter their programs or face retrenchment or termination. For example, by the 1970s, many YMCAs and YWCAs were depending increasingly on fee-based recreation and exercise programs for middle-class people but found their resources imperiled by the rise of profit-oriented exercise centers.[38] Many Ys were forced to retrench when they were unable to develop alternative programs.

Most social agencies establish partnerships with other agencies. They may jointly fund specific programs. They may contract with other agencies to provide specific services. They may establish cooperative referral patterns. They may merge with another agency when they have overlapping missions. They may share space or facilities with other agencies.

To secure resources in the harsh era of the 1980s and 1990s, agencies had to negotiate and manage relations with their political and economic environments by building relationships with existing and potential funders; by developing services that appealed to sufficient numbers of clients to provide revenues; by satisfying external funders that their services met specific evaluative criteria; by developing public relations campaigns to attract funders and clients to the agency; and by modifying their services as competitors encroached on their traditional sources of clients. Many social agencies experienced funding challenges during the deep recession from 2007 to 2010 due to sharp drops in private donations and public funding. Funders and clientele shape organizations' policies, as do agencies' adjustments to their turbulent environment. Although rarely reaching the levels described in Policy Advocacy Challenge 4.4, conflict can occur in agencies as people develop different positions in the context of their values and the agency.

Policy Advocacy Challenge 4.4

Agency in Policy Turmoil

Samuel H. Taylor, DSW

Exactly one year ago, Dr. George Breeze came to San Marcos, a metropolitan suburb of Los Angeles with a population of 60,000 people, to direct the recently established San Marcos Community Mental Health Center. Dr. Breeze had previously worked in Philadelphia, where he had acquired a reputation as the innovative, inspiring, and flexible director of Manford University's Outreach Mental Health Services Department.

When Dr. Breeze was initially interviewed for his position, several board members expressed reservations about how he would fit in, because he did not wear a tie and seemed overconfident. Dr. Sedgwick, the retiring director, calmed the board by saying that, as a young psychoanalyst, he too had been fairly unconventional. The board had to keep in mind that this was no longer the San Marcos Clinic; it was a new mental health center, and it needed new ideas and the dedication of the youth. "He will work out," Dr. Sedgwick reassured them.

Shortly after George Breeze arrived at the San Marcos Community Mental Health Center, he made it clear to the staff that waiting lists, long-term therapy, and supervision were outdated. In the following months, he

1. urged short-term, crisis-oriented management of cases.
2. requested and received permission to establish an advisory board of citizens from the catchment area and another board composed of consumers.
3. abolished the supervision system and established a flexible peer-consultation system.
4. asked staff members to work evenings in order to see families.

5. got into an argument with the chief of police about how officers were handling youngsters and emotionally ill persons.
6. hired paraprofessionals from a human services program of a community college to serve as community aides.
7. told the staff that he wanted to know personally about the service and disposition of each case that involved a racial or ethnic minority client because he suspected that the staff members were allowing biases to influence case management.

Within six months, the staff in the agency had become deeply divided. Three major groups had formed and developed leaderships. First, some of the original clinic staff members (who had helped Dr. Sedgwick prepare the mental health center application) resented Dr. Breeze's nontraditional ways and felt that they had no chance to introduce their ideas. They rallied behind a Dr. Jones, met privately, and decided that they must take their case to other agencies in San Marcos and to local civic leaders and then must present their complaints to the agency board with the support of these other groups and leaders.

The staff hired by Dr. Breeze (young activist professionals and community aides) learned of the strategy and immediately alerted Asian, black, and Chicano groups in San Marcos and rallied behind a Dr. Smith, who contacted both the National Institute of Mental Health (the prime federal funder of the center) and the Citizen and Consumer Advisory boards. They were ready to ask for termination of federal and state funds if Dr. Breeze was dismissed.

Finally, a number of agency supervisors formed a group behind a Dr. Virtue that advocated "responsible change." They were not opposed to all the changes instituted by Dr. Breeze but particularly opposed to those that deprived "professionals" of their rightful positions of authority and prestige within the agency. They wanted restoration of the supervisory system and curtailment of hiring of new careerists.

The issue reached crisis proportions when a patient being cared for by a community aide committed suicide in a most sensational manner. A reporter from a newspaper interviewed a member of the original staff and was told that "this would never have happened if Dr. Sedgwick had been there; Dr. Breeze's ideas just don't work." The board decided to hold a meeting to settle the issue, and they agreed to allow representatives of all sides to present their evidence. They felt that Dr. Breeze had introduced some good programs but also felt that he was unconventional. At this meeting, they hoped to reach a final decision as to whether Dr. Breeze should be fired, retained (but only after placing limits on the reforms he had issued), or given a vote of complete confidence.

"Traditionalists," then, rallied behind Dr. Jones and wanted to restore the traditional mission of the agency—long-term therapy with white and middle-class clients. "Insurgents" supported Dr. Breeze and his various reforms with no qualifications. "Advocates of responsible change" wanted some innovations but not at the expense of the traditional prerogatives of professionals. The board wished to bring unity to the agency as soon as possible to avoid further adverse publicity as well as possible loss of funds.

Source: This case was developed by Professor Samuel H. Taylor. Names and locations have been altered.

We do not mean to suggest that political and economic factors wholly determine organizations' actions. Not-for-profit agencies have latitude in deciding, for example, which public contracts or grants to seek. Governmental policies that descend on public and nonpublic agencies are often vague or ill-defined on many points, so the staff in these agencies has considerable discretion in shaping many details of their services. While noncompliance with governmental policies poses legal and ethical questions, agencies sometimes flout specific policy requirements or bend the rules.

The description of the harsh atmosphere for social agencies in the 1980s and 1990s as well as the recession from 2007 to 2010 that extended into 2012, such as funding restrictions, should not suggest that they cannot maintain humane, caring services. Even when such restrictions stretch staff resources to the limit, many agencies deliver effective services. Skilled leadership allows many agencies to keep up staff morale even in difficult circumstances.

EP 2.1.9b

As they manage and plan relations with their environment, agencies must also attend to their internal operations: They have to build and maintain a staff, design programs, mediate internal disputes and conflicts, develop decision-making processes, produce budgets, attend to logistical tasks, and maintain their facilities. Indeed, social agencies may be unable to obtain a steady flow of resources if they lack a reputation for delivering quality services. In the case of not-for-profit agencies, for example, foundations often ask community leaders about a specific agency's reputation in the community. This reputation depends on people's perceptions of the services and staff of the agencies they interact with or hear about.[39]

The executive of an agency, then, must juggle many tasks if the agency is to flourish, devoting attention to the agency's relations with its environment while trying to develop internal processes that enable the agency to maintain quality services. Of course, executives often delegate tasks, as when they use fund developers and planners for external relations and program directors for internal matters.

The Political Economy of Programs and Social Work Units

EP 2.1.9a

We have discussed social agencies' political economy, but many social workers operate in large organizations dominated by other professions, as in hospitals, public welfare departments, corporations, and schools. Others work in specialized units within a broader social service organization, such as adoption units within child welfare departments, programs for homeless persons within mental health clinics, and programs to help single mothers within family counseling agencies.[40]

Our discussion of social agencies' political economy applies in double measure to these units or programs that exist within larger organizations. They depend on their host organizations for resources and for permission to perform specific roles or functions. In turn, the political and economic factors that impinge on the host organization influence the subsidiary programs' ability to command resources and mandates from that host organization.

To illustrate, consider the case of a social work unit in a hospital. Such a unit must hire sufficient staff to help patients in many parts of the hospital, including the emergency room and the oncology and outpatient departments. It also needs permission from various units of the hospital, as well as the top management of the hospital, to assign personnel to these areas. To obtain these resources and permissions, the social work unit must be exceedingly adroit in managing its relationship with the hospital's officials and staff; indeed, the hospital is a key part of the social work unit's political economy. (A more detailed discussion of the political strategies the social work unit can use to obtain resources appears in Chapter Ten.) In turn, the hospital's willingness to allocate resources to the social work unit hinges on factors in its political and economic environments, such as hospital accreditation standards and the extent to which Medicare and private insurance will or will not fund social work services.[41]

Some program units within larger agencies derive funds from both the host organization and special external funders. A project for homeless persons in a mental health clinic, for example, might receive funds from a governmental agency or a foundation and funds or supplies from the host organization. The directors and staff of such a program would need to be attentive to both sets of funders to ensure the program's survival. If the external funding ended or decreased, the program's staff would have to try to convince the clinic itself to increase its funding of the program.

Mapping Agencies' Policies

Our discussion of social agencies' political and economic context leads us to consider the nature, varieties, and content of agencies' social policies. To better understand the nature of agency policies, try to imagine a social agency without policies. In such an agency, the staff members would be compelled to act without the guidance of agency rules, regulations, protocols, or priorities. There would be no written mission statement and no manual to define procedures. It would be impossible for the staff members to describe the agency's activities to outsiders, such as clients and funders. And how would clients using an agency with no policies know which services they could obtain and for how long? How would they know their rights, or what protections or safeguards were in place?[42]

Policies govern the relationships among agency staff members as well, so staff members in an agency lacking policies would find themselves in a chaotic and unpredictable environment. There would be no personnel policies to establish staff's duties and rights, rules for termination, or protection from arbitrary treatment. Nor would such an agency have clear priorities established by the agency budget, which is itself a kind of policy.

Although policies cannot shape every detail of an agency's internal organization or internal dynamics, they typically provide an agency with a central direction, priorities, and guidance for its operating programs, and some protections for staff and clients.

Figure 4.4 maps the variety of agency policies. It is a complex diagram because of the wide range of policies, which cannot be easily summarized.

Policy Advocacy Challenge 4.5

Map of Agency Policies

Ron McClain, J.D., MSW, LCSW
Go to
www.cengage.com
to watch this video clip.

Using Figure 4.4 as an orienting framework, select a specific program in a social agency. Trace the following:

- Its history
- What combination of policies exist within it or define it
- What money streams are relevant to it
- How it is (or is not) supported or shaped by informal policies in the agency
- Whether it has implications for relations between the agency and other agencies
- How it might be changed or reformed in the context of agency politics so that it provides better services

Watch the video clip for this policy advocacy challenge, where Ron McClain discusses how Hurricane Katrina's destructive effects on New Orleans powerfully shaped and transformed the map of his agency. Please answer these questions:

1. What changes took place in his agency's mission and why?
2. How did the programs of the agency change?
3. Speculate whether he was able to tap into new funding sources that helped his agency implement its transformed mission.

FIGURE 4.4 Map of Agency Policies

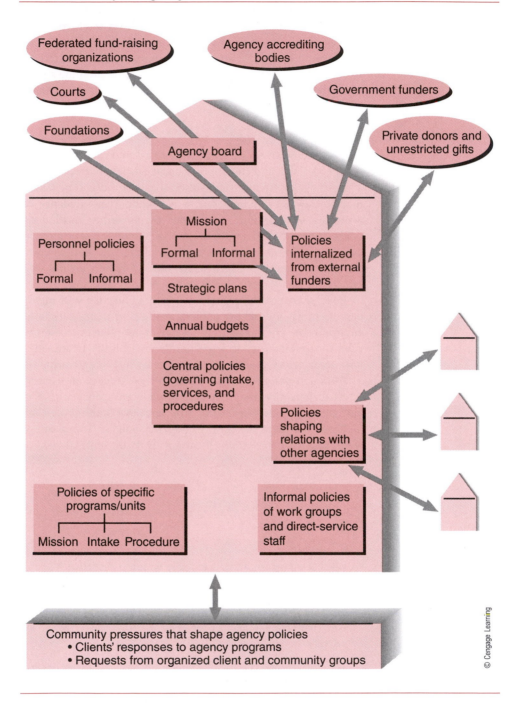

© Cengage Learning

The missions and programs of many social agencies are not static. Not only do funding sources change through time, but so also do flows of clients. In the wake of Hurricane Katrina, these shifts in funding and clientele occurred rapidly, whereas they may change more gradually at other times. Effective executive directors and agency boards of directors work hard to position agencies in their environments so that they can not only thrive fiscally but meet important community needs.

Some policies are originally external to agencies but are then internalized, like the policies agencies accept when they take funding from governmental programs.

These internalized policies establish specific rules, such as intake procedures, staffing requirements, content of services, reporting mechanisms, and a general statement about the program's purposes. An agency that has a number of externally funded programs (not-for-profit agencies now receive the majority of their funds from the government and from foundations) will have multiple sets, or clusters, of these externally established policies. Some details of funded programs are left relatively vague, so the agency's staff must fill the gaps with their own policies. (Of course, agency staff may ignore or even violate some of the funder's policies, at the risk of their violations being detected during audits.)

Court rulings shape agency policies as well. For example, the *Tarasoff* decision requires social workers to inform intended victims when a client tells the worker that he or she intends to inflict bodily injury on them. Social workers who fail to inform the threatened targets may be sued.[43]

The stipulations of nongovernmental agencies that purchase services that reimburse agencies (or their clientele) for specific kinds of services, such as health insurance companies, also affect agency policies.

Other agency policies are centrally established, even though external economic and social forces may influence their content. For example, most not-for-profit agencies have a mission statement that defines their priorities and strategy.[44] One agency defines its mission as "a career and job resource center created to serve a broad spectrum of women by helping them recognize and attain their employment and earnings potential in the work world through providing job and career resources in a supportive environment."

As you can see, mission statements are relatively vague; nonetheless, they establish the agency's general philosophy. In this example, the mission statement affirms certain activities, such as providing job and career resources, but not others, such as counseling services or mental health services. In addition to a mission statement, the staff often has certain objectives, goals, or priorities in common. For example, a staff member who says, "What makes us unique is that we like preventive services" or "We like to use outreach," suggests an overall approach to services that, she thinks, distinguishes her agency from other agencies.

Agencies' annual budgets also serve as policy statements, at least in part. They shape agencies' priorities by distributing resources to various programs, perhaps cutting funds for one program while increasing them for another. To fully understand an agency's policies, then, one must examine both its present and its previous budgets to determine its priorities and how they have changed.[45]

For services that are self-funded, the agency must establish its own internal policies, such as intake procedures and the content of services. For example, a not-for-profit mental health clinic might receive 50 percent of its annual operating funds from external funders (which shape the policies for those programs) and make up 50 percent of its budget from its own funds. The clinic would decide internally how to govern the intake, services, and other details of those programs funded with its own money.

Many nonprofit agencies receive funds from federated fund-raisers, who then impose some of their own policies. They monitor the agency regularly and may make recommendations about the agency's internal priorities.[46]

In complex organizations, such as hospitals or government bureaucracies, many policies exist at the level of the unit, the bureau (or department), or the program. These smaller units often have their own mission statements. The following is the mission statement of one social work unit in a hospital:

> It is the mission of the Social Service Department to enhance the delivery of comprehensive health services by providing social services to the patients and their families of the University of Minnesota Hospitals and to assist in the resolution of social and emotional problems related to illness, medical services, and rehabilitation.[47]

These units usually have their own budgets, which the staff of the host organization review and approve, and their own policies. A social work department in a hospital may decide, for example, to fund social work services in one unit, such as the emergency room, but not in another, such as the neurology unit.

In addition to the budgets; mission statements; and official policies of agencies, units, or departments, many other policies are fashioned through informal systems and networks. While not documented, informal policies shape staff's actions and choices at many points in their work and deliberations. Informal policies may vary from official written policy, but they may also fill gaps when official policy is ambiguous.[48]

To illustrate the importance of informal policy even in the higher reaches of an agency, we will return to the discussion of an organization's mission. A written mission statement conveys a unity that is usually absent from organizations, because different staff members often have diverse and subjective notions concerning their organization's mission. While the official mission may, for example, stress services to families with single heads of households, some staff may want the agency to place more stress on serving intact families. Staff members may also disagree about the extent to which the agency should seek or accept governmental funds or about how intake policies should be structured. Sometimes, divergent notions of the agency's mission erupt into conflict, as when the organization selects a new director or when it deliberates over the agency's budget.[49] In other cases, however, staff may sublimate their differences and may even be unaware of some of them.

And on a very basic level, each agency employee will have a set of personal policies, or approaches, to his or her work. When confronting virtually identical client problems, for example, one staff member may provide services based on traditional psychotherapy, while another may emphasize survival skills, advocacy, and empowerment.

Personal interpretations of policy, as well as binding informal policies that many staff share, are neither good nor bad; they must be judged by their specific outcomes for the clients and the agency. If policy advocates decide that a worker's personal policy preferences or the informal policies of a group of staff result in prejudices against certain kinds of clients, such as gays, they will want to modify them. But sometimes these preferences and policies lead to positive outcomes, such as advocacy and outreach, constructive efforts to help clients, and extraordinary efforts to assist clients above and beyond the call of duty.[50] In addition, they sometimes help place legitimate limits on official policies, as when elderly patients are under pressure by hospital and Medicare administrators to leave the hospital as soon as possible after medical treatment. Disoriented by surgery and medications, such older persons often resist early discharge and find ready allies in social workers who help delay their discharge for one or more days. While operating in apparent violation of higher-level policy, these social workers can often justify their actions as being necessary for the well-being of their clients.

The Players in Organizational Settings

Anyone who seeks to change organizational policies encounters hierarchies and divisions of labor. These are the formal and structural characteristics of organizations that Max Weber emphasized in his classic writings.[51] A hierarchy is the chain of command that gives high-level executives such powers as creating high-level policies, hiring staff, and making budgets. The division of labor, or specialization, divides staff into units that focus on specific tasks, such as protective services, adoptions, and foster care in a child welfare office. While many organizational theorists have sought ways to soften hierarchy and specialization within organizations, they remain enduring, important features.

Some may associate these structural characteristics with control, rigidity, and fragmentation, but they also serve positive purposes. As productive collectives, organizations need powerful officials who focus on functions such as developing overarching policies, a mission, budgets, and planning. The complexities of the tasks in the modern welfare state often require specialization, both in the work of specific units or departments within the larger organization and in the work of the individuals within the units or departments.

Figure 4.5 provides useful clues to hierarchy and division of labor in a sample organization. The organizational units include those that provide specific kinds of services to clients and those that perform work for the entire organization, such as research and accounting. The figure also shows the distribution of power within the organization: The people toward the top of the hierarchy have certain formal powers.

Were we to attend only to the organizational chart, however, we would have an incomplete and distorted conception of the organization. Policy practitioners often want to know how power is distributed in organizations with respect to certain issues. While the organizational chart offers clues, it may overstate or understate the power of specific individuals.[52] The director of a relatively small unit, for example, may have considerable power with respect to certain issues and less power with respect to others.

To obtain a more complete understanding of power within organizations, and other organizational dynamics and processes, we need to understand the interactions among

FIGURE 4.5 Sample Organizational Chart

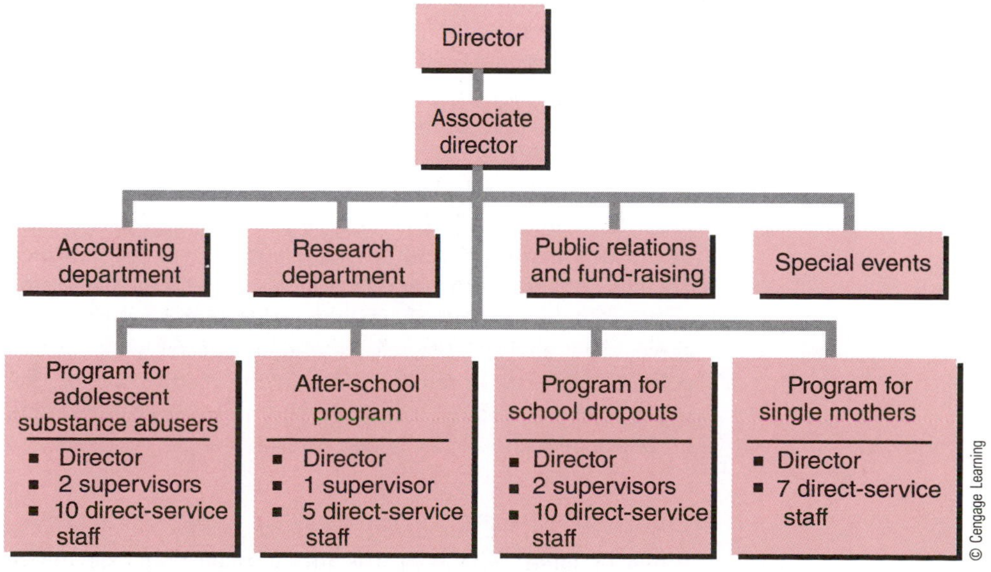

the staff of an organization. We can conceptualize organizations as transparent overlays, placed on top of one another, that depict (a) the formal organizational chart, which displays the official hierarchy and division of labor; (b) the resources allocated to specific units, programs, or functions within the organization; (c) employees and internal programs that generate revenue, clientele, and prestige for an organization; and (d) informal relationships and patterns of consultation between members of the organization.[53] Of course, such overlays do not exist in the real world, but they provide a useful means of conceptualizing power and relationships within organizations. Together, these overlays provide useful, important information that allows us to build a fuller understanding of the dynamics of a specific agency.

Overlay 1: The Organizational Chart

Organizational charts tell us a great deal about the players in a specific organization. As we have discussed, people at high levels in the hierarchy, whether in specific units of the organization or in the broader organization, usually have powers and prerogatives that enable them to shape decisions. They help make budgets; participate in hiring, dismissing, promoting, and supervising lower-level staff; obtain access to information about the personnel, programs, and budgets of the agency; and have access to information about the resources and institutions in the agency's external environment.

We can sometimes infer a person's perspective from her or his position in an organization.

Top executives are often concerned about the budget implications of specific choices, whereas lower-level professional staff often emphasize budget implications for clients and staff workloads. As intermediaries between management and direct-service staff, supervisors often share the perspectives of both higher-level and lower-level personnel. Those who direct or work in a specific program often view policy choices and agency budgets only from the perspective of that program.

The board of directors of nongovernmental agencies makes many important policy decisions. The board establishes an agency's high-level policies, such as its mission; hires its executive director; oversees the development of personnel policies; examines the agency's budget; and serves as the general overseer. Some public, or governmental, agencies also have advisory boards that offer suggestions to the top staff of the agency.[54] (The top executives of public agencies are ultimately responsible to those elected officials who appoint them, as discussed earlier in this chapter.)

An organizational chart, however, may be misleading. Some people in the higher ranks of organizations defer to persons who are horizontal to them or even below them in the formal chart. Organizational charts do not tell us which units or programs in an organization have considerable resources, and which ones the top executives favor. In addition, organizational charts imply that high-level persons make most general policy choices, but they do not tell us who has power with respect to specific issues. Many political scientists have observed that the distribution of power often varies with the issue; persons who are exceedingly powerful concerning certain issues may have little or no power regarding other issues.[55]

Overlay 2: Budget Priorities

We have noted that a budget is an important policy document because it establishes an organization's priorities. People who oversee program units with considerable resources, for example, often have more power than those who oversee units with relatively few resources. Examining budget trends in organizations can prove useful; if one unit has been losing staff positions while another has been gaining them, we can deduce that the power of each unit has changed. However, when considered individually, budgets may give us misleading impressions. Some persons who direct units with relatively small budgetary resources may have extraordinary power that derives, for example, from their close personal ties with other persons in the organization.

Overlay 3: Boundary Spanners and Mission Enhancers

Some persons are boundary spanners who have links with institutions, officials, and agencies that can bring substantial resources to an agency. They may have links to funders, such as staff in a foundation; a knowledge of funding sources or grant-writing skills; connections to elected officials (or their aides) who have power over the funds that go to the agency; a seat on an important committee in the host organization or in the community; or connections with key sources of referrals to an agency. Such people, who enhance agencies' resources and clientele, often derive power from these roles.[56]

Mission enhancers promote goals that highly placed persons in organizations favor. If the top officials in a hospital want to increase the number of older clients, they are likely to view with favor those units or officials within their hospital who they believe can advance this goal. Conversely, we can assume that units or staff whose activities are peripheral to the organization's central objectives are likely to have less power.

Overlay 4: Informal Relationships Among Organizational Members

Some of the connections between persons in organizations are predicted by the organizational chart, but proximity in the organization's hierarchy does not tell us about real-world patterns of friendship and trust, enmity, or social distance. Nor does it tell us about human contacts that span different units of an organization or cut across levels of the hierarchy. Policy practitioners need to know about these relationships to understand processes and choices in organizations.

The formal organizational chart cannot tell us which persons will band together to enhance their power within an organization. Groupings take many forms. Some are ongoing informal clusters of persons who share knowledge and who support one another. Other groupings are constructed during specific controversies or crises, such as to oppose the termination of a program. Some groupings are relatively large; others consist of only a few staff members.

The Political Economy of Communities

EP 2.1.9a

Many kinds of communities exist. They may be so heterogeneous that they cannot easily be described, or they may be dominated by a specific group. Most neighborhoods within communities can be described by social class or economic variables, as well as by ethnic, racial, and age characteristics.[57]

As sociologists have long noted, communities have vertical and horizontal dimensions. When we discuss their vertical dimensions, we analyze the economic, political, and social institutions that descend on communities from the outside, such as supermarket chains, corporations, state or federal policies, the mass media, and social movements with local chapters or supporters. When we discuss their horizontal dimensions, we examine local civic associations (groups that advance a neighborhood's well-being), advocacy groups (local groups that promote specific causes), social agencies, public agencies, neighborhood groups, and churches. Moreover, social movements—that is, broad movements that foster social change, such as the civil rights movement of the 1960s and the Rainbow Coalition in the 1980s—sometimes develop local offshoots or chapters.[58]

When addressing specific issues in communities, such as where to place social service institutions or how to mobilize opposition to certain policies, policy advocates need to discover which community residents, leaders, politicians, and institutions have traditionally focused on this issue. Rather than a single power elite that controls all issues, most communities have a series of elites that specialize in specific issues.

In seeking specific reforms in communities, policy advocates often affiliate with, consult, or enlist the support of community-based groups. These groups may include civic associations; advocacy groups; local chapters of national groups, such as NOW or the National Association for the Advancement of Colored People (NAACP); or local offshoots of social movements. Policy practitioners sometimes form coalitions representing social agencies and community groups when they want to oppose a specific measure, such as a cut in welfare benefits, or when they want to establish new programs, such as programs to help abused children.[59]

The mass media, including local papers, television stations, and radio stations, often assume a pivotal role in local communities. Of course, the mass media may be relatively conservative in local areas, and so astute policy practitioners cultivate relationships with sympathetic reporters.

Many kinds of policy issues develop in communities. Some pertain to where buildings are, or are not, placed, such as whether a half-way house for persons with specific problems is placed in a certain neighborhood. Some pertain to the policies of institutions, such as local schools. Advocates might question, for example, whether a particular school provides sufficient tutoring to certain kinds of students, sufficient outreach to truants, or sufficient public health services. Some pertain to a local government's budget: Should it allocate greater resources to specific programs or needs? Still other issues involve patterns of citizen participation in decision making, such as whether certain boards are representative of the jurisdiction's population. Advocates sometimes seek establishment of task forces to analyze problems such as inadequate child care, lack of after-school recreation programs, or gangs.

The community politics of many issues can be highly conflicting. For example, when a county welfare office wanted to establish a branch office in a certain community, remarkable conflict ensued that pitted policy advocates against persons and businesses who feared the office would lower property values and bring undesirable people into the area. Only after protracted conflict and court rulings was the branch office finally established.

Different Layers of Government and Policy

We have discussed policy within specific levels of government, such as federal, state, city, and community levels. Different policies and resources exist at each of these levels in the American federal system. Policies that are germane to homelessness exist, for example, at each level. The federal government funds programs for homeless persons run by local jurisdictions or nongovernmental groups, such as shelters. Some federal programs exacerbate homelessness, such as inadequate funding of construction of affordable housing,

When different units of government have different policies for addressing problems like homelessness, policy advocates have to try to get them to work together. Listen to the online video, where Bob Erlenbusch, member of the Board of the National Coalition Against Homelessness in Washington, DC, discusses his challenges in trying to link programs and policies of Los Angeles County with those of the City of Los Angeles when trying to end homelessness in southern California.

failure to enact a sufficient minimum wage, and insufficient funding for substance abuse and mental health programs. States, too, fund service programs, housing and social-service programs. Local units of government sometimes cooperate with advocates who seek to end homelessness, but often enact policies that harm homeless persons, such as by local ordinances that allow the police to place them in jails. States have assumed larger policy roles in recent decades with the devolution of federal policy to them, for example, through block grants and federal mandates that require states to address specific problems.

When addressing issues like homelessness, policy advocates have to understand specific policies and funds that exist at each level of government so that they not only can tap resources but know what policies they wish to change.

Nor should we forget the private sector. In the case of homelessness, for example, some foundations fund programs to help or empower homeless persons. Not-for-profit groups that build affordable housing are often key resources in specific communities. Advocacy groups and some churches work to eradicate homelessness in specific communities. Some private developers, particularly if required to do so by local or state ordinances, include affordable housing in their projects—or can be pressured to do so.

The multiplicity of policies that bear on specific social problems like homelessness often presents challenges to policy advocates, who need to get officials from different levels of government, and from the public and private sectors, to collaborate (see Policy Advocacy Challenge 4.6).

Maneuvering in a Multi-Layered Policy Ecology

Americans have created a complex policy ecology that involves policies from different levels of government, including federal, state, and local levels, as well as public and private sectors. This complex policy ecology shapes how specific jurisdictions develop policies germane to their homeless population. We discuss this context in Policy Advocacy Challenge 4.7.

Take a jurisdiction of your choosing, such as the city or town where you live, and discuss how its multi-layered policy ecology shapes how policy is made with regard to homelessness. Specifically, consider the following factors:

- Who are the key players that influence policy related to homelessness? Which elected officials, civil servants, lobbyists, and advocates in your chosen jurisdiction influence policy related to housing, shelter, or social services for this population?
- What special interest groups might get involved in efforts to pass or defeat a bill related to supportive housing for the homeless, and why?
- What role does the legislative branch of your chosen city, state, or federal government have in addressing the needs of homeless individuals within its jurisdiction?
- What legislative committees within the local, state, and federal government might be involved in addressing the problem of homelessness?
- How might the political economy of a social agency, such as a homeless shelter or a soup kitchen, impact the homeless clients it serves (or could potentially serve)?
- In your opinion, what should be the mission statement of a homeless shelter in your chosen jurisdiction? Would it include policy advocacy with or on behalf of the disadvantaged population?
- How might public opinion influence the creation of policies to address the problem of homelessness in your chosen jurisdiction?
- What laws currently impact the homeless population in your chosen jurisdiction? You might wish to perform an Internet search to look for legislation that criminalized this population, such as anti-panhandling ordinances.
- What charities or foundations might fund social services for the homeless, such as shelters or a soup kitchen? What about advocacy efforts to ameliorate homelessness; what charities or foundations might fund these types of activities?

What You Can Now Do

Chapter Summary

You are now equipped to do the following:

- Understand how governments are structured.
- Understand relations among legislators, lobbyists, interest groups, public opinion, and members of the executive branch.
- Find names of key committees in state and federal jurisdictions.
- Understand the mindsets of elected officials such as legislators and heads of government.
- Know the mindsets of nonelected officials such as civil servants and political appointees.
- Understand the political economy of social agencies.
- Understand the political economy of programs and social work units within agencies.
- Be able to map agencies' policies.
- Be able to draw an organizational chart.
- Use four overlays to develop a dynamic understanding of a specific social agency.
- Understand the political economy of communities.

Competency Notes

EPA 2.1.1b   Practice personal reflection and self-correction to assure continual professional development (p. 113): Social workers reflect to decide if they want to become public officials.

EPA 2.1.5a   Understand forms and mechanisms of oppression and discrimination (p. 120): Social workers learn how specific statutes oppress vulnerable populations.

EPA 2.1.5b   Advocate for human rights and social and economic justice (pp. 119, 121): Some social workers seek public office to advocate for human rights.

EPA 2.1.5c   Engage in practices that advance social and economic justice (pp. 114, 119, 120): Some social workers seek public office to advance social and economic justice—and collaborate with public-interest attorneys.

EPA 2.1.9a   Continuously discover, appraise, and attend to changing locales, populations, scientific and technological developments, and emerging societal trends to provide relevant services (pp. 101, 114, 122, 126, 133): Social workers must learn about the context of policy-making, including officials in government, agency, and community settings.

EPA 2.1.9b   Provide leadership in promoting sustainable changes in service delivery and practice to improve the quality of social services (p. 126): Social workers seek to sustain quality services during budget cuts.

Endnotes

1. See James McGregor Burns, *The Power to Lead* (New York: Simon & Schuster, 1984).

2. For discussion of the budget roles of the president, see Aaron Wildavsky, *The New Politics of the Budgetary Process* (Glenview, IL: Scott, Foresman, 1988), pp. 166–186.

3. Abraham Holtzman, *Legislative Liaison: Executive Leadership in the Congress* (Chicago: Rand McNally, 1970).

4. Hedrick Smith, *The Power Game: How Washington Works* (New York: Ballantine Books, 1988), pp. 388–428.

5. Wildavsky, *The New Politics,* pp. 165–212.

6. Smith, *The Power Game,* pp. 41–57.

7. Smith, *The Power Game,* pp. 145–150. For a classic discussion of the different orientations of conservative and liberal constituencies to social legislation, see Lewis Froman, "Interparty Constituency Differences and Congressional Voting Behavior," *American Political Science Review* 57 (March 1963): 57–61.

8. Marilyn Bagwell, *A Political Handbook for Health Professionals* (Boston: Little, Brown, 1985), pp. 63–64.

9. Ibid., pp. 64–66. See also Richard Cheney and Lynne Cheney, *Kings of the Hill* (New York: Continuum, 1983).

10. Bagwell, *Political Handbook,* pp. 67–68.

11. Judith Meredith, *Lobbying on a Shoestring* (Dover, MA: Auburn House, 1989), pp. 65–78.

12. Lewis Froman, *The Congressional Process: Strategies, Rules, and Procedures* (Boston: Little, Brown, 1967).

13. Glenn Abney and Thomas Lauth, *The Politics of State and City Administration* (Albany: State University of New York Press, 1986), pp. 130–212.

14. Laurence Lynn, *Managing Public Policy* (Boston: Little, Brown, 1987).

15. Smith, *The Power Game,* pp. 270–326.

16. For a discussion of links between legislatures and civil servants, see J. Weatherford McIver, *Tribes on the Hill* (New York: Rawson Wade, 1981), pp. 87–111.

17. Interactions between lobbyists and legislators are discussed throughout Jeffrey Birnbaum and Alan Murray, *Showdown at Gucci Gulch* (New York: Vintage Books, 1987).

18. See Policy Advocacy Challenge 11.1 for a detailed discussion of the tactics used by lobbyists.

19. The role of funds from special interest groups and affluent Americans in campaigns and politics is discussed by Thomas Edsall, *The New Politics of Inequality* (New York: Norton, 1984).

20. See, for example, James Smith, *Brookings at Seventy-Five* (Washington, DC: Brookings Institution, 1991).

21. McIver, *Tribes on the Hill*, pp. 87–111.

22. See R. Douglas Arnold, *The Logic of Congressional Action* (New Haven, CT: Yale University Press, 1990), pp. 1–87.

23. Lynn, *Managing Public Policy*, pp. 68–73.

24. Arnold, *The Logic of Congressional Action*, pp. 60–87.

25. Ibid.

26. Smith, *The Power Game*, pp. 119–159.

27. Ibid., pp. 119–159; and Willard Richan, *Lobbying for Social Change* (New York: Haworth Press, 1991), pp. 53–54.

28. Smith, *The Power Game*, pp. 270–284.

29. Arnold, *The Logic of Congressional Action*, pp. 141–144.

30. For a discussion of the need not to write off conservatives when developing coalitions, see Nancy Amidei, "How to Be an Advocate in Bad Times," *Public Welfare* 40 (Summer 1982): 41.

31. As an example of the ambiguous signals that high-level political appointees often receive from heads of government, see the roles of Elliot Richardson and Edward Zigler in my case study titled "An Extended Policy-Practice Case: Child Development and Daycare," in *Social Welfare Policy: From Theory to Practice* (Belmont, CA: Wadsworth, 1990), pp. 350–377.

32. Richan, *Lobbying for Social Change*, pp. 60–62.

33. See Ron Dear and Rino Patti, "Legislative Advocacy: Seven Effective Tactics," in Maryann Mahaffey and John Hanks, eds., *Practical Politics: Social Work and Political Responsibility* (Silver Spring, MD: National Association of Social Workers, 1982), pp. 107–108.

34. An example of a civil servant's resistance to a policy advocate is provided by William Bell and Budd Bell, "Monitoring the Bureaucracy: An Extension of Legislative Lobbying," in Mahaffey and Hanks, *Practical Politics*, pp. 128–130.

35. Yeheskel Hasenfeld, *Human Service Organizations* (Englewood Cliffs, NJ: Prentice Hall, 1983), pp. 43–49.

36. Economic pressures on human service organizations in the 1980s and 1990s are discussed by Stephen Webster and Mary Wylie, "Strategic Planning in a Competitive Environment," *Administration in Mental Health* 15 (Fall 1988): 25–44.

37. Hasenfeld, *Human Service Organizations*, pp. 50–83.

38. Mayer Zald, *Organizational Change: The Political Economy of the YMCA* (Chicago: University of Chicago Press, 1970).

39. Jean Potuchek, "The Context of Social Service Funding: The Funding Relationship," *Social Service Review* 60 (September 1986): 421–436.

40. Bruce Jansson and June Simmons, "The Survival of Social Work Departments," *Social Work* 31 (September 1986): 339–344.

41. Bruce Jansson and June Simmons, "The Ecology of Social Work Departments," *Social Work in Health Care* 11 (Winter 1985): 1–16; and Bruce Jansson and June Simmons, "Building Department or Unit Power within Human Service Organizations," *Administration in Social Work* 8 (Fall 1984): 41–56.

42. Robert Goodin, *Reasons for Welfare* (Princeton, NJ: Princeton University Press, 1988), pp. 190–193.

43. See *Tarasoff v. Regents of the University of California*, 1976. 17 Cal. 4d 425.

44. Hasenfeld, *Human Service Organizations*, pp. 84–109.

45. For a discussion of the politics of money in organizations, see Burton Gummer, *The Politics of Social Administration: Managing Organizational Politics in Social Agencies* (Englewood Cliffs, NJ: Prentice Hall, 1990), pp. 46–67.

46. For a critical view of federated fund-raising, see Stanley Wenocur, "A Pluralistic Planning Model for United Way Organizations," *Social Service Review* 50 (December 1976): 586–600. See also Eleanor Brilliant, *The United Way: Dilemmas of Organized Charity* (New York: Columbia University Press, 1990).

47. Murray Gruber, ed., *Management Systems in the Human Services* (Philadelphia: Temple University Press, 1981), pp. 87–96.

48. A case study of the divergence between high-level official policy and the actual operative policies in agencies is provided by Franklin Chu and Sharland Trotter, *The Madness Establishment* (New York: Grossman, 1974).

49. Gummer, *The Politics of Social Administration*, pp. 10–11, 19–20, 162–163.

50. Goodin, *Reasons for Welfare*, pp. 190–193.

51. Hans Gerth and C. Wright Mills, eds., *From Max Weber: Essays in Sociology* (New York: Oxford University Press, 1946).

52. Gummer, *The Politics of Social Administration,* pp. 11–13.

53. Existing organizational theory, which presents a variety of factors that shape outcomes and behavior, is suggestive of the concept of overlays. Different authors emphasize different structural, political, and economic factors, as well as the informal culture of organizations. While placing organizational behavior in a political–economic framework, for example, Hasenfeld discusses these various factors in *Human Service Organizations.*

54. See, for example, Sheldon Gelman, "The Board of Directors and Agency Accountability," *Social Casework* 64 (February 1983): 83–91.

55. Robert Dahl, *Pluralist Democracy in the United States* (Chicago: Rand McNally, 1967).

56. Hasenfeld, *Human Service Organizations,* p. 8.

57. For a discussion of neighborhoods, see James Cunningham, "Are Neighborhoods Real? A Review Essay," *Urban Resources* 1 (Winter 1984): 19–22.

58. Roland Warren, *New Perspectives on the American Community* (Homewood, IL: Dorsey Press, 1977), pp. 260–365.

59. Milan Dluhy, *Building Coalitions in the Human Services* (Newbury Park, CA: Sage, 1990).

Suggested Readings

Legislatures

R. Douglas Arnold, *The Logic of Congressional Action* (New Haven, CT: Yale University Press, 1990).

J. Weatherford McIver, *Tribes on the Hill* (New York: Rawson, Wade, 1981).

Hedrick Smith, *The Power Game: How Washington Works* (New York: Ballantine Books, 1988), pp. 119–160, 270–326.

Government Bureaucracies

Laurence Lynn, *Managing Public Policy* (Boston: Little, Brown, 1987).

Interest Groups and Lobbyists

Marilyn Bagwell, *A Political Handbook for Health Professionals* (Boston: Little, Brown, 1985).

Hedrick Smith, *The Power Game: How Washington Works* (New York: Ballantine Books, 1988), pp. 215–269.

Policies of Social Agencies

Burton Gummer, *The Politics of Social Administration: Managing Organizational Politics in Social Agencies* (Englewood Cliffs, NJ: Prentice Hall, 1990).

The Political Economy of Services

Michael Fabricant and Steve Burghardt, *The Welfare State Crisis and the Transformation of Social Service Work* (Armonk, NY: Sharpe, 1992).

Yeheskel Hasenfeld, *Human Service Organizations* (Englewood Cliffs, NJ: Prentice Hall, 1983).

5 Expanding Policy Advocacy Across National Borders

Policy Predicament

No one would have guessed that globalization would shape events in New Orleans in the years following Hurricane Katrina, but, as we shall discuss in Policy Advocacy Challenge 5.8 at the end of this chapter, globalization did vastly augment the city's homeless and migrant populations, as well as its Latino population even into 2012 and beyond.

Chapter 4 focused on policy institutions and processes within the United States. This chapter broadens the horizon to include global realities and institutions—not only as they contribute to social problems abroad but also within the United States. This chapter is germane to Task 2 of the policy framework presented in Figure 3.1, that is, *navigating policy and advocacy systems* in the interdependent world in which we live.

LEARNING OUTCOMES

By the end of the chapter, students will be able to discuss:

1. Globalization's role concerning social, economic, and political issues in America
2. The relationship between globalization and global warming
3. Reasons behind the economic gap between developing and developed nations
4. Specific international institutions and treaties that have shaped trade and economic relations among nations
5. The impact of globalization in developing nations
6. How policy advocates can use various options to address problems caused by globalization at home and abroad

Social Problems in an Interdependent World

Globalization is a broad and complex phenomenon that impacts almost every aspect of life in the United States and most nations, including their economies, educational systems, health and human service systems, relations among ethnic groups, patterns of immigration and emigration, mass media, and cultures. Even though many definitions of globalization exist, most of them emphasize the massive movement in recent decades of capital, jobs, labor, and culture across national boundaries. (Such movements have long existed, but their magnitude has vastly increased to the point that virtually all nations are deeply enmeshed in these global movements.)

Banks and financiers in industrialized nations make loans, for example, to governments and entrepreneurs in developing nations. American firms outsource jobs to developing nations, such as having personnel in India respond to inquiries from American consumers about credit applications. America and other industrial nations set up automobile plants and garment factories in developing nations such as Mexico and Thailand. Often lured by the prospect of jobs, millions of migrants have crossed international borders from developing nations to industrial nations in the last decade—just as entrepreneurs in industrial nations often relocate in developing nations to gain access to their markets. Even diseases and pollution cross national boundaries—and the world risks the effects of global warming that will impact all nations in coming years.

The Internet represents the most dramatic example of globalization. Persons in remote parts of developing nations who have Internet access can reach thousands of websites that give them music, news, and entertainment from many other nations. Improvements in transportation across national boundaries have also speeded globalization as persons routinely fly between distant nations.

Globalization has brought many benefits to nations and citizens. It has created jobs in many developing nations. It has fostered the sharing of technology and information across national boundaries—allowing citizens in developing nations to obtain a considerable portion of their education from industrial nations via distance education on the Internet. It has created markets for industries in industrialized nations. It has stimulated technological innovation.

But globalization has a darker side. For example, in industrialized nations like the United States, it has led to the loss of jobs or to reductions in workers' pay and benefits. It has undermined some American trade unions. In some regions of the United States, it has widened the gap between relatively well-educated and skilled workers and many relatively uneducated and unskilled workers whose jobs have migrated abroad. It has sometimes degraded environmental standards and working conditions. It has increased the vulnerability of some Americans to illnesses that spread across international boundaries. It has led to huge migration flows to the United States, and these immigrants are often victimized by American employers in agribusiness, tourism, construction, restaurants, and other businesses.

Globalization has had a darker side in many developing nations also. It has sometimes destabilized their economies, exposed workers to harsh working conditions and low pay, and encouraged child labor. It has sometimes contributed to growing inequality. It has undermined indigenous traditions with American culture, whose music and films have dramatically impacted other nations. It has increased pollution in some nations. It has fostered such rapid migrations from rural to urban areas that huge numbers of rural migrants face poverty and disease in urban areas in nations that lack resources and human service systems to help them. It has fostered, as well, massive movements of persons across borders—with some of them occupying a marginal and illegal status that has accentuated their poverty and other problems in their destination nations.

In the coming decades, policy advocates must therefore expand their horizons to include issues and problems that cross international boundaries if they wish to help vulnerable populations that are impacted by globalization—both at home and abroad. They need to develop social policies that will prevent or offset some of globalization's negative consequences while embracing some of its positive impacts.

Why Globalization Sometimes Harms Vulnerable Populations in the United States

Many Americans view globalization as a positive phenomenon, but significant numbers view it in neutral or negative terms. Reservations about it may partly stem from the belief that is has contributed to growing economic inequality in the United States that derives from the migration of many corporate jobs to developing nations, such as China and India. In 2007, 37.3 million people, or 12.5 percent of the total population, were living under the federal poverty level, including 13.3 million children (almost 1 in 5) and 3.6 million seniors.[1]

The exodus of jobs from the United States began in the 1960s when automobile companies began to place their plants in such nations as Mexico, dealing a mortal blow in succeeding decades to the economies of such cities as Flint and Detroit, Michigan. Other industries followed suit, including textile, steel, furniture, and many other manufacturing jobs. More recently, service jobs, such as certain clerical, customer service, and engineering jobs, have been outsourced to companies in other nations.

Many American workers and trade unions became even more worried when several free-trade agreements, such as the North American Free Trade Agreement (NAFTA), and additional trade agreements were ratified during the presidency of Bill Clinton. Also, many of the protective tariffs, which had hitherto shielded American companies from lower-cost foreign goods, were markedly reduced or even terminated in the 1990s and during the administration of George W. Bush.

Some benefits, however, have accrued from economic globalization. American consumers reduced their cost of living by purchasing inexpensive imported goods. The United States found new markets for its products in developing nations. Globalization spurred many nations to pay greater attention to their shared pollution risks—even though the United States failed to sign the groundbreaking Kyoto Treaty in 1997, which required assenting nations to reduce carbon dioxide gas emissions, widely believed to cause global climate change. (The administration of Barack Obama, as well as the Congress, has moved toward developing "cap and trade" policies, which will provide economic incentives to corporations to cut these emissions, and signing international agreements that establish goals for cutting them—topics that led to initial agreements among the world's nations at an international conference in Copenhagen in December 2009 where President Obama assumed a critical role.)

If optimists contend that "all boats rise" during globalization, experts predict a "race to the bottom" among nations. In such a scenario, nations generally cut corporate taxes, protections for labor, and protections for the environment to lure corporations to their shores. As they cut corporate and other taxes, nations are forced to cut their funding on social programs. Some experts fear that this competitive dynamic has increased economic inequality in many nations, not to mention the well-being of their vulnerable populations (see Policy Advocacy Challenge 5.1).

Policy Advocacy Challenge 5.1

Issues Raised by Wal-Mart in a Global Context

Bruce Jansson, Ph.D.

EP 2.1.5a

A fierce debate about the merits of Wal-Mart, the giant of American retailing, exemplifies the emerging controversy within the United States about globalization and corporate responsibility. Founded in 1962 in Rogers, Arkansas, Wal-Mart has developed a world-wide chain of discount stores, grocery stores, and hypermarkets that produces revenues of more than $315 billion annually and is the largest private employer in the United States and Mexico. One of its founders, Sam Walton, viewed its corporate mission as providing products at discounted prices to consumers—viewing it as a friend of low-income persons who could save resources by purchasing its products.

Its critics contended, however, that Wal-Mart achieved its low prices by purchasing many of its products from contractors and producers in developing nations, who underbid other producers by paying excessively low wages and giving poor working conditions to their employees. Critics argued, as well, that Wal-Mart followed similar policies with its own employees, not only paying low wages but also denying many of them health and other benefits. These purchasing and employee policies, they argued, often forced more ethical competing companies out of business because they could not successfully compete against Wal-Mart.

Wal-Mart is not the only American corporation to be criticized for aggressively obtaining its products from contractors and manufacturers in developing nations that underpaid workers and subjected them to poor working conditions. Nike, the seller of athletic shoes, has also been widely criticized for underselling competitors by using similar tactics. Nike mitigated this criticism by monitoring the labor policies of contractors and manufacturers abroad. However, Wal-Mart was not able to quell controversy surrounding it, as competing groups argue for and against Wal-Mart. Wal-Mart supported its policies by forming a group called Working Families for Wal-Mart in late 2005 with the former civil rights activist Andrew Young as its chairperson. Trade unions, in turn, formed several organizations that sought to change Wal-Mart's labor policies at home and abroad, including Wake Up Wal-Mart (the United Food and Commercial Workers) and Wal-Mart Watch (the Services Employees International Union).

The groups formed by trade unions mostly criticized Wal-Mart's labor policies, as well as the aggressive strategies it used to obtain approval from local areas to construct its stores. They criticized, for example, its low wages and its refusal to provide many employees with health insurance—policies that often contributed to local poverty and that required American taxpayers to foot the bill for programs such as Medicaid, widely used by Wal-Mart employees. They also criticized Wal-Mart's exploitation of labor in other nations. In Bangladesh, where the average annual income of citizens is only $400, approximately 2 million workers produce clothing exports worth $5 billion, with most of it purchased by American companies such as Kmart, GAP, and Wal-Mart.[1]

These companies *did* require contractors and manufacturers not to use child labor in Bangladesh, after opposition from human rights groups in the 1990s. But many abuses have remained. When NBC News set up a fictional American company wanting to purchase clothing from manufacturers in Bangladesh, they discovered that manufacturers' promises to comply with working and pay regulations for their workers were often broken. Workers were frequently denied breaks, required to sit on stools with no backrests, and provided with no air conditioning so that temperatures often exceeded 90 degrees Fahrenheit. Employees were often given excessive production quotas with

---

[1]See the NBC Dateline hidden camera investigation of labor practices in Bangladesh, "The Human Costs Behind Bargain Shopping," at http://msnbc.msn.com/id/8243331/

(continued)

the stipulation that they had to work overtime with no pay if they failed to meet them. Many workers were required to work more than 70 hours per week—or 10 hours more than permitted by local laws. Some workers were required to work 18 hours straight to meet production deadlines. When American companies sent inspectors to check on working conditions, workers often gave them false information for fear they would be dismissed.

Nor were workers reimbursed at levels often promised to American companies. In one factory, for example, workers were paid 12 cents per hour to start, rising to 19 cents when they became "senior operators." These low wages, in turn, placed workers in extreme poverty, with more than 30 families sometimes sharing one cooking area, with little nutritive value in their diets.

While many contractors and manufacturers in Bangladesh are greedy, some *are* prepared to raise wages if they receive even slightly higher purchase prices from companies like Wal-Mart. Intent on keeping its prices low and increasing its profits, however, Wal-Mart often refuses to accept products even a cent more costly—as a matter of fact, it often insists that manufacturers in Bangladesh *lower* their prices each year.

Such hard-fisted purchasing policies by corporations like Wal-Mart not only allow them to undersell other American corporations but also to pocket huge profits. When a worker from Bangladesh visited the United States, she was astonished to find that a single pair of pants sold for the equivalent of a single week's pay for her—$12.84.

Wal-Mart's spokespersons, in turn, argue that its hard-fisted purchasing policies led to lower prices for its hard-pressed American consumers, many of whom cannot make ends meet. They contend, as well, that "the wages and benefits we provide have helped improve the lives of many thousands of workers of the world." They also deny that they require lower prices each year from manufacturers in developing nations. Not only did Wal-Mart deny allegations against it but it also sought to convince the WTO in late 2005 at its meeting in Hong Kong to pass a regulation forbidding any nation from restricting the placement of foreign-owned businesses in specific neighborhoods—attempting to stop other nations from following the example of many American communities that refused to allow Wal-Mart stores to be constructed in their neighborhoods.

The chair of the Wal-Mart group formed to defend its policies, Andrew Young, resigned in August 2006 after apologizing for a statement he made that Wal-Mart had emancipated low-income African American persons from Jewish, Arab, and Korean shop grocery-store owners who had "ripped off" urban communities for years by "selling us stale bread and bad meat and wilted vegetables.... You see those are the people who have been overcharging us [before] they sold out and moved to Florida."

In fairness to Wal-Mart and other corporations, such as Nike, they have begun monitoring companies that supply them in developing nations more rigorously in the past several years. Wal-Mart increased health coverage for many of its employees in 2008 and 2009. Unlike Nike, however, Wal-Mart failed to publish lists of its foreign suppliers by 2011. New York City pension funds pressed it to have its vendors publish annual lists reporting on working conditions in factories producing its goods in developing nations (T. A. Frank, "Whipping Wal-Mart Into Shape," *New Republic*, June 7, 2011: Retrieved on December 15, 2011, from www.tnr.com/article/environment-energy/89430/walmart-china-labor-new-york-congress-nike).

The computer company, Apple, became the subject of controversy in 2012 when the media ran lurid accounts of working conditions in a Chinese factory that assembled many of its products. For example, many employees suffered from chemical hazards in the plant. Still others committed suicide within the plant by jumping to their deaths. Apple secured major wage and working-condition improvements by February 2012 and instituted greater surveillance of the plant, but many activists wanted more evidence of progress.

Controversies surrounding Wal-Mart and Apple illustrate how corporations from industrialized nations are enmeshed in globalization. Consider these questions:

1. Can responsible corporations that truly insist upon ethical human labor practices abroad compete with corporations that do not? If not, what kinds of international regulations, such as ones stated in treaties, are needed—and what kinds of monitoring procedures?

2. To the extent that the United States as a developed nation has relatively high levels of poverty, is it ethically correct for Wal-Mart to lower prices through purchasing policies abroad that create hardships for workers in developing nations?

3. Mass media coverage of the controversies surrounding Wal-Mart and similar corporations has drastically waned since 2006. Do you think this is because these problems have been corrected or because the media has moved on to other stories?

4. Do you know of any corporation in your area that relies upon similar types of labor practices or purchasing policies in order to provide goods at reduced prices? If so, what can you do as a consumer to combat these types of practices and policies?

Why an Economic Gap Developed Between Developing and Developed Nations

We need to understand why a substantial economic gap developed between developing and developed nations. As recently as 1820, virtually the entire world was impoverished: The average income of European nations was only about 90 percent of the current income of African nations, and Europeans' average life expectancy was merely 40 years. The world population barely grew between 1000 AD and 1800 AD, from its base of roughly 1 billion persons.

Then everything changed. World population zoomed upward, increasing by six times between 1800 and the present. Average per capita income in the world climbed by nine times in the same period (15 times in Europe and 25 times in the United States). Total world economic output increased 49 times.

This revolution in the world's economy and growth in population created a new phenomenon: a gap between relatively affluent and less affluent nations. If in 1800 average income had been roughly the same in different nations, by 2000, for example, the gap between American average income had become 20 times greater than the African average income—and Europe and Japan had developed similar disparities with most other nations in Africa, Asia, Central America, and South America. These disparities between developed and developing nations did not grow overnight, but over the long haul, as more affluent nations grew annually two to three times more rapidly than African nations, yielding an enormous discrepancy over a period of 200 years.

Many scholars argue convincingly that the economic gap between developed and developing nations was *not* caused by intrinsic differences between their citizens, such as in their intelligence or other personal characteristics. Instead, some nations moved forward economically as compared to others because they gained access to technology, which enabled them to produce and harness power primarily from fossil fuels such as coal and (later) petroleum. They used this power to create the industrial revolution that enabled them to mass produce a wide array of products in factories. They used it to greatly increase agricultural produce. They harnessed power, moreover, to develop mass transit, to make machines with which they farmed large tracts of land with relatively little labor, to manufacture ships driven by engines, to build infrastructure, and to distribute electricity to large segments of their populations. They also used power to mine minerals such as iron ore and copper, which they used to make steel and many other products that were essential to the construction of machines and the transmission of energy. They developed market economies as they created systems of banking and currency that allowed businesses to get loans and to invest their resources.

EP 2.1.9a

These technological advances, in turn, led to a geometric increase in per capita wealth in industrializing nations. Emancipated from reliance on manual labor to farm and to make goods, persons could mass-produce goods and could farm large tracts of land with relatively little labor. With the growing profits that they received, entrepreneurs could hire large workforces and reimburse them at steadily increasing rates, even if recessions often led to periodic economic turndowns.

Europeans obtained access to technology by a series of fortuitous events. Even before the industrial order began, Europeans benefited from inventions and practices in the Middle East, where cattle, horses, goats, pigs, and sheep had been domesticated. These animals, in turn, not only gave them relatively large quantities of food and fiber but also enabled them to cultivate crops relatively efficiently (horses, mules, and oxen). (Close proximity to these animals also immunized them to those many diseases that spread from animals to people—diseases that would soon kill as much as 90 percent of the populations of indigenous persons in South and North America in the aftermath of European immigration to these areas because they lacked this immunity, partly because they had not domesticated many animals.) Europeans learned from Middle-Easterners how to smelt iron ore to make iron and how to make gunpowder, swords, and guns, which helped them conquer large areas in Africa, South and Central America, and North America, where they got access to gold and timber and other commodities that fueled their economic growth.

Great Britain was particularly well placed to industrialize even in the latter part of the 17th century. With its traditions of political liberty, it was relatively open to new ideas, which led to breakthroughs in science, mathematics, and technology, which in turn realized many inventions. Because it protected property rights, entrepreneurs had an incentive to increase their holdings. Because it was an island and had a powerful navy, it could protect its emerging industries from invasion. It had copious quantities of coal and iron ore, which it could transport by its many rivers and canals—and then with its railroads. It could feed its urbanized citizens with a robust agricultural sector due to its climate and soils as well as an emerging agricultural technology.

With similar advantages, other European nations, as well as the British colonies and the United States, replicated Britain's surge toward industrialization, as steam engines, railroads, telegraphs, ocean steamers, electrification, and the internal combustion engine followed in rapid succession.

After two world wars in the first half of the 20th century and marked economic downturns that included the Great Depression of the 1930s, it seemed that Europe, the United States, and former British colonies, as well as Japan, would squander their economic advantage over the rest of the world. As we will discuss, however, they evolved various international organizations and treaties, as well as internal banking systems and economic policies, that allowed them to mitigate the economic chaos caused by these difficult periods.

As Europe, the United States, and other nations made this transition from reliance on human labor to one on machines, large parts of the rest of the world failed to gain access to technology, so their economies remained powered primarily by human labor rather than machines and fossil fuels. Their per capita incomes barely rose. They were victimized by Europeans who invaded them, colonized them, plundered them, took their timber and minerals, and killed vast numbers of them with diseases to which they had little immunity. They mostly provided raw commodities to industrialized nations rather than trading with them as equals; indeed, colonizers often exported goods to them at prices that undercut prices of indigenous businesses.

A series of interrelated factors enmeshed these developing nations in poverty. Many of them did not possess minerals, or their lands were arid or landlocked. People who lived in tropical areas were often devastated by tropical diseases. Lacking resources that industrializing nations developed as their economies grew, the governments of developing nations could not invest in infrastructure and educational systems. They often had governments that were relatively corrupt—and they lacked judicial systems and ways of protecting property rights for those persons and corporations that might invest in their domestic economies or develop innovations. They often denied women basic rights, diminishing their contributions to the economy. They had such small local markets that few incentives existed to develop innovations. With high fertility rates, women could not contribute to economic growth because they were mired in family roles—and these large families often lacked the resources to invest in their children's education.

Large parts of the world were relatively poor as compared to Europe, former British colonies, the United States, and Japan during the 20th century. (Japan had industrialized before and after World War II.) Even the Union of Soviet Socialist Republics, before its dissolution in 1991 into separate republics, was relatively poor—although it developed an industrial order in the middle and latter part of the 20th century.

Considerable differences nonetheless existed among developing nations by 2000. Some of them, such as India and China, had made considerable economic progress. Others, such as Bangladesh, had promoted growing numbers of small businesses. Yet others, such as Malawi, remained mired in deep and persistent poverty. Jeffrey Sachs, a leading development economist, estimates that about one-sixth of the world's population resembles Malawi whereas one-half of the world's population is relatively poor but making progress toward less infant mortality, more education, and better sanitation.[2]

The World Bank estimated that about 1.4 billion persons lived in poverty using cost-of-living measures in 116 developing nations in 2005. It estimated that 2.6 billion persons consumed less than $2 a day in 2005 prices. Yet progress occurred between 1981 and 2005 as the percentage of persons in developing nations consuming less than $1.25 a day was halving—and aggregate poverty fell by one percentage point per year.[3] Progress has occurred most dramatically in East Asia and China, but poverty for Sub-Saharan Africa has shown no sustained downward trend, almost doubling from 200 million to 380 million between 1981 and 2005. (For information about how to learn more about developing nations, (see Policy Advocacy Challenge 5.2). Even at this current rate of progress, roughly 1 billion persons will live below $1.25 per day in 2015.

The challenge facing the world is to cut extreme poverty—and then to end it. When endorsing the UN Millennium Development Goal in 2000, 191 nations pledged to cut world poverty by one-half by 2015 and to end extreme poverty by 2025. To accomplish this goal, however, such nations as the United States will have to pledge far greater resources to other nations than they do currently.

Policy Advocacy Challenge 5.2

Using the Web to Find International Data

Rachel Katz, MPP

Researching international social policy issues can be difficult because the quality and quantity of information available varies widely across sources. Some websites contain comparative country data that enable you to examine differences and similarities between countries. These tend to be websites of international organizations, which collect data from individual countries and compile it in a central location. Other websites, specifically national websites, provide only data limited to specific countries. Because national websites vary in content and quality, it may be difficult to find the information you need, and you should assess the reliability of the data. An additional challenge when accessing national websites may be language, because a country's website is likely available only in the national language of that country.

Here are some sources of international data.

ORGANISATION FOR ECONOMIC CO-OPERATION AND DEVELOPMENT This is an international organization with 30 member nations. It is a good source of information on economic and social issues in these countries, with data on social and welfare indicators and policies as well as analyses of social conditions. You can access comparative data or data by country.
www.oecd.org

UNITED NATIONS The United Nations currently has 193 member nations, and its website is a good source for comparative data on social indicators. The UN website also contains a database listing that may provide links to organizations involved in advocacy efforts, including humanitarian relief agencies and international NGOs.
www.un.org

CIA The Central Intelligence Agency publishes *The World Factbook* every year, which provides a basic set of data on every country, including statistics related to population, government, and health systems.
https://www.cia.gov/library/publications/the-world-factbook/index.html

U.S. CENSUS BUREAU Within its Population Division, the Census Bureau operates an International Programs Center, which provides demographic and socioeconomic statistics on 227 countries or "independent states" and "areas" of the world. The international database offers historical data dating back as far as 1950 and projections available up to 2050.
www.census.gov/ipc/www

GOVERNMENT WEBSITES You may search for data through national websites. Here are two websites that provide links to the websites of individual countries:
www.psr.keele.ac.uk/official.htm
www.library.northwestern.edu/govpub/resource/internat/foreign.html

NATION MASTER This site enables users to access a broad range of economic and social indicators from the world's nations, and to generate graphs and make comparisons between specific countries.
www.nationmaster.com/index.php
Some national websites offer links to statistical databases. For example, Mexico has a National Institute of Information, Statistics and Geography, which can be accessed at **www.snieg.org.mx** (available in Spanish only). Taiwan has a Government Information Office, with information available in English at **www.gio.gov.tw**.

UNIVERSITY LIBRARY RESOURCES Many university libraries subscribe to database services that can provide additional international data sources. Visit the reference or database listing section of your university library's website or talk to a reference librarian for assistance. Here is a listing of some of the databases with information on international topics that your university library may subscribe to:

Columbia International Affairs Online. CIAO offers basic comparative data on all countries, including birth rates, mortality rates, GDP, and so forth.

Economist Intelligence Unit. EIU offers data on approximately 200 countries, including information on social issues in its Country Reports and Country Profiles.

Statistical Universe. This database is accessed through LexisNexis, and enables you to search for comparative data on a wide range of topics.

EXERCISE

Visit the website of the U.S. Census Bureau International Programs Center and collect data for all available years on the infant mortality rates of Latin America and the Caribbean, eastern Europe, and western Europe. Look at how the rates have changed over time and how they have been projected to change over the next several decades in these three regions. Which region has the highest infant mortality rate today? Which has the lowest? Which region is projected to have the highest infant mortality rate in the year 2050? Which is projected to have the lowest? On the basis of this data, think about what types of efforts a policy advocate interested in public health might undertake in one or more of these regions to decrease the incidence of infant mortality.

EP 2.1.6b

Why Globalization Sometimes Harms Vulnerable Populations in Developing Nations

When globalization accelerated in the 1980s, it was accompanied by a policy consensus known as the Washington Consensus among top officials in the United States, as well as some European nations, about ways to foster it. They wanted to promote it in ways that would advance an *economic model of "free market capitalism"*—a theory widely credited to the British economist David Ricardo, who postulated that free trade should be developed so that specific nations specialize in producing only those goods and services that afford them a competitive advantage, producing these goods not only for internal consumption but also for export. In turn, they should import products that are produced more efficiently elsewhere. In his best-selling book on globalization, *The Lexus and the Olive Tree*, New York columnist and Pulitzer Prize recipient Thomas Friedman (2000) wrote, "Those countries that are most willing to let capitalism quickly destroy inefficient companies, so that money can be freed up and directed to more innovative ones, will thrive in the era of globalization" (p. 11).[4]

If advocates of the Washington Consensus favored eventual elimination of tariffs, they also believed that nations should gradually reduce special subsidies or corporate tax concessions that might give their products—and their manufacturers—an unfair advantage in a free-trade world. They favored, as well, fiscal discipline in government spending so that nations had relatively little budget deficits and debt, reduction of marginal tax rates, free movement of capital from developed to developing nations, privatization of public enterprises, and development of private-property rights.

Many of the advocates of the Washington Consensus wanted to use international organizations and treaties to pressure developing nations to adopt these economic principles—including Russia and China as well as many nations in Latin and South America, Africa, and Asia. They could seek assistance from the International Monetary Fund (IMF), instituted in the wake of World War II to rebuild Europe by providing loans and grants—assimilated by contributions of different nations—to nations in need. The IMF is dominated by the major developed nations—and particularly by the United States, which is the only nation that has a veto over its decisions. The IMF was supplemented by the World Bank, which lent money to nations for infrastructure projects like roads and dams. The General Agreement on Tariffs and Trade (GATT) was also established after World War II, to promote tariff-reduction agreements between nations. Wanting even greater reduction in tariffs, policy makers established the World Trade Organization (WTO) in 1995, to serve as a forum for trade negotiations between nations, as well as to enforce its decisions through specific penalties and fines. (Member nations can file grievances against other nations that they believe are unfairly seeking international-trade advantages for their corporations through protective tariffs or governmental subsidies.)

In his *Globalization and Its Discontents*, Joseph Stiglitz (2002), a Nobel-Prize-winning economist, documents how the IMF, the World Bank, and the WTO were often dominated not only by the United States but also by the Washington Consensus, particularly from the 1980s onward.[5] (Both the IMF and the World Bank have their headquarters in Washington, DC.) Prigoff (2000) discusses how British economist John Maynard Keynes had lost the fight to locate the World Bank in London because he felt that "the fund might be more independent of the U.S. government than it would be in Washington, DC" (p. 116).[6]

Imposition of the views of the Washington Consensus on developing nations often exacerbated their economic problems, partly because these nations faced a catch-22 dilemma. In order to stimulate economic growth, they had to invest considerable resources in their infrastructure (such as roads, public buildings, and dams) as well as their citizens (such as schools, human services, and health services). Yet they often possessed relatively meager tax revenues to cover these expenditures because their national economies were relatively small. When they sought loans and grants from the IMF and World Bank to help them fund these expenditures, they often discovered that these institutions would give them resources *only* if they cut their spending markedly to reduce their budget deficits—a policy that forced them to cut spending on programs for vulnerable populations and their infrastructure. These spending cuts not only increased inequality in their nations but also curtailed programs needed to stimulate their economic growth.

EP 2.1.5a

Stiglitz (2002) contends, moreover, that the IMF and World Bank wrongly pressured some developing nations to privatize publicly held firms, such as banks, energy-producing companies, and utilities. This policy sometimes led, he argues, to acquisition of these concerns by criminal elements at cut-rate prices—a development likely to occur in nations that did not yet possess law enforcement and monitoring procedures comparable to those in more advanced economies. Better, he contends, to move more gradually toward private property than to impose this policy all at once.[7]

The IMF, World Bank, and WTO sometimes stimulated greater inequality in developing nations, as well, when they demanded deep reductions in some of their tariffs. In the case of agricultural products, for example, large American agricultural concerns, which operate efficiently because of their very size and their use of expensive equipment, have an economic advantage over the small agricultural producers of developing nations, such as peasants in the Chiapas region of Mexico. When pressured to cut tariffs on agricultural products, peasants were often forced into bankruptcy—hastening their migration to cities or across borders where they often faced extreme poverty, as in shanty towns that ringed many Mexican cities. To add insult to injury, the United States sometimes gave its agricultural producers large subsidies at the very time that it asked developing nations to end their agricultural tariffs, giving the American producers an even greater advantage over their counterparts in developing nations.

Other forms of victimization of developing nations took place. As corporations shift their production facilities to these countries, they also focus their sales efforts in these emerging markets. Unfortunately, they sometimes sell "lower-quality products or products that are outright toxic and thus banned in the industrialized countries."[8] Such products include pharmaceutical drugs or contraceptives banned in Europe, the United States, or Japan; cigarettes with high tar or nicotine content; and diluted or contaminated baby formulas.

Corporations also victimized many of their workers in developing nations. They often used child labor; exposed workers to unsafe working conditions; paid excessively low wages; made workers work for excessive hours per week; did not give workers benefits; and laid workers off with no advance notice. They often failed to install antipollution equipment on their factories.

Another Vulnerable Population: Migrants Within and Between Nations

EP 2.1.5a

Globalization has been associated with unprecedented movements of people in the last five decades—both within a nation and between nations. For example, with the rapid industrialization of China, roughly 300 million of its rural persons will migrate to urban areas from 2010 to 2025 according to China's Ministry of Housing and Urban-Rural Development. Migrants from rural to urban areas have often experienced great hardships in China because they were denied public education, health care (aside from brief emergency care), adequate housing, and other amenities. Such migrations have taken place in all developing nations, with similar adverse consequences for many migrants. Yet these migrants choose to move to urban areas because their economic situation is intolerable in rural areas, where population increases often mean that insufficient arable land or jobs exist to support them. (Even the low wages of many factories in developing nations far exceed the incomes persons receive in rural areas.)

Migrants to urban areas in many developing nations have uncertain legal status. In China, for example, migrants who move to urban areas without required permits lack residency status, so many of them are not even allowed to use public schools or receive benefits from many government programs. Huge shanty towns have developed on the periphery of Mexico City, Beijing, and Caracas, where migrants live in unhealthy settings and dire poverty.

The United States has been an immigrant nation from its origins to the present. A dramatic shift in immigration occurred in the 1960s in the United States. The Immigration Act of 1965, the 1975 Indochina Migration and Refugee Assistance Act, and the 1980 Immigration Act revolutionized inflows of immigrants to the United States by abolishing quotas of specific nations and regions as well as discriminatory Asian restrictions. As a result, the Asian American population grew from 1 million to 5 million between 1965 and 1985. Large numbers of refugees from Vietnam, Central America, and the Caribbean were admitted from a wide range of social backgrounds, as well as from the Middle East, Russia, and Eastern Europe. The Immigration Act of 1986 granted amnesty to three million undocumented immigrants, mostly from Mexico and Central America. The legislation became merely a stop-gap measure, however, because migration to the United States accelerated after its enactment, leading to roughly 12 million undocumented workers by 2011.

Many immigrants are *pushed* by intolerable economic and social conditions in their native lands that included violations of human rights, wars between nations, civil wars, genocide, tribal or sectarian conflict, and famine. We can distinguish among *refugees, asylum seekers*, and *internally displaced persons*. Refugees "can document that they have been persecuted for reasons of race, religion, nationality, membership in a particular social group, or political opinion" and are unable or unwilling to return to their country (http://en.wikipedia.org/wiki/Refugee). Some lesbian, gay, bisexual, and transgender (LGBT) persons seek refugee status due to discrimination and physical attacks in their native lands. Refugees also include internally displaced persons (IDPs) by wars, natural disasters, tribal conflicts, or internal discord. (Asylum seekers are persons whose claim to be refugees and IDPs has not yet been documented.) The United Nations High Commissioner for Refugees (UNHCR), which coordinates refugee protection, estimated that 10.5 million refugees existed in 2010 (http://unhcr.org/4dfa11499.html). Most refugees flee to neighboring nations, but many seek refuge in distant lands.

Many immigrant women come to other nations, including the United States, due to human trafficking—"an extreme form of labor exploitation" that includes sex trafficking and use of persons for labor or services through use of force, fraud, or coercion (ACLU, undated). Many persons emigrated to the United States during civil wars in Nicaragua, El Salvador, Cuba, Afghanistan, and Iraq—while many others came to the United States in the wake of the Vietnam War. Some parents insist that their oldest child migrate to provide them with needed resources. Droughts, floods, tsunamis, and earthquakes have often led to the destruction of food and housing in many nations—leading many persons to flee to other nations or to refugee camps funded by NGOs, the UN, or specific governments.

Migrants to other nations are a heterogeneous group with respect to their legal status. Many of them are "undocumented," i.e., cross borders without the approval of host nations. Persons need visas to legalize temporary stays through petitions filed with the U.S. Citizenship and Immigration Services or USCIS (http://FAQ.VisaPro.com/). *Family visas* include ones for persons with close relations with a U.S. citizen, such as fiancées, spouses, and children—as well as visas for persons with more distant family relationships with a U.S. citizen. *Green cards* grant lawful permanent residency to persons including permission to live and work in the United States (http://en.wikipedia.org/wiki/Permanent_residence_United_States). Holders must maintain permanent resident status and can be removed from the United States if certain conditions of this status are not met. Roughly 140,000 *work visas* are issued each year, such as ones for business visitors; registered nurses; persons of extraordinary ability in the arts, athletics, business, education or science; and agriculture. Some work visas are only given to temporary immigrants who are sponsored for a specified period by an American employer (http://travel.state.gov/visa/immigrants/types/types_1323.html). A system of priorities exists: first priority is given to persons with extraordinary ability, researchers, professors, and multinational managers or executives. Second priority goes to professionals holding advanced degrees. Third priority is given to skilled workers, professionals, and unskilled workers. Fourth preference goes to certain special immigrants, including Iraqi and Afghan interpreters and translators and persons recruited for U.S. armed forces outside the nation. Fifth priority goes to immigrant investors and entrepreneurs.

Student visas are given to academic or language students, exchange visitors, or vocational or nonacademic students. *Other visas* include ones for persons seeking asylum from persecution by governments in other nations as well as ones for persons who come to the United States from human trafficking. Some persons have uncertain immigration status, such as persons who wait for extended periods in the United States as they seek citizenship—waits that can months or years. American citizens petition the USCIS who wish to adopt children from other nations.

Family members and some employers file petitions to help persons emigrate to the United States. Under the 1996 welfare law, they must often become their financial "sponsors" by filing an "affidavit of support" where they promise to support the immigrant and even to repay certain benefits that the immigrant uses.[9] Sponsors' income is sometimes added to immigrants' income to determine their eligibility for specific public benefit programs, even for 10 or more years after immigrants enter the nation under the 1996 legislation. (Exceptions include survivors of domestic violence and immigrants who would become hungry or homeless without assistance.)

We confront important ethical issues when analyzing unauthorized or undocumented immigration or time-limited immigration through workers' visas. The United States benefits from the work of immigrants as they often take positions that naturalized Americans do not seek, particularly in low-paying and undesirable jobs in agriculture, tourism, health care, and industry. These positions often expose immigrants to health and other risks. These immigrants often contribute to the nation through sales taxes and Social Security taxes. Many researchers conclude that immigrants contribute more resources to the American economy than they take from it because they make relatively little use of Americans safety-net programs, whether because they are ineligible to use them or because they fear deportation if they *do* use them. With looming labor shortages due to the aging of the American population, the economic necessity of labor from immigrants will become even greater.

The United States *invites* undocumented immigrants because it fails to develop rules and visas needed to provide legal workers sufficient for the nation's economy. The visas that it provides to immigrants are far fewer than ones actually needed to fill jobs that immigrants uniquely fill—and this shortage of legal visas creates a vacuum that undocumented persons fill. This vacuum is sustained not only by immigrants' need for work and income, but employers' nondisclosure of the legal status of many of their workers—and pressure from them to curtail "raids" by federal immigration officials on their workers to detect and deport undocumented workers.

Undocumented immigrants are often victimized because the perpetrators realize that law enforcement and government officials often will not come to their defense or enforce their rights *because* they are a marginalized population—and because immigrants often do not assert their rights for fear of deportation. Immigrants are abused by many employers who pay them even less than the minimum wage and expose them to dangerous work conditions, poor housing, and lack of basic services in this legal limbo. They are subject, as well, to hate crimes. Their marginal legal status invites hostile actions from many legislators at all levels of American society as reflected by welfare and immigration legislation in 1996 by the Congress and harsh policies recently enacted by legislatures in Arizona, Georgia, Alabama, and South Carolina.

Sweeping immigration reform is needed that legalizes immigrants sufficient to meet the nation's economic needs by granting temporary work visas—and that makes raids by federal immigration officials unnecessary. It should protect their economic, legal, and social rights. It should provide amnesty to millions of immigrants who have "paid their dues" by working in the United States for extended periods. It should promote unification of families by refraining from deporting undocumented parents whose children are U.S. citizens.

Policy Advocacy Challenge 5.3

Websites Pertaining to Migrants or Immigrants in the United States and Abroad

Dennis Kao, Ph.D.
Assistant Professor, School of Social Work, University of Houston

UNITED STATES

ASIAN AMERICAN JUSTICE CENTER Founded in 1991, AAJC (formerly the National Asian Pacific American Legal Consortium) works to "advance the human and civil rights of Asian Americans through advocacy, public policy, public education, and litigation." In addition to immigrants' rights and immigration issues, AAJC works on affirmative action, hate crimes prevention and race relations, census, language access, and voting rights.

www.advancingequality.org

CENTER FOR IMMIGRATION STUDIES CIS, founded in 1985, is an independent, nonpartisan, not-for-profit research organization devoted to research and policy analysis dealing with the economic, social, demographic, fiscal, and other implications of immigration for the United States. Its mission is "to expand the base of public knowledge and understanding of the need for an immigration policy that gives first concern to the broad national interest."

www.cis.org/

FEDERATION FOR AMERICAN IMMIGRATION REFORM FAIR is a national not-for-profit organization of more than 198,000 members, which "seeks to improve border security, to stop illegal immigration, and to promote immigration levels consistent with the national interest."

www.fairus.org

NATIONAL COUNCIL OF LA RAZA As the "largest national Hispanic civil rights advocacy organization in the United States," NCLR is a not-for-profit organization that strives to improve opportunities to the nation's Hispanic American population. Through a network of nearly 300 community-based organizations in 41 states, Puerto Rico, and the District of Columbia, NCLR works on five key issue areas: assets/investments, civil rights/immigration, education, employment/economic status, and health.

www.nclr.org

NATIONAL IMMIGRATION FORUM The forum's mission is to "embrace and uphold America's tradition as a nation of immigrants" and advocates for public policies that "welcome immigrants and refugees and are fair and supportive to newcomers in the United States."

www.immigrationforum.org

NATIONAL IMMIGRATION LAW CENTER Founded in 1979, NILC is "a leading expert on immigration, public benefits, and employment laws affecting immigrants and refugees." Committed to protecting and promoting the rights of immigrants and their families, NILC's work includes policy analysis and advocacy, impact litigation, coalition building, technical assistance, publications, and training.

www.nilc.org

NATIONAL NETWORK FOR IMMIGRANT AND REFUGEE RIGHTS Committed to the rights of immigrants and refugees in the United States, NNIRR is a national organization that "serves as a forum to share information, to educate communities and the general public, and to develop and coordinate plans of action on important immigrant and refugee issues."

www.nnirr.org

INTERNATIONAL

MIGRATION POLICY INSTITUTE Founded in 2001, MPI is an independent, nonpartisan, nonprofit research organization, which conducts research on the movement of people worldwide and provides analysis, development, and evaluation regarding local, national, and international migration and refugee policies. In 2002, MPI launched the Migration Information Source, which provides up-to-date data on international migration.

  www.migrationpolicy.org and **www.migrationinformation.org**

INTERNATIONAL ORGANIZATION FOR MIGRATION Established in 1951, IOM is the world's primary intergovernmental organization focused on the issue of migration and is dedicated to "promoting humane and orderly migration for the benefit of all." With 146 member states as of March 2006, IOM focuses on four areas: migration and development, facilitating migration, regulating migration, and addressing forced migration.

  www.iom.int

MIGRANTS RIGHTS INTERNATIONAL MRI—founded during the 1994 United Nations International Conference on Population and Development in Cairo—is a membership organization of migration and human rights experts and practitioners.

  www.migrantwatch.org

POPULATION REFERENCE BUREAU PRB works to "inform people around the world about population, health, and the environment, and empower them to use that information to advance the well-being of current and future generations." PRB's work is focused around four themes: reproductive health and fertility, children and families, population and the environment, and population futures (which include migration).

  www.prb.org

OFFICE OF THE UNITED NATIONS HIGH COMMISSIONER FOR REFUGEES Established on December 14, 1950, the Office of UNHCR was created and mandated by the UN General Assembly to "lead and coordinate international action to protect refugees and resolve refugee problems worldwide" and "safeguard the rights and well-being of refugees." Since its inception, the agency has helped approximately 50 million refugees looking to restart their lives.

  www.unhcr.ch

UNITED NATIONS POPULATION FUND The UN Population Fund (UNFPA) is an international development agency which "promotes the right of every woman, man, and child to enjoy a life of health and equal opportunity." UNFPA works with governments to develop policies that lead to reduced poverty and improved sustainable development and also assists countries with their population data collection and analyses.

  www.unfpa.org

Ideological Conflict over Immigration

Animus toward immigrants has often occurred in American history due to prejudice against immigrants, such as Irish and Asian immigrants in the 19th century. It has often peaked during economic downturns when Americans have feared they would lose jobs to immigrants. It has been fed by myths such as the belief that immigrants use American social programs extravagantly when (in fact) they use them at low rates.

Recent conflict over immigration began with passage of Proposition 187 in California in 1994 that prohibited undocumented immigrants from using health care, public education, benefits from public programs, and other social services until they had been verified as citizens or as lawfully admitted aliens. Law enforcement agents were required to investigate arrestees' immigration status. Schools were required to verify the legal status of each enrolled child and that child's parent or parents. Many churches, leaders of the Latino community, and liberals contended that it was xenophobic—leading to lawsuits filed against it the day after its passage by the Mexican American Legal Defense and Educational Fund (MALDEF) and the American Civil Liberties Union (ACLU). It was supported by many Republicans, including Governor Pete Wilson (http://en.wikipedia.org/wiki/California_Proposition_187_(1994). It was never implemented due to the ruling of a federal court that it was unconstitutional on grounds the U.S. Constitution vests the federal government, not state governments, with regulating migration across national boundaries. Provisions of welfare reform legislation in 1996 banned undocumented immigrants from using many federal grant programs.

Bipartisan support for more moderate policies developed by 2005, leading to the development of the Comprehensive Immigration Reform Act of 2007 that proposed to grant amnesty to roughly 12 million undocumented immigrants, allow millions of persons to obtain short-term work visas, and increase priority for visas for high-skilled workers. Democratic Senators Harry Reid and Ted Kennedy joined with Republican Senator John McCain and President George W. Bush to support it. It assuaged conservatives by strengthening interdiction at borders, including 20,000 more border patrol agents and increasing barriers, including installation of cameras and radar towers. The legislation failed to come to a vote in the Senate, however, due to opposition from conservatives who opposed granting citizenship to undocumented workers— and from some liberal activists who feared that a large group of persons with short-term work visas would become "underclass workers" with no benefits (http://en.wikipedia.org/wiki/Comprehensive_Immigration_Reform_Act_of_2007). The defeat of the legislation triggered mass marches in many cities led by Latinos.

EP 2.1.5b

Barack Obama promised to seek immigration reform during his presidency in 2008, but was unable to make place for it on his legislative agenda in his first two years in office as he focused on stimulus, health and financial reforms. The pendulum swung back to conservatives in the wake of their regaining control of the House of Representatives in 2010 Congressional elections with passage of restrictive laws in Arizona, South Carolina, Alabama, Georgia, Indiana, and other states. These laws variously required law enforcement officers to apprehend persons who appeared to be undocumented immigrants and to require schools to check the immigration status of children and their parents. Liberal organizations sought to block implementation of these laws by alleging they authorized unlawful search and seizure, invasion of privacy, racial profiling, and usurpation of federal immigration roles. Conservatives blocked enactment, as well, of the federal DREAM Act that proposed to allow federal education assistance to undocumented youths who had been brought to the United States by undocumented parents, often as infants or children.

Conservatives have overlooked some social and economic facts: minus their labor, large sections of the American economy would markedly decline, including agriculture, tourism, construction, and food processing industries where millions of immigrants work for low wages and often in harsh working conditions. They do not understand that the United States will need to augment its workforce as baby boomers retire.

Globalization's Impact on the Environment

Recent global issues, such as the depletion of the atmospheric ozone layer, global climate change due to the greenhouse effect, and the depletion of the earth's natural resources (e.g., forests and land), have gained increasing attention. Scientists differ in their estimates of the rate of global climate change, but they mostly agree that the huge releases of carbon dioxide from industrial use of fossil fuels have already led to increases in global temperatures and accelerated the melting of glaciers and ice caps. Many scientists offer dire predictions of consequences that nations will suffer if carbon dioxide emissions are not slowed and capped, as advocated by the Kyoto Treaty of 1997, which the United States refused to sign. If just the ice cap over Greenland were to melt, for example, the seas around North America could rise by more than 20 feet, inundating such areas as New Orleans, coastal areas of Florida, and some of Manhattan. This has been predicted to occur sometime in the coming century, although experts differ in their estimates.

Were the oceans to rise markedly, citizens in coastal regions around the world would have to evacuate to higher ground, causing massive migrations, huge industrial losses, and the destruction of hundreds of ports that undergird the world's economy. Global climate change would cause large sections of the globe to have insufficient rain to support agriculture, possibly contributing to famine in many nations. Global climate change will have unknown consequences for the world's oceans and fisheries, but some evidence already exists that it will disrupt them by endangering some of the organisms that form the diets of various species of fish.

Globalization when coupled with rapid industrialization in many nations will pose other problems for the world's economy. While abundant fossil fuel reserves still exist, they will probably become increasingly expensive during the 21st century—not to mention the cost of many other minerals, like copper, iron ore, and bauxite. Unless other means of generating power are invented that can produce power at levels comparable to those of fossil fuels, such as solar- and wind-generated energies, a meltdown of the world's economy could take place because the world is currently heavily reliant on use of fossil fuels. Escalating prices for fossil fuels could, as well, incite conflict between nations for control of deposits of oil, gas, and coal—and could widen the gap between affluent nations and poor nations, as industries in affluent nations outbid industries in developing nations for fossil fuels.

Nations will have to grapple with the difficult issue of sustainability. To what degree can escalating industrialization and consumption of goods be sustained with the world's existing stock of fossil fuels and minerals—particularly when global climate change and the world's population is considered? (See Policy Advocacy Challenge 5.4.)

Threats to Public Health

Similar to environmental problems, public health problems—such as communicable diseases—are not bound by national borders, as evidenced by recent scares about severe acute respiratory syndrome (SARS), bird flu, and swine flu epidemics. With increased movement of both goods and people, preventing the spread of potentially deadly diseases has become increasingly challenging for national governments. The U.S. Office of Travel and Tourism Industries estimates that the number of international travelers to the United States was nearly 51 million in 2000. In the month of January 2008 alone, 3.4 million international visitors arrived in the United States, a marked increase from the previous year. The Harvard Working Group (HWG) on New and Resurgent Diseases argues that "increased travel and trade have greatly increased the opportunities for

Policy Advocacy Challenge 5.4

Threat of Global Climate Change to New Orleans and Other Coastal Areas

Bruce Jansson, Ph.D.

The flooding of New Orleans after Hurricane Katrina in 2005 was shaped by an array of erroneous decisions made by the Army Corps of Engineers, as well as by international oil companies.

The Army Corps had built incorrectly designed levees around New Orleans, often not giving them a deep enough base to withstand rising waters from a Category 5 hurricane. Nor had it sufficiently maintained the levees over a period of many decades, so that cracks had developed in many of them.

Both the Army Corps and oil companies had made yet another set of errors, by their construction of canals and water diversion projects. These structures prevented soil from washing down the Mississippi River and sustaining the extended delta, wetlands, and islands south of New Orleans that had buffered the city from upsurging water from hurricanes. As a matter of fact, this buildup of soil and land had protected New Orleans from hurricanes for centuries, but it had become increasingly depleted in the decades preceding Hurricane Katrina. Many scientists contended that, useful as levees were, they would prove insufficient to protect New Orleans if environmental policies were not put in place to rebuild these wetlands, the delta, and offshore islands.

Many experts believe, however, that *neither* the levees *nor* rebuilding of wetlands would be ultimately effective if nations of the world failed to contain and place a ceiling on carbon dioxide emissions from the burning of fossil fuels, thereby arresting global warming. If the seas rose more than 25 feet *just* from the melting of the ice cap over Greenland at some point in the 21st century or later—you may add many more feet when the Artic and Antarctic ice caps are considered—New Orleans and the entire Gulf region would be inundated with water, forcing mass and permanent evacuations. This would occur not all at once, as happened with Hurricane Katrina, but over great periods of time.

The United States and 33 other industrial countries in the Organization for Economic Co-operation and Development (OECD), now use less than half of the world's primary energy sources as developing nations have rapidly increased their consumption of oil, natural gas, coal, nuclear energy, and hydroelectricity.[1] As India and China rapidly industrialize, not to mention other nations like Brazil and Mexico, carbon dioxide emissions will accelerate as the world's stock of forests, which slow global climate change, rapidly decline with deforestation in Asia, South America, and elsewhere.

The international trading system, as well as international regulations regarding pollution caused by fossil fuels, remains ill-prepared to address these difficult issues. For example, nearly 80 percent of the world's international trade is carried by ocean ships that use an enormous amount of fossil fuel and are highly polluting.[2] The push for free trade has often led to the "ratcheting-down" of environmental regulations, which are viewed as costly obstructions to deregulation, even leading the WTO in one of its earliest actions to rule against the United States' Clean Air Act on grounds that its guidelines for controlling pollution were excessively strict.[3]

Global climate change is a manifestation of globalization because carbon dioxide emissions cross international boundaries and nations share the world's atmosphere. Only international treaties and policies that mandate and fund the use of alternative fuels, the installation of antipollution devices in factories, and fuel-efficient cars, among other initiatives, can control and prevent global climate change. Rising seas will imperil the

EP 2.1.6b

[1]Shell Oil Company (2010). Shell Energy Scenarios to 2050. Retrieved on December 15, 2011, from http://www.static .shell.com/static/aboutshell/downloads/aboutshell/signals_signposts.pdf.
[2]JerryMander, "Intrinsic Negative Effects of Economic Globalization on the Environment," in James Gustave Speth, ed., *Worlds Apart: Globalization and the Environment* (Islander Press Washington, DC, 2003): pp. 109–129.
[3]Ibid.

coastal regions around the world, where the bulk of the world's population lives. The future of coastal regions such as New Orleans is linked to these global realities.

Visit www.climatehotmap.org to view a map of the world illustrating the local consequences of global warming. What parts of the world are already affected by ocean warming, rising sea levels, and coastal flooding? Are there any "fingerprints" (i.e., direct manifestations of a widespread and long-term trend toward higher global temperatures) or "harbingers" (i.e., events that foreshadow the types of impacts likely to become more frequent and widespread with continued warming) in your area?

EP 2.1.6b

pathogens and vectors (e.g., insects) to spread to new areas. This problem is not a new one—but the rapidity with which goods and people now move around the globe has augmented the likelihood of 'microbial traffic'" (pp. 164–165).[10]

Despite advances in knowledge of and technology related to health care and public health, infectious diseases remain a leading cause of death globally, accounting for a quarter to a third of the world's deaths in 1998.[11] The international community has seen not only the emergence of new diseases but also a resurgence of old diseases. In a recent television series and Web-based educational program, entitled *Rx for Survival: A Global Health Challenge*, the Public Broadcasting Corporation (PBC) found that "some 38 new diseases—including avian flu, West Nile virus, SARS, and mad cow disease—have appeared since 1973. Further, 20 diseases that had been suppressed—including malaria and tuberculosis—are again on the rise."[12] These reemerging diseases are also spreading to new geographic areas. With globalization leaving many countries and communities behind economically, these populations face extreme poverty, malnutrition, and lack of access to safe drinking water, thus making them more vulnerable and susceptible to disease.[13]

Creating a Monoculture?

Harvard University professor Marcelo Suarez-Orozco (2001) writes that "globalization decisively undermines the once imagined neat fit between language, culture, and the nation" (p. 346).[14] Not surprisingly, this "global monoculture" generally reflects the values and lifestyles of the United States, "from Big Macs to iMacs to Mickey Mouse".[15] Similarly, Barnet and Cavanagh (1996) write that "the entire planet is being wired into music, movies, news, television programs, and other cultural products that originate primarily in the film and recording studios of the United States.... American culture products are sweeping the globe" (p. 72).[16]

The Great Caveat: Globalization's Positive Effects

Countries that have entered the global economy have often experienced overall higher standards of living. Marber (2004/2005) writes that "no matter how one measures wealth—whether by economic, bio-social, or financial indicators—there have been gains in virtually every meaningful aspect of life in the last two generations.... Most people are living longer, healthier, fuller lives" (p. 29).[17] In fact, overall improvements can be shown in a broad range of measures: life expectancies; literacy rates and public education; economic output and trade; poverty, per capita income, and income equality; access to technology (e.g., televisions and automobiles); quality of life (e.g., work hours per year); and political participation (i.e., the right to vote). In its 2002 report, *Globalization,*

Growth, and Poverty, the World Bank shows that the "more globalized" developing countries, such as China and Mexico, fared better on several of these indicators than "less globalized" countries, such as Pakistan and Kenya. For example, in the newly globalized countries, the number of individuals living in extreme poverty (less than $1 per day) declined by 120 million in the five-year period between 1993 and 1998.[18]

It is clear, however, that this prosperity has not been shared by everyone or every country. Even the World Bank—one of the key institutions driving globalization—admits that "the fact that globalization does not on average increase inequality within countries disguises the reality that there are specific winners and losers in each society" (p. 2).[19] After touting the benefits of globalization, Marber writes that "even with its positive trends, globalization is not a perfect process. It is not a panacea for every problem for every person at every moment in time" (p. 37).[20] A critic of some aspects of globalization, Joseph Stiglitz argues that "those who vilify globalization too often overlook its benefits," while then proceeding to state that

> [T]he proponents of globalization have been, if anything, even more unbalanced. To them, globalization (which typically is associated with accepting triumphant capitalism, American style) is progress; developing countries must accept it, if they are to grow and to fight poverty effectively. But to many in the developing world, globalization has not brought the promised benefits (p. 5).[21]

Policy Advocacy for Populations Harmed by Globalization

Policy advocates need to develop and secure the enactment of an array of policies that decrease the negative impact of globalization upon vulnerable populations in the United States and abroad by working with advocacy groups that seek to address social problems abroad or in the treaties and international organizations that regulate or deal with issues associated with globalization. A few illustrative examples follow.

Policy Options in the United States

EP 2.1.5c

Local, state, and federal governments need to invest more resources in relatively unskilled workers so that they can rebound when they lose their jobs as corporations close plants or move abroad. These workers need job training assistance and relocation assistance. In some cases, they need financial assistance so that they can obtain educational credentials from high schools, community colleges, and colleges.

Policy advocates need to enact policies that require corporations to give advance notice of their intention to close or move their operations—and require them to help fund assistance to workers who become unemployed. To the extent some corporations undercut American corporations by selling low-cost imports that rely on victimization of workers in developing nations, policy advocates need to place pressure on them to set and enforce minimum-wage and work-safety standards in the developing nations where their products are manufactured.

Policy advocates need to develop policies to help migrants. Persons who are defined as "illegal" or "undocumented" immigrants are subject not only to prejudice but also to victimization by landlords, criminal elements, and employers who realize that they cannot easily seek protection from the police or courts for fear of deportation. The United States needs to give substantial groups of these persons—without whom the American economy cannot function at its current level—a combination of amnesty and other legal protections—as a concerted social movement for immigration reforms, like the one sought by widespread demonstrations in the United States in 2006. Because efforts to keep such persons from entering the United States are futile as long as the economic gap is large between the countries of origin and the destinations of immigrants, efforts to rely exclusively on strengthening border patrols may not succeed in keeping many persons from crossing borders.

For an example of policy advocacy for immigrants, see Policy Advocacy Challenge 5.5, in which Dennis Kao discusses his advocacy for immigrants to the United States.

Policy Advocacy Challenge 5.5

Serving as an Intermediary Between Immigrant Communities and Sacramento: Lessons Learned

Dennis Kao, MSW and Ph.D. Assistant Professor, School of Social Work, University of Houston

Like other disadvantaged groups, immigrants and their families often feel disconnected from the policy-making process. However, immigrants also encounter another layer of unique barriers. For example, while other disadvantaged groups may be perceived to be low-propensity voters, immigrants, by definition, cannot vote and consequently are often unable to participate in public elections or legislative decisions. Many immigrants also may not yet have attained a strong grasp of the English language and therefore often lack knowledge regarding their basic rights and have difficulty communicating their needs and concerns. Depending on the current political climate and/or their own experiences in their home countries, many immigrants may also feel a sense of fear or distrust toward the government. Given these challenges, it is often difficult for immigrant families to feel that they can have a voice. For several years, I had the opportunity to work for a not-for-profit immigrant rights organization in Los Angeles County, which was also part of a statewide coalition of organizations. Our primary role was to serve as an intermediary, that is, to facilitate communication between the immigrant communities we served and the policymakers in Sacramento. Here are some of the lessons I learned during my time there.

ENGAGING COMMUNITY LEADERS AND ORGANIZATIONS

We felt that a single organization could not possibly outreach to or engage the broader immigrant community, given its diversity and size. Much of our time, therefore, was spent working closely with community leaders and organizations (i.e., service agencies, churches, and membership organizations), who can then work to engage their own members or clients. To help build their advocacy capacity, we conducted ongoing advocacy trainings (e.g., legislative/budget processes, advocacy skills, and lobbying rules for nonprofits). We also held monthly regional meetings that pulled in many of our partner organizations, as well as other groups. The purpose of these meetings was to discuss current policy issues that were important to the local organizations and to strategize regional campaigns.

INVESTING IN COMMUNITIES LONG TERM

We often found that the community work necessary to build capacity and momentum operated on a much slower timeline than the fast and unpredictable policy-making process. It was important, therefore, to establish short-term policy goals and campaigns, but to always keep in mind the longer-term goal of capacity-building. In our case, it was also important to redefine what "policy success" meant to us. In most circles, policy success simply means achieving legislative victories. While this obviously was important to us, we also felt that we were successful if more organizations or individuals were meaningfully engaged in the process each year. The challenge then is how we measure this type of success. Examples of outcome measures included were number of advocacy trainings/workshops, number of legislative visits organized, number and types of

(continued)

organizations who participated in those legislative visits, attendance at regional meetings, response to our policy updates (see following text), and the extent we are engaging immigrants and their families.

FACILITATING ONGOING COMMUNICATION

Before the start of each legislative session, we conducted surveys and consulted with key partners to assess the key state policy issues for that year. On the basis of this process, these issues became a part of our policy agenda for that legislative session. We established a rapid-alert network, which at one point grew to about 400 organizations and individuals in the county. Either through fax or email, we would provide timely state policy and budget updates regarding the issues on our agenda, as well as other issues impacting immigrants. These updates often included simple actions that individuals and organizations could take, for example, writing a letter or making a call (in which case, a sample letter or script would also be included). Having a presence in Sacramento can be important, and in our case, our statewide coalition had established an office in Sacramento with a full-time policy advocate who provided us with timely information and updates. Understanding that this is not possible in most cases, there are also a number of Sacramento-based organizations that would be open to working closely with local groups.

PROVIDING SPACE FOR INDIVIDUALS TO TELL THEIR STORY

The most important lesson for me was to learn that everyone has a story to tell if given the chance and that these personal stories or testimonies can be extremely effective in conveying a strong message and influencing policy. In addition to providing opportunities for individuals to express their concerns via letters or phone calls, we coordinated group visits with state legislators in their district office. Depending on the issue, these groups could consist of community leaders, providers, advocates, and immigrants themselves. We also compiled the stories of immigrants directly impacted by specific policies and distributed them (e.g., in a brochure, weekly fax, or a larger report) to legislators. Finally, each year in May (a crucial time in the state budget process), we and our statewide partners coordinated an "immigrant advocacy day" in the state capitol, which pulled together hundreds of advocates and immigrants. Throughout the day, participants would take part in a number of activities, such as legislative visits, rallies, and training. For many, this day was the first opportunity to speak directly to a policy maker.

Policy Options to Help Vulnerable Populations Abroad

Policy advocates need to pressure international organizations, such as the IMF and World Bank, as well as the WTO, to implement policies that do not victimize vulnerable populations in developing nations. For example, policies that require developing nations to reduce their spending on social programs harm their vulnerable populations. The latter's discontent with the WTO was apparent when thousands of demonstrators disrupted the WTO's 1999 ministerial meeting in Seattle, Washington, and for the most part, shut down the city.[22] Policy advocates should support efforts to eliminate barriers to imports from developing nations that curtail the well-being of their vulnerable populations. This was illustrated when some policy advocates sought a detailed agreement at the WTO meetings in mid-December 2005 to eliminate all duties and quotas on the exports of at least 32 of the world's poor countries—with considerable support for this policy coming from Europe and Japan. (Faced with pressure from such states as North Carolina over cuts in American quotas on cotton imports, the Bush administration withheld its support for such far-reaching policies.) They can, moreover, support or work with groups that provide assistance to vulnerable populations in developing nations. They can support projects to help developing nations retain some of their protective tariffs when their removal would excessively harm vulnerable populations such as peasants (see Policy Advocacy Challenge 5.6). Policy advocates can lend support to advocacy groups that pressure governments to include minimum standards for wages and working conditions in trade treaties approved by the WTO, NAFTA, Free Trade Area of the Americas (FTAA), and GATT.

Protecting Human Rights

EP 2.1.5b

Human rights are defined by Article 1 of the United Nations Universal Declaration of Human Rights as "basic rights and freedoms to which all humans are entitled"—a non-binding declaration of the UN General Assembly in 1948 that partly emanated in response to the atrocities committed during World War II. The Geneva Convention of 1949 formalized laws of war and war crimes under the leadership of the International Committee of the Red Cross. Many additional international laws have been enacted in ensuing years, such as the UN Convention on the Elimination of all Forms of Discrimination Against Women in 1981, the UN Convention Against Torture in 1984, and the International Convention on Protection of the Rights of All Migrant Workers and Members of Their Families in 1990. Article 39 of the UN Charter designates the UN Security Council, or its appointed authority, as the sole tribunal that can determinate a UN human rights violation. The UN Security Council, in turn, oversees the UN Human Rights Council and many other UN committees, all of which investigate violations of human rights and can refer cases to the International Criminal Court. (This court, established in 2002 and meeting at The Hague in the Netherlands, recently indicted 14 persons for genocide and similar crimes.) Wars of aggression, war crimes, and crimes against humanity, such as genocide, are the most serious violations of human rights, but many experts include in this category the death penalty, torture, police brutality, violations of reproductive rights, such as the rights to have children as well as legal and safe abortions, and violations of rights of the LGBT population.

Despite efforts to outlaw genocide in the wake of World War II, as well as oppression of dissidents, violations of human rights took place in many nations from the 1940s to the present. Civil wars and dictatorships existed in Central and South America, including Argentina, Cuba, El Salvador, and Guatemala. President Bill Clinton orchestrated major American and NATO involvement in Bosnia to curtail genocide of Bosnians and Croats by Serbs and in Kosovo to curtail genocide of indigenous Albanians by Serbs. He and the UN failed to intervene in Rwanda where roughly 800,000 Tutsis were killed by Hutu groups in 1994. Genocide took place in Uganda over a 20-year period when the Lord's Resistance Army and the Ugandan government killed and terrorized members of the Acholi Tribe leading to 1.5 million IDPs living in camps with deplorable conditions (Daniella Boston, "Genocide in Uganda: The African Nightmare Christopher Hitchens Missed," Retrieved on 12/15/2011 from www.huffingtonpost.com/daniella-boston/genocide-in-uganda-the-af_b-21150.html). A civil war led to 2 million deaths and 4 million displaced persons in the Sudan from 1983 to 2011.

Mass uprising took place in Algeria, Tunisia, Libya, Egypt, and Syria in the so-called Arab Spring as residents demanded the ouster of dictators and the development of democratic institutions in 2011. The outcome of these uprising appeared positive in Algeria and Tunisia in late 2011, but remained uncertain in the other nations. Mass killings or repression of dissidents persisted in Syria, Yemen, and Bahrain. Libyan insurgents overthrew and killed the Libyan dictator, Muammar Qaddafi, in 2011, only to face the challenge of establishing a new democratic government.

**Policy
Advocacy
Challenge 5.6**

Factors to
Consider in
Rebuilding
Areas Stricken
by Natural
Disasters

Imagine trying to rebuild a nation when virtually all of its public buildings were destroyed; when 1 million persons were made homeless, 316,000 persons perished, 300,000 were injured often leading to serious disabilities; when 250,000 residences and 300,000 commercial buildings were destroyed or seriously damaged.* Imagine, too, that the nation was the poorest one in the Western Hemisphere, ranking 149th of 182 nations on the Human Development Index that measures life expectancy, literacy, education, and living standards. Also imagine that its medical infrastructure was devastated by the earthquake, including key hospitals and clinics, its major port, many of its schools, and many of its roads. Imagine, too, that it possessed a dysfunctional government hobbled by corruption and nepotism.

Assume that considerable assistance flowed to this nation in the earthquake's wake, but that it was far less than other nations had promised in the first year following it— and that more than 1 million persons remained displaced in crowded camps where persons had no work, lived in tents, and had virtually no health or other services.

Would you give priority to health, housing, development of economic growth, social services, or political reforms? Would you try to develop community groups to bring political reforms? Who would assume leadership of these tasks?

For ideas, go the Web and look at the role of the Inter-American Development Bank (IDB) in a forum it held on December 8, 2011 in Miami at http://defend.ht/money/artiles/economy/2178-idb-held-the-haiti-reconstruction-forum-in-miami.

---

*Some experts question these numbers, contending the government inflated them to get more resources from other nations, the UN, and other sources; see http://en.wikipedia.org/wiki/2010/2010_Haiti_earthquake.

Surmounting Natural Disasters

EP 2.1.5c

Already facing economic and social challenges, some developing nations must also cope with natural disasters, as illustrated by nations rebuilding from the tsunami of 2004 in the Indian Ocean that devastated large portions of South and East Asia and a catastrophic earthquake that devastated Haiti in 2010. (Developed nations also encounter natural disasters of epic proportions, as illustrated by the tsunami in 2011 in Japan.) Lacking revenues to fund massive rebuilding of their nations, developing countries rely on external donors and technical assistance in a protracted process of development. Their task is made even more difficult when they possess governments that are corrupt, lack skilled civil servants, and do not have technical expertise. Haiti encounters these and other challenges as it seeks to rebuild (see Policy Advocacy Challenge 5.6).

Crucial Role of Nongovernmental Organizations

Nongovernmental organizations (NGOs) have assumed significant roles in recent decades in safeguarding human rights, including Amnesty International, Human Rights Watch, the Global Fund for Women, Oxfam, and many NGOs in specific nations. They include NGOs in developing nations that "may deploy their activities within domestic frameworks or that … influence international decision-making procedures" such as by asking the Human Rights Council (HRC) or the General Assembly of the United Nations to intervene.[23] Civil rights groups sometimes emerge spontaneously, such as during the so-called Arab Spring. The uprisings in North Africa in spring 2011 spawned the Saudi Women for Driving Internet Campaign where Saudi women defied the ban on

EP 2.1.5b

driving imposed by the government of Saudi Arabia. Attorneys often assume central roles in civil rights campaigns, such as the Lawyers Collective in Mumbai, India that drafted comprehensive antidiscrimination legislation in behalf of persons with HIV-AIDS. Nor is the United States immune from criticism: Amnesty International and other NGOs have cited the United States for police brutality, sentencing in some states of adolescents to prison without the possibility of parole, inhumane treatment of prisoners, the death penalty, including disproportionately large number of executions of persons of color, and interrogation methods and torture of prisoners, as at the Guantanamo Bay detention center.

NGOs assume other functions, as well. They help developing nations cope with natural disasters. They assist refugees. They organize community development projects. They provide health clinics. They introduce technological innovations in agriculture and health.

Policy Advocacy Challenge 5.7

International Advocacy Organizations

Rachel Katz, MPP

Many international organizations work as advocates for socially vulnerable groups across the globe. Some work at the community level to provide direct relief services or empower people and groups in developing nations to fight for social justice at the community level, while others focus on political campaigns and lobbying to effect broader policy changes. In the following text are descriptions of several organizations involved in international advocacy efforts.

OXFAM INTERNATIONAL Oxfam is a group of 17 humanitarian organizations around the world, which together work to fight poverty and social injustice. Oxfam engages in three types of advocacy work: (1) leading organizing efforts for people living in poverty around the world, (2) conducting political lobbying, and (3) building alliances across organizations and groups.
   www.oxfam.org

COOPERATIVE FOR ASSISTANCE AND RELIEF EVERYWHERE CARE is a humanitarian organization made up of 12 member organizations in different nations around the world. CARE member organizations work to fight poverty in over 70 nations. Like Oxfam, CARE advocates both through empowerment initiatives and lobbying for policy changes.
   www.care.org

UNITED NATIONS CHILDREN'S FUND UNICEF advocates for the rights of children in 157 nations around the world. UNICEF's focus areas are education, health, environmental safety, and violence and abuse. UNICEF provides direct services within these areas, and also conducts policy analysis and other research, which it disseminates throughout its partner organizations. UNICEF does not affiliate itself with political parties, and does not engage in political lobbying efforts.
   www.unicef.org

UNITED STATES AGENCY FOR INTERNATIONAL DEVELOPMENT USAID is an independent agency of the U.S. federal government. USAID carries out U.S. foreign aid projects in many areas, including health, humanitarian assistance, and conflict prevention. Because USAID is a federal agency, it does not engage in political lobbying, though it does publish reports on strategies to address global issues.
   www.usaid.gov

GLOBAL TRADE WATCH GTW is an international organization that advocates against what it calls "corporate globalization," arguing that free trade does more harm than good. GTW conducts both grassroots advocacy and political lobbying efforts in many areas of globalization, including the environment, health, and responsible governance.
   www.citizen.org/trade

(continued)

THE WORLD FOOD PROGRAM WFP is the United Nations' frontline agency in the fight against global hunger.
www.wfp.org/

THE WORLD HEALTH ORGANIZATION WHO is the United Nations' specialized agency for health. It provides leadership on global health matters, shapes the health research agenda, sets norms and standards, articulates evidence-based policy options, and monitors and assesses health trends.
www.who.int/en/

THE INTERNATIONAL FEDERATION OF RED CROSS AND RED CRESCENT SOCIETIES The world's largest humanitarian organization, the society has programs grouped into four core areas: promoting humanitarian principles and values; disaster response; disaster preparedness; and health and care in the community.
www.ifrc.org/index.asp

INTERACTION The largest alliance of U.S.-based international development and humanitarian nongovernmental organizations. With more than 160 members operating in every developing country, this diverse coalition of organizations works to overcome poverty, exclusion, and suffering by advancing social justice and basic dignity for all.
www.interaction.org/

Just as many organizations advocate protecting vulnerable populations in developing nations from the effects of globalization, other groups actively promote globalization with the argument that it spurs economic growth and improves living standards around the world. These groups tend to be business associations, which focus on the economic and trade aspects of globalization. Some examples include the Business Roundtable (www.businessroundtable.org), an association of business leaders in the United States with an international focus; the International Chamber of Commerce (www.iccwbo.org), an association of business executives from over 130 countries; Amnesty International (www.AmnestyUSA.org), a nongovernmental organization that monitors human rights violations around the world; and Human Rights Watch (http://hrw.org), another nongovernmental organization that monitors human rights violations around the world.

Policy advocates also need to seek enactment of legislation in the United States that protects migrants from victimization by employers and citizens. The need for these protections was illustrated during 2011 and 2012 when conservative legislators in many states enacted legislation that gave local police extraordinary power to apprehend persons who "looked like" undocumented persons. In such states as Arizona, this legislation gave police authority to apprehend *any* persons of Latino appearance, even U.S. citizens and persons with Green Cards or other kinds of legal status. When the Supreme Court ruled in 2012 that the Arizona legislation was unconstitutional because it preempted authority given to the U.S. government to regulate immigration, the momentum behind such legislation was blunted—but even this court ruling was likely to lead to additional controversy over the rights of state to enact legislation impacting immigrants.

Policy advocates should consider measures extending amnesty to persons who have resided in the United States for a specific period and policies that guarantee and monitor rights of immigrants who have guest-worker status, including decent wages, access to education, and access to medical services extending beyond the emergency medical services currently available to them. Because large numbers of undocumented persons live in the United States, many of them are likely to be victimized as they lack rights given to

EP 2.1.5b

citizens or to persons with visas. As fugitives, they cannot easily report crimes done to them or use medical programs when they need them. Nor are they likely to report employers' unfair treatment of them. National immigration legislation was almost enacted in 2008, partly due to nationwide marches by hundreds of thousands of citizens. Policy advocates need to pressure whoever wins the presidential election of 2012 to support immigration legislation that puts an end to these kinds of discrimination.

Policy Advocacy Challenge 5.8

Two Examples of the Interconnectedness of Globalization, Immigration, and Social Problems

Bruce Jansson, Ph.D.

THE REBUILDING OF NEW ORLEANS

When a huge portion of New Orleans's population evacuated the city in the wake of Hurricane Katrina—and when many of them chose not to return to the city even years later—the city encountered a major labor shortage. Vast amounts of debris had to be collected and moved. Many of the city's structures had to be demolished. Those structures that could be salvaged often had to be gutted to remove mold- and mildew-infested plaster, drywall, and wood. The electrical and plumbing systems of houses often had to be replaced. Roads and bridges had to be repaired or rebuilt. Levees had to be repaired or rebuilt.

One source of labor was African American evacuees and residents—because they had comprised about 67 percent of the population of New Orleans prior to Hurricane Katrina.[1] So also would have been African American contractors who had been a vital part of New Orleans's business community before Katrina. Other sources of labor included not only the Caucasian residents and evacuees but also sizeable numbers of immigrants from Vietnam and Honduras, who had settled in New Orleans before Hurricane Katrina.

Once the city had been devastated by the hurricane, however, local employers and companies were often supplanted by out-of-state contractors, such as construction firms with links to powerful public officials in Louisiana and in Washington, DC. These firms wanted to reap the benefits of substantial contracts from the federal government—benefits that would be greatly increased if they could pay low wages, offer few or no benefits to workers, and ignore work-safety regulations.

It is not surprising, then, that the contractors obtained the enactment of many policies that relaxed regulations protecting workers' rights and safety. President Bush suspended by executive order provisions of the Davis-Bacon Act, which required federal construction contractors to pay no less than the prevailing wage rates for private construction workers in September 2005—allowing them to cut their pay even below the already low rates in Louisiana. Only pressure from unions and others forced the president to restore these provisions in November 2005. The Occupational Safety and Health Administration (OSHA) suspended enforcement of work-safety and health standards in August 2005. The Department of Labor assigned virtually no staff to monitoring whether employers actually paid their employees.

Any hope that African American contractors would obtain many contracts were dashed when the Department of Labor suspended affirmative action requirements. While it lifted this suspension in late 2005, the tone had been set: few contracts went to

---

[1] I draw heavily on a report titled "And Injustice for All: Workers' Lives in the Reconstruction of New Orleans" (2006) issued by the a Washington legal aid group called the Advancement Project, co-authored by Judith Browne-Dianis and Jennifer Lai of the Project, as well as Marielena Hincapié of the National Immigration Law Center and Saket Soni of the New Orleans Worker Justice Coalition. The report can be found online at www.advancementproject.org/reports/workers-report.pdf. I also used a 2011 report from National Public Radio (NPR) at www.npr.org/2011/12/10/143390961/latinos-get-little-credit-for-rebuilding-new-orleans.

(continued)

Policy Advocacy Challenge 5.8 (continued)

EP 2.1.5a

these firms. Then many contracts were given to specific contractors without using a competitive bidding process—again putting minority contractors at a disadvantage as compared to contractors with links to powerful government officials. Nor did the Small Business Administration (SBA) give many loans or grants to small businesses so that they could resume work after many had lost their equipment and supplies after Hurricane Katrina. Many African Americans could not get jobs, moreover, because of job discrimination by employers, either because they were racially prejudiced or because they believed that they could pay immigrants from abroad lower rates. Some African Americans alleged, as well, that employers systematically discriminated against them in favor of hiring migrants, thinking that migrants would be less likely to complain to government officials about working conditions and low pay for fear of being deported.

Out-of-state contractors aggressively sought workers in Mexico and some Asian nations such as Thailand by advertising in newspapers, where they promised housing and relatively high wages. Believing these advertisements, immigrants went to American consulates and obtained H-2A visas for "nonimmigrant workers," which gave them the right to temporarily enter the United States if they were sponsored by a specific employer. This kind of visa allowed them to stay in the United States only as long as they worked for *this* employer. Many other undocumented Latinos came to New Orleans to seek work.

Louisiana had never been a pro-labor area, lacking even a minimum wage law unlike most other states. It became even less so in the wake of Katrina when vast sums of money were dispatched to contractors in a short span of time. Between 30,000 and 100,000 persons streamed into New Orleans to get work—roughly half of them from Mexico. Many of these persons became embroiled in a "national crisis of civil and human rights." Many of them received meager pay. They often worked in toxic environments in areas with mold, mildew, and chemicals, and with little or no protective gear. They often discovered that they were not paid, or only partially paid for their work, were not reimbursed for overtime, and sometimes given checks that bounced. They often lived in motels with as many as 10 persons in a room—or were homeless. Even when they possessed temporary-worker visas, they were often harassed by police and immigration officials. Many of these laborers received no health insurance and no worker's compensation—and some were even dismissed when they developed illnesses, such as eye infections from working in toxic areas. Some migrants were told that they would be reported to immigration officials if they complained to authorities about their working conditions.

Tragically, Latino and African American workers seldom made common cause against their victimization, partly because many of them subscribed to beliefs that pitted them against one another. If many African Americans often viewed themselves as the rightful residents of New Orleans who were overrun by Latinos, Latinos often subscribed to the view that African Americans were too lazy to work. Mayor Ray Nagin contributed to this view when he said on October 10, 2005, "How do I make sure that New Orleans is not overrun by Mexican workers?" In the same vein, Senator Mary Landrieu said about the same time, "they [Mexicans] aggravate our employment crisis and depress earnings for our workers." Both public officials might better have focused on the victimization of workers of both racial and ethnic groups by federal contractors—a practice that was promoted by the laxness of the Bush administration in enforcing federal wage, work-safety, and wage-payment policies and not moving even faster to get affordable child care, housing, and medical care back into New Orleans.

The inability of African Americans to obtain jobs in New Orleans was frustrated, as well, by the post-Katrina decisions of some corporations based in New Orleans to relocate their facilities abroad in developing nations where they could pay lower wages, use child labor, and avoid American environmental and work-safety regulations.

THE ECONOMIC RECESSION OF 2007–2009 AND BEYOND

When the economic recession hit a few years later, the situation of poor residents—both native and immigrant—in New Orleans and beyond was worsened. Many people expected that immigrants would pour back into their home countries en mass as they encountered a tightening American economy and fewer job opportunities. Although fewer undocumented persons are in fact arriving in the United States as a result of the ailing economy, immigrants who were already here appear to be staying. Remaining in the United States may be the result of a lack of funds to make the trip home, but more likely it is attributable to the global nature of the recession. Not only is the U.S. economy ailing but so also are developing regions. Undocumented workers do not perceive that their situation will improve if they return to their home countries.

The demography of New Orleans had markedly changed. Since Katrina, the Latino population in New Orleans had increased by more than 33,000 people—or a 57 percent increase during the preceding decade. Because the demolition and construction work lasted for several years, they made New Orleans their home and had no intention of leaving, even though many became unemployed and still found that they often were not paid for their work by employers when they did work. Many African Americans still resented Latinos because they believed they had taken jobs from them. Many Latinos, in turn, felt unappreciated by Americans, as expressed by Jordan Shannon, a spokesperson for Puentes, an advocacy group representing them: "the city … has really been built on the back of Latinos" (www.npr.org/2011/12/10/143390961/latinos-get-little-credit-for-rebuilding-new-orleans).

To make matters worse, immigrants who remain in the United States are finding their earnings sinking to the point that they are unable to send remittances home. These remittances are often not only a large source of income for their families back home but also are a substantial part of the economy of the home country. For example, in 2005, remittances from Mexicans living abroad were valued at $18 billion, and represented 2.5 percent of the nation's gross domestic product (GDP). When workers in the United States are unable to send remittances home, their families and the national economy of their home countries suffer.

Considering the circumstances surrounding the rebuilding in New Orleans and the economic recession that began in 2007, discuss the following questions.

1. What social problems did both immigrants and natives of New Orleans face during efforts to rebuild the city as a result of the policies and practices discussed?
2. How did Katrina change the demography of New Orleans for years to come, not just the size of its overall population, but the relative mix between African Americans and Latinos?
3. How did globalization shape the opportunities of the residents of New Orleans to participate in the rebuilding of their city? What policies would you have put in place to ensure worker protections and rights?
4. Considering that the rebuilding of New Orleans was such a massive undertaking, do you think it was ethical for many of the bids to go to out-of-state contractors? Was it fair for a large portion of the jobs to be given to immigrants?
5. Why is it often difficult for African Americans and Latinos to make common cause?
6. How is the global economic recession impacting immigrants currently in the United States, as well as would-be immigrants who are opting not to leave their home countries? How are the social problems faced by immigrants in the United States impacting their families and communities back home?
7. What other examples can you think of that illustrate the interconnectedness of globalization, immigration, and social problems?

Policy advocates need to work to increase the amount of foreign aid that the United States gives to developing nations, such as for infrastructure, technology, health and education programs, job-training programs, and family planning services. To the extent that this foreign aid reduces poverty and unemployment in the developing nations, it will cut rates of migration of poor persons into the United States. The United States ranks low among developed nations in its foreign aid, giving less than 1 percent of the federal budget even after significant increases during the presidency of George W. Bush. Time will tell whether President Barack Obama will increase foreign aid above this meager level.

Policy advocates also need to work on environmental and public-health fronts. They should pressure the U.S. government to sign treaties like the Kyoto treaty and successor treaties that commit nations to reduce carbon dioxide emissions threatening global warming—and to reduce other international problems such as overfishing of the seas and air pollution. They need, as well, to pressure the government to increase its fiscal commitments to public health so that the nation has an infrastructure that can protect Americans from diseases that spread across national boundaries.

EP 2.1.5b

As you consider this case, ponder the following questions:

1. To what extent does globalization pit low-income groups against one another in the United States—or to what extent do immigrants take jobs that residents would not seek?
2. To what extent can Americans help create economic growth in Mexico and other developing nations through the provision of foreign aid?

What You Can Now Do

Chapter Summary

You are now equipped with knowledge about social problems caused by globalization, as well as the role that policy advocates can assume in addressing them. You can do the following:

- Define globalization.
- Identify specific problems caused by globalization in the United States.
- Identify links between globalization and global warming.
- Understand why a large economic gap arose between developing and developed nations.
- Identify specific international institutions and treaties that have shaped trade and economic relations among nations.
- Identify specific problems caused by globalization in developing nations by international organizations.
- Know where to gain more information about developing nations.
- Identify some policy options that policy advocates can use to address problems caused by globalization at home and abroad.
- Identify key international advocacy groups.

Chapter Six will enable you to place specific issues on the agendas of decision makers in organizational, community, and government settings.

Competency Notes

EPA 2.1.5a **Understand forms and mechanisms of oppression and discrimination** (pp. 143, 150, 151, 168): Social workers analyze why disparities exist in the wealth of different nations and why immigrants often face discrimination.

EPA 2.1.5b **Advocate for human rights and social and economic justice** (pp. 156, 163, 165, 167, 170): Social workers advocate for immigrant rights and support policies to enhance human rights in developing nations.

EPA 2.1.5c **Engage in practices that advance social and economic justice** (pp. 160, 164): Social workers support policies to help immigrants in the United States and victims of natural disasters.

EPA 2.1.6b **Use research evidence to inform practice** (pp. 149, 158, 159): Social workers use health and climate data to guide social programs.

EPA 2.1.9a **Continuously discover, appraise, and attend to changing locales, populations, scientific and technological developments, and emerging societal trends to provide relevant services** (p. 146): Social workers analyze why large disparities exist in the wealth of different nations.

Endnotes

1. Steven Kull, Clay Ramsay, Stefan Subias, and Evan Lewis, *Americans on Globalization, Trade, and Farm Subsidies* (Washington, DC: Program on International Policy Attitudes, January 22, 2004).

2. Jeffrey Sachs, *End of Poverty: Economic Possibilities for Our Time* (New York: Penguin Press, 2005).

3. Shaohua Chen and Martin Ravallion, The Developing World is Poorer than We Thought, But No Less Successful in the Fight Against Poverty, Poverty Research Working Paper, World Bank. Retrieved December 15, 2011, http://econ.worldbank.org/docsearch. The World Bank, *Globalization, Growth, and Poverty: Building an Inclusive World Economy* (Washington, DC: World Bank and Oxford University Press, 2002).

4. Thomas L. Friedman, *The Lexus and the Olive Tree: Understanding Globalization* (New York: Anchor Books, 2000), p. 11.

5. Joseph E. Stiglitz, *Globalization and Its Discontents* (New York, NY: W. W. Norton & Company, 2002).

6. Arline Prigoff, *Economics for Social Workers: Social Outcomes of Economic Globalization with Strategies for Community Action* (Stamford, CT: Brooks/Cole Thomson Learning, 2000): p. 116.

7. Stiglitz, *Globalization and Its Discontents*.

8. Martin Khor, "Global Economy and the Third World," in Jerry Mander and Edward Goldsmith, eds., *The Case Against the Global Economy and for a Turn Toward the Local* (San Francisco, CA: Sierra Club Books, 1996), pp. 47–59.

9. National Immigration Law Center, *Overview of Immigration Eligibility for Federal Programs: Resource Manual: Low-Income Immigrant Rights Conference* (2005).

10. Harvard Working Group on New and Resurgent Diseases, "Globalization, Development, and the Spread of Disease," in *The Case Against the Global Economy and for a Turn Toward the Local*, pp. 160–170.

11. Erica Barks-Ruggles, "The Globalization of Disease: When Congo Sneezes, Will California Get a Cold?" *The Brookings Review* 19(4) (2001): 30–33; and Harvard Working Group on New and Resurgent Diseases, "Globalization, Development, and the Spread of Disease."

12. Public Broadcasting Corporation, *Rx for Survival: A Global Health Challenge*, October 2005, http://www.pbs.org (accessed November, 18, 2005).

13. Erica Barks-Ruggles, "The Globalization of Disease: When Congo Sneezes, Will California Get a Cold?"; and D. Yach and D. Bettcher, "The Globalization of

Public Health. I. Threats and Opportunities." *American Journal of Public Health* 88(5) (2001): 735–738.

14. Marcelo M. Suarez-Orozco, "Globalization, Immigration, and Education: The Research Agenda," *Harvard Educational Review* 71(3) (2001): 345–635.

15. Friedman, *The Lexus and the Olive Tree.*

16. Richard Barnet and John Cavanagh, "Homogenization of Global Culture," in *The Case Against the Global Economy and for a Turn Toward the Local*, pp. 71–77.

17. Peter Marber, "Globalization and Its Contents," *World Policy Journal* 21(4) (2004/2005): 29–37.

18. The World Bank, *Globalization, Growth, and Poverty: Building an Inclusive World Economy.*

19. Ibid.

20. Marber, "Globalization and Its Contents."

21. Stiglitz, *Globalization and Its Discontents.*

22. Jay R. Mandle, *Globalization and the Poor* (Cambridge, United Kingdom: Cambridge University Press, 2003).

23. C. Tomuschat, *Human Rights: Between Idealism and Realism* (New York: Oxford University Press, 2008).

PART 4

Committing to Problems and Solutions by Building Policy Agendas and Engaging in Policy Analysis

Policy advocates are driven by a desire to improve society. As a prelude to their work, they need to identify specific problems or issues in which they believe they can make a difference—and get them placed on the policy agendas of decision makers. They also need to find meritorious solutions by engaging in policy analysis, as well as ones that appear to have a reasonable chance of enactment and implementation. (We will discuss in Part 5 how policy advocates get policies enacted or approved and in Part 6 how they implement and assess them.)

Chapters Six through **Nine** discuss this preparatory work, which often determines whether policy advocates will succeed in changing existing policies and implementing policy innovations.

Chapter Six discusses how advocates place issues, problems, or solutions on policy agendas of decision makers so that they will take them seriously.

Chapter Seven introduces a six-step model of policy analysis that policy advocates can use to develop policy proposals. The chapter focuses upon the first step of this model, in which policy advocates familiarize themselves with a social problem or issue.

Chapter Eight focuses on the second, third, and fourth steps of the six-step model of policy analysis, wherein policy advocates develop specific policy proposals by identifying various policy options and then selecting one.

Chapter Nine focuses on the fifth and sixth steps of the policy analysis model, wherein policy advocates seek to persuade other persons to accept or fund specific proposals, by making presentations to them, engaging in negotiations or debates, or writing grant proposals.

6

Committing to an Issue: Building Agendas

Policy Predicament

According to the nonpartisan Congressional Budget Office (CBO), income of the richest 1 percent of American households rose 275 percent from the 1970s to 2008 compared with an increase of only 18 percent for the lowest 20 percent of the population. Yet little attention was given to economic inequality in the United States during this period. We discuss in Policy Advocacy Challenge 6.7 at the end of this chapter how policy advocates developed and implemented strategy to place inequality on decision makers' agendas in 2011 and 2012 in diverse locations in the United States.

This chapter discusses Task 3 of the model of policy practice and policy advocacy depicted in Figure 3.1. Experienced policy advocates realize that their first challenge is to get a specific policy issue on decision makers' agendas in agency, community, or legislative settings. Before an issue can advance into the later phases of policy practice, where proposals are actually refined, enacted, and implemented, decision makers must decide that a specific issue is important enough to merit serious consideration. It must compete with myriad other issues for the scarce time and resources of staff, executives, boards of directors, governmental officials, legislators, mayors, boards of supervisors, community leaders, and presidents. Policy advocates often have to use a combination of political, interactional, and analytic skills to place their issues on decision makers' agendas.

LEARNING OUTCOMES

Students will be equipped to discuss:

1. The importance of agenda-building processes to policy practice
2. The three stages of agenda building: diagnosing, softening, and activating
3. How social problems and solutions reach agendas of decision makers
4. How political processes shape agendas of decision makers
5. How windows of opportunity and policy entrepreneurs shape agendas
6. How direct-service staff can build agendas
7. The challenges policy advocates face in shaping agendas

How do we as policy advocates know when an issue is on the agenda? In legislative settings, this has happened when legislation has been introduced into the legislative process and referred to a committee, and has attracted the serious attention of some legislators—preferably ones with clout. In agency settings, an issue is on the agenda when it has become part of the agency's deliberations. Perhaps the executive director has formed a task force or committee to study it. Maybe the staff or the agency's board plans to discuss the issue in a meeting. A group in the agency may have decided to rally support for a policy change. In communities, an issue is on the agenda when community leaders and decision makers have decided to take it seriously enough to convene meetings to consider solutions.

Of course, placing issues or proposals on these agendas does not necessarily have a positive outcome; many factors, such as opposition, can defeat them. Indeed, many issues never reach the agenda because opposing groups successfully use tactics to keep them off the agenda.[1] Also, placement on the agenda does not tell advocates precisely what kind of proposal or solution will finally emerge, because proposals are finalized in the give-and-take of deliberations. But placement on the agenda does tell them that a proposal is well positioned to receive serious attention and that it has received an initial impetus, unlike many issues that do not even achieve this status. Were we *not* to discuss agenda building, it might seem that policy reforms can be easily initiated without any preliminary work, such as discussing the proposed reform, analyzing its feasibility, convincing others that it merits attention, considering who might get the ball rolling, and deciding on the right time to introduce the issue to others.

In this chapter, we discuss some policy-practice skills that help get proposals onto agendas.

Taking the First Step

Assume that you work in an agency that provides job referrals and career assistance to women. You are perturbed because the agency provides little service to a specific client group, such as single teenage mothers. While some services are available to them, none of the services, you decide, focuses on their employment needs. While your distant challenge is to develop a proposal to help this population and perhaps secure funding for this help, your immediate challenge is to convince others, preferably decision makers at the agency, that the problem merits their serious attention. At this very moment, you are engaged in building an agenda. In this preliminary phase, you must place the issue on the agenda so that someone—perhaps an executive, a staff committee, or a committee of the agency's board—will examine the issue in more detail or delegate it to others for further exploration.

EP 2.1.10a

Agenda building is a critical phase of the policy development process. Skillful policy practitioners who are building an agenda try to create favorable conditions, interest, and support for a policy reform at the outset.

Why Agenda Building Is Needed

Legislatures

It is easy to see why most proposals fall by the wayside when we consider some simple realities that confront legislators and agency executives. Legislators must limit the number of issues they consider and must prioritize them. Thousands of pieces of legislation are introduced into each session of state legislatures and Congress, conceived by lobbyists, citizens, professional associations, or the legislators themselves (see Policy Advocacy Challenge 6.1).

Policy Advocacy Challenge 6.1

Finding Emerging Legislation in State and Federal Jurisdictions

Stephanie Davis, Research Librarian, University of California, Irvine

FEDERAL GOVERNMENT INFORMATION

In 1995, a team of librarians and technologists from the Library of Congress created THOMAS, under a federal mandate from the 104th Congress to make federal legislative information freely available to the public via the Internet. THOMAS, located at http://thomas.loc.gov, is named for Thomas Jefferson, and provides access to many types of political and government information:

- Legislation: text of bills and information about those bills introduced into the House and Senate, text of laws passed by Congress, record of how members of Congress vote on bills, motions, and more (roll call votes)
- Congressional Record: an index to and full text of the official record of the speeches, remarks, issues, and other happenings in Congress
- House and Senate Committee Information: membership, charges, schedules, text of hearings
- Senator/Representative Directories: links to homepages with contact information, constituency information, profiles, legislative agendas; finding aids for locating a specific member by ZIP code and state
- Other Congressional Internet Services: the Government Printing Office, the General Accounting Office, the Congressional Budget Office, and others
- Links to guides on the legislative process in the House and Senate, database of historical documents, and more

Your library may have access to a subscription database called *Congressional Universe,* which provides much of the same information as THOMAS. Both are excellent resources for finding federal legislative information.

STATE LEGISLATIVE INFORMATION

Finding state information is, in general, not as streamlined as finding federal information. States generally do not have the same mandate to place their legislative information on the Internet. Often the best way to find state information is to look for Web links on your state's homepage to government, legislature, agencies, elected officials, and state libraries or archives. You might also wish to explore websites of the National Council of State Legislatures, at www.ncsl.org/, and the National Governors Association, at www.nga.org/. These are excellent starting points.

EXERCISE

First, spend some time getting acquainted with THOMAS. Select a topic of interest to you, and search for bills or laws on that topic (i.e., health care, welfare, children).

Next, using the search engines we discussed in Chapter One, find your state's homepage, and then find your state legislature's website. If the website allows for searching introduced and passed legislation, repeat the search you did in THOMAS.

- Compare the results of your searches—how are the bills or laws similar? Do they address the same or similar problems? How is the state's approach different from the federal, and vice versa?
- Who introduced or sponsored each piece of legislation? Find their homepage and compare their legislative agendas.
- From your perspective, is the solution to the problem addressed in the legislation a good solution or a poor solution? Critique each piece of legislation as if you were a member of the state legislature faced with voting on that piece of legislation.

Were legislators to debate a large fraction of these proposals, they would work themselves to exhaustion and not give careful attention to any of them. When many people with different perspectives and constituencies are involved, it takes time and effort to consider even simple pieces of legislation. In each chamber of Congress, for example, subcommittees consider the policies and forward them for further debate and votes to the full legislative committee, which forwards them to the full chamber for floor debates and votes. If each chamber enacts a different version, they may have to be sent to a conference committee composed of members of both chambers, and then to the president. Moreover, during this process, many legislators must spend endless hours with lobbyists and other citizens. It is no wonder, then, that leaders of legislatures decide not to put most measures on the legislative agenda, thus reserving their scarce time for those pieces of legislation they want to concentrate on.

Legislators often avoid issues that appear to give them little or no political advantage in reelection, for example, not selecting issues that will not help them obtain or retain constituents' support. A particular issue may seem too controversial or may antagonize an important faction or interest group, even if it pleases other people. Yet legislators sometimes do select issues that they realize will be difficult to enact or controversial. So it is important not to assume that such issues cannot attract attention from those legislators who may be willing to invest political capital on them, such as when various presidents from both parties sought to enact national health insurance when they knew it would be controversial.

Unlike agency executives who often want to avoid contentious issues that could disrupt their agency, politicians are often attracted to issues associated with conflict if such issues can gain them support among their constituents. For example, liberal politicians may deliberately support an issue to anger conservatives and thus prove their ideological leanings to their liberal supporters. Legislators may opportunistically select issues that will give them media exposure and a resultant advantage over their opponents in an upcoming election battle. On other occasions, however, specific legislators decide not to invest their limited time and resources in issues that stand little or no chance of success.

Agencies

Agency executives must manage organizations, raise funds, hire staff, adjudicate conflicts, and plan—tasks that occupy most of their working hours. Executives also confront myriad policy issues, such as deciding what kinds of clients to serve and which social problems fall within the purview of the agency, naming overarching objectives or goals, developing policies and procedures within specific grant proposals, deciding whether to be advocates for their clients in the broader community or in a legislature, determining what kind of staff to hire, and developing policies and procedures to guide their staff. Some of these policies concern internal, procedural matters, while others concern the goals or mission of the organization in its political and funding contexts.

In light of these many tasks, executives must ignore or defer many issues, even ones that seem important to a staff member, a board member, or a client. Were executives to try to examine each issue in considerable detail, they would become exhausted and frustrated.

Executives also ignore or defer certain issues because they would embroil the agency in conflict. Even seemingly mundane issues such as changing an agency's intake procedures may impassion people who want the issue left alone. Often, they act only when they are convinced that an issue merits attention in spite of possible political conflict and the time and effort it may take. Perhaps they like an existing policy because it furthers their own interests, as when it facilitates a steady flow of certain kinds of clients to their units. Often more than staff, executives take a strategic view of their agencies, wanting policies that will give them a competitive advantage over other agencies. Policy advocates who can argue that a specific policy innovation will help an agency increase its resources and clientele may attract more support to it than if the policy is perceived as diminishing or having no effect on an agency's ability to survive.[2]

Executives may like an existing policy or one that is proposed by a policy advocate for ideological reasons. They may be committed, for instance, to serving a specific vulnerable population and be unwilling to diminish services for it. Or they may be committed to a specific approach to serving a specific population, believing it most effectively and efficiently meets their needs.

Policy advocates must develop a strategy to convince agency executives that their issues merit attention. When policy advocates succeed in placing an issue on the agendas of executives and agency boards, they do not necessarily succeed in getting them to enact new policies or to accept policy innovations, but at least the proposals have a better chance of success than if these executives and boards develop little or no interest in the issue.

Communities

Agenda building also occurs in community settings as various issues vie for attention. Community activists may introduce ideas to community groups, the media, city or town councils, school boards, and other community influentials. These ideas could include blocking a freeway that will split the community, expanding a school, securing approval for a community park, or opening a counseling program for substance abusers. Activists may draw attention to a policy proposal by getting a story in the mass media, holding a community forum, or staging a protest. Or they may inject the issue into a campaign for city council or school board elections, with the ultimate objective of persuading community decision makers to prioritize it in their deliberations.

Three Challenges in Agenda Building

Agenda building can be conceptualized as a funnel (see Figure 6.1). We will discuss this agenda-building framework from the top down. Policy practitioners face three challenges when considering specific reforms: they (or their allies) must *diagnose* the context as they *listen* to others, *soften or moderate* the context, and *activate* change.

The top funnel illustrates the process that policy practitioners use to winnow a few issues from the multitude of issues that could be presented for active consideration. At the top of the funnel are the context and the practitioner's diagnosing role. Just beneath these are the modified context and the policy practitioner's softening or moderating role. The numbers 1 through 10 just above the funnel represent the many potential issues that exist in any setting. Policy entrepreneurs, discussed in more detail later, engage in the activating role when they pull a specific issue (in this case, number 8) into the funnel, where it is placed on the decision agenda when someone or some group prioritizes it for systematic deliberation. (See the decision agenda at the bottom of the top funnel in Figure 6.1.)

After an issue is placed on the decision agenda, such as on to the agenda of a meeting or committee, it enters policy deliberations wherein it is waylaid, defeated, or enacted. (See the bottom funnel in Figure 6.1.) This is a second winnowing process; relatively few policies are actually enacted after they enter policy deliberations.

From Figure 6.1, we can tell the stage at which an issue is by asking several questions: Has the issue been floated with little or no discussion? If so, it is in the original context or the modified context. Has the issue been forwarded to a committee, a task force, or

FIGURE 6.1 The Agenda Funnel

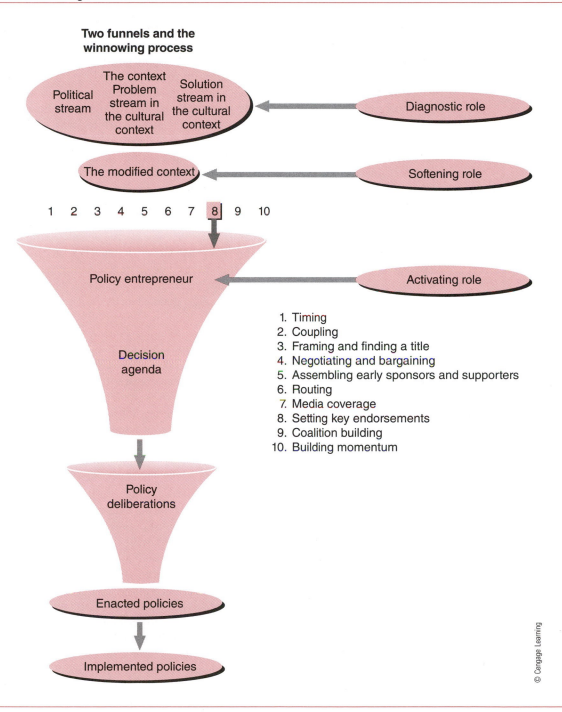

Two funnels and the winnowing process

Political stream

The context Problem stream in the cultural context

Solution stream in the cultural context

Diagnostic role

The modified context

Softening role

1   2   3   4   5   6   7   8   9   10

Policy entrepreneur

Activating role

Decision agenda

1. Timing
2. Coupling
3. Framing and finding a title
4. Negotiating and bargaining
5. Assembling early sponsors and supporters
6. Routing
7. Media coverage
8. Setting key endorsements
9. Coalition building
10. Building momentum

Policy deliberations

Enacted policies

Implemented policies

© Cengage Learning

some other deliberative entity for further discussion? If so, it is on the decision agenda. Have systematic deliberations begun? If so, it is in policy deliberations. Has the issue been enacted by decision makers? If so, it is positioned for implementation at the bottom of the second funnel.

Policy advocates need to diagnose the context to identify contextual constraints and opportunities as they listen to others. If they decide that specific policies will be extremely difficult to change, they must do considerable work to change the context or to focus on alternative policy changes. When they decide that the contextual opportunities far outnumber constraints, they can initiate a policy-changing strategy at once. In some cases, the prognosis will be guarded or unclear.

Having diagnosed the context, policy advocates must soften or moderate it; that is, they must make it more amenable to a specific policy initiative. Even when the context appears bleak, they may discover that engaging strategically placed persons will make the prognosis more optimistic or will indicate that their pessimistic forecast was unwarranted. Or they may work with a coalition or advocacy group to pressure decision makers to take interest in a specific issue, such as by sending a delegation to them or by getting the issue placed on the meeting of a city council or school board.

At some point, of course, policy advocates need to activate change. They need to get a community decision maker or legislator to put an issue on the agenda of the other decision makers in the agency, community, or legislative setting. The chairperson might place the issue on the agenda of an agency committee or staff meeting. Perhaps a legislator drafts a piece of legislation and initiates a search for cosponsors. Or maybe a state's director of health and human services presents a detailed analysis of a particular problem in the administration of his or her program.

Agenda building is, then, often a precursor to other policy-practice tasks, although in some cases policy advocates may proceed with other tasks, such as developing a policy proposal, even before decision makers have shown an interest in a specific issue. Even in this case, however, policy advocates must return to agenda building to get the issue on decision makers' agendas lest they find their issue stymied for lack of interest by them. And if policy advocates have successfully softened or moderated the context, they may make ultimate success in placing an issue on decision makers' agendas more likely.

In our discussion of agenda building, I rely heavily on the pathbreaking work of political scientist John Kingdon. Before Kingdon wrote his classic work, *Agendas, Alternatives, and Public Policies,* many people had ignored the agenda-building task altogether, conveying the misleading impression that policy reforms magically appear with no prior work by policy practitioners.[3] Or they used simplistic explanations. Some *rationalists* assumed, for example, that decision makers placed issues on agendas whenever they received technical reports or data that recommended a specific change. While this assumption is sometimes true, issues are often placed on agendas without empirical studies—and technical reports often gather dust in agency, community, and legislative settings. Indeed, legislators and even agency executives sometimes retain policies that they know to be ineffective if they are supported by powerful lobbyists or bring revenues to an agency. Some *incrementalists* assumed that administrators and legislators often introduced modest changes in existing policies in response to complaints or pressures, as when federal legislators expanded the Head Start program to include children with physical and mental disabilities in response to lobbying by groups representing these children. While incremental change often takes place, Kingdon rightly argues that decision makers, in both agency and legislative settings, often support major changes in existing policy.[4] Legislators sometimes seek a major overhaul of a program or the enactment of a major social reform. Agencies sometimes launch new programs that diverge markedly from their existing programs.

Another theorist developed the *garbage can theory* of agenda building. Emphasizing organizations, he noted that many ideas bubble up regarding problems (e.g., social problems, service delivery problems, and administrative problems) and solutions (e.g., service delivery, program, or administrative innovations).[5] These problems or solutions may surface at staff or committee meetings, or at a retreat of the executives and the board. Even when agency members and executives consider an issue fleetingly, these problems and solutions often retain a place in their memories, remaining in a state of limbo—a figurative garbage can—until they are placed on the agendas of decision makers at a later point in time as they recall them. Similarly, we can say that myriad problems and solutions exist in the "garbage cans" of legislatures. These problems and solutions derive from such sources as lobbyists, reform-minded legislators, think tanks, professional associations, and citizens. The garbage can theory suggests a more fluid and dynamic process than the rationalist or incrementalist theories, but it does not discuss in sufficient detail how certain issues are activated or placed on policy agendas.

EP 2.1.3b

While we draw on Kingdon's theory, we also modify it. We include more factors in the context than he does, and we add the diagnosing (or listening), softening (or moderating), and activating stages because they clarify the roles of policy advocates in bringing issues to the agenda.

As can be seen in Figure 6.1, agenda building is a precursor to actual deliberations. Agenda building merely gets specific issues or policies on the table, to be followed by actual deliberations, where they are processed by committees and legislatures. In this deliberative process, some of the issues and policies are also sifted out. Some are defeated. Some are cast aside. Some are tabled. What we have, then, are two funnels that each winnow issues and policies. What is actually enacted or approved—a small fraction of the issues and policies that began this trip at the top of the first funnel—comes out by the bottom of the second funnel.

EP 2.1.3a

Even though many issues, problems, or solutions do not emerge from the bottoms of the funnels—or only make it through one of them—it is important to realize that an equal number of them do emerge from both funnels, as is illustrated by the many policies that are enacted or approved by legislatures, communities, and agencies.

The Diagnosing or Listening Stage

When diagnosing the context, policy advocates must analyze streams of problems and solutions, recent professional decisions and trends, and political realities.

Streams of Problems and Solutions   When policy advocates begin their work, they must carefully consider the kinds of problems and solutions that have already been considered in a setting. Indeed, we can use Kingdon's language, as he refers to problem and solution "streams" in specific settings.[6]

In many agencies, one needs to merely examine developments in the agency during, say, the last five years to see whether a problem stream exists. Take the earlier example of a small agency that provides job placement and career counseling services to women. The social worker who directs these services also founded the agency. In the beginning, the agency had a relatively narrow set of services, consisting mostly of posting job openings from area firms on a bulletin board and holding career-planning seminars for women. In the 10 years since its founding, the staff, the executive director, and the members of the board have identified problems that the agency could address. They initially discussed some of these ideas in meetings or in personal conversations, but over time, many of the ideas have led to new programs, funded grant proposals, and cooperative projects with other agencies. The agency has added special job placement and career planning services for Latinos, single teenage mothers, and displaced homemakers; a job placement program for unemployed women funded by the federal Job Training Partnership Act; and job fairs for high school women in a local school district. Each of these programs stemmed from a problem that someone placed in the agency's general problem stream in conversations or meetings. Of course, many other problems have been discussed that never reached solution. For example, the agency staff decided not to pursue a suggestion to provide a support group for unemployed women with a mental health orientation, because they believed it fell outside their mission, which emphasizes concrete services like job referral, job search, and career development services.

A stream of problems exists in legislative settings, too. Policy practitioners interested in reforming the child welfare system of a specific county, for example, would be likely to interview advocates and highly placed officials to find out what kinds of problems concerning the child welfare system have already been discussed. (See Policy Advocacy Challenge 6.2 for ways to search for legislative proposals that are in the hopper.)

Similarly, a stream of solutions exists in agency, community, and legislative settings. In our women's job placement agency, the staff, the board, and the executive director have considered decentralizing services, adopting a sliding-fee schedule, merging with a local YWCA, developing joint programs with a community college, and developing a computer lab to help job seekers. In a specific county, the board of supervisors and child welfare officials may consider new management systems, new record-keeping systems, partnerships with local schools, use of evidence-based practice, and different ways of recruiting foster parents.

We can classify solutions into three broad groups. Some propose specific programs, such as interventions to help children, single mothers, or older people. Others aim to correct institutional problems, such as financing a program, changing an agency's fee structure, or enhancing the collaboration of different agencies in serving a specific client group. Still others propose methods of making decisions, such as setting up a task force, establishing a committee, or organizing an interagency planning committee.

**Policy
Advocacy
Challenge 6.2**

Using the
Mass Media
to Discover
Issues That
Might Be
Placed on
Policy
Agendas

Bruce Jansson,
Ph.D.

Over a period of several weeks, collect stories in a local newspaper that suggest items, problems, or solutions that might be candidates for policy agendas in your jurisdiction. Group them under issues, problems, and solutions. Also analyze which public officials, parties, high-level officials, or advocacy groups might be candidates to champion them, and at what level of government or in the private sector. Are persons and parties with different ideologies likely to approach the issues differently?

Policy advocates rarely begin policy practice with a blank slate. By examining streams of problems and solutions in specific settings, policy advocates discover where their issue fits into this larger picture. They might discover, for example, that others have already introduced the issue, but that it failed to progress because of budgetary implications. Or they might discover that their issue has never been discussed, but that related issues were the subject of initial discussion several years ago. By piecing together the history of streams of problems and solutions, policy advocates get a better sense of their issue's prognosis.

Recent Professional Developments and Trends   Fads and trends can powerfully shape the prognosis of a policy reform. For example, partnerships and collaborations between agencies became popular in the mid-1990s, partly because many professionals, public officials, and funders came to believe that their clients required more intensive and sophisticated services than specific agencies could give. A policy reform encouraging collaboration would have fared better in this environment than if it had been introduced a decade earlier, when less attention was given to collaboration. More recently, evidence-based practice has been widely emphasized in professional literature—making it more feasible for policy advocates to put forward policies that are grounded in research, such as proposals for different or new interventions in a specific agency. Fads and trends can be discerned by examining professional journals, conversing with professionals, and analyzing the kinds of innovations that funders (such as foundations and government agencies) prioritize.

Problem and solution streams exist in a cultural context, whether in nations or in specific settings. "Problems" in one setting are not perceived to be problems in other settings. Americans are less likely to view great discrepancies in wealth as a problem as compared with many Europeans. High levels of conflict between staff may be viewed as problematic in one agency but not in another. Similarly, some solutions, such as national health insurance, are widely accepted in European nations but not in the United States. It is important, then, to be familiar with the culture of specific settings to better understand the kinds of innovations that are relatively feasible in them, while also realizing that decision makers sometimes make policy choices that are discrepant with these traditions.

Political Realities   Background political developments powerfully influence whether specific issues will be placed on policy agendas, as our discussion of the big picture in Chapter Four suggests. Let's start with legislative settings. When working on a policy issue or reform, policy advocates need to consider the viewpoint of important officials by finding out what position they have taken on similar issues or reforms in the past. This consideration should include the following:

- The viewpoints of heads of government or chief executives
- The viewpoints of legislators, particularly those who have official positions (like majority speaker or committee chairperson) or who have influential roles in specific caucuses such as a women's caucus
- The viewpoints of the legislators from one's own district because they often support proposals made by their constituents
- The viewpoints of legislators who have assumed leadership on similar issues in the past, such as legislators who have taken a personal interest in child welfare issues
- The viewpoints of key members of government bureaucracy, whether political appointees or civil servants, particularly those who oversee programs and policies relevant to the present issue

- The viewpoints of lobbyists or the heads of interest groups that are active on the issue or policy
- The viewpoints of the public as reflected in polls or in recently contested elections
- The extent to which a policy reform is likely to receive sympathetic coverage in the mass media as reflected by media coverage of similar issues in the past

Read Policy Advocacy Challenge 6.3 for an example of how policy advocates capitalized on the sympathetic viewpoints held by the Democratic majority in the House and Senate in 2008–2010 to pass legislation to address homelessness.

Policy advocates also need to consider court rulings that are germane to their issue. With respect to homelessness, for example, court rulings have required some local jurisdictions to provide shelters for homeless people.

In agency settings, policy advocates must consider a range of factors that shape the prognosis of a specific reform or issue, including the following:

- The extent to which a policy reform is consonant with the agency's mission
- The state of the agency's budget, whether it is running a deep deficit or is balanced
- The amount of interest that specific agency funders are likely to have in a specific issue or problem
- The viewpoints of the key agency officials, such as the director, top administrators, or members of the board of directors, and the directors of important agency programs, as surmised from their position in previous years on similar issues

Policy Advocacy Challenge 6.3

Combating Homelessness Through Policy Advocacy at the Federal Level

Gretchen Heidemann, MSW

Policy advocates at the National Coalition for the Homeless (NCH) saw a silver lining in the economic recession that began in 2007, which wreaked havoc in the lives of thousands of Americans who lost their jobs and their homes. Advocates saw a unique opportunity to bring the issue of homelessness to the forefront, pushing it onto the policy agenda of Congress and the Obama administration, and accomplishing significant gains.

With a Democratic-controlled Senate and House of Representatives, these advocates were met with sympathetic ears when they came to the table to share the results of a study they had conducted: "Foreclosures to Homelessness: The Forgotten Victims of the Subprime Crisis." Their efforts in Congress resulted in the passage of S. 896—Protections for Tenants in Foreclosed Properties—that was signed by President Obama on May 20, 2009. This bill includes a nationwide 90-day pre-eviction notice requirement for tenants in foreclosed properties. This provision will prevent countless renters from being forced into homelessness.

In addition, the NCH, along with other national homeless advocacy organizations, provided comments to the Obama administration that led to $1.5 billion of federal stimulus going to the Homeless Prevention and Rapid Re-Housing Program (HPRP). The $1.5 billion in HPRP funding was distributed throughout the nation to homeless prevention and assistance programs, making it the largest investment in homeless prevention and eradication in history.

Finally, NCH and the National Low Income Housing Coalition are working to capitalize the National Housing Trust Fund, which was established as a provision of the Housing and Economic Recovery Act of 2008. The housing trust fund is a permanent program not subject to the annual appropriations process. Once capitalized, it will provide communities with funds to build, preserve, and rehabilitate rental homes that are affordable for very low income households.

- The viewpoints of the agency officials or staff who are likely to be most impact
  reform or issue
- The viewpoints of union leaders (if staff are unionized)
- The likely effects of a specific reform on an agency's clientele
- The likely position of the agency's accrediting bodies

In community settings, policy advocates must consider the following:

- The viewpoints of key community leaders
- Local public opinion
- The perspectives of the local media

When considering the prognosis of policy changes in any setting, several factors often suggest when specific policy innovations will be relatively difficult to achieve:

- The sheer magnitude of a policy change: Large changes are often more difficult to obtain than more modest changes.
- Whether an issue is already politicized: If the issue has already excited considerable political conflict, it is likely to be associated with political conflict when it is reintroduced.
- Whether persons with considerable power believe that specific policy changes will harm their economic, professional, or political self-interest: If they have this negative orientation, policy reform will be more difficult.
- Whether a specific reform will be expensive or difficult to implement: Policies that present logistical or funding problems are often opposed by agency executives.

When engaging in diagnostic work, policy advocates should not prematurely abandon an issue when they believe it has a negative prognosis. Reforms that will help powerless or oppressed populations, for example, often encounter opposition. Had Martin Luther King, Jr., abandoned the civil rights movement in the 1950s because of its poor prognosis, the subsequent enactment of civil rights legislation in the United States would have been significantly delayed.

The Softening or Moderating Stage

Policy advocates can sometimes attempt to improve the prognosis of a policy reform even before it enters policy deliberations by working in problem and solution streams and by building political support.

Working in Problem and Solution Streams As Kingdon suggests, those who want decision makers to take their problem seriously have to convince them that it is a problem and not merely a condition.[7] Unlike a condition, a problem poses a threat or danger to someone, whether a group in the population, an agency, or politicians. When a condition is perceived as a problem, legislators, agency officials, and others are more likely to view it as important—and believe that someone (or they themselves) will suffer dire consequences if it is not addressed. If agency executives believe that their agency will suffer important consequences if they do not support a reform, such as loss of resources or clientele, they will be more likely to support it. If proponents of measures to end homelessness can persuade public officials in a specific jurisdiction that they will save resources by helping homeless persons find affordable housing and jobs—such as by cutting welfare costs and the use of emergency rooms—they increase the odds that they will support reforms.

But how do we as policy advocates convince other people that certain conditions *are* problems? We can use data to argue that a condition is serious by virtue of absolute

EP 2.1.10d

numbers involved, that some subset of the population is afflicted far more than other portions of the population, or that the problem is steadily worsening.[8] Absolute numbers, such as the percentage of women with inadequate or no child care, can shock decision makers into believing that a condition is a problem. Someone with data indicating that Latinos lack adequate child care in far greater numbers than white women may be able to use these data to persuade legislators to fund day care for Spanish-speaking children. Data showing that a problem is worsening may convince legislators that it will reach crisis proportions without governmental intervention.

Policy advocates can use data to demonstrate that a specific social problem has important implications that extend beyond a specific issue or population. If persons who want greater federal support for measures to protect wetlands and offshore islands in the Gulf region can convince public officials that specific environmental measures will save the nation billions of dollars by preserving Gulf Coast fisheries and other businesses, they will be more likely to succeed in obtaining support.

Advocates for corrective action often use words such as *crisis* to describe a condition. Because this word is overused, the advocate needs some evidence or rationale for its use. Take, for example, the dramatic spread of tuberculosis in the United States in the 1990s, which particularly affected AIDS patients and immigrants. When drug-resistant strains of the disease spread because many persons failed to take the prescribed medications long enough, advocates of greater funding for tuberculosis programs were able to convince federal, state, and local officials to prioritize funding for public health programs.

Policy advocates also need to demonstrate that a problem is not hopeless and can be ameliorated. For example, advocates have often found it difficult to secure support for inner cities, the underclass, and people who are homeless, because many legislators see these problems as unsolvable, in contrast to simpler ones. Advocates can buttress their cases by citing research or finding successful pilot projects that demonstrate that specific reforms could well yield positive outcomes.

EP 2.1.5b

In addition, policy advocates can appeal to values such as the ethical principles of beneficence, social justice, and fairness by arguing that society (or a legislature) has a duty to address an issue. They can use value-based arguments, and they can illustrate them with specific case studies of persons who suffer from problems. In the case of Hurricane Katrina, for example, the testimony of persons who suffered grievous harm made a compelling case for policy reforms that would provide them with resources, services, and opportunities.

Because politicians often consider the effect of corrective action on their careers, advocates often try to state problems in relatively broad terms. They may stress the absence of child care for working women, the increased incidence of Alzheimer's disease among all social classes and races, or inadequate sex education in American schools. By presenting problems in general terms, advocates increase the likelihood that more politicians will see the problem as important to significant segments of their constituencies.[9]

Terminology is important when describing problems. For example, some policy advocates may refer to a social program as "investing" in human needs rather than merely "spending" resources. Legislators and citizens are more likely to respond to the word *investing* because it suggests that society will receive a return on its expenditure of funds. Nomenclature can also take advantage of socially acceptable symbols.[10] The Obama Administration named its major health reforms The Patient Protection and Affordable Care Act of 2010 to underscore how health consumers would be protected from health insurance companies and from lack of health insurance.[11]

Policy advocates often have to ponder how to "frame" issues so that other persons are more likely to take them seriously. They have to decide what symbols, words, values, and proposed outcomes will compel other persons to take note of them. Listen to the video in this Policy Advocacy Challenge, in which Bob Erlenbusch, chair of the Board of the National Coalition Against Homelessness and the executive director of the Los Angeles Coalition to End Homelessness and Hunger, discusses how he is trying to make homelessness an issue that persons who own their own homes can understand.

When faced with harsh fiscal realities, policy advocates try to show that a specific policy, such as increasing Head Start funding, will avert subsequent costly problems, such as welfare and crime. They may propose a pilot program and hope to expand it later.

Advocates encounter a double-edged sword when they use the word *prevention* to seek support for a problem. Prevention is, on the one hand, a culturally acceptable symbol because everyone prefers preventing a problem to fixing it afterward. On the other hand, decision makers often perceive preventive programs negatively. They may wonder if a specific problem, such as teenage pregnancy or drug use, can be prevented. They may want to prioritize services for persons who are already afflicted with a specific problem rather than to fund prevention programs. Those advocating preventive programs, then, need to find evidence that they can successfully avert problems when proposing a specific innovation.[12] For example, a significant body of research has emerged in the last two decades that demonstrates that preschool programs prevent cognitive and other problems and decrease drop-out rates in high schools.

Our discussion suggests that policy practitioners need to anticipate likely objections or opposition to a specific policy so they can diminish or rebut them. They should develop arguments to counter claims that a particular problem is not solvable or cannot be prevented, that a remedy is too expensive or too difficult to implement, that a particular issue does not fall within an agency's mission, that a specific problem is unimportant, or that voters will punish legislators who support a specific reform. When they successfully counter these objections, they soften the context, making it easier not only to get an issue placed on the agenda but also to get a reform enacted.

The media can serve as an important educational tool in policy practice. Stories in the press, on the radio, and on television about social problems can create powerful images in the minds of citizens and elected officials, who may decide to give them serious attention. A social worker in an agency found, for example, that a reporter from a local paper became a frequent ally.[13] When the social worker wanted the city administration to replace junkyards with low- and moderate-income housing in a specific neighborhood, several stories in the newspaper about the blighted area prompted local politicians to take the neighborhood's problems seriously, and to help find federal and state programs to build affordable housing and recreation areas in it.

Social workers can help shape agendas by using the mass media (see Policy Advocacy Challenge 6.5). This is not easy to do because the media ration their scarce time among many claimants. With their proximity to many social issues and problems, however, social workers should increasingly seek air time and print space in local and national media.

As with social problems, only certain solutions make it to agency or legislative agendas. Those who examine solutions often test their fiscal, administrative, and political feasibility.[14] Assume that a staff person in a job-counseling agency for women is not only referring women to jobs but also actually training them. Some staff may be skeptical about this idea's feasibility. They may ask whether the agency, which has emphasized job referrals and job search, can develop training programs in fields such as computer literacy. Can it find facilities to house these services, the needed staff, foundations, or government funders to fund them? Can it place the graduates in actual jobs? Because this program represents a marked departure from current programs, it is likely to encounter political opposition from some staff, as well as some board members, who will question whether the proposal falls within the agency's mission. Some staff may fear as well that the proposed service will detract from existing services. Decision makers also judge a solution's likely effectiveness and technical merits. Will a proposed program actually help clients, and will it be sufficiently inexpensive to prove feasible in light of the agency's budget? Policy advocates can counter such skepticism, of course, by citing evaluative research or by showing how a solution has been successfully used in model programs elsewhere. They can find possible funding sources for the proposed policy innovation.

Our discussion suggests that policy advocates must try to place a solution in a favorable light if they want it to get onto decision makers' agendas. They must accomplish this task, moreover, in settings where specific solutions vie with one another for the scarce space on agendas. They should also recognize that they may encounter opposition from persons or groups that do not like their solution and want to cast it in an unfavorable light.

Policy Advocacy Challenge 6.5

Using the Mass Media to Place Issues on Agendas

Bob Erlenbusch, Ph.D.

Go to **www.cengage.com** to watch this video clip.

Policy advocates increase their chances of getting media coverage if they develop a compelling story that has human interest. They need to be able to express the basic theme of this story in a few sentences because they will not often have the luxury of an extended story in the media. They can seek coverage from a single reporter with whom they have contact or who they call, telling him or her about their story. Additionally, they can make a press release to many print and visual media outlets, where they may convey in a succinct but compelling way what they will discuss during the press release, and who will make the presentation. They need to remember, however, that intensive competition exists for media space in light of the many possible stories that the media can cover. Their chances for coverage increase if the presenter or interviewee is a well-known community leader. For more discussion of strategies relating to the use of media, see the video in this policy advocacy challenge, in which Bob Erlenbusch, member of the Board of the NCH, discusses strategies for getting media coverage.

EP 2.1.10b

Building Political Support   Policy advocates can also soften the context by diminishing opposition to a specific reform. They can engage persons in strategic positions to educate them about the need for a specific reform. They can directly address the concerns or objections these persons have, and they can correct erroneous information.

As Tip O'Neill, the late Democratic Speaker of the House, suggested, it is often effective to co-opt others by asking for their suggestions.[15] Policy practitioners can ask people to offer suggestions about getting a policy reform on the agenda. As these people offer guidance about how to proceed, they sometimes unwittingly become part of the change effort.

When softening the political context, it is important not to prematurely dismiss some people on the basis of their ideology or previous positions. To the extent they can, policy advocates often want to construct a "big tent" that contains an array of persons, even those with divergent perspectives, to build a coalition that can support a policy reform. To achieve this objective, they must be open to input from a variety of people, have good listening skills to understand various perspectives, and be willing to compromise.[16]

Of course, this approach is not always feasible in highly polarized situations, wherein policy advocates sometimes have to rely on the support of a specific faction. Indeed, in some situations, policy advocates have to create a ruckus to get decision makers to pay attention to an issue, such as organizing demonstrations, picketing, or sit-ins. Disruptive activities sometimes backfire by hardening decision makers against a proposal or issue, but they can also mobilize popular opinion if used skillfully.

When an agency staff member wants to make the political context more favorable to a problem or solution, he or she can point to funding trends, court rulings, or professional developments that support a specific change in agency policy.

The Activating Stage

Now we turn our attention to the activating stage, which appears inside the top funnel in Figure 6.1. A policy entrepreneur is a decision maker, a legislator, a chairperson, an executive, or another person who has the power to pull an issue onto an agenda so that it will receive serious consideration.[17]

To pull an issue into the decision funnel, policy entrepreneurs use tactics that often include timing, coupling, negotiating, assembling early sponsors and supporters, and routing.

EP 2.1.9a

Timing and Windows of Opportunity   Calling key periods "windows of opportunity," Kingdon suggests that they represent relatively brief moments when "the time is ripe" for specific initiatives. In legislative settings, key events often sensitize legislators to a specific issue. Dramatic and publicized stories, such as a homeless person's death from exposure or a flagrant example of child abuse, may make them suddenly alive to specific needs. A task force may issue a report that alerts people to a specific problem, such as the one issued in 2006 that described the extent construction workers in New Orleans were victimized by their employers through low wages, unpaid wages, unreimbursed overtime, and unsafe working conditions. When the media cover such events extensively, public opinion may encourage legislators or heads of government departments to consider a legislative proposal.

Pivotal events in the political stream stir up support for a specific problem or solution. With Barack Obama's victory in November 2008, after eight years of Republican rule, many people hoped that issues that had lain dormant would now reach congressional agendas, such as national health care reforms, immigration reforms, job-training initiatives, changes in military policies concerning gay men and lesbians, and pro-choice issues. With renewed hope that their issues would now reach decision or choice agendas, people invested time and resources in publicizing and championing them. As this example suggests, though, the placement of issues on decision agendas does not mean they will be successfully resolved. Political opposition and budget deficits stopped many of Obama's reforms. This example also illustrates how windows of opportunity often close rapidly. When the Republicans captured control of the House of Representatives in 2010, the federal government experienced gridlock between the two parties in 2011 and 2012.

The election of Barack Obama to the presidency in 2008 opened the door to such issues as national health insurance—which had not been seriously considered since its defeat in 1994 in the Clinton administration. The deep economic recession of 2007 to 2009 and beyond made Americans more sympathetic to medically uninsured persons—because so many of them had lost it when they became unemployed or when their employers rescinded or cut their health benefits.

However, regular, predictable windows of opportunity exist in legislative settings during annual budget preparations, when advocates can seek a discussion of expanded resources for specific programs.[18] When legislation is being reauthorized—that is, renewed—advocates sometimes obtain reforms in the legislation. When tax revenues increase more rapidly than had been expected, more resources exist for spending on social programs at home and abroad.

Pivotal events in social agencies also create opportunities for changing policy. A governor, a mayor, or a large foundation might announce a new program for dealing with a problem related to an agency's mission, thereby creating a positive milieu for policy changes. Dramatic events may sensitize an agency's executive director or board members to a problem that the agency does not currently address; Hurricane Katrina forced the federal government to pay more attention to the levees in New Orleans after neglecting them for decades. An affluent person may unexpectedly bequeath funds to an agency, enabling it to start a new program. In contrast, fiscal crises sometimes force an agency to reconsider its priorities or to search frantically for resources from new funding sources. Perhaps an accrediting agency is about to make a visit, causing the agency to make some changes that will guarantee a favorable report.

New tides in an agency's politics also create opportunity, such as the arrival of a new executive director or other high-level staff.[19] While executives are not omnipotent, their critical position enables them to chart new directions for agencies. Changes in the leadership of an agency's board of directors may also create a positive milieu for policy changes. When agencies engage in systematic planning about their mission and programs—often called *strategic planning*—their staff and boards are often open to program and policy reforms. Indeed, strategic planning is a formal planning approach to finding issues, problems, and solutions that should be placed on agendas (see Policy Advocacy Challenge 6.3).

Similarly, a change of presidents and governors or a shifting of majorities from one party to another in one or both legislative branches of the federal government or state government can signal a window of opportunity for a policy. Not only did Democrats win the presidency in 2008, for example, but they also obtained large majorities in both the House and the Senate, sufficient to enable them to enact many pieces of legislation that would have been unthinkable before the 2008 elections.

Good timing enables policy entrepreneurs to capitalize on windows of opportunity. Their strategy involves (a) preparing for a possible opportunity by analyzing an issue or problem, (b) recognizing when a window of opportunity augurs well for the specific solution, and (c) seizing the moment by placing it on the decision agenda.[20]

EP 2.1.9a

In government settings, the policy entrepreneur is often an enterprising legislator with persistence, creativity, respectability, and good timing skill, or a creative lobbyist or an advocate who convinces a legislator that the time is ripe to draft and introduce legislation on a specific issue before the window of opportunity closes. In agency settings, policy entrepreneurs can come from anywhere within the organization, recognizing a window of opportunity for a specific issue and persuading others to place it on the decision agenda.

Alas, windows of opportunity often close in a relatively short time. Perhaps crises emerge that divert attention of public officials to other issues. Perhaps leaders change, people think that a problem has been adequately addressed by some other measure, and new issues supplant older ones. Perhaps the momentum of a specific policy proposal is lost as persons haggle over the details of a suggested reform, as opposition emerges, as budget exigencies intervene, or as other issues surface. In the case of New Orleans, policy advocates had to try to keep many of the problems that they confronted before federal and state legislators, who often wanted to move onto other issues when newspaper headlines about Katrina's destruction had vanished. Indeed, the editors of the *Times-Picayune,* the New Orleans newspaper, chose to put their newspaper online (www.nola.com) so that public officials and the news media in other parts of the nation would possess nonstop coverage about the many needs of citizens of New Orleans even many months after Hurricane Katrina.

Coupling   Policy practitioners sometimes try to make imaginative connections among the solution, problem, and political streams depicted in Figure 6.1. Perhaps someone in an agency has discussed decentralizing services (a solution), while someone else has noted the relative lack of services to the Latino population (a problem). A policy entrepreneur in the agency may suggest writing a grant proposal to develop outreach stations for the Latino population, a proposal that would couple the problem with the solution.[21] Or perhaps someone links the many problems of public schools in New Orleans prior to Hurricane Katrina, including high drop-out rates and poor student achievement levels, with the solution "charter schools," wherein schools are placed under the control of parents and administrators rather than the public bureaucracy. Quite apart from whether it was good policy to do so, the vast bulk of public schools in New Orleans had become charter schools within a year of Hurricane Katrina because of this coupling. President Barack Obama coupled his 2009 stimulus package with many social programs, such as alleviating homelessness, building infrastructure, and reforming the health system.

Framing and Finding Titles   Policy entrepreneurs put a twist on proposals to make them appealing to decision makers. For example, they may portray a benefit as an *earned* benefit to make it difficult for opponents to argue that it is a *welfare* benefit. This strategy is illustrated by arguments used to support the enactment of the Earned Income Tax Credit in 1973, given to families with working parents, and to increase its coverage so that it is now the largest antipoverty program funded by the federal government. Had the Earned Income Tax Credit been framed as a *welfare* program, it probably would not have been enacted in light of widespread political opposition to welfare. Even critics of George W. Bush's program No Child Left Behind would agree that the title cleverly makes it difficult for opponents to marshal opposition to it because we would all agree that no child *should* be left behind.

Negotiating and Bargaining   Even before an issue appears on the decision agenda, policy entrepreneurs need to accommodate different points of view. Even though policy proposals are not fully developed until an issue has entered policy deliberations (see the bottom of the funnel in Figure 6.1), policy entrepreneurs often develop their tentative outlines even before this stage. They often try to create a *win-win* atmosphere that allows different people and factions to believe they will each have a piece of the action. President Barack Obama tried in 2009 to secure bipartisan support for national health insurance, particularly in the Senate where he knew that he needed to keep conservative Democrats and some moderate Republicans supportive of it. When that failed, he used the same strategy within the Democratic Party to gain all of its 60 Senate votes to prevent a filibuster by Republicans who had decided to vote in unison against the legislation. By contrast, if a *win–lose* atmosphere exists even before an issue reaches policy deliberations, public officials are more likely to have a combative mood that will sometimes imperil the policy's enactment.[22]

EP 2.1.8b

Negotiating and bargaining take place in agency and community settings as well. Assume, for example, that a planning commission in a city is deciding whether to approve the placement of a residential treatment center for substance abusers in a specific neighborhood. If the supporters of this center give residents a chance not only to discuss the proposal but also to offer suggestions about how the proposed center might be administered (so that it does not cause crime or other neighborhood problems), opposition to it is likely to decrease—and the planning commission is more likely to approve it.

Assembling Early Sponsors and Supporters In legislative arenas, policy entrepreneurs actually enlist people to sponsor a legislative proposal by placing their names on it. The characteristics of these sponsors are important: If they are powerful politicians who also represent an array of perspectives, the chances of the legislation passing are much better than if the legislation is sponsored by only a narrow range of politicians who lack power.[23] For example, President Barack Obama supported the leadership of Senator Ted Kennedy for a national health insurance program because he knew that many senators in both parties respected him. Even in agency settings, policy entrepreneurs often enlist an array of persons during the agenda-building process by soliciting their advice and making them part of the planning process.

To return to our example of the residential treatment center, a policy advocate would be well advised to invite persons in the neighborhood to come to meetings about it. This would cultivate highly respected neighborhood leaders, whose support would be most helpful to getting residents to support it.

Routing Policy entrepreneurs must find a home base for their issue by routing it to decision makers who want to resolve it in ways that the entrepreneurs find acceptable. When a choice exists in legislative settings, they have to decide which committee should get jurisdiction. Naturally, a policy entrepreneur does not want an issue routed to a committee whose chairperson or members do not want to act on it or have contrary views. By discussing the routing with highly placed politicians and members of a special committee (called the Rules Committee in the U.S. House of Representatives), policy entrepreneurs can sometimes influence routing decisions.[24] Policy entrepreneurs influence routing decisions in agency settings as well; they may seek jurisdiction by a specific committee, the general staff, the agency's board, an ad hoc committee, or the executive director. Of course, some issues, such as fundamental changes in agency policies, have to be considered by the agency board.

Media Coverage Timely coverage of proposals is often critical in projecting them onto decision agendas in the case of legislation and community decisions. Policy entrepreneurs who are state or federal legislators often use the media to get stories about their activities printed or placed on television in their home districts.

**Policy
Advocacy
Challenge 6.6**

The Competi-
tion for Policy
Agendas—
and Diver-
sions from
Them

Bruce Jansson,
Ph.D.
Go to
www.cengage.com
to watch this video clip.

The scramble for scarce resources in the wake of Hurricane Katrina illustrates the challenge that policy advocates often encounter. All experts agreed that the hurricane's wrath was most concentrated in New Orleans, as well as in specific cities in southern Mississippi and Alabama such as Gulfport, Biloxi, and Mobile. Yet considerable Federal Emergency Management Agency (FEMA) assistance was given to counties and cities that experienced only tropical storm-force winds of speeds less than 74 mph. Jackson, Mississippi, for example, received $21 million, where only 50–60 homes were declared uninhabitable. Mississippi requested the Bush administration to broaden the initial disaster area to extend as far as 220 miles inland. The Red Cross followed FEMA's example and gave extensive aid to outlying and relatively undamaged areas, some of it to persons who fraudulently claimed damage when none or little existed. A large amount of resources directed toward New Orleans actually went to repairing military facilities—resources not taken from the already-large military budget.

Some policy advocates feared that large amounts of federal loans and grants would go to private commercial interests intent on rebuilding New Orleans as a tourist center—thus bleeding funds needed for affordable houses, schools, and other basic needs of vulnerable populations.

Policy advocates in New Orleans had to contend, then, with intense competition for space on policy agendas. Wanting to prioritize the needs of vulnerable populations whose housing had been destroyed, they found that other claimants for resources often succeeded in getting on policy agendas even when their needs were not as dire as those of vulnerable populations and even when their resources could have come from existing military and other budgets.

Policy advocates also had to contend with diversion of resources—by fraud and corruption—from resources supposedly dedicated to meeting the needs of vulnerable persons. Government investigators revealed in June 2006 that over $1 billion of FEMA resources was fraudulently claimed by criminals. Still other resources were wasted because FEMA staff miscalculated the benefits that specific persons were due. All told, the overall estimate of $2 billion in fraud and waste amounted to nearly 11 percent of the $19 billion spent by FEMA on Hurricanes Katrina and Rita by June 2006. According to Senator Susan Collins (R–Maine), who chaired the U.S. Senate's Homeland Security and Governmental Affairs Committee, "The blatant fraud, the audacity of the schemes, the scale of the waste—it is simply breathtaking."[1]

The scramble for resources in New Orleans continued into the Obama Administration. Activists in New Orleans were aware that President Obama has many pressing domestic and international issues to address. They faced an uphill battle in pressuring Congress and the administration to focus resources on the Gulf Coast areas. Yet they had considerable success. Temporary trailers were replaced with affordable housing units. A vast rebuilding of infrastructure to protect New Orleans from future hurricanes proceeded ahead of schedule and was nearly complete by 2012. Tourists and conventions greatly increased, augmenting the city's economic growth, Large numbers of young people flocked to New Orleans to teach in local schools and to participate in various projects of AmeriCorps. New Orleans was a far smaller city than prior to Katrina, but it was on an economic and social upswing by late 2012.

Listen to Russell Henderson, MSW, LCSW, in the online video, as he discusses competition for policy agendas and waste in New Orleans.

---

[1]Eric Lipton, "Breathtaking Waste and Fraud in Hurricane Aid," *New York Times* (June 27, 2006): A1, A13.

Can Direct-Service Staff Help Build Agendas?

Our discussion suggests that policy advocates in agency and legislative settings can diagnose and soften the context, as well as search for a policy entrepreneur.

Is agenda building restricted to legislators and high-level agency staff, such as executive directors? To be sure, these persons are best situated to assume pivotal roles in building agendas, but direct-service staff can participate in agenda building in both agency and legislative settings. They can begin by working within their agencies and agency networks, by locating unaddressed or poorly addressed community needs. They can read professional literature and find evidence-based practices that could be—but are not—implemented in specific settings, drawing this to the attention of other staff members as well as executives. They can join coalitions and advocacy groups that already exist in the community and lend them volunteer and other support. As individuals who directly serve the public, they gain credibility from their direct observations of persons and communities that their agency or program seeks to serve.

EP 2.1.10a

Direct-service staff ought, as well, to move beyond their agencies into the broader policy world. They can engage legislative aides about specific unaddressed or poorly addressed issues that they have seen in their work. They can encourage their clients to call high-level officials within agencies and agency networks, and within legislatures or commissions at the local, state, and federal levels. They can help their clients draft letters to these officials.

To the extent that their agency is not involved in trying to shape policies that are relevant to its clientele or to the community, direct-service staff can ask whether voter registration projects can be organized by their agency or by other agencies in their area, or whether informational materials can be distributed by agencies about specific propositions or initiatives on the ballot. Agencies cannot endorse specific candidates, but they can endorse propositions or initiatives.

Persons do not have to—and should not—wait to become policy advocates until they have risen to executive positions in agencies. If they limit their work only to clinical practice at the outset of their careers, they risk limiting their horizons thereafter as well. If it is ethically meritorious to be a policy advocate, as we discussed in Chapter Two, why not begin this trajectory while in a school or department of social work, and in the initial phases of one's career?

To find windows of opportunity, staff can identify strategic times in the workings of agencies or legislatures when conditions will favor advancing specific initiatives. Finally, staff can search for policy entrepreneurs who can place a specific issue on their agency's or a legislature's agenda, or on the agenda of a city council, school board, commission, or county board of supervisors.

Policy Advocacy for Powerless Populations and Unpopular Issues

Thus far, our discussion about agenda building has emphasized how agenda processes work and how a pragmatic policy practitioner can use these processes to reach policy goals. When we discuss how agenda processes actually work, however, it is important to remember that they are often skewed against unpopular issues and powerless groups. For example, the Children's Defense Fund, established in 1973, sought for more than 15 years to convince Congress to place day care on its agenda, finally succeeding in 1989. Advocates of initiatives to end homelessness have made considerable success, but still have a long way to go as homeless populations in major cities—and even some

EP 2.1.10e

suburban and rural areas—suggest. Those who want to change the American federal tax structure to truly reduce economic inequality have been relatively unsuccessful for decades, although they have succeeded in taking many persons with low income off federal tax rolls, even if they must continue to pay Social Security and Medicare taxes.

Groups that plug away for unpopular issues and populations may be laying the groundwork for subsequent policy changes. In the case of day care and the Children's Defense Fund, advocates' diligent and sustained lobbying, as well as their assistance to grassroots reform groups throughout the United States, doubtless educated many politicians about the specific problems and needs of children. When pressure from feminist groups and corporations that hired large numbers of women finally placed day care on Congress's decision agenda in the 1980s, the Children's Defense Fund spearheaded a coalition to seek specific legislation. Had they not promoted the issue in the preceding two decades, however, they might not have been successful in the legislation they enacted in 1990. Had they not been active over an extended period, this legislation, which was hardly adequate in its funding and scope, might have been even more limited.

We have mostly discussed policy change through conventional channels, such as by working with public officials in legislative settings or with executives in agency settings. We should note, however, that some policy advocates conclude at specific points in time and in specific places that they cannot secure policy initiatives working solely through conventional channels. Abolitionists in the 1850s, suffragettes in the early part of last century, and civil rights advocates in the 1950s and 1960s used nonviolent protest strategies to force neglected issues onto public officials' agendas, as did a national movement of persons seeking reforms in immigration legislation in 2006. They persisted despite criticism that their tactics were unethical or unwarranted, or that they were counterproductive.

Policy advocates who use protests as a part of their strategy to secure policy changes should realize that they can sometimes harden the positions of some public officials against the reforms that they seek, and that protests can sometimes lead to a backlash by persons who oppose their policies. Yet some policy advocates believe they must use nonviolent protests and demonstrations because decision makers will not otherwise pay attention to them, and the general public will remain ignorant or opposed to their positions. The organizers of nationwide protests to secure more human immigration policies in the United States came to this conclusion in 2006, leading to a series of massive, nationwide demonstration of hundreds of thousands of persons. Consider public demonstrations, then, to be an arrow in policy advocates' quivers, but realize, too, that they are not a panacea and must, in any case, be supplemented with efforts to work through conventional channels to get specific proposals enacted.[25]

Electoral Processes

Agenda setting often takes place within electoral politics as politicians, parties, and activists try to find issues that can be used to distinguish themselves from their opposition. They want issues that will appeal to their natural constituencies while also allowing them to appeal to swing voters. Sometimes they want issues (so-called wedge issues) that will divide the opposing party. If they do not find new issues and their opponents do, they lose a strategic advantage in upcoming elections.

The search for new issues is particularly intense after a party loses an election. Bolstered by support from the so-called Tea Party's emergence in 2009, Republicans won control of the House of Representatives and many governorships and local elections in 2010. Democrats, led by Barack Obama, had to decide what issues to prioritize to allow them to regain the House and retain the presidency and the U.S. Senate in 2012, while burdened with high unemployment. In this context, Obama decided by late 2011 to contrast his (and the Democrats') vision of society with Republicans' vision, i.e., to pit his relatively liberal philosophy with (in his view) the outdated conservative philosophy of the Tea Party and Republican leaders who had subscribed to it. He sought to link his vision with specific policies, such as increasing taxes on millionaires, funding job development programs, extending payroll tax cuts for working Americans, not deporting immigrant youth who had been brought to the United States by their parents, and cutting defense spending. In turn, Republican leaders favored policies and arguments to convince voters that Democratic policies had worsened the Great Recession that had begun in 2007. They argued that Obama's policies would slow economic growth—favoring, instead, to retain tax cuts for wealthy persons that President George W. Bush had initiated, cut social spending, repeal the Affordable Care Act of 2010.

Local candidates also engage in agenda building as they seek issues that will generate support for themselves as compared to their opponents.

In this nonstop process of agenda setting, ideology assumes a key role partly because the two major parties have somewhat different bases of political support. A large segment of Republicans' constituencies derives from relatively affluent segments of the population, farmers, and southerners, as well as residents of so-called red states in the Midwest and Rocky Mountain area. In contrast, the more urban, northern, and working-class population, as well as the so-called blue coastal states, such as New York and California, provide a base of support for Democrats. Republicans' natural base of support is relatively more conservative than Democrats', so the two parties gravitate toward somewhat different ideologies and, therefore, positions on issues.

Developing Links with Advocacy Groups

Policy advocates who wish to build agendas in the broader community, but who do not know how to get started, should consider connecting with an established advocacy group (see Box 2.1). Effective advocacy groups try to shape public officials' agendas by pressuring them to consider solutions or problems, presenting research that underlines the importance of addressing specific social needs, and publicizing stories in the mass media that dramatize certain issues. Would-be advocates can join a local group or a local chapter of a national group, meet the director of the advocacy group, subscribe to its newsletters and other materials, volunteer to work on its outreach and education projects, help its staff conduct research, and help the group lobby public officials. Those who want to be involved can work with local and state chapters of the National Association of Social Workers (NASW), whose leaders and lobbyists pressure legislators. Both advocacy groups and the NASW not only generate ideas for policy agendas, such as specific pieces of legislation, but also pressure politicians to move these ideas toward choice or decision agendas. They often try to convince the chairpersons of pivotal legislative committees, for example, to hold hearings and discuss proposals, rather than let them slip into oblivion.

EP 2.1.10a

Policy advocates can also campaign for politicians they believe will put certain issues on policy agendas. For example, PACE, the political action arm of NASW that backs politicians who support issues favored by NASW, regularly canvasses NASW members to work for the candidates it supports.

Using Multiple Skills in Agenda Building

EP 2.1.7a

Policy advocates use the four skills discussed in Chapter Three when they try to influence policy agendas. They use *political skills* to analyze and engage in the political stream; *analytic skills* to develop and use data in the problem and solution streams; *interactional skills* to help problems and solutions reach policy deliberations in agency and legislative settings, persuade people to consider specific problems and solutions, participate in committees and task forces, and organize coalitions; and *value-clarifying skills* to decide whether to invest energy in promoting an issue in the first place and to decide how to frame it.

Policy Advocacy Challenge 6.7

Using the Agenda Funnel to Propose Legislation to Reduce Economic Inequality

President John F. Kennedy surprised the nation in 1964 when he proposed a War on Poverty because poverty had hardly been discussed in the United States since the Great Depression of the 1930s. Poverty virtually disappeared from national discourse in the 1970s, 1980s, 1990s, and through the first three years of Barack Obama's presidency. A constellation of factors led to its resurfacing. The Great Recession of 2007 to 2009 and beyond dramatized the sheer number of poor people in the United States—whether persons who were chronically poor or moderate- and middle-income persons who had descended into poverty as they lost their jobs and their houses. The mass media publicized problems associated with poverty: homelessness, unemployment, and increased use of food banks and food stamps. It ran many stories about the sheer number of persons who had been unemployed for 18 months or longer, as well as young persons who could not find jobs when they graduated from high school or college. Republican presidential contenders made statements that dramatized insensitivity of top leaders to poverty. If Newt Gingrich called President Obama "the food-stamp president," Mitt Romney stated that he "was not concerned about the very poor" on two occasions. The extent of inequality in the nation was dramatized by Democrats' failed attempt to decrease the nation's deficits and debt by increasing taxes on persons earning over $1 million—a proposal that was endorsed by billionaire Warren Buffett who had revealed that his secretary paid a higher proportion of her income in taxes than did he. Occupy Wall Street dramatized the differences in wealth between the top 1 percent and the bottom 99 percent of the nation. President Obama was pressured from the left, such as by television talk-show host Tavis Smiley, to use the words "poor people" rather than being content with "defending the middle class."

Using the agenda-building framework in Figure 6.1, discuss what would need to happen to convert this new interest in poverty into legislative proposals that might actually be enacted. What developments might thwart efforts to help impoverished people? What actually happened?

What You Can Now Do

Chapter Summary

You are now equipped with skills to do the following:

- Diagnose agendas in legislative, agency, and community settings.
- Enhance support for a problem or solution by softening the context.
- Develop support for a problem or solution by using such tactics as timing, coupling, negotiating, finding sponsors, and routing.

- Place items on the agenda as a direct-service worker.
- Be able to engage in agenda building at different levels of government as well as in the private sector.

We will discuss methods of analyzing problems in Chapter Seven.

Competency Notes

EP 2.1.3a   Distinguish, appraise, and integrate multiple sources of knowledge, including research-based knowledge and practice wisdom (p. 181): Social workers must consider various streams of information.

EP 2.1.3b   Analyze models of assessment, prevention, intervention, and evaluation (p. 181): Social workers can navigate the different models issued by rationalists, incrementalists, and garbage can theorists.

EP 2.1.3c   Demonstrate effective oral and written communication in working with individuals, families, groups, organizations, communities, and colleagues (p. 178): Social workers should tailor their policy strategies and communicate specific points after listening to other parties' constraints and opportunities.

EP 2.1.5b   Advocate for human rights and social and economic justice (p. 186): Social workers can appeal to values such as beneficence, social justice, and fairness.

EP 2.1.7a   Utilize conceptual frameworks to guide the process of assessment, intervention, and evaluation (p. 197): Social workers can use political, analytic, interactional, and value-clarifying skills to influence policy agendas.

EP 2.1.8b   Collaborate with colleagues and clients for effective policy action (p. 192): Social workers negotiate and bargain with those of different points of view when drafting legislative proposals.

EP 2.1.9a   Continuously discover, appraise, and attend to changing locales, populations, scientific and technological developments, and emerging societal trends to provide relevant services (pp. 189, 191): Social workers should identify windows of opportunity to determine the best time to advocate for change.

EP 2.1.10a   Substantively and affectively prepare for action with individuals, families, groups, organizations, and communities (pp. 175, 194, 196): Social workers must perform the agenda-setting task in order to bring focus to an issue.

EP 2.1.10b   Use empathy and other skills (p. 189): Social workers can build political support by engaging with opponents.

EP 2.1.10d   Collect, organize, and interpret client data (p. 186): Social workers can use data to highlight problems that client populations face.

EP 2.1.10e   Assess client strengths and limitations (p. 195): Social workers should understand the challenges faced by unpopular and powerless populations.

Endnotes

1. Marc Ross and Roger Cobb, *The Cultural Strategies of Agenda Denial* (Kansas City: University of Kansas, 1997).

2. Robert Eyestone, *From Social Issues to Public Policy* (New York: Wiley, 1978), pp. 20–21; and Frank Baumgartner and Bryan Jones, *Agendas and*

Instability in American Politics (Chicago: University of Chicago Press, 1993), pp. 250–251.

3. John Kingdon, *Agendas, Alternatives, and Public Policies* (Boston: Little, Brown, 1984).

4. Ibid., pp. 83–88.

5. Michael Cohen, James March, and Johan Olsen, "A Garbage Can Model of Organizational Choice," *Administrative Science Quarterly* 17 (March 1972): 1–25.

6. Ibid., pp. 95–121.

7. Kingdon, *Agendas, Alternatives, and Public Policies*, p. 115.

8. Ibid., pp. 95–108.

9. The work of policy advocates to place Alzheimer's disease on national policy agendas illustrates how they seek to dramatize the severity or pervasiveness of a social problem—even when precise data are lacking. See Julie Kosterlitz, "Anguish and Opportunity: Alzheimer's Disease," *National Journal* 24 (July 25, 1992): 1727–1732.

10. See Reich's use of the term *investment* rather than *spending* in Robert Reich, *The Work of Nations: Preparing Ourselves for 21st-Century Capitalism* (New York: Knopf, 1991), pp. 252–261.

11. Bruce Jansson, *Improving Healthcare Through Advocacy: A Guide for the Health and Helping Professions* (Hoboken, NJ: John Wiley & Sons, 2011), pp. 253–296.

12. The political problem of securing funds for prevention is illustrated by the AIDS epidemic; see Julie Kosterlitz, "AIDS Wars," *National Journal* 24 (July 25, 1992): 1727–1732.

13. For uses of the media to place issues on an agenda, see Hedrick Smith, *The Power Game: How Washington Works* (New York: Ballantine Books, 1988), pp. 331–387; and Baumgartner and Jones, *Agendas and Instability in American Politics*, pp. 103–125.

14. Ibid., pp. 138–139.

15. Chris Matthews, *Hardball: How Politics Is Played* (New York: Summit Books, 1988).

16. Donald deKieffer, *The Citizen's Guide to Lobbying Congress* (Chicago: Chicago Review Press, 1997), pp. 19–20.

17. Kingdon, *Agendas, Alternatives, and Public Policies*, pp. 174–193.

18. Ibid., pp. 110–115.

19. Ibid., pp. 160–162.

20. Ibid., pp. 188–193.

21. Ibid., pp. 181–188.

22. Clinton decided not to use the single-payer Canadian system not only because health care provider groups opposed it but also because the federal government would have been required to fund the entire package of benefits just as Clinton was trying to reduce the federal deficit. Ibid., pp. 1, 9.

23. Ron Dear and Rino Patti, "Legislative Advocacy: Seven Effective Tactics," *Social Work* 26 (July 1981): 289–297.

24. Ibid.

25. Kingdon, *Agendas, Alternatives, and Public Policies*, pp. 134–138.

Suggested Readings

Joel Best, ed., *Images of Issues: Typifying Contemporary Social Problems* (New York: Aldine de Gruyter, 1989).

John Kingdon, *Agendas, Alternatives, and Public Policies* (Boston: Little, Brown, 1997).

Julie Kosterlitz, "Anguish and Opportunity: Alzheimer's Disease," *National Journal* (April 28, 1990): 1008–1015.

Marc Ross and Roger Cobb, *The Cultural Strategies of Agenda Denial* (Lawrence: University of Kansas, 1997).

Jeffrey Schmalz, "Whatever Happened to AIDS?" *New York Times Magazine* (November 28, 1993), pp. 55–86.

Hedrick Smith, *The Power Game: How Washington Really Works* (New York: Ballantine Books, 1988), pp. 331–387.

Rochelle Stanford, "Child Care Quagmire," *National Journal* (February 27, 1993): 55–86.

CHAPTER

7

Analyzing Problems in the First Step of Policy Analysis

Policy Predicament

Public housing was created as a response to the Great Depression in the 1930s. Today more than 1.3 million units of public housing exist in the United States. Some argue that these areas of concentrated poverty are riddled with drugs, crime, and other social problems, and residents should therefore be removed and assimilated into "mainstream" communities. To illustrate policy analysis, we discuss at the end of this chapter the debate surrounding whether very low-income persons, particularly African Americans, benefit when they are relocated from areas of concentrated poverty and integrated into mixed-income, largely Caucasian communities. We also discuss how vast populations of destitute persons have migrated from rural to urban areas in many developing nations, but mostly live in segregated communities on their periphery with scant economic, educational, and medical services.

LEARNING OUTCOMES

By the end of this chapter, you will be able to discuss how:

1. Policy advocates use a six-step approach for developing and defending policy proposals
2. During the first step, policy advocates familiarize themselves with a specific social problem or issue or interrelated problems or issues
3. During the first step, policy advocates analyze the causes of social problems or issues
4. During the first step, policy advocates develop interventions and programs
5. During the first step, policy advocates develop preventive programs
6. During the first step, policy advocates measure the magnitude of problems and locate problems spatially
7. During the first step, policy advocates contend with the slippery nature of many social problems
8. During the first step, policy analysts can use visual aids, such as flowcharts, to map out a social issue in the context of familial, community, and economic factors.

FIGURE 7.1 Developing and Defending Policy Proposals Using a Six-Step Policy Analysis Framework

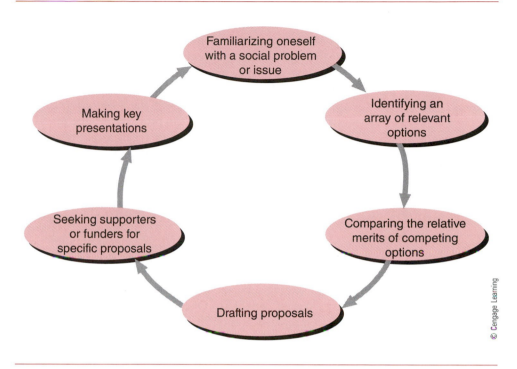

© Cengage Learning

Putting It All Together: A Six-Step Policy Analysis Framework

Please recall that our Policy Practice Framework that we presented in Chapter Three in Figure 3.1 identified eight tasks that policy advocates undertake. Now that we have discussed the first three of these tasks in preceding chapters (deciding what is right and wrong, navigating policy and advocacy systems, and agenda-setting), we are ready to turn to the fourth and fifth tasks in our Systems Approach to Policy Making framework, i.e., analyzing problems and writing proposals. These two tasks lie at the heart of policy advocates. They allow them to improve society by developing and defending policy proposals that will prevent or address major social problems.

We engage these two tasks by using a six-step policy analysis framework that is portrayed in Figure 7.1. We summarize the six steps in this chapter and then discuss the first of these steps in the remainder of this chapter, i.e., familiarizing oneself with a social problem or issue. We discuss the remaining five steps in the next two chapters.[1]

A Six-Step Policy Analysis, Proposal-Writing, and Presentation Framework

1. *Familiarize oneself with a specific social problem or issue or interrelated problems or issues.* Policy analysis begins with the selection of a specific social problem or issue that can include victimization of persons by landlords and others; inability of

persons to meet their basic or survival needs; inability of persons to obtain opportunity-enhancing services; inability of persons and families to get help with specific needs or issues; infringement of the rights of members of specific vulnerable populations by employers or others; excessive levels of inequality; inability of persons to acquire needed assets such as housing and savings; insufficient access to loans, capital, and resources by specific geographic areas; and inequities in the political process such as unfair electoral districts. It can involve ways to rebuild disaster-torn areas, such as the Gulf Coast after the BP oil spill, the devastation of communities in Missouri and Alabama in the wake of tornadoes in 2011, or Haiti after its catastrophic earthquake. Or the problem or issue can involve defects in the implementation of specific programs or regulations. Perhaps a specific program, such as medical services in the Latino community, fails to connect with substance abuse programs even when a substantial number of Latinos possess this problem. Perhaps public schools do not implement the mainstreaming of developmentally challenged youth in their classrooms as required by federal law.

EP 2.1.3a

Policy advocates need to ask the following questions:

- What political, fiscal, cultural, or other factors led to a specific festering problem or issue, which can often be stated by using such words as "too many people possess XYZ condition or problem" such as homelessness, poverty, or lack of access to specific services. Or "too few persons with depression receive optimal services for their condition." Or they can use a value-based perspective to state a specific problem, such as by contending that too many low-income persons lack adequate housing when compared with the broader population.
- What remedies or solutions (if any) currently exist for the social problem or issue, and why are they insufficient in strategy, relative size, or implementation? Can they be reformed or changed, and, if so, how, or are new remedies or solutions needed?
- What is the magnitude of current expenditures on the program or issue? From what sources do these funds come? Are they sufficient or insufficient?
- What adverse consequences does the current problem or issue pose for specific persons, communities, and society? What is the level or amount of these consequences? Do the adverse consequences suggest that the problem requires urgent action? (If policy advocates cannot make a strong case that the problem or issue is trivial or unimportant, they will find it difficult to generate support for solutions from decision makers.)

When developing proposals that address specific social problems, policy advocates need to use social science and other literature to better understand how they evolve or develop in specific populations. They need to understand where these populations go for assistance with these problems or issues both within organized programs and from nontraditional agencies. They need to understand how specific populations perceive specific conditions and whether they even view them as "problems." They need to examine an array of strategies currently used to redress or solve them, such as empowerment approaches, remedial strategies, use of regulations, or some combination of these approaches.

Policy advocates sometimes develop strategies for preventing specific problems. They might propose specific policies to curtail exposure to toxic substances such as smoke or pollution. They might seek greater funding for child care as it helps children prepare for school or avoid neglect. They need to examine social science, public health, and other literature, as well as Internet sites, that discuss prevention strategies.

EPA 2.1.6b

They also need to ask what policy solutions might be considered:

- In what specific policy arenas can remedies for this social problem or issue be developed and enacted, including local, state, or federal legislatures; specific local, state, or federal bureaucracies; the courts; the private sector; specific social agencies, whether public ones or nongovernmental organizations; and nonpublic entities such as faith-based or for-profit organizations.
- Or should the issue or problem be addressed by a combination of these organizations, such as by a strategy that links public and nonpublic agencies?

Even at the outset, policy advocates often involve other persons in their work. Policy advocacy usually involves collaborative work by task forces, teams, coalitions, or advocacy groups that seek solutions to specific social problems or issues.

2. *Policy advocates brainstorm an array of relevant policy, programmatic, and resource options that, singly and together, might define a strategy for addressing the social problem or issue.* These can include several options depending on the complexity of the proposal that is ultimately developed during the analytic process, including:

- The elements of a new social program, such as its intake procedures, the content of its services or benefits, where the program is positioned in an existing or new agency, the nature of its staff, and how it is linked to other social programs
- The content of a proposed or modified regulation, such as ones that protect rights of members of specific vulnerable populations
- The proposed modifications in an existing social program or in the way it is implemented
- A proposed change in the amount of resources dedicated to a specific program or issue, such as a proposal to increase these resources
- A proposed modification in a specific protocol or procedure for helping specific persons, such as a proposal to require social workers' involvement in end-of-life decision making

To identify and compare options, policy advocates collect information from a variety of sources, including interviews with persons knowledgeable about existing programs and policies. They use social science and other research and theory to develop options that appear promising for addressing or solving a specific social problem such as homelessness or substance abuse.

EPA 2.1.3a

3. *Policy advocates analyze the relative merits of competing options so that, on balance, they can select a specific one from two or more options.* To compare the options, they must first identify specific criteria they will use to contrast the options and to decide, on balance, which of them is meritorious.

Several kinds of criteria are commonly used in policy analysis. Value-based criteria are critical since they provide a normative basis for comparing options. A policy analyst might want to consider, for example, whether and to what extent specific options meet social justice or fairness criteria and whether they preserve persons' confidentiality or self-determination rights. To underscore the importance of values, imagine a proponent of free-market capitalism developing a proposal for rebuilding areas of the South and Midwest that were hit by deadly tornadoes in April 2011. The free-market advocate might not even include such values as "social justice" or fairness in his or her analysis, and this decision would lead him or her to favor such policy options as letting private developers decide how to rebuild specific areas, even if their housing was primarily purchased by affluent persons. Contrast this free-market advocate with a policy advocate who believes that government must intervene when private markets will not suffice. She would want government to offer disaster relief to poor people, housing subsidies to help low- and moderate-income families build or rent housing, and monies to make repairs to damaged infrastructure to hasten economic recovery. As this example reveals, *the selection of criteria pivotally shapes the recommendations of policy analysts, so they must be chosen with care.*

Most policy analyses also include criteria that deal with the effectiveness of specific options. Decision makers usually want to know whether a specific option will actually prevent, address, or solve an issue or problem effectively, particularly given the competition for programs for scarce resources. In the case of rebuilding New Orleans, for example, federal HUD officials would want to know how to get affordable housing constructed in a timely way in key parts of the city. In the case of social problems such as homelessness or substance abuse, policy analysts *have to* use available social science research and theory to make the case that a specific option will effectively address a specific social problem. (We use the term *evidence-based policy* in Chapter Fourteen when discussing how policy analysts use research to buttress the case for specific policies.)

They would also want to compare policies by their cost. If the cost of a specific option is prohibitive in light of available resources, decision makers may reject it even if it scores high on other criteria.

Decision makers sometimes combine criteria, such as by asking if the options are *cost effective*. In this case, they favor policy options that are *both* effective *and* relatively inexpensive.

Still other criteria have to do with practical political and implementation considerations. Assume, for example, that a specific option is cost effective, but will attract such opposition from legislators that it has no chance of passage. In this case, a policy analyst might recommend a policy option that is less cost effective, but that has a greater chance of being enacted. Policies that cannot easily be implemented may also be rejected. Perhaps, for example, a policy option is sufficiently complex that implementing agencies will be unlikely to understand it, much less to put in place some of its provisions. Here, too, an otherwise meritorious option may be rejected by decision makers on implementation grounds.

The term *trade-offs* is used to describe how policy analysts deal with the fact that a specific policy often ranks higher on one or more criteria but lower on others. Faced with this situation, a policy analyst might conclude that *on balance* he or she prefers a specific policy option, even though it does not rank high on all criteria.

Criteria often include:

- Cost
- Effectiveness
- Political feasibility
- Ease of implementation
- Specific values such as social justice, fairness, confidentiality, and self-determination

In simple proposals, such as changing an intake procedure in an agency or a protocol for helping certain kinds of persons, such as battered women in hospital settings, relatively few options will need to be considered. Policy advocates who advance more complex proposals may need to examine a variety of options with respect to several facets of this larger proposal. (We discuss how proposals are fashioned in more detail in Chapter Eight.)

4. *Policy advocates draft a specific policy proposal that flows from their brainstorming and conceptual work during the preceding three stages of policy analysis.* The proposals can be relatively simple or complex, modest or ambitious, inexpensive or costly. Policy advocates can propose new policies or modifications of existing ones, such as new programs or improvements. The proposals often include proposed budgets.

Policy advocates often get feedback during the drafting process from other policy advocates and decision makers and modify their proposals as needed. They might decide, for example, to downsize or upsize proposals. They might decide to delete certain contentious provisions from them or add some if they think they have sufficient political support for them.

5. *Policy advocates seek supporters for their proposals.* As we noted in Step 1, they will have involved other persons in their work from the outset.

6. *Policy advocates make key presentations* to public officials or decision makers to persuade them that their policy proposal is meritorious as they enter the policy-enacting phase of the policy-advocacy process as discussed in Chapters Nine, Ten, and Eleven.

Do Policy Advocates Have to Analyze Problems?

Some people may believe that policy advocates do not have to analyze problems because their work is driven by their progressive values, such as their commitment to social justice and fairness. In fact, advocates must analyze problems for several reasons. Were they not to base their recommendations (at least in part) on hardheaded analysis of specific problems, including the use of up-to-date research, they would often find their proposals dismissed as lacking a substantive base (see Policy Advocacy Challenge 7.1). Moreover, a candid assessment of the social reforms of prior eras suggests that they have often not worked, partly because their advocates lacked sufficient knowledge of specific problems when they proposed specific reforms. The classic example is public housing for low-income persons. Believing that they were providing a long-term solution, reformers in the late 1930s and the next two decades obtained federal funding for huge public housing

---

Policy Advocacy Challenge 7.1

Using the Web as a Tool in Policy Analysis

Stephanie Davis, Research Librarian, University of California, Irvine

Analysis is an essential part of policy work and advocacy. Analysis can take many forms, such as statistics, reports, case studies, and so on. The goals of analysis (in part) establish a definition for the problem; investigate the causes, history, and impacts of the problem; and determine who the problem affects. Your research will lead you to ask these questions and more. A few examples of websites that present analysis are listed as follows:

- Center on Budget and Policy Priorities: **www.cbpp.org**
- Fedstats: **www.fedstats.gov**
- John F. Kennedy School of Government at Harvard University: **www.hks.harvard.edu**

Using these sites and others that you find for your specific issue or problem, assess how well the sites address your topic or issue.

Websites are also useful for finding statistics. Why are statistics important? First of all, they provide a picture of our country—information about our population, pastimes, habits, how we spend our money, where we work, and the problems we face as a nation. Using statistics to back up your words or show the impact of a specific problem on a population can be powerful.

As part of your research, you may be asked to find statistics, such as the number of children in foster care or the percentage of women without health care. You can find statistics in many places, online and in print sources such as books and journal articles.

(continued)

Here are a few resources to get you started:

- *Dictionary of U.S. Government Statistical Terms.* Alfred N. Garwood and Louise Hornor. 1991.
- *Historical Statistics of the United States: Colonial Times to 1970.* 2 vols. 1975.
- *Social Work Almanac.* Leon Ginsberg. 1995.
- *Statistical Abstract of the United States.* U.S. Bureau of the Census. 1878–.
- *The World Almanac and Book of Facts.* 1923–.

In addition, three indexes provide comprehensive access to statistical information, available in print and through the subscription database *Statistical Universe*:

- *American Statistics Index* (U.S. Federal Government Statistics)
- *Index to International Statistics* (international statistics from intergovernmental organizations, including the United Nations)
- *Statistical Reference Index* (statistics collected by states, private agencies, nonprofit organizations, and research organizations)

ONLINE SOURCES:

- USA.gov, the Federal Government Search Engine: **www.usa.gov**
- Fedstats, One-Stop Shopping for Federal Statistics: **www.fedstats.gov**
- University of Michigan Documents Center Statistical Resources: **www.lib.umich.edu/ govdocs/stats.html**
- United States Census Bureau: **www.census.gov**
- NationMaster: www.nationmaster.com/index.php
- The World Factbook: https://www.cia.gov/library/publications/the-world-factbook

EVALUATING STATISTICS: Locating your statistics is only the first step. You need to evaluate this information critically as you would a journal article, report, or book.

Here are criteria to consider when evaluating statistics:

- Where does the information come from—the government, corporation, private agency, state agency, or regional agency?
- Did the government pay for the study that produced the statistics? If not, who paid?
- How old is the statistical information? Is it based on the current or the previous census?
- What was the sampling size and sampling error?

EXERCISE

Go to the library and find the most recent edition of *Statistical Abstract of the United States.* (It is published every year.) Find statistics about your research topic or an issue that interests you. Then look at the Appendix titled "Limitations of the Data" (usually Appendix III). Do these limitations have a possible impact on the data you found? Give three reasons how the data you found could be incorrect or inconsistent.

projects, not fully realizing that they would become segregated by class and race and bedeviled by high rates of crime and drug use.

When searching for new solutions to problems, policy advocates must realize that persons, groups, and institutions often select policies that will enhance their prestige, revenue, and power, sometimes with scant regard for citizens who need assistance. Tradition often shapes policies, even when existing policies are obviously outmoded and

EPA 2.1.4a

ineffective. Professional wisdom, which often fosters effective services, sometimes promotes dysfunctional policies, such as many surgeons' excessive reliance on radical mastectomies, hysterectomies, and heart bypass operations. Policy makers are not immune to societal prejudices and misconceptions as well as fads and presumed panaceas. So policy advocates must subject their policy choices to careful deliberation to minimize the effects of power, tradition, fuzzy intentions, and intuition.

Using a Flowchart to Analyze Some Social Problems in Step 1

It is useful to diagram social problems so that we can develop solutions or ameliorating policies. Flowcharts are particularly useful when seeking policy solutions to social problems that social workers emphasize, such as welfare reform, homelessness, and substance abuse, since they place the problems in a developmental context. Let us begin with an overarching diagram that can be used, in whole or part, to analyze many social problems. Then let us develop a diagram specifically geared to the welfare-to-work problem to show how to apply the overarching diagram to a specific problem.

Using a Flowchart in Step 1

As can be seen in Figure 7.2, our flowchart begins with the context that includes familial, community, and economic factors. The context is identified in numerous places at the periphery of Figure 7.2 because of its importance to social problems and human services.

EPA 2.1.10i

Family members, peers, and social networks powerfully shape how people address their needs, whether they seek organized services, how they respond to organized services, and whether they develop specific problems and how they deal with them. Persons in affluent communities with outstanding schools and services, for example, have a head start compared with those in low-income communities with poor schools, poor housing, and high rates of crime. We should also not forget cultural factors that influence how people define specific problems and whether they seek help from organized institutions and programs.

The cell at the far left of Figure 7.2 represents the prevention arena, which describes persons who have not yet developed a problem such as substance abuse, mental illness, poverty, or diabetes. The prevention arena shows interventions we can use to stop persons from developing such specific problems. We can sometimes identify risk factors that allow us to target interventions that decrease the odds of a specific person developing a specific problem. In some cases, we find out by luck that specific interventions prevent certain problems, such as when medical researchers discovered that the daily intake of small amounts of aspirin lessened persons' likelihood of contracting colon cancer. In other cases, we have no idea how to prevent certain problems, and sometimes considerable controversy exists about the effectiveness of specific interventions. Preventive strategies sometimes require the active involvement of people, for example, changing their lifestyles (such as diet) in an effort to avert a specific social problem. In addition, society sometimes attempts to prevent certain social problems, by instituting changes in peoples' environment, such as decreasing pollutants, improving the safety of automobiles, or preventing cigarette sales to youth.

If we are successful in preventing specific problems, or if some people simply do not develop them, they stay within the preventive arena. People who do develop specific problems move into one of the three cells in the middle of the diagram, which we call the *problem development arenas*.

FIGURE 7.2 An Ecological Model of Social Problems

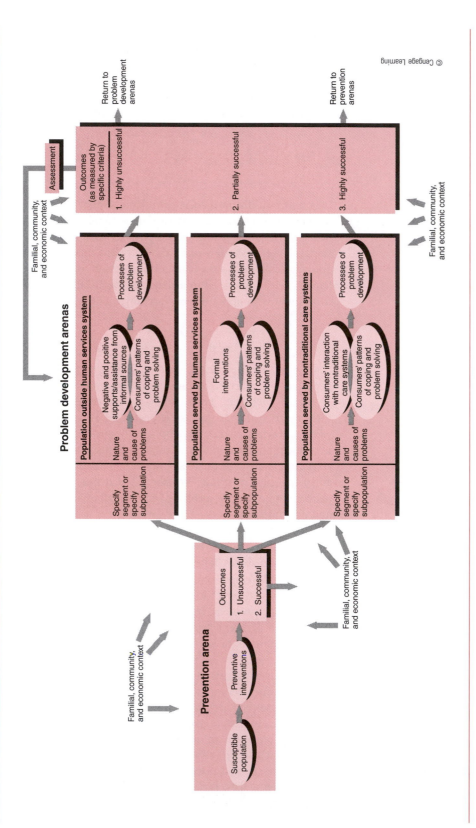

Prior to pursuing a masters degree in social work, I worked with lesbian, gay, bisexual, transgender, queer, and questioning youth (LGBTQQ). I became shocked by the prevalence of homelessness among these youth.

According to a report by the Lambda Legal Defense and Education Fund, LGBTQQ youth make up 20 to 40 percent of the national youth homeless population each year.[1] LGBTQQ youth become homeless for a number of reasons both related and unrelated to their sexual orientation or gender identity. Many become homeless due to forced departure from their homes as a result of family rejection of their sexual orientation or gender identity. In addition, LGBTQQ youth become homeless due to family discord, abuse, neglect, and religious or cultural conflict. Some LGBTQQ homeless youth do not identify as LGBTQQ upon becoming homeless, but discover their identities through exposure to the LGBTQQ community while they are homeless.[2]

After they become homeless, LGBTQQ youth under the age of 18 are funneled into the foster-care system, oftentimes to families who are not affirming their identities. Consequently, many LGBTQQ youth run away from their foster-care placements, beginning an endless cycle in the child welfare system.[3] These youth may be placed in congregate care settings where they are often verbally and physically harassed by youth and/or staff and are unable to access the services they need.[4]

After emancipation from foster care at age 18, a disproportionate number of LGBTQQ youth end up back on the streets.[5] While the experience of homelessness often allows LGBTQQ youth to explore their identities and attain a sense of belonging through membership in the larger LGBTQQ community, they face a number of challenges while they are homeless, including emotional distress, depression, post-traumatic stress disorder (PTSD), suicidal ideation, drug and alcohol abuse, coming out issues, homophobia, and invisibility. They often struggle to come to terms with the withdrawal of love and acceptance from their families. Research shows that these youth are more likely to engage in prostitution and report higher rates of sexual victimization than their heterosexual peers. They are more likely to contract HIV while homeless than heterosexual youth.[6]

Broad-based structural change is needed within the child welfare system to prevent homelessness in this population. First, LGBTQQ family reunification programs must be created. Second, child welfare agencies must offer training for foster parents and child welfare workers to improve their skills in working with this population to promote greater success in placements. Third, child welfare agencies must recruit foster parents interested in helping these youths and create additional LGBTQQ congregate care settings. Fourth, child welfare agencies must offer transitional housing services, life skills training, education, substance abuse treatment and preventive programs, and mental health services. Fifth, child welfare agencies must offer mentorship programs to LGBTQQ homeless youth to help them develop support networks.

[0]C. Sullivan and S. Sommer, "Youth in the Margins: A Report on the Unmet Needs of Lesbian, Gay, Bisexual and Transgender Youth in Foster Care." (New York: Lambda Legal Defense and Education Fund, 2001).

[0]S. Pendergast, G. A. Dunne, and D. Telford, "A Story of 'Difference,' A Different Story: Young Homeless, Lesbian, Gay, and Bisexual People," *The International Journal of Sociology and Social Policy*, Vol. 21, 2001, 4–6, 64.

[0]National Center for Lesbian Rights, *LGBTQQ Youth in the Foster Care System.* Retrieved March 1, 2006, from http://www.nclrights.org

[0]M. Freundlich and R. J. Avery, "Gay and Lesbian Youth in Foster Care: Meeting Their Placement and Service Needs," *Journal of Gay and Lesbian Social Services*, Vol. 17, 2005, 4.

[0]G. P. Mallon, "There's No Place Like Home: Achieving Safety, Permanency, and Well-Being for Lesbian and Gay Adolescents in Out-of-Home Care Settings," *Child Welfare*, Vol. 51, 2002, 2.

[0]R. C. Savin-Williams, "The Disclosure to Families of Same-Sex Attractions by Lesbian, Gay, and Bisexual Youths," *Journal of Research on Adolescence*, Vol. 8, 1998, pp. 49–68.

(continued)

Policy Advocacy Challenge 7.2 *(continued)*

Social workers are uniquely able to design and deliver these preventive services in the child welfare system to prevent many LGBTQQ youth from becoming homeless. See Policy Advocacy Challenge Video 7.2 in which Jessica Van Tuyl discusses prevention strategies for LGBTQQ youth. Discuss the following:

- Causes of homelessness in this population
- Remedies that Jessica Van Tuyl identifies both from reunification within the child welfare system and through services given to homeless youth

- The top-middle cell describes persons who remain outside the orbit of all organized systems of care. To the extent they get help from others, it is from family and neighborhood members, persons at their place of employment, the clergy, and others in their support systems.
- The middle-middle cell describes organized systems of care, such as social agencies, hospitals, clinics, schools, job-training programs, and professionals.
- The bottom-middle cell describes programs that operate on an empowerment or self-help perspective such as Alcoholics Anonymous, programs for persons who are physically challenged, and community-based programs for persons with persistent mental problems.

This distinction between those who remain outside institutions and programs and those who remain in them is critical to understanding social policy. In many cases, only a small percentage of persons with specific problems actually seek organized services for them. For example, huge numbers of persons with mental illness, medical problems, poverty, reading disorders, and delinquency are not helped by organized institutions and programs—because they do not know about them, they believe they are not eligible, they do not want to present a stigmatized condition to others, they drop out of services, or they do not perceive themselves as having a problem.

We should not prematurely conclude that persons outside the orbit of organized programs do not cope with or even solve their problems. Many people solve problems on their own or with help from support networks in their own communities, and a certain number of people, such as substance abusers, mature out of their problems over the course of time.

Yet some persons clearly harm themselves by not using organized programs. People with diabetes or cancer, for example, may die from their malady if they do not get medical help—as may persons with clinical depression. Persons with severe reading disorders are unlikely to deal with their condition without assistance. It is important to ask why some people do not avail themselves of organized programs. Some people lack the resources needed to use organized programs as in the case of medically uninsured Americans. Some may not know about organized services, and others may be given services that they perceive to be intrusive, demeaning, or ineffective. Finally, organized services may be so severely underfunded that people cannot gain access to them, as is true with substance abuse counseling.

Other people do use organized services and programs to address specific problems, either voluntarily or because they are required or coerced into using them by judges or correctional systems. Voluntary entrants use organized services because they want assistance with specific problems and believe that organized services can help them. To understand how they fare during such service transactions, we need to understand not only what is provided to them, but how other factors (such as family and support networks, economic conditions, and peer factors) shape how they perceive and benefit from services.

Involuntary entrants are forced to get certain services, often by the courts, which require persons to use them to avoid incarceration or other penalties. Implied, stated, or perceived threats can also lead some persons to seek services, such as a parent who fears that he or she will lose custody of his or her children if he or she does not solve a substance abuse problem or accept services from a child welfare agency.

Some people turn not to organized programs, but to programs or activities that use a self-help or empowerment paradigm. Examples include community-based programs to help physically, mentally, or developmentally challenged persons, Alcoholics Anonymous, and community-based programs that help people purchase their own houses. In each of these cases, people have problems, physical disabilities, substance abuse, or poverty, but these programs focus on persons' strengths in dealing with them. (Many programs that help physically challenged persons do not even use terms such as *disability*, *clients*, *patients*, or *diagnosis* because they view them as disempowering them.) They want to mobilize people's existing skills and motivation or help develop them. For example, asset-building programs operate under the assumption that poverty can best be averted by helping persons obtain assets, such as houses or savings accounts, that middle- and upper-class people commonly use to advance their well-being. These empowerment programs not only use different language and different strategies, but they are not structured like traditional social agencies. They are more likely to have informal organizational structures and less likely to have charts on their clients. In addition, their staff are less likely to be credentialed professionals.

Consider the case of a self-help agency that assists persons with persistent mental problems such as schizophrenia. Psychiatrists, mental institutions, and professional counselors comprise the central thrust of traditional mental health services. By contrast, community-based programs with an empowerment perspective aim to inculcate problem-solving skills in persons with persistent mental problems. They may provide them with low-cost housing, encourage them to seek employment while providing job training and referral services, and give them skills to develop social supports such as going to specific organized activities. They are taught to monitor their medications so that they can seek technical assistance when certain symptoms emerge. The community-based program establishes an advisory council, comprising persons with persistent mental problems, to develop additional empowerment strategies.

Typologies Within the Middle Cells   It is important to remember that populations with specific problems are not homogeneous in the prevention. Indeed, considerable evidence suggests that specific interventions often do not work for many people, who may respond to different approaches. Later we discuss in more detail, using welfare reform as our example, how policy advocates need to develop typologies identifying subgroups within a larger population that possesses a specific problem.

Relationships Among the Cells   People move among the three cells in the middle of Figure 7.2 in interesting and complex ways. For example, someone may begin in organized services, drop out of them, and then be helped by a community-based empowerment program. Someone else may solve a problem with the assistance of family members and move back into the prevention arena. Or people can use organized institutions and empowerment programs simultaneously, such as when a physically challenged person uses traditional health services while getting help from a community-based organization run by physically challenged people (see Policy Advocacy Challenge 7.3).

An important issue in social policy is whether the organized system of services can successfully draw upon family and neighborhood resources (the top-middle cell in Figure 7.2) or the work of agencies using an empowerment paradigm (the bottom-middle cell). It would seem advisable for social agencies, for example, to use community leaders and caregivers, such as barbers and beauticians, to refer cases (such as depressed persons) to

Policy Advocacy Challenge 7.3

Diagramming a Social Problem in Step 1

Bruce Jansson, Ph.D.

Take a social problem that interests you and diagram it following the format of Figure 7.2. Be certain to include the prevention arena and persons who are not part of and do receive help from the organized service-delivery system. What does this exercise teach about the following?

- The relative numbers of persons who remain outside the human services system
- The roles of families, communities, and self-help groups
- The potential promise of preventive strategies
- The sheer number of outcomes that are possible for clients, patients, and consumers of service
- The sheer number of policies that influence whether and how persons move through and access the organized human services system

trained professionals working in agencies and even to use them to give therapeutic services that supplement professional ones. It would also seem logical for organized systems of care to organize support networks for persons with mental and other problems, since considerable research suggests that persons with social supports fare better than many others in addressing their problems.

However, these courses of action need to be taken with the awareness of certain risks, as a number of researchers and theorists suggest. Social supports are not always helpful to clients, such as when dysfunctional relationships exist within them that may even exacerbate someone's problems. When family and neighborhood persons relate to professionals, they may lose their natural way of relating to a client. It takes time for professionals to organize and relate to community and family supports, and it is not always clear how to do it.

Nor is it easy for organized systems of care to relate to empowerment-focused programs such as those for persons who are physically challenged. Empowerment-focused groups are often suspicious of professionals, such as physicians, who they believe label them and treat them paternalistically. They may fear overmedication and excessive use of surgery. In some cases, traditional organized systems of care incorporate units or programs with an empowerment perspective, such as a birthing clinic in a hospital that uses midwives and places less emphasis on traditional medical ways of delivering babies.

Assessment of Outcomes   On the far right side of Figure 7.2, *outcomes* are depicted. Successful outcomes can include eradicating a problem or lessening its severity or impact. If we use an empowerment approach, successful outcomes would include mobilizing persons' personal strengths to allow them to cope with specific issues in their lives or overcome such challenges as physical disability. Unsuccessful outcomes can include failure to solve or redress a problem or develop personal coping strategies. We sometimes try to assess the effectiveness of specific programs by using techniques of program evaluation, either quantitative or qualitative approaches as we discuss in more detail in Chapter Fourteen.

Illustrating a Flowchart with Welfare Reform

We will illustrate a flowchart with the welfare-to-work issue. We do not have to use all the cells in Figure 7.2 because we focus on organized systems of care in this case; we use only the prevention arena, the center-middle cell, and the right-hand cell (see Figure 7.3).

By way of background, recall that President Bill Clinton and Congress revolutionized the American welfare system when they approved the Personal Responsibility and Work

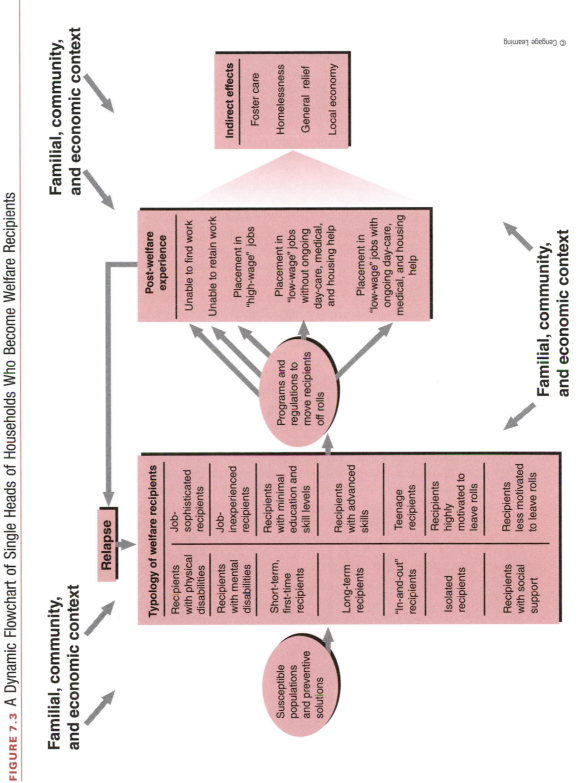

FIGURE 7.3 A Dynamic Flowchart of Single Heads of Households Who Become Welfare Recipients

Opportunity Reconciliation Act in 1996. It replaced Aid to Families with Dependent Children (AFDC) with state-run welfare programs to be funded by a combination of federal block-grant funds and state resources. (Grants under the new state-run program were called Temporary Assistance for Needy Families [TANF] grants.) The legislation ceded virtually all decisions to the states. Only prohibiting them from reducing their current spending on welfare more than 20 percent, it even allowed them not to fund welfare for specific families if the state's allotted funds ran out, to replace cash payments with in-kind assistance (such as food items), and not to provide fair hearings if recipients believed their rights had been violated.[2]

Rather than establishing statewide rules, as under the AFDC program, states could let each of their counties establish their own programs drawing on state block-grant funds. The federal government did not add significant training and day-care funds to the federal block-grant funds. The legislation also cut food stamp allotments deeply, ended welfare payments under the Supplementary Security Income (SSI) program for legal immigrants, and proposed the removal of many disabled children from SSI rolls. This welfare reform legislation set in motion developments that would profoundly shape the well-being of millions of women and their children, requiring 50 percent of single-parent recipients to be participating in work or work-related activities by the year 2002.

Welfare reform is an excellent example of how policymakers analyze social problems, using such methods as quantitative research. Yet it also demonstrates that perceptions of social problems, as well as proposed solutions, are profoundly shaped by such nonrational factors as values, culture, and politics. Indeed, persons with radical, liberal, and conservative perspectives disagreed sharply about the advisability of the welfare reform legislation. Certainly, these divergent perspectives will come into play whenever Congress reauthorizes welfare legislation in the coming years.

We use welfare reform throughout this chapter as a case example of policymaking in the United States. It demonstrates that policy advocates must assert their analyses of social problems, lest other analyses prevail.

Figure 7.3 presents a flowchart of single heads of households who are susceptible to joining welfare rolls, who currently use welfare, or who have left welfare rolls. It includes various *stages of development*, as seen from an analysis of the model from the left to the right, moving from a susceptible population not yet using welfare to an array of users of welfare to former users who have left the rolls. Policy advocates are also interested in understanding the *dynamics* of a problem, such as patterns of movement between the different phases as depicted in Figure 7.3 by arrows between the different stages. They might ask, for example, what percentage of susceptible persons actually seek and obtain welfare benefits, what percentage of recipients obtain jobs and for how long, how many recipients leave the welfare rolls permanently, what percentage of former recipients find themselves with a net income lower or higher than when they were on the welfare rolls, and how many recipients move repeatedly between welfare and work during a brief period.

A typology of welfare recipients can classify them with respect to their manifestations, chronicity, and demographic characteristics (see the center portion of Figure 7.3, titled "Typology of welfare recipients"). *Manifestations* are outward behaviors, symptoms, or characteristics that differentiate people with specific problems. They are widely used to establish typologies of illness in medicine and mental health, as illustrated by the diseases and illnesses listed in any medical encyclopedia or in the *DSM-IV* to become *DSM-V in 2013*.[3]

We can develop a typology of welfare recipients based on such characteristics as whether they have extensive or little job experience, whether they possess job-related skills, and the extent of their education. Or we could establish categories based on recipients' views about job seeking, such as "discouraged job seekers versus optimistic job seekers."[4]

Policy advocates often examine the *chronicity* of problems. For example, welfare recipients can be classified as chronic users, in-and-out or oscillating users, brief onetime users, and occasional users.

By using manifestations, chronicity, and demographic factors, policy analysts develop typologies of persons who have a specific problem. Typologies are useful because they make clear that populations with a specific problem are not homogeneous and consist of specific subgroups with distinguishing characteristics. Some single heads of households who receive welfare, for example, have had extensive working experience, and others have never been employed. Some of them are teenagers, and others are considerably older. Some have physical or mental disabilities, and others have no disabilities. Some are highly educated, and others have not completed the eighth grade.

Policy Advocacy Challenge 7.4

Developing a Typology of Homeless Persons in Step 1

Anne Milder, MSW

When my fellow students and I were required to advocate for the homeless in Los Angeles and Orange counties as part of our first-year policy sequence at University of Southern California School of Social Work, many of us followed the individual passions that had influenced our decision to become social workers. For instance, a student previously interested in women's rights looked at homeless women, another previously interested in LGBTQQ youth looked at homeless LGBTQQ youth, and as I was previously interested in young children, I investigated the needs of and services offered to homeless children, ages 0–5, in Los Angeles county and the policies that govern them.

As social work students, we knew that the face of homelessness is quite different from the cliché, more than the popular image of the disheveled and smelly old man living on a park bench, taking swigs from a bottle, and too lazy to work. We knew that the population is multifaceted, and we soon became aware that describing our particular homeless population of interest, their numbers and needs, and the policies affecting their status is important, in order to think about advocating for them and, ultimately, developing preventive strategies and securing services for them.

It took us, or at least me, longer to understand that any discussion of the subgroups under the umbrella of the term *homelessness* assumes that there is a uniform working definition of homelessness, a commonly agreed-upon definition. How homelessness is defined is a legal and political battle in and of itself. The legal definition of homelessness determines literally who is counted, how monies are distributed, and who is eligible for support and services. Thus, an essential point of advocacy must be to determine the legal definition of who is homeless.

The legal definition of homelessness varies across federal law and is currently the subject of much political debate. A USC professor indicated that there are something like 14 different federal definitions of homelessness. But, as Barbara Duffield, policy director at the National Association for the Education of Homeless Children and Youth, indicated to me, "what is at issue is not so much the number of definitions, but the extreme limitation of the HUD definition of homelessness." According to the HUD website, "[g]enerally speaking, homeless individuals and families are those who are sleeping in places not meant for human habitation, such as cars, parks, sidewalks, and abandoned buildings, or those who are sleeping in an emergency shelter as a primary nighttime residence."

While the HUD definition may sound perfectly reasonable (homeless people lack homes), it excludes many homeless subgroups, and it disproportionately excludes families and children. Unlike the education subtitle of the McKinney-Vento Act, the HUD definition excludes those who are living with relatives or friends (commonly called "doubled-up"), those who are

(continued)

"couch surfing" (moving from the home of one relative or friend to another), and those living in motels or hotels because they lack other options. As a result, the HUD definition excludes a number of families who opt not to live on the streets, for child safety reasons, or to avoid the involvement of child-protective services, or, as in the city of Los Angeles, because public policy prevents them from doing so (the new policy of the Los Angeles Board of Supervisors is one of "zero tolerance" for families on skid row).

When designing programs and services, of course, one cannot simply assume that all homeless people need the same services or even that all homeless people need shelter. When touring skid row, we were told that certain individuals refuse shelter because the shelter regulations are more than they can endure. One homeless individual said that he just wanted to live as he is, on the street; he did not want any more people trying to help; he thought a section of the city should be available for those wanting to live unhoused. Yet, there are various subgroups of homeless people, and if we treat them all as one homogeneous group, the needs of many will be neglected. An elderly woman recently homeless due to the lack of affordable housing will need different services from a pregnant teen kicked out of her parents' home, or from a veteran with PTSD. If public officials limit homelessness to only one type of person, then only one type of homeless person will be served. The HUD definition is so limited that it focuses services only on one type of persons, chronically homeless persons.

Since I am biased toward the care of young children, I, of course, am advocating that the current HUD definition be made more inclusive.

Typologies are useful for several reasons. Because they divide people with specific social problems into smaller subgroups, they force policy practitioners to develop an array of interventions rather than relying on a single approach.[5]

Indeed, many theorists in social marketing contend that policy advocates must segment populations into smaller groups, much as we have done in Figure 7.3.[6] As these theorists identify smaller groups, they can use so-called focus groups to find out what kinds of services or resources the members of these groups believe they need. A policy advocate forms a focus group of five to eight people who fit into a subgroup such as those in Figure 7.3, choosing people who are likely to articulate the needs of this subgroup.

A policy advocate develops five or six broad questions framed to capture the subgroup people's definitions of their problems and the interventions that they believe will be effective. He or she poses the questions, allowing 15 to 25 minutes of discussion per question and carefully eliciting the views of all group members. Taking careful notes or recording the session, he or she analyzes the group's responses at a later time to develop policies and programs geared to this group's needs[7] (see Policy Advocacy Challenge 7.5).

Typologies also facilitate evaluations of programs and policies. A welfare-to-work program may be highly successful with a specific subgroup, such as highly educated recipients who have had prior work experience, but may have poor rates of success with less educated recipients with scant work experience. Were policy practitioners to rely on global evaluations of welfare-to-work recipients, they would fail to detect variations between subgroups, thwarting efforts to propose strategies designed to address their specific needs.

Typologies also allow policy practitioners to establish priorities. If research suggests that certain subgroups are most likely to become long-term users of welfare, for example, state authorities can prioritize programs to assist them. Typologies help us understand not only welfare populations but also people who have other social problems, such as mental illness, poverty, child abuse, and marital discord.

**Policy
Advocacy
Challenge 7.5**

**A Focus
Group in
Action in
Step 1**

Bruce Jansson,
Ph.D.

A social worker wants to establish outpatient services for older citizens in a major hospital but wants to obtain their perspectives. She segments this population into ambulatory but relatively healthy older people and those with more acute rather than chronic conditions. Realizing that older people in her hospital's service area are Caucasian and Asian, she draws well older people from these two groups to form two focus groups.

The social worker develops the following broad questions:

1. What kinds of medical problems or issues do you (well older people) have?
2. Where do you currently receive outpatient medical services?
3. What problems do you experience with the services that you currently receive?
4. If you could establish the ideal outpatient agency for well older people, what would it be like?
5. What dangers or pitfalls would you advise the staff of this outpatient agency to avoid?

The policy advocate gains important insights from the older people she has consulted. For example, she finds that they value continuity of care (i.e., having a regular doctor) more than promptness of service.

Armed with insights from her use of focus groups, she develops a proposal for outpatient services that she hopes will be accepted by the hospital's board of directors.

EXERCISE

Now imagine that you are conducting a focus group with evacuees from the Ninth Ward of New Orleans, and you want to know what they would want in terms of amenities and quality of life to induce them to return to New Orleans from another city. Develop a set of questions that you might ask.

Of course, typologies are not a panacea, as we discuss at more length later. Critics may ask, for example, whether the subgroups in Figure 7.3 are mutually exclusive, since welfare recipients often fall into several of them. Persons who construct typologies often encounter a dilemma regarding the breadth of their categories. If relatively few categories are used, it is difficult to develop specialized programs that focus on the needs of specific subgroups. If too many categories are used, policy practitioners may fail to see the commonalities of persons in different subgroups, such as the common problems that welfare recipients confront as they enter job markets.[8] In the case of mental health typologies, such as those in the *DSM-IV*, many critics wonder whether some of the categories have been invented by psychiatrists or actually describe existing mental conditions.[9]

Analyzing the Causes of Social Problems in Step 1

EP 2.1.10d

Problems are caused by physiological, personal, familial, community, and societal factors. (See Box 7.1 for various causes of welfare dependency.) Welfare dependency is linked to such personal and familial factors as levels of education, job-related experiences, family size, whether a woman has been divorced or widowed or has had children out of wedlock, how much child support a woman receives, personal orientations toward welfare, the physical or mental disabilities of a head of household, and whether a woman has a child or children with disabilities.[10] These personal factors operate not only singly but also together to cause welfare dependency. A woman's risk of welfare dependency

BOX **7.1**   **Some Causes of Welfare Dependency**

- Physiological and mental causes
- Physical disabilities
- Developmental disabilities
- Mental disabilities
- Personal and familial causes
- Age (e.g., teenage mothers)
- Educational deficits
- Skill deficits
- Lack of work experience
- Lack of role models that facilitate job entry
- Lack of child support
- Subjection to abuse by spouse or others
- Environmental causes
- Lack of jobs in local area
- Lack of jobs in local area that pay sufficiently to allow economic independence
- Lack of job placement and training programs
- Lack of public or subsidized transportation to job sites
- Discrimination by employers against welfare recipients
- Competition for scarce jobs from other people, such as unemployed persons, new job entrants, persons reentering the labor force, and immigrants
- Interacting causes placing some people at higher risk of welfare dependency
- Persons associated with two of the preceding at-risk factors
- Persons associated with three of the preceding at-risk factors
- Persons associated with four or more of the preceding at-risk factors

increases, for example, if she is the single head of a household, does not receive child support, and has a child with disabilities.

Welfare is also shaped by a host of community factors, such as rates of unemployment, wage levels, the availability of child care, the receptivity of employers to hiring welfare recipients, and the availability of transportation and job-training programs.[11] The likelihood of high rates of welfare in a community increases as multiple factors interact, such as low-wage employment, unavailability of day care, and high rates of unemployment.

Various personal, familial, and environmental factors often act together to place some people in higher-risk categories than persons who are exposed to only one factor. A woman may experience short-term risk, for example, when her husband leaves, rendering her economically dependent on government programs. But her chances of securing employment that pays enough to allow her to leave the welfare rolls increase if she has prior work experience, has a college degree, lives in a neighborhood with expanding economic opportunities, and has access to affordable transportation and child care. By contrast, a woman who lacks all these advantages and who is also left by her husband is less likely to find employment that pays enough to make her economically independent.

Policy advocates use both quantitative and qualitative research to analyze the causes of specific problems. Four approaches are common. First, they compare persons with a social problem with those who do not have it, to infer from their differences why only certain persons develop the problem. Because welfare dependency is strongly associated with single-parent families, for example, we can infer that persons in families with single wage are more vulnerable to poverty, and welfare, than those in families with dual wages.[12] Second, they follow people through time to discover why they develop a problem, such as following teen women to discern why some of them become pregnant and join welfare rolls. To conduct the second kind of research is more difficult, because it requires gathering data at many intervals from participants who must agree to participate for an extended period.[13] Third, they evaluate existing programs to find clues to a problem's causes. If recipients who received ongoing and substantial daycare subsidies after they left the rolls have lower rates of recidivism than those who did not receive them, policy practitioners can surmise that daycare expenses force many women onto the rolls.[14] Fourth, they get information directly from persons who are experiencing a specific problem, by observing (as in anthropological studies) or interviewing them.[15]

Rather than limiting ourselves to examining the immediate causes of welfare dependency, we can analyze a sequence of factors that causes dependency. If low wages cause welfare dependency for many single mothers, for example, we can ask what causes low wages. If many poverty-stricken inner-city persons do not live near job sites, we can ask what caused residential segregation by race and social class. The answers to these kinds of questions force us to consider social reforms that might address the economic and social forces that ultimately cause welfare dependency, such as raising the minimum wage or securing housing for low-income persons in suburban areas, where jobs are increasingly located.[16]

When researchers examine the causes of social problems, their perspectives influence their work, such as whether they emphasize personal, psychological, economic, biological, or environmental causes. Researchers with *public health* or *ecological perspectives* emphasize occupational, economic, familial, peer, and neighborhood factors.[17] When examining the causes of welfare, for example, these researchers implicate low-wage industries, the sheer cost of day care, the lack of transportation, and the placement of many jobs in suburban areas that are distant from inner-city residents. They also cite discrimination against welfare recipients by many employers.

EPA 2.1.4b

Persons with *radical perspectives* implicate economic and social inequalities, the reduced economic opportunities of certain populations, and the practices of corporations as causes of specific social problems.[18] With the globalization of the economy, for example, corporations often place their factories in low-wage nations in the developing world, thereby eliminating jobs in the United States that might have employed some welfare recipients. In addition, corporations have often relocated their plants to suburban sites, making it difficult for inner-city residents to get to them. Corporations stand to benefit, moreover, from welfare reforms that force hundreds of thousands of people into the competition for jobs, allowing them to depress wages even further for relatively unskilled persons.

Analysts who use *medical* or *disease models* explore the physiological factors associated with specific problems.[19] Considerable numbers of welfare recipients are disabled or must care for children with disabilities. Medical or disease models dominate the medical and, increasingly, mental health fields, where physiological and pharmaceutical causes and solutions dominate.

Persons who emphasize *intrapsychic factors* explore personal and familial causes of social problems. Some researchers contend, for example, that teen pregnancy is often caused by a constellation of personal and familial dynamics, such as abusive parents, truancy, and poor school performance.

In a departure from traditional approaches, some persons adhere to *behavioral frameworks*, contending that certain social problems can be redressed only by providing rewards and disincentives that make welfare less attractive than employment. Persons who favor disincentives advocate reducing the levels of welfare grants or requiring teen mothers to live with their parents except when they are abused by them. Persons who favor rewards often favor allowing recipients to retain some assistance from the government even after they leave welfare so that their postwelfare income will exceed their welfare income.

Some people emphasize *deterrent strategies* that penalize persons with social problems. Deterrents might include time limits for welfare or ending welfare altogether for certain groups of persons, such as legal immigrants.

These different approaches often cause vigorous debates among theorists, analysts, and researchers. Persons who implicate economic and environmental factors often contend that counseling is an ineffective strategy. Radicals contend that, without remedying the inequalities in American society and the stress that poverty causes, many social problems cannot be significantly alleviated. Contending groups often selectively cite research evidence to support specific remedies and attack the proposals of persons who use different paradigms.

These various frameworks and causal factors are not mutually exclusive, because various causes interact. Sophisticated policy practitioners and theorists believe that social problems are caused by an array of factors that combine the traditional approaches.[20] The risk of dependency increases when someone has not completed high school, has had no prior work experience, lives in a geographic area with high unemployment, has been subjected to parental abuse, and is sexually victimized by an older male. Such theorists as William Julius Wilson analyze these kinds of intersecting factors that shape complex phenomena such as welfare dependency.[21] Indeed, policy advocates should take leading roles in critiquing social policies that are premised on simplistic analyses of social problems.

Developing Interventions and Programs in Step 1

EPA 2.1.8a

Having established a typology and analyzed causation, policy advocates devise interventions to solve specific social problems. They develop curative strategies and preventive programs, measure the prevalence of specific problems, and conduct research to locate persons with specific problems.

Some policy initiatives emphasize a deterrent approach, but many policy advocates favor a public health and radical approach. Single women have children for many reasons, due to coerced sex, lack of knowledge of contraception, a desire for companionship, or a desire to form a family unit. (In many cases, women believe that the father of the children will remain part of the family, only to find that he deserts, divorces, or fails to marry the mother of his children.) Research does not suggest that a diminution of welfare benefits markedly diminishes the number of single-headed families because women do not base childbirth decisions primarily on economic calculations.[22]

Once women do have children and once they are single heads of households, economic realities force them into poverty when they confront low-wage jobs and the sheer cost of day care, transportation, health care, and housing. Many of them realize from personal experience or from discussions with other women who have tried that they cannot support their families with income from low-wage jobs. So, many women stay on the rolls for extended periods or resort to on-and-off patterns as they enter and leave jobs that cannot finance their basic needs. Many women who cannot obtain sufficient money to support their families do not, or cannot, return to welfare because of lifetime limits in the TANF legislation. The decision to seek welfare in these economic circumstances is often a meritorious strategy used by women who care about their children enough to want them to have sufficient food, clothing, medical care, and housing.[23]

What is needed, then, is not deterrence but a constructive approach to make work pay enough to (at least) bring families to a poverty standard. This can be accomplished by giving all families in the lowest economic quintile in-kind help through day care, health care, and housing subsidies that continues as long as families remain below the poverty level. These in-kind subsidies need to be supplemented by direct income subsidies, such as an expanded earned income tax credit (EITC) that gives families tax rebates as long as they remain below the poverty level.

Programs that help people employed at low wages to upgrade their earning potential are also needed. Persons with minimal skills and limited education must be prepared for jobs that are geared to their abilities and must receive sophisticated job placement services. To the extent that their skills and education can be enhanced to improve their long-term prospects, they should receive extended services, education, and job training. Some recipients need help moving to areas with less unemployment and those with disabilities might need jobs geared to their capabilities.

Even these remedies, however, ignore the reality of growing inequality in the wage structure of the United States. Dramatic increases in the minimum wage, as well as an increase in the power of American trade unions, are needed to raise wage levels for low-wage workers whose economic status has been eclipsed by the dramatic growth of wages for highly skilled and educated workers. Many advocates participate in a movement to require "living wages" in jobs that flow from government contracts.

Another set of interventions must be directed to employers in the private and public sectors. It is tempting to portray private employers as villains, but it is understandable that they would try to fill specific slots with job seekers who already have the requisite skills and job experience, which many welfare recipients do not possess. Without economic incentives for employers to hire them, many welfare recipients will not get jobs except during booming economic periods, and they are likely to be the first persons laid off when the nation enters a recession.[24] Moreover, federal, state, and local governments must create large numbers of public service jobs and retain them as long as the private sector does not absorb welfare recipients. These public service positions are needed particularly by recipients who are physically or mentally challenged. The government also ought to offer massive tax incentives to corporations that locate in low-wage areas, rather than the minor incentives offered under the current tax code.

Of course, booming economic growth will reduce the welfare rolls in some states even without these ameliorative policies. It will make deterrent strategies appear successful in the short term because employers, facing labor shortages, will hire many welfare recipients into low-wage jobs and will even promote some of them into moderate-paying ones. In the long term, however, the deterrent approach to welfare is not likely to be effective because it does not upgrade the skills and education of recipients; consequently, they will be vulnerable to layoffs when economic growth slows. Services and policies tailored to the needs of specific subgroups are needed rather than a single set of policies (see Policy Advocacy Challenge 7.6).

To protect the rights of single heads of households and safeguard their children, the welfare reforms of 1996 should have included a *bill of rights* for welfare recipients. If they participate in activities that prepare them for work, diligently seek employment, and secure employment, they should not fall beneath poverty standards or the combined AFDC, food stamp, housing, and health benefits that welfare recipients received just before the enactment of welfare reforms. The bill of rights is

Policy Advocacy Challenge 7.6

Designing Services for Homeless Children in Step 1

Anne Milder, MSW

When I learned, last December, that I, like every other first year MSW student at the University of Southern California School of Social Work, would be required to advocate for a specific homeless population in Los Angeles or Orange counties, to do real policy analysis and advocacy, I complained and I complained loudly. *This was not what I had signed up for when I enrolled in the program; I just wanted to be a practitioner, working with infants and toddlers and their mothers. How could I, a student, know enough to tackle a problem as large and seemingly unsolvable as homelessness? Besides, wasn't it obvious that the homeless just needed homes? I couldn't provide houses....* The task felt not only unrelated to the conceptualization of social work practice I held at the time, but, worse, it seemed like a futile exercise.

Given my ongoing interest in young children, from the prenatal stage through age five, and the crucial brain development that takes place at this juncture (and its interrelationship, at least according to the postulations of affective neurobiology, with attachments to primary caregivers), I chose homeless children under the age of five as my area of focus.

None of my roughly 250 fellow students were looking at the 0–5 age range, and, in my studies, I was surprised to discover the many ways in which the 0–5 age homeless population is commonly overlooked. For instance, at the time I began my analysis, I was told that First 5 LA, a public institution created by funds from Proposition 10 in Los Angeles County by a statewide ballot initiative designed to increase and improve services for children 0–5, had not yet designed programs specifically for homeless children. Also, I was told that LAUP, the institution created by First 5 LA to promote universal preschool, was not yet specifically thinking about preschool issues for homeless children. And I was told that ICARE, a network coordinated by the Department of Mental Health, specializing in children from birth to five years of age, had not yet concentrated on homeless children. I was told that many frontline staff in local schools do not understand the McKinney-Vento definition of homelessness and do not know that children who are "doubled-up" with other relatives or friends are legally homeless. Most surprising to me was that the homeless count often did not include these children or lumped them in a broader group of youth from birth to age 18, thus not recognizing them as a subgroup with its own needs.

I believe this is a particularly good example of just how subtle, insidious, and pervasive is the prejudice embodied by the HUD definition of homelessness. Even though I had come to USC precisely because of my interest in young children, studied the work of Emmi Pikler's Budapest orphanage the summer before starting school, and spent the first semester thinking about relief efforts for young children relocated to Los Angeles due to Hurricane Katrina, I had never thought of children as homeless persons, even though many orphans and Katrina children evacuees become homeless.

Without knowing the depth of the problem, in terms of numbers, it was difficult to do a full analysis and advocate for services. I was, however, able to speak with the Department of Mental Health, specifically the coordinators of their 0–5 program group, and propose the possibility that my School of Social Work might survey their providers to see how many homeless children they serve and determine the needs of those children. (Perhaps some students from next year's policy class will take on this task.) I was able to propose to the Los Angeles County McKinney-Vento Coordinator that a question be asked on the intake forms at all schools about the ages of all siblings, a practice I was told by those working at the controversial Pappas School in Phoenix, Arizona, is very good for identifying younger, homeless siblings who are not yet in school. Via my professor, Ralph Fertig, I was able to advocate to the Los Angeles Homeless Services Agency (LAHSA) that homeless children 0–5 be included as a separate category in the next homeless count and also that the count adopt a broader definition of homelessness, substituting the McKinney-Vento definition for the HUD definition.

It now seems obvious to me that these children are part of at least two vulnerable populations. Not only are they children, thus not voters or adults with a vote or a voice, but they are homeless, another usually voiceless population, and many of them are homeless in a way not recognized or counted by HUD.

What I learned stirred me enormously, both emotionally and intellectually. These homeless children, and all children, exist within a continuum of nested systems, from the family system, the community systems, to the sociopolitical systems. To do the work I originally envisioned when enrolling in an MSW program, to work with young children and their mothers and to work at bettering those relationships, I must also become a policy advocate.

Having identified the number and location of these children, we must then go to the next step and design services that will speak to their needs and prevent them from becoming homeless in the first place.

needed to prevent the victimization of recipients by states that push recipients into poverty by insisting they take low-wage jobs, while cutting off the child care, health, housing, and transportation.

Developing Preventive Programs in Step 1

Both Figures 7.2 and 7.3 show prevention arenas at their left edges. Prevention is akin to apple pie and motherhood, yet Americans devote scant resources to the prevention of most social problems, including the need for welfare. The challenge is to find preventive strategies that are sufficiently effective for funders to devote resources to them.

EPA 2.1.10i

The Promise of Prevention We should make a distinction at the outset among primary, secondary, and tertiary prevention. We emphasize primary prevention in Figures 7.2 and 7.3 because it prevents persons from experiencing important problems in the first place. Were we to prevent some people from ever getting cancer by cutting use of pesticides, for example, we would achieve *primary* prevention. In *secondary* prevention, persons with a specific problem are given assistance in its early stages, thus averting a full-blown or serious problem. When medical and mental health screening problems locate persons with early-stage cancer or early-stage depression, for example, they can avert life-threatening cancer and depression through early interventions, even though they failed to prevent cancer and depression altogether. *Tertiary* prevention aims to arrest a well-developed problem by using interventions that stop it from evolving further into a catastrophic condition. For example, the progression of clinical depression can often be stopped in persons treated with new medications as compared with persons who receive only counseling. (We can now update Figures 7.2 and 7.3 by noting that, although primary prevention occurs in the left-most circle, secondary and tertiary prevention occur in the middle circles of the diagram as persons are engaged with organized services or with community-based empowerment programs.)

Many preventive strategies have been shown to be effective at primary, secondary, and tertiary levels. With respect to primary prevention, for example, we know that lifestyle changes such as exercise, reduction of fat intake, reduction of alcohol consumption beneath certain thresholds, and weight control can markedly change health and mental health outcomes. We know that the requirement that automobile riders use seat belts and that bicycle and motorcycle riders use helmets have saved tens of thousands of lives. We have good evidence that Head Start improves school performance years after children have graduated from it. We know that educational credentials, such as a community college or a college degree, markedly increase earnings (and therefore reduce poverty) in succeeding years. With respect to secondary and tertiary prevention, we have good evidence that early treatment stops the progression of an array of medical, mental health, school, and job performance problems.

All these examples share certain characteristics. Research had established links between specific causal factors and specific problems. Prevention interventions could be targeted to persons with identifiable at-risk factors, such as obesity, sedentary lifestyles, poor diets, and lack of educational credentials, thus allowing society to focus its interventions on persons with these at-risk characteristics. Or, in the case of seat belts, society targeted everyone who rides in cars with clear evidence that the preventive intervention, seat belts, would increase the percentage of persons who survive car accidents. In each case, the cost of prevention was not so prohibitive that opponents could contend that society could not afford it.

Yet the promise of prevention is often unfulfilled. Certain interventions are poorly funded and implemented even when data suggest their effectiveness. Relatively few resources are devoted to helping persons make lifestyle changes, for example, even when sedentary lifestyles and obesity are strongly linked to various diseases and shortened life expectancy. We often invest too little money in programs that might prevent poverty, such as tutoring and preschool programs.

We lack good research on some preventive strategies, such as whether we can prevent many mental health problems from occurring in the first place. We do not yet know whether certain asset-building strategies actually work in the long term, such as helping low-income persons to establish savings accounts or own their own homes, though early results are promising. Therefore, we need to examine an array of factors that impede greater emphasis on prevention.

We can decrease economic dependency as well as poverty by enhancing income through a variety of income-enhancing programs as depicted in Box 7.2. The importance of these safety-net programs was illustrated by the economic hardships endured by tens of millions of Americans during the Great Recession of 2007 to 2009 and beyond—with the national unemployment rate remaining above 8 percent even at the end of 2012. (Unemployment rates were far high for vulnerable populations, including Latinos, African Americans, and persons with disabilities.) Many single mothers lost their employment or had their wages cut during this recession, forcing some of them on to TANF rolls or to take multiple jobs in a desperate effort to meet their family's survival needs.

Factors That Impede Prevention   A series of barriers discourage prevention, including the problem of efficiency, difficulties in marshaling evidence of the effectiveness of preventive programs, the power of special interests, and competition with curative programs.

The Problem of Efficiency   To understand the problem of efficiency, let us assume that we know precisely which persons will develop social problems, such as which teenage women will have out-of-wedlock births in high school and enter the welfare rolls. Our knowledge would be based on research about at-risk indicators, such as the various causes of welfare dependency listed in Box 7.1. Assume that this research allows us to predict with complete accuracy *true positives* (women who will join the rolls) and *true*

BOX 7.2   **An Array of Interventions to Increase the Resources of Low-Wage Earners**

1. Direct economic assistance
2. Expanded EITC
3. In-kind economic assistance
4. Child-care, health, transportation, and housing subsidies
5. Food stamps
6. Indirect strategies to elevate wages for low-wage employees
7. Increases in the minimum wage and enactment of a living wage
8. Encouragement of trade unions
9. Job creation
10. Public subsidies of private wages
11. Public service jobs
12. Expanded tax concessions to industries that locate in areas with high unemployment
13. Encouragement of mobility
14. Relocation assistance to promote migration from areas of high unemployment
15. Tailoring of services to the needs of subgroups
16. A bill of rights for welfare recipients

---

negatives (women who will not join the rolls). Under these circumstances, we will direct our prevention efforts exclusively to the true positives, excluding true negatives from our project because we have accurately predicted that they will not join the welfare rolls. Were policy advocates able to predict accurately which women would become welfare recipients and which would not, they could develop a highly efficient prevention program that targeted its preventive services and resources only to true positives and provided no preventive services to true negatives.

In the real world, however, our ability to predict which people will develop a specific problem is imperfect.[25] Some women have characteristics that are frequently associated with pregnancy in high school, such as low school achievement, abusive parents, and sexual victimization by an older male, but defy the odds and do not become pregnant. These women are *false positives* because they do not become welfare recipients, even though they have at-risk characteristics. Conversely, some women do not have these at-risk characteristics and do become pregnant. These women are *false negatives*. To the extent that a prevention program makes incorrect predictions about who will develop a problem, it wrongly directs some of its resources to false positives and fails to direct its resources to some true positives. As it wastes resources in this manner, the prevention program's efficiency declines. (See Figure 7.4 for examples of a relatively inefficient prevention program, Program B, and a relatively efficient prevention program, Program A.)

Prevention programs further decline in efficiency, moreover, if they cannot help persons actually avert a problem. Assume, for example, that a program asks teenagers in a high school who the school staff believe are at high risk of becoming pregnant to take a pledge to be abstinent. Also assume that the staff later discovers that this intervention

FIGURE 7.4 An Efficient and Inefficient Preventive Intervention

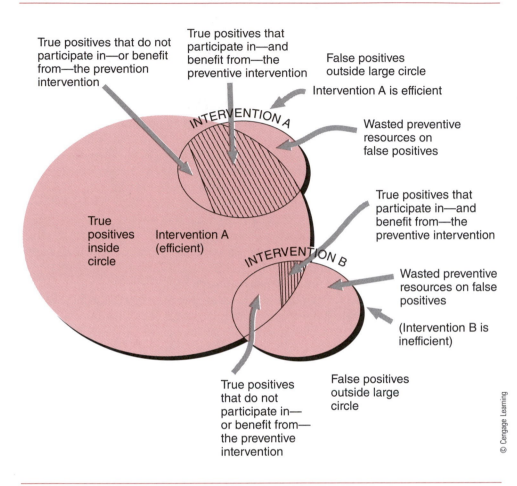

is relatively ineffective in averting teen pregnancy. Even if this program had correctly predicted which teens would become pregnant, it would be inefficient because its intervention, getting teens to pledge abstinence, is relatively ineffective in averting teen pregnancy. This situation is not unusual: Prevention programs must both direct resources to true positives *and* develop effective interventions.

Problems in Getting People to Participate   Efficiency also declines when prevention programs cannot persuade people who are at risk to participate. Some teens refuse to participate because they do not want to make the effort, dislike the intervention, fear the motives of its staff, or are persuaded by peers not to participate.

We need not be excessively pessimistic: Some prevention programs are highly efficient and effective (see Figure 7.4). For example, the Ford Foundation funded a system of mentoring for high school students deemed to be at high risk of truancy and dropping out. High school graduates were assigned students to whom they were mentors for at least three years, aggressively monitoring the attendance and performance of these students, immediately finding them when they were truant, and getting them tutorial assistance when they received failing grades. The mentors visited the homes of their students frequently to secure the cooperation of parents and address familial factors that impeded school attendance. In schools with dropout rates exceeding 50 percent, the mentoring program reduced dropout rates to less than 10 percent.[26]

It is also useful to discuss the importance of passive prevention in social policy, as it is distinguished from active prevention. If active prevention helps people make corrective lifestyle changes or personal decisions to forestall a disease or problem (such as changing diets, engaging in exercise, using birth control, or stopping smoking), passive prevention changes the environments of people to diminish the likelihood that they will develop a problem. Examples of such changes are installing seat belts in cars (to prevent injuries or deaths from crashes), removing pollution from the air (to prevent lung diseases), and persuading food manufacturers to reduce the saturated fat in certain foods (to prevent heart disease). In each of these cases, people passively receive the benefits of these environmental changes without having to alter their lifestyle or make different choices.[27] As in the case of active prevention, however, advocates must convince decision makers that the cost of these measures will be balanced by the benefits to society. For example, many advocates had to pressure legislators for years before convincing them that the cost of seat belts would be offset by the number of deaths they would prevent.

Many prevention measures fall between the active and passive poles. Banning smoking advertisements from billboards near schools, for example, is effective only if teenagers decide not to smoke.

Difficulties in Marshaling Evidence of the Effectiveness of Preventive Programs   To marshal the empirical evidence that specific programs actually prevent specific problems is often difficult. Researchers must follow subjects over a significant period of time to demonstrate that preventive interventions actually reduce such problems as teen pregnancy or alcoholism. They also have to rule out the effects of other factors that have affected the lives of their subjects during this period. And they must demonstrate a magnitude of prevention that justifies the costs of the preventive program. The problems in demonstrating the effects of preventive programs are well illustrated by the controversy in the health field over the efficacy of dietary supplements such as vitamin C; researchers remain uncertain despite myriad studies. Yet some interventions have been demonstrated to have remarkable success, such as the aforementioned mentoring program for students at risk of not finishing high school.

The Unproven Efficacy of Genetic Testing   Genetic testing has enormous promise for conditions linked to genetic factors, such as many health problems and possibly some mental health problems. If researchers can identify genetic predispositions to certain problems, they can involve persons with them in preventive programs, such as lifestyle changes for persons with a disposition for heart disease. But the efficacy of genetic testing is now limited to relatively few conditions, and it remains to be seen if persons with genetic predispositions will commit themselves to prevention programs that could allow them to avert certain problems.

The Power of Special Interests   Special interests often oppose meritorious prevention projects. Cigarette companies have successfully thwarted efforts to prevent teenagers from smoking because cigarette manufacturers consider teenagers a lucrative and growing market. Automobile manufacturers fought the installation of seat belts for years because of the cost. Right-to-life and moral majority groups have prevented many schools from providing effective sex education programs as well as birth control services. Professionals who are socialized to medical models tend to focus on curative rather than preventive remedies.

Yet determined reformers often overcome the power of special interests. Laws requiring the use of helmets by motorcyclists and bicyclists have saved thousands of lives, even though they were strenuously opposed by motorcyclists. Even cigarette companies, despite opposition, have been required to comply with many governmental regulations.

Competition Between Curative and Preventive Programs   Preventive programs must compete for funds with programs that help people who already have specific problems. In the case of welfare programs, for example, states and localities must expend vast resources to sustain dependent families, by providing them with welfare benefits, helping them get jobs, subsidizing child care, or providing health care. Advocates who want significant resources to prevent teenage girls from joining the rolls have to convince legislators to divert scarce resources from curative to preventive programs.

We should not be deterred from developing preventive programs just because they are often inefficient, difficult to evaluate, or opposed by special interests or they compete with curative programs. To the extent that we can prevent problems, we not only forestall human suffering but also avoid future costs (see Policy Advocacy Challenge 7.7).

Measuring the Magnitude of Problems in Step 1

To measure the magnitude of welfare dependency among single women with children is relatively simple because public authorities issue data about the number of persons who receive welfare checks. Other problems, such as homelessness and substance abuse, are more difficult to measure because people who have these problems often do not seek public services. Policy advocates often have to demonstrate that specific problems are sufficiently important to merit the attention of agency staff, funders, government officials, and legislators.

Legislators, funders, and agency executives are likely to invest scarce resources in programs that they believe address widespread problems. Rates, prevalence, and incidence are commonly used to measure the relative magnitude of social problems.[28] *Rates*

Policy Advocacy Challenge 7.7

Developing a Prevention Program and Convincing Decision Makers to Adopt It

Bruce Jansson, Ph.D.

Try to develop an intervention program for an inner-city school that seeks to diminish teen pregnancy. As you plan the program, discuss whether it should do the following:

- Try to increase teenagers' self-esteem.
- Emphasize career and employment planning in hopes that teenagers who believe they have an economic future will be less likely to have children.
- Seek to change behaviors of teenagers or attempt to change behaviors of males, to the extent that teenagers become pregnant because they are raped or pressured to have sex by older men.
- Include the parents of teenagers in their project in hopes that improvements in family functioning will avert pregnancies.
- Provide birth control information and devices.

Assuming that you lack resources to provide your intervention to all teenagers in the school, what at-risk factors might you use to decide whom you would try to reach?

Once you have developed a tentative strategy, discuss what strategies you might use to persuade teenagers to participate in your intervention.

Discuss some problems you might face in trying to convince the local school board to adopt your intervention for the entire school district. Discuss the problem of efficiency in this context.

(expressed as percentages), for example, measure the ratio of a group of persons, such as white males between the ages of 18 and 25 who were arrested for drunk driving in a specific year, to a larger reference group, such as the total number of white males in this age bracket in the population that year. *Incidence* (also expressed as percentages) measures the ratio of new cases, for example, the number of new arrests of white males aged 18 to 25 in 2001, to a larger reference group, such as the total number of white males in the population that year in that age bracket. *Prevalence* (again, expressed as percentages) measures the ratio of persons who are currently experiencing a social problem to the total population. A policy practitioner might want to compare the number of persons currently being prosecuted for drunk driving to the total number of drivers on a specific day. Each measure provides a somewhat different estimate of the problem's seriousness. These kinds of data are often available from city, county, state, or federal agencies or research literature in the social and health sciences.

EPA 2.1.7a

Practitioners can use a variety of technical approaches when measuring the magnitude of social problems. When data are not available from government agencies or the research literature, policy practitioners measure social problems in other ways. Jonathan Bradshaw contrasts measures of felt need, expressed need, expert need, and comparative need.[29] *Felt need* measures persons' belief that they have a problem. An agency might interview a sample of working mothers with preschool children, for example, to assess their belief that they cannot afford day care. Of course, persons sometimes exaggerate their actual needs or, in the case of stigmatized conditions such as substance abuse, underreport them.

Expressed need measures persons' actual search for specific services. A policy practitioner might examine the length of the waiting lists at drug treatment centers, for example, or the number of calls that a hotline receives about substance abuse. Although the knowledge of clients' service-related behaviors is useful, these behaviors may not accurately reflect people's actual needs. Some persons do not seek services, for example, because they believe they cannot afford them, do not like social agencies, are unaware of the services, think they will receive ineffective services, fear they will be prosecuted, or fear they will be subjected to punitive services because of their stigmatized condition.

Policy advocates sometimes assess *expert needs* by asking experts, such as social scientists, social work practitioners, local agency executives, or government officials, for their estimates of the severity of specific problems. Experts can draw convincing evidence from current research, such as the extent of alcoholism among women. Of course, experts' biases and values may influence their position and credibility; someone who defines alcoholism as consuming many drinks each day will provide a lower estimate of the problem's seriousness than someone who uses a more stringent standard, such as consuming only a few drinks a day.

A *comparative need* approach measures unmet needs by comparing the services offered in different communities. Assume, for example, that certain neighborhoods have many drug treatment programs, but others with similar demographic characteristics have a few. We can infer a larger unmet need for drug treatment services in the neighborhoods with fewer treatment programs. One should interpret comparative need measures with caution, however, because they rely on inference rather than a direct measure of need. For example, a neighborhood with few drug treatment programs will appear to have a shortage of services when compared with those that have too many such programs.

Using several or all of these means of assessing needs helps us gauge the importance of specific social problems. If we were trying to promote drug treatment programs in a specific neighborhood, for example, we might look into the length of the existing programs' waiting lists (expressed need), ask high school students for their perceptions of the seriousness of adolescent substance abuse (felt need), discover whether similar neighborhoods have more programs (comparative need), and get information from selected experts (expert need).

Measurements of social problems become more dramatic when they include trend data suggesting that a specific problem is becoming more serious. Such data may come from felt-, expressed-, comparative-, or expert-need sources or from rising rates, prevalence, or incidence of specific problems. A dramatic increase in a community's substance abuse problems, for example, would be documented by a rising rate of deaths from overdose and longer waiting lists for drug treatment programs (felt need).

Policy decision makers, however, do not spring into action merely because policy advocates present them with data about the prevalence of a problem or the need for specific services. Legislators often ignore overwhelming data about a problem, particularly when they are not subjected to strong pressure by voters and interest groups or when powerful interests oppose ameliorating measures. Despite large numbers of deaths and injuries from guns in inner-city areas, for example, politicians in most jurisdictions have not enacted stringent measures to control guns because of opposition by the National Rifle Association. Politicians sometimes take action not when a problem is becoming more serious, but when the public believes it is becoming more important or when party leaders believe they can improve their political fortunes by taking action. In the case of welfare reform in 1996, for example, the cost of AFDC had risen from $15.5 billion in 1970 to $22.3 billion in 1993, not a marked increase after adjusting for inflation. Yet a welfare crisis was proclaimed, leading Congress and the president to rescind the AFDC program and devolve welfare assistance to the states.[30]

Locating Problems Spatially in Step 1

It does little good to determine that a problem is relatively widespread if we cannot locate and reach its victims or, in the case of preventive programs, its potential victims. Social science tools are one way to locate people with certain problems. The U.S. census, done every 10 years, does not collect data about social problems such as substance abuse and mental illness but instead states demographic, economic, and housing data in aggregate terms for specific geographic regions.[31] Nonetheless its data are important to social workers because social scientists have linked demographic and economic factors with social problems. For example, poor persons are more likely than affluent persons to experience specific medical problems, to be unemployed, to have poor housing, and to be pressured by dealers to use illegal drugs. Members of certain ethnic groups are more likely than others to have some medical conditions, such as sickle cell anemia and Tay-Sachs disease. Using economic, housing, demographic, and ethnic data, policy practitioners can infer high rates of certain social problems in specific geographic areas.

EPA 2.1.3a

Policy advocates need not confine themselves to census material. Local public health offices, various state agencies, municipal and county authorities, and some federal agencies, such as the National Institute of Mental Health, regularly collect and compile various kinds of population-based data.[32]

Census and other public data can also shape marketing, outreach, and advertising strategies. An agency could publicize its services in certain neighborhoods with a high concentration of specific groups. For example, the agency could market its services to areas with working women (day care), adolescents (substance abuse), or elderly people (home health care services). Policy advocates can even inspect neighborhoods to decide where persons with specific kinds of problems live. As a tenant organizer, for example,

Listen to Bob Erlenbusch, member of the Board of the National Coalition Against Homelessness, in Policy Advocacy Challenge Video 7.8 as he discusses why policy advocates must often collect data from the census or from other sources to buttress their case to decision makers that a specific issue or problem should receive priority. Please ask the following questions:

Why is a map showing the distribution of homeless persons in a jurisdiction an important device when talking with elected officials in that area?

Why is a map important, as well, to providers and other agencies?

I discovered that I could easily locate substandard housing by observing the window frames in specific neighborhoods; from flaking paint and the absence of putty, I could often predict the overall condition of the rental unit.

Understanding Social Problems as Slippery Concepts in Step 1

Flowcharts such as the ones in Figures 7.2 and 7.3 are useful, but they do not reveal the subtle distinctions and philosophical issues that confront policy advocates. Social problems are human constructs, not purely objective phenomena. Indeed, by referring to social phenomena as social problems, people define them as requiring human intervention to be solved. They invent terms and classification systems, sometimes even when demonstrable problems do not exist or when it is unclear how many people have them. Part of the subject of this chapter, then, the analysis of problems, is a consideration of the basic concept of *social problem*. Let us analyze some ambiguities and philosophical issues that most social workers will confront during their careers.

When Are Social Problems Real, and When Are They Invented?

Because social problems are social conditions invested with human meaning, all of them are "invented."[33] Pestilence and famine were regarded in medieval times as inevitable and not solvable, but they are widely regarded in contemporary society as problems that demand solutions, at least in developed nations where the resources and technology exist to address them. Myriad conditions, such as dyslexia, many mental disorders, and such physiological conditions as menopause, have only recently been called problems. (Successive versions of the *DSM*, which describes mental conditions for mental health professionals, have included scores of additional conditions, often with no credible evidence that they are important mental problems.[34])

Most of us would agree, however, that we can be relatively confident in declaring some conditions to be problems. Such conditions as malnutrition, heart disease, cancer, and severe mental depression bring demonstrable suffering and death to their victims. Moreover, human service and health workers diagnose these conditions with high levels of reliability by using diagnostic tests that have been perfected through decades of research. But other social conditions are called problems without evidence that they are regular and identifiable phenomena in the real world. Critics of *DSM-IV* contend, for example, that research demonstrates that qualified clinicians cannot reliably make distinctions among many of the disorders listed.[35]

Social workers should view problems with healthy skepticism. As they proliferate with scant evidence that they are truly problems, human service workers are likely to treat subjects unnecessarily, label them, and apply remedies to conditions that do not require treatment. Indeed, the attitude toward some problems must be reversed, as is illustrated in the medical field by childbirth. For centuries, when childbirth was viewed as a normal condition rather than as a problem, women delivered their babies at home with the help of a midwife, a practice still prevalent in some European nations. Once childbirth was declared a medical problem by American obstetricians, women were taken to hospitals for delivery, drugged heavily, and subjected to extraordinarily high rates of cesarean section, policies that vastly increased the cost of childbirth without lowering the infant death rate.[36] Only recently has the pendulum reversed, as increasing numbers of women use midwives, either in hospitals or in their own homes.

Some social conditions are so complex that it is difficult to know when they are problems. Take the case of teen pregnancy, which is widely viewed as a problem. Considerable medical evidence suggests that when girls of 12 or 13 give birth, they imperil themselves and their infants, who experience high rates of birth defects. Such risks diminish sharply, however, as girls enter their mid and late teens. One researcher contends, moreover, that on a variety of indicators, including wages and amount of schooling, low-income women who have children in their mid to late teens are not worse off than those who wait to have children.[37] (The researcher contended that because they do not have to interrupt their careers with pregnancies and child rearing, women who have children early may be more able than those who wait to concentrate continuously on work and careers.) Even this cursory discussion suggests that teen pregnancy may not always be a problem. Indeed, we might well ask whether the decision of some teen mothers to have children is a legitimate lifestyle choice, particularly in light of evidence that some of them do not harm themselves or their children.

Many Social Problems Defy Simple Solutions, but Many People Favor Panaceas

Most social problems are complex phenomena that do not lend themselves to simple solutions. Yet people frequently demand panaceas, as American history amply suggests.[38] This familiar pattern reasserted itself with respect to welfare reform in the mid- and late 1990s with the adoption of a deterrent strategy to deal with a complicated problem. Because of its roots in the social and economic fabric of American society, welfare dependency cannot be solved by deterrence; it is caused by such factors as low-wage jobs; residential segregation; and the high cost of day care, housing, medical care, and transportation.

Moreover, solving problems requires persistence rather than time-limited crusades. As existing welfare recipients enter the job market, additional women will require job-seeking assistance or welfare when they have children and can find only low-wage jobs. Many women who secure jobs will lose them during recessions. When welfare recipients do receive jobs, they will displace some current workers (male and female) from the labor force, particularly in areas that do not have high rates of economic growth. As even this brief discussion suggests, many social problems cannot be solved but merely ameliorated through continuing efforts.

The panaceas are sometimes promoted by class and racial prejudice. Because they have not experienced the actual circumstances of living in many inner-city and rural areas and are not subject to the structural factors that cause and sustain such social problems as high levels of crime, unemployment, disease, delinquency, welfare dependency, bad housing, homelessness, and dropping out of school, many affluent Americans seek simple solutions aimed at changing the values and viewpoints of low-income persons. Some believe that sex education programs preaching abstinence will eradicate teen pregnancy. Some favor the widespread use of volunteers to teach children to read or to offer middle-class models to impoverished children. Some support deterrent policies to diminish crime rates and welfare dependency in inner-city communities. These solutions do not take into account the realities of living in these communities.

Priorities Are Not Chosen Rationally

The literature on policy analysts sometimes conveys the misleading impression that decision makers rely on research to shape public priorities. We have already mentioned, for example, that policy analysts often try to gauge the costs to society of specific problems, such as the work absenteeism, death, and lost wages that derive from alcoholism. However, the reality that politics ultimately shapes the selection of priorities can be shown by two examples: antismoking policies and the magnitude of the resources devoted to children's programs. An extraordinary body of research has implicated smoking in hundreds of thousands of deaths annually, yet strong gains were made in regulating tobacco as a drug only in the late 1990s. Many researchers have argued that interventions directed at children, such as children's health programs, have a high benefit-to-cost ratio. Yet the United States devotes only a small fraction of its domestic budget to children and continues not to fund medical coverage for many of them.

Solving One Problem Can Create Others

Even if some problems can be solved, others often emerge in their wake, as in the case of welfare reform. While saving money by paying reduced welfare costs, society incurs new costs as some (or many) former recipients receive lower resources from employment or general relief. As some become homeless, they require shelter care and develop health problems that local authorities have to fund. Foster care costs rise as some mothers become unable to provide adequately for their children. Economic desperation is likely to bring increases in family violence, crime, and substance abuse. As some recipients exceed their allotted time on welfare and still are unemployed, counties and cities will have to expend more funds for general relief.[39]

The precise amount of these new costs to society will depend partly on rates of economic growth. In parts of the country with robust growth, job creation will absorb large numbers of former welfare recipients, but they will compete with other unemployed people, new job seekers (such as recent graduates from high school), and immigrants for scarce jobs in other areas. When former recipients do find jobs, some other job seekers will not find work and will be forced onto general relief. Were a recession to occur, moreover, the relief and unemployment rolls would vastly expand.

Variations in Problems

When pointing to the issues in defining, measuring, and conceptualizing social problems, many policy advocates stress the differences between groups in the population. Alcoholism appears, for example, to have different causes and take different forms in men and women.[40] Unlike men, whose alcoholism often stems from occupational stress and peer pressure, many women develop alcoholism during times of family crisis, such as marital discord, divorce, or a child's death. Unlike alcoholic men, who tend to drink in public—in bars or with friends—many alcoholic women drink secretly. These differences in both the causes and the manifestations of alcoholism suggest that men and women need different kinds of treatment as well as different kinds of preventive services.

Moreover, cultural differences affect people's responses to services. Spanish-speaking families, for example, often defer to male heads of household before seeking assistance for specific problems. In white families, women often take the initiative in seeking services for specific problems. If they want to be successful, social service agencies that serve Latinos must try to include male heads of household in service transactions.[41] Some ethnic groups require bilingual and bicultural staff who can interpret nuances of expression and probe for the meaning of verbal and nonverbal cues that would escape staff from the dominant culture. Some persons respond favorably to one approach, such as a specific kind of counseling, whereas others respond to behavior modification or membership in support groups, such as Alcoholics Anonymous. Deterrent measures, such as increasing the cost of alcohol or cigarettes, appear to decrease some people's use, but they may be even more effective when supplemented with counseling programs and reductions in advertising.

EPA 2.1.4a

The vast literature that has recently evolved on "culturally sensitive practice" and "multidiversity" stresses the need to adapt programs to specific populations.[42] This sensitivity must occur on two related levels. First, we need to examine the differences in specific social problems in different populations, as our discussion of alcoholism among males and females suggests. Second, services must be adapted to the culture and norms of specific ethnic and racial groups.

We should also remember that the problems of oppressed populations are often caused or exacerbated by the hostile environments and extreme poverty that many of their members encounter, particularly in inner-city communities. The rules of mental health, for example, whether in diagnosis or in treatment, must be modified when social workers are helping persons who live in areas that look like bombed-out cities, who are exposed to violence daily, who cannot obtain secure jobs that will allow them to escape poverty, and who can obtain amenities such as health care only by waiting for days in clinics. Terms such as *paranoia, inability to make long-term plans*, and *flight*, which can be used in the diagnosis and treatment of mental conditions or problem-solving deficits in middle-class citizens, must be used cautiously in labeling persons in these high-stress environments, where trust, planning, and permanent social arrangements are less feasible.

The term *empowerment* helps us reconceptualize some of the services that social workers provide to persons in high-stress environments. (While empowerment is not limited to persons in high-stress environments, it may have particular relevance for them.) When seeking to empower persons, social workers often emphasize survival skills, such as helping persons cope with the fragmentation of services, understaffed services, and hostile bureaucrats. Rather than focusing on pathology, empowerment helps people develop personal plans to improve their lives. Indeed, some people favor such terms as *consumers of service* rather than *patient* or *client* to avoid labeling people. Some social workers advocate placing less reliance on mental health diagnostic categories, such as those in *DSM-IV*, that label persons on the basis of deficits rather than strengths.[43]

Challenges for Policy Advocates in Step 1

We have noted that policy advocates who help oppressed populations encounter particular challenges in policy arenas because their issues are frequently unpopular. Certain kinds of issues and populations have a relatively privileged position in American culture, as can be seen by their success in securing a disproportionate share of resources. Fund-raisers for hospitals, certain cultural undertakings, and privileged educational organizations such as private schools have an enviable job in raising funds compared to shoestring organizations that help stigmatized populations.[44]

Moreover, the broader population views the problems of stigmatized conditions, such as homelessness or AIDS, through prejudiced lenses. Rather than viewing homelessness as stemming from an absence of halfway houses, decent social services, and affordable housing, many persons stress the personal failings of those who are homeless as the major, even the sole, cause of this condition. Rather than viewing AIDS as an epidemic, similar to cholera in prior eras, some persons view many who have this disease through the lens of homophobia, seeing it as stemming from an aberrant lifestyle choice. Problems of oppressed populations are, moreover, often viewed as relatively hopeless and unsolvable, unlike those of more powerful populations.

When policy advocates suggest that inequalities in American society, such as discrepancies in the incomes and opportunities of the social classes, should be rectified, they are often dismissed as left-leaning radicals. In a society that lacks a strong radical tradition, the rhetoric of social equality is often dismissed. But advocates for powerless populations and unpopular issues often realize that without a fundamental redistribution of resources and opportunities, specific groups, such as inner-city African Americans, will remain on the periphery of American society. They will be unable even to imagine themselves significantly improving their lives.

EPA 2.1.5b

These common perceptions of the problems of oppressed populations underline the need for their advocates to educate people, whether through the mass media or through personal discussions with highly placed officials. They must contest the definitions and conceptualizations of specific social problems, such as equating welfare with bad character rather than with limited, low-paying jobs. They have to resist people's stereotypes by arguing that certain groups do, in fact, have different needs and problems.

What You Can Now Do to Analyze Problems in Step 1

Chapter Summary

You are now equipped to do the following:

- Identify the six steps of the policy analysis, proposal-writing, and presentation framework (Figure 7.1), and understand how this framework combines Tasks 4 and 5 of the policy practice and policy advocacy framework in Figure 3.1.
- State why policy analysis is often needed in policy advocacy.
- Develop flowcharts to understand the development of social problems and enhance policy analysis.
- Use typologies to identify subpopulations within a broader population of persons with specific social conditions.
- Identify multiple causes of social problems.
- Identify different perspectives or models that shape the solutions that persons develop for specific social problems.
- Develop preventive solutions to specific social problems.

- Measure the magnitude of specific social problems and their spatial distribution.
- Grapple with nonrational factors that shape how persons view specific social problems and the kinds of solutions that they propose.
- Develop policy solutions that take into account the culture, ethnicity, race, and social class of specific populations.

We discuss strategies for defending and presenting policy proposals in Chapter Eight.

Policy Advocacy Challenge 7.9

Analyzing Effects of and Solutions to Concentrated Poverty in the United States and Globally

Bruce Jansson, Ph.D.

Some social scientists and public officials have long hypothesized that persons in neighborhoods with concentrated poverty would be better off if they resided in mixed-income areas.[1] Their logic seemed unassailable since the residents would have better housing, schools, medical facilities, grocery stores, and other amenities in mixed-income areas. They would live closer to places of employment and have more employment options than in areas of concentrated poverty. African American youth would, they hypothesized, benefit from living in neighborhoods with sharply lower rates of crime, school dropouts, and availability of illicit drugs, and they would be more likely to obtain employment as they established networks with relatively affluent youth.

Jonathan Crane's research, published in 1991, appeared to confirm the deleterious impact of "ghettoes" on their residents.[2] His data indicated that such problems as dropping out from schools and teen pregnancy rapidly escalate once they reach a certain threshold. He conjectured that teens spread these problems to their peers once they reach high thresholds, growing to "epidemic levels."

Based largely on such theories, relocation of low-income persons to mixed-income areas has been implemented in cities throughout the nation for decades. To settle a class-action suit against the Chicago Public Housing Authority 1969, for example, 7,100 African American families were relocated from areas of concentrated poverty to integrated or largely Caucasian areas with the use of housing vouchers. Congress funded the movement of 4,600 low-income families to more affluent areas in five cities in so-called Moving to Opportunity demonstrations in the mid-1990s. And beginning in 1992, President Bill Clinton's Housing Opportunities for People Everywhere (HOPE) VI program converted tens of thousands of public housing projects into mixed-income ones in 166 cities throughout the country.

Unfortunately, however, data that were gathered at these various sites could not definitively show that the relocation of low-income persons had necessarily been responsible for encouraging outcomes, such as increased income, lower rates of dropouts, and less drug usage. Since an experimental design had not been used, it was possible that the persons who agreed to be relocated were already more motivated than those who chose to remain in their neighborhoods. Some data also suggested that some relocated persons did not fare better than those who remained, particularly among African American male adolescents who sometimes developed relatively high rates of drug usage and were prone to dropping out of school.

Quite apart from social science theory and data, however, an excellent ethical rationale could be articulated for giving low-income African Americans a range of choices so that *they* can decide where they want to live. It seems only fair to give these low-income

---

[0]Julie Kosterlitz, "The Katrina Experiment," *National Journal*, November 5, 2005, 3436–3441.
[0]Jonathan Crane, "The Epidemic Theory of Ghettos and Neighborhood Effects on Dropping Out and Teenage Child-bearing," *American Journal of Sociology*, Vol. 96, March 1991, 1226–1259.

residents choices that more affluent residents possess. With use of housing vouchers and Section 8 rent subsidies, they ought to be able to choose whether to live in mixed-income areas or in low-income areas. These choices could not exist, however, if the federal government was not determined to fund mixed-income housing projects or to help low-income African Americans find rental housing or even to purchase homes with subsidized mortgages, in mixed-income areas.

Segregation of persons by social class is a global problem as tens of millions of persons move into urban cities from rural areas in developing nations such as China, India, Mexico, and Brazil. Living in segregated communities, these impoverished persons often exist at the periphery of these nations. They often cannot find work. Their children are often denied education. They often lack medical services and are subject to legal and other forms of discrimination. Often possessing relatively small budgets for social spending, these nations mostly ignore the problems of this vast population.

Explain how this case example illustrates:

1. How public officials and policy advocates need to engage in problem analysis in order to determine the best course of action for residents in areas of concentrated poverty.
2. How definitive data often do not exist when important policy decisions must be made, but public officials often need to proceed anyway using best information about the issue at stake.
3. Why public policy should often seek to give vulnerable populations choices that more affluent persons take for granted.
4. Why developed nations should augment foreign aid to developing nations so that they can help destitute rural populations that have migrated to their cities.

Competency Notes

EPA 2.1.3a   Distinguish, appraise, and integrate multiple sources of knowledge, including research-based knowledge and practice wisdom (pp. 202, 203, 230): Social workers should consider various political, fiscal, and cultural factors regarding social problems.

EPA 2.1.4a   Recognize the extent to which a culture's structures and values may oppress, marginalize, alienate, or create or enhance privilege or power (pp. 207, 234): Social workers realize that different groups select policies that will enhance their prestige, revenue, and power.

EPA 2.1.4b   Gain sufficient self-awareness to eliminate the influence of personal biases and values in working with diverse groups (p. 219): Researchers' perspectives influence their work, such as whether to emphasize personal, psychological, economic, and biological causes.

EP 2.1.5b   Advocate for human rights and social and economic justice (p. 235): Social workers obtain and implement laws that protect members of vulnerable populations.

EPA 2.1.6b   Use research evidence to inform practice (p. 202): Social workers should examine social science, public health, and other literature before developing strategies for prevention.

EPA 2.1.7a   Utilize conceptual frameworks to guide the process of assessment, intervention, and evaluation (p. 229): Social workers can use a variety of technical approaches when measuring the magnitude of social problems.

EPA 2.1.8a **Analyze, formulate, and advocate for policies that advance social well-being** (p. 220): Social workers devise interventions, strategies, and preventative programs to solve specific social problems.

EPA 2.1.10d **Collect, organize, and interpret client data** (p. 217): Social workers are interested in understanding the dynamics of a problem.

EPA 2.1.10i **Implement prevention interventions that enhance client capacities** (pp. 8, 24): Social workers can identify at-risk factors that enable them to target interventions to those predisposed to certain problems.

Endnotes

1. For an eight-step model of policy analysis, see Eugene Bardach, *The Eight-Step Path of Policy Analysis: A Handbook of Practice*, (Berkeley, CA: Berkeley Academic Press, 1998).

2. Mary Jo Bane, "Welfare as We Might Know It," *American Prospect* 30 (January–February 1997): 47–53.

3. The *DSM-IV* is the fourth edition of the *Diagnostic and Statistical Manual of Mental Disorders*, published in 1994 by The American Psychiatric Association.

4. See the testimony of David Ellwood in the U.S. Senate, *Hearings*, Subcommittee on Social Security and Family Policy of Committee on Finance (March 2, 1987), pp. 105–111.

5. See John Kenneth Wing, *Reasoning about Mental Illness* (London: Oxford University Press, 1978), Chap. 2.

6. Phillip Kotler, *Principles of Marketing*, 4th ed. (Englewood Cliffs, NJ: Prentice Hall, 1989), pp. 42–46.

7. Richard Krueger, *Focus Groups: A Practical Guide for Applied Research* (Newbury Park, CA: Sage, 1990).

8. See David Mechanic, *Mental Health and Social Policy*, 3rd ed. (Englewood Cliffs, NJ: Prentice Hall, 1989), pp. 16–44.

9. Stuart Kirk and Herb Hutchins, *The Selling of DSM: The Rhetoric of Science in Psychiatry* (New York: Aldine de Gruyter, 1992).

10. Bane, "Welfare as We Might Know It."

11. Claude Fischer et al., *Inequality by Design: Cracking the Bell Curve Myth* (Princeton, NJ: Princeton University Press, 1996), pp. 102–128.

12. David Ellwood, *Poor Support: Poverty in the American Family* (New York: Basic Books, 1988).

13. Irving Piliavin et al., "The Duration of Homeless Careers: An Exploratory Study," *Social Service Review* (December 1993): 57–69.

14. Richard Berk et al., "Social Policy Experimentation," *Evaluation Review* 9 (August 1985): 387–431.

15. Claire Renzetti and Raymond Lee, eds., *Researching Sensitive Topics* (Newbury Park, CA: Sage, 1993).

16. Bane, "Welfare as We Might Know It."

17. U.S. Department of Health and Human Services, *Alcohol and Health: Report to U.S. Congress* (Washington, DC: Government Printing Office, 1987), pp. 97–119.

18. Steven Wineman, *The Politics of Human Services: A Radical Alternative to the Welfare State* (Boston: South End Press, 1984).

19. For a critique of the medical model in substance abuse, see Dorothy Nelkin, *Methadone Maintenance: A Technological Fix* (New York: Braziller, 1973).

20. William Miller and Hester Reid, "Matching Problem Drinkers with Optimal Treatments," in William Miller and Nick Heather, eds., *Treating Addictive Behaviors: Processes of Change* (New York: Plenum Press, 1986), pp. 175–204.

21. William Julius Wilson, *When Work Disappears: The World of the New Urban Poor* (New York: Knopf, 1996).

22. Melissa Healy, "Welfare 'Family Cap' Fails to Cut Birthrate in New Jersey," *Los Angeles Times* (September 12, 1997), pp. 1, 16.

23. David Zucchino, *Myth of the Welfare Queen* (New York: Scribner, 1997).

24. Louis Uchitelle, "Welfare Recipients Taking Jobs Often Held by the Working Poor," *New York Times* (April 1, 1997), pp. 1, 10.

25. Martin Bloom, *Primary Prevention: The Possible Science* (Englewood Cliffs, NJ: Prentice Hall, 1981).

26. Jonathan Smith, "Quantum Opportunities Program," *New York Times* (March 9, 1995), pp. 1, 2.

27. Bloom, *Primary Prevention*.

28. Ibid., pp. 173–174.

29. Jonathan Bradshaw, "The Concept of Social Need," *New Society* 30 (March 1972): 640–643.

30. Mary Ellen Hombs, *Welfare Reform: A Reference Handbook* (Santa Barbara, CA: ABC-CLIO, 1996), p. 54.

31. See National Institute of Mental Health, *A Working Manual of Simple Evaluation Techniques for Community Mental Health Centers* (Washington, DC: Government Printing Office, 1976), pp. 99–146.

32. Ibid.

33. Arnold Green, *Social Problems: Arena of Conflict* (New York: McGraw-Hill, 1975), pp. 67–115.

34. Kirk and Hutchins, *The Selling of DSM*, pp. 199–218.

35. Ibid.

36. Barbara Ehrenreich and Deirdre English, *For Her Own Good: 150 Years of the Experts' Advice to Women* (New York: Anchor Books, 1979).

37. See the discussion of Joseph Hotz's work in Richard Cooper, "Contrary Message on Teenage Pregnancy," *Los Angeles Times* (May 24, 1997), pp. 1, 14.

38. Bruce S. Jansson, *The Reluctant Welfare State*, 3rd ed. (Pacific Grove, CA: Brooks/Cole, 1997), pp. 352–353.

39. Wolch and Sommer, *Los Angeles in an Era*, pp. 78–80.

40. Vasanti Burtle, ed., *Women Who Drink: Experience and Psychotherapy* (Springfield, IL: Charles C Thomas, 1979).

41. Vicente Abad, "Mental Health Delivery Systems for Hispanics in the United States: Issues and Dilemmas," in Moises Gaviria and Jose Arana, eds., *Health and Behavior: Research Agenda for Hispanics* (Chicago: Simon Bolivar Hispanic American Psychiatric Research and Training Program, 1987).

42. See, for example, Wynetta Devore and Elfriede Schlesinger, *Ethnic-Sensitive Social Work* (St. Louis: Mosby, 1981), and Donna Ferullo, *Cultural Diversity in Social Work Practice* (Boston: Social Work Library at Boston College, 1991).

43. Barbara Solomon, *Black Empowerment* (New York: Columbia University Press, 1976).

44. Jean Potuchek, "The Context of Social Service Funding: The Funding Relationship," *Social Service Review* 60 (September 1986): 421–436.

Suggested Readings

Developing Typologies

David Ellwood, *Poor Support: Poverty in the American Family* (New York: Basic Books, 1988).

Controversies in Defining and Conceptualizing Social Problems

Mary Jo Bane, "Welfare as We Might Know It," *American Prospect* 30 (January–February 1997): 47–53.

David Ellwood, "Welfare Reform as I Knew It," *American Prospect* 25 (May–June 1996): 22–29.

Claude Fischer et al., *Inequality by Design: Cracking the Bell Curve Myth* (Princeton, NJ: Princeton University Press, 1996).

Stuart Kirk and Herb Hutchins, *The Selling of DSM: The Rhetoric of Science in Psychiatry* (New York: Aldine de Gruyter, 1992).

How Culture and Values Influence Definitions of Social Problems

Joel Best, ed., *Images of Issues* (New York: Aldine de Gruyter, 1989).

Malcolm Spector and John Kitsuse, *Constructing Social Problems* (Menlo Park, CA: Cummings, 1977).

Technical Approaches to Analyzing and Measuring Social Problems

Jonathan Bradshaw, "The Concept of Social Need," in Neil Gilbert and Harry Specht, eds., *Planning for Social Welfare* (Englewood Cliffs, NJ: Prentice Hall, 1977), pp. 290–297.

Christopher Jencks, *The Homeless* (Cambridge: Harvard University Press, 1994).

Irving Piliavin et al., "The Duration of Homeless Careers: An Exploratory Study," *Social Service Review* (December 1993): 57–69.

Developing Policy Proposals in the Second, Third, and Fourth Steps of Policy Analysis

Policy Predicament

The economic recession that began in 2007 led to a significant rise in the number of homeless individuals and families. As discussed in Policy Advocacy Challenge 8.4, advocates used the recession as an opportunity to push the Obama administration to authorize $1.5 billion of federal stimulus spending for the Homelessness Prevention and Rapid Re-Housing Program (HPRP). At the end of this chapter, you will be provided an exercise that requires you to develop a proposal to implement the HPRP. Much larger initiatives are needed, as well, in developing nations to provide affordable and quality housing for tens of millions of destitute persons, sometimes living in cardboard shacks at the periphery of their cities.

LEARNING OUTCOMES

By the end of this chapter, you will be able to:
1. Identify different stakeholders as well as the perspectives they bring to specific issues
2. Discuss nine kinds of substantive issues that policy advocates consider when they are developing policy proposals
3. Develop two or more policy options for addressing specific social problems or issues
4. Identify alternative criteria that policy advocates can use to compare the relative merits of different policy options
5. Select a preferred policy option by selecting one that is preferable to others with respect to selected criteria
6. Develop qualitative rankings
7. Use different policy skills in tandem when developing policy proposals

Returning to the Six-Step Policy Analysis, Proposal-Writing, and Presentation Framework with Steps 2, 3, and 4

We discussed Step 1 of the six-step policy analysis, proposal-writing, and presentation framework presented in Chapter Seven (see Figure 7.1). We now discuss Steps 2, 3, and 4 that allow policy advocates to draft policy proposals as they develop promising policy and programs options for addressing specific social problems or issues, compare their relative merits, and draft proposals.

Intersecting Arenas and Stakeholders

Proposals are fashioned through deliberations and discussions of stakeholders—key persons, groups, and institutions with an interest in a particular policy issue. They comprise administrators, consumers, advocacy groups, government officials, persons from the private sector (such as business leaders), and persons from so-called NGOs (nongovernmental organizations) as described in Figure 8.1.

Stakeholders have various motivations and perspectives as they consider the merits of specific policies. We have discussed ideology at many points. Some stakeholders bring their ideological preferences to the table, such as when some conservatives insist that homeless persons be subjected to relatively harsh policies such as placing them in jails. Businesspeople and shopkeepers sometimes want streets cleared so that pedestrians and their would-be customers are not deterred. Developers of downtown housing often fear that a significant homeless population will deter persons from purchasing their units. Policy advocates, in turn, are often somewhat more likely to support spending on a variety of medical, social service, housing, child-care, job training, substance-abuse counseling, and mental health services for homeless persons. Courts have issued a number of rulings that set limits on the actions of local police. Some stakeholders want to advance their self-interest, such as medical providers that want special reimbursements for the costs of treating homeless persons in emergency rooms and outpatient departments. Some stakeholders advance their political self-interest, such as elected officials who seek re-election.

FIGURE 8.1 Intersecting Arenas and Stakeholders

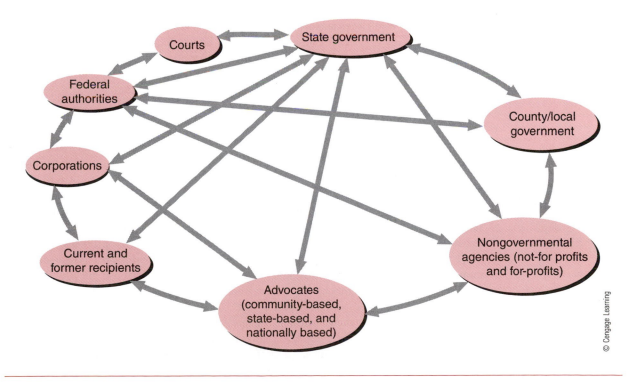

© Cengage Learning

We can use the wheel of interaction shown in Figure 8.1 to understand the proposal preferences of specific stakeholders by placing them in the center of the wheel. In the politics addressing various forms of inequality (educational, housing, fiscal, etc.) in your state or local jurisdiction, for example, place community-based advocates in the center of the wheel. What demands or requests might they make of other stakeholders?

What perspectives might they possess about how to address these problems? Contrast their likely demands or requests with stakeholders who want to advance their financial or political self-interest.

Identifying Recurring Policy Issues and Policy Options in Steps 2, 3, and 4

EPA 2.1.3a

When designing policy proposals, policy advocates must consider a range of issues.

They can be placed in nine groups that establish the following:

1. A mission for a proposal
2. How a proposal's services will be structured
3. The resource path of a proposal
4. The content of a proposal's services
5. How a proposal's resources will be rationed
6. How agencies associated with a proposal will be linked
7. How a proposal's services will be linked to communities
8. How the implementation of a proposal will be monitored
9. How a proposal's services will be assessed

EP 2.1.9b

As they encounter each of these nine issues, policy advocates must choose among competing alternatives or options.

To illustrate our discussion, we will consider a hypothetical policy advocate in Washington, DC, who wants to develop a federally funded program for victims of domestic violence.[1] She thinks abused women need the immediate protection that shelters afford and realizes that many women lack the resources to find alternative sources of safe shelter. She works for a shelter in Baltimore and is connected with a coalition of service providers, feminists, victims of domestic violence, and professionals who want the federal government to take a more active role in addressing this problem.

(The group is called the Stop Domestic Violence Coalition.) This policy advocate knows that several local programs have been initiated for this purpose, mostly by underfunded not-for-profit agencies that have sought assistance from foundations, private benefactors, and public sources, such as the U.S. Department of Housing and Urban Development. Despite their founders' determined efforts, these centers have proved woefully inadequate in helping the rising number of women who seek relief from domestic violence. The coalition tentatively calls its proposed program the Federal Shelter Program.

Establishing a Mission in Steps 2, 3, and 4

While developing this program, the policy advocate must create some objectives for the Federal Shelter Program. We have noted that policies usually contain explicit or implicit objectives that provide programs with an overarching direction. Often, the preambles of legislation also provide such a rationale.

When discussing the shelters with legislators' aides, our hypothetical policy advocate finds no consensus on the federal government's mission in responding to domestic violence. Some legislators are uninterested in the issue, believing that advocates grossly exaggerate its importance and magnitude; indeed, one aide contends that domestic violence is a "figment of the imagination of do-gooder social workers, who want to create more jobs for themselves." Other legislators favor a "get-tough" strategy that would provide federal funds and policy requirements to local governmental units to find, prosecute, and imprison offenders. However, they object to direct federal assistance to shelters, which they think local jurisdictions should fund. Still other legislators want to provide federal assistance to a national network of shelters for victims of domestic violence and their children.

While believing that better law enforcement is also needed, our policy advocate and other participants in the Stop Domestic Violence Coalition decide to emphasize federal assistance to shelters. The coalition also wants the shelter program to offer a service to help women cope with their predicament and link them to legal, welfare, job placement, and other services.

Their objectives, then, emphasize federal funding to establish shelters and serve the women who seek protection there. This mission has important consequences for the policies they will develop; had they adopted a mission that emphasized prosecuting perpetrators, their proposal would have taken an entirely different form.

Designing the Structure of Service in Steps 2, 3, and 4

Having established a general direction, this policy advocate and her allies encounter some practice questions: Who should ultimately oversee the new program? What kinds of agencies should receive funds for the program?

Fixing Ultimate Responsibility   Programs and agencies are typically classified into policy sectors, such as mental health, health, child welfare, public welfare, and gerontology. Assigning a specific program to a sector is often arbitrary and sometimes contentious. For example, the federal Office of Education and the federal Office of Economic Opportunity (OEO) vied for the Head Start program at its inception. In truth, it could have been placed in either sector because it has educational components as well as the parent and community participation that OEO emphasizes.[2] Ultimately, it was placed with the OEO because its key founders feared that placing it in the Office of Education would render it a mere educational program that lacked advocacy, parent-participation, and child-development dimensions.

Returning to our example, the policy advocate has to decide who should have ultimate responsibility for the program. For example, had the Federal Shelter Program been assigned to the National Institute of Mental Health, its major focus would have become providing counseling services, with less emphasis on providing shelter services. Had it been assigned to the Department of Housing and Urban Development, social services might have been ignored. Of course, the policy advocate could try to make the program an independent agency that reports directly to the president and is possibly linked to other programs that assist victims of violence.

EPA 2.1.8b

She not only needs to decide which governmental department should receive ultimate jurisdiction but must also develop policies about implementation. In doing so, she must ask the following questions: Should state officials (perhaps from a state agency) or federal authorities oversee the program, and who should choose which agencies are to receive federal funds? Who should collect statistics about how the shelters use their funds, to keep legislators informed? Who should attend to program problems, such as misuse of funds or failure to comply with local building codes? Who should determine the shelters' eligibility policies within a specific state? Should these policies be contained within the federal legislation, be defined by federal officials after the legislation has been enacted, or be left to the discretion of state officials?

In the 1960s, legislators made federal officials responsible for many funding and operational decisions. Indeed, in many federally funded programs in the War on Poverty, local agencies applied directly to federal authorities for funds, and federal officials inspected and audited local projects. Since then, authority increasingly has been vested in state, regional, or county officials, who ultimately report some details of local programs, such as program statistics, to federal funders. (In the Reagan administration, this reporting was minimized because the president wanted to eliminate federal roles in favor of state and local ones.)

Our policy advocate must weigh the advantages of using the various levels of government.[3] If she believes that many local units will be particularly unreceptive to the needs of domestic violence victims, she can vest responsibility in the federal government.

However, it is difficult for federal officials to superintend the operational details of thousands of shelters—and the political climate bodes ill for policies that propose augmenting federal power. Alternatively, she can choose a middle course, by directing the federal funds to state authorities, but requiring them to follow specific standards and report specific information to federal authorities.

Kinds of Agencies Receiving Funds   The policy advocate has to decide which kinds of agencies can receive federal funds. Should not-for-profit, public, or profit-oriented agencies, or some combination of these, receive funds?[4] Not-for-profit agencies have boards of directors, but their members are not allowed to have a financial stake in the agency, nor do the boards have shareholders or other investors who receive dividends. (Agency surpluses must be reinvested in the agency, whose staff receive fixed salaries.) Not-for-profit agencies are exempt from state and federal taxes, and contributors can usually deduct donations from their income, provided the agencies have a tax-exempt status with the Internal Revenue Service and with the state authorities that oversee not-for-profit agencies. Profit-oriented agencies are owned by private investors, either owners or stockholders, who expect a financial return on their investment. (Owners may assume a major role in overseeing their agencies or may cede management to outside managers who work under their general direction.) Public agencies are usually funded exclusively by public authorities and clients' payments. In actual practice, though, complex hybrids exist. Virtually all not-for-profit agencies and some profit-oriented agencies receive contracts from public authorities; indeed, most not-for-profits receive more than 60 percent of their revenues from public contracts and grants. Some not-for-profits even have profit-oriented subsidiaries.

The policy advocate then has to compare these kinds of agencies when deciding whom to recommend funds for. Because public agencies lack a profit motive, they have no economic incentive to deceive or shortchange clients. Many critics have assailed public agencies, however, because they are often bedeviled by red tape, and by civil service and unionized employees who cannot be easily removed if they are ineffective. Although ultimately accountable to elected officials, many public agencies do not make extensive use of community resources, such as volunteers and support groups. Because public agencies often have emphasized services to poor persons, they often are shunned by working- and middle-class citizens, who may also believe them to be excessively bureaucratic.[5]

Not-for-profit agencies are perceived as more innovative than public agencies because fewer regulations constrain their programs.[6] As they tend to be smaller than public agencies and have boards composed of residents, some of them are likely to be more responsive to the needs of specific communities. Some critics nonetheless question whether not-for-profit agencies are actually more innovative than public agencies, noting that their boards are often dominated by community elites, with scant participation by ordinary citizens.[7] Some of them engage so aggressively in marketing and fundraising that they are indistinguishable from profit-oriented agencies, which have their own defenders and detractors. Many persons advocate privatizing human services by giving profit-oriented organizations an expanded role in delivering services. They contend that private markets enhance the efficiency of human services and the gearing of services to clients' needs. Wanting to instill market efficiency into the human services sector, they contend that public agencies that are inefficient or unresponsive to consumers should be supplanted by for-profit or not-for-profit agencies.[8] Many critics of such a view point out that profit-oriented nursing homes and day-care centers sometimes attract clients with deceptive advertising, cut the quality of their services to increase their profits, and refrain from serving persons who cannot pay their fees.[9]

Planning the Extent of Devolution and the Resource Path in Steps 2, 3, and 4

Our policy advocate realizes that fiscal resources are the lifeblood of the human services system and that shelters desperately need funds to survive. She must choose a funding source for social programs, determine how much money to give specific programs, and select a funding channel—and she must make these choices in the context of existing policy realities.

Extent of Devolution   Intense controversy exists about the respective roles of federal and state governments. Indeed, a movement to devolve federal programs and policies to state and local levels has taken place during the last three decades. After establishing federal social insurance and welfare programs during the Great Depression, the United States vastly enlarged a federally directed welfare state in the following four decades; federal domestic spending rose from a paltry 2 percent of the gross national product (GNP) in 1930 (before the depression) to 17 percent by 1979.[10] This growth in the federal spending was a result of widespread cynicism about the ability of state and local governments to address their social problems. Even as liberals took the lead in developing this welfare state, conservatives chafed at the rise in federal power and launched three successive assaults on it. Richard Nixon, Ronald Reagan, and Newt Gingrich attempted in the early 1970s, the 1980s, and the mid-1990s, respectively, to cut federal spending and to devolve federal programs to state and local governments using so-called block grants. (Unlike categorical programs such as Head Start, which the federal government funds, defines, and regulates, block grants distribute funds to states or localities with relatively few restrictions.) Reagan succeeded in establishing nine block grants in 1981, which redirected funds for 77 categorical programs to block grants, and Gingrich and his allies, with some cooperation from Bill Clinton, ended the AFDC (Aid to Families with Dependent Children) as a federal program and entitlement and converted it to a block

TABLE 8.1 Orienting Framework Criteria for Placing Social Policies on the Federal-to-State Continuum

CRITERIA	SOLE FEDERAL	DEVOLVED WITH FEDERAL TILT	DEVOLVED WITH STATE/ LOCAL TILT	SOLE STATE OR LOCAL
Extent to which federal tax code is used	X			
Extent to which program addresses survival needs	X	X		
Likelihood that states will discriminate	X	X		
Extent to which problem requires large resources	X	X	X	
Extent to which economic competition among states inhibits socially responsive policies	X	X	X	
Extent to which problem is linked to global competitiveness	X	X	X	
Extent to which local inputs and partnerships are needed		X	X	X
Service-intensive programs		X	X	X

© Cengage Learning

grant called TANF (Temporary Assistance for Needy Families). Devolution continued through the presidency of George W. Bush. His successor, Barack Obama, revived a stronger role for the federal government in health reforms, bank regulations, and federal spending to revive the economy during and after the Great Recession of 2007 to 2009 and beyond.

While conservatives have often framed relationships between federal and nonfederal governments in either-or terms, many permutations are not only possible but also desirable (see Table 8.1). Where programs should be placed on a continuum extending from sole federal to sole state or local depends, I contend, on how the programs rank on eight criteria.[11] (Of course, many people might disagree with my recommendations, such as some conservatives who would like to turn virtually all social programs over to the state and local governments.)

National authorities should fund programs that meet survival needs, such as SSI (Supplemental Security Income), the Supplemental Nutrition Assistance Program (SNAP, formerly the food stamp program), social insurances, and the now-devolved AFDC program. Not only do these programs require huge resources but also, for several reasons, they are unlikely to be funded sufficiently by state and local governments. The nationwide total of state and local tax revenues is only half the total of federal tax revenues; thus, state and local governments lack the resources for large programs, particularly as they must also fund schools, highways, prisons, and the local share of such federal programs as Medicaid. Moreover, many policy experts fear a "race to the bottom" as states compete to cut their safety net programs.[12] Fearing that low-income persons will immigrate if they offer safety net programs that are more munificent than those of other states, some states offer miserly benefits. Many states restrict their tax revenues, moreover, by keeping their tax rates lower to entice corporations. These constrictions of their tax revenues diminish their resources for social programs.

Many other programs can be devolved with a federal tilt so the federal government provides some funds and considerable oversight and regulations, or they can be devolved with a state/local tilt so the federal government provides fewer resources, less oversight, and fewer regulations. Many social service programs that require local input and partnerships and that need to be tailored to local needs fit into these two models. But many of these programs should not be completely devolved because they will be poorly funded. Moreover, the nation has a stake in many state and local services, such as job training, that keep American citizens competitive in job markets as the economy globalizes.

Some programs should continue to be funded and administered by local and state governments, such as large components of secondary education and correctional institutions. Also, states and localities can and should fund many social programs that fill the gaps in federal and state programs.

Sources of Funds for Social Programs   Policy advocates must choose from a variety of funding options.[13] The extensive general revenues of local, county, state, and federal governments fund many programs. Since the 1930s, the federal government has emerged as the major funder of social welfare programs because, as we know, it raises roughly two times the combined tax revenues of state and local governments, by state income taxes; state (or local) property taxes; and state (or local) sales, excise, and license taxes, to name a few. General revenues provide a useful source of funds for social programs because they are generally unrestricted. However, fierce competition exists over appropriation of general revenues, as many groups, thousands of existing social programs, and the Department of Defense all seek them. When taxes are periodically cut, access to general revenues becomes even more difficult.

Payroll taxes fund Social Security and Medicare programs. These taxes take a certain percentage of employees' or employers' payrolls, or both. While payroll taxes are a predictable and stable source of revenues, it is virtually impossible to develop new payroll taxes because Social Security and Medicare already preempt a considerable share of people's income.

Clients' payments for services fund a significant share of the nation's social programs run by agencies or private practitioners. Requiring payment discourages clients from the unnecessary use of social and medical services. In the case of sliding fees, relatively affluent persons shoulder a substantial part of programs' operating costs. However, charging fees often deters poor persons from seeking needed services.

Special taxes, such as taxes on marriage licenses, auto licenses, and alcoholic beverages, are often earmarked for specific programs, as when states use taxes on marriage licenses to fund shelters for victims of domestic violence. Like payroll taxes, special taxes provide a stable source of revenues for specific programs, but political interests, represented by, for example, liquor companies, often oppose them, fearing the taxes will raise the cost of their products and erode their markets.

Private philanthropy, of, for example, federated community fundraising drives (such as United Way and appeals for Jewish and Catholic agencies), corporations, foundations, and individual donors, remains a major funding source for social programs, even though it has been eclipsed by governmental funding since the late 1950s.[14] Private philanthropy provides funds that are often less restricted than government funds because they are not usually earmarked for specific programs. As with general government revenues, however, agencies and programs compete fiercely for scarce philanthropic funds, particularly since the cuts in government funding in the 1980s and 1990s. The bulk of private philanthropic dollars is, moreover, given to educational, medical, and cultural groups rather than to agencies serving persons with stigmatized conditions or from low-income groups.

Determining Levels of Funds

Euphoric after the enactment of legislation, policy advocates often discover that the programs they have championed have received inadequate funding. The funding of public programs usually follows a two-step procedure.[15] First, legislatures authorize funds by stipulating an upper limit to the funds a specific program can receive in a given year. Second, the legislature appropriates a specific amount of money to the program for a specific year. Alternatively, as illustrated by Medicare, Medicaid, and Social Security, legislatures provide open-ended funding for some programs, in which they agree to fund whatever costs those programs incur in a specific year. However, most programs must battle for their funds in the appropriations process, often receiving far less money than was authorized for them because of competing demands for the available funds.

We should realize that choices about the funding of social policies occur in a broader context, whether at county, state, or federal levels. Using the federal level as an example, assume that you wanted federal resources for a so-called discretionary program. (The funding of discretionary programs is determined annually in the push-and-pull of the budget process, unlike interest on the federal debt and entitlements—or mandatory spending—like Medicare, Medicaid, food stamps, SSI, the Earned Income Tax Credit (EITC), and Social Security, which are automatically funded to the level of claimed benefits in a given year.) When mandatory spending is subtracted from budget totals, about 36 percent of federal budget revenues remain. In turn, more than one-half of these revenues are absorbed by military spending, meaning that about 13 percent of the entire federal budget is available for domestic discretionary spending. Many claimants that are not social programs vie for these discretionary dollars, including transportation, the National Park Service, environmental clean-up, road and bridge construction, public works programs, and foreign policy expenditures. About 5 percent of the total federal budget exists for discretionary social programs of the Department of Health and Human Services, so advocates of increased funding for specific programs must realize that they play in a crowded field—and they must use considerable pressure and lobbying to convince legislators to increase funding for the program they favor. Even in agency settings, policy advocates who want greater resources for a specific program must understand the agency's budget so they can make a good case for shifting resources from existing programs to one that they favor—assuming they cannot find new resources, such as by writing a grant proposal.

Some legislative committees are authorizing committees that, essentially, decide the maximum amount of resources that can be expended on a particular program in a given year. (An example is the House Committee on Economic and Educational Opportunities, which authorizes resources for the Social Services Block Grant.) Appropriations committees decide how much money will actually be given to a specific program in a given year. So advocates need to get both sufficient authorizations and sufficient appropriations for specific programs.

Funding Channels

Once funds exist for a social program and some combination of public, not-for-profit, and profit-oriented agencies has been chosen to receive the money, funding channels need to be devised to distribute these resources. We can visualize the funds as flowing through channels, or routes, from various levels of government to agencies or consumers (see Figure 8.2).

Federal funders often provide money directly to agencies, as shown in Route 1, Figure 8.2. Funding may take the form of *project grants,* in which the federal government

FIGURE 8.2 Possible Funding Channels

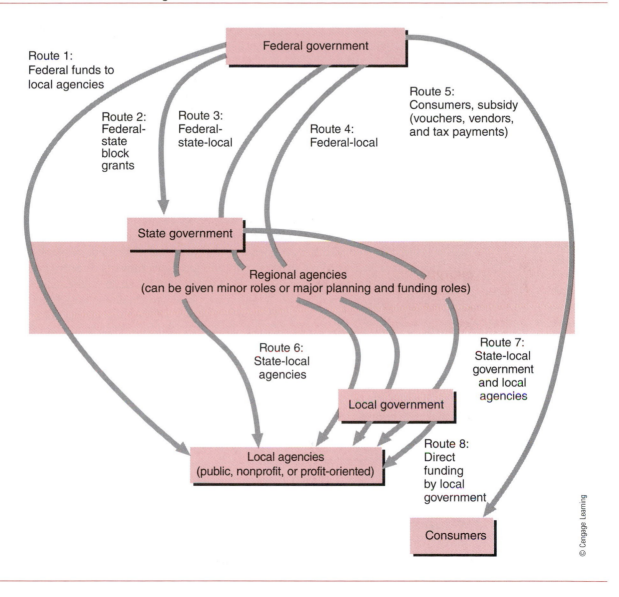

gives funds to a shelter to provide services to domestic violence victims. If project grants usually give agencies considerable latitude, government *contracts* specify the precise services the government wishes to provide, such as "5,000 days of residential services, for victims of domestic violence in Fargo, North Dakota."[16]

Alternatively, some persons argue that federal funders should provide resources directly to consumers (Route 5). For example, some persons favor the use of *vouchers*, that is, funds consumers can use to purchase specific services, such as day care. Government may place limits on the kinds of commodities that can be purchased and may require providers to meet certain licensing standards. Government funds may also take the form of *vendor payments* that reimburse providers for their services to specific clients.[17] For example, the Medicaid program directly reimburses hospitals and physicians for the medical services they provide to low-income patients.

In the federal-to-state channel (Route 2), the federal government distributes funds to the states, which then distribute the funds to specific agencies. Advocates of state government support this policy because it gives the states an enhanced role in the human services system. Indeed, advocates of block grants, which are relatively unrestricted funds that the federal government gives states or local units of government, argue that they give recipients the flexibility to use the funds as they wish and to adapt their programs to local need. Opponents of block grants contend that they provide local jurisdictions with carte blanche use of federal funds for trivial or misdirected programs, and might allow them to underserve specific groups.[18] These opponents favor the federal funding of specific programs that requires the recipient to use the money for specific purposes and to adhere to numerous federal regulations. These programs, such as the Head Start program, are often called *categorical programs.* In the Reagan administration, a number of large block-grant programs were established, including ones for maternal and child health and for social services. While the federal government placed some restrictions on how the states could use these funds, there were fewer constraints than in the 57 categorical programs that these two replaced. (As we discussed in Chapter Seven, welfare reform legislation in 1996 replaced the categorical AFDC program with a federal block grant.)

Alternatively, the federal government can fund local governments directly (Route 4), a tactic favored by some mayors and county supervisors who chafe at the extraordinary power of the federal government. In this case, local governments would use federal funds to fund shelters for victims of domestic violence within their jurisdictions.

Similarly, the states use many channels when they distribute their funds to local programs. They may distribute the funds directly to agencies (Route 6) or they may use local governments to distribute funds to agencies (Route 7).

Each funding channel has its critics and defenders. Those who favor the use of vouchers contend, for example, that it promotes healthy competition among agencies for clientele and decreases the need for government bureaucracy. Critics, however, point to many defects in market schemes. Although armed with vouchers, many low-income consumers cannot find quality providers because relatively few of them have agencies or practices in low-income areas.[19]

Indirect Financing

We have focused on how federal and state governments finance social welfare programs directly. Social welfare services can also be financed indirectly through the tax system, as when clients are given *tax deductions* that allow them to deduct specific health, housing, or social welfare expenditures from their pretax income. In the case of interest payments on their mortgages, for example, millions of Americans receive tax deductions for their housing. *Tax credits* are direct cash rebates from the U.S. Department of the Treasury to taxpayers who meet specific eligibility standards after they have filed their taxes, such as cash received by low-income families through the EITC. Some taxpayers receive tax credits by subtraction of payments for specific programs from their federal taxes; for example, many working women fund only a part of their day-care expenditures, by subtracting a child-care credit from the taxes they would otherwise pay. *Tax exemptions* allow taxpayers not to pay taxes on part of their income. For instance, people can subtract from their taxable income an exemption for each dependent, which lowers their taxable income.

By these indirect methods of financing social welfare, then, citizens receive money not by direct government appropriations but through tax concessions.[20] The advantage of using the tax system to finance social welfare is that it does not require appropriations and thus avoids political uncertainties. However, tax concessions often benefit wealthy persons and corporations disproportionately (see Policy Advocacy Challenge 8.2). For instance, the tax deductions for mortgage interest payments on expensive homes vastly exceed the deductions for modest homes, and tenants generally receive no assistance from the tax codes. Although the government gives persons with tax-subsidized benefits a free hand in choosing their services, it does not usually regulate or monitor them. For example, persons who receive day-care credits may use services that do not meet basic standards.

<table>
<tr>
<td>

Policy Advocacy Challenge 8.2

The Upside-Down Welfare State[1]

Mimi Abramovitz, DSW, Professor, School of Social Work, Hunter College School of Social Work; Director of Social Welfare Program, The Graduate Center, City University of New York

</td>
<td>

It is commonly accepted that government tax and spending policies create more equality because they cushion the blows of the market economy for the poor. But a broader look at spending levels, benefit amounts, and vulnerability to budget cuts reveal that, by and large, government programs favor the haves over the have-nots. Contrary to popular wisdom, as it is currently configured, social policy reinforces inequality.

SOCIAL WELFARE SPENDING FOR THE MIDDLE CLASS

In 2000, the federal government spent more than $1 trillion on social welfare programs, or 61 percent of all federal spending, including welfare, food stamps, SSI, the EITC, Social Security, and Medicare, among numerous other programs. Paradoxically, the majority of these dollars ended in the pockets of the well-to-do. While $235.9 billion dollars went to means-tested public assistance program for the poor, we spent a much larger $793.9 billion for programs that do not use poverty or need as a criterion for receiving aid. Programs for the have-nots absorbed 23 percent of all entitlement spending compared to 77 percent for the more affluent.[2] While the latter comprise more of the U.S. population, they profit from less restrictive and more generous programs and from the belief that they are more worthy of aid.

TAX EXPENDITURES FOR THE AFFLUENT

When tax expenditures are factored into the equality calculation, it turns out that the government spends even more on the more well-to-do. Tax expenditures—revenue losses stemming from provisions of federal tax laws that reduce income taxes that need to people pay[3]—represent taxes the government chooses not to collect. Few people think of the tax code as a social welfare system, yet these dollars address the same common human needs as social welfare spending, including family support, retirement, health care, housing, child care, and education but are targeted to the needs of the middle and upper class.

Between 1965 and the late 1990s, the number of tax expenditures grew from 50 to 166. The cost to government in lost revenues rose from $36.6 billion in 1967 to an estimated $587 billion in 2000—$292 billion more than the $295 billion allocated to the military that year. Projections indicate that from 1996 through 2002, taxes not collected amounted to $3.7 trillion—more than enough to have paid off the $3.4 trillion national debt in 2000.[4] This tax spending on the gilded welfare state for the upper class often exceeds

</td>
</tr>
</table>

---

[1]Title adapted from D. Huff, "Upside-Down Welfare," *Public Welfare* (Winter 1992): 36–40. See also M. Abramovitz, "Everyone Is Still on Welfare: The Role of Redistribution in Social Policy," *Social Work* 46 (4) (October 2001): 297–308.
[2]Congressional Budget Office, *The Economic and Budget Outlook: Fiscal Years 2002–2011* (Washington, DC: U.S. Government Printing Office, January 2001).
[3]U.S. Joint Committee on Taxation, *Estimates of Federal Tax Expenditures for the Fiscal Years 2001–2005* (Washington, DC: U.S. Government Printing Office, April 6, 2001), pp. 2–3.
[4]Congressional Budget Office, *The Economic and Budget Outlook: Fiscal Years 2002–2011* (Washington, DC: U.S. Government Printing Office, January 2001).

(continued)

**Policy
Advocacy
Challenge 8.2**
(continued)

similar programs for the poor. The U.S. Joint Committee on Taxation in 1989[5] projected that in 1998 the federal government would spend some $72.2 billion on housing subsidies for the rich (mortgage interest tax deductions, property taxes, and capital gains on home). This contrasts sharply with the $24 billion spent by the Department of Housing and Urban Development on low-income housing and rental subsidies for the poor. On a larger scale, the $587 billion tax expenditure bill for 2000 was $352 billion more than the $235 billion allocated to means-tested programs for poor people; $118 billion more than the $406 billion for Social Security; and just $378 billion less than the total $966 billion spent on entitlement benefits.[6]

Remarkable conflict developed between Republicans and Democrats about the advisability of increasing taxes on affluent Americans during the presidency of Barack Obama. If Obama sought higher taxes on persons earning more than $250,000 and especially on millionaires, Republicans insisted that taxes on affluent Americans should be markedly cut.

The benefit levels of both the social welfare and tax benefit systems also favor the affluent over the poor. Tied to the cost of living, social insurance programs serving the middle class pay significantly higher benefits than the public assistance programs for poor people that lack this built-in protection against erosion from inflation.[7] Tax benefits are even more class-biased. The 1999 tax cut amounted to nearly $32,000 more a year for the wealthiest 1 percent of the U.S. households, while the bottom 60 percent suffered a $166 cut.[8] The 2001 Bush administration's $1.3 trillion, 10-year tax cut continued this uneven pattern.[9]

The differential vulnerability to budget cuts furthers the systemic inequalities resulting from government policies. The nation's leaders readily cut spending for the needy—who lack political clout and who are deemed unworthy of government aid—while protecting programs used by the better-off middle class. In the mid-1990s, low-income programs received 23 percent of all mandatory funds but suffered 93 percent of the cuts. Low-income programs received 21 percent of discretionary spending but absorbed 43 percent of the cuts.[10] Tax expenditures are particularly *in*vulnerable to the budget ax. Less visible to the wider public than direct social spending and less subject to the perils of the budget process, they win Congressional approval more easily and remain on the books longer than direct spending programs.

CORPORATE WELFARE

Government aid to business and industry intensifies the affluent bias of social policy. As reported by the conservative Cato Institute, every major government department is a repository for government funding of private industry.[11] The editors of *Time Magazine* estimated that the government dispenses about $125 billion a year to companies to help them advertise their products, build new facilities, train their workers, and write off the cost of perks.[12] Corporate welfare also includes direct government grants, tax reductions, support for research and development, and discounted user fees for public resources,

[5]U.S. Joint Committee on Taxation, *Estimates of Federal Tax Expenditures for the Fiscal Years 1999–2003* (Washington, DC: U.S. Government Printing Office, December 14, 1998), Table 1, pp. 17–18.
[6]Congressional Budget Office, *The Economic and Budget Outlook: Fiscal Years 2002–2011* (Washington, DC: U.S. Government Printing Office, January 2001).
[7]House Committee on Ways and Means, *Overview of Entitlement Programs* (2000 Green Book) (Washington, DC: Government Printing Office, 2000).
[8]I. J. Lav and R. Greenstein, *Tax Bill Contains Only Modest Benefits for Middle Class Despite Its High Cost* (Washington, DC: Center on Budget and Policy Priorities, August 29, 1999), p. 1.
[9]L. Shapiro and J. Sly, *Bush Tax Cut and House Rate Cuts Widen Record after Tax Income Disparities* (Washington, DC: Center on Budget and Policy Priorities, 2001).
[10]R. Greenstein, R. Kogan, and M. Nichols, *Bearing Most of the Burden: How Deficit Reduction During the 104th Congress Concentrated on Programs for the Poor* (Washington, DC: Center on Budget and Policy Priorities, 1996).
[11]R. D. Hershey, Jr., "A Hard Look at Corporate Welfare," *New York Times* (March 7, 1995), p. D1.
[12]D. L. Bartlett and J. B. Steel, "Corporate Welfare," *Time Magazine* (November 8, 1998), p. 38.

among others. But the vast bulk of government largesse to big business appears in special tax abatements, which in fiscal 2000 cost the government approximately $195 billion—far, far larger than direct-spending business subsidies.[13]

In sum, everyone is on welfare, but the class biases of both the highly visible social welfare system and the hidden welfare state embedded in the tax code ensure that government tax and spending policies do not benefit everyone equally. To make government a better deal for ordinary Americans in the United States—whose gap between the rich and the poor exceeds that of any other industrialized nation—social workers can help expose the gilded welfare state as undemocratic and unfair and call for a system based on real distributive justice for all.

EXERCISE

List and discuss the ways in which you and your family have benefited from the American welfare state. How have your socioeconomic status, gender, and race impacted the types of welfare or assistance that you and your family have received?

---

[13]Statement of Robert S. McIntyre, director, Citizens for Tax Justice, before the House Committee on the Budget Regarding Unnecessary Business Subsidies, June 30, 1999.

Some Funding Choices   Our policy practitioner has to state in her legislative proposal how much funding she is requesting, to what extent the states should match federal funds, whether the states should receive funds with relatively few restrictions, and whether in some states taxes on marriage licenses should be used to fund shelters.

When examining funding channels, she has to review her approach toward the various levels of government. If she decides to emphasize the states' role in superintending the program, she will propose that federal authorities direct funds to states, which will then fund the shelters. If, by contrast, she wants to emphasize the role of the federal government, she will have federal authorities directly fund local agencies, or she will develop a categorical program providing funds to states, which follow specific guidelines in using the funds.

She decides, let us assume, to ask for an authorization level of $450 million in the first year, with authorizations to rise to $600 million within three years. Although she wants more funds than this for the program, she realizes that conservatives, as well as some moderates and liberals, will object to a larger program during a period of federal budgetary deficits. She selects Route 2 from the funding channels, that is, the federal government is to give funds to the states, which then fund local shelters. She would have preferred direct federal funding of shelters, but decides that this alternative is not politically feasible.

Defining Services in Steps 2, 3, and 4

As she develops an initial outline of the Federal Shelter Program, the policy practitioner must provide direction for the shelters' services, decide what mix of preventive and curative services to offer, and determine how to ration scarce resources.

Establishing an Orienting Framework

We can return now to our discussion of conceptual frameworks in Chapter Seven, wherein we contrasted public health, intrapsychic, deterrent, and other paradigms frequently used in social policy. The policy practitioner has to articulate an orienting framework on which to base her services.

The policy advocate realizes that women who have been subjected to abusive behavior often have multiple problems, such as legal, psychological, familial, medical, and economic issues. Many of them contend with divorce suits and police protection, suffer from anxiety and depression, have children traumatized by family violence and disruption, have serious physical injuries from the violence, and face a loss of income after separating from their spouses. These considerations prompt the policy practitioner to favor multifaceted services integrated with residential services. As she struggles to define the services, she decides she wants some combination of advocacy, crisis intervention, and referral services, integrated by a case management system.

EPA 2.1.7a

She is certain, however, that some shelters will not provide any social services because they will lack the funds or will be preoccupied with the residential services. Therefore, she decides to specify in the legislation the services that shelters receiving federal subsidies will need, including crisis intervention, referral services, and case management services, to attend to the multiple needs of victims of domestic violence. She does not want the shelters to become merely places of residence for women fleeing domestic violence; indeed, she wants to link the shelters to their surrounding community and local feminist organizations. Moreover, she wants the shelters to be advocates, not only for individuals but also for domestic violence victims in general. She wants the shelters to support policies that increase the prosecution of perpetrators and that include domestic violence victims in the existing state programs that provide financial reimbursement to the victims of violent crimes. Besides case management and other services, she decides to require advocacy for domestic violence victims, the use of volunteers, and residents' participation on the shelters' governing or advisory boards (to be discussed later). Even with these stipulations, she realizes that many shelters will seem to offer only a residence, not a multiservice center, because it is far simpler to define facilities' formal attributes than it is to shape their informal qualities, such as sensitivity, advocacy, or responsiveness to community needs.

Staff and Licensing

The policy advocate realizes that implementing these plans requires competent staff. She also knows, however, that considerable competition may develop among social service professionals if she favors certain kinds of professionals, such as social workers, in her legislation.

Before we can understand her predicament, we need to discuss how professions, including social work, develop their power and credibility.[21] Professions develop out of both altruism and self-interest. Members of specific professions want to protect consumers from incompetent persons (altruism), but they also want to reserve certain jobs and private practices for persons who meet certain requirements (self-interest). Both altruism and self-interest encourage monopolies from which professionals exclude outsiders who have not received specific training.

Professions must establish minimal education and training requirements, both to be certain that their members have certain competencies and to distinguish their members from the general public and from other professionals. (If no minimum requirements existed, anyone could use the title of the profession and pose as a member of it. This would undermine the profession's credibility because consumers and employers would be likely to believe the title meant nothing.) To protect their members, then, professions specify minimal training and education and develop methods for monitoring them. In the case of social work, graduate schools, whose graduates receive an MSW degree, cannot be accredited by the Council on Social Work Education (CSWE) unless they follow minimal classroom and fieldwork requirements.[22] Similarly, persons who claim they have the BSW degree must have completed specified undergraduate education and fieldwork requirements that CSWE specifies. Programs not accredited by CSWE can graduate students, but they would have difficulty recruiting faculty, and their graduates might have trouble finding jobs.

However, professional organizations are rarely content, again for reasons of altruism and self-interest, to rely exclusively on accreditation to enhance their status. They also want government to use its licensing powers to reserve certain titles, tasks, and positions for their members.[23] Licensing of titles means that by state law, people can use titles such as *licensed clinical social worker, physician,* or *attorney at law* only when they have met certain training requirements, including graduating from an accredited program and engaging in postgraduate training. For example, in some states, the requirements for the title licensed clinical social worker (LCSW) include working for a specified number of hours under an LCSW's supervision.

Licensing of tasks or functions requires people to complete certain training before performing specified tasks, such as surgery or prescribing drugs. This kind of licensing represents an even more potent form of protection for a profession because—unlike the licensing of titles, which merely regulates the terms that persons use to describe themselves—it limits certain tasks to members of a profession.[24] Imagine the power that LCSWs would suddenly gain if all counseling were limited to them, just as surgery is limited to surgeons!

Professions often try to keep certain positions in government agencies to themselves by having them *classified.* When government authorities require certain credentials for a civil service position, such as a master's degree in social work, they prevent members of other professions from competing for that position. It is small wonder that professional social workers have been perturbed by declassification, which removes the requirement that one must have a master's degree, or even a bachelor's degree, in social work for positions in child welfare agencies, welfare programs, and other programs. Licensing and classification are often controversial because rival professions vie to reserve certain positions for themselves or to prevent other professions from monopolizing them.[25]

Our policy advocate, therefore, must decide whether to require the shelters that receive federal funds to hire certain kinds of professionals. The legislation could stipulate, for example, that each shelter's director of social services must have an MSW degree and that only members of specific professions with a supervised practicum in clinical work can provide certain counseling and case management services. Such requirements may enhance the quality of the shelters' social services and make their services billable to insurance. But the policy practitioner realizes that such staffing requirements have some disadvantages. They will substantially increase the cost of maintaining the shelters because the shelters will have to pay the higher salaries that professionals command. Professionals excluded from directing the shelters, such as marriage and family counselors and psychologists, may oppose the legislation.

Some people may even argue that professionalizing the shelters will detract from their use of volunteer and community support; many feminists seek to increase the contributions of nonpaid women to programs that help women. Our policy advocate decides that the shelters' directors should have an MSW degree and that the direct-service staff have had a supervised practicum but decides not to specify their professional affiliation.

Preventive Versus Curative Services

When contemplating whether to incorporate a major preventive component, the policy advocate confronts difficult dilemmas (see Chapter Seven). The number of women on waiting lists for shelters makes it difficult to justify spending large sums on prevention, and it is difficult to know how to prevent abusive behavior in light of the complexity of the problem and the absence of definitive research. Abusive behaviors probably stem from some combination of exposure to abuse as a child, marital discord, substance abuse, cultural factors, sexism, situational stressors such as unemployment and poverty, ownership of a gun, a national culture that promotes violence, and possibly a genetic predisposition toward violence. While large-scale national reforms could address some of these causes, the policy practitioner cannot easily address them in her legislative proposal. If *primary prevention*, which is directed to persons not yet having a social problem, is difficult to accomplish, she nonetheless wonders whether her legislation could engage in *secondary prevention*, which aims at averting the further progression of problems that are in their early stages. As members of her coalition brainstorm the issue, they decide that properly advertised local hotlines would encourage women to seek early assistance. Thus, the policy advocate includes in her proposal a section qualifying shelters to apply for funds to set up a hotline.

Rationing Scarce Resources in Steps 2, 3, and 4

There are always many people who need assistance, so every social agency and social program must engage in some form of rationing.[26] Our policy practitioner must grapple with this issue as she plans the legislation because the resources that Congress might authorize will not be sufficient to address the large demand for services by victims of domestic violence, who have formed long waiting lists for the existing shelters. Moreover, if the Federal Shelter Program is enacted and advertised, it is likely that many women who do not currently use services will seek them.

Formal or Direct Methods of Rationing

One of the most common methods of restricting access is giving free services only to those who fall beneath a minimum level, such as the official poverty line. This method is called *means testing*. Using income measures poses some problems, however.[27] Means testing requires shelter staff to check applicants' financial records, a time-consuming task. Many victims of domestic violence are, moreover, in a chaotic financial situation in the wake of leaving their spouses or partners, losing access to joint banking accounts, and lacking independent sources of income. Can shelter staff accurately identify actual available income, as opposed to total family income, in these circumstances? Income-based eligibility, however, has some advantages. It enables social agencies to focus scarce resources on those who are least able to purchase services.

In addition to, or instead of, basing eligibility on income, the policy advocate can use diagnostic criteria, such as the level of danger, the frequency or severity of the abuse, or the extent of the applicants' personal trauma. Like mental health institutions, which often limit access or at least involuntary commitment to persons who are a danger to themselves or others, the policy practitioner can limit use of the shelters to women who have been physically abused rather than those who have only received verbal threats. Diagnostic criteria have the advantage of limiting the programs to the persons who appear to have the most serious problems. This is an important consideration when dealing with domestic violence victims, whose lives are sometimes in danger. However, these criteria place applicants at the mercy of intake staff, who may misread the seriousness of a woman's problem or who may allow their own preferences to shape their judgments.[28] Indeed, intake staff may be more sympathetic to certain persons, such as members of their own racial or ethnic group or women with certain kinds of problems. When analyzing her options, the policy advocate might choose to use a number of eligibility

EPA 2.1.2a

criteria. She could, for example, limit free service to persons earning less than a certain amount and require shelter staff to give priority to women in danger of serious injury.

The policy advocate cannot resolve rationing issues without considering certain values and her original mission. If she wants a national network of federally subsidized shelters that will serve most victims of domestic violence, she may establish eligibility policies that are relatively nonexclusionary. She could even aim to make the shelters an entitlement, much like Medicare or Social Security, which will receive automatic funding for whatever services they provide to domestic violence victims during a given year. This option would have bleak political prospects, however, because of its high cost.

We should note that buck passing is common with respect to eligibility. In order not to make difficult and sometimes controversial choices, federal legislators, for example, may yield eligibility decisions to states or agencies, as in some block-granted programs. Such ceding of decisions on eligibility standards has some merit because standards of living and demand for services vary in different parts of the nation. Critics contend, however, that more conservative and poorer states restrict eligibility excessively when given this power.

Indirect Methods of Restricting Access

Social agencies and programs devise policies that indirectly influence clients' access. One method of rationing is to place upper limits on the intensity or duration of services. To enable more persons to receive assistance, a program administrator may decide, for example, to limit residence in a shelter to a certain number of months. When placing limits on services, policy practitioners must balance effectiveness with equity. If the intensity, duration, or number of services or benefits is markedly reduced, more consumers will receive program benefits (equity is increased), but the services may be distributed so thinly that they are ineffective or inadequate. Policy practitioners must make difficult choices when considering the relative intensity or number of program benefits.

EPA 2.1.3c

Another common method of rationing resources in social agencies and programs is to adopt a first-come, first-served policy, in which consumers receive services in the order of their application. This approach appears at first glance to be equitable because no favoritism is possible. However, this policy has its own liabilities. People with serious problems may need preferential access, and certain clients may drop off waiting lists.

Some critics argue that social agencies should reserve resources for underserved populations, much as affirmative action has reserved employment slots for women and racial minorities. According to this argument, social agencies should also develop outreach to these populations and examine service utilization patterns in order to reach consumers who leave the service prematurely.

Some social agencies ration services by discouraging specific populations from using them. Overt discrimination is probably less serious than subtler forms.[29] Low-income populations with economic and social problems who want tangible assistance will probably not use some service approaches, such as extended talking therapies. Similarly, a lack of bilingual and ethnic-minority staff will deter ethnic minorities from using services. Agency personnel may not fully realize that their forms of service or their staffing patterns powerfully influence who does or does not use the program.

Agencies ration services indirectly in many other ways, including the location of facilities, the use of specific program titles, and the selective use of outreach. Facilities located in low-income areas promote use by poor persons, just as facilities in many suburban areas favor affluent populations. The importance of titles becomes obvious when one examines the difference between "free clinic" and "women's free clinic": the latter clearly would encourage female users and discourage male users. Patterns of outreach and

EPA 2.1.2d

advertising also influence access; if an agency advertises its program to relatively affluent populations, for example, it biases access toward these persons and away from other populations.

Charging fees is another way to restrict access. As fees increase, low-income consumers are less likely to seek services and more likely to terminate early. Some policies, such as restricting services to regular hours, impose a hidden but substantial burden on working persons and poor persons, who must, in effect, pay a fee by taking time from their employment.

Our policy advocate reluctantly decides that she has to ration the services financed by the Federal Shelter Program because of the enormity of the unmet needs. She decides to restrict access to three months of residence in the shelters unless a woman remains in imminent danger of physical abuse. She also decides to require the shelters to disseminate information about their services to a broad range of community groups, and she establishes a sliding-fee schedule that can be waived when family finances are disrupted by dislocation.

Addressing Agency Network Issues in Steps 2, 3, and 4

In the 1950s, it was customary to conceptualize a social agency as an autonomous entity providing services more or less in isolation from other agencies. But in the succeeding decades, many policy theorists came to realize that agencies had to develop links with one another if they were to provide quality services. Child welfare agencies maintain hundreds of thousands of children in foster care, while serving the natural families of many of these children and the dysfunctional families whose children have not been removed.

No matter how dedicated its staff, the child welfare agency cannot provide quality services unless it links these children and families to schools, mental health agencies, job-training agencies, job-search agencies, substance-abuse clinics, adult education agencies, health providers, Social Security offices, and government welfare agencies. Indeed, linkage must occur on several levels simultaneously. At a case management level, child welfare staff need to develop individualized plans for children and families that identify an array of services, make referrals, and monitor referrals to be certain that children and families actually receive them. If a child welfare agency lacks funds to purchase services, moreover, children and families will sometimes fail to receive them from referral agencies that are overwhelmed by current demands on their services. So, case management has to be supplemented with purchase-of-service resources.

At a more ambitious level, however, a child welfare agency must develop partnerships and collaborations with other agencies. In some cases, it must subcontract with other agencies to help specific kinds of families and children. A child welfare agency might subcontract with a family-counseling agency, for example, to provide family support and empowerment services for dysfunctional families that show promise of improving their parenting sufficiently so that children can remain in the family. Or a child welfare agency might establish a *collaborative project* with other agencies to which each contributes staff and resources. It might, for example, establish a collaboration with a substance-abuse agency and a job-training agency, creating a new program that combines substance-abuse, job-training, job-referral, and family-counseling services. The substance-abuse, job-training, and family-counseling staff would not only meet separately with families but have frequent case conferences, both among themselves and with the families.

Links among agencies were also fostered by a *managed-care* revolution in the 1990s. It began in the health service industry in response to the double-digit annual increases in costs that confronted government funders, corporations, and insurance companies.[30] By 2002, the United States was spending about 16 percent of its gross domestic product (GDP) on health care—far more than any other industrialized nation. Before the advent of managed care, autonomous physicians were reimbursed for each test or service, such as $1,000 for removing an appendix. Few limits were placed on their fees, and insurance companies usually reimbursed physicians and hospitals for whatever fees they charged. Such *fee-for-service* reimbursement was very costly because it encouraged physicians to do excessive surgeries and diagnostic tests, as their incomes were based on the number of services they provided.

Determined to establish limits on these costs, insurance companies formed managed-care organizations and placed physicians and hospitals under tight controls. To participate in managed care and to get reimbursed, physicians and hospitals had to agree to limit their charges and to get approval for diagnostic tests and surgeries. Variously called *health maintenance organizations*, these organizations sharply restricted the autonomy of physicians and hospitals.

It seemed at first that managed care, which began with health services, would not affect social workers, but it was soon extended to mental health services, which employ tens of thousands of social workers. Because, originally, they had provided some mental health benefits, health insurance companies placed mental health practitioners under controls similar to those on physicians: If they wanted to be reimbursed, mental health practitioners had to agree to certain fee levels and had to get approval if they wanted to provide treatment that exceeded, as in many cases, 10 sessions.[31] This trend toward managed care in the mental health services was accelerated by federal legislation in 1996 that required health insurance plans to include mental health coverage. Managed care in mental health quickly spread to the public sector as well. For example, the Los Angeles County Mental Health Department, which is charged with caring for persons with chronic conditions who receive SSI, decided to subcontract its services to not-for-profit and for-profit agencies, giving them specific payment amounts per patient. This method of financing care, called *capitation*, differs markedly from fee-for-service. Whereas mental health providers had often billed insurance companies and public authorities by the hour for the clinical services they provided, capitation meant that they received a flat amount per year for each patient in their care, say, $1,500 per patient. As with managed care generally, capitation removes any incentive to overextend services because the more treatment provided, the less return on the time expended.

As clients soon discovered, the movement toward managed care had both positive and negative consequences. By placing providers under the control of insurance administrators and by setting limits on their fees and services, it fostered greater efficiency in health and mental health. Some managed-care health facilities, however, chose to underserve their patients and clients, increasing their revenues per capita, for example, by deciding to deny diagnostic tests, surgeries, and mental health services even to patients and clients who clearly needed them.[32]

EPA 2.1.10h

Indeed, policy advocates in many states introduced legislation that placed restrictions on managed-care insurance companies, such as diminishing the power of their administrators to force providers to restrict their services excessively, or that gave consumers the right to appeal treatment decisions that denied them services or tests.

In some cases, policy advocates work to create regional organizations to fund local agencies and shape policy choices. For example, the Ryan White legislation provides federal funds for AIDS treatment and prevention programs.[33] This legislation created regional boards across the nation that distribute funds to agencies in their area, monitor these agencies' services, and create new programs when gaps or omissions exist. While critics view these regional organizations as yet another layer of bureaucracy, their proponents note their ability to locate unserved needs, promote joint programs, and advocate for the needs of underserved populations.

Addressing Community Factors in Steps 2, 3, and 4

We noted earlier that our policy advocate wants to embed the shelters in her program in the community. She inserts provisions in the legislation to encourage shelters to spread word of their services to local self-help groups; local professionals who have extensive contact with women (such as hair stylists); female community leaders; and agencies that link women to schools, job placement, medical services, free clinics, and other social agencies. She also requires the shelters to provide advocacy services, such as seeking greater protection by local police departments for women who have been abused.

Because shelters' staff and boards will define priorities and objectives, the policy advocate requires the boards to select 51 percent of their membership from survivors of domestic violence, female leaders in the community, and local professionals who work in self-help and other agencies. These kinds of board members, she believes, should be more sympathetic to her objectives than the businesspeople and professionals who usually dominate agencies' boards. To give the boards even greater powers, the policy practitioner also requires them to review programs and budgets in the hope that they will promote the full range of services in the legislation, including advocacy and outreach.

Guiding and Overseeing Policy Implementation in Steps 2, 3, and 4

As we discuss in more detail in Chapter Thirteen, implementation is a critical part of the policy process. Were policy advocates not to consider implementation in their proposals, they would ignore a vital aspect of the policy-making process. They must consider two issues: Who will establish the detailed policies that will guide the implementation of their proposal, and who will monitor their proposal's implementation?

Most proposals do not attempt to define the myriad administrative policies that will shape their implementation. While they may discuss a broad strategy for determining eligibility, for example, they may not describe detailed policies, such as how current income will be calculated if a means-tested sliding-fee approach is used. These kinds of details are frequently decided through *administrative regulations* that a high-level agency establishes. Our policy practitioner decides to give the responsibility for establishing these detailed policies to the states rather than vesting them with the federal government, partly because she fears that conservatives will oppose her Federal Shelter Program if it gives the federal government this role.

She must also decide whether the programs of specific shelters will be monitored by higher authorities to see if their services are in compliance with the policies in the legislation and the states' administrative regulations.[34] In addition, she must decide whether shelters will be given technical assistance to help them implement these federal and state policies. She decides they will and gives state agencies the task of monitoring the shelters and providing them with technical assistance. Realizing that monitoring and technical assistance can be costly because staff must be hired and reimbursed to travel widely, she decides to earmark some of the Federal Shelter Program's resources for these two functions.

Assessing Implemented Policies in Steps 2, 3, and 4

Policy proposals often discuss how programs or services they establish will be assessed. In the case of the Federal Shelter Program, the policy advocate must decide who will perform these assessments and how they will be funded. As with monitoring and technical assistance, she decides to give this responsibility to the state agency that oversees the shelters.

An Overview of a Proposal to Fund Domestic Violence Shelters

We have watched our policy advocate face a number of policy options and make some tentative choices. Here is an overview of her decisions.

She has established a mission by proposing a nationwide system of domestic violence shelters. The shelters will provide abused women with a range of social services. She has designed the structure of service to place the Federal Shelter Program in the U.S. Department of Health and Human Services, to use only not-for-profit agencies, and to set some standards at the federal level. However, each state is required to appoint a lead agency to administer the funds to the local shelters. She has planned the disbursement and circulation of resources by establishing an authorization level of $450 million, which will increase to $600 million within three years, using Route 2 from Figure 8.2. She has defined the services to be offered by using an ecological paradigm, requiring that they include referral, crisis management, case management, advocacy, legal help, and outreach. She has proposed a regional hotline in designated regional areas, and will require that the shelter directors have an MSW degree and direct-service staff to have had a supervised practicum.

She has rationed scarce resources by (a) establishing a sliding fee that can be waived when family finances are disrupted by dislocation; (b) limiting residence to a period of three months, which can be extended when the resident remains in imminent danger of physical abuse; and (c) giving admittance priority to women in imminent danger of physical abuse. She has included local coordinating boards to link the work of different shelters. The proposal addresses community factors by requiring outreach to underserved segments of the population, links with community support systems, and advocacy; and by requiring 51 percent of the board to consist of survivors of domestic violence, female community leaders, and professional staff in agencies or support groups for this population. Finally, she has arranged for overseeing policy implementation by earmarking 3 percent of funds for state agencies to monitor the shelter programs.

As we will see in Chapter Nine, it is relatively simple to list policy options and to make preliminary choices, as our practitioner has done. But she and other members of her coalition have not yet encountered the difficulties of the political process or persons who are not favorably disposed to the proposal. At that point, she will have to make some agonizing choices.

The Anatomy of Policy Proposals

We can conceptualize proposal writing as choosing from the competing options on various policy issues. The policy advocate maps a proposal by drawing lines between alternative options on a diagram that displays the issues and the competing options. See Figure 8.3, which illustrates the choices made by the policy practitioner who has constructed the Federal Shelter Program. The shaded items are the options.

FIGURE 8.3 The Anatomy of the Federal Shelter Program Proposal

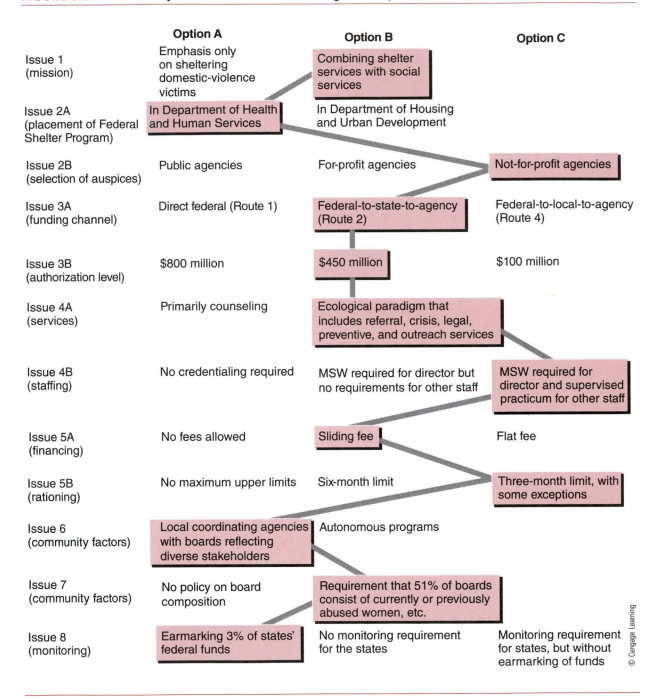

Trade-Offs: Systematically Comparing Policy Options in Step 3

EPA 2.1.8a

Policy advocates sometimes use a systematic process to compare the relative merits of competing options like the ones discussed earlier in this chapter. To make systematic comparisons of policy options, policy advocates often proceed deliberately; they identify options, select and weigh criteria and rank options, and develop a decision-making matrix.[35] You should know about this analytic style of reasoning because it is often used in policy deliberations.

Identifying Options in Step 2

Policy analysts rarely feel comfortable with a single policy approach, wanting to compare and contrast alternative policies before making a final selection. Someone seeking to end malnutrition in certain segments of the population, for example, might examine the merits of distributing food directly to certain persons, changing the food stamp program, and changing existing welfare programs to give low-income persons more funds to purchase food. These three policy choices might be contrasted with expanding income tax credits to poor persons to enable them to purchase more food. By identifying these four options, the policy analyst hopes to avoid being prematurely committed to a specific policy.

2.1.2c

Let us consider the systematic process of examining trade-offs by using as our example an MSW student intern who discovered that Spanish-speaking patients in her hospital placement had very few translation services available to them. She observed that some newly admitted patients had been hospitalized for as long as 24 hours without receiving any explanation of their medical condition or treatment. Many hospital staff were not informed about nuances of Latino culture, moreover, that powerfully shaped patients' responses to medical treatments. For example, a Latina signed an informed consent form for a hysterectomy. Her physician, knowing that her bilingual son had served as her interpreter, assumed that she favored the treatment plan, only to discover the next day that she was so irate that a hysterectomy had been performed that she was threatening to sue the hospital. Only later was the physician informed that it is culturally inappropriate for a Latino son to discuss private parts with his mother—and that the embarrassed son had told his mother that a tumor would be removed from her abdomen! In turn, the mother was furious, not only because she had not been informed about the procedure but also because hysterectomies are considered taboo procedures by some segments of the Latino community.

The intern's challenge was to develop a proposal to address this situation. To do so, she had to compare alternative strategies and gauge which one would be most effective in getting translation services to Latinos. She did not take this task lightly; she realized that the well-being of many Latinos depended on getting translation services.

The social work intern identified four options:

1. Develop a cultural awareness course for new medical residents to instill sensitivity to the culture and language of Spanish-speaking patients. In particular, the course would help the residents understand the need to engage these patients in extended discussions and caring services to offset their fear of the medical system and their inability to express their needs in English.

2. Develop a computerized list of all hospital employees and residents who speak Spanish, allowing them to be contacted by medical staff when translations are needed, thus easing the burden on the seven full-time interpreters employed by the hospital.

3. Hire more interpreters.
4. Recruit 40 bilingual Latino undergraduate students to serve as volunteer interpreters two hours per week, assigning them to the nurses' station in each unit of the hospital.

Selecting and Weighing Criteria in Step 3

In order to select an optimal policy, policy advocates must first identify the criteria to use as a basis of comparison. In simple cases, a single criterion suffices; given three policy options, for example, with the single criterion being cost, the cheapest policy option would be selected. In most cases, however, advocates identify several criteria. For example, they might consider costs, administrative feasibility, and effectiveness in addressing consumers' needs.

Policy advocates can select a variety of criteria. As was discussed in Chapter Two, *value-based criteria* are reflected in terms such as *equality*, *equity*, *social justice*, and various freedoms, such as the right to free speech, the right to privacy, the right to receive accurate and honest information, and the right to self-determination. (Moral philosophers and religious leaders discuss these value-based criteria, which are also discussed in the due process clause of the Fifth and Fourteenth Amendments to the U.S. Constitution and in the Bill of Rights.)

Consumer-outcome criteria define specific policies' effectiveness in ameliorating social problems. In the social services, for example, people often scrutinize how various policy options will affect clients' well-being.

Terms such as *efficiency* and *cost* reflect *economic criteria*. Having limited resources, policy advocates must assess the relative cost of competing options. *Feasibility criteria* pertain to the political and administrative practicality of specific policy options. An option may seem quite attractive but may be rejected because it cannot be implemented or is not politically feasible. For example, some people believe we should decriminalize certain drugs, such as cocaine, by selling them at low prices in state-regulated stores. However, many practical details confound the administration of this policy. If cocaine were legalized, what about countless other substances, including some that have not even been invented? If cocaine were legalized, the state-regulated stores might offer a wide assortment of mood-altering substances. Who would pay for growing or manufacturing the currently illegal drugs? Should poor persons be allowed to use their food stamps to purchase them? Could federal authorities easily override state laws that declare mood-altering substances illegal? Would authorities have to limit the amount of a drug someone could purchase, or could persons obtain unlimited quantities? Could drugs in such an open market be kept from adolescents or schoolchildren, or would older friends, siblings, or even some parents supply them? Some politicians would very likely assail this policy for threatening to corrode youths' morals by making drugs too accessible.

Externalities criteria are used to assess how a policy option would affect institutions or persons who initially appear to be unrelated to the policy. If drugs, including hallucinogens, were decriminalized, policy analysts would have to ask whether driving accidents would markedly increase. This externality could not be dismissed as trivial because as many as 35,000 Americans die each year from accidents caused by driving while under the influence of alcohol, which some consider as similar to a decriminalized and accessible drug. However, some positive externalities might offset these negative ones. The reduced price of drugs and their increased availability in state-regulated stores would drive criminal elements, gangs, and foreign profiteers out of drug dealing and would make it unnecessary for addicts to steal to support their habit. It would also save the federal government the millions it currently spends on combating drug smugglers, money that could well be used to fund social programs.

Terms such as *cost effectiveness* reflect how we can combine several criteria into single measures.[36] In cost-effectiveness studies, analysts want to know which policy will most benefit consumers at the lowest cost. One policy option may yield considerable benefit to consumers, but at a prohibitive cost; another option may yield few benefits, but at a low cost; and a third option may provide considerable benefits at a relatively modest cost. A policy analyst who wants a cost-effective policy would probably select the third option because it balances cost and effectiveness.

When selecting more than one criterion, policy advocates need to weigh their relative importance. This is not a scientific undertaking; it reflects the values of the policy practitioner. For example, when discussing alternative criteria for evaluating welfare reform (see Chapter Seven), many policy advocates would be more likely than conservatives to emphasize welfare reform's effects on the economic well-being of former recipients, whereas many conservatives would emphasize its effects in reducing the welfare rolls.

Our social work intern decided to select four criteria, assigning a numerical value to each of them. To force herself to determine the relative importance of these four criteria, she decided to make the four scores add up to 1.0. She gave the most weight to cost and effectiveness in helping patients with translation needs, wanting to help patients immediately but realizing that funds were short in her hospital. (Each of these criteria was scored as 0.3.) She included the criteria of political feasibility and ease of implementation, realizing she would need high-level approval that would stem partly from the administrators' belief that the project could be easily implemented. (Each of these criteria was scored as 0.2, so the total score for the four criteria was 1.0.) Of course, someone else might have weighted the criteria differently.

Creating a Decision-Making Matrix in Step 3

To help them select policies, advocates often construct a decision-making matrix that graphically portrays the options and the criteria.[37] Our social work intern placed her four options and her four criteria on a decision-making matrix that organized her options and criteria into a table (see Table 8.2).

Recall that she had already rated the criteria by giving scores of 0.3 to cost and effectiveness and scores of 0.2 to political feasibility and ease of implementation. (See the criteria at the top of Table 8.3, which shows how she rated the criteria and the options.)

She then rated the policy options by the criteria (Table 8.3). She decided to rank each of the options from 1 (poor) to 10 (outstanding), using information gleaned from physicians and administrators, as well as her own best guesses. She rated the cultural course as 6 with respect to cost because it would require the development of curriculum and staff to teach it. Because the computerized list would be relatively inexpensive to produce, she gave it a ranking of 8. She ranked the hiring of more interpreters as 1 because it would require more paid hospital staff. The recruiting of undergraduate volunteers was ranked 7; while they would provide free labor, staff time would be needed to recruit, train, and coordinate them. She then ranked the four policy options by the remaining three criteria. As shown in Table 8.3, she gave the lowest score on effectiveness in helping patients with translations to the cultural course (3) on the grounds that it might sensitize residents to the culture of Latinos, but it would not provide new

TABLE 8.2 A Decision-Making Matrix

| POLICY OPTIONS | CRITERIA | | | |
	COST	EFFECTIVENESS IN HELPING PATIENTS WITH TRANSLATIONS	EASE OF IMPLEMENTATION	POLITICAL FEASIBILITY
Cultural course for new residents				
Computerized list of Spanish-speaking employees				
Hiring more interpreters				
Recruiting 40 bilingual undergraduate volunteers				

© Cengage Learning

translation services. Regarding political feasibility, she ranked the option of hiring new translators the lowest, giving it only a score of 3 because she doubted that the hospital administrators would fund this proposal. All of the options were relatively easy to implement, she decided, not giving any of them a score lower than 6.

She discovered that each option had at least one weakness: The cultural course would not make an immediate impact on the translation needs of patients; the computerized list would not prove easy to implement because bilingual staff could not interrupt their

TABLE 8.3 Scoring Policy Options by Using Policy Criteria

| POLICY OPTIONS | CRITERIA | | | | |
	COST (0.3)	EFFECTIVENESS IN HELPING PATIENTS WITH TRANSLATIONS (0.3)	EASE OF IMPLEMENTATION (0.2)	POLITICAL FEASIBILITY (0.2)	TOTAL
Cultural course for new residents	$6_{1.8}$	$3_{.9}$	$8_{1.6}$	$6_{1.2}$	5.5
Computerized list of Spanish-speaking employees	$8_{2.4}$	$7_{2.1}$	$8_{1.6}$	$6_{1.2}$	7.3
Hiring more interpreters	$1_{.3}$	$9_{2.7}$	$3_{.6}$	$8_{1.6}$	5.2
Recruiting 40 bilingual undergraduate volunteers	$7_{2.1}$	$9_{2.7}$	$9_{1.8}$	$6_{1.2}$	7.8

© Cengage Learning

regular assignments and become translators on the spur of the moment; hiring new translators was too costly; and training and coordinating undergraduate volunteers might prove difficult to implement.

The student intern now had to calculate scores that combined her ranking of the options for each criterion and the relative importance of each criterion (the number in parentheses next to each criterion in Table 8.3). She multiplied the option rating in each cell by each criterion score, arriving at a final score for each cell (the subscript number in italics). To score the recruiting of undergraduate volunteers by the cost criterion, for example, she multiplied 0.3 times 7, arriving at a score of 2.1 in the lower-left-hand cell.

Then, she added the scores for each option across the table to discover the total score for each option. She concluded that using undergraduate volunteers was the best solution, because it received a total score of 7.8, compared with the next closest option, the computerized list, which received a score of 7.3. (See the total scores for each option in the right-hand column of Table 8.3.) She hoped she could get a local foundation to provide funds for a part-time coordinator to recruit and train these volunteers. She was excited about this option for educational reasons as well: It would provide an excellent opportunity for the students to learn about the health care system.

The term *trade-off* refers to assessing the comparative advantages of policy options. The policy practitioner seeks to discover which option has the most weight, that is, the greatest net score on the criteria that the policy analyst has identified and ranked.[38] Thus, the student intern selected the fourth policy option, even though other options had received higher scores on specific criteria.

When reviewing this example of a decision-making matrix, it is important to dwell not on the details of the scoring rules but on the style of analytic reasoning. Other approaches to scoring could easily have been used to rank the criteria and the various options and to compute the final scores. When using an analytic style of reasoning, the policy analyst breaks the selection process into a series of sequential steps that eventually lead to an overall score for specific options.

Using a policy matrix does not necessarily eliminate conflict; persons may disagree about the criteria selected, their relative importance, and specific options' scores for those criteria. When policy analysis occurs before a policy is enacted, as in this hospital case, policy practitioners must predict the outcomes, costs, and consequences of options. Such predictions often turn out to be partially inaccurate; in this case, the student intern might later discover that she had underestimated the costs of a policy option or its effectiveness in solving a social problem.

Assume, for example, that another policy analyst came to a strikingly different conclusion than this student intern. The intern did not realize that hospitals are required by federal civil rights legislation to give translation services to consumers who have limited English proficiency (LEP). Nor was she aware that translation services can be accessed through telephone connections that link a health provider and an LEP consumer with a translation-using technology. This policy analyst, too, realized that bilingual undergraduate students lacked sufficient familiarity with medical terms—even with considerable in-service training. How might this knowledge have led this policy analyst to reconfigure Table 8.3 and possibly reach new policy recommendations?

Qualitative Rankings

Had the student intern not been quantitatively inclined, she could have ranked her four policy options qualitatively. Some critics of quantitative techniques would readily support this tactic on the grounds that the existing data do not allow accurate quantitative rankings. However, persons making qualitative rankings (such as high, medium, and low)

TABLE 8.4 Trade-Offs in Policy Options

POLICY OPTIONS	ADVANTAGES	DISADVANTAGES
Using intensive rather than extensive services	Provides in-depth services with greater impact	Denies services to large numbers of consumers
Developing community-based rather than agency services	Decreases stigma of service; helps integrate consumers into mainstream	Is difficult to orchestrate several community services and involve transient populations
Using generalist rather than specialized services or staff	Focuses on client as a whole person	Staff members lack specialized expertise relevant to consumers' specific needs
Providing preventive rather than curative services	Allows early detection and treatment of social problems and educates consumers to forestall development of problems	May neglect the needs of people who already have a serious problem
Using universal rather than selective eligibility	Allows staff to serve all applicants; makes imposing means tests unnecessary	Makes it difficult to target scarce resources on those with particularly serious problems
Using decentralized rather than centralized services	Makes outreach to consumers possible; improves access to services and use of community networks	Is more expensive to operate than centralized facilities
Using multiprofessional teams rather than single-profession teams	Allows many professions to contribute to service	May promote interprofessional conflict

© Cengage Learning

would still have to develop options and criteria and weigh the criteria to judge the relative merits of the policy options.

Table 8.4 shows some trade-offs that social workers in agencies often encounter. Indeed, the student policy advocate discussed earlier in the chapter who developed legislation to help victims of domestic violence would have encountered each of the trade-offs in Table 8.4 when designing shelter programs at the local level (see Policy Advocacy Challenge 8.3).

Policy Advocacy Challenge 8.3

Micro-Level Policy: Examining Policy Trade-Offs in Agencies

Bruce Jansson, Ph.D.

Take any social agency with which you are familiar and any of the policy options listed in Table 8.4. Discuss how the administrators and staff of the agency have wrestled with that option and what solutions they have chosen in the context of trade-offs. If possible, interview some agency staff about their choices concerning the option; otherwise, use your knowledge of the agency to speculate about the possible trade-offs they had to consider when they made their choices.

Using Different Policy Skills in Tandem in Steps 2, 3, and 4

The evolution of the Federal Shelter Program proposal demonstrates that effective policy advocates combine analytic skills in identifying, comparing, and selecting policy options with other policy practice skills. Our policy advocate *also* had to develop and maintain a coalition and make ethical choices as she (and her allies) decided whether to make compromises to get the proposal enacted.

As our example of the proposed legislation to fund domestic violence shelters suggests, policy advocates must *also* be acutely aware of political realities as they construct proposals. In drafting the legislation, our policy advocate decided at several critical junctures to modify some of the provisions to accommodate political realities. She chose, for example, to propose a fiscal authorization at the rather limited sum of $450 million in the first year. She also chose to use the states to administer the funds (Route 2, Figure 8.2), rather than give federal authorities a more expansive role. In making these concessions to conservative and moderate politicians, she had to wrestle with an ethical dilemma: Is half a loaf better than none? Recall our Chapter Two discussion of ethical dilemmas that arise when ethical principles, such as social justice, are pitted against pragmatic factors, such as political realities.

<table>
<tr>
<td>

Policy Advocacy Challenge 8.4

Developing a Proposal to Address Homelessness Nationwide

Gretchen Heidemann, MSW and Doctoral Candidate, School of Social Work, University of Southern California

</td>
<td>

On February 17, 2009, President Obama signed the American Recovery and Reinvestment Act of 2009, which includes $1.5 billion for the HPRP. Imagine you are a high-level official in the Obama administration. Using Figure 8.3 as a guide, develop a proposal to implement HPRP. You will need to decide what types of services will be emphasized, which federal agency will oversee the program, under what auspices the services will be rendered, what types of qualifications will be required of staff, whether caps or time limits will be placed on those receiving services, whether services will be provided autonomously or in collaboration, and how the program will be monitored. Keep in mind the various contributing factors and unique circumstances of homeless subpopulations, as presented in Policy Advocacy Challenge 2.9 and Figure 2.3 as you construct your proposal.

As an additional exercise, assume that a developing nation wished to provide decent housing to some rural migrants who had migrated to the periphery of a large city. What particular challenges would its public officials confront, do you think, as compared to those of a developed nation in providing housing to its homeless persons?

</td>
</tr>
</table>

What You Can Now Do

Chapter Summary

You are now equipped to undertake the second, third, and fourth steps of the policy analysis framework presented in Figure 7.1, including the following:

- Identifying stakeholders and understanding how their vantage points affect their perspectives.
- Identifying a range of policy options that often recur in policy advocacy work.
- Diagrammatically representing a proposal in the context of alternative options that occur with respect to specific issues.
- Examining trade-offs using both quantitative and qualitative approaches.
- Understanding how analytic skills must often be coupled with political, interactional, and value-clarifying skills.

Having discussed how we meld an array of options together to form a policy proposal, we next discuss how we present and defend policy proposals in Chapter Nine.

Competency Notes

EPA 2.1.2a   Recognize and manage personal values in a way that allows professional values to guide practice (p. 257): Advocates cannot resolve rationing issues without considering the original mission and their own values.

EPA 2.1.2c   Tolerate ambiguity in resolving ethical conflicts (p. 263): Advocates must make difficult choices when striking the balance between effectiveness and equity.

EPA 2.1.2d   Apply strategies of ethical reasoning to arrive at principled decisions (p. 258): Advocates oftentimes must reluctantly decide to ration services based on the most urgent needs.

EPA 2.1.3a   Distinguish, appraise, and integrate multiple sources of knowledge, including research-based knowledge and practice wisdom (p. 242): Social workers must consider a range of issues, including the mission, the resource path, how resources will be rationed, and how implementation will be monitored.

EPA 2.1.3c   Demonstrate effective oral and written communication (p. 257). Advocates must communicate effectively with audiences in organizational, community, and government settings.

EPA 2.1.7a   Utilize conceptual frameworks to guide the process of assessment, intervention, and evaluation (p. 254): Policy advocates must articulate an orienting framework on which to base services.

EPA 2.1.8a   Analyze, formulate, and advocate for policies that advance social well-being (p. 263) Advocates must engage in policy analysis.

EPA 2.1.8b   Collaborate with colleagues and clients for effective policy action (p. 243). Advocates must collaborate with others to obtain policy changes.

EPA 2.1.9b   Collaborate with colleagues and clients for effective policy action (p. 242): Social workers work with different allies, entities, agencies, and channels to advocate for services.

EPA 2.1.10h   Initiate actions to achieve organizational goals (p. 259): Advocates work to create regional organizations to fund local agencies and shape policy choices.

Endnotes

1. For an overview of one effort to secure federal legislation to fund shelters for victims of domestic violence, see the *Congressional Quarterly Almanac*, vol. 35 (Washington, DC: Congressional Quarterly Service, 1979), pp. 508–509. Also see Liane Davis and Jan Hagen, "Services for Battered Women: The Public Policy Response," *Social Service Review* 62 (December 1988): 649–667.

2. Bruce Jansson, "The History and Politics of Selected Children's Programs and Related Legislation" (PhD dissertation, University of Chicago, 1975), pp. 66–67, 76–77.

3. See Paul Gorman, "Block Grants: Theoretical and Practical Issues in Federal/State/Local Revenue Sharing," *New England Journal of Human Services* 4 (Spring 1984): 19–23; Robert Fulton and Ray Scott, "What Happened to the Federal/State Partnerships?" *New England Journal of Human Services* 4 (Fall 1984): 38–39; and Allen Imershein, "The Influence of Reagan's New Federalism on Human Services in Florida," *New England Journal of Human Services* 5 (Spring 1985): 17–24.

4. Some overview literature on auspices includes Ralph Kramer, *Voluntary Agencies in the Welfare State* (Berkeley and Los Angeles: University of California Press, 1981); and Bruce Jansson, "Public Monitoring of Contracts with Nonprofit Organizations: Organizational Mission in Two Sectors," *Journal of Sociology and Social Welfare* 6 (May 1979): 362–374.

5. For an overview of some criticisms of public agencies, see Ralph Kramer, "From Voluntarism to Vendorism: An Organizational Perspective on Contracting," in Harold Demone and Margaret Gibelman, eds., *Services for Sale* (New Brunswick, NJ: Rutgers University Press, 1989), pp. 101–102.

6. For a critical overview of the emergence and roles of not-for-profit agencies in the federally funded welfare state, see Eleanor Brilliant, "Private or Public: A Model of Ambiguities," *Social Service Review* 47 (September 1973): 384–396.

7. For criticisms of voluntary agencies, see Kramer, "From Voluntarism to Vendorism," pp. 102–103.

8. For a defense of profit-oriented agencies, see Emanuel Savas, *Privatizing the Public Sector: How to Shrink Government* (Chatham, NJ: Chatham House, 1982).

9. For criticism of profit-oriented agencies, see Harold Demone and Margaret Gibelman, "Privatizing the Acute Care General Hospital," in Barry Carroll, Ralph Conant, and Thomas Easton, eds., *Private Means—Public Ends: Private Business and Social Service Delivery* (New York: Praeger, 1987), pp. 50–75.

10. Alice Rivlin, *Reviving the American Dream: The Economy, the States, and the Federal Government* (Washington, DC: Brookings Institution, 1992).

11. Bruce Jansson and Susan Smith, "Articulating a 'New Nationalism' in American Social Policy," *Social Work* 41 (September 1996): 441–451.

12. Paul Peterson, "State Response to Welfare Reform: A Race to the Bottom?" in Isabel Sawhill, ed., *Welfare Reform: An Analysis of the Issues* (Washington, DC: Urban Institute, 1995), pp. 7–10.

13. For an overview of funding options, see Paul Terrell, "Financing Social Welfare Services," in Neil Gilbert and Harry Specht, eds., *Handbook of the Social Services* (Englewood Cliffs, NJ: Prentice Hall, 1981), pp. 392–394.

14. Ibid., pp. 398–399.

15. Classic accounts of the authorizations and appropriations processes are found in Richard Fenno, *Power of the Purse* (Boston: Little, Brown, 1966); and Aaron Wildavsky, *Politics of the Budgetary Process* (Boston: Little, Brown, 1964).

16. See Demone and Gibelman, *Services for Sale*.

17. John Coons and Stephen Sugarman defend voucher and vendor payments in *Education by Choice: The Case for Family Control* (Berkeley and Los Angeles: University of California Press, 1978). Frederick Thayer criticizes them in "Privatization: Carnage, Chaos, and Corruption," in Carroll, Conant, and Easton, *Private Means—Public Ends*, pp. 146–170.

18. Various points of view on block grants appear in Richard Nathan and Fred Doolittle, "Federal Grants: Giving and Taking Away," *Political Science Quarterly* 100 (Spring 1985): 53–74; and Richard Williamson, "The 1982 New Federalism Negotiations," *Publius* 13 (Spring 1983): 11–33.

19. Thayer, "Privatization."

20. Herman Leonard, *Checks Unbalanced: The Quiet Side of Public Spending* (New York: Basic Books, 1986).

21. Bruce Fretz and David Mills, *Licensing and Certification of Psychologists and Counselors* (San Francisco: Jossey-Bass, 1980).

22. David Hardcastle, "The Profession: Professional Organizations, Licensing, and Private Practice," in Neil Gilbert and Harry Specht, eds., *Handbook of the Social Services* (Englewood Cliffs, NJ: Prentice Hall, 1981), p. 677.

23. Ibid., pp. 679–683.

24. Ibid., pp. 666–687.

25. S. K. Khinduka, "Social Work and the Human Services," *Encyclopedia of Social Work*, vol. 2, 18th ed. (Silver Spring, MD: National Association of Social Workers, 1987), p. 691.

26. For a discussion of rationing, see Richard Frank, "Rationing of Mental Health Services: Simple Observations on the Current Approach and Future Prospects," *Administration in Mental Health* 13 (Fall 1985): 22–29.

27. A general discussion of means tests appears in Neil Gilbert and Harry Specht, *Dimensions of Social Welfare Policy*, 2nd ed. (Englewood Cliffs, NJ: Prentice Hall, 1986), pp. 82–84.

28. For a discussion of staff discretion, see Robert Goodin, *Reasons for Welfare: The Political Theory of the Welfare State* (Princeton, NJ: Princeton University Press, 1988), pp. 184–228.

29. For subtle forms of discrimination and rationing, see Sharon Sepulveda-Hassell, *An Assessment of the Mental Health Treatment Process: Eliminating Service Barriers to Mexican Americans* (San Antonio, TX: Intercultural Development Research Association, 1980); and David Ramirez, *A Review of Literature on Underutilization of Mental Health Services by Mexican Americans: Implications for Future Research and Service Delivery* (San Antonio,

TX: Intercultural Development Research Association, 1980).

30. John Iglehart, "The Struggle between Managed Care and Fee-for-Service Practice," *New England Journal of Medicine* (July 7, 1994): 63–67.

31. Wes Shera, "Managed Care and People with Severe Mental Illness: Challenges and Opportunities for Social Work," *Health and Social Work* 21 (August 1996): 196–201; and Susan Rose and Sharon Keigher, "Managing Mental Health: Whose Responsibility?" *Health and Social Work* 21 (February 1996): 76–80.

32. Marc Rodwin, "Conflicts in Managed Care," *New England Journal of Medicine* (March 2, 1995), pp. 604–606.

33. John Fleishman et al., "Organizing AIDS Service Consortia: Lead Agency Identity and Consortium Cohesion," *Social Service Review* (December 1992): 547–560.

34. For a discussion of monitoring, see Bruce Jansson, "The Political Economy of Monitoring: A Contingency Perspective," in Demone and Gibelman, eds., *Services for Sale*, pp. 343–359; and Kenneth Wedel and Nancy Chess, "Monitoring Strategies in Purchase of Service Contracting," in Demone and Gibelman, eds., *Services for Sale*, pp. 360–370.

35. The analytic process of identifying and selecting options is discussed by Eugene Bardach, *The Eight-Step Path of Policy Analysis* (Berkeley, CA: Berkeley Academic Press, 1996).

36. Ibid., p. 27.

37. See, for example, Robert Francoeur's "decision making matrix," in *Biomedical Ethics: A Guide to Decision Making* (New York: Wiley, 1983), pp. 127–137.

38. Bardach, *The Eight-Step Path*, pp. 49–54.

Suggested Readings

Federal, State, and Local Relationships

Bruce Jansson and Susan Smith, "Articulating a 'New Nationalism' in American Social Policy," *Social Work* 41 (September 1996): 441–451.

Paul Peterson, *The Price of Federalism* (Washington, DC: Brookings Institution, 1995).

Alice Rivlin, *Reviving the American Dream: The Economy, the States, and the Federal Government* (Washington, DC: Brookings Institution, 1992).

Profit-Oriented, Not-for-Profit, and Public Agency Relationships

Barry Carroll, Ralph Conant, and Thomas Easton, eds., *Private Means—Public Ends: Private Business and Social Service Delivery* (New York: Praeger, 1987).

Harold Demone and Margaret Gibelman, eds., *Services for Sale* (New Brunswick, NJ: Rutgers University Press, 1989).

Sheila Kamerman and Alfred Kahn, *Privatization and the American Welfare State* (Princeton, NJ: Princeton University Press, 1984).

Lester Salamon and Alan Abramson, *The Nonprofit Sector and the New Federal Budget* (Washington, DC: Urban Institute Press, 1986).

Stan Smith and Deborah Stone, "The Unexpected Consequences of Privatization," in Michael Brown, ed., *Remaking the Welfare State* (Philadelphia: Temple University Press, 1988), pp. 232–252.

Organizational Issues in the American Welfare State

Darlyne Bailey and Kelly Koney, "Interorganizational Community-Based Collectives: A Strategic Response to Shape the Social Work Agenda," *Social Work* 41 (November 1996): 602–611.

John Fleishman et al., "Organizing AIDS Service Consortia: Lead Agency Identity and Consortium Cohesion," *Social Service Review* (December 1992): 547–560.

John O'Looney, "Beyond Privatization and Service Integration," *Social Service Review* (December 1993): 501–534.

Fiscal Issues

Harold Demone and Margaret Gibelman, eds., *Services for Sale* (New Brunswick, NJ: Rutgers University Press, 1989), pp. 101–102.

Herman Leonard, *Checks Unbalanced: The Quiet Side of Public Spending* (New York: Basic Books, 1986).

Paul Terrell, "Financing Social Welfare Services," in Neil Gilbert and Harry Specht, eds., *Handbook of the Social Services* (Englewood Cliffs, NJ: Prentice Hall, 1981), pp. 380–410.

Professional and Staffing Issues

Bruce Fretz and David Mills, *Licensing and Certification of Psychologists and Counselors* (San Francisco: Jossey-Bass, 1980), pp. 9–29.

David Hardcastle, "The Profession: Professional Organizations, Licensing, and Private Practice," in Gilbert and Specht, eds., *Handbook of the Social Services,* pp. 666–688.

Allocation Issues

Richard Frank, "Rationing of Mental Health Services: Simple Observations on the Current Approach and Future Prospects," *Administration in Mental Health* 13 (Fall 1985): 22–29.

Prevention

Thomas Frieden et al., "Tuberculosis in New York City: Turning the Tide," *New England Journal of Medicine* (July 27, 1995): 229–233.

Dennis Poole, "Achieving National Health Goals in Prevention with Community Organization: The Bottom-Up Approach," *Journal of Community Practice* 4 (November 2, 1997): 77–92.

P. J. Porter, "Ways and Means of Providing Primary and Preventive Health Services," *Journal of Health Care for the Poor* 6 (1991): 167–173.

Staff Discretion

Robert Goodin, *Reasons for Welfare: The Political Theory of the Welfare State* (Princeton, NJ: Princeton University Press, 1988), pp. 184–228.

Michael Lipsky, *Street-Level Bureaucracy* (New York: Russell Sage Foundation, 1980).

Policy Analysis

Eugene Bardach, *The Eight-Step Path of Policy Analysis* (Berkeley, CA: Berkeley Academic Press, 1996).

CHAPTER 9

Presenting and Defending Policy Proposals in Step 5 and Step 6 of Policy Analysis

Policy Predicament

Policy practitioners need presentation skills. You can access the speeches of many world and national leaders in Policy Advocacy Challenge 9.6 to analyze their strengths and weaknesses using concepts discussed in this chapter.

LEARNING OUTCOMES

We can analyze policies with great skill, but we must write creative policy proposals and convince others to accept them if we are to be successful. We will help you become an effective policy advocate by discussing in this chapter how to:

1. Engage in combative persuasion such as debates and hardball negotiations
2. Establish specific objectives with specific audiences
3. Diagnose audiences
4. Develop a persuading strategy
5. Devise tactics for apathetic, hostile, and expert audiences
6. Develop friendly communication strategies in debates and mediation
7. Write grant proposals

EPA 2.1.3c

Having developed meritorious proposals, policy advocates also need to defend them, in one-on-one discussions, presentations to larger audiences, or debates. Without policy persuasion skills, they cannot attract sufficient support for their ideas to be effective (see steps 5 and 6 of the policy analysis framework in Figure 7.1).

We distinguish between friendly and adversarial communications. In friendly communications, policy advocates try to decrease opposition to a proposal with conflict-reducing techniques. For example, they stress commonalities with the audience or engage in win–win negotiations that emphasize shared interests. In adversarial communications, a policy advocate tries to *best* a person or group with opposing points of view through debates or hardball negotiations. Naturally, most of us would like to use friendly communications, but adversarial ones are sometimes needed. Communication that combines friendly and adversarial elements is also often needed.

EPA 2.1.9a

To overstate the role persuasion plays in policy advocacy would be difficult. While enacting policies, advocates often face significant challenges from people who are deeply opposed to their position or who are apathetic. No matter how loudly persuaders shout or how articulately they make their case, their efforts will come to naught unless the audience sees merit in the message and decides to heed its prescriptions. People highly skilled in the art of persuasion tailor their messages to specific audiences and situations.[1]

Policy advocates try to influence people through interpersonal discussions, proposals, speeches to large audiences, memoranda, formal reports, debates or arguments, messages (such as editorials), or the mass media.

The social context is often important. One persuader may be successful in interacting with people in relative isolation. However, he or she may find his or her work frustrated by external noise, such as peer pressure or competing messages from other senders. For instance, political campaigners seldom have the luxury of engaging in extended personal discussion with voters. As they try to reach voters with *their* messages, they must compete with opposing candidates' messages as well as messages from their families and friends. They must also contend with voters' traditional political loyalties, such as when voters have voted with an opposing candidate's political party in previous elections.[2]

Ideology and Policy Positions in Step 5 and Step 6

Proposals and Ideology

Ideology powerfully shapes proposals in legislative settings as well as the content and tenor of policy debates. As a general rule, policy debates are more likely to be adversarial if protagonists' positions are shaped by ideological differences.[3]

Ideology manifested itself markedly during the presidency of Barack Obama with respect to numerous issues. Republicans made unanimous or near-unanimous votes against the Affordable Care Act (ACA) of 2010, for example, insisting that it gave excessive power to the federal government, represented a "socialist model" of health care, and interfered excessively with the private market. President Obama and his Democratic supporters strongly endorsed the legislation on grounds it gave medical care to roughly 32 million uninsured persons and regulated private insurance companies so that they could not deny coverage to persons with preexisting conditions.

Legislators from both parties realize that the "devil is in the details." It is in legislative details that broader ideologies are often manifested. In the case of complex legislation, conservatives, moderates, and liberals may battle over scores of legislative details, as they did concerning the ACA. They battled over whether the legislation would fund abortions and birth control. They fought over the extent the federal government could regulate private insurance companies. They argued over the ACA's likely cost, with Republicans disputing Democrats' claims that cuts in Medicare and government oversight would mean that the ACA was cost neutral. Ideological conflict continued after the ACA was enacted as Republicans challenged the so-called individual mandate that required persons to obtain insurance in federal courts, leading to litigation in the U.S. Supreme Court.

The political context strongly influences the outcomes of these grand debates. Democrats prevailed with respect to passage of the ACA only because Democrats controlled both Chambers of Congress in 2010 just before Republicans gained control of the House of Representatives in November 2010.

Unless one party has a huge majority in legislative chambers, compromise versions of legislation usually emerge in the course of negotiations. One party or faction will make concessions on specific points in return for concessions from another party or faction on other points. Each party or faction will want to convey the impression to their constituents that, on balance, they won or at least received major concessions from opponents. Sometimes a party or faction will want to delay the outcome if they think that delay will strengthen their position, such as when public opinion polls or trips to their home districts suggest widespread support for their positions. On other occasions, a party or faction may decide to resolve the conflict so that they are not seen as sabotaging an eventual solution. They may also decide to do so if they think opponents are besting them in the polls, or with their own constituents or independent voters.

The effects of ideology on policy debates are sometimes muted by other factors. We should not forget that legislators often get tangible benefits from specific policies or programs. Even the most ardent conservative, for example, may favor certain big spending programs because his or her constituents benefit from them, such as when conservatives support major increases in food stamps because this program benefits farmers in their districts. Similarly, many liberals vote for huge and sometimes unnecessary weapon systems because they provide jobs to their constituents or secure campaign contributions. Personal experiences often assume a major role, such as when a conservative supports large increases for mental health programs because a close relative has a serious mental problem. So policy advocates should not assume that they cannot find allies even among legislators who they might expect to be ideologically opposed to specific proposals.

Electoral Politics and Proposals in Step 5 and Step 6

Policy proposals and policy persuasion lie at the heart of political campaigns as opposing candidates try to assemble a winning strategy. Candidates need to identify which issues will resonate positively with their natural constituents as well as with sufficient numbers of swing voters to give them a winning margin.

Various possibilities ensue. Candidates sometimes avoid issues they perceive as no-win, such as when some Democrats in relatively conservative districts chose not to support immigration reforms in 2007 and 2012. They sometimes avoid issues that they think will polarize their potential supporters, such as when some Democrats in 2010 did not support President Obama's decision to make huge cuts in Medicare spending as part of the ACA.

In other cases, candidates address issues but take only fuzzy positions, fearing that highly specific positions would antagonize key groups of their intended supporters. President Obama supported comprehensive immigration reforms in 2012, for example, but did not release details—an approach that angered some Latino immigration advocates who were partly mollified by other reforms he supported unlike virtually all elected Republican officials who staunchly opposed immigration reforms.

Candidates sometimes take contradictory positions on specific issues, emphasizing different points to different audiences. A Democrat might, for example, favor cuts in government spending with relatively conservative constituents, while favoring many new programs with more liberal ones. This tactic can backfire, of course, if opponents charge him or her with waffling on the issues.

Candidates often use combative persuasion in which they try to best their opponents. By drawing distinctions between themselves and their opponents, they can build support for themselves. Democrats forced House Republicans to enact an extension of reduction of payroll taxes in early 2012, for example, by contending that the Republicans opposed tax cuts for middle class persons while supporting them for millionaires.

Combative Persuasion in Step 5 and Step 6

In combative persuasion, presenters use confrontational strategies to modify the opinions and actions of those who oppose them.[4] Three kinds of combative situations exist. In the first type, persuaders debate an adversary hoping to convince observers to choose their point of view over that of the adversary. In a staff meeting, for example, a presenter might argue with another person to win over staff members, just as candidates for political office often debate their opponents on television. In the second type, persuaders use coercive, one-on-one confrontation to change an adversary's position. For example, the presenter might demand that an agency executive make the agency's services more responsive to a specific population's needs. In the third type, persons negotiate with other persons in a kind of extended debate where contending parties decide whether and when to make concessions to opponents and when to accept ones that their opponents put forward. Negotiations often culminate with an agreement that represents the views of both participants, unless they stalemate with no resolution.

EPA 2.1.10k

Adversarial Debates in Step 5 and Step 6

Three parties exist in adversarial debates: the persuader, the adversary, and an audience of observers. Debates rarely follow a structured format (except when school debate teams meet), and arguments often arise.[5] For instance, a staff member presents a proposal in an agency meeting, one or more persons criticize it, and its initiator then defends it. Persuaders sometimes hope to change the minds of both their immediate adversary and the audience that hears their argument, or, if they cannot change the views of their immediate adversary, to secure the support of the audience or influential persons within it.

To better understand adversarial debates, assume that Harry Johnson, a lobbyist for an AIDS advocacy group, is attacking a conservative legislator's proposal to require all testing services, both public and private, to give state public health officials the names of all persons who test positive for HIV. He is debating the legislator before a student audience in the mid-1990s before many states had antidiscrimination statutes outlawing discrimination against gays and persons who were HIV positive or had AIDS. In this context, many AIDS advocates feared that requiring testing centers to give state public health officials the names of all persons who tested positive for HIV (so they, in turn, could inform their sexual partners) could lead to discrimination against HIV-positive persons and persons with AIDS. With the so-called cocktail of drugs not yet widely used in the mid-1990s, many AIDS activists were less likely to believe that sexual partners who had become HIV positive *could* be medically helped. It was in this context, then, that Harry Johnson debated a conservative legislator to oppose his proposal. To illustrate the array of arguments that debaters can use, Policy Advocacy Challenge 9.1 presents 12 arguments Johnson used in his debate.

Participants in social policy debates can also use arguments drawn from the analysis of social problems that we discussed in Chapters Two and Seven. Recall from the

**Policy
Advocacy
Challenge 9.1**

Attacking
Someone
Else's
Proposal

Bruce Jansson,
Ph.D.

Johnson can do the following:

- *Attack the values that are implicit or explicit in the proposal.* A debater can contrast any value premise with an alternative value premise. While the legislator values control to protect the public's health, Johnson favors protecting the privacy and freedom of people who test positive for HIV. Such privacy, he contends, conforms to the traditions embedded in the Bill of Rights. Persons who are HIV positive but might remain free of AIDS symptoms for many years particularly need privacy to protect them from discrimination.

- *Attack the proposal's feasibility.* Public health departments would ask HIV-positive individuals to list persons with whom they have had sexual relations. Department officials would then alert each of those partners to their possible infection with HIV. However, it is extremely time-consuming to develop these lists and contact the persons on them, and health departments lack sufficient staff. "If public health officials lack the staff to adequately accomplish their existing functions, how can we expect them to assume these added functions?" Johnson might ask.

- *Attack the legislator's motives* by saying, "He wants a witch hunt, not humanistic services for those who are HIV positive."

- *Attack some unanticipated or adverse consequences of the proposal.* People who fear they carry the virus may avoid testing if the results are not confidential. Many people would forgo testing, fearing that their identity would be revealed to employers, landlords, and others.

- *Attack the legislator's use of specific analogies.* The legislator contends that public health departments have long required divulging the names of persons with syphilis and gonorrhea. The legislator says that this information has led to successful efforts to alert their sexual partners to their possible infection. To attack this analogy to other sexually transmitted diseases, Johnson notes that syphilis and gonorrhea are currently epidemics despite these practices. Moreover, discrimination against people with these treatable diseases is not nearly as marked, he might argue, as against persons who are HIV positive. Unlike syphilis and gonorrhea, the initial infection with HIV is often followed by a lengthy period, sometimes more than 10 years, when the person has no serious symptoms, much less AIDS. "If we breach the confidentiality of persons with a disease of such duration," Johnson argues, "we risk extended damage to their careers and reputations that does not occur with treatable diseases, such as syphilis."

- *Attack the legislator's uses of data and analytic assumptions.* The legislator contends that such action has already been successful in Colorado. Johnson criticizes specific quantitative studies that the legislator uses to buttress this claim. Johnson attacks the methods used to collect the data, the applicability of the Colorado data to his state, and the way the legislator has interpreted the data. (We discuss methods of criticizing quantitative studies in more detail in Chapter Fourteen.)

- *Attack implicit models of human motivation* in the legislator's rationale for the proposal. Requiring that testing centers report HIV-positive persons' names to the public health department implies that most HIV-positive persons will not voluntarily cooperate with public health officials. This assumption suggests that most HIV-positive persons lack a strong sense of social responsibility. Johnson asserts that many HIV-positive individuals are (or can become) concerned about former and current sexual partners if given access to high-quality counseling that does not infringe on their confidentiality. When they receive their test results, for example, they can be told about voluntary counseling and the need to inform current and previous sexual partners of their risks. Johnson also reframes the issue, moving away from forcing

HIV-positive persons to assume social responsibility to providing assistance to HIV-positive persons to help them arouse their inherent altruism. The gay men's community's remarkable generosity to people with AIDS and the proliferation of support networks they have established support this contention.

- *Attack the legislator's conception of the chain of events that would follow the enactment of his proposal.* The legislator assumes that testing centers will provide the names of HIV-positive people to the state's public health department; this department will contact HIV-positive people; HIV-positive people will agree to provide the names of previous sexual partners or persons with whom they shared needles when using drugs; public officials will contact these partners; and the partners will agree to be tested for HIV, will practice safe sex, and, if they test positive, will provide public officials with the names of their partners. Johnson contends that this chain of events will often be broken at one, two, or more points. We have noted that public health departments often lack the staff to make these contacts. When forced to divulge names, some HIV-positive persons may decline to be cooperative because of the violation of their privacy and the imposition of mandatory procedures. In the case of casual sexual encounters or needle sharing, HIV-positive persons may be unable to supply names. Because of the population's mobility, locating some of the partners will be difficult, even if authorities have their names.
- *Expose the vagueness in the legislator's proposal,* which may make it seem less attractive to other people. Perhaps the legislator's proposal fails to describe how the testing services, some of them being private ones, will be linked to the state's public health department. Perhaps the proposal fails to discuss how the mandatory reporting policy will be evaluated for its effectiveness in slowing the spread of HIV.
- *Attack the unacceptable trade-offs in the legislator's proposal.* Johnson commends the legislator for wanting to stem the spread of HIV (a desirable objective) but argues that, noble as it may be, this objective should not cost tens of thousands of individuals their privacy (a valued objective) or cost the government exorbitant amounts. When making this kind of argument, the lobbyist says, in effect, that we need to stem the spread of HIV with methods that do not violate personal privacy and that are not so costly.
- *Argue that the legislator's proposal will be rendered ineffective by other events.* Argue, for example, that technology that allows individuals to test themselves for HIV in the privacy of their homes renders moot the mandatory reporting law because many people bypass public or private testing centers.
- *Offer a counterproposal.* Because tracking partners is expensive, Johnson argues that scarce public resources ought instead to be invested in public education projects, such as efforts to promote safe sex by the use of condoms. Perhaps scarce resources should be invested in teaching addicts and prostitutes how not to become infected and how not to spread the disease to other people. The lobbyist might conclude that the state will get a far better return on funds invested in an educational program than in a mandatory reporting program.

EPA 2.1.6b

discussion at the end of Chapter Two that Claude Fischer and many of his sociologist colleagues at the University of California at Berkeley attacked the assertion by Richard Herrnstein and Charles Murray that African Americans had lower intelligence than white non-Latinos as measured by a specific test (the Armed Forces Qualifying Test (AFQT)) and that their lower intelligence scores caused them to have higher rates of such social problems as unwed pregnancies, dropping out of school, and crime. Had they debated Herrnstein and Murray in person, Claude Fischer and many of his sociologist colleagues would have used arguments drawn from social science research and theory that would have included contentions that Herrnstein and Murray had:

- Not sufficiently considered the effects of various environmental factors that caused some persons to be more likely to have these social problems, including effects of school, their adolescent community environment, years of schooling, and academic track
- Used a variable ("intelligence" as measured by the AFQT) that did not measure intrinsic intelligence, but was deeply influenced by the schooling and social class of persons who took the test
- Placed undue emphasis on a single alleged cause (AFQT scores) of many social problems rather than a network of factors
- Failed to test their theory with various populations, such as those within Africa, and with other marginalized groups in the United States
- Failed sufficiently to test their theory with low-income persons who were *not* African American
- Used erroneous statistical procedures to analyze their data

Social science research and theory, then, can and should be used extensively in social policy debates as well as evidence-based research that assesses or evaluates specific policies as we will discuss in Chapter Fourteen. Such research and theory is not a panacea, however. Persons can differ about the quality of specific research projects when citing them or when attacking opponents' use of them. Research findings sometimes conflict as is amply illustrated in the field of medicine when conflicting results emerge from efforts to test the efficacy of specific medications or treatments. Yet, social science theory and research can provide valuable clues about the kinds of social policies that will effectively prevent or address specific social problems. In some cases, evidence-based policies can be identified from existing research, and some policies can be attacked in policy debates on grounds that they conflict with this research.

Policy Advocacy Challenge 9.2

Debating Johnson's Arguments in a Changed Environment

Bruce Jansson, Ph.D.

As an exercise in attacking someone else's policy proposal, attack Harry Johnson's arguments in light of the extraordinary progress that had been made against AIDS by mid-1998. New drug therapies had appeared that markedly cut death rates from AIDS. Strong legal protections had lessened discrimination against people with AIDS. In early 1997, New York began a program to test newborns for AIDS and to tell their mothers of the results, rather than (as previously) telling their mothers only when they asked. Many public health officials around the nation had begun to urge the reporting of persons who tested HIV positive to public health officials. Colorado and New York State had begun more aggressively to implement a partner notification system even in 1998 so that partners of persons with HIV could get testing. By 2002, many AIDS advocacy groups came to support partner notification systems—and they existed in most states by 2012.

To hone your debating skills, assume that you are now debating against Johnson's position in the preceding debate—from the vantage point of someone deeply committed to eradicating this cruel disease and helping persons with it to get effective medical treatment. What arguments would you use, and where would you attack Johnson's positions?

Coercive Messages in Step 5 and Step 6

Policy advocates may use coercive messages when they believe that decision makers will oppose their position and that cooperative messages will not work because of decision makers' political and ideological stance, discriminatory attitudes, vested interests, and traditions. In addition, decision makers may feel that existing resources are already so committed to other programs that they cannot support a new program.[6]

Coercive messages are often used when persons make a formal demand that includes a threat, for example, to take further steps, such as litigation, protests, sending delegations to even higher authorities, or publicizing the issue through the mass media.[7]

EPA 2.1.9a

Persons who use coercive messages often try to use the social context in ways that will place additional coercive pressure on decision makers. They may insist that they listen to a delegation, rather than to one person. They may physically surround them with members of their group. They may inform the mass media of an encounter before it has occurred to place even more pressure on decision makers or seek favorable media coverage in the wake of a specific confrontation.

Using coercive messages is effective in those situations where decision makers capitulate—either because they accept the merits of the arguments of persons who confront them or because they fear political or other costs to themselves if the confrontation is not quickly resolved.

But using coercive messages also has drawbacks. Perhaps decision makers become so angered at the tactics of persons who use them that they dig in their heels. Perhaps they retaliate against them.[8] For example, staff in an agency who use coercive messages with their executive director may be fired or demoted. Moreover, once coercive messages have been initiated by one side in a dispute, a vicious circle of escalating intransigency and reprisal may begin that makes it increasingly difficult for the opposing sides to cooperate. Both sides then begin to view the conflict as win–lose, rather than win–win, so that any concession to the other side becomes a personal defeat.[9]

Negotiations: Hardball and Win–Win Options in Step 5 and Step 6

We have discussed both friendly and adversarial approaches to communication. Either approach, or some combination of the two, can be used in negotiations where different participants engage in an extended discussion to try to reach an agreement that will resolve an issue under contention. Let us start with a friendly approach.[10] Directors of two different programs in an agency must decide which of them will administer a new program that will bring considerable prestige and revenue to the person who wins. Rather than staking out a position at the outset, Mary Jones (who wants an amicable solution) encourages mutual discussion of the situation.

She encourages Jack Hoopes, the other administrator, to acknowledge that he would benefit from the added revenues and the challenge of running a new program, just as she would. Rather than moving toward rapid closure and a hardening of positions, Jones moves the discussion toward brainstorming, in which each of them imagines alternative solutions:

1. The new program goes to only one director.
2. The two directors jointly administer the new program.

3. One director receives basic authority for the program but gives the other director key roles in the new program, while retaining the program's revenue for his or her unit.

4. A rotational system is devised to give each of the directors a chance to administer the program.

To Jones's delight, Hoopes's initial adversarial stance has diminished by their third meeting. Already overburdened by other programs, he wants responsibility for only one facet of the new program. To underscore her desire to reach a conciliatory solution, Jones offers to cede to Hoopes one of her current programs that closely resembles other programs that he directs, and she makes this concession without a request by Hoopes. After only five meetings, Jones and Hoopes have not only concluded this negotiation, but achieved a win–win style that heightens their sense of mutual respect.

This win–win approach can be contrasted with a hardball or win–lose approach.[11] Assume that Jones and Hoopes strongly dislike each other, have already had repeated battles over turf and revenue, and both want jurisdiction over the new program. Both believe that they will lose significant prestige to the other party if he or she gets control of the new program. In their first meeting, both of them state that they want control of the new program because it fits in with their existing programs and, fearing to appear weak, stick to this position during the next four meetings. The agency director then tells them that she will decide if they cannot reach an agreement, and Jones reluctantly implies that she will consider ceding the program to Hoopes, but only if she receives some of his existing programs in return. Convinced he has Jones at a disadvantage, Hoopes makes no concessions during the next three meetings, finally agreeing to cede a small program. Unsatisfied with this concession, Jones demands a larger program instead. Only after several additional stalemated meetings and another threat by the agency director to intercede, Hoopes agrees to Jones's request. Both parties leave the negotiations with renewed animus toward each other, determined not to yield any ground in future negotiations.

Hardball negotiations usually begin with each side presenting an initial position. As the negotiations proceed, each side decides whether and when to grant concessions to the other side—as a means of testing their intentions, as a sign of good faith, or as a quid pro quo for a concession the other side has made. Each side has to decide how tolerable a stalemate would be, whether the other side will match its concessions, and when to make concessions. If both sides believe that resolving the conflict is necessary, each party will gradually reveal where it is willing to make concessions. The two sides often use delays, veiled or open threats, and inducements to persuade the other side to make concessions.

We should not forget the role of mediators, who operate between contending factions. Assume that two opposing factions in your agency have been embroiled in conflict for a sustained period. They want to resolve the conflict but do not know how to achieve this resolution. You approach both parties with an offer to mediate the dispute, and they accept. After talking with both sides to better understand their position, you set up a meeting wherein you will act as a mediator. During this meeting, your role is not to suggest solutions, but to facilitate a discussion in which both sides state their concerns and wishes, brainstorm possible solutions, and move toward a settlement. Several meetings may be needed. In more complex mediations, such as those between members of a union and those of management in a social service agency, the two parties may meet separately and communicate only through the mediator. For mediation to be successful, each party to a conflict has to believe that the mediator will not manipulate the situation to the other's advantage, but will merely help the two sides to come to a settlement.[12]

In both adversarial and friendly negotiations, a positive outcome is not guaranteed. Even after a friendly start, two parties may become sufficiently stalemated so that no solution emerges. Or a solution may have to be imposed by a higher-level person or an official *arbitrator* who is appointed to reach a solution. Arbitrators are frequently used in stalemated negotiations between labor and management.

Adversarial or Friendly Communication: Which Is Preferable in Step 5 and Step 6

Let there be no doubt: Friendly communications and negotiations are preferable to adversarial ones in many situations. Parties to conflict can usually settle issues more rapidly when they accommodate each other and are more likely to emerge from friendly communications with respect for each other and develop creative solutions. Indeed, an extensive literature urges policy practitioners to make greater use of collaborative techniques.[13]

Yet, friendly communications are not always possible. In Table 9.1, we identify some situations wherein friendly and adversarial approaches are used. Policy advocates should first attempt conciliation to see if the opposing party will engage in collaborative problem solving. But if their conciliation fails and their opponent tries to steamroller them, they may have to use hardball strategies (see Policy Advocacy Challenge 9.3).

TABLE 9.1   Situations Favoring Friendly and Adversarial Approaches

SITUATION	FRIENDLY APPROACHES	ADVERSARIAL APPROACHES
Relations between parties	Amicable	Hostile
How this issue has been discussed in the past	With low conflict and mutual concessions	With high conflict and few concessions
Extent to which one or both parties have a rigid position based on ideology or self-interest	Neither party has a fixed position at the outset	Both parties have fixed positions at the outset
Extent to which parties attach symbolic importance to issue (e.g., view a loss or victory as having extraordinary consequences)	Neither party attaches symbolic meaning to the outcome	Both parties believe a victory is vital to their well-being, to advance their self-interest or their ideology
Role of onlookers or followers	Onlookers do not pressure the parties to best each other	Onlookers pressure each party to best the other side
Extent to which parties value conciliation	Both parties value conciliation	Both parties value hardball tactics
The effects of the negotiating style	Low conflict and mutual concessions reinforce a win–win style	High conflict fosters more conflict and reinforces a win–lose style

**Policy
Advocacy
Challenge 9.3**

Using Hardball
and Softball
Styles of
Negotiation
in Reforming
the Nation's
Immigration
Policy

Bruce Jansson,
Ph.D.

During the presidential campaigns of 2008 and 2012, President Barack Obama promised immigration reform. The issue was placed on the backburner in his first four years in office as other issues, like health and banking reforms, as well as stimulating the economy during the Great Recession, took precedence. While many Republicans have opposed immigration reform, others displayed considerable interest like Senator John McCain and President George W. Bush who almost enacted it in concert with some leading Democrats in 2007. Many of these Republicans come from districts with considerable numbers of Latino voters—and some of them are pressured by agricultural, tourism, and industrial enterprises to allow them to have continued access to low-wage immigrants.

The prospects for negotiations between the two parties over immigration markedly worsened with Republican electoral successes in the Congressional elections of 2010 when many members of the Tea Party gained office. Even Senator McCain changed his mind after supporting comprehensive immigration reforms in 2007. As Republicans moved toward the right, Obama and many Democrats moved cautiously to the left as they supported the DREAM Act to help undocumented immigrant youth, who had been brought to the United States by their parents, obtain college educations in the United States After deporting record numbers of undocumented immigrants in his first three years in the presidency, President Obama markedly decreased deportations except for undocumented persons with criminal records.

Try out conciliatory and hardball negotiating strategies between Congressional Democrats and Republicans with respect to a comprehensive immigration reform proposal. Create the negotiating situation by assigning different persons to the two sides. Assume that the two sides have still not resolved how to reform immigration. Assume that conservatives want more emphasis placed on interdiction at borders and deportation than liberals who place more emphasis upon giving many undocumented persons amnesty and creating legal status for millions of persons who can be temporary workers. Address these preparation issues first in a hardball manner and have the two sides negotiate for, say, 40 minutes. (You can begin with a period in which both sides state their entering positions for 5 minutes each and then negotiate across a table for another 30 minutes.) Ask whether these hardball negotiations were successful.

Then try negotiating these issues in a softball manner for 50 minutes. Have each side, in its opening presentation during the first 10 minutes, ask conciliatory or open-ended questions of the other side. Then have members of each side discuss the issues in a non-confrontational manner *outside* the official negotiations, while seated in a circle, for 15 minutes. Then have the two sides reconvene in an official negotiation to see if a plan can be developed that is acceptable to both sides. Ask whether these softball negotiations were successful. What differences existed between the processes and outcomes associated with them as compared to those associated with the hardball negotiations?

Discuss which style works best in different situations. Was it difficult to shift styles in midstream? What interpersonal skills are needed for each style?

Persuading Specific Audiences in Step 5 and Step 6

We have mostly emphasized combative persuasion thus far, even though we discussed softball negotiations as an alternative to hardball ones. Now we turn to *friendly persuasion*, which rests on techniques for changing an audience's beliefs and actions by engaging it in a cooperative transaction rather than by confronting it. When such persuasion is used skillfully, audiences are hardly aware that its perspective has changed or that the persuader has been using a carefully developed strategy.

We discuss several kinds of persuasion: written, verbal, and PowerPoint presentations.

Determining Objectives

Before persuaders can decide how to fashion a message, they have to establish objectives. Objectives can be ranked on a continuum extending from ambitious to modest. At the most ambitious level, persuaders hope both to markedly modify the audience's beliefs and to convince it to take specific actions, such as helping change a policy, performing specific tasks, or pressuring decision makers to support a proposed policy. At a somewhat more modest level, a persuader may be content, at least in the short term, merely to modify others' beliefs, perhaps as a precursor to having them take action. (As we will discuss later, changing people's beliefs does not necessarily cause them to change their actions.) Hoping eventually to convince an agency executive to support a new policy, a staff member might send him or her information about an unmet need in the community or a promising pilot project in another agency.

EPA 2.1.10f

At any even more modest level, a policy advocate may wish merely to maintain an audience's beliefs and actions. Assume that some agency staff fear that someone will soon question a favored program, and they want to head off this attack by maintaining, or even strengthening, their director's support for the program. Assume as well that the director has funded the program relatively generously in the past. These staff members need to send messages that reinforce the program's importance so that the director will not be unduly influenced by the impending attack.[14]

At a similarly modest level, a policy advocate may wish merely to educate or sensitize other persons about an issue or problem—perhaps as a preliminary step so that they will support a policy proposal at a subsequent point.

We also need to distinguish between the short- and long-term objectives of persuasion. When planning a message on one occasion, a policy advocate may have a relatively modest objective, such as sensitizing an audience to an issue. However, he or she may anticipate relaying a series of messages to an audience that will ultimately change its beliefs and rally its support of a new policy. Indeed, policy advocates often hope to persuade people bit by bit. A campaign might consist of interpersonal discussions, a memorandum, and a formal presentation, each planned to move an audience toward support of a policy.

To develop a series of presentations is, of course, more difficult than to make a single presentation. In a series of presentations, the policy advocate must decide when to proceed beyond educating the audience to seeking its support for new policies and beliefs. The policy advocate does not want to proceed too cautiously or too rapidly from modest to ambitious objectives.

Diagnosing Audiences

EPA 2.1.9a

Policy advocates often try to diagnose the audience. They want to know the audience's beliefs, degree of motivation on an issue, fears and hopes, and the extent to which situational or historical factors may influence its response to a message.[15]

When examining the audience's beliefs, policy advocates gauge the degree of opposition to their message. Audiences are most hostile to a message when they oppose both its value premises and its fundamental argument. When policy advocates seek to persuade a conservative audience to support softening some of the deterrent provisions of welfare reforms, for example, the audience is likely to disagree with their value premises that society is obliged to help impoverished people, that it should expand its social welfare roles, and that unemployment and low-paying jobs, rather than the size of the existing welfare grants, are the primary causes of expanding welfare rolls.

Audiences are less hostile when the value premises and logic of the message approximate their own beliefs or when they have a flexible or undefined position. When an audience has a broad zone of tolerance, it is open to new ideas, values, or perspectives. Advocates encounter a difficult challenge when the audience's zone of tolerance is relatively narrow.[16]

When an audience is hostile to a policy, persuaders have to try to figure out the reason. Indeed, theorists suggest that audiences are most receptive to messages relevant to their own fears and hopes. When a new agency program is proposed, for example, some staff may fear that it will jeopardize their current responsibilities; divert funds from favored projects; or cause new burdens that they do not wish to shoulder, such as learning new skills or working longer hours. Skillful persuaders try to allay these kinds of fears in their messages, such as by contending that the new program will increase agency revenues, increase the agency's prestige, and allow some staff to migrate to challenging and interesting positions in the new program.[17] They might also appeal to the staff's commitment to the well-being of community residents by showing how the new program will help the agency's clientele.[18]

Audiences also differ in their levels of involvement in specific topics. All of us have been part of audiences that are disinterested in a message. Perhaps we have been inundated with boring messages about the same subject or do not perceive its relevance to us. In such cases, a novel or unusual argument is sometimes effective (see Policy Advocacy Challenge 9.4).

Policy Advocacy Challenge 9.4

Using a Novel Message

Patsy Lane, MSW, Director, Department of Human Services, City of Pasadena

During the time I was a member of the statewide Child Development Policy Board, state legislators and administrators were considering "loosening" the regulations for licensing child-care centers as a cost-saving measure. One proposed change was to reduce child-care licensing staff by decreasing the required number of licensing staff's on-site visits to child-care programs. Such site visits were already perceived by the social service and child-care providers as dangerously few—in many cases, only once every few years. Various child and family advocacy groups tried to educate state decision makers that any reduction in such regulations would be detrimental to the quality of child care and would place children at risk. It was a challenge to find an effective way to communicate to legislators how problematic such a regulatory change would be: Often, the objections were dismissed as overly protective of children.

Finally, a staff person of the Child Development Policy Board submitted an effective one-page chart: a comparison of inspection requirements for child-care facilities with those for dog kennels. Dog kennels, it seemed, averaged a regulatory site visit every six months, while child-care facilities averaged one such visit every two years. This comparison created a dilemma for elected state officials and administrators: Would they be perceived as valuing the safety and care of dogs in kennels much higher than those of children in licensed child care?

OUTCOME Shortly thereafter, the proposed reduction in regulatory visits to child-care facilities was dropped.

LESSONS LEARNED A key lesson in this case was the importance of how a message is communicated. Sometimes, the logical, professional, well-researched, well-documented approach (i.e., regular site visits prevent problems and promote good child-care practice) does not succeed in advancing good policy and practice, so look for other creative ways to frame and illustrate the issue.

The social context may influence the audience's response to a particular measure. If a social agency is cutting costs, for example, its staff members are unlikely to support a costly new program. Audience's responses are also influenced by prior events. If, for example, a specific issue has been presented previously to some members of an audience, their recollections of prior discussions, which they may communicate to those who were not present, can powerfully shape the whole audience's responses. If an issue was divisive, it may generate extensive conflict when it is reintroduced. By contrast, policy issues associated with positive traditions often have a good chance of gaining a positive audience response.[19]

Until now, we have assumed that the audience's viewpoints are relatively homogeneous. In fact, the audience usually contains a range of perspectives; one faction may support a new policy, while another faction may oppose it. Practitioners must identify a mixed audience's factions.[20] They should decide how to address the subgroups in their messages, perhaps appealing first to one segment of the audience (Some of you fear that …) and then to another (Others of you believe that …). Even when audiences have divergent perspectives, policy advocates can identify and appeal to common values, hopes, or aspirations, saying, for example, "Despite our differences on this issue, we all agree that this agency needs to diversify its services."

Tailoring Objectives to the Audience   Policy advocates often establish objectives that are either too modest or too ambitious. Persuaders may falsely believe that an audience is so hostile to their message that they can hope to achieve only minor changes. By contrast, persuaders establish unrealistic expectations if they falsely believe that their audience is similar to themselves. Those with liberal perspectives, for example, may unrealistically expect to make an extremely conservative audience accept a policy that stems from liberal premises, only to find that the message merely unites the audience in its preexisting opposition to knee-jerk liberals.

EPA 2.1.3c

Strategies of Persuasion in Step 5 and Step 6

With objectives, the audience, and situation in mind, policy advocates must develop a persuading strategy by selecting a medium, a sequence of presentations, a format, and a presentation style. After discussing these components, we will discuss tactics for specific audiences.

Selecting a Medium

Persuaders rely on symbols, such as words and visual aids, to influence the audience's ideas and actions, but they can present these symbols in many ways: through speech, documents, graphic aids, or some combination of these methods. Because these modes of communication are so familiar, we often do not consider their relative merits.

PowerPoint presentations have become ubiquitous in the United States. Persuaders couple verbal content with PowerPoint slides. They can also include video content and music in a format that can powerfully influence the views of an audience. We present an example of a PowerPoint presentation in Policy Advocacy Challenge 9.10.

Public speaking allows presenters to interact with the audience. Oral communication allows persuaders to be flexible; if they are skilled at thinking on their feet, they can change their message midway through to respond to perceived fears and hopes that will impede or facilitate a positive response. When persuaders want an audience to become emotionally involved in an issue, they often use arguments that culminate in a call to audience members to support a cause actively.[21]

Written communications, such as memoranda, letters, and reports, allow precision, unlike spoken communication, in which definitions and details are often relatively vague. When presenters want audiences to commit themselves to a course of action, they can elicit relatively binding agreements with documents; a memo, for example, may ask people to check a specific category, such as "agree or support," "disagree," or "undecided." Written communications are useful in explaining technical subjects, such as the implementation details for a specific policy or a summary of existing research; conveying technical subjects in brief addresses is difficult.[22]

Graphic materials, such as graphs and slides, simplify complex materials and often help capture the attention of a hostile or indifferent audience. Someone seeking support for vulnerable populations, for example, can use pictures or slides to promote sympathy or interest. If used to excess, however, graphic materials can lose an audience's attention.[23]

Certain rules should be observed when using PowerPoint slides or other graphic materials. The slides themselves must be relatively simple. Indeed, some persons contend they should contain no more than five or six words. If they are complex and contain too many words, members of the audience become so absorbed with reading them that they lose touch with the central themes that the presenter seeks to emphasize. Moreover, the presenter often succumbs to the temptation to read them to the audience—often not even looking at the members of the audience. Slides are merely used as *aids* for a presentation and should not divert the audience excessively from the presenter and his or her message. It is often fine to augment PowerPoint slides with pictures drawn from the Internet, diagrams, or audio effects such as music—but such augmentation must itself be done with caution so that the slides should not detract the audience from the presenter or his or her message.

When using PowerPoint slides, then, considerable attention must be given to the text that the presenter gives as he or she displays the slides. The presenter should devote some or considerable time during the presentation to words that are *not* on the slides, even perhaps leaving the screen blank during portions of the presentation to reinforce his or her relationship with the audience.

These provisos should not suggest that the PowerPoint slides cannot be highly effective—merely that they must be viewed as only a part of a larger message. Presenters want audiences to emerge from their presentation impressed by the slides—but, even more important, by them and their messages.

Using a Sequence of Presentations

When we envision presentations, we customarily think of one effort to convince an audience to take a specific position on an issue. In fact, skilled persuaders realize that they will be more effective if they use a sequence of persuasive encounters—a variety of written, interpersonal, and other communications, perhaps culminating in a formal presentation. A persuader might first use some informal personal encounters to discover where people stand on an issue and what they fear or dislike to initiate the process of changing the audience's knowledge or beliefs.[24] The persuader might then plan a meeting to educate his or her audience about an issue as a prelude to a meeting to take action.

Selecting a Format

When you do a formal presentation to an audience, the format is critical. Every speech has a beginning, a middle, and an end. Your challenge is to command your audience's attention at the outset, impart important substantive information in the middle, and conclude with the presentation's essential purpose (such as persuading the audience to take action, set up a committee, or take a specific problem seriously).

It is essential to decide what you want the audience to do as a result of your presentation, for example, to set up a committee to study an issue, to take a condition seriously, or to gain new knowledge. Once you have decided on your objective, you can develop a format that will achieve it.

Do not lock yourself into a single format prematurely. Try different versions of your speech. Think about novel points you can make at the outset or in the conclusion that will appeal to your audience. Brainstorm to develop alternative outlines.

Skilled policy advocates use basic formats tailored to specific kinds of communications. These formats establish an integrating logic for a presentation. Seven such formats are given in Box 9.1.[25]

Our discussion suggests that policy presenters should tailor their outline to the subject they are discussing. While outlines can take different forms, they need to include a logical sequence of topics that structures the presentation for both the presenter and the audience.

Fine-Tuning a Presentation   Once presenters have developed a medium, analyzed the audience, and developed an outline, they can fine-tune the presentation in numerous ways and, in the process, revise the outline. Presenters often use specific techniques to make a presentation more interesting to the audience. They may add case examples to capture the audience's attention. They may elicit audience participation during part of the presentation by asking, "Which of these options do you prefer?" or "Can you think of an option I have not considered?" They may use a particular visual aid, such as a chart distributed to the audience or presented by overhead projector.

The following is an illustrative presentation to the staff of an agency about its flawed intake procedures. The speech is based on an outline and uses a criticism structure.

- Initial statement, an overview of the presentation: "I will discuss three reasons why I think our intake policies are flawed."
- Supporting arguments: "Why do I think they are flawed?"
- Certain clients with serious conditions have to wait long periods. (Discuss Client A as an example.)
- Certain kinds of people drop off the waiting list disproportionately. (Discuss Client B as an example.)
- Our waiting-list procedures frustrate certain clients. (Discuss Client C as an example.)
- Ask the audience to share any experiences they have had with the intake procedures.
- Recommendation: Establish a committee to find alternative ways to structure our intake procedures.

Developing an Effective Presentation Style

Your effectiveness as a presenter is based not only on the substantive content of your presentation, but also on your *delivery style*, including your relationship with the audience, your speech patterns, and your use of gestures.[26]

You have to feel comfortable with your basic outline before you begin your presentation, and you need to have rehearsed it so that you need to look only at the bold headings from time to time as you make the presentation. Most audiences like presenters to make eye contact with them.

To offset the fear that you will ramble, you may start by explaining the presentation's basic logic, that is, the basic points you will discuss. Select an interesting case example,

EPA 2.1.3c

BOX **9.1** Alternative Formats for Policy Advocates

To discuss how a problem developed, use a time structure of the sequence of events that caused the problem. Begin, "I want to discuss how the problem with our agency's intake procedures developed by taking you through a sequence of events."

A. Intake procedures in 1985.
B. Revisions of intake procedures in 1986.
  1. Why revisions were made.
  2. The nature of the revisions.
C. Changes in the composition of our agency's clients between 1987 and 1991.
D. Intake problems caused by these changes in clientele.
E. Options we should consider in revising our intake procedures again.
  1. Option 1.
  2. Option 2.
F. Call for a task force or committee to make recommendations.

To explain a problem, use a topical structure that discusses a problem's components. Begin, "I want to discuss operating problems in our agency as a prelude to some policy recommendations."

A. We are experiencing a number of problems in our agency's program for school dropouts.
  1. Problem 1.
  2. Problem 2.
  3. Problem 3.
B. Relationships among these three problems.
C. Options we should consider to address these problems.
  1. Option 1.
  2. Option 2.
  3. Option 3.

To establish that a problem exists and needs attention, use a criticism structure to describe the problem and the criteria for demonstrating that it is a problem. Say, "Our intake procedures are faulty because clients with serious problems do not receive prompt attention and because the procedures are unfair."

A. An overview of our intake procedures.
B. Why our intake procedures need to be overhauled.
  1. Problems of fairness.
  2. Problems encountered by clients who are denied immediate service.
  3. Administrative problems.
  4. Staffing problems.
C. The need to collect more information about Problems 2 and 4.
D. Call for a committee to collect the information and make some recommendations.

To show a cause–effect relationship, use an association structure. Say, "I want to discuss how the problem with our intake procedures stems from the rapid increase in our waiting list."

A. Discuss problems with the intake policy.
B. Discuss specific changes in the nature of the clientele using the agency during the past five years.

    C. Link the problems with the changes in clientele.
    D. Discuss possible implications for changing intake policy.

To gain acceptance of a plan, use an argument structure in which you present the elements of the problem and the central features of your corrective plan. Begin, "I want to discuss why our intake policies are faulty and then present a five-part plan to deal with the situation."

    A. Discuss problems with the intake policy.
    B. Provide solutions.
    C. Discuss how the solutions address specific criteria.
       1. Administrative feasibility.
       2. Fairness.
       3. Cost.

To criticize someone else's statement of a problem or plan, use a refutation structure in which you state his or her central tenets and then present your arguments about why they are flawed. Say, "I want to discuss why the plan Susan Smith offered to correct our intake system is flawed."

    A. Provide an overview of the intake problems.
    B. Describe the central elements of Smith's plan.
    C. Discuss how it fails to address certain criteria.
       1. It is not administratively feasible.
       2. It is not fair to certain kinds of clients.
       3. It would be too costly.
    D. Discuss an alternative approach and state why it is better.

To influence people to take action, use a directive structure, in which you state the reasons why immediate emergency action is needed. Say, "This situation is urgent. We should send a delegation at once to see the head of the welfare agency."

    A. Why this problem has taken on urgency.
       1. Effects on clients.
       2. Possible political ramifications.
       3. Implications for our funding.
    B. Why a delay in addressing it would be calamitous.
    C. Alternative courses of action.
       1. Write a letter.
       2. Contact the head of the welfare agency by telephone.
       3. Send a delegation.
       4. Other actions.
    D. A call to action.
       1. Send a delegation.
       2. Have the delegation make the following arguments.
       3. Supplement the delegation with other actions.
          a. Call the mayor.
          b. Contact a member of the county board of supervisors.

visual image, or analogy to gain the audience's attention at once. Make clear transitions as you move from topic to topic with such statements as, "Having discussed why intake procedures are flawed, we can now move to possible remedies." Wrap things up with a thoughtful conclusion that draws on the preceding sections of your presentation.

Try to avoid distracting habits, such as fumbling with papers, using excessively rapid or slow speech patterns, or pacing back and forth. Some experts videotape themselves before making presentations to discern the unconscious, distracting mannerisms that they have.

What do you do if you are frightened about making speeches? Most important, try not to run away from public speaking opportunities, as difficult as they may seem. Some of us develop fright instincts when making speeches, and we can break these patterns only with practice. Many people find it useful to pause momentarily before speaking to gain equilibrium, to collect their thoughts, and to remind themselves of the presentation's outline.

Tactics for Specific Audiences

You will want to modify your outline as you consider the likely nature of your audience, which may be hostile, apathetic, or expert.

Policy advocates sometimes encounter *hostile audiences* with values or beliefs that predispose them to oppose a specific message. Various techniques can decrease hostility. You can identify common values, perspectives, and practical concerns that link you to the audience. These links may be common group memberships, educational affiliations, or demographic traits. Or you can appeal to higher values that you share with the audience, by saying, for example, "All of us share concern for the homeless people we see on the streets." Some policy advocates seek conservatives' support for social programs by appealing to their patriotism; if Americans want the nation to remain competitive in international markets, these advocates may argue, they need to address the high dropout rate in schools.[27]

You can establish your credibility with hostile audiences by citing authorities or experts the audience is likely to respect and by discussing your own credentials or experiences that increase your credibility. To seem reasonable, you can present both sides of complex issues and freely admit that alternative viewpoints are inevitable. Rather than beginning with your conclusion, you can build a case, hoping that your evidence will gradually change the audience's view of an issue. You might reach your eventual proposal only after rejecting or refuting alternative positions.[28]

Humor often defuses tense situations. Some persuaders make fun of themselves so that the audience perceives them as unceremonious and unpretentious. If told with skill, anecdotes at the start of a presentation may ease audiences into subjects they find difficult or stressful.

Apathetic audiences present similar challenges. It is important not to overwhelm apathetic audiences with complex arguments or data, which will intensify their apathy. Nor is it wise to tell the audience that they should care about an issue, an intrusive technique likely to make them retreat even further into apathy. The skillful persuader makes the presentation interesting and lively, stresses few themes or arguments, presents a simple argument, and offers interesting and unusual evidence that the audience has not heard before.[29]

The members of *expert audiences* perceive themselves to be well versed in the presentation topic. Presenters need to offer an array of perspectives and evidence to such audiences, admitting that the existing knowledge is imperfect and that choices are difficult. They need to discuss the merits of alternative options and not move quickly to a single solution. The presenter should pay tribute to the audience's expertise by recognizing that they have thought extensively about the subject and, perhaps, by eliciting their opinions or suggestions.[30]

Other Tactical Choices

Additional tactics help presenters modify their outlines.

Single-Sided or Two-Sided Arguments? Should persuaders present the strongest possible argument for a specific policy (a single-sided argument), or should they consider both sides of an issue (a two-sided argument)? Some social psychologists suggest two-sided arguments for critical or hostile audiences because the persuader anticipates and defuses some criticisms and therefore appears reasonable and open-minded. Single-sided arguments are more effective with audiences that share the values of the speaker.[31]

How Much Dissonance? All persuaders want to change their audience's beliefs, but they have to decide how much dissonance, or discrepancy between the audience's beliefs and the proposal, to introduce. If they ask for massive changes, they risk alienating the audience. If they ask for minor changes, they risk undermining the audience's possible support for more extensive change.

When persuaders anticipate hostility, they should probably not begin by suggesting massive changes. Several presentations should be scheduled, the first one seeking to educate the audience, rather than to secure a commitment to major change. A sympathetic audience is more immediately open to a commitment to major change.[32]

Climax or Anticlimax? Social psychologists' findings on whether the beginning of a presentation or the end makes the strongest impression are contradictory, but either the introductory or the concluding portion of a speech should be the strongest, and the weakest points should be inserted in the middle sections.[33]

Who Should Present? When a choice exists, persuaders need to ponder carefully who should present information to a specific audience. Presenters to hostile or apathetic audiences should have either high credibility with them or styles of communication suited to overcoming hostility and apathy. It is sometimes useful for multiple presenters to give different portions of a presentation.[34]

Adapting the Setting Skillful persuaders sometimes find or create a setting conducive to reaching a specific audience. Intimate settings may be chosen over formal ones to increase rapport. Seating arrangements may be devised to facilitate exchanges between the presenter and the audience. Graphic aids, such as slides, may overcome an audience's apathy. Sometimes, an audience is broken into smaller groups that later reconvene to share their solutions to a specific problem.[35]

Honoring Protocols and Expectations Audiences often have specific expectations about a presentation. Legislators, for example, expect testimony to legislative committees to be relatively brief—not more than 10 or 15 minutes.[36] (Detailed materials and the text of the presenter's comments are submitted separately.) An audience may have certain expectations regarding the formality, tenor, and style of a presentation. Audiences of persons who consider themselves experts on a subject expect the presenter to offer alternative viewpoints, whereas an audience of activists often expects a call to action. To understand these expectations, presenters need to speak with audience members before their presentation or with people familiar with the audience.

Assembling a Strategy in Step 5 and Step 6

To illustrate persuading strategy, let us examine how Harry Johnson, our lobbyist for an AIDS advocacy group who was introduced in Policy Advocacy Challenge 9.1, develops strategy to secure support for legislative reforms for people with AIDS.

The Hostile Audience

Suppose that Harry wants to convince some conservative Republicans—the people most likely to be critical of the gay community and to believe that people with AIDS "brought it on themselves"—to support a major legislative initiative. The legislation would expand the state's funding of home health care programs to serve people with AIDS. It would cover homemaker, visiting-nurse, and physical therapy services. Both Medicaid recipients and people considerably above the poverty line would receive these services. (Currently, counties fund most state home health services, but only for individuals who meet restrictive income standards.) Admittedly, the new program will be expensive because many people with AIDS who are not eligible for existing county programs will need extended home health services.

Even before the presentation, Harry enlists the assistance of several sympathetic Republican legislators, who agree to moderate the sessions and expedite discussion. He wants his introduction to make at least some of the conservative legislators perceive the problem in human, personal terms rather than abstract, ideological ones. He decides to present several case histories of HIV-positive people who have encountered difficulty when seeking home-based services. To decrease the audience's perception of the problem as belonging only to gay radicals, he relates several cases of conservative Republicans who have contracted the disease. He also makes analogies with older people and people with disabilities to communicate that the AIDS population's home health needs and problems are similar to those of other, more accepted populations. He concludes the first presentation with a question-and-answer session about the dimensions of the problem.

Johnson wants the audience to be favorable to a legislative proposal that a bipartisan group has tentatively drafted. He decides to use a format with a two-sided argument. He acknowledges that some persons in the audience may believe that existing policy is sufficient, and he does note that it is less expensive simply to use the home health services currently funded by Medicaid in his state. But he then discusses why an expanded home health program, with broader eligibility criteria than Medicaid, would be worth considering. Even here, he discusses different options and their likely cost to the state and their pluses and minuses. He wants to project an image of reasonableness and attentiveness to cost, since he knows that his conservative audience values these attributes. At the end of the presentation, he makes the best case possible for the legislative proposal that the bipartisan group has tentatively drafted. He encourages questions from the audience at the end of the presentation, showing how the bipartisan group considered them when drafting the legislation. He concludes by seeking the support of the group for the proposal, while also planning to seek some revisions in the proposal from the bipartisan group so that the proposal can be altered to make it more appealing to some conservative legislators.

In developing this plan for his presentation, Johnson rejects other alternatives, such as a call to action, a format that allows no give-and-take with the audience, and a discussion that does not focus on the likely cost of the proposal. He hopes later to reconvene this group of conservatives when he can show them that he has secured some changes in the bipartisan draft that will draw upon their comments.

The Sympathetic Audience with Some Hostile Members

The legislative proposal is introduced into a legislative committee with many sympathetic members but some hostile ones. Johnson, who hopes to intensify support for the proposal, encounters the dilemma of addressing a mixed audience. Should he write off the minority and direct his comments to the sympathetic members, or should he target his comments to the hostile minority because he already expects the majority to support the proposal?

Johnson decides to focus his comments on those who are sympathetic but to include points in his presentation that will attract some votes from those who are hostile. (The sympathetic do not need an extended argument and want only a brief, dramatic message to energize them to support the proposal.) Indeed, he focuses his presentation on a particularly poignant case. To appeal to the hostile members, however, he selects a case that illustrates how providing a homemaker and other services will allow some people with AIDS to remain productive workers (and hence taxpayers) for a longer period than if these services are unavailable.

The Expert Audience

Johnson also seeks support for the proposal from hospital administrators, whose professional association wields power within the state. Unlike most legislators, who have scant knowledge of the intricacies of the health care programs, hospital administrators are familiar with the existing programs. Therefore, Johnson decides to emphasize practical cost and administrative issues, such as how the proposal will be implemented, how the state will monitor it, and how it will affect the duration of hospitalization of people with AIDS.

To enhance his rapport with this audience, Johnson cites evidence and arguments obtained from a hospital administrator and some hospital social workers who specialize in discharge planning. Because the proposal's funds will be funneled through nonprofit agencies, he discusses how these agencies will coordinate their services with hospitals. Throughout his presentation, Johnson elicits input from the experts, both to obtain their insights and to make it clear that he respects their expertise. (See Policy Advocacy Challenge 9.5 for an exercise in developing a persuasion strategy to city officials about a specific policy proposal.)

Interpersonal Discussions

As this legislation progresses from initial proposal to drafted legislation to (it is hoped) enacted legislation, Johnson will have countless discussions with foes and friends of the legislation, officials in the state's bureaucracies, local officials, and community activists. These discussions will take many forms. In some of them, Johnson will solicit information about people's positions, biases, and perspectives, thus maintaining a fact-finding posture. Of course, his patience will be tested when individuals are hostile toward people with AIDS, such as the legislator who maintains that "persons who contract AIDS should bear all the costs of home health care even if it makes them destitute." As Lewis Dexter suggests, the lobbyist should remain "benevolently neutral" in some of these hostile discussions.[37] While he need not agree with these legislators, he need not attack them either. Indeed, he might say, "We share a desire to bring this epidemic under control. What are your ideas about how to help people with AIDS remain productive members of society in the interim?"

In some of these discussions, Johnson uses a directive format, seeking support for the proposal. He asks the leader of an advocacy group to mobilize support for the legislation by obtaining letters and phone calls from key legislators' constituents. He also uses a

Persuading City Hall to "Ban the Box"

Gretchen Heidemann, MSW, Doctoral Candidate, School of Social Work, University of Southern California

More than 13 million people in the United States have criminal conviction records, and upwards of 800,000 people are added annually to this growing population. Formerly incarcerated people experience a host of barriers to successful re-entry into society, including barriers to employment, housing, voting, education, and public assistance. Employment plays a critical role in the re-entry process, as it helps formerly incarcerated people be productive, take care of themselves and their families, develop valuable life skills, establish a positive role in the community, strengthen social connectedness, and avoid recidivism. Despite this critical link, however, formerly incarcerated people increasingly face barriers to employment, including employer aversion and discriminatory hiring practices. People with felony records are twice as likely to be denied employment as those without past criminal records. As a result, an estimated 70 to 90 percent of formerly incarcerated people are unemployed.

One specific hiring practice may provide an explanation for the high rate of unemployment among formerly incarcerated people. The question "Have you ever been convicted of a crime?" appears on most applications for employment. While intended as a measure of public safety and employer liability protection, research has shown that it is used widely as a screening mechanism to the detriment of formerly incarcerated people who are attempting to acquire legal employment and rebuild their lives. When employers see that the box is checked "yes," they toss the application without considering such important factors as the type of crime committed, how long ago it occurred, or whether the applicant has completed a rehabilitation program. Formerly incarcerated people and their allies have approached private employers and local jurisdictions and tried to persuade them to "Ban the Box" on employment applications. The policy advocates argue that the question regarding prior conviction should be removed from the initial application and instead asked after the applicant's experience and qualifications have been considered. As a result of their efforts, several major U.S. cities have revised their hiring procedures.

Boston City Council passed an ordinance that went into effect on July 1, 2006, that restricts the City of Boston and its 50,000 private vendors from conducting a criminal background check as part of their hiring process until the job applicant is found to be "otherwise qualified" for the position. The ordinance requires that the final employment decision, which includes information about the individual's criminal record, also takes into account the age and seriousness of the crime. In addition, it creates important appeal rights for those denied employment based on a criminal record.

The City and County of San Francisco passed a similar resolution, which took effect in June 2006. The resolution seeks to prevent discrimination on the basis of a criminal record by removing conviction history information from the initial application. Instead, an individual's past convictions are not considered until later in the hiring process when the applicant has been identified as a serious candidate for the position. The only exception is for those jobs wherein state or local laws expressly bar people with convictions from employment. Unlike the Boston ordinance, San Francisco's policy applies only to public employment, not to private vendors that do business with the City or County of San Francisco.

Other cities are considering similar measures. Chicago, Los Angeles, Philadelphia, Newark, and Indianapolis are all moving toward changing their hiring practices relative to persons with criminal conviction histories.

EXERCISE

Imagine that you are a policy advocate working with formerly incarcerated people to "Ban the Box" on employment applications in your city. Your task is to make a presentation to two liberal, five conservative, and two moderate city council members to try to convince them to adopt an employment resolution similar to the ones in Boston and San Francisco. Develop a persuasion strategy, carefully considering what medium(s) you will use and what format structure your presentation will take (i.e., criticism, argument, directive, or some combination). How might your strategy be different if the city council were majority liberal? Now imagine that you are the city's district attorney and you oppose removing the question about prior convictions from applications. What might your presentation look like utilizing a refutation format?

A compilation of the top 100 speeches in American history with persons ranging the full political spectrum from Martin Luther King, Jr., and Jesse Jackson to Ronald Reagan and Richard Nixon is available at www.americanrhetoric.com/top100speechesall.html.

Select and listen to one of them (your computer will need audio capabilities). Ask the following questions:

- What goal or objective did the speechmaker seem to have?
- What audience did he or she address, and how was the speech tailored to them?
- How was the speech organized?
- What did the speechmaker emphasize at the beginning of the speech?
- What middle-speech content did he or she have?
- How did the speechmaker finish the speech?
- How did the speechmaker's style of presentation enhance or detract from the speech?
- Summarize briefly why you think this speech was ranked as one of the top 100 in recent American history?

combination of flattery and emotional language: "We've turned to you many times in the past, and you have never let us down. How do you think we can place pressure on these five legislators who are possible swing votes?"

Other discussions follow a substantive format, such as those with health experts. In these conversations, Johnson seeks assistance in defining the home health needs of people with AIDS, the potential cost of specific provisions in the legislation, and the administrative considerations.

We can often improve our communication skills by observing speeches of successful communicators (see Policy Advocacy Challenge 9.6).

Gaining Support for Grant Proposals

When constructing proposals, such as legislative proposals, proposals to establish new programs in agencies, and grant proposals, policy advocates find that specific strategies often make their proposals more enticing to decision makers and funders. We focus here on a grant proposal written from an agency site. At first glance, some readers may wonder whether grant proposals are policy proposals, since they do not involve legislation. In fact, grant proposals are part of policy advocacy. They seek resources, after all, to fund innovative policies of agencies and agency networks. In many cases, they allow expansion of services to underserved populations. They often establish new programs. They are, in fact, agency counterparts to legislative proposals. Let us return to our discussion from Chapter 8 of the social work intern who wanted resources to expand translation services for Latinos in the hospital where she had her internship.

EPA 2.1.8a

Writing an Imaginative Title

Policy advocates should develop creative, eye-catching titles for their proposals—titles that will attract support from a wide range of persons. In naming her proposal in a foundation grant, for example, the student intern could select a purely descriptive title, such as "Increasing Translating Services to Latinos in XYZ Hospital." Alternatively, she could select a more imaginative title, such as "Linking the University with a Hospital to Help Latinos Navigate the Health System."

Giving a Compelling Rationale

Proposal writers have to provide a compelling rationale, or decision makers and funders will perceive their proposal as addressing trivial problems.[38] Bear in mind that most proposals must compete with many others, and in the winnowing process, proposals that are perceived to be unimportant are likely to be discarded.

The student intern should provide dramatic instances of harm to Latino patients caused by the lack of translation services. She should present data that show the desperate shortage of translating services as well as the likelihood that this shortage will not be redressed by the hospital in the near term. She could provide quotations from physicians, nurses, and social workers that confirm the shortage of translators as well as the adverse effects of this shortage on patients.

EPA 2.1.6b

Drawing on Research Findings

Some innovative policies hinge on the research and conceptual work we discussed in Chapter Seven. The student intern might find data demonstrating that Latino patients without adequate translation services suffer specific consequences in medical transactions. Or she might find data from a pilot project in another setting wherein student volunteers have successfully served as interpreters.

Setting Clear Objectives

Proposals fare best when they contain clear objectives.[39] The student intern ought to estimate the number of patients who would be helped annually by her student volunteers, both overall and on specific units. She should estimate how many students would be recruited to be volunteers. Objectives are often made clearer when they are linked to specific time lines. Perhaps the intern would allow three months to recruit and train her 40 students as a prelude to moving ahead with the translation services.

Including an Evaluation Component

EPA 2.1.7a

Policy advocates often include an evaluation component in their proposals to gauge whether their innovation has been successful.[40] The student intern might propose gathering data directly from Latino patients who have used the volunteer students. Or she might propose gathering data from medical staff, nurses, and social workers. She might also ask the students to evaluate the project, asking whether they have received adequate training and whether they have expanded their knowledge of the health care system.

Demonstrating Feasibility

Laudatory as a proposal may be, decision makers and funders must believe that it is feasible.[41] The student intern would need to answer such questions as the following: Do top hospital and university administrators favor the proposal, and will they cooperate with it? Who will be in charge of the program's implementation? Has the student intern already located a competent coordinator whose qualifications are included in her proposal? Where will the project be housed? How will the volunteer students be trained? In what accounts will the project's funds be kept? Who will audit or oversee the budget? And how long will it take to get the program up and running?

Establishing Partnerships

Many policy innovations are not accepted by legislatures or private funding sources because they are not clearly linked to other programs through joint planning, referral networks, joint programs, or shared facilities. These partnership links must be clearly articulated. The student intern should discuss how she would gain the cooperation of local colleges and hospital administrators in her project and how she would get these administrators to work together.

Demonstrating Support

Proposals are rarely approved if they lack substantial support.[42] The student intern should attach letters of support for her project from top college and hospital administrators as well as from community leaders. When people introduce legislative proposals, they often try to get a range of legislators to be cosponsors.

Proposals are strengthened, moreover, if they demonstrate tangible support. Perhaps the hospital and university will agree to provide some funding for the project and make in-kind contributions such as donating office space, equipment, supplies, and staff time.

Many foundations also want evidence that other institutions will contribute to a project once foundation or government funding ceases. Perhaps the student intern could obtain assurances from university and hospital staff that they will assume a larger share of the project's funding after several years.

Developing a Realistic Budget

Policy advocates must develop realistic budgets that clearly state what magnitude of resources is needed and how they will be used. If advocates seek excessive funding, foundations and legislators may see their proposals as wasteful. If they seek funding that is clearly inadequate, funders may regard the proposal as unrealistic. The student intern would need to write a so-called line item budget that shows the precise funds needed for different categories of expenditures, such as salaries, supplies, transportation, rent, mailings, and telephone.[43]

Finding Funders

The student intern has to search for potential foundation funders for her proposal. These foundations include corporate foundations, small family foundations, large foundations, and community foundations. Corporate foundations typically give small grants to projects where their corporate headquarters (or major installations) are located. They are particularly fond of sponsoring events, such as luncheons, and giving in-kind contributions, such as supplies or copy machines. Small family foundations are established by wealthy individuals who typically give relatively few grants each year compared with large foundations. Some large foundations, such as the Ford and Rockefeller Foundations, usually fund ambitious proposals with national implications, unlike other large foundations that emphasize grants to specific parts of the country. Community foundations, such as the Rhode Island Foundation, the Milwaukee Foundation, or the California Community Foundation, are quasi-public entities that have some public officials, as well as community leaders, on their boards (see Policy Advocacy Challenge 9.7). Their charters require them to make grants exclusively in their local jurisdictions.[44]

Revising the Proposal

Proposals rarely emerge full-blown from first drafts; they are gradually developed in an evolutionary process. Amendments to bills are written in successive committee deliberations during the legislative process. Grant proposals to foundations, government authorities, and other funding bodies are also extensively revised as they are drafted. In some cases, the framer will write a one-page version and circulate it to other persons, including a staff

Policy Advocacy Challenge 9.7

Finding Funders via the Web

Stephanie Davis, Reference Librarian

Some useful references for fundraising and grantwriting in the human services are as follows.

INTERNET:

Foundation Center maintains a database of more than 95,000 foundations, corporate donors, and grantmaking public charities in the United States.

http://fconline.fdncenter.org

Center for Nonprofit Management provides training, consulting, and resources for emerging nonprofits, including workshops and events on fundraising, grantseeking, proposal writing, and building a donor base.

www.cnmsocal.org

The Nonprofit Resource Center provides a comprehensive list of resources for nonprofit organizations, including fundraising, grantwriting, and donor resources.

www.not-for-profit.org

Flexibility is critical in finding funding sources, as discussed in Policy Advocacy Challenge 9.8.

member in a foundation or a government agency. A later version, which may be four or five pages long, will be circulated for comments again as a prelude to a lengthier final version.

Translating complex ideas into fluent prose requires considerable skill. Excessive jargon, long-windedness, complex sentences, and poor syntax diminish interest in a proposal. Many decision makers, such as legislators, who lack technical understanding, are disinclined to read dense, lengthy materials. Policy practitioners sometimes err, of course, in the opposite direction; if their proposal is too brief and fails to address important issues, their work may be discarded as superficial.

We provide an example of a grant proposal in Policy Advocacy Challenge 9.9 that Gretchen Heidemann developed.

Policy Advocacy Challenge 9.8

Creatively Seeking Funding Sources

Patsy Lane, MSW, Director, Department of Human Services of the City of Pasadena

While serving as an administrator for VOALA (a large nonprofit organization), we were seeking funds to rehabilitate an old, deteriorated Skid Row hotel and convert it to a new alcohol detoxification, recovery, and support service site. Funding specifically for such a project was very limited, but in our search, we learned that the federal Department of Housing and Urban Development had a grant called an Urban Development Action Grant (UDAG). At first glance, UDAG funding did not seem relevant to our proposed creation of an alcohol recovery and social service site, but as we reviewed the category called "Neighborhood Revitalization," we began to rethink our project. It seemed apparent that rehabbing a deteriorated Skid Row hotel and creating a new hub offering a range of social and health services (including addressing local problems with public inebriates) would eliminate an area of "urban blight" and revitalize a neighborhood—key criteria for UDAG funding. We redesigned the concept, broadening the range of health, housing, and social services and including information and education activities to further enhance the neighborhood.

OUTCOME Our organization submitted the grant proposal, and the project was awarded $1.6 million in UDAG funds.

LESSONS LEARNED Most human service programs have multiple outcomes, address multiple issues, and fit into more than one funding category. Flexibility and creative design are keys to making a project fundable by a variety of potential sources. If you view a potential project from a limited perspective or as a single-category item, you may miss out on key opportunities for funding, partnerships, collaboration, and other resources.

Policy Advocacy Challenge 9.9

Writing a Grant Proposal: The "Empowering Women for Change" Project

Gretchen Heidemann, MSW, Doctoral Candidate, University of Southern California, School of Social Work

PROBLEM STATEMENT

The female prison and parole populations in California have risen dramatically in the past two decades, largely as a result of mandatory sentences for drug-related crime. According to the Little Hoover Commission, as of December 2004, 10,000 women were in California's prisons and 12,000 on parole. And while approximately 80 percent of women offenders have a substance abuse problem, drug treatment is available for just a fraction of incarcerated offenders and parolees. Most will return to prison within a year of their release. One-third of female parolees returned to custody for parole violation are charged with a drug-related offense.

Under the 1996 federal Welfare Reform Act, anyone with a felony drug conviction is banned for life from receiving government aid for herself and her children. The Sentencing Project found that over 37,825 women in California (40 percent of the total 92,000 women affected by the national ban) have been declared permanently ineligible for welfare benefits since 1996. This welfare ban inevitably dooms many formerly incarcerated women and their children to living on the street where they are subject to hunger, malnutrition, disease, sexual assault, and physical abuse. The ultimate victims of this lifetime ban are the more than 54,000 California children who are now at risk because their mothers are without access to income supports and food stamps.

The welfare ban is a short-sighted public policy approach that is already causing long-term damage to families and entire communities. We believe that we can create social change by training and organizing formerly incarcerated women to be active participants in the movement to advocate for policies that would remove the barriers to re-entry for women prisoners. We intend to show policy makers the faces and voices of real women who are impacted by inhumane policies and practices that continue to punish former prisoners (and their families) long after their release from behind bars.

Our vision is for all women and girls to be able to live positive, fulfilling lives free of the ensnaring cycle of violence and involvement in the criminal justice system. Through the Empowering Women for Change project, formerly incarcerated women will be empowered to speak out against policies that are inhumane and damaging not only to women prisoners but also to their children and families. Formerly incarcerated women will understand the public policy process and will insert themselves into this process as representatives of the largely unheard voices of prisoners, former prisoners, and the re-entry community. Through our efforts, formerly incarcerated women will gain a sense of self-worth and strength in the knowledge that they possess the power to improve societal conditions for themselves and others like them.

AGENCY DESCRIPTION

Women's Re-Entry Project is a grassroots, nonprofit organization founded as a sober-living home for women by a former prisoner who understands the challenges that women face after leaving prison. Our mission is to assist women and girls to break the cycle of entrapment in the criminal justice system and lead healthy and satisfying lives. The goals of the Women's Re-Entry Project are to:

- Provide a clean, safe, sober-living home environment where formerly incarcerated women and their children can feel welcomed and supported in their transition to becoming independent members of the community.
- Offer education, job training, and skill-building opportunities for women to prepare them for self-sufficiency.

(continued)

- Provide leadership as a community advocate for the rights of women inmates and ex-offenders and their families.

The agency is located in South Los Angeles and is the only sober-living facility in the urban Los Angeles area designed to serve women returning from prison. Women's Re-Entry Project provides a safe, sober, re-entry home for up to 20 indigent women ex-offenders and their children and gives them the skills to live independent, fulfilling lives. The agency is unique in that it has a director who was entrapped in the criminal justice system until the late 1990s and has since dedicated her life to helping other women break the cycle of incarceration, homelessness, addiction, and despair. Since its founding, the organization has succeeded in transforming the lives of over 180 paroling women.

PROPOSED PROGRAM
DESCRIPTION

Women's Re-Entry Project proposes to implement the Empowering Women for Change project. We plan to develop the leadership skills of formerly incarcerated women organizers who will develop a statewide media strategy and plan a Southern California Re-Entry Conference. This project will involve the planning and coordination of a two-day leadership training retreat wherein 20 formerly incarcerated women will gain leadership, public speaking, and community-organizing skills. We will also coordinate a series of workshops in which these same women organizers will devise a statewide media strategy to educate the public about the needs of women returning home from prisons and to improve the image of formerly incarcerated women in the media. Finally, the same group of organizers will plan and implement a Southern California Re-Entry Conference that will bring together formerly incarcerated women with policy makers to devise solutions to the barriers that women face upon their release from prison.

OBJECTIVES

The objectives of the "Empowering Women for Change" project are to:

- Increase the leadership skills and the ability of formerly incarcerated women in our community by providing the tools that will allow them to effect social change.
- Increase positive media coverage around the need for re-entry services and reunification support for formerly incarcerated women.
- Influence local and state policy makers to address the needs of formerly incarcerated women.

ACTIVITIES

The Empowering Women for Change project will entail the following four core activities:

- Recruit 20 formerly incarcerated women who desire to engage in community organizing around prisoner re-entry.
- Coordinate a two-day leadership training for 20 formerly incarcerated women focusing on outreach, media, and communication skills to help them plan a Southern California Re-Entry Conference.
- Coordinate a series of workshops with formerly incarcerated women organizers to develop a statewide media strategy with consistent and clear messaging around the needs of formerly incarcerated women.

- Convene a Southern California Re-Entry Conference to educate city, county, and state policy makers about the needs and barriers to re-entry for formerly incarcerated women and work with them to devise strategies for addressing those needs.

OUTCOMES

We will achieve the following three outcomes during the grant period:

1. A trained corps of 20 formerly incarcerated women organizers
2. A statewide media strategy with consistent and clear messaging around the needs of formerly incarcerated women designed by formerly incarcerated women organizers
3. Commitments from policy makers to address the needs of formerly incarcerated women

EVALUATION

Measures of success will include attendance and retention records for leadership training sessions and workshops, written documentation outlining the statewide media strategy, sign-in sheets at the Southern California Re-Entry Conference, and written commitments from policy makers addressing the needs of formerly incarcerated women.

We will distribute and collect written assessments at the beginning and ending of the leadership retreat to assess participants' familiarity and past experience with the topics being discussed as well as the extent to which they benefited from the training. We will also collect written assessments for each media workshop to ascertain their effectiveness and to incorporate participant feedback into future workshops. Finally, we will distribute evaluations for our Re-Entry Conference to assess the impact on community participants as well as policy makers.

EXERCISE

Pretend that you are a grant officer at a foundation that has just received this proposal. Imagine that you have a pile of 200 other grant proposals on your desk and that you can pick only 20 of them for funding. Having a skeptical orientation, ask tough questions about this proposal. What do you think this proposal would cost?

To get yourself into the mind-set of a foundation staff person, make a list of key questions that you would be likely to ask about all grant proposals. (*Hint:* Draw on the discussion of qualities of good policy proposals in the preceding section of this chapter—but feel free to add other questions that may be germane to your foundation.) How does this proposal stack up on these questions? Would you fund it?

EPA 2.1.3c

PowerPoint presentations are widely used to provide audiences with an overview of a policy issue and make policy recommendations. A PowerPoint presentation that was developed by MSW students to persuade a panel of public officials in Los Angeles County to support a "housing first" policy for homeless persons is discussed in Policy Advocacy Challenge 9.10.

**Policy
Advocacy
Challenge 9.10**

Making a
PowerPoint
Presentation
to Public
Officials with
Respect to
Homeless-
ness in Los
Angeles
County

Michele Baggett,
MSW; Robert
Hernandez,
MSW; Ali
Wagner, MSW;
Laura Koonin,
MSW; Carolyn
Ryan, MSW; and
Alicia Case,
MSW

In the spring semester of 2006, 13 classes of policy advocacy students in the MSW Program at the School of Social Work of the University of Southern California addressed various aspects of the homelessness issue in Los Angeles County. A panel of city and county officials came to the school at the end of the semester to hear the findings and recommendations of each of the classes. I discuss here the presentation that my group, composed of Robert Hernandez, Ali Wagner, Laura Koonin, Carolyn Ryan, Alicia Case, and me, made.

My student group partnered with the not-for-profit advocacy group LAMP that favored a "no strings attached" policy that would seek *immediately* to give each homeless person a place to live regardless of whatever drug, mental health, health, or other issues that they might have. (Of course, many homeless persons are simply poor and unable to afford rent.) We wanted not just to *manage* homelessness but to *end* it.

We wanted to develop a presentation that had a clear message to *end* homelessness in Los Angeles County within the next 10 years by providing sufficient housing along with supportive services for those homeless persons needing them. We knew we had only a limited time slot of roughly 10 minutes.

We chose Bob Hernandez to make the presentation from our group, since we knew he could speak passionately without being overly emotional—and he was very versed in the issue because he had been an MSW intern at LAMP. We were certain that he could connect on a personal level with members of the audience and yet provide them with the central ideas we wished to convey.

Our group also had a member, Ali Wagner, who had designed PowerPoint presentations professionally. She was skilled in making PowerPoint slides that focused on the major concepts we wished to present, while not being excessively cluttered.

With contributions from all members of our group, then, a presentation strategy emerged. We would start with an agenda for our presentation so that the audience would know what to expect. We would then show them a map of Los Angeles's primary Skid Row in downtown Los Angeles. We would share our values with the group that led us to prioritize ending homelessness in the first place. We would then contrast the current punitive approach to dealing with homeless persons—and the cycle of homelessness—that it engendered with our housing first strategy. We would demonstrate that our approach would cost no more per homeless person than the current policy. We would conclude with a piece of model legislation that could put "housing first" into place. To show the public officials that our ideas actually work, we decided to end the presentation with a specific example of a renovated apartment building with supportive services. We would urge the county and city to develop a unified single plan that would link public and private sectors.

We knew that public officials were often moved to action by specific case stories. So we selected "Nancy's Story" to move them to action before making a final plea for permanent supportive housing.

Here is our 10-minute presentation with our PowerPoint slides and the text that went with each of them.

Slide 1

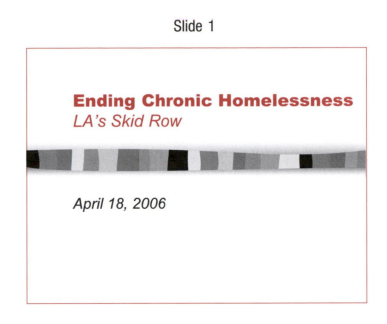

Text That Accompanies Slide 1

- Thanks to the panel.
- Our role as social workers is to create awareness, educate, and advocate on behalf of our clients.
- Our goal, today, is to provide a voice for the chronically homeless on Skid Row in downtown Los Angeles. The chronically homeless are defined as individuals who have one disability, or more, and have been homeless for a year.
- We want to express concerns and advocate on their behalf.

(next slide)

Slide 2

(continued)

Policy Advocacy Challenge 9.10
(continued)

Text That Accompanies Slide 2

- First, we would like to explain the characteristics of the Skid Row population.
- Second, we would like to express concerns about the cycle of homelessness and how, we believe, the criminalization of the homeless is not the solution to ending homelessness.
- Next, we would like to offer insight on possible solutions to ending the cycle of homelessness.
- Our closing thoughts will offer hope that we can end homelessness.
- For references, we have included the names of specific studies on the relevant slides and we would like to note that we are highlighting several points made in the recent report issued by Bring LA Home, "The Campaign to End Homelessness."

(next slide)

Slide 3

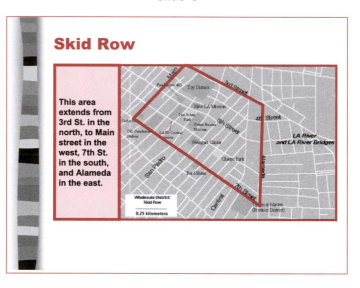

Text That Accompanies Slide 3

- Today we are focused on the homeless population on Skid Row in downtown Los Angeles.
- Skid Row is a 50 square block area on the eastern side of downtown. On any given night, approximately 10,000–12,000 people call Skid Row home. These individuals are either living in shelters, jail, hospitals, or literally on the streets.

(next slide)

Slide 4

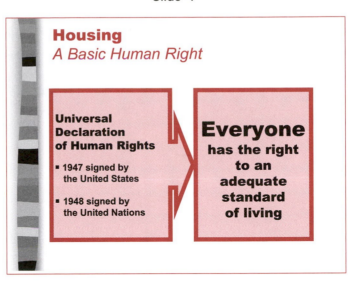

Text That Accompanies Slide 4

- Article 25 of The Universal Declaration of Human Rights states in part, "Everyone has the right to a standard of living adequate for the health and well-being of himself and of his family, including food, clothing, housing and medical care, and necessary social services."
- Our work is to ensure that the chronically homeless population on Skid Row are afforded this right.
- Our belief is that everyone wants to end homelessness, but not everyone agrees on how to end it.

(next slide)

Slide 5

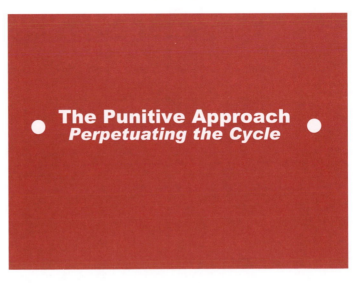

(continued)

Text That Accompanies Slide 5

There are those who support the punitive approach, or the criminalization of the homeless, which we suggest perpetuates the cycle of homelessness.

(next slide)

Slide 6

Text That Accompanies Slide 6

- We are concerned about the pending legislation put forth by Senator Gil Cedillo. Although well-intended, we believe the bills supporting sentence enhancements and a downtown narcotics recovery zone will:
- Not deter crime, but will enhance the number of people caught in the cycle of homelessness.
- Create an opportunity for racial profiling.
- Further contribute to the overcrowding in jails.
- We are concerned that homeless individuals convicted of drug crimes, once released, will not be allowed to return to Skid Row, the area in which they are arrested, which is the very area that provides them with the housing and services they need. This sets them up for homelessness again, in another city.
- Both of these bills, we believe, trap individuals in the cycle of homelessness.

(next slide)

Slide 7

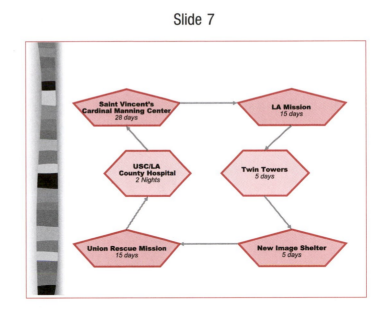

Text That Accompanies Slide 7

- For these people, it is a revolving door as they cycle from the streets to costly acute care services such as hospitals, city shelters and jail, and then back to the streets.
- We suggest that the cost of doing nothing to stop this cycle is, in reality, quite costly.

(next slide)

Slide 8

Text That Accompanies Slide 8

- Using city and county services such as jail, hospitals, and shelters to house the mentally ill homeless is not cost effective.

(continued)

- For these homeless individuals caught in this cycle, the total cost per person per year is $40,449.
- This cycle is costly, ineffective, and it perpetuates homelessness.
- We believe it is time to break that cycle.

Cite: Bring LA Home

(next slide)

Slide 9

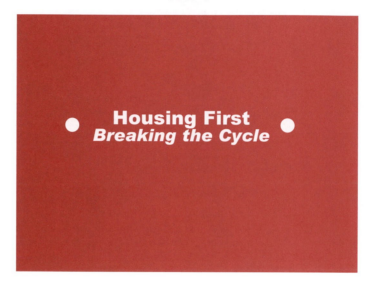

Text That Accompanies Slide 9

The way to break that cycle is to provide housing first.

(next slide)

Slide 10

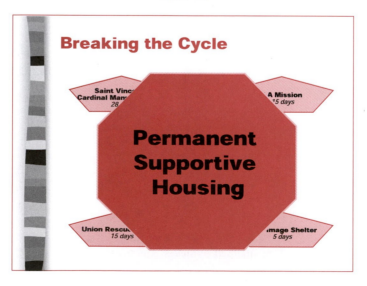

Text That Accompanies Slide 10

The housing first approach provides permanent, affordable housing that is linked to services to enable tenants with special needs to live as independently as possible.

Providing permanent supportive housing for the homeless is a proven model that:

- Provides stable housing with services that support the individual and help prevent them from returning to the street.
- Creates a foundation on which the process of recovery can begin. Having a place of one's own may—in and of itself—serve as a motivator for consumers to seek counseling, job training, and refrain from drug and alcohol abuse. Having a home motivates a potential homeless person in doing whatever it takes to keep a home.

(next slide)

Slide 11

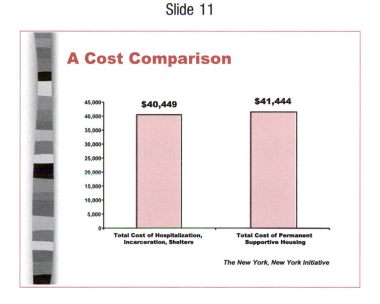

Text That Accompanies Slide 11

- These totals are taken from a New York study that compares the costs of acute services to the costs of permanent supportive housing. As you can see, the cost for acute services (or doing nothing) is roughly $40,000 per person per year.
- The cost of providing housing with supportive services is only about $1000 more per person per year—essentially, we break even.
- The critical point to remember here is that over the course of time, the cost of acute services will rise while the cost of permanent supportive housing will decrease. Once we have individuals, in housing, with services, the costs per person per year will decrease to almost half of the cost of acute services.

(next slide)

(continued)

**Policy
Advocacy
Challenge 9.10**
(continued)

Slide 12

What does it really cost?

- Hospitalization is **49 times more costly** than supportive housing
- Jail is **47% more costly** than supportive housing
- **One month's** stay in a mental hospital could pay for about **20 months** in supportive housing
- **One day** in the hospital could pay for **more than 45 days** in supportive housing

Bring LA Home

Text That Accompanies Slide 12

In comparison, housing the homeless through the permanent supportive housing approach is less costly than using city and county services.

- Hospitalization is 49 times more costly than supportive housing.
- Jail is 47% more costly than supportive housing.
- One month's stay in a mental hospital could pay for about 20 months in supportive housing.
- One day in the hospital could pay for more than 45 days in supportive housing.

Cite Bring LA Home

(next slide)

Slide 13

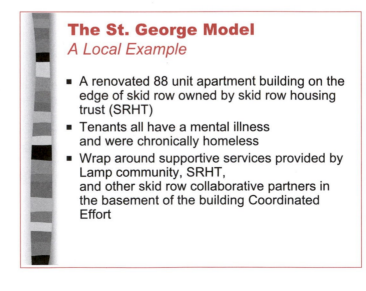

The St. George Model
A Local Example

- A renovated 88 unit apartment building on the edge of skid row owned by skid row housing trust (SRHT)
- Tenants all have a mental illness and were chronically homeless
- Wrap around supportive services provided by Lamp community, SRHT, and other skid row collaborative partners in the basement of the building Coordinated Effort

Text That Accompanies Slide 13

Another example of how we can end chronic homelessness is the St. George model—an effective and creative approach to housing:

- A renovated 88 unit apartment building on the edge of Skid Row owned by Skid Row housing trust (SRHT).
- Tenants all have a mental illness and were chronically homeless.
- Wrap around supportive services provided by LAMP community, SRHT, and other Skid Row collaborative partners in the basement of the building.

    There are other creative strategies that provide housing. For example:

- Master leasing
- Informal agreements with landlords
- Purchasing and rehabilitating existing units and working with developers to create new ones

(next slide)

Slide 14

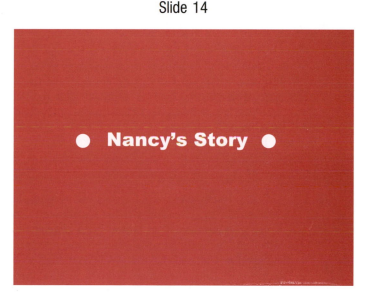

Text That Accompanies Slide 14

I have a letter here from a client whose life has been changed by the model we are suggesting. I would like to highlight parts of her story that speak to what we are discussing here today.

Nancy …

(next slide)

(continued)

**Policy
Advocacy
Challenge 9.10**
(continued)

Slide 15

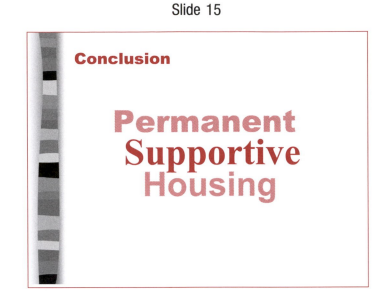

Text That Accompanies Slide 15

In conclusion, we hope that the numbers speak for themselves. We propose that the permanent supportive housing approach is the most cost-effective way to end the cycle of homelessness. This approach gets the homeless individual off of the street, into housing, with services that support their effort to remain in housing and off of the streets.

Thanks to panel.

The end.

Our presentation received a standing ovation due to the combination of a very convincing delivery, impactful visuals, a clear policy message, use of data, a case study of Nancy who represented a pathway for a better future, and a strong conclusion. We succeeded in showing that social workers can offer practical solutions by connecting needs and services with stakeholders. We learned that social workers can influence policy even as they offer clinical and other services and that presentations are a critical component of policy practice and policy advocacy.

Some questions to ponder as you view the PowerPoint presentation:

- Why is it important to have relatively little text on PowerPoint slides?
- Why is it important for presenters of PowerPoint presentations not to look excessively at the screen and to focus mostly on the audience?
- Why is it important not to mechanically read the text on the slides to the audience, but, rather, to have "fresh" text that is not identical to the text on the slides?
- What other positive attributes of this PowerPoint presentation can you identify?

What You Can Now Do

Chapter Summary

Our discussion in this chapter suggests that communication skills are a key part of policy advocacy—whether oral presentations (such as debates, negotiations, or speeches) or written presentations (such as succinct policy memos or grant proposals). You are now equipped to do the following in the fifth and sixth steps of the policy analysis, proposal-writing, and presentation framework:

- Engage in debates on affirmative or negative sides.
- Use hardball and win–win options in negotiations.
- Develop strategy for making presentations to audiences, such as diagnosing them, setting objectives, selecting a medium, and developing a format.
- Improve your presentation style.
- Write grant proposals.

In the next three chapters, we turn to tactics for developing and using power resources in policy advocacy as well as for participating in electoral politics.

Competency Notes

EPA 2.1.3c   Demonstrate effective oral and written communication in working with individuals, families, groups, organizations, communities, and colleagues (pp. 274, 287, 289, 303): Social workers must develop policy persuasion skills to gain support.

EPA 2.1.6b   Use research evidence to inform practice (pp. 279, 298): Participants in social policy debates can use arguments drawn from the analysis of social problems.

EPA 2.1.7a   Utilize conceptual frameworks to guide the process of assessment, intervention, and evaluation (p. 298): Policy advocates often include an evaluation component in their proposals to gauge whether their innovation has been successful.

EPA 2.1.8a   Analyze, formulate, and advocate for policies that advance social well-being (p. 297): Social workers gain support for grant proposals that advocate for increased resources.

EPA 2.1.9a   Continuously discover, appraise, and attend to changing locales, populations, scientific and technological developments, and emerging societal trends to provide relevant services (pp. 275, 281, 285): Advocates should be aware that the social context is important when persuading different audiences.

EPA 2.1.10f   Develop mutually agreed-on intervention goals and objectives (p. 285): Before persuaders can decide how to fashion a message, they have to establish objectives that appeal to their audience.

EPA 2.1.10k   Negotiate, mediate, and advocate for clients (p. 277): Social workers use confrontational strategies to modify the opinions and actions of those who oppose them.

Endnotes

1. Willard Richan, "A Common Language for Social Work," *Social Work* 17 (November 1972): 14–22.
2. Herbert Simons, *Persuasion*, 2nd ed. (New York: Random House, 1986), pp. 18–21; and Donald Cegala, *Persuasive Communication: Theory and Practice*, 3rd ed. (Edina, MN: Bellwether, 1987), pp. 13–15.
3. Michael Barone, "The 49 Percent Nation," *National Journal* (June 9, 2001): 1710–1716.

4. Simons, *Persuasion*, pp. 253–254.

5. Ibid., pp. 190–192.

6. George Brager, Harry Specht, and James Torczyner, *Community Organizing*, 2nd ed. (New York: Columbia University Press), pp. 355–357.

7. Simons, *Persuasion*, pp. 253–256.

8. Ibid., pp. 259–261.

9. Ibid., pp. 253–256.

10. Roger Fisher and William Ury, *Getting to Yes: Negotiating Agreement without Giving In* (New York: Penguin Books, 1991).

11. Ibid. Also see Herb Bisno, *Managing Conflict* (Newbury Park, CA: Sage, 1988), pp. 99–147.

12. See Jay Folberg and Alison Taylor, *Mediation* (San Francisco: Jossey-Bass, 1984).

13. Fisher and Ury, *Getting to Yes*.

14. Simons, *Persuasion*, pp. 23–24, 141–142.

15. Karlyn Campbell, *The Rhetorical Act* (Belmont, CA: Wadsworth, 1982), pp. 69–118.

16. Ibid., pp. 101–116.

17. Ibid., pp. 69–118.

18. Stan Paine, G. Thomas Bellamy, and Barbara Wilcox, *Human Services That Work* (Baltimore: Paul Brooks, 1984), pp. 42–44.

19. Morton Deutsch, *The Resolution of Conflict: Constructive and Destructive Processes* (New Haven, CT: Yale University Press, 1973), pp. 124–152.

20. Segmentation is discussed extensively in marketing literature; see Philip Kotler, *Principles of Marketing*, 4th ed. (Englewood Cliffs, NJ: Prentice Hall, 1989), pp. 42–46. Also see Simons, *Persuasion*, pp. 143–146.

21. George Brager and Stephen Holloway, *Changing Human Service Organizations* (New York: Free Press, 1978), pp. 199–203.

22. Ibid.

23. See Marya Holcombe and Judith Stein, *Presentations for Decision Makers* (New York: Van Nostrand Reinhold, 1983).

24. Ibid., pp. 16–25.

25. Ibid., pp. 11–13.

26. Simons, *Persuasion*, pp. 124–129, and Robert Reid, *Work of Nations: Preparing Ourselves for the 21st Century* (New York: Knopf, 1991), pp. 154–168.

27. Hedrick Smith, *Rethinking America* (New York: Random House, 1995).

28. Simons, *Persuasion*, pp. 148–154.

29. Ibid., pp. 153–154.

30. Ibid., p. 153.

31. Cegala, *Persuasive Communication*, p. 136.

32. Simons, *Persuasion*, p. 153.

33. Cegala, *Persuasive Communication*, p. 134.

34. See Brager et al., *Community Organizing*, pp. 342–343.

35. Paul Ephross and Thomas Vassil, *Groups That Work* (New York: Columbia University Press, 1988), p. 157.

36. George Sharwell, "How to Testify before a Legislative Committee," in Maryann Mahaffey and John Hanks, eds., *Practical Politics: Social Work and Political Response* (Silver Spring, MD: National Association of Social Workers, 1982), pp. 85–98.

37. Lewis Dexter, "Role Relationships and Conception of Neutrality in Interviewing," *American Journal of Sociology* 62 (September 1956): 153–157.

38. Craig Smith and Eric Skjei, *Getting Grants* (New York: Harper & Row, 1980), pp. 173–181.

39. Armand Lauffer, *Grantsmanship and Fund Raising* (Beverly Hills, CA: Sage, 1983), pp. 238–246.

40. Ibid., pp. 80–84.

41. Ibid., pp. 236–246.

42. Smith and Skjei, *Getting Grants*, p. 152.

43. Soraya Coley and Cynthia Scheinberg, *Proposal Writing* (Newbury Park, CA: Sage, 1992).

44. Ibid.

Suggested Readings

Policy-Persuading Strategies

Austin Freeley, *Argumentation and Debate*, 6th ed. (Belmont, CA: Wadsworth, 1986).

Willard Richan, "A Common Language for Social Work," *Social Work* 17 (November 1972): 14–22.

Herbert Simons, *Persuasion*, 2nd ed. (New York: Random House, 1986).

Negotiations and Mediation

Herb Bisno, *Managing Conflict* (Newbury Park, CA: Sage, 1988), pp. 98–147.

Roger Fisher and William Ury, *Getting to Yes: Negotiating Agreement Without Giving In* (New York: Penguin Books, 1991).

Jay Folberg and Alison Taylor, *Mediation* (San Francisco, CA: Jossey-Bass, 1984).

Margaret Gibelman and Harold Demone, "Negotiating a Contract: Practical Considerations," in Harold Demone and Margaret Gibelman, eds., *Services for Sale* (New Brunswick, NJ: Rutgers University Press, 1989), pp. 131–148.

Developing Grant Proposals

Soraya Coley and Cynthia Scheinberg, Proposal Writing (Newbury Park, CA: Sage, 1992).

Jean Potuchek, "The Context of Social Service Funding: The Funding Relationship," *Social Service Review* (September 1986): 421–436.

PART 5

Advocating for Change

No matter how skilled policy advocates are in accomplishing agenda building, problem analyzing, and proposal writing, their work comes to naught if they cannot get their recommendations enacted in agencies, communities, or legislatures. Policy advocates have to know how to develop and use power, and they need skills in developing strategy.

Chapters Ten, Eleven, and Twelve pertain to the sixth task—the policy-enacting task—in the Systems Approach to Policy Making described in Figure 3.1. Chapter Ten discusses how to develop and use power. **Chapter Eleven** discusses how to develop political strategy and how to develop and implement it in legislative, community, and agency settings. **Chapter Twelve** discusses how to change the composition of government by participating in electoral politics.

10 Developing and Using Power in the Policy-Enacting Task

Policy Predicament

A social work intern in a mental health agency discovers that no mental health services are provided to children whose parents have been institutionalized for psychiatric problems. She soon discovers numerous political obstacles to the development of such services. What political tactics would she devise? Her case is presented in Policy Advocacy Challenge 10.2 after briefly discussing power and politics. In Policy Advocacy Challenge 10.7, we discuss how low-budget lobbyists in the field of social welfare can nonetheless be effective in influencing the state legislature and changing policies.

Now that we have discussed how to analyze policies, write proposals, and defend them in debates and presentations, we are ready to move to the policy-enacting task (Task 6) of the policy practice and policy advocacy framework presented in Figure 3.1. This task is critical to policy advocacy because it allows us to secure the approval of specific policies that we favor in specific settings.

Power and politics have a bad reputation among some professionals, who regard them as unseemly, even unethical. However, power and politics can often be used for ethical purposes, and each of us can develop and use power resources to help stigmatized groups and unpopular causes.

LEARNING OUTCOMES

By the end of this chapter, you will be prepared to discuss:

1. The positive functions of politics in policy deliberations
2. The transactional nature of power relationships
3. Person-to-person and substantive power resources
4. Ways to shape policy outcomes indirectly by using decision-making procedures, processes, and contexts
5. Personal characteristics that enhance political effectiveness
6. Issues of autonomy, discretion, compliance, and whistleblowing
7. The importance of power differentials
8. External and internal vantage points when making policy changes
9. Ways in which policy practitioners develop power resources, including use of the Internet

10. Ways in which members of vulnerable groups or vulnerable populations encounter challenges when seeking and using power
11. The psychology of power as illustrated by intimidation and assertiveness
12. The dynamics of task groups, including coalitions and networks

In Defense of Politics

People sometimes call those who are preoccupied with political realities opportunistic, power-hungry, or wedded to special interests. Some truth exists in these assertions, but they obscure how important politics are to policy advocacy. Before discussing some of these functions, we define the word *politics* more precisely. Some people equate politics with government policy making; indeed, one part of Webster's definition declares it "the conducting of or participation in political affairs, often as a profession."[1] Certainly, government and party functions belong in a definition of politics, but what about politics in other settings, such as social agencies, professional associations, and communities? Webster's comes to our aid by including in its definition, "political methods, tactics, etc.; sometimes … crafty or unprincipled methods."[2] Webster's choice of words, *crafty* and *unprincipled methods*, suggests a disdain for political activity, though the definition includes power-related struggles in any setting. We need a definition that does not cast aspersions on persons who develop and use power, because leaders such as Franklin Roosevelt, Robert Kennedy, and Marian Wright Edelman have used power for noble ends.

At the risk of rewriting the dictionary, let us hazard our own definition. Politics represents efforts by people in governmental and nongovernmental settings to secure their policy wishes by developing and using power resources. When defined in this manner, politics becomes relevant not only to highly placed officials, but also to anyone who tries to influence policy making.

It is difficult to imagine a world in which politics does not exist, because political processes are endemic in social interactions (see Policy Advocacy Challenge 10.1). Without political recourse, people who lack formal authority would have to obey existing policies or seek remedies through other means, such as force.

Information about politics at the federal, state, and local levels can be found at an array of websites like the following:

THE U.S. SENATE This site gives the name and state of all U.S. senators, along with links to their offices to view what issues they are currently focused on. It details what the Senate as a whole is working on, and it offers an opportunity to contact your state's senators via email to voice your own opinion.

   www.senate.gov

THE U.S. HOUSE OF REPRESENTATIVES This site gives the name and state of all U.S. representatives, along with links to their offices to view what issues they are currently working on. It also details what the House as a whole is considering. It offers an opportunity to contact your representative via email to voice your own opinions.

   www.house.gov

THE WHITE HOUSE The homepage for the president and the vice president, this site gives you the opportunity to visit the pressroom and see what daily activities are

(continued)

**Policy
Advocacy
Challenge 10.1**
(continued)

occurring at the White House. It also offers an email link for writing to the president or the vice president on issues of importance to you.

www.whitehouse.gov

THE NATIONAL COUNCIL OF STATE LEGISLATURES NCSL is a bipartisan organization that serves the legislators of the nation's 50 states, its commonwealths, and its territories. NCSL's website provides an opportunity for you to get involved in a number of issues of concern to state governments, including health, immigration, criminal justice, and labor and employment.

www.ncsl.org/

NATIONAL GOVERNORS ASSOCIATION NGA is also a bipartisan organization representing the nation's governors. NGA's committees (such as health and human services and education, early childhood, and workforce) work to influence action by the federal government on various issues of concern.

www.nga.org/

NATIONAL ASSOCIATION OF COUNTIES With a membership of more than 2,000 counties, NACo is the only national organization that represents county governments in the United States. NACo's legislative action center provides opportunities to get involved in a wide range of issues of concern to county governments.

www.naco.org/

NATIONAL LEAGUE OF CITIES NLC provides links to more than 1,600 member cities' websites, as well as statistics and information about government structures, elections, and finances. It also hosts a legislative action center where you can learn about and get involved in a number of issues that impact our nation's cities.

www.nlc.org/

UNITED STATES CONFERENCE OF MAYORS The USCM is a nonpartisan organization of 1,201 cities with populations of 30,000 or more. USCM holds an annual conference to discuss and vote on policy resolutions that are then distributed to the president of the United States and Congress. The mayors' annual reports provide valuable information on a range of social work issues, such as homelessness, prisoner reentry, unemployment, gangs, and environment. You can learn about a number of legislative issues on its website.

http://usmayors.org/

The political process in a democracy provides a way for people with conflicting values or opposing positions to resolve their differences. Some policy analysts claim to be purely objective and scientific in their approach, but even they make many value-laden choices in their analyses.[3] Therefore, even an analytic position often requires negotiation through the political process.

Analytic and Political Approaches to Policy Advocacy

The political model differs markedly from the analytic approaches we discussed in the preceding chapters. If the analyst wants to discover technically superior solutions to a problem by using quantitative and qualitative techniques, the adherent of the political approach wants to understand existing political realities to select

| BOX **10.1** | A Political Model |

Distribution of power

- What persons, interests, and factions are likely to participate in certain policy deliberations?
- What are their power resources?
- What are their likely positions on a proposal?
- How strongly do they hold these positions?

Political stakes in an issue

- What political benefits and risks will I encounter if I participate in certain policy deliberations?
- Should I be a leader, a follower, or a bystander?

Political feasibility

- What patterns of opposition and support are likely to be associated with specific policy options?
- Which position, on balance, should I support?

Political strategy

- What power resources do I (or my allies) currently have that are relevant to these deliberations?
- What power resources might I (or my allies) develop that will be relevant to these deliberations?
- What strategies will we use as the deliberations proceed?

Revising strategy

- How should I change my strategy in light of evolving political realities, including my opponents' likely moves?
- As the political realities change, how should my role change?

feasible options and develop an effective political strategy to outmaneuver likely opponents.[4] If the analyst assumes that the truth will win out, the politician assumes that might will prevail. If analysts devote most of their time to technical tasks, political practitioners devote their time to gauging patterns of support for and opposition to specific issues, developing power, and implementing political strategies. (Of course, sophisticated policy practitioners can creatively couple analytic and political approaches in specific situations, as discussed in Chapter Three.) Policy advocates who use a political approach ask questions like those presented in Box 10.1.

Let us now consider the policy predicament encountered by the social work intern who wanted to develop innovative services for the children of parents who have been institutionalized for psychiatric reasons (see Policy Advocacy Challenge 10.2).

In this case, a social work intern tries to develop an innovative program in a mental health agency. She notes that the agency, which considers itself an advocate for children's mental health needs, lacks a program to help children whose parents have been institutionalized for psychiatric problems. She hopes to obtain approval for an eight-week crisis model of services to these children but soon realizes that she has encountered numerous political barriers. She narrates her experience in this policy advocacy challenge.

It is curious that the Mountain View Child Guidance Clinic considers itself an advocate for children's mental health needs when it neglects children of the psychiatrically hospitalized parent. Such children are in crisis and experiencing extreme family disequilibrium. They need immediate assistance in understanding and dealing constructively with feelings and thoughts associated with this experience. It is preferable that this intervention occur at or near the time of the crisis, when defenses are most fluid and before maladaptive patterns of functioning have solidified. To meet this need, I am trying to develop, in addition to the brief services offered by the clinic, a crisis group for the children of psychiatrically hospitalized parents.

The coordination and cooperation necessary for such a program would be a landmark in the clinic's history. Its success would depend on the referrals of psychiatrists who assist patients admitted to local public and private psychiatric hospitals. If the clinic bypasses the physician's authority and accepts referrals directly from hospitals' social service departments, we would alienate some physicians, who might imperil the program by boycotting it.

Announcements could be sent to the hospitals, their social service departments, and specific physicians. The service must offer support to both the physician and the hospital.

The politics of this agency dictates that the new program not be called preventive, lest funders and policy makers not favor it. This program will be called crisis intervention because funders and policy makers believe that no room exists in the budget for prevention.

We could approach four local hospitals with announcements of the new clinic program. A follow-up phone call would add a personal touch and hopefully clinch the process. As a staff member, I would persuade physician friends of the program's merit and solicit their support.

There are a number of barriers to change in this agency. The clinic focuses its energy on the quantity rather than on the quality of services. Of primary importance to the executive director is avoiding a waiting list. To this end, he mobilizes all forces and automatically shelves any program change that would conflict with this aim. Further, staff are usually inundated with work and have little time for innovative services. Similarly, the agency values efficiency in programming and expenditures. Clinic executives believe that they cannot afford to risk any revenue by applying funds to areas other than those directly funded and approved. Another barrier to innovation is the agency staff's disinclination to participate in program development, which deprives the agency of new program ideas. Staff members seek fulfillment in their routine work and leave the business of the clinic to the bureaucracy.

I am only a student intern in this agency, but I want to get this innovation off the ground before my field experience ends. Considering the nature of the agency, it is essential to introduce the change in an administratively sanctioned way through approved channels. Therefore, I initially broached the idea of the innovation to the director of outpatient services, Mr. Jones, who is my preceptor for short-term and intake cases. On first mentioning the plan, I was careful to make it appear to be an idea that I had developed in the course of discussions with him. I told him I saw the idea as consistent with comprehensive mental health care for children, an ideal he often espouses. Underscoring that the services would take only eight weeks, which he likes, and stressing its efficiency in terms of the waiting list, I ventured to actually propose a pilot plan. He groaned and suggested that I "write it up," with no explanation of what that meant. Rather than irritate him further, I did not mention the project for several weeks. I then told my regular field instructor that I was discussing with Mr. Jones a new program for the children of hospitalized patients, and I received her approval to use this project as a learning experience in program design.

Several weeks later, I found that Mr. Jones had completely forgotten my plan. But in further discussion, he expressed strong interest and even brainstormed an initial strategy with me that would help the innovation gain gradual support in the Mountain View Child Guidance Clinic. He suggested that we should develop a two-phase strategy. In phase one, I would develop a pilot project. Because I am a student intern, it would not need formal clearance by high-level executives or the agency board. He would simply notify the executive that a student intern was establishing a pilot group for children of institutionalized parents. He urged a low profile during this initial period. After we initiated the project, he would develop a strategy for a formal proposal that would go to the executive director and hopefully eventually to the board. That would be phase two. If all went well, the agency would formally earmark funds for the program. He hoped that my experience with the pilot project would provide useful information for writing the formal proposal and presenting it orally to the executive and the board. He concluded our meeting by saying, "You know you will have to do the entire program in the pilot phase. All the screening and everything." He seemed tantalized by the idea of obtaining increased service with no additional expenditure of staff time.

To date, I have succeeded in involving Mr. Jones in planning sufficiently to encourage his sense of investment in the program. I have abided by the rules in recognizing his authority and decision-making powers and deemphasizing my own initiative. My short-term strategy, then, is to begin the program myself. But a number of obstacles could still interfere with program acceptance by key decision makers, even during the pilot phase.

One obstacle is the issue of community coordination. Currently, the clinic has superficial coordination with local mental health agencies, exchanging cases only sporadically. No clear plan exists for coordination of services. This program necessitates an intermediate type of coordination, a case-planning coordination organized into a whole-family approach. The current fragmentation in the treatment of families with a disturbed member would be a danger to this program because it would undermine the purpose of comprehensive care. What factors are involved in this coordination process?

First, there is the issue of goal conflict. On the surface, there appears to be little; both the psychiatric hospitals and the clinic serve and are concerned with families' mental health needs. But is that really the case? In fact, the hospitals view the treatment of the parent-patient from a pathology, rather than a family systems, perspective. Therefore, they may choose to refer the child not for group, but for individual treatment as an "impaired" family member. It will be important to impress on these staff members that the groups help the child in crisis, rather than provide long-term therapy. With regard to the power relationships between agencies, the major snare seems to be the physicians' autonomy. The administrators of local psychiatric hospitals may perceive the children's group as highlighting their own program deficiencies and therefore may choose to provide a similar service themselves.

At present, the agencies do not consider themselves interdependent. Instead, they coexist in separate realms of the psychiatric community and rarely communicate with each other. More positively, though, they may cooperate with this project, not only because of the children's emotional needs, but also because child and adult agencies are complementary community services that do not usually compete for the same clientele.

To alleviate some of the tension between agencies and to facilitate the common goal of improved community mental health, I will plan individual visits to each hospital's social

(continued)

services department. I may be invited to present this program to the monthly meeting of hospital psychiatrists, an opportunity for a direct encounter with most of the staff physicians. In addition, I will invite representatives of each hospital to the clinic for an orientation and open house, which should improve relationships between the clinic and the hospital and emphasize the community nature of the project.

Within the clinic itself, a political process will follow the initiation of this program. When Mr. Jones seeks its official approval, he must submit it to the medical director for confirmation; the director, in turn, will take it to the executive committee for approval, and the committee will then present it to the board of directors for final approval. However, because Mr. Jones is the most powerful person in the agency, his approval should lead to its acceptance.

A complicating factor is the director of training, Ida Brown. To be candid, she does not particularly like Mr. Jones and often opposes any proposals he initiates. She may interfere in the decision-making process by pushing for a nondecision; that is, she may suggest that the plan be initiated only after lengthy study or pending the location of special sources of external funding. Another problem may arise because many in the agency focus on the child of an institutionalized adult as a patient, a view that clashes with the program's preventive mission.

I also see several other groups developing in relation to the program. One such group consists of the senior administrator and the chief of program development (also the director of support services). These two men are allied in their unstated mission to increase clinic prestige and influence in the community. They will probably support the program from their stated position of commitment to enriching the quality of the services available to the community. This position would appear reasonable and would underscore the senior administrator's interest in the efficient business operation of the clinic.

The executive director himself will probably support the program in deference to Mr. Jones, to whom he defers on all issues pertaining to the outpatient services of the agency. The outpatient service functions virtually independently of the day-treatment and other components of the agency.

The medical director is also a figurehead, whose medical degree is valued by the agency. He will most assuredly remain neutral lest he find himself in the middle of a political battle. He appears to have little power in the agency.

The board of directors also has little power in this agency. The members are most concerned about what mural is painted on which wall and how chairs are grouped in the waiting room. Program development is not their expertise, and they usually abide agreeably by decisions made by the executive director.

In the future, I see this program as an integral part of the clinic's services, if it can survive the pilot and approval stages. The children served during their first experience with a parent's hospitalization may choose to return to us if the parent is rehospitalized. Children who have experienced numerous parental hospitalizations will be able to compare previous episodes with the one eased by clinic services. We may then see self-referrals by children and families, reducing the need for physician referrals.

Mr. Jones wants me to assist him in writing the formal proposal after my pilot project has been in operation for five months. The project has made me realize that good clinical skills need to be supplemented by program design and political skills. How else can social workers develop and institute innovative services?

EXERCISE

List both barriers to this innovation and potential sources of support. Remember, of course, that some barriers can be eliminated or partly addressed by the strategy of the social work intern.

If you had encountered this situation and had wanted to obtain this mental health innovation, would you have persevered, or would you have decided not to proceed because too many political barriers existed? Does a danger exist of prematurely deciding that the "glass is half empty"? In the case of the children who needed help while a parent was institutionalized, what ethical implications might the intern have faced had she decided to discontinue her effort?

How does this case illustrate the adage that many people fail to secure their policy objectives because they prematurely discount their power resources? What power resources did this intern have?

Source: This case is adapted from one by Stacy Stern, MSW. Names and locations have been altered.

The Nature of Power in the Policy-Enacting Task

If politics is both inevitable and, at least in some cases, beneficial, policy advocates have to understand political power and develop skill in using it. We will first discuss the transactional nature of power relationships and then analyze the power resources that people use in these relationships. We will also discuss other kinds of power that use decision-making procedures, processes, and contexts. We will use the case presented in Policy Advocacy Challenge 10.2 to illustrate power and how it is used.

When the social work intern wanted to develop an innovative program to help children, she realized at once that various barriers to preventive programs existed in the agency. In this simple two-person situation, in which X "sends" power and Y "receives" it, X succeeds in exercising power by convincing Y to take an action that he would not otherwise have taken. The social work intern has exercised power with her preceptor, Mr. Jones, if he assents to a program that he would not otherwise have supported.[5] (The intern has not exercised power if Mr. Jones would have initiated the innovation anyway.)

If X uses physical coercion, Y has virtually no choice—for example, when a criminal suspect is forced to enter a police car at gunpoint. In some situations, it is difficult to determine the line between voluntariness and coercion; for example, people in desperate economic straits may feel forced to accede to requests if they fear the loss of their jobs. However, some people do leave jobs to follow the dictates of their conscience.[6] Were the intern to make Mr. Jones support the innovation by holding a gun to his head, she would be forcing him to make this decision. We agree with Peter Bachrach and Morton Baratz that force is not power, because it gives people little or no choice.[7]

Real power involves transactional rather than unilateral relationships and choices.[8] The receiver (Y) in a power transaction can choose whether to accede to the sender's (X's) suggestions. Y has many options; for example, he or she could refuse to follow X's suggestions, voice indecision, agree but not really mean it, agree enthusiastically, or respond ambiguously. The social work intern had to discuss the program innovation with Mr. Jones on two occasions before he formally committed himself to her project. He gave only symbolic support on the first occasion (probably not wishing to discourage the intern) and had completely forgotten the plan when the intern reintroduced the idea several weeks later. However, he seemed to support the idea enthusiastically on the second occasion, even initiating ideas about strategy. If the exercise of power is transactional, the actions of both partners must be examined. We can portray power relationships graphically by placing arrows between X and Y, as in Figure 10.1.

FIGURE 10.1 Direct Power Transactions

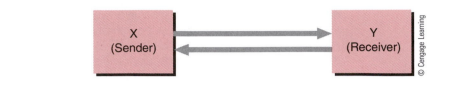

Power's transactional nature has important consequences for political strategy. Even in this simple two-person example, success in using power hinges on a number of considerations. X first has to decide that a particular issue warrants the expenditure of power. The intern's commitment to children's well-being, as well as to preventive mental health, led her to put effort into securing the innovation. (We discuss the intern's power resources later.)

Power often enters into transactions that involve more than two persons (see Figure 10.2). We first discuss the transactional nature of power to provide an overview and then move on to power resources. As a person with little formal power, the intern realized that officials in the upper reaches of the organization ultimately would have to approve the plan. Because she could not shape their actions directly, she had to work through Mr. Jones, hoping that he would convince them to support the innovation.[9] In this case, two sets of transactional relationships exist; the intern (X) tries to convince Mr. Jones (now Z) so that he will persuade, say, the director of medical services (Y). See Figure 10.2, in which the dashed line signifies the intern's exerting power over the medical director by using Mr. Jones as an intermediary. (Intermediaries are commonly used in legislatures and agencies.) We will now discuss the various power resources people use with other people in power relationships, including person-to-person power, substantive power, and indirect power.

FIGURE 10.2 Indirect Power Transactions

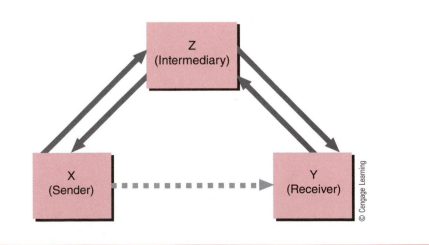

Person-to-Person Power in the Policy-Enacting Task

EPA 2.1.3c

Policy advocates sometimes exert power in personal discussions with others. We call this *person-to-person power*. In their classic article, John French and Bertram Raven discuss expert, coercive, reward, referent (including charisma), and authority (or legitimate) power resources.[10] Other theorists have identified yet other kinds of power resources. We discuss nine kinds of these power resources: expert, coercive, reward, referent, authority-based (or legitimation), position, information, connections, and value-based.

When using *expert power*, senders display their personal credentials and knowledge to convince others. They might, for example, argue that a specific policy recommendation that they make is supported by empirical evaluations, that is, an evidence-based policy. Or they might suggest that they have expertise that led them to select this policy. For such entreaties to be effective, of course, the receivers have to believe that the senders *are* experts. The student intern in Policy Advocacy Challenge 10.2 realized that high-level officials would be more likely to approve her innovation after its successful implementation as a pilot project. After this success, they could argue, as experts, "We know how to implement this kind of innovation."

Policy advocates use *coercive power* when they threaten penalties, for instance, by hinting at the loss of a job, a promotion, or a desirable position if another person does not support a specific policy. Politicians may threaten to punish opponents by opposing legislation that the opponents want, cutting programs or funds from their districts, or not granting them positions on key committees. Threats may backfire as well, because they may alienate people. Also the recipient of a threat must believe its sender can actually implement the threat.

When using *reward power*, policy advocates promise inducements, such as promotions, pay increases, financial or other support in upcoming campaigns, and bribes. They may also promise a quid pro quo: They will support someone's policy request in return for that person's support.[11] Like coercive power, reward power backfires if people believe they have been offered a bribe or other unethical inducement. Here, too, the receivers must believe the sender can and will give them the promised reward when they have taken the actions he or she requests.

Referent power "originates from being seen as someone associated with people or groups that other people identify with or want to belong to."[12] Members of specific professions or specific racial or ethnic groups often respect the views, for example, of members of their own profession or group. *Charismatic power* can be viewed as a subset of referent power.[13] Persons who possess personal qualities of leadership, moral authority, and persuasiveness can often stimulate others who admire these qualities to follow their policy wishes.

The *power of authority (or legitimation)* stems from one's position in an organization's hierarchy: Followers hope to receive rewards and avoid sanctions by following their superiors' suggestions. Persons who use the power of authority try to influence the actions of subordinates in several ways. They may imply that it is the duty of employees to follow the wishes of persons with higher rank. They may suggest that persons who deviate from their wishes will suffer repercussions, such as demotion or loss of employment. Or they may reward persons who accede to their wishes. In practice, then, power that derives from the organizational hierarchy is often coupled with coercive and reward power.

The power of *position* gives certain persons power resources because of their strategic location in an agency or legislature with respect to its workflow. As Sager notes, for example, intake workers in social agencies possess power by virtue of their ability to create rules and procedures for intake, as well as their implementation of these rules.

Because flow of clients into an organization is vital to its survival and (in some cases) revenues, intake workers possess considerable power resources. Others view them as indispensable to the organization and will listen to their perspectives because of this.[14]

Information power is derived from a person's control of critical information in specific situations.[15] As an example, take a so-called majority (or minority) whip in the U.S. House of Representatives. This person not only has records about how legislators have voted in the past, but also keeps tabs on their current policy preferences. A policy advocate who wants to get legislation through the House might consult the whip—and his or her advice about the feasibility of getting a specific measure enacted might influence whether and how the policy advocate chooses to proceed. In similar fashion, intake workers in agencies possess important knowledge about why specific persons come to the agency and what they need—information that could be used by higher-level staff to decide whether to initiate a specific new program.

Connections power is derived from the particular networks or key contacts of specific persons.[16] Assume, for example, that a policy advocate wants to get a policy enacted in a specific legislature, but has no key contacts among its legislators or legislative staff. Contrast this person with another policy advocate who had devoted the past 20 years to mixing and dealing with legislators and staff on myriad issues. The latter policy advocate would likely be more effective in getting the policy enacted—unless the former advocate, realizing he or she lacked such networks, compensated for this disadvantage by drawing into his or her coalition some key persons who *did* possess them. We discuss the use of Internet power later in this chapter—a key kind of connections power.

Value-based power is derived from a person's ability to appeal to others based upon their shared ethical commitments. (Sager called this "commitment to purpose.")[17] We discussed in Chapter Two a variety of ethical principles, as well as the use of utilitarian ethical arguments for supporting specific policies. We also discussed different ideologies that emphasize specific values such as equality or fairness (in the case of liberals) or liberty and autonomy (in the case of conservatives and libertarians). Persons will often heed the advice of those people who share their values and ideologies.

We have discussed nine kinds of person-to-person power. Our discussion suggests that policy advocates can draw upon many kinds of power resources when seeking policy changes—or can draw into their coalitions persons who possess power resources that they personally lack.

We have discussed person-to-person power in dyads and triads, but it is also used when a sender gives presentations to groups. An executive might say to his or her whole staff, for example, "Support this policy or our agency will suffer severe financial repercussions" (coercive power), or a politician might say to a neighborhood group, "Have people vote for me if you want this proposed neighborhood project to be funded" (reward power).

Person-to-person power is most effective when the sender selects the kind of power that the receiver is likely to honor. The receiver may respond to expertise, for example, but not to coercion. Effective users of power learn as much as they can about the predispositions of the people they seek to influence. Power is also most effective when it is applied skillfully. Practitioners who use expertise as a power resource, for example, have to marshal persuasive evidence sufficiently skillfully so that the receiver believes that the *expert* is an expert.[18]

Power resources can be used singly or in tandem. (See Policy Advocacy Challenge 10.3 that discusses how lobbyists for New Orleans would need to use many of these various person-to-person power resources.) An advocate may use both a carrot (reward power) and a stick (coercive power) in persuasion. A policy advocate might use one power resource a specific point in time, and use another one at a later point in time. When

Cities and towns need lobbyists in their state capitols and in Washington, DC, to get the resources that they need to meet the urgent needs of their citizens. Take as an example the small city of Treasure Island, Florida, to show what lobbying can accomplish.[1] Its leaders had tried for years to obtain funds to rebuild a major bridge, but succeeded only when they hired a lobbyist who had known their congressman for decades. They soon learned from the congressman that he had obtained a $50 million appropriation by slipping an earmark into a larger piece of legislation. Paying $5,000 per month for a lobbying firm, they received in the next three years $500,000 to fix a sewage plant, $625,000 to repair wooden walkways over the dunes, and $450,000 for pedestrian crosswalks.

To be successful, lobbyists astutely use a variety of power resources in combination. They possess expertise on the issues that are of concern to the clients. They donate resources liberally to the campaign funds of those congresspersons who help them. They have connections with influential legislators and their staff. They know the staff of important congressional committees, including the appropriations committees.

These power resources are particularly effective with legislators. They lack the time to gain expertise in the issues that the lobbyists represent because of the many pieces of legislation and the many claimants for public resources. Because the cost of political campaigns has greatly risen, they need campaign contributions. They want to be able to boast in the next round of elections that they obtained key resources for cities and towns in their jurisdiction. They are, in short, as dependent on lobbyists as the lobbyists are upon them.

Some questions to ponder:

- Why do many legislators depend heavily on lobbyists?
- Is it ethically correct for cities to hire lobbyists that they fund with taxpayers' dollars?
- Why do many chapters of the National Association of Social Workers (NASW) hire their own lobbyists?

[1] Jodi Rudoren and Aron Pilhofer, "Hiring Lobbyists for Federal Aid, Towns Learn that Money Talks," *New York Times* (July 2, 2006): 1, 14.

viewed in tandem, the use of power resources constitutes a policy advocate's *strategy*, which we discuss in the next two chapters.

Power Resources That Stem from Policy Maneuvering in the Policy-Enacting Task

If we stopped with person-to-person power resources, we would ignore a wide range of other power resources that policy advocates develop and use during policy maneuvering. These power resources develop from specific actions that policy advocates take during policy deliberations—often in response to the actions of other persons. They stem less from the specific characteristics of power users themselves, as in the case of person-to-person power resources, and more from give-and-take with other persons in the policy-making process.

Substantive Power

People often form opinions about a policy, not because they have been encouraged to support or oppose it, but because of how they view its substantive content. Policy practitioners exercise *substantive power* when they shape the content of policies to elicit support from specific persons. For example, two persons favor providing low-income housing subsidies in a government program, but one wants the subsidies to go only to people below poverty standards, while the other wants the subsidies to go also to people with moderate incomes. The initiator of the housing-subsidy proposal might decide against a precise definition of the income levels, hoping that both persons will vote for it. Indeed, the use of *vagueness* is often an effective tactic when persons disagree about the specific details of a proposal.[19] Of course, vagueness also can be counterproductive because an excessively vague proposal will arouse the opposition of those who strongly favor specific measures. Moreover, when key points of legislation are not defined, the implementers of the legislation have more leeway. If one party believes the other party will control the presidency (and thus the top appointive positions in implementing agencies), they will want to make key points specific so their political foes cannot implement the legislation contrary to their wishes. For example, in 1988, some Democrats, fearing that Republicans would not insist on minimum child-to-staff ratios when implementing a national day-care proposal, tried to place specific ratios in the federal legislation.[20]

EPA 2.1.10k

Policy advocates exercise substantive power when they change a policy's content to enhance specific decision makers' support for it. In the aforementioned day-care proposal, its advocates inserted many provisions to counter conservatives' opposition, such as putting a modest ceiling on the program's costs and giving the states a significant role in shaping the programs within their boundaries. These changes may be made when a proposal is initially drafted, during deliberations, or when the proposal goes before a legislature or other decision-making body. Substantive power often involves compromises; one faction may modify one provision in exchange for another faction's changing another provision.

Policy advocates encounter dilemmas when using substantive power. They may change a policy proposal to obtain one person's support, only to find that they have alienated someone else. When they make numerous concessions to obtain opponents' support, proposals may become so diluted as to be, in the words of Bachrach and Baratz, "decisionless decisions" or merely symbolic measures.[21]

For example, Senator Hubert Humphrey and Representative Augustus Hawkins initiated a legislative proposal in the 1970s requiring the federal government to create jobs whenever the national unemployment rate exceeded 3 percent. By the time the legislation was enacted, it was only a vague statement that the federal government would seek full employment. It required no specific actions, such as developing public works when considerable unemployment existed.[22] Skillful policy practitioners often refrain from offering changes in a proposal until they are certain that compromises are needed for its passage.

A policy advocate using substantive power also may couple a relatively unpopular proposal with more popular ones. In "Christmas-tree legislation" (so named because of the "gifts" many legislators place in it for certain persons or interest groups) in Congress, politicians insert various previously unenacted proposals in a larger piece of legislation just before the yearly congressional session finishes at the end of December. Politicians who oppose these inserted measures nonetheless vote for the legislation because it contains some of their own measures.[23] A controversial proposal may be swept to victory when it is attached to a popular proposal. Foes of abortion, for example, won prohibition of the use of Medicaid funds for abortions when they attached it to the appropriations bill for the Department of Health and Human Services.[24]

Proponents have many ways to shape a proposal so that it is nonthreatening to potential opponents. A program may be designed and portrayed as a pilot project to defuse opposition.[25] Proponents may place a proposed program under a specific government unit's jurisdiction to make it more appealing to potential opponents. Proponents enhanced support for the Supplementary Security Income (SSI) program, which provides income to destitute older people and people who are disabled, by proposing that it be placed under the jurisdiction of the Social Security Administration, because that unit of government was more acceptable to conservatives than units that administer welfare programs.[26] Proposals' titles are often selected to make them more acceptable to conservative politicians. Senator Daniel Patrick Moynihan emphasized family support payments rather than welfare payments when discussing a welfare reform initiative in 1988.[27]

Christopher Matthews contends that many successful politicians avoid discussing basic principles when considering legislation.[28] Realizing that mentioning fundamental principles often alienates valuable allies with different perspectives from their own, they focus instead on the precise details of the legislation. It is better, they reason, to win battles over the content of legislation than to have shouting matches about ultimate purposes. On the other hand, an enunciation of basic principles is needed in some cases to rally support for a measure.

We discussed negotiations—both softball and hardball ones—in Chapter Nine. In fact, negotiations and bargaining also illustrate the use of substantive power resources. Advocates yield on some points while insisting on others in a give-and-take process with opponents—hoping that such bargaining will convince many persons to support specific legislation or policies.

Power in Decision-Making Procedures

Policy is often fashioned by *decision-making* or *procedural power* during deliberations. In legislatures, for example, numerous people and committees, and finally the full body, must assent to a policy before it can be enacted.[29] (Recall Figure 4.3 depicting the normal course of legislation through both chambers of the Congress.)

There are many parliamentary techniques and strategies for increasing a proposal's chances of enactment, or for blocking a proposal: bypassing persons, committees, and meetings unfavorable to the proposal, while routing the proposal to those more favorable; persuading party officials to steer a proposal to the committee most favorably disposed or to leapfrog a meeting or procedure; and using person-to-person power with key decision makers, such as chairs of important committees, not only to obtain their support but also to secure their assistance with logistic details. A committee chair can place a proposal in a preferred position on a meeting agenda, insist that policies undergo further subcommittee deliberations, or abbreviate lengthy deliberations to help or prevent a specific measure's enactment. Clever strategists are well versed in such tactics.[30]

Procedural tactics are sometimes counterproductive, however, provoking accusations of unfairly stifling dissent by rushing a proposal through a legislature, stacking the cards for or against a proposal, or bypassing normal channels. Ethical objections may also be raised when concerned persons are excluded from policy deliberations.

When initiating proposals, it is necessary to know who the key decision makers are, whether they favor a proposal, and whether the opposition can be overcome. During the first six years of the administration of George W. Bush, Republicans chaired the committees of both the House and the Senate because they had majorities in both chambers. White House staff members and these Republican chairs mobilized party support for bills that Republicans favored. Disgruntled Democrats discovered that many of their legislative initiatives never made it beyond these committee chairs. So they hoped that they could regain majorities in either or both the Senate and the House in the elections of 2006 in hopes that their policy proposals would receive more attention (see Policy Advocacy Challenge 10.4).

Policy Advocacy Challenge 10.4

How National Politics Works—the Wrong Way

Bruce Jansson, Ph.D.

It is sometimes instructive to study how politics works—the wrong way. In the eyes of Norman Ornstein, a person who had studied Congress for 25 years, a "culture of corruption" had established itself in Washington—a culture that manifested itself in relationships among lobbyist Jack Abramoff, House Majority Leader Tom DeLay, Congressman Bob Ney, and others. View the documentary "Capitol Crimes" that was narrated by Bill Moyers on PBS at **www.pbs.org/moyers/moyersonamerica/capitol/index.html**. (It lasts about one and one-half hours—time well spent because it so graphically discusses how Congress and other political institutions work—at their worst.) The documentary traces how Abramoff used a variety of power resources—many of them illegal—to get favors for his clients, including owners of sweatshops abroad. At the time of the documentary, Abramoff had been indicted for various crimes, but chose to cooperate with federal investigators by giving them information about his dealings with various congressmen. Congressman DeLay had been indicted for illegal funneling of corporate funds into Texas legislative contests. Congressman Ney had been indicted for bribery.

As you watch this documentary, ask these questions:

- What power resources did Abramoff use to secure assistance for his clients?
- Why did it take so long for federal investigators to uncover his—and the others'—illegal activities?
- How does the documentary prove the saying, "money corrupts, but power corrupts absolutely"? Also ask whether many persons use power ethically—and cite some examples.
- What makes some power transactions unethical?
- Why are politicians sometimes able to curtail corruption, such as the bipartisan Congressional agreement in 2012 to stop "insider trading" where politicians purchase stocks or land likely to escalate in price due to impending Congressional actions? (Hint: CBS ran a story on "60 Minutes" in November 2010 that documented that many members of Congress conduct insider training including House Speaker John Boehner and former Speaker Nancy Pelosi. While they denied the allegation, members of Congress feared they might be turned out of office when a poll found that 56 percent of registered voters favored replacing all members of Congress prior to this allegation. The legislation will require members of Congress to disclose purchases of stocks, bonds, commodities, and other securities within 30 days of their purchase, with purchases posted on the Web [Larry Margasak, "Congress Weighs Insider Trading Bill, *Huffington Post*, January 29, 2012; Robert Pear, "Senate Approves Ban on Insider Trading by Congress," *New York Times* (February 2, 2012)].)

Decision-making procedures also exist in agencies. A staff member, a committee, or an executive may propose a new agency program, which is then developed by a staff committee and brought to the full staff for consideration. The executive then may take it to the board of directors, which may refer it to a board committee before taking a final vote. Or simpler procedures might be used: For example, a hospital social services director wants to develop social work services on the neurology ward and only seeks the agreement of the medical director of neurology. After the services have been in effect for some time, the staff member obtains formal approval from a higher hospital official, perhaps when he needs additional funding from the hospital's budget.

In Policy Advocacy Challenge 10.2, the social work intern carefully considered procedural options as she developed a strategy for her program innovation. Because of barriers to this

EPA 2.1.7a

innovation in the agency, such as tight budgets, the intern and her preceptor decided the innovation would be doomed if they began with a formal proposal to the executive director. Therefore, they planned a two-phase strategy: first to develop a pilot project without securing formal high-level clearance, and then, after proving the program workable, to develop a formal program proposal that would go through the executive director to the board for approval. The intern and the preceptor improved their proposal's chances not through efforts to convince other people of its merits, but by shaping the decision-making process.

Process Power

EPA 2.1.10b

Policies are shaped in the give-and-take of deliberations, which are characterized by their tenor, tempo, and scope of conflict. The *tenor* is the level of conflict; the *tempo* is the timing, pace, and duration of deliberations; and the *scope of conflict* is the number and kind of people who participate in them. Policy advocates use *process power* when they influence the tenor, tempo, or scope of conflict of deliberations in order to get a specific proposal enacted.

Let us begin with the crude analogy of a schoolyard dispute to illustrate tenor, tempo, and scope of conflict. After the two parties develop their positions in the dispute, they must decide how to resolve it. First, they must shape the tenor of deliberations: Should they use brute strength (a fight), have an amicable discussion, or take some middle course in which they shout at each other but do not fight? Next, each must decide what tempo of deliberations will help their cause: Should they seek a speedy settlement or protracted deliberations? Finally, they must determine who should participate in the conflict: Do they want a narrow scope of conflict that will exclude outsiders from their interaction or should they invite others to join the fray, in the belief that a broad scope of conflict will help their cause?[31]

A bully with physical superiority might decide to initiate a fight that involved only himself and a proverbial 90-pound weakling, whereas the weakling might want to enlarge the scope of conflict to include powerful allies, including some bystanders. The bully might want to resolve the issue speedily so the weakling would not have time to organize an attack—favoring a rapid tempo. The weakling, realizing he had no chance in the event of actual combat, might wish to convert the impending battle to a lower tenor, such as "settling our differences by talking things out."

The social work intern in Policy Advocacy Challenge 10.2 used process power to increase her chances of getting her innovation accepted. She wanted to keep it low profile during its pilot phase so it would not create controversy because she feared that it would otherwise be rejected by agency staff. She wanted to wait until she had initiated the pilot project before even developing a formal proposal with Mr. Jones that might be forwarded to the executive director and the board. Contrast this strategy with one that emphasized confrontation, a rapid tempo, and a broad scope of conflict.

We can usefully contrast win–lose politics with win–win politics. In win–lose politics, each side in the contest believes that it loses each time the other side wins and therefore wants to contest every point. In win–win politics, the two sides believe they will obtain mutually beneficial concessions. While they do not want to concede all points, they are open to compromise so they will both emerge better off than before deliberations. It would be a more pleasant world if people perceived win–win possibilities in more conflicts and transformed these conflicts into win–win situations. In many cases, however, this approach is not feasible. Parties may have conflicting values, may not trust their opponents, and may believe they will suffer severe losses if they make concessions.

Individuals can sometimes influence the level of conflict. People who wish to intensify discord, for example, can use emotion-laden words; refer to conflicts in the fundamental values at stake; enlarge the scope of conflict by publicizing the issue; use unusual tactics, such as the filibuster in the U.S. Senate; or clearly state that they do not want amicable resolution: "We plan to fight to the finish," or "We will accept no significant changes in our proposal!"[32] People who believe that conflict will be detrimental to their cause will try to diminish conflict, for example, by emphasizing a proposal's technical features, by identifying the common interests of all the parties, and by discouraging the participation of those who will raise the level of conflict. These different tactics were used by Democrats and Republicans in 2009 and 2010 when considering national health insurance. If Democrats often wanted to decrease conflict to get the legislation enacted, Republicans often sought to increase it to block its passage.

Timing is another kind of process power. The timing of a disputed proposal often favors a specific side. If someone introduces a proposal at an inopportune moment, its chances may be imperiled, no matter how skillful its defenders or how great its merits are. Whether in agency or legislative settings, such background factors as budgetary deficits, a crowded agenda, or an unsympathetic executive provide a harsh environment for a policy proposal. When a favorable context exists, a proposal defeated earlier may suddenly sail through the political process.[33]

In the give-and-take of policy deliberations, policy advocates use other power resources to increase their odds of success. They may try to co-opt other persons by giving them credit or by involving them in key tasks. In the case of Policy Advocacy Challenge 10.2 for example, the intern co-opted Mr. Jones by giving him credit for developing the innovation even when she had first thought of it. Policy advocates may try to intimidate opponents by giving the impression that they have the momentum and are certain to prevail.

Unfortunately, policy advocates sometimes have limited power to influence the political process because of limited control over the actions of their opponents. Someone who wants to limit conflict, for example, may find his or her goal sabotaged by opponents who succeed in escalating conflict or enlarging the scope of conflict by publicizing it in the mass media—as the frequent leaks to the press about government business suggest. Even skillful policy advocates miscalculate. Someone who introduces a proposal at a seemingly opportune moment may later become aware of background factors that will scuttle it. Moreover, policy processes often develop a momentum that cannot be slowed, no matter what advocates do.[34] Tradition also frustrates policy advocacy: Issues that have previously generated high conflict, such as national health insurance, are sure to stir up conflict if reintroduced.[35] The dimensions of a proposed change also shape the course of conflict; proposals for massive changes are more likely to polarize liberals and conservatives than more modest proposals.[36]

Shaping Contexts Including Use of the Internet

EPA 2.1.10a

We have already noted that power transactions occur within a context that includes public opinion and interest groups. Policy advocates can increase their odds of success in many situations if they place pressure on decision makers from external sources, such as by involving interest groups, by forming coalitions, or by using the Internet to solicit support from persons likely to be sympathetic with their policy initiative.

With respect to the Internet, consider these realities. More than 75 percent of Americans had Internet access at home in 2006; 29 percent of American adults used the Internet in the 2004 election to get political news (up from 4 percent in 1996). Many more adults used the Internet to get political news in 2009, and young persons especially use cell phones, wireless emails, the Internet, websites, instant messaging, and social network sites like Facebook, MySpace, and YouTube. We are entering an era of "connected activism" in which technology helps advocates form networks that provide information to large numbers of persons and involve them in specific advocacy projects. Technology is not a panacea—for example, opponents of policy advocates can also use it—but it can be hugely helpful to specific advocacy projects.

Policy Advocacy Challenge 10.5

The Internet as an Advocacy Tool

Gretchen Heidemann, MSW & Doctoral Candidate, University of Southern California, School of Social Work;

Bruce Jansson, Ph.D.; and

Elaine Sanchez, MPP

Internet advocacy has revolutionized many causes including, but not limited to, health care reform, marriage equality, mental health parity, child welfare, gun violence prevention, media reform, wildlife preservation, and global warming. From political blogs to online fundraising, and from virtual town halls to podcasting, the Internet now is a key tool in any advocacy organization's or political party's toolkit. You have probably participated in Internet advocacy if you receive email alerts from organizations that work on issues important to you, or if you have signed an email petition, sent an electronic letter to your elected representative, watched a virtual town hall meeting, viewed a campaign speech on YouTube, or donated money to a cause via a website.

The following is a partial list of the various Internet advocacy tools that organizations and political parties are using to advance their agenda:

Email alerts, "tweets," text messages, and mobile messages to constituents/supporters

Electronic petitions

Electronic letters to elected representatives

Online fundraising

Event publicizing

Blogging

Video streaming

Citizen journalism

Virtual town halls

Podcasting

Virtual pressrooms

Social network sites

The power of social media and its ability to fuel advocacy campaigns was exemplified in the February 2012 battle between the Susan G. Komen for the Cure foundation and Planned Parenthood. The Komen organization had announced its plans to cease its funding of Planned Parenthood's breast cancer screening program, after a politically motivated Republican Congressman commenced his own investigation into Planned Parenthood's use of grant money.[1] Komen's controversial decision sparked an immediate backlash, which played out in the Internet. As news spread, women across the country—politicians, advocates, celebrities, and citizens alike—flocked to Twitter and Facebook to decry Komen's actions. According to a social media analytics tool from a Washington-based public relations firm, three-quarters of persons who posted commentary regarding the decision on social media channels expressed negative feelings toward Komen, and more than one-fifth of persons indicated they would go so far as to boycott the foundation[2] In 24 hours, more than 19,000 people circulated a Planned Parenthood online letter titled "I Stand with Planned Parenthood," and $400,000 was raised online, alone, in support of the organization.[3] Planned Parenthood's official Facebook page drew nearly 20,000 new "likes," and more than 10,000 supporters gave personal monetary

---

[1]Gardiner Harris and Pam Belluck, "Uproar as Breast Cancer Group Ends Partnership with Planned Parenthood," *The New York Times* (February 1, 2012). Taken from **www.nytimes.com/2012/02/02/us/uproar-as-komen-foundation-cuts-money-to-planned-parenthood.html?pagewanted=all**.
[2]Jennifer Preston, "Komen Split With Planned Parenthood Draws Fire Online." *The New York Times*. Taken from http://thelede.blogs.nytimes.com/2012/02/01/komen-split-with-planned-parenthood-draws-uproar-online/.
[3]Ibid.

(continued)

**Policy
Advocacy
Challenge 10.5**
(continued)

contributions.[4] An estimated 250,000 people visited MoveOn.org to sign a petition that called for Komen's reversal.[5] In a victory for the Internet advocates, Komen reversed its decision to eliminate its Planned Parenthood funding. Due to the firestorm of public criticism, Karen Handel, Komen's vice president for public policy, also resigned from the organization.

EXERCISE

Select an issue or a topic that concerns you. Perform an Internet search to see if there are any organizations working to advocate for this cause. If so, what type of Internet advocacy is this organization conducting? Make a list of the various forms of Internet advocacy it utilizes to advance its platform. What other tools might it use to help it accomplish its advocacy objectives? To the extent that this organization is not utilizing Internet advocacy tools, how would you recommend it begins to do so? If you were to design an Internet advocacy campaign for a cause of concern to you, which tools would you use, and why?

[4]Louise Radnofsky, Anna Wilde Mathews and Melanie Grayce West, "Charity Does an About-Face," *The Wall Street Journal* (February 4, 2012). Taken from **http://online.wsj.com/article/SB10001424052970203889904577201010816706778.html**.
[5]Elizabeth Lopatto and Anna Edney, "Planned Parenthood Gains Online Push for Komen Funds," *Bloomberg Businessweek* (February 14, 2012). Taken from: www.businessweek.com/news/2012-02-14/planned-parenthood-gains-online-push-for-komen-funds.html.

EPA 2.1.8b

Politicians are also more likely to take the advice of an advocate who is backed up by affiliation with a recognized group or coalition. Such affiliations give advocates several advantages. Recognized groups or coalitions can mobilize external pressure by activating their members and those of affiliated organizations. As a result, they are more likely than solo advocates to get attention from the mass media, particularly as they develop long-standing associations with reporters and officials in television and the print media. Because they can obtain funds from foundations and other sources more easily than solo advocates can, advocacy groups and coalitions can conduct more sophisticated research than solo advocates—research that enhances their standing with legislators and government officials. And because advocacy groups are long-standing organizations, their staff can develop ongoing associations with government officials and legislators, as well as close working relationships with the staff of other advocacy groups that allow them to pool resources, share contacts, and form coalitions around specific issues. It is not sufficient only to develop advocacy groups and coalitions, however; policy advocates need also to enlist them in well-conceived campaigns to secure policy reforms.

Sometimes policy advocates can use a low scope of conflict, relying on personal relationships with policy makers to bring policy changes. In such cases, advocates do not mobilize external pressure on legislators because they believe they can secure policy reforms without it. In other cases, however, they do need to mobilize external pressure in a well-coordinated campaign that includes letter writing, coverage by the mass media, and even demonstrations.

Policy advocates should try, then, to work with and through advocacy groups and coalitions whenever possible. If such groups do not exist, policy advocates should form them. (We discuss strategies for organizing coalitions in Chapter Eleven.)

External pressure can also be placed on social agencies. As Yeheskel Hasenfeld and other organizational theorists with a political economy perspective note, organizational policies are shaped by many forces.[37] Funders, courts, community groups, and community leaders all can shape organizations' internal policies. Just as policy advocates sometimes pressure legislators, these forces sometimes pressure social agencies to modify specific policies or to consider program innovations.

Hedrick Smith argues that television has revolutionized political tactics in Congress, especially since the decline in power of political party leaders and legislative committees. The committees have lost power because of procedural changes and an increase in party members' power to choose their committee memberships.[38] Viewing themselves as quasi-independent of their party and seeking a national as well as a local constituency, many politicians regularly make videotapes that they forward to the media in their constituencies. Through the mass media, then, politicians increase public support for issues they believe will enhance their popularity. Advocacy groups and coalitions also need to make skillful use of the mass media, as we discuss in Chapter Twelve, by having press conferences, writing editorials, briefing reporters, and staging media events.

Successful Power Users in the Policy-Enacting Task

Personal characteristics—*persistence,* for example—increase some persons' ability to shape policy outcomes. Jane Addams and Martin Luther King, Jr., persevered over decades despite repeated failures in their quest for social justice. Even our student intern, who might have been discouraged by her preceptor's initial irritation about her proposed innovation, brought up the issue again several weeks later and secured a positive response. As we noted in Chapter Six when discussing agenda building, some issues float for years and then resurface when someone is sufficiently persistent to reintroduce the measure.

Policy advocates who focus on an issue's content and avoid attacking the motivations or character of their opponents are often viewed more positively than those who make personal attacks.[39] As we point out in Chapter Eleven, even though we often have to respond to unfair attacks on our intentions or motivations, we do not usually enhance our personal power by initiating such attacks.

Although skillful policy advocates are flexible, they do not bend with every breeze. Personal credibility, which is essential to the effective use of power, will be eroded if they seem excessively opportunistic. They must be able to stick to their basic convictions, even in the face of opposition.

However, successful policy advocates also are skilled in fashioning compromises, which are frequently needed to obtain support in agency and legislative settings.[40] A fine line sometimes exists between having convictions and being able to compromise.

Power in Organizations in the Policy-Enacting Task

EPA 2.1.2a

We have discussed power relationships and power resources, using many examples from legislative settings. As our example of the social work intern suggests, power relationships and power resources also are used extensively in social agencies as advocates try to improve services for clients. We now discuss a special kind of policy issue that many social workers confront at some point in their professional work: when to challenge policies or practices that they believe to be unethical and that are supported by higher level staff and officials.

Discretion, Compliance, and Whistleblowing

The interrelationship of discretion, compliance, and whistleblowing confronts direct-service and other social service staff throughout their careers. Considerable controversy may exist in an agency about how much discretion, or autonomy, policy makers and administrators should grant human service workers. Under what circumstances should social workers be able to disobey policies they believe are unethical? When should social workers take their disagreements about internal agency matters to external parties, such as the mass media?

Defining Zones of Discretion

When analyzing policy implementation, we often think in broad terms, such as agency budgets and leadership, taking a top-down perspective. We also can take a bottom-up perspective by beginning with the line worker, who translates policy into action.

High-level policies may seem to dictate virtually all the actions of direct-service staff. However, much of their work occurs within zones of discretion in which their own judgments and choices shape their actions.[41]

Why do agencies cede so much discretion to their direct-service staff? Assume that you are a high-level administrator and are quite certain about the intake policies you want in your agency's program for children with learning disorders. You can write some definitive admission standards, such as "Only children from families with XYZ income shall obtain admittance to this program." Because this kind of policy is quantitative, it is clear-cut and allows no exceptions. However, when you come to "learning disorders," you despair of writing an exact definition, and you must cede to those who will implement this policy considerable discretion in selecting children with learning disorders. Moreover, you must let professional workers determine when a child has reached sufficient learning competence to make her or him ineligible for continuing service. Realizing that some people will need extended help and others may overcome their problems quickly, you decide against a blanket rule that establishes a maximum period of service.

Our discussion suggests that professionals are given so much discretion because they often are required to use their own judgment on complex social problems, human motivation, and clients' progress. High-level officials may also decide that professionals need the latitude to make exceptions to policies. Assume, for example, that legislators are aware that some psychotic patients need to be committed to institutions, even though they are not suicidal and have not physically threatened other persons, the criteria usually used for involuntary commitment. Legislators may add professional judgment to those criteria, even though such discretion may sometimes lead to unnecessary commitment.

In connection with the autonomy of direct-service workers, we must note as well that the location and nature of their work precludes detailed oversight. Direct-service workers conduct much of their work in private interactions with clients. Moreover, many human services agencies do not conform to the bureaucratic models discussed by Max Weber; rather than having tight controls in centralized structures, many of them are "loosely coupled" organizations with several quasi-independent programs, units, and branches. In such organizations, it is difficult for top administrators to regulate the work of direct-service staff.[42]

Ceding discretion to professionals bears some risks and may lead to discrimination against certain clients in the name of professional judgment. A professional may decide that people with specific learning disorders should not be allowed into a program, because he or she is prejudiced against them and has erroneous perceptions of their condition.[43]

Some professionals take advantage of the discretion allowed them to further their own material interests or their own narrow approach to service delivery. Franklin Chu and Sharland Trotter discovered that many mental health professionals failed to implement federally legislated policies because they were uninterested in working with psychotic or low-income persons.[44] A few social workers have even siphoned clients from their public agency for their private practice, despite the widely held ethical norms that prohibit this practice.

There is a constant tension between maximizing professional discretion and making binding rules to prevent discrimination against particular clients and to protect the public interest. If professionals often want to expand their discretion, policy makers often want to constrict it.

Issues of Compliance

A social worker in a public welfare setting dislikes specific, punitive policies. A social worker in a child welfare office objects to pressures to reunify families that have not been adequately analyzed or helped. Social workers who do not want to implement specific policies can adopt several strategies. First, they can keep their noncompliance secret even from their supervisors by bending or ignoring rules, by enforcing rules halfheartedly, or by counseling clients in ways that circumvent specific policies. Second, they can comply with official policy but use every available means to seek exemptions for specific persons. For example, to help an older person avoid early discharge from a hospital, they might claim that no nursing home beds can be found, after a halfhearted look for a bed, or they may even lie about a bed's availability. (Such deception returns us to the first strategy.) Third, they may comply with official policy in every respect, even while believing it to be defective. Fourth, they may comply with official policies while trying to change them.

No easy answers exist for such dilemmas. The duty to obey official policy cannot be dismissed lightly; professionals' credibility would be severely jeopardized if they routinely flouted the rules. Yet some policies are unethical or harmful to clients, either to all clients or just to those with idiosyncratic needs. Beneficence requires us to consider disobeying policies that appear to be inimical to clients' needs or to be in violation of professional ethics. However, it is difficult to protest policies when high-level officials strongly promote them or when agency officials fear that higher authorities, such as legislators, will retaliate if they discover noncompliance.

By the same token, direct-service social workers sometimes find that their colleagues do not implement good policies. (Social workers may fail to implement meritorious policies because they have narrow helping philosophies that deemphasize such activities as outreach, they believe they lack the necessary expertise or resources, they feel burned out, or they are prejudiced against certain kinds of clients.) In such cases, social workers should try to change their colleagues' behavior through educational techniques or technical assistance, or even by alerting higher management to the noncompliance.

Changing peers' behavior can pose a formidable challenge, however, particularly when the agency atmosphere is not conducive to challenging the norms.

Whistleblowing

Individual staff members should try to work through normal channels, but what if they find specific policies or other staff members' actions (such as corruption) so morally flawed that they cannot abide their continuation? And what if they fear that open opposition will cause their dismissal or other penalties? An emerging literature suggests that staff members can ethically publicize flawed policies and actions by divulging information to persons outside the organization, such as members of the mass media, legislators, state authorities, regulators, or funders.[45] They can reveal this information to outsiders, either using their own names or speaking on condition of anonymity in order to prevent personal reprisals. However, whistleblowers who make their names public are sometimes perceived as more credible than those who leak charges anonymously. They also can give the information to the NASW, which will protect their identity while making the information public.

Whistleblowing is an attempt to correct lapses by calling external parties into the conflict. It is ethical if the policies or actions are major, not trivial, violations of ethics or professional standards; if the whistleblower has extremely good evidence that he or she cannot modify policies by conventional means; and if the whistleblower has excellent evidence that he or she will be subjected to serious penalties as a result of raising questions about the policies or conduct. (Despite recent legislation in some states that protects whistleblowers, as well as sanctions that the NASW can exact against employers who fire whistleblowers, persons sometimes have justifiable reason to believe that they will be in jeopardy if they engage in whistleblowing.) At the same time, whistleblowing is abused when persons raise trivial issues, such as minor indiscretions in an agency, or when they have not fully considered alternative means of changing policies.[46]

Our prior discussion of discretion suggests that social workers often encounter not objectionable high-level policies, but vague policies that require them to develop means of filling the policy vacuum.

Power Differentials in the Policy-Enacting Task

So far, our discussion may falsely suggest that all of us have an equal opportunity to wield power, and that if we just put our minds to the task, we will succeed in having policy proposals enacted. This optimistic conclusion ignores harsh realities, such as the power differentials that give some people a significant advantage over others.

Legislators and high-level government officials have *formal authority*, which gives them the power to approve or disapprove certain policy initiatives; to make proposals; and to obtain access to program, budget, and technical information. They have access to other highly placed people who yield information and assistance that are not available to others, and they often command obedience from others when they issue directives or make recommendations. Executives of agencies and government bureaucracies have considerable power over their subordinates, as well as experience and knowledge. Technical experts on specific topics often have extraordinary power in governmental and agency settings.

The leaders, staff members, and lobbyists of groups that have large constituencies, such as interest groups, professional associations, and social movements, derive power from these constituencies that can exert influence on decision makers who do not heed policy suggestions. These leaders, staff members, and lobbyists also have useful expertise that helps them cultivate personal relationships with decision makers that further enhance their power. Some interest groups increase their power by making large campaign contributions to politicians who support their position. In a compelling account of how the mass media and large interest groups (such as the American Association of Retired Persons and political action committees) influence policies, Hedrick Smith contends that well-organized, grassroots constituencies with extraordinary resources and access to the mass media are wielding increasing power in legislative settings.[47]

Individuals who help shape and enact budgets, such as legislators on appropriations committees and officials who control budgets in bureaucracies, often have extraordinary power because "those who pay the piper call the tune." A professor of mine once lamented social workers' tendency to seek jobs in organizations' personnel sections because the staff in the fiscal departments usually have more power to shape the policies and programs of bureaucracies. Officials in the federal Office of Management and Budget (OMB) are key players in establishing the nation's domestic policy because they shape the president's budgetary recommendations.

In some cases, authority figures command obedience even when their suggestions are ethically flawed.[48] The impulse to obey authority figures may stem from peer pressure, loyalty to the organization, lack of information about specific issues, or fear of sanctions.

We should not overlook the role cultural symbols play in giving certain persons and groups more power than others. Officials affiliated with socially acceptable issues, such as children, health, and education, are often more influential than people associated with socially stigmatized groups, such as people who are mentally ill, welfare recipients, or ex-offenders.[49]

EPA 2.1.5a

Discrimination patterns in the broader society influence power transactions. Rosabeth Kanter suggests that women are often excluded from decision making in large organizations because of gender-based prejudice and because they lack access to old-boy networks. Members of minority groups often encounter similar problems.[50]

Although few people would deny that power differentials exist, some theorists, such as C. Wright Mills, have suggested the existence of a power elite, such as the leaders of well-financed interest groups, that monopolizes power and consigns other people and interests to marginal roles.[51] On the other hand, "pluralist" theorists, such as Robert Dahl, have suggested that many interests and people shape policy choices.[52] These theorists point to the multiple interest groups that shape policies in municipal, county, state, and federal jurisdictions.

Who is right? Each theory applies in some situations. In some areas, specific people and interests have the power to dominate policy making, whereas in others, policy choices stem from a political process in which almost anyone can participate. In still other situations, certain people and interests have the power to set agendas and shape choices, but determined and well-organized groups can force them into important concessions. As we discuss in Chapter Eleven, policy practitioners need to be realistic in assessing the distribution of power in specific settings.

The case of the student intern illustrates how persons with little formal power can be surprisingly successful. By taking the initiative, working through an intermediary (Mr. Jones), developing an effective innovation, and securing support for the innovation from psychiatric hospitals, the intern mapped a sophisticated strategy to secure a major policy change in her agency.

Ethical Issues in the Policy-Enacting Task

Some social workers believe that developing and using power is unprofessional. We argued in Chapter Three, however, that although they may be unaware of it, social workers use power frequently in their work, including their direct-service work. Whenever they guide, direct, or suggest options to clients, they use power. When they make recommendations to supervisors or external authorities, such as the courts, they use power. Indeed, we argued in Chapter Two that it may be unethical not to use power in certain situations, such as questioning defective policies or seeking policy changes. In such cases, we said, social workers (and other professionals, such as teachers, attorneys, and physicians) may fail to advance beneficence, social justice, and fairness.

Power can be used unethically—dishonestly or manipulatively—but we cannot make simple, easy-to-follow ethical rules. Someone who is blatantly dishonest to gain a strategic advantage is clearly behaving unethically, but there are grayer areas in ethics. For example, should someone volunteer to an opponent that she will attack his position in a forthcoming meeting? Is withholding this information the same as lying? As discussed in Chapter Two, we may also encounter ethical dilemmas when we use power, as when honesty and social justice conflict. For example, what if enacting a measure to help low-income persons hinges on your telling a falsehood to an opponent of that measure? Faced with this ethical dilemma, you would certainly want to reflect carefully and seek consultation before acting.

The use of manipulation is also an ethical issue. Assume that you want to win and are convinced that you cannot win unless you use a devious parliamentary maneuver that will place your opponent at a disadvantage, use a threat to gain an opponent's support, or suppress data that would make your position appear less tenable. All of these behaviors are manipulative because they will give you an advantage at the expense of open discourse and free choices. Such tactics are usually unethical and even counterproductive because they may cause others to distrust you and even oppose your position.

However, certain manipulative behaviors, such as some forms of dishonesty, can be justified in limited situations. You might rightly decide that ethical principles, such as social justice and beneficence, are at stake; that your opponents are using hardball tactics, so you must use them, too; and that you will lose without some form of manipulation. Here, too, you will want to reflect and seek consultation. (See Policy Advocacy Challenge 10.6 for a discussion of manipulation in political communication.)

Policy Advocacy Challenge 10.6

The Use of Manipulation in Political Communication

Bruce Jansson, Ph.D.

Members of both political parties have at times used manipulative rhetoric to accomplish their objectives. We provide two examples below, one from each side of the aisle.

Democrats contend that President George W. Bush engaged in manipulative rhetoric on the eve of the 2006 congressional elections. The stakes for this election were high for both sides: if the Democrats prevailed, they might regain control of both the House and the Senate for the first time in decades. Background political conditions seemed to favor the Democrats. Widespread discontent existed with respect to the war in Iraq. A scandal occurred in early October involving a Republican congressman alleged to have made suggestive advances to male pages in the Congress.

Following the strategies of the presidential election of 2004, however, Republican strategists wanted to portray Democrats as soft on terrorism. It was difficult to do this on a factual basis because Democrats had supported huge budgets for the Homeland Security Agency—and had even challenged Republicans to approve more funds for protection of the nation's ports and its chemical factories, as well as to screen baggage on airlines.

But Republicans *could* use manipulative rhetoric to make it appear that the Democrats *were* soft on terrorism. President Bush had recently told an interviewer, for example, that "Most people want us to win."[1] He had said at a fundraising event, "I need members of Congress who understand that you can't negotiate with these folks." He had characterized Democrats as "cut and run" and "defeatocrats." He had said that he needed help from lawmakers who "understand you can't negotiate with terrorists."

What made these words manipulative, Democrats contended, was that these words failed to say to whom they applied. Nor did they give specific examples. So the statements left impressions that a large group of unnamed persons—implied to be Democrats—were not concerned about terrorism or wanted to leave Iraq on a moment's notice. The statements often took Democrats' criticisms of the war in Iraq to their logical but extreme conclusion—far more extreme than Democrats' arguments had actually been.

On the flip side, Democrats have been known to conduct their fair share of "spin." During the presidential election campaign season of 2004, some liberal Democrats

---

[1] Quotes in this Policy Advocacy Challenge can be found in Jim Rutenberg, "For the White House, War of Words, at Least, Is Battle Where It Excels," (September 26, 2006): A21.

"indulged in inflammatory and unsubstantiated attacks on the right" by comparing the Bush administration to Nazi Germany, associating the Republican Party with a racist fringe candidate, and alleging—without evidence—that Bush advisor Karl Rove was the mastermind behind the attacks on John Kerry's Vietnam war record.[2] These occurrences of manipulative rhetoric lead one commentator on political spin to conclude that, "in the heat of the campaign, reasonable debate is again falling by the wayside."[3]

Some questions to ponder:

- When is rhetoric "manipulative"?
- Is there ever a time when this type of political "spin" is appropriate or justified?
- What remedies do persons possess who believe they are unfairly attacked?

---

[2]Nyhan, B. (2004). "Outrageous Rhetoric from a Trio of Liberals." Posted September 7, 2004, on www.spinsanity.org.
[3]Ibid.

Engaging in the Policy-Enacting Task in Situations Where Advocates Are Disadvantaged as Compared to More Powerful Players

In some situations, policy advocates have less power than more advantaged players. Members of oppressed vulnerable populations, such as women, gay men and lesbians, and racial minorities, may be challenged to obtain and use power in specific settings. Yet we should not assume that they cannot achieve significant successes as is illustrated by tactics of low-budget lobbyists in Policy Advocacy Challenge 10.7. Indeed, it is remarkable how much can sometimes be achieved with minimal power resources.

Policy Advocacy Challenge 10.7

How Low-Budget Lobbyists Get Power

Kathy Beasley, California Journal

The phone rang a dozen times before a harried Rand Martin could grab it. He disconnected the caller when he tried to put the line on hold so he could finish another call. Such is life when you are between secretaries and cursed with a cheap, quirky phone system.

He would probably receive little sympathy from Sherry Skelly, who lacks not only a secretary but also, until recently, a desk, a typewriter, and an office. Until she managed to scrape up the money, she had been using a donated hallway as her headquarters. She still makes do with a single phone line and an answering machine.

Martin and Skelly are lobbyists, Martin for the AIDS-oriented Lobby for Individual Freedom and Equality (LIFE) and Skelly for the California Children's Lobby. You can tell they are lobbyists because they work bills, meet with legislators and consultants, and testify at hearings. Their pictures are also in the secretary of state's *Directory of Lobbyists*.

But if you look for other signs that signify "lobbyist" to most of the public, you will not find any. The organizations they represent never show up on the lists of heavy campaign contributors. They keep their fingers crossed when they send their cards to legislators on the floor, hoping to speak with them, for, unlike their heavyweight counterparts, Martin and Skelly are unable to command an audience. They do not have legions of staff to keep them posted on the dozens of bills they must track. If they hit the Sacramento hot spots at night, it is to relax and enjoy themselves; their budgets do not allow for the drinks or dinner that might further connections with lawmakers and legislative staff. In short, what these two lack is money.

(continued)

Of course, they are not alone. The Fair Political Practices Commission lists 762 registered lobbyists. Ranking lobbyists by affluence, there are only 11 big operators at the top. Those 11 receive in excess of $500,000 in client fees and spread around hundreds of thousands of dollars more in campaign contributions.

Much lower in the rankings are the lobbyists for public interest groups—California Common Cause, Consumers Union, American Civil Liberties Union—along with lobbyists for state agencies, departments, and commissions. Although they have no money to grease the wheels of power, they usually have enough resources to track bills, produce position papers, and rally the public.

Scraping dead bottom are a subgroup of public interest entities, such as LIFE and California Children's Lobby, whose annual budgets detail how many stamps may be used and how many photocopies may be made in one month. Martin runs his operation on a budget of $80,000, including office rent, his salary, and that of a secretary. Skelly makes it on $63,000. Clearly neither of them is in it for the money. If it is true that money turns the wheels in the capital, then one would expect Martin's and Skelly's work to be mostly futile. So who are these penny-pinching lobbyists, how do they get by, and what can they possibly accomplish?

"A lobbyist is a be-all," says the 27-year-old Skelly. "I feel like I'm a mediator and a resource who can provide expertise on an issue. If you have no money, you end up working closely with consultants, and consultants are very detail-oriented."

Expertise, a flair for detail, credibility—these are the tools a low-budget lobbyist brings to work every day. Some of the weight such a lobbyist carries is personal, earned over years of consistently giving good advice and testimony; some of it comes from the organization he or she represents.

California Children's Lobby, for instance, is an umbrella group for child-care providers, child-care educators, and parent groups around the state. Skelly says the lobby has a 20-year track record of grassroots activism that makes it an effective advocate on children's issues.

"It's a very sophisticated network," she says. "With the phone tree we have, we can get 40 calls into a member's office on a particular bill within an hour. These people know the [legislative] members in their areas; they write letters, make phone calls, and involve the parent groups. This committed network has been developing for the past 10 or 20 years, and now it's primed and ready to go."

Skelly, who has been with California Children's Lobby for almost a year, says she is the only full-time lobbyist for children's issues in Sacramento. Although that has the drawback of spreading one person too thinly over hundreds of bills, it does mean that Skelly has become a focal point for children's issues and a natural funnel for information, studies, and trends.

But beyond the clout of her organization, Skelly works on developing her own ties and credibility. She knows about one-quarter of the members of both houses. "When I meet a member, I don't just talk about my bills," she says. "Education bills, minimum wage—if I know a certain member is interested in something this year, then I talk about that. Then they know I'm interested in their concerns and views and not just pushing my agenda." Just as important are her consultant contacts. "Consultants tap into [lobbyists] as a resource. You have to prepare good amendments for bills and make good suggestions well in advance of hearings if you are going to influence the outcome."

The 34-year-old Martin, who has been a lobbyist on health issues for three years, says he is always working on his recognition and credibility with both legislators and consultants. Unlike Skelly's organization, Martin's group is still learning to flex its political muscles.

While children's issues may be simmering on a front burner this year, Martin's issue has been boiling at high speed for a couple of years.

Martin was instrumental in forming the LIFE, an umbrella organization for 42 California organizations concerned about AIDS. He has been its sole lobbyist since it began.

During the first full year of operation, he felt swamped, working out of his living room to track 65 bills. Confronted with 142 bills this year, Martin is beginning to feel last year was calm in retrospect.

"The number of bills, so many legislators and staff to get to know, plus keeping a fledgling organization afloat—it's been difficult," Martin says.

The difficulties are not just in the part of the job that deals with bills. He has learned quickly that a discount lobbyist not only needs to keep an eye on developments in the capital but also needs to educate, guide, and cajole the groups he represents. One of his biggest tasks is forming his backers into a cohesive, effective voice.

"Gays and lesbians have always been very adept at turning people out on a single issue, but they've been unable to do it on a consistent basis," Martin says. "LIFE has been working to build that kind of network. LIFE illustrates a new political maturity that acknowledges the need for a group to have continuous visibility."

Networking and consensus-building are slow processes, however, and the AIDS epidemic is moving very quickly. "Building a network takes longer than gaining personal access to an individual legislator, but it's every bit as important," Martin says.

Important, yes; comfortable, no. Martin is often caught between a legislative agenda that threatens to move ahead without LIFE and purists on his board who believe compromise is synonymous with evil. "It puts us in a tough position, because we have liberal legislators who want to side with us telling us we have to give on some things," Martin says. "But then we have those who believe LIFE needs to maintain a pure image in the gay-lesbian community. And there's a need for those kinds of people: they create such a pure position, we look like moderates in comparison."

So Martin frequently finds himself in the role of an educator, not just to consultants and legislators, but to his own group members, who need to understand how the process works and what is probable, feasible, and impossible.

Skelly agrees with the vision of a lobbyist as an educator. She conducts seminars and attends the monthly meetings of a half-dozen child-oriented organizations. It is important for the folks back home to understand how Sacramento works and how they can affect what comes out of the capital.

"The Children's Lobby network can produce a teen parent and her partner, holding a baby, to give testimony at a hearing," Skelly says. "We can call on experts in the field and find out anything a legislator might want to know. These people are on the scene where state programs are actually working, so they are in a good position to know what's wrong and what needs to be done. They need to be able to convey that information to the legislature."

Skelly says that such personal testimony at hearings can have a "significance beyond dollars."

But dollars do count, no matter how optimistic or well-armed with statistics a lobbyist may be.

"A lobbyist without money just doesn't have the access," Martin says. "It's most visible when lobbyists are giving testimony. The committee members sit up and listen when it's someone with clout or money; they pay attention."

Martin says this matter-of-factly, with little bitterness in his voice. He regretfully accepts reality; lobbyists without the big bucks have to be more diligent in preparing arguments, supplying statistics, and proposing improvements—sometimes to no avail.

"You take a lot of frustration home. But then there have been people we've turned around on a particular issue," Martin says. "I think we've had a lot of impact on Dr. Filante (Assemblyman William Filante) and helped build his leadership on the AIDS issue among Republicans."

(continued)

**Policy
Advocacy
Challenge 10.7**
(continued)

Skelly says her biggest victory came last year when she helped secure $500,000 in the state budget for California State University child care. The governor had already vetoed a $1.2 million expenditure, so getting the partial funding past his blue pencil was a plus. "These campus centers had been struggling along for 20 years without any state funding, and many of them were on the verge of closing," she says. "So this was the first time general-fund money was ever committed to campus child care, and I was very excited about it."

The upbeat Skelly cannot remember a defeat that left her depressed in the past, but even an optimistic nature will not block reality this year. California Children's Lobby's top priority is a statutory cost-of-living adjustment for child care. The governor has already vetoed similar legislation in the past. The governor also placed an equitable cost-of-living adjustment in his budget proposal this year, cutting the ground out from under Skelly's arguments by removing the need for immediate action. "I have to admit I'm beginning to anticipate a problem," she says.

Like all lobbyists, Martin has experienced both victories and defeats. His biggest victories have been killing two of GOP State Senator John Doolittle's ten-bill AIDS packages, and his worst defeat was the passage of a bill to test prostitutes for AIDS.

Victories that come by defeating bills are often fleeting. One of Doolittle's bills would have substantially relaxed AIDS test confidentiality laws, including turning results over to public health officials, and the other would have allowed widespread testing in psychiatric institutions. Those two are dead, but other measures this year are likely to accomplish at least some of Doolittle's goals.

The prostitute bill's passage was the type of fluke that leaves lobbyists with nightmares. The bill swept out of the assembly, not as a well-reasoned policy decision, but on a Gang-of-Five tidal wave while Martin watched helplessly. "It happened so fast, and most of it was behind closed doors," Martin says, "so we really couldn't do much about it."

Had the Gang of Five, a group of dissident Democrats, not been trying to find common ground with Republicans so they could successfully challenge Speaker Willie Brown, the prostitute bill would have stayed buried or at least could have been modified to be less objectionable to LIFE, Martin says. But it is just one of several bills on which Martin expects defeat, leaving him feeling stressed and making his shoestring-budget operation all the more depressing.

"Burnout is common with public interest lobbyists," Martin says. "The ones you see around the building who have been here for 20 or 30 years work for industries, big-buck clients."

So if Martin received an offer from a big-time lobbying firm, would he switch?

"I couldn't leave LIFE dangling in midsession," says Martin, who is gay and deeply committed to the fight against AIDS. "But in the longer term, yes, I'd probably move on. You can have a deep personal commitment to an issue, but it only lasts until burnout hits."

Martin, whose father is a Washington, DC, lobbyist, is already well sidetracked from the theater career he had planned. He keeps his hand in acting and directing with a Davis community theater group, but his future is in the capital. "It's in my blood," he says simply. "The more I've been involved in government activities, the more I've been fascinated with what is going on in Sacramento."

The fascination is still there for Skelly, as well. "I really enjoy lobbying. It's exciting and stimulating."

Skelly did not start out as a lobbyist. An active role in starting a child-care program at University of California, Santa Barbara, put her in the limelight when the university's student association needed a lobbyist. Two years there and another year with the California Children's Lobby have satisfied her itch to do something professionally that focuses on children.

"I have a bottom-line commitment to education and children's issues. I might move on to something else in the future. But I'm pretty dedicated to children's issues and, right now, I couldn't imagine doing anything else."

Some questions to ponder:

- How do policy advocates compensate for their meager resources in state capitals, where well-heeled lobbyists, with many times their resources, compete with them for the attention of legislators?
- What kinds of power resources do they have?
- How can they achieve some successes even when they cannot wine-and-dine legislators extravagantly?
- Do they have any advantages when contrasted with well-heeled lobbyists?

Obtaining Power Resources in the Policy-Enacting Task

EPA 2.1.8b

To this point, we have discussed the kinds of power resources that policy advocates use in agency, community, and legislative settings. We now turn to tactics for developing power resources in the first instance. To do this, policy advocates must build their personal credibility, learn how to network, and create links with groups that can help them in their policy practice. Please read Policy Advocacy Challenge 10.7 because we will refer to it as we discuss how two policy advocates (Sherry Skelly and Rand Martin) developed and used power resources as lobbyists for child care and persons with HIV/AIDS in a state legislature.

Building Personal Credibility

Whether they are attorneys, physicians, or social workers, professionals require personal credibility to be effective with their clients. Similarly, the personal credibility of policy advocates influences the degree to which others will listen to them[53] (see Policy Advocacy Challenge 10.8).

Several tactics can enhance individuals' personal credibility. Such tactics can emphasize that the individuals are reasonable and pragmatic team players affiliated with successful institutions, who have integrity and authoritativeness and a positive track record. People often use Machiavellian tactics as well to enhance their personal credibility, although not without ethical and practical risks.

Appearing Reasonable and Pragmatic   Policy advocates sometimes increase their credibility with decision makers who have different values by not emphasizing a proposal's underlying principles and by focusing instead on its substantive provisions.[54] Assume, for example, that a policy advocate who has a radical perspective wants to redistribute resources to poor people by substantially increasing the benefits of the food stamp program. When dealing with the aide of a conservative legislator, this policy advocate will downplay his radical ideology and emphasize instead both the details of the reform and the objective of increasing distressed farmers' revenues. By downplaying his ideology, which is dissonant with the ideology of conservative politicians, the policy advocate will seem more credible to the aide.[55]

Policy advocates who sacrifice their preferences excessively in their zeal to appear reasonable and pragmatic may find this strategy counterproductive if other people perceive them as disingenuous.

Appearing to Be a Team Player   Adherents of power-dependence theory suggest that others view us as credible when they depend on us.[56] Let us consider the social work units in two hospitals. The unit in Hospital 1 contents itself with providing crisis intervention services to patients, whereas the unit in Hospital 2 fills several functions besides traditional counseling. The staff members assume a highly visible role in discharge planning, providing financial counseling for patients, providing social services to rape victims, serving as intermediaries between the hospital and the state's department of children's services in suspected cases of child abuse and neglect, operating a substance abuse clinic, and providing home-based services to frail, older persons. Top decision makers in Hospital 2 depend on the social work staff for these services. Indeed, they cannot imagine how their hospital would function without this unit. By contrast, top decision makers in Hospital 1 hardly know that the social work unit exists, much less that it is vital to the hospital. According to power-dependence theory, decision makers are more likely to heed suggestions of the director or other staff of the expansive social work unit at Hospital 2 than at Hospital 1.[57]

Power-dependence theory suggests, then, that policy advocates can increase their stature by assuming multiple functions beyond their narrow job descriptions. As the director of a social work unit once said to me, "I might even consider washing windows!" These expanded functions serve several purposes; they make high-level administrators feel beholden to the units and individuals who perform these many positive tasks for the institution, and they make these units and individuals appear to be team players who care about the institution's broader interests.

Policy advocates also can enhance their credibility by taking the initiative to make changes within an organization. Assume, for example, that in a casual conversation with a social worker, a hospital administrator remarks on "the turnover of nursing and social work staff in the pediatrics unit during the past five years, which has severely jeopardized the quality of services and staff morale." If the social worker seizes the initiative and offers to survey the staff before discussing possible causes of the turnover, she makes the administrator dependent on her by performing a necessary task. Volunteering this service makes her appear to be a team player. If she assumes additional roles on this project, such as chairing a committee, she continues this proactive and positive role. We can imagine that these assertive actions would enhance her credibility on this issue.

People can also increase their image as team players, and thus their credibility, by shaping policy proposals germane to an organization's mission.[58] Of course, ethical concerns limit the use of this tactic because we should not make proposals based on morally objectionable values. If a hospital does not wish to serve any poor patients who lack insurance, even those with emergency conditions, a social work unit should not seek funds for additional staff to screen out such people.[59]

EPA 2.1.9b

Personal Integrity   Some people may rightly wonder whether some of these tactics for increasing personal credibility will imperil practitioners' integrity. If we constantly appear to be reasonable and to be team players, when should we speak out for specific causes or not be team players when we think the team needs fundamental reforms?

Policy advocates may take as models many effective legislators who have combined moderate approaches with principled and outspoken positions on certain issues. When he was president, Bill Clinton often hewed to a moderate course, but he often tangled with such conservative opponents as Representative Newt Gingrich, refusing to back down when challenged at key points. Yet he enjoyed considerable popularity and was overwhelmingly re-elected in 1996. Perhaps one reason for his credibility in the area of budget politics—despite his personal scandals—was that many people perceived him as having integrity on budget issues, such as not making sweeping cuts in entitlements and as being able to draw the line when his most fundamental beliefs were challenged.[60]

Authoritativeness When we want to change a policy in an agency, community, or legislative setting, opposition may arise from people who say the change is not warranted. The policy advocate often can diminish such inertia by demonstrating authoritativeness on the subject and offering evidence that supports the policy change, whether by citing important research, documenting similar changes in other settings, or quoting reputable experts.[61] In the case mentioned previously of the high rate of staff turnover in the hospital's pediatrics service, the social worker might conduct her survey of the situation by using a well-known standardized instrument that measures staff morale. As individuals appear to be authoritative on a specific issue, they increase the likelihood that they will be perceived as authoritative on future occasions.

Developing a Positive Track Record One cannot develop credibility merely by using rhetoric; people have to observe firsthand, or hear secondhand, that someone is competent, trustworthy, or authoritative, or that a department performs indispensable services.

Secondhand reports may be quite helpful in establishing credibility. As people initiate useful policies and try to change existing policies, they obtain a good reputation not only with those they encounter directly but also with those who hear positive feedback about them.

Affiliating Oneself with Successful Institutions Credibility stems not only from individuals' actions and attributes, but also from their affiliations. Assume that a hospital administrator receives requests for additional funding from the directors of two units. The first director's unit has been marked by chronic and repeated turmoil, and the administrator does not perceive it as providing quality services. The second director's unit is widely viewed as outstanding; the hospital administrator has received many positive reports about its services and staff. Although the directors may have similar personal characteristics, we can guess whose request the hospital administrator is more likely to heed.

The lesson for social workers who work in bureaucracies is simple. Personal credibility stems in part from being associated with a well-regarded and effective unit. That unit, in turn, derives its reputation from the quality of its work and its staff.[62] Practitioners can enhance their credibility indirectly by improving the services of the unit that employs them.

Using Machiavellian Tactics Some individuals try to enhance their credibility by using negative tactics, such as harming others' reputations, buck-passing, sandbagging, and turf or empire building. Those who use Machiavellian tactics often assume that they can enhance their own reputation only by diminishing the reputations of their colleagues. Buck-passing means blaming others for one's own failures,[63] and sandbagging means diminishing another's accomplishment by contending that others, perhaps even oneself, were really responsible for it.[64] As any participant in bureaucratic politics can confirm, many people excel in turf or empire building, which means accumulating power and responsibility by wrestling them from others.[65] People malign colleagues to diminish their initiatives by suggesting that the proposals reflect ulterior and evil motivations, such as a desire for status or power.[66]

These negative tactics are quite effective in some political campaigns, and some administrators obtain power by using them. But the credibility of those who use them can suffer, because they can be perceived as immoral.

Illustrations from Policy Advocacy Challenge 10.7 Policy Advocacy Challenge 10.7 illustrates how many interactional skills low-budget lobbyists need to develop power resources. Rand Martin tells us that his power depends on his being reasonable and pragmatic in dealing with legislators, though he finds it is difficult to make concessions that he and his allies do not want to make. He discusses building a reputation for personal integrity and authoritativeness by providing well-researched, accurate information to legislators. Both he and Sherry Skelly mention the need to develop a track record of timely and responsible contributions to legislators.

Networking

EPA 2.1.3a

A network is the number and range of supportive relationships a person has.[67] Networks are important to policy practitioners in several ways. Individuals with broad networks develop early-information systems through which they learn about issues, problems, and trends relevant to their work, and they have many sources of advice as they develop policies and strategies.

There are many kinds of networks. *Lateral networks* consist of relationships with colleagues; *vertical* and *subordinate networks* consist, respectively, of persons who are superior to and beneath a person in an organization's hierarchy. People have *heterogeneous networks* when they have supportive relationships with others in a range of positions both within and outside their work. A social worker in a hospital has a heterogeneous network, for example, when it includes members of different units or departments and different professions. Some relationships in networks are short term, perhaps fashioned in response to a specific problem, while others are long standing.

Strategies that help expand a person's networks include enhancing visibility, seeking inclusion in decision-making bodies, cultivating mentors, obtaining access to informal groups, and developing links with social movements.

Enhancing Personal Visibility Some people develop networks by increasing their visibility in bureaucratic, community, legislative, and social settings.[68] An example is the young Lyndon Johnson, who lived in a boardinghouse when he first arrived in Washington, DC, as an aide to a legislator. To meet other aides who lived in the same boardinghouse, he brushed his teeth three or four times each morning and took several showers. In these encounters, he asked the other aides about their jobs and their interests, a tactic that convinced each aide that Johnson cared about him.[69]

Indeed, politicians often employ a tactic that others can use. Although exchanging information is important, both as an end in itself and as a method of establishing a relationship, it should be supplemented by actively seeking advice, support, or suggestions from others. As Christopher Matthews notes, people like to be asked for advice; it makes them feel important and wanted.[70]

Obtaining Inclusion in Decision-Making Bodies To examine specific problems, agencies often establish either ongoing committees or time-limited ad hoc committees.

Membership on these committees is sometimes controlled by top officials in the organization. However, individuals can seek membership by showing interest or by suggesting the formation of a committee to examine a problem. Committee membership is an excellent opportunity to obtain an inside position on important issues, improve one's credibility, and extend one's network.

Seeking Mentors and Inclusion in Informal Groups In her research on why women have difficulty obtaining promotions in corporations, Rosabeth Kanter implicates their exclusion from mentoring relationships and old-boy networks.[71] Males, she observes, develop informal relationships with high-level male officials, who become their mentors, giving advice and information about the internal workings of the corporation, its politics, taboo subjects, informal factions, upcoming policy issues, and strategies for obtaining promotion. Mentors also introduce these neophytes to important officers of the corporation and into informal cliques and relationships, and go to bat for them when they need high-level assistance.

As J. McIver Weatherford notes with respect to legislatures, old-boy networks span the legislative, bureaucratic, and lobbying spheres of government as people move among them in their employment.[72] In both state and federal capitals, powerful legislators have an intricate network of acquaintances, many of them former aides, in lobbying and the bureaucracy. They tap into these rich networks at many points in their work—when contemplating whether to introduce legislation, when seeking to help a constituent with a specific problem, and when searching for issues that will enhance their reputation as initiators of new legislation.

These old-boy networks contain a wide-ranging set of contacts that provide their members with assistance, information, business connections, and job possibilities. Many high-level decisions are made during social encounters among the people in these networks; those outside such networks are not consulted about these decisions and therefore have no advance notice of future policy changes.[73]

The workings of the mentor system and the old-boy network are manifestly unfair to those not included in them. Lacking allies within such networks, many women and racial minorities are excluded, as are loners and those disinclined to maintain a network of relationships.[74] Declarations about the evil nature of these networks, however, will not make them disappear, nor will the moral victories of those who avoid them erase the disadvantages this exclusion brings.

EPA 2.1.8a

Developing Links with Social Movements   Some policy advocates develop links with groups that take interest in issues such as AIDS, reforms for children, and persons with physical or mental disabilities. The members of such groups, who often have minimal resources, are highly knowledgeable about specific issues and deeply committed to them. Other people become active in local chapters of professional organizations, such as the NASW, or form relationships with politicians or civil servants.

Such connections increase a person's power within her or his own organization because those who have them are often viewed as more credible than those who lack them. They bring into an organization ideas and information from these external contacts.[75] In turn, to help these external groups or movements, the members sometimes recruit other staff or even clients as volunteers, though they must be certain that their clients should not feel that services have a price tag attached to them.[76]

Power Challenges Encountered by Members of Vulnerable Populations in the Policy-Enacting Task

We have already alluded to Rosabeth Kanter's pioneering work on problems that female executives confront when seeking power in organizations. Her observations apply as well to persons of color, gay men and lesbians, people with disabilities, and members of any groups that confront prejudice.[77]

Members of these groups use the techniques we have already discussed, such as networking, but they must be even more diligent and persistent. They can also develop relationships with other members of their own group in their workplace, such as women who have attained positions of power, to provide special assistance, support, and advice. When such contacts are lacking, they should seek help from mentors outside the organization, in similar or related organizations.

Members of vulnerable populations can also find allies among mainstream persons, who may, for example, take the lead in diversifying an agency's staff or including a broader range of staff in supervisory positions.

The case of a formerly incarcerated woman turned policy advocate illustrates how persons with marginal power resources can gain significant power (see Policy Advocacy Challenge 10.8).

Policy Advocacy Challenge 10.8

From Powerless to Powerful: Susan's Story

Gretchen Heidemann, MSW & Doctoral Candidate, University of Southern California, School of Social Work

Susan Burton is the founder and executive director of A New Way of Life Re-entry Project, a nonprofit organization whose mission is to help women and girls break the cycle of entrapment in the criminal justice system and lead healthy and satisfying lives. Susan is a former prisoner and drug addict who was in and out of the California prison system six times before turning her life around and opening her arms and her doors to other women.

Growing up in poverty-stricken south Los Angeles, Susan endured child abuse, molestation, and family dysfunction. At age 15, she was gang-raped. She began skipping school, running away, and experimenting with drugs and alcohol. But it was not until years later, when her five-year-old son was killed by a police officer, that Susan was sent spiraling out of control, and into a life of drugs and crime.

Susan describes her years in and out of prison as lonely, desperate years. She was never offered drug treatment or counseling inside the prison, but left to deal with all she had experienced in silence. Each time she was released, she made a promise to herself never to go back. Yet when she would get off the bus at the Los Angeles terminal, she was instantly confronted with drug dealers, pimps, and others who preyed on the vulnerable women coming home. With little family support, and no money to pay for rehabilitation, she relapsed many times.

Susan finally got the help she needed in 1998. Through a combination of drug treatment, intensive therapy, and sheer determination, Susan was able to heal her childhood wounds, make amends for her wrongs, and recover from the effects of having been locked up. A strong believer in the 12-step philosophy, Susan felt a calling and obligation to give back to others. She struggled and saved enough from what she earned working as nurse for the elderly to buy a modest three-bedroom house in the Watts section of Los Angeles. Immediately, she began opening her doors to other women coming out of prison.

Recognizing that the women sharing her home were in need of more than just a roof over their heads, Susan began seeking out other forms of support. One day, a friend told her she could get some bus tokens to help the women get to their appointments, if only she had nonprofit status. So, on her own, Susan embarked on the difficult process of filing the paperwork to found a nonprofit organization. At the time, she had no idea that bus tokens were just the tip of the iceberg! Through her nonprofit organization—A New Way of Life Re-entry Project—Susan now operates four homes for women returning home from prison and their children, offering an array of services and support. Since 1998, the lives of over 200 women and children have been transformed through the programs and services of A New Way of Life Re-entry Project.

But Susan did not stop there. She began to make connections between the neighborhood conditions of south Los Angeles, the circumstances of the men and women she knew who were being locked up, the treatment they faced inside prison, and the lack of support services and barriers they faced upon release from prison. Susan began to organize. She got together with a group of other former prisoners to help found All of Us or None—now a national network of formerly incarcerated people and their allies who work to combat the many forms of discrimination that people face as the result of felony convictions. Susan is the lead organizer of the southern California chapter, which is currently working to pressure the city and county of Los Angeles to "Ban the Box" and to remove the question about prior convictions from applications for employment (see Policy Advocacy Challenge 9.5 for more information).

Susan also acknowledged the complete lack of housing options for people returning home from prison, and began to network with other sober living home operators in impoverished south Los Angeles, knowing that sober living was often the choice of last resort for people being released from prison who had nowhere else to go. She is now the coordinator of the south Los Angeles chapter of the Sober Living Coalition, which advocates for the needs of sober living consumers and works to improve the public image of sober living as a safe and viable housing option for those in need. The coalition is currently working to change the structure of resource allocation in the county of Los Angeles such that its most vulnerable citizens—the homeless, formerly incarcerated, drug-addicted, and mentally ill—are provided the housing and other support services they need to recover and rebuild their lives.

In the 13 years since being released from prison, Susan has worked tirelessly to become a voice for poor women of color and formerly incarcerated people. In 2004, she provided testimony to the California Little Hoover Commission on the mistreatment of women in prison and the lack of reentry services, which resulted in the report "Breaking Barriers for Women on Parole." The next year, she was invited by California's governor to serve on the Gender Responsive Strategies Committee of the Little Hoover Commission, a group that advises prison authorities on best practices for women in the criminal justice system. In 2004, Susan became a fellow of the California Women's Policy Institute, and in 2006, she received a very prestigious Justice Advocacy Fellowship from the Soros Foundation. She has served as a member of the Prison Advisory Committee of the Fund for Nonviolence, as well as a board member for the Los Angeles Coalition to End Hunger and Homelessness and Stop Prisoner Rape. She has received numerous awards and recognition for her service.

Susan Burton is a leader, a voice for the voiceless, and a source of hope for women and formerly incarcerated people who have nowhere else to turn. She has devoted her life to the cause of helping others and creating a better world. Discuss the following questions:

- What strategies did Susan use to build power resources?
- How does her example dispute the assertion that marginalized persons cannot develop power resources?

Becoming Appropriately Assertive in the Policy Enacting Task

Policy advocates sometimes fail to seize strategic opportunities to shape policies because they assume they cannot win. In some cases, as our discussion of power differentials suggests, the deck is stacked against them. In many other cases, however, individuals undermine their own effectiveness by becoming fatalistic.

To use power effectively, people must first decide that they possess power resources, that they can use them successfully, and that they want to use them. The word *assertiveness* describes this proclivity to test the waters, rather than to be excessively fatalistic.

Assertiveness is undermined, however, by two dispositions. The first is a victim mentality that disposes people to believe that others will conspire to defeat their preferences.[78] A director of a hospital's social work department might believe, for example, that the nurses and physicians will systematically oppose any proposals by social workers. The second is fatalism about using power in a more general sense; some people believe that only high-level persons or powerful interests can wield power successfully and that people outside these exalted categories cannot effectively participate in policy deliberations.

Both the victim mentality and fatalism create self-fulfilling prophecies. People who believe that others will conspire against them and that only a restricted group can use power effectively will fail to use their personal power resources; those who see them as disinclined to participate in policy deliberations are likely to ignore their occasional suggestions and to exclude them from policy deliberations, further reinforcing the victim mentality and fatalism.[79] Fatalistic practitioners ignore the diversity of potential power resources and assume that they cannot increase theirs even by enhancing their credibility, finding allies, establishing networks, developing expertise, and obtaining information.

To understand this problem, recall our discussion of the sender of power (X) and the receiver of power (Y), as illustrated in Figure 10.1. Assume that you are Y, that you work in an agency, and that your program director intimidates you. Through his demeanor toward you, his intimidating remarks, and even his veiled threats, your director seeks to dissuade you from trying to make changes in the program.

What can you do? You can realistically assess both the risks and the benefits of trying to change defective policies. Those who intimidate others derive power from convincing them that they have no recourse but to follow the intimidator's suggestions that he or she has won. Ask yourself, "Is my program director's power as extensive as he suggests, or can I use my own power resources without incurring unacceptable penalties, such as losing my job?" Ask other people how they perceive a specific policy to see if your perceptions have merit, and find out whether they also feel intimidated or whether your director is singling you out. You can try direct communication with your program director, focusing on substantive issues and the specific issues on which you differ with him to see if he is more bark than bite. Accusing someone of seeking to intimidate you usually makes the situation even worse.[80]

If you are truly subject to intimidation, you should not expect easy answers. An assertive person does not passively accept a situation but tries to diagnose it, identifying possible strategies and then trying several options in search of one that works.

Here is an example of assertiveness. The director of a hospital's social work department requested a budgetary increase for her department but was denied. She noticed, however, that even unsuccessful entreaties served to educate top officials about social work programs and that some officials actually felt guilty about denying well-presented and justified requests. She decided not to be intimidated and to make further requests for funds for her department. She discovered that skillfully and frequently requesting funds brought increases in her unit's budget. Unlike departments with more timid executives, her department gained size and stature as she assertively sought resources, even after a number of unsuccessful requests.[81]

Illustration from Policy Advocacy Challenge 10.7 Policy advocates with minimal resources must combat burnout and fatalism. Despite the overwhelming advantage of the lobbyists with munificent resources, these two low-budget lobbyists in our examples have asserted themselves, persevered, and obtained notable successes.

Can Direct-Service Staff Use Power Resources in the Policy-Enacting Task?

EPA 2.1.8b

Our discussion of vulnerable population members' special problems and of assertiveness leads naturally to the question: Can people at the bottom of the heap, like direct-service staff members, use power resources, or does their subordinate position in the organizational hierarchy make them powerless? Organizations vary considerably; some executives elicit and even expect input from direct-service staff, and other executives are authoritarian.[82]

Direct-service staff members already have considerable power stemming from their personal knowledge of an agency's problems. Many supervisors and executives value suggestions from direct-service staff about a range of agency matters and respond readily to well-conceived suggestions for changing existing services. Executives depend on direct-service staff for the agency's reputation, efficiency, revenues (when the agency charges for services), and public relations with clients and other agencies. Most agencies would cease to exist if they lacked competent frontline staff.

Direct-service staff members who belong to unions can imply or state that their work will be disrupted if certain demands are not met; such demands usually involve salary and workload, but unions sometimes also seek changes in policy. Even without union backing, direct-service staff can vigorously protest some policies by taking their case directly to high-level staff.

Direct-service staff often have access to at least some agency decision-making processes, such as staff meetings, retreats, unit meetings, and meetings with supervisors. Developing their power through the strategies we discussed earlier in this chapter (such as enhancing personal credibility and visibility, networking, and developing relationships with external groups) is likely to increase their power in these agency deliberations. Moreover, they can seek membership on specific agency committees or even suggest that a committee be formed to examine a specific issue.

Direct-service staff can also wield power indirectly as in Policy Advocacy Challenge 10.2 by influencing a supervisor to initiate a suggestion. They can also form coalitions within the agency to pressure administrators to modify specific policies. However, staff members should be realistic about the limits of such power.

Direct-service staff members often derive power from their autonomy.[83] Although regulations may govern the length and intensity of services, recommend procedures, and establish priorities, they are difficult to enforce because the details of direct-service work are hard to supervise. Moreover, it is possible to bend some rules without technically violating them. Carried to an extreme, autonomy brings anarchy but, in moderation, represents an important kind of power.

In addition to their participation in decision making, direct-service staff members can shape outcomes by helping to build agendas, define problems, and construct proposals, as discussed in Chapters Six through Nine.

Direct-service staff do not, of course, have the power resources of executives, funders, or legislators, so they must enhance their power resources imaginatively and select the issues on which they will use their influence.

What You Can Now Do

Chapter Summary

You are now equipped to engage in Task 6 of the policy practice and policy advocacy framework in Figure 3.1, including the following:

- Define power and politics.
- Engage in power relationships.
- Use an array of power resources, including direct and indirect ones.
- Use power in organizational settings through normal channels and, rarely, through whistleblowing.
- Surmount power differentials in certain circumstances.
- Grapple with ethical issues when using power resources, understanding that power can be used both ethically and unethically.
- Develop power resources.
- Network.
- Develop skills in assertiveness.

In Chapter Eleven, we discuss how we use our power resources to develop political strategy, in legislative, agency, or community settings.

Competency Notes

EPA 2.1.2a   Recognize and manage personal values in a way that allows professional values to guide practice (p. 339): Social workers should learn when to challenge policies or practices they believe to be unethical even though they are supported by higher level staff.

EPA 2.1.3a   Distinguish, appraise, and integrate multiple sources of knowledge, including research-based knowledge and practice wisdom (p. 352): Social workers with broad networks develop early-information systems through which they learn about issues relevant to their work.

EPA 2.1.3c   Demonstrate effective oral and written communication in working with individuals, families, groups, organizations, communities, and colleagues (p. 329): Policy advocates sometimes exert power in personal discussions with others.

EPA 2.1.5a   Understand forms and mechanisms of oppression and discrimination (p. 343): Advocates understand that discrimination patterns in the broader society influence power transactions.

EPA 2.1.7a   Utilize conceptual frameworks to guide the process of assessment, intervention, and evaluation (p. 334): Social workers consider procedural options as they develop strategies for policy proposals.

EPA 2.1.8a   Analyze, formulate, and advocate for policies that advance social well-being (p. 353): Social workers develop links with groups that take interests in social movements.

EPA 2.1.8b   Collaborate with colleagues and clients for effective policy action (pp. 338, 349, 357): Advocates should collaborate with groups or coalitions to gain support from politicians.

EPA 2.1.9b   Provide leadership in promoting sustainable changes in service delivery and practice to improve the quality of social services (p. 350): Social workers can demonstrate authoritativeness on subjects and offer evidence to support policy changes.

EPA 2.1.10a **Substantively and affectively prepare for action with individuals, families, groups, organizations, and communities** (p. 336): Advocates can increase their odds of success if they place pressure on decision makers from external sources.

EPA 2.1.10b **Use empathy and other interpersonal skills** (p. 335): Advocates use process power to get a specific proposal passed.

EPA 2.1.10k **Negotiate, mediate, and advocate for clients** (p. 332): Social workers use substantive power when compromising a policy's content.

Endnotes

1. Victoria Neufeldt, ed., *Webster's New World College Dictionary,* 3rd ed. (New York: Macmillan, 1996), p. 1045.
2. Ibid.
3. Martin Rein, "Value-Critical Policy Analysis," in Daniel Callahan and Bruce Jennings, eds., *Ethics, the Social Sciences, and Policy Analysis* (New York: Plenum Press, 1983), pp. 96–100.
4. William Coplin and Michael O'Leary, *Everyman's Prince* (North Scituate, MA: Duxbury, 1976).
5. Peter Bachrach and Morton Baratz, *Power and Poverty* (New York: Oxford University Press, 1970), pp. 17–38.
6. For a discussion of the dilemmas of those who receive power resources, see Stanley Milgram, *Obedience to Authority* (New York: Harper & Row, 1975).
7. Bachrach and Baratz, *Power and Poverty,* pp. 17–38.
8. Ibid.
9. Edward Banfield, *Political Influence* (New York: Free Press, 1961), pp. 307–314.
10. John French and Bertram Raven, "The Bases of Social Power," in Dorwin Cartwright and Alvin Zander, eds., *Group Dynamics: Research and Theory* (New York: Harper & Row, 1968), pp. 259–269.
11. Doris Kearns, *Lyndon Johnson and the American Dream* (New York: Harper & Row, 1976), pp. 190, 224–227.
12. Jon Sager, "Sources of Power," in Jack Rothman, John Erlich, and John Tropman, eds., forthcoming 7th edition of *Strategies of Community Intervention,* Wadsworth, 2007.
13. Sager, "Sources of Power," p. 24.
14. Sager, "Sources of Power," p. 7.
15. Sager, "Sources of Power," p. 16.
16. Sager, "Sources of Power," p. 21.
17. Sager, "Sources of Power," p. 24.
18. See Christopher Matthews, *Hardball: How Politics Is Played* (New York: Summit Books, 1988), pp. 21–43.
19. Bruce Jansson, *Theory and Practice of Social Welfare Policy: Analysis, Processes, and Current Issues* (Belmont, CA: Wadsworth, 1984), p. 184.
20. Julie Rovner, "Daycare Package Clears First Hurdle in House," *Congressional Quarterly Weekly Report* 46 (July 2, 1988): 1833–1836.
21. See Bachrach and Baratz, *Power and Poverty,* pp. 17–38.
22. *Congressional Quarterly Almanac,* vol. 34 (Washington, DC: Congressional Quarterly Service, 1978), pp. 272–279.
23. Jansson, *Theory and Practice,* p. 184.
24. Joseph Califano, *Governing America* (New York: Simon & Schuster, 1971), p. 67.
25. Gerald Zaltman and Robert Duncan, *Strategies for Planned Change* (New York: Wiley Interscience, 1977), p. 100.
26. Vincent Burke and Vee Burke, *Nixon's Good Deed: Welfare Reform* (New York: Columbia University Press, 1974), pp. 195–204.
27. Congress, Senate, Committee on Finance, *Hearings before the Subcommittee on Social Security and Family Policy* (January 23, 1987), pp. 2–14.
28. Matthews, *Hardball,* pp. 144–154.
29. Lewis Froman, *The Congressional Process: Strategies, Rules, and Procedures* (Boston: Little, Brown, 1967).
30. Eugene Bardach, *The Skill Factor in Politics* (Berkeley and Los Angeles: University of California Press, 1972), pp. 234–240.

31. Eric Schattschneider, *The Semisovereign People* (New York: Holt, Rinehart & Winston, 1980), pp. 20–46.

32. Morton Deutsch, *The Resolution of Conflict: Constructive and Destructive Processes* (New Haven, CT: Yale University Press, 1973), pp. 124–152.

33. John Kingdon, *Agendas, Alternatives, and Public Policies* (Boston: Little, Brown, 1984), pp. 1–22.

34. Deutsch, *The Resolution of Conflict,* pp. 124–152.

35. Ibid., p. 368.

36. See Theodore Lowi's discussion of the politics of redistributive measures in "American Business, Public Policy, Case Studies, and Political Theory," *World Politics* 16 (July 1964): 677–715.

37. Yeheskel Hasenfeld, *Human Service Organizations* (Englewood Cliffs, NJ: Prentice Hall, 1983).

38. Hedrick Smith, *The Power Game: How Washington Works* (New York: Ballantine Books, 1988), pp. 388–444.

39. Matthews, *Hardball,* pp. 144–154.

40. Ron Dear and Rino Patti, "Legislative Advocacy," in *Encyclopedia of Social Workers,* vol. 2 (Silver Spring, MD: National Association of Social Workers, 1987), p. 37.

41. Michael Lipsky, *Street-Level Bureaucrats: Dilemmas of the Individual and Public Service* (New York: Russell Sage Foundation, 1980), pp. 16–18.

42. Kenneth Weick, "Educational Organizations as Loosely Coupled Systems," *Administrative Science Quarterly* 21 (March 1976): 1–9.

43. Robert Goodin, *Reasons for Welfare* (Princeton, NJ: Princeton University Press, 1988), pp. 184–228.

44. Franklin Chu and Sharland Trotter, *The Madness Establishment* (New York: Grossman, 1974).

45. Sissela Bok, "Blowing the Whistle," in Joel Fleishman, Lance Liebman, and Mark Moore, eds., *Public Duties: The Moral Obligations of Government Officials* (Cambridge: Harvard University Press, 1981), pp. 200–215.

46. Ibid.

47. Smith, *The Power Game.*

48. Milgram, *Obedience to Authority.*

49. Richard Fenno, *The Power of the Purse* (Boston: Little, Brown, 1966), pp. 366–390.

50. Rosabeth Kanter, *Men and Women of the Corporation* (New York: Basic Books, 1977), pp. 129–163.

51. C. Wright Mills, *The Power Elite* (New York: Oxford University Press, 1956).

52. Robert Dahl, *Pluralist Democracy in the United States* (Chicago: Rand McNally, 1967).

53. See Herbert Simons, *Persuasion,* 2nd ed. (New York: Random House, 1986), p. 130. Also see discussion of credibility by George Brager, Harry Specht, and James Torczyner, *Community Organizing,* 2nd ed. (New York: Columbia University Press, 1987), pp. 342–347.

54. Matthews, *Hardball,* pp. 144–352.

55. Rochelle Stanford, "Beleaguered Lobbyists for the Poor—Taking Allies Where They Can Find Them," *National Journal* 12 (September 20, 1980): 1556–1560.

56. Richard Emerson, "Power-Dependence Relations," *American Sociological Review* 27 (February 1962); 31–40; and D. J. Hickson et al., "A Strategic Contingencies Theory of Organizational Power," *Administrative Science Quarterly* 16 (June 1971): 216–229.

57. For research findings on power-dependence theory in hospital settings with social work departments, see Bruce Jansson and June Simmons, "Building Department or Unit Power within Human Service Organizations: Empirical Findings and Theory Building," *Administration in Social Work* 8 (Fall 1984): 41–44, 49–50.

58. See Bruce Jansson and June Simmons, "The Ecology of Social Work Departments: Empirical Findings and Strategy Implications," *Social Work in Health Care* 11 (Winter 1985): 1–16.

59. Bruce Jansson and June Simmons, "The Survival of Social Work Units in Host Organizations," *Social Work* 31 (September 1986): 342.

60. Joel Fleishman, "Self-Interest and Political Integrity," in Joel Fleishman, Lance Liebman, and Mark Moore, eds., *Public Duties: The Moral Obligations of Government Officials* (Cambridge: Harvard University Press, 1981), pp. 67–77.

61. Eugene Bardach, *The Skill Factor in Politics,* pp. 204–206, 216–220.

62. Jansson and Simmons, "Survival of Social Work Units," p. 341.

63. Matthews, *Hardball,* pp. 207–209.

64. Ibid., pp. 203–204.

65. J. McIver Weatherford, *Tribes on the Hill* (New York: Rawson, Wade, 1981), pp. 87–111.

66. Matthews, *Hardball,* pp. 194–211.

67. Noel Tichy, *Strategic Change: Technology, Politics, and Culture* (New York: Wiley, 1983), pp. 69–94.

68. Weatherford, *Tribes on the Hill,* pp. 20–24. Also see Tom Peters and Nancy Austin, "MBWA

(Managing by Walking Around)," *California Management Review* 28 (Fall 1985): 9–34.

69. Matthews, *Hardball,* pp. 21–33.

70. Ibid., pp. 59–73.

71. Kanter, *Men and Women of the Corporation,* pp. 181–184.

72. Weatherford, *Tribes on the Hill,* pp. 87–111.

73. Ibid.

74. Ibid., pp. 250–253.

75. See how a social movement led to legislative reform in Wyoming in William Whitaker, "Organizing Social Action Coalitions: WIC Comes to Wyoming," in Maryann Mahaffey and John Hanks, eds., *Practical Politics: Social Work and Political Response* (Silver Spring, MD: National Association of Social Workers, 1982), pp. 136–158.

76. See Frances Piven and Richard Cloward, "New Prospects for Voter Registration Reform," *Social Policy* 18 (Winter 1988): 2–15.

77. Kanter, *Men and Women of the Corporation.*

78. Ibid., pp. 158–160, 196–197.

79. Ibid., pp. 196–197.

80. Linda MacNeilage and Kathleen Adams discuss various strategies in *Assertiveness at Work* (Englewood Cliffs, NJ: Prentice Hall, 1982).

81. Jansson and Simmons, "Survival of Social Work Units," pp. 339–340.

82. David Mechanic, "Sources of Power of Lower Participants in Complex Organizations," *Administrative Science Quarterly* 7 (December 1962): 349–364.

83. Michael Lipsky, *Street-Level Bureaucrats: Dilemmas of the Individual and Public Service* (New York: Russell Sage Foundation, 1980), pp. 13–18.

Suggested Readings

Building Personal Credibility

Richard Emerson, "Power-Dependence Relations," *American Sociological Review* 27 (February 1962): 31–40.

Bruce Jansson and June Simmons, "Building Department or Unit Power within Human Service Organizations: Empirical Findings and Theory Building," *Administration in Social Work* 8 (Fall 1984): 41–50.

Bruce Jansson and June Simmons, "The Ecology of Social Work Departments: Empirical Findings and Strategy Implications," *Social Work in Health Care* 11 (Winter 1985): 1–16.

Christopher Matthews, *Hardball: How Politics Is Played* (New York: Summit Books, 1988).

Networking

Rosabeth Kanter, *Men and Women of the Corporation* (New York: Basic Books, 1977), pp. 129–163, 181–197.

Noel Tichy, *Strategic Change: Technology, Politics, and Culture* (New York: Wiley, 1983), pp. 69–94.

J. McIver Weatherford, *Tribes on the Hill* (New York: Rawson, Wade, 1981), pp. 87–111, 250–253.

Working with Task Groups

Milan Dluhy, *Building Coalitions in the Human Services* (Newbury Park, CA: Sage, 1990).

Paul Ephross and Thomas Vassil, *Groups That Work* (New York: Columbia University Press, 1988).

Irving Janis, *Victims of Groupthink* (Boston: Houghton Mifflin, 1972).

John Tropman, Harold Johnson, and Elmer Tropman, *The Essentials of Committee Management* (Chicago: Nelson-Hall, 1979).

The Nature of Power

Peter Bachrach and Morton Baratz, *Power and Poverty* (New York: Oxford University Press, 1970).

Varieties of Power

John French and Bertram Craven, "The Bases of Social Power," in Dorwin Cartwright and Alvin Zander, eds., *Group Dynamics: Research and Theory* (New York: Harper & Row, 1968), pp. 259–269.

Lewis Froman, *The Congressional Process: Strategies, Rules, and Procedures* (Boston: Little, Brown, 1967).

Christopher Matthews, *Hardball: How Politics Is Played* (New York: Summit Books, 1988).

Hedrick Smith, *The Power Game: How Washington Works* (New York: Ballantine Books, 1988).

A Defense of Politics

Eric Schattschneider, *The Semisovereign People* (New York: Holt, Rinehart & Winston, 1960).

Using Power from Internal Vantage Points

Burton Gummer, *The Politics of Social Administration: Managing Organizational Politics in Social Agencies* (Englewood Cliffs, NJ: Prentice Hall, 1990).

Bruce Jansson and June Simmons, "The Survival of Social Work Units in Host Organizations," *Social Work* 31 (September 1986): 339–344.

Using Power from External Vantage Points

Donald deKieffer, *The Citizen's Guide to Lobbying Congress* (Chicago: Chicago Review Press, 1997).

Power Resources of Direct-Service Staff

Michael Lipsky, *Street-Level Bureaucrats: Dilemmas of the Individual and Public Service* (New York: Russell Sage Foundation, 1980).

David Mechanic, "Sources of Power of Lower Participants in Complex Organizations," *Administrative Science Quarterly* 7 (December 1962): 349–364.

The Problem of Assertiveness

Rosabeth Kanter, *Men and Women of the Corporation* (New York: Basic Books, 1977), pp. 158–197.

Linda MacNeilage and Kathleen Adams, *Assertiveness at Work* (Englewood Cliffs, NJ: Prentice Hall, 1982).

Stanley Milgram, *Obedience to Authority* (New York: Harper & Row, 1975).

Ethical Issues in Politics

Chauncey Alexander, "Professional Social Workers and Political Responsibility," in Maryann Mahaffey and John Hanks, *Practical Politics: Social Work and Political Responsibility* (Silver Spring, MD: National Association of Social Workers, 1982), pp. 22–25.

George Brager, Harry Specht, and James Torczyner, *Community Organizing,* 2nd ed. (New York: Columbia University Press, 1987), pp. 316–339.

Joel Fleishman, "Self-Interest and Political Integrity," in Joel Fleishman, Lance Liebman, and Mark Moore, eds., *Public Duties: The Moral Obligations of Government Officials* (Cambridge: Harvard University Press, 1981), pp. 52–92.

Developing Political Strategy and Putting It into Action in the Policy-Enacting Task

Policy Predicament

The conservative governor of Virginia, George Allen, decided to transfer the Virginia Department of Aging—a freestanding agency—to another department of government. Policy advocates for older people quickly decided that this transfer would have grave implications for the department. What political tactics could policy advocates such as an Emeritus Professor of Social Work at the School of Social Work at Virginia Commonwealth University use to block the governor's strategy? We discuss these strategies in Policy Advocacy Challenge 11.5. Concerned about the failure of his city to pay a living wage to employees, Professor Manny Gale, Emeritus Professor of Social Work and Gerontology at California State University in Sacramento, developed a campaign to pressure public officials to require one, which we discuss in Policy Advocacy Challenge 11.13.

LEARNING OUTCOMES

This chapter continues discussion of the policy-enacting task (Task 6) of the policy practice and policy advocacy model in Figure 3.1. We discussed the nature and varieties of power in Chapter Ten. Now we turn to how policy advocates use their power resources to create political strategy in agency, community, and legislative settings. *Political strategy* is a sequence of actions and verbal exchanges that advocates believe will increase the likelihood that a proposal will be enacted. We discuss the following in this chapter:

1. How to establish objectives and positions
2. How to gauge who supports and who opposes specific policies
3. The importance of situational and contextual factors to policy strategy
4. How we build alternative scenarios to select and revise political strategy
5. Seven recurring steps in strategy building
6. How to organize a campaign to secure the enactment of a specific legislative proposal
7. How to use an array of interventions that puts pressure on legislators, including use of the Internet
8. How to organize or participate in an effort to change an agency policy
9. How to organize or participate in a community-based effort to change a community policy
10. Ways to work with task groups to seek policy changes in legislatures, agencies, or communities

Establishing Some Objectives in the Policy-Enacting Task

To develop intelligent strategy, policy advocates first have to answer this question: Why am I participating in the political process? Then they must decide which side they are taking and the degree and kind of policy changes they seek.

Determining a Position

Strategists must first decide whether to do the following:

1. Initiate their own proposal (an affirmative position)
2. Change others' proposals (an amending position)
3. Oppose others' initiatives (an opposing or blocking position)
4. Assume no role (a bystander position)

These choices are important because they commit the strategist to certain obligations and risks. People who *initiate* their own proposals have to invest considerable time in research, discussion, meetings, and negotiations. They have an advantage, however: Their ideas are likely to figure prominently in ensuing policy deliberations. By taking the initiative, they can shape discussion at the outset by giving prominence to their analysis of a specific problem and their policy proposals. Were they *not* to take the initiative, they realize that some important problems or proposals would never be addressed. By taking the initiative, policy practitioners exercise leadership in agency, community, and legislative settings.

Yet initiators expose themselves to criticism by placing their ideas in front of a larger audience. Opponents may question their motives, such as contending they seek to further their own interests. Or they may attack their analysis of a problem or their policy proposals. For many initiators, however, these perils pale beside the benefits of initiating proposals.

Unlike those who initiate proposals, policy advocates who agree generally with the initiators' position confine themselves to *amending* a proposal to advance their preferences for specific changes. Amenders often play a key role in policy deliberations. If they do not like a policy proposal, they can change its direction in fundamental ways by changing its details—even gutting it. If someone dislikes a policy, for example, he or she can try to get others to cut the amount of resources devoted to it. If amenders like a policy proposal but want to make it even better, they can change specific provisions to seek this result, such as increasing the amount of resources devoted to it.

It is easier in some respects to *block* proposals than to develop them, because opposers need only pinpoint their flaws or use procedural maneuvers to defeat them. Because of the sheer number of sequential points through which legislative proposals must pass, blockers need only defeat them at a single point to prevail. They can also block them by cutting off their funding, obtaining a legal injunction against them through litigation, or not renewing them in the case of policies that must be periodically reauthorized.

Yet blockers may be perceived merely as naysayers who lack constructive alternatives. They may be accused of inciting "gridlock" rather than being responsible contributors to policy deliberations. Congressional Republicans ran this danger during the first four years of Barack Obama's presidency because they opposed so many of his initiatives. To the extent they are perceived to have the power to block specific initiatives, factions that might block them often intimidate initiators who decide it is folly even to try to get a specific policy enacted.

Strategists may adopt a *bystander* role because they believe they lack the power to influence the outcome, want to save their political resources for a future issue, believe their involvement in deliberations will antagonize one or both sides in the controversy, or expect to assume a mediating role later. Bystanders are not truly neutral in many situations, however, because their nonparticipation often tilts power toward one or another faction in policy deliberations. Those legislators who absent themselves from key votes often shape outcomes as much as those legislators who *do* vote, particularly when votes are closely divided. Bystanders also can be accused of lacking courage of their convictions.

Strategists' roles often depend on their analysis of a proposal's prospects. If they believe the prospects to be extremely bleak, for example, advocates may be reluctant to initiate a proposal. If they believe a policy will be enacted, they may be reluctant to try to block it. However, policy advocates sometimes oppose objectionable policies or initiate proposals in the face of overwhelming odds, because they believe fundamental principles are at stake, want to educate voters about the issue, or want to please some segment of their supporters who are deeply committed to a specific proposal. Over the objections of many members of his administration, for example, President Barack Obama chose to support health reform in 2009 and 2010—and prevailed with enactment of the Affordable Care Act (ACA) in 2010.

At national and state levels of government, the leaders of the two major parties must frequently decide which issues to champion, which ones to oppose, and which ones to leave alone. They realize, of course, that the leaders of the opposing party must make the same kinds of choices, because both parties want a competitive advantage in forthcoming elections (see Policy Advocacy Challenge 11.1).

Policy Advocacy Challenge 11.1

Finding Information about National Political Strategy

Stephanie Davis, Research Librarian, University of California, Irvine

Political parties must strategize constantly to make their stance on issues known to the population in order to gain votes and win elections. One strategy is to gain endorsements from an organization, a specific political party, or other politicians in order to swing supporters' votes to a certain candidate. Take any important political race in congressional or presidential elections. Find out from opposing candidates' websites which community organizations, state officials, trade unions, public officials, and professional organizations endorsed which candidates—and then speculate why they made these endorsements. Which policies did the candidate support that contributed to support for his or her candidacy from specific groups or persons? Candidates use websites, political advertisements, and speeches to gain votes. Candidates also often publicize how they tried to *block* certain proposals, such as when a candidate brags that she opposed "big oil interests" when she seeks the votes of environmentalists or persons troubled by the high cost of gasoline.

More can be learned about political strategy in the form of party platforms, agendas, policy issues, and educational information on the following websites of political parties in the United States. While there traditionally have been two major parties in the United States, others are gaining ground.

1. Democratic Party **www.democrats.org**
2. Republican Party **www.gop.com**
3. Green Party **www.gp.org**
4. Libertarian Party **www.lp.org**
5. Constitution Party **www.constitutionparty.com/**
6. Reform Party **www.reformparty.org**

EXERCISE

Visit the websites above and compare each party's stance on a topic of interest to you.

Selecting the Extent of Policy Changes

Policy advocates must decide whether to seek major or incremental changes, a choice that is often difficult. Policy advocates sometimes want major changes in those policies that they believe are fundamentally flawed, or when they want to appeal to a segment of the population or key interest groups that dislike it. They may seek only incremental changes when they believe that major changes are not politically feasible, require large investments of time and energy, or will antagonize key supporters.[1]

Selecting a Time Frame

Policy advocates often ask the following: Do we want specific changes to be enacted in the short term (during an upcoming meeting, the present year, or the present session of a legislature), or will we accept an extended time frame?[2] They sometimes want immediate results because they believe urgent action is needed, want to be able to claim a specific policy victory in an upcoming election, or believe it will be more difficult to get them enacted at a later point in time, such as after a specific election. President Barack Obama wanted his stimulus package enacted early during the first year of his presidency, for example, because he believed its passage was urgently needed to counter the deep recession that he had inherited—just as he hoped his health reforms would be enacted in the first year of his presidency. He was not able to meet this goal but sought passage in early 2010. Policy advocates realize that it is more difficult to get a policy enacted when they lose momentum, because other issues may intrude. In other cases, however, policy advocates select a longer time frame, deferring action on a policy proposal until times are more propitious. They may believe they will have greater support for a policy after a specific election. They may not want to defer action on a proposal until other issues are resolved. It is often difficult to maintain interest in a specific issue over a long period of time, however.

Grounding Strategy in Current Realities in the Policy-Enacting Task

Political strategy must be firmly linked to existing realities, including power distribution, contextual factors, past stances, vested interests, cohesion of likely opponents and proponents, situational realities, and the setting.

The Power Distribution

Kurt Lewin, the noted social psychologist, pioneered the concept of force field analysis to assess the distribution of power in specific situations.[3] To obtain a rough estimate of the support for a proposal, Lewin suggests enumerating persons by name and indicating the strength of their support or opposition in a diagram in which the line lengths correspond to the level of their opposition or support. Figure 11.1 depicts a power distribution that is relatively evenly balanced between supporters and opposers.

Useful as a force field diagram is, it lacks key information. It does not tell us the relative power of a person to shape policy on a specific issue. The chair of a committee that is considering a proposal, for example, often has more power than any other member of the committee. It does not tell us the salience (or importance) that specific individuals attach to an issue. Someone who has strong convictions about an issue and is well positioned to affect policy, for example, may not see it as very important. Perhaps he or she is more interested in other issues, does not think it can be enacted, or lacks the time to invest in it.

Nor does force field analysis tell us to what extent advocates can mobilize persons who will support a policy initiative—not just persons who are decision makers but

FIGURE 11.1 Support of and Opposition to a Measure

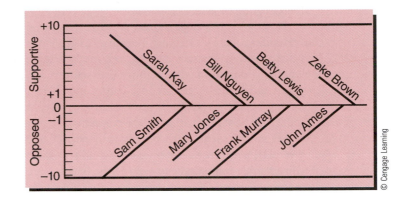

persons external to them. As we discuss in many chapters, for example, the Internet is an important tool in mobilizing persons to participate in advocacy coalitions around key issues. So we could add to Figure 11.1 another line not with the name of a specific person, but a category called "potential supporters" of a measure, for example, persons and advocacy groups who might be enlisted in a particular advocacy project through the Internet or by other means.

William Coplin and Michael O'Leary have developed a simple system for scoring the distribution of sentiment, salience, and power on specific issues.[4] To illustrate their approach, let us take a simple situation—a family of four that must consider two issues: whether to ask the grandmother to move into the house after a recent illness and whether to allow the 18-year-old son, Sam, to own his own car. The parents (Mary and Frank) and the two children (Sam and Diane) have decided to reach these decisions democratically, but as we know, policy making does not usually occur on a level playing field. Assume that we know the family well enough to construct Table 11.1, which

TABLE 11.1 Estimating the Distribution of Sentiments, Salience, and Power

	ISSUE 1: GRANDMOTHER				ISSUE 2: CAR			
	M	F	S	D	M	F	S	D
Positions on the issues (−10 to +10)	10	−5	2	4	4	2	10	8
Salience (1 to 10)	8	8	3	4	7	7	7	7
Power to influence the outcome of this issue (1 to 4)	3	3	1	1	3	3	2	1
Totals for each participant (multiply the numbers down each column)	240	−120	6	16	84	42	140	56
Grand total for each issue (add the totals for each person)	142				322			

© Cengage Learning

represents the sentiment, salience, and power of each of the family members. (The initials *M, F, S,* and *D* stand for the mother, Mary; the father, Frank; the son, Sam; and the daughter, Diane, respectively.)

First, we give each person a score for his or her sentiment on the two issues (extending from −10, very negative, to +10, very favorable). Table 11.1 shows that Mary strongly favors allowing her mother to live in their home (her score is 10), whereas Frank opposes the move (his score is −5). The children are mildly supportive (their scores are 2 and 4). All family members support allowing Sam to have a car, having scores of 4, 2, 10, and 8; predictably, the two children support this policy more strongly than either of their parents.

Second, we score each person with respect to the salience, or importance, that they give each issue on a scale from 1 (low salience) to 10 (high salience). Both parents attach considerable importance to each of the issues; hence, their scores of 8 on the issue of the grandmother and 7 on the issue of Sam's car. The children attach much more importance to the issue of the car (they both score a 7), while attaching less importance to the grandmother's residence in their home (their scores are 3 and 4).

Third, we estimate the family members' relative power to influence choices on a scale from 1 (low power) to 4 (high power). The parents have far more power than the children; thus, they score a 3 on each issue, while the children score a 1 or 2 on each issue.

To obtain an overall reading of the distribution of sentiment, salience, and power, we multiply each person's scores on each issue. Mary's score is 240 ($10 \times 8 \times 3$) on Issue 1 and 84 ($4 \times 7 \times 3$) on Issue 2; Frank's scores are –120 ($-5 \times 8 \times 3$) on Issue 1 and 42 ($2 \times 7 \times 3$) on Issue 2. The two children have considerably higher (more favorable) scores of 140 and 56 on Issue 2 than on Issue 1, where their scores are 6 and 16.

Now, we total the participants' scores on each issue. Because a higher score indicates a more favorable prognosis for a proposal, it appears that Sam is more likely to have a car ($84 + 42 + 140 + 56 = 322$) than is grandmother to be asked to move into the family home ($240 + −120 + 6 + 16 = 142$). Table 11.1 shows that a single negative score for a powerful participant (father or mother) markedly decreases the likelihood that a specific proposal will be approved. A numbers approach to force field analysis may seem farfetched, but politicians in legislative bodies sometimes use this kind of numeric analysis, crude and imperfect as it may be, to determine the prognosis for pieces of legislation.[5] If a proposal has an extremely low or unfavorable score, policy practitioners may decide the situation is hopeless, unless they can develop strategy that will enable them to change the sentiment, alter the salience, or modify the power of those who oppose their proposal.

Moreover, identifying the important participants, as well as their sentiment, salience, and power, helps policy practitioners develop strategy.[6] The data in Table 11.1 suggest several strategy options. Assume that Mary wants the grandmother to move into her home. She may try to bring Frank to at least a neutral sentiment, she may hope to reduce the salience he attaches to the issue, or she may try to isolate him from the decision-making process, thus reducing his power to influence the outcome. She may also seek to alter the children's sentiment, salience, and power, perhaps by promising them support for the car in return for their support on the grandmother issue.

Table 11.1 does not include coalitional power in which advocates augment their power by teaming with others. Mary may increase her power by forming a coalition with her children. She may also try to add new participants to the struggle such as by getting other relatives to become participants or by securing the family physician's support.[7]

We have already mentioned, moreover, that force field analysis must include a category of persons and groups called "potential supporters" of a specific measure—persons and groups that might be enlisted to a cause through the Internet using techniques that we discussed in Policy Advocacy Challenge 10.5.[8] We should realize that policy advocates rarely achieve policy victories acting by themselves. They must usually work with others to get progressive changes because individuals usually lack sufficient power to obtain them.

Force field analysis is not a panacea, even though it is often highly useful to policy advocates. Others' positions might be falsely judged. Persons may change their positions abruptly. Some persons may become bystanders when an advocate thought they scored high on salience. Someone who the advocate thought was well positioned to shape outcomes with respect to an issue might be unable to influence the course of policy deliberations.

Force field analysis can, then, lead advocates to commit two kinds of errors: refraining from pursuing a proposal that could be enacted when they predicted it could not and supporting a policy only to find that it cannot be enacted. Had President Barack Obama refrained from seeking health reform in 2009 and 2010 on the erroneous predictions of many of his staff that he would be unsuccessful, he would later have regretted his inaction. Predicting policy outcomes is often frustrated by the fluid nature of many policy deliberations as persons change their positions or take actions that were not predicted by the policy advocate in advance.

Despite these cautionary notes, force field analysis is often very helpful. Without efforts to gauge our support and opposition, we may blindly commit ourselves to proposals that are not politically feasible. Or we may fail to take actions that can change the positions of participants in policy deliberations. Force field analysis also helps us to estimate the time and political resources required to get a specific policy enacted. If we face a difficult battle, better to know that up front so that we can be prepared for likely realities that we will confront. (See Policy Advocacy Challenge 11.2 in which Bob Erlenbusch discusses how he used force field analysis on many occasions.)

Policy Advocacy Challenge 11.2

How I Used Force Field Analysis in Helping Develop a Plan to End Homelessness

Bob Erlenbusch, Ph.D.
Go to
www.cengage.com
to watch this video clip.

In the real world, policy advocates must frequently determine what positions persons hold prior to key meetings. They need to know, for example, if a large number of attendees will agree or disagree with specific proposals that will be discussed in the meeting. In some cases, they may try to change their views prior to the meeting. See Policy Advocacy Challenge 11.2 video in which Bob Erlenbusch, member of the board of the National Coalition on Homelessness, discusses his use of force field analysis before key meetings of a Blue Ribbon Commission on Ending Homelessness that developed a plan to end homelessness in Los Angeles County.

Some questions to ponder:

- Why did Bob Erlenbusch need to know the positions of persons prior to key planning meetings of the Blue Ribbon Commission?
- Did he try to change some persons' views prior to the meeting?
- Why are "one-on-one" meetings often critical when conducting force field analysis?

Identifying Contextual Factors

Although knowing a policy's relative support and opposition is useful, we need to know also why people take certain positions and how they are likely to act when an issue enters policy deliberations. Analyzing participants' past stances during deliberation, vested interests, and cohesion of likely opponents and proponents enables a more accurate prediction of people's likely actions than does merely estimating their current position.

Past Stances

Many issues may have been deliberated previously. The responses of decision makers, interest groups, and the general public to policies depend on their recollections or accounts of the prior deliberations.[9] Deliberations are more likely to be conflictual, for example, when an issue has previously been associated with ideological polarization, as illustrated by the controversy that arises whenever Congress considers national health insurance, gun control, or abortion. Indeed, many politicians avoid such issues because they do not want to become embroiled in controversies among their constituents or in an extended legislative battle with an uncertain outcome. In other organizations, too, participants may avoid reintroducing issues or policies that are associated with prior controversy.

Policy advocates sometimes erroneously conclude that the controversies associated with an issue will continue. After Congress defeated President Clinton's national health measure in 1994, many people thought major health reforms could not be enacted for years, but Clinton managed to get Congress to approve a measure to fund health coverage for more than 5 million uninsured children in 1997.—and President Barack Obama enacted the ACA in 2010. Indeed, skillful policy advocates try to offset the negative effects of past stances by emphasizing developments that now make a change more feasible. Clinton's proposal was strengthened, for example, by his argument that, with the exodus of hundreds of thousands of single-headed families from the welfare rolls after the welfare reforms of 1996, many children would need to be medically insured because many mothers would no longer be eligible for Medicaid once they had left welfare—and many of their employers would not offer health insurance to them. Obama's quest for national health reform was strengthened by the deep recession of 2008 into 2010, which left many persons without health insurance in the wake of losing jobs or finding that their employers had canceled their health insurance.

EPA 2.1.7a

Vested Interests

People often base their position on an issue on their own interests.[10] Politicians may worry, for example, that a certain policy will antagonize some of their constituents or enable the other party to expand its constituency or obtain an electoral advantage. An executive of a social agency or a government bureaucracy may fear that a proposal will shift resources or program responsibilities to rival agencies, impose controls or regulations on their activities, or diminish their revenues. Alternatively, people may support a policy because they believe it will enhance their power, prestige, or resources. It is no secret that many politicians support some policy proposals to obtain campaign contributions from special interests that will benefit from them. If Democrats are more likely to receive contributions from trade unions, Republicans are more likely to receive resources from corporations. If Democrats are more likely to seek votes from women and persons of color,[11] Republicans are more likely to seek them from relatively affluent persons. Both parties cater to independent voters and moderates because they realize they often are swing voters who can determine the outcome of pivotal elections.

Cohesion of Likely Opponents and Proponents

Although we can sometimes calculate with considerable precision specific individuals' positions on an issue or policy, our analysis is incomplete if we fail to examine their relationships. For example, evenly balanced support of and opposition to a proposed policy should end in a stalemate. The proponents may still win, however, if their close working relationship enables them to evolve a strategy and to work together to implement it, while their opponents remain splintered. Moreover, if leaders with knowledge, commitment, political expertise, and considerable power support a specific proposal, it is more likely to be successful because they are often adept at assembling and maintaining supportive coalitions.

Situational Realities

Situational realities often shape the course of policy deliberations. In legislative settings, for example, the success of proposals is often influenced by coming elections, the balance of power between the contending parties, rivalries among powerful legislators and among members of the two legislative chambers, the budget, changes in leadership, the other proposals vying for attention, and the time remaining in a legislative session.[12]

These kinds of situational factors influence decision makers' interest in a proposal and the extent of the conflict associated with it. When national elections are imminent, for example, politicians of both parties begin to jockey for position; they want to take conspicuous positions that will consolidate their existing support and also draw some of their opponents' constituents to their side. Liberal Democrats from northern cities may support social programs and publicly oppose conservative initiatives, such as efforts to privatize Social Security. Conservatives not only promote issues that will solidify their traditional support but also advance social measures that will attract some moderates to their cause. By the same token, impending elections may make all politicians avoid issues offering no advantage or that are fraught with significant political risks. For example, some liberal Democrats who normally support the federal financing of abortions may avoid this divisive issue in an election year.

Personal and institutional rivalries also influence efforts to initiate proposals. Legislative committees may jealously guard their jurisdiction over certain issues and, when they hear rumors that another committee is developing a proposal, may hurriedly frame their own proposal. This kind of rivalry may exist between committees within a legislative chamber or between rival committees in the two chambers. As one example, the House Committee on Economic and Educational Opportunities and the Senate Committee on Labor and Human Resources each developed rival versions of national health reform early in the Clinton administration, as well as during the Obama administration in 2009.

Situational factors also influence the political process in social agencies. Some policy proposals fare well when a new leader is selected who favors them.[13] Just as in legislatures, internal institutional and personal rivalries sometimes determine who will support or initiate a specific policy proposal. Budget realities and external funding can significantly influence the politics of specific proposals, such as favoring ones that enhance funding.[14]

Adapting Strategy to the Setting

Skillful policy advocates realize that they have to adapt their strategy to the setting. (We discuss later in this chapter how agency politics differ from legislative politics.) In legislative settings, two legislative committees may have entirely different norms and operating procedures. If the members of the House Committee on Economic and Educational Opportunities are accustomed to wide-open conflict between liberals and conservatives, for instance, the members of the House and Senate Appropriations Committees have traditionally prided themselves on quiet, private deliberations, in which they seek behind-the-scenes solutions to budgetary issues.[15] Policy practitioners must adapt their tactics to such idiosyncrasies.

Developing Alternative Scenarios

EPA 2.1.9a

We have discussed to this point a variety of considerations that policy advocates may consider as they move toward developing political strategies to secure the enactment of specific policy proposals. We have discussed not only force field analysis, but also other situational, institutional, and historical factors that can give us clues about how to proceed to get support for a specific policy.

Policy advocates sort through a series of political options much as a quarterback considers the possible plays to use in a tight situation. Indeed, creative strategists run through successive what-if scenarios in which they explore whether various actions or statements may help them obtain their policy preferences.[16] Imagine three what-if scenarios. In Scenario 1, the policy advocate asks, "What would happen if I made a *single* presentation to a decision maker, suggesting a course of action?" This presentation might involve a request that a problem be taken seriously enough to be placed on a committee agenda, or a suggestion that a policy option be seriously considered. In some cases, this single presentation (a modest strategy) will suffice, particularly if the practitioner correctly assesses the current environment as supportive.

Policy advocates often develop at least two additional scenarios. Scenario 2's strategy is somewhat more ambitious; perhaps the single presentation will be coupled with discussions with key decision makers to make them more sympathetic to a proposal. Scenario 3 is even more ambitious; it may involve creating a coalition, cultivating a constituency, coupling presentations with many personal discussions, allocating specific roles and tasks to a range of people, and mixing internal pressure with external pressure. An example of an ambitious strategy occurred in the early 1990s. A coalition of organizations, in which the National Organization for Women (NOW) was a central participant, developed a legislative proposal that would allow employees to obtain unpaid leave from work following the birth of a child, because of a parent's illness, or because of the death of a family member or close relative. NOW's members not only had personal liaisons with legislators and government officials but also exerted extensive external pressures on congressional members through letter writing and articles in the mass media.

We contrast the three preceding scenarios with an improvised one. In some cases, policy advocates decide not to formulate a strategy, but to seize opportunities as they arise.[17] At an opportune moment, they may inject an idea into committee discussions, a staff meeting, or a conversation with an official in their organization. Improvisational strategies are sometimes useful when policy advocates lack the time or knowledge of the situation to develop more refined strategies. However, unlike the three preceding strategy scenarios, improvisational strategies do not enable the policy advocate to mobilize and use power resources systematically.

Policy advocates need not invest major resources in this preliminary development of strategy scenarios because they need only the broad outlines of strategy at this point. In effect, they ask: Does this issue now require a major investment of resources and time, or should we address this issue with a modest or improvisational strategy?

Selecting a Strategy

Pragmatic considerations and stylistic preferences shape the selection of strategy. Policy advocates review strategy options in light of the realities we have discussed in this chapter. If their force field analysis suggests that there is extraordinary opposition to their proposal, for example, they may select an ambitious, complex strategy that requires a significant investment of time and energy. However, they must also consider the limits of their resources and time. If a proposal can be enacted with a relatively simple strategy that requires few resources and little time, most policy practitioners will select it.[18] Even when they fear a more ambitious one is needed, they may select a relatively modest strategy because they lack time or they place a higher priority on another issue.

Policy advocates' strategy choices are also influenced by their stylistic preferences. Some of us state our positions directly, whereas others discuss them in private deliberations. Some people like to precipitate conflict by advancing controversial positions, and others serve as mediators. Some initiate policies; others prefer to amend or oppose proposals.

Different styles have different advantages and disadvantages. Mediators facilitate compromises, but are sometimes accused of failing to take a solid position. Champions of ideological positions initiate proposals for bold changes but sometimes lack the compromise skills necessary for enactment. Persons who select only sure winners or who avoid controversial issues can be seen as lacking courage or leadership.

Revising the Strategy

Strategies often need to be revised. Perhaps a policy proposal attracts far greater support—or opposition—than advocates anticipated. Perhaps opponents developed an effective coalition to oppose a specific proposal—or supporters were far more cohesive than was anticipated. Perhaps new situational factors arise, such as an improvement in the finances of an agency or a state. Perhaps new leaders arise in the wake of elections, or there is a leadership succession in an agency, which either hinders or promotes the enactment of a specific policy proposal. After assuming a relatively passive role in emerging health insurance proposals in Congress, for example, President Barack Obama developing a stronger role in developing pressure on legislators to enact a proposal as he feared loss of momentum in summer and fall 2009 and in early 2010.

Seven Recurring Steps in Strategy in the Policy-Enacting Task

We have discussed various factors that policy advocates must consider when they develop strategy, such as the need to establish objectives, to select the extent of policy changes, to select a time frame, to examine the distribution of power, to identify contextual factors, to examine situational factors, to construct alternative scenarios, and to develop strategy. With this as a backdrop, we can now discuss seven recurring steps (see Box 11.1) that policy advocates take when they develop strategy, even if they do not take these steps in any particular order. These steps in legislative, organizational, and community settings are illustrated further in this chapter.

Specific policy advocates must also decide what role they wish to assume in a policy advocacy project. Do they wish to be part of the leadership team? Do they wish to be volunteers to the project, such as engaging in fundraising, hosting events, organizing email or letter-writing campaigns, or undertaking other activities? These decisions hinge on the time and resources of specific policy advocates.

| BOX **11.1** | Seven Steps in Formulating and Implementing Strategy |

Organizing a team or coalition

- How will proponents organize a leadership team that will develop and coordinate strategy?
- To the extent resources are needed, either money or supplies, how will they be obtained?
- To the extent a division of labor is required, such as committees or leaders focusing on specific tasks, how will it be worked out?

Establishing policy goals

- What do proponents wish to achieve?

Specifying a proposal's content and getting early sponsors

- What minimal features or content should the policy proposal contain?
- On what points can proponents negotiate or compromise?
- Can early sponsors be found, such as key legislators, who will support the proposal?

Establishing a style

- What level and scope of conflict will proponents seek?

Selecting power resources and framing strategy

- What kinds of person-to-person, substantive, decision-making process and context-shaping power resources will be used? To what extent can the Internet be used to mobilize support?
- Who will use these power resources and in what situations?

Implementing strategy

- How will the strategy be put into action?
- When might it be necessary to improvise?

Revising the strategy

- How should the game plan be revised in light of the opponents' strategies?
- What new events or background factors suggest a change in strategy?

Organizing a Team or Coalition

Particularly in an ambitious project, policy advocates need to organize themselves into a coherent unit. As events unfold and opposition emerges, it is important that a proposal's proponents develop a common strategy so they will not disintegrate in the face of conflict or give out contradictory messages, and will implement strategy effectively. They can either establish a new group or work with an existing advocacy group. Whatever approach they take, policy advocates have to devote time and skill to keeping their team or coalition functioning effectively (see Policy Advocacy Challenge 11.3).

Policy Advocacy Challenge 11.3

Keeping a Coalition Together in Guilford County, North Carolina

Gretchen Heidemann, MSW & Doctoral Candidate, University of Southern California, School of Social Work

It is often challenging to keep coalitions functioning once they have been established. Yet coalitions are often critical to the success of policy advocates, because they allow the policy advocates to pool power resources and financial resources in a common cause.

The Partners Ending Homelessness coalition in Guilford County, North Carolina, was created to develop and implement a 10-year plan to end homelessness. Numerous obstacles, such as intergovernmental conflict and territorialism, had to be surmounted in order to form a functioning coalition in Guilford County. What makes the coalition strong today, says K. Jehan Benton, the director, is the leadership of the United Way, the assistance of local volunteers, the commitment of their "community champion," and the relationships among the various individuals and institutions. Within the first two years of implementation, Guilford County saw a significant drop in the number of chronically homeless people, and the number far surpassed the coalition's annual goal of providing permanent, supportive housing for 20 homeless individuals or families.

Revisit Guilford County's Partners Ending Homelessness website at **www.partnersending homelessness.org/**, and discuss the following questions: In your opinion, what are the elements of a highly functioning coalition? What do you think makes the Partners Ending Homelessness coalition successful? If you were to form a coalition to end homelessness in your community, what steps would take to keep all parties engaged and working effectively?

Establishing Policy Goals

Early in the process, policy advocates have to establish policy goals within the context that they encounter. Do they want basic change or incremental change? Who are the likely proponents and opponents? Will the proposal meet major resistance or be widely accepted?

Policy advocates often align themselves with existing advocacy groups and volunteer to help them as they can. In such situations, fundamental decisions about policy goals, as well as some of the other seven steps in political strategy, are made by others. Volunteers often ask what they can contribute to this larger effort, such as by fundraising, hosting events, helping to organize letter-writing and email campaigns, and visiting legislators from their hometown districts.

Specifying a Proposal's Content and Getting Early Sponsors

Policy advocates aim ultimately to have their proposal enacted, but they often must ask: precisely what proposal? They have to decide what points of a proposal are most important to them and resist efforts to change or delete them. If they are willing to compromise excessively, they risk ending up with nothing, but if they are too rigid or dogmatic, the proposal may not be enacted at all. President Obama had to decide in 2009 and 2010, for example, what elements of national health insurance he strongly wanted and which ones he might sacrifice in order to get a measure enacted.

Early in the process, policy advocates need to find sponsors who will agree to support the proposal. If possible, such sponsors should include some influential people who sit on key committees or hold important positions.

Policy Advocacy Challenge 11.4

A Web Crusader in Egypt

Elaine Sanchez, MPP

In early 2011, protesters in Egypt banded together in an uprising that led to the eventual resignation of then-President Hosni Mubarak, who had headed the country for 30 years. Emerging as a voice—and later a face—of the opposition movement, Google marketing executive Wael Ghonim used his Internet prowess to organize a series of anti-government demonstrations. Specifically, Ghonim anonymously created a Facebook page called "We Are All Khaled Said," in reference to a young Egyptian activist who had been brutally and fatally beaten by police. The page drew 100,000 supporters in just one week. It also drew the attention of Egyptian authorities, who detained Ghonim for interrogation for 11 days. After his release, Ghonim revealed his involvement with the cause and was subsequently hailed a national hero. He continued to post entries onto the social media feed, which featured protest dates and locations, photographs of the resistance, and messages of hope and inspiration. Highlighting his advocacy efforts, *Time* magazine named him one of the world's 100 most influential people in 2011.

EXERCISE

Watch this video of an interview with Wael Ghonim, featured on 60 Minutes: www .cbsnews.com/video/watch/?id=7346812n.

- What characteristics does Ghonim possess that make him an effective policy advocate?
- Why was he successful in his ability to reach out to so many supporters?
- What are the advantages and limitations of Internet activism?

[1] Sam Gustin, "Wael Ghonim Rejoins Egypt's 'Internet Revolution' as Mubarak Clings to Power," *Wired* (February 10, 2011). www.wired.com/epicenter/2011/02/ghonim-ready-to-die/ (accessed on January 16, 2012).
[2] Benjamin Wallace-Wells, "The Lonely Battle of Wael Ghonim," *New York Magazine* (January 22, 2012). http://nymag .com/news/features/wael-ghonim-2012-1/ (accessed on January 15, 2012).
[3] "We are all Khaled Said," *Facebook* page. https://www.facebook.com/elshaheeed.co.uk (accessed on January 15, 2012).
[4] "Who is Wael Ghonim?" *CBS News* (February 8, 2011). www.cbc.ca/news/world/story/2011/02/08/f-wael-ghonim.html (accessed on January 16, 2012).

Establishing a Style

To be effective, a strategy needs an overarching style. Will behind-the-scenes and nonconflictual deliberations suffice, or is more conflictual and publicized interaction advisable? Of course, the style may change: If a low-conflict approach is unsuccessful, policy practitioners may wish to use a higher-conflict approach. For an example of a policy advocate who selected a higher-conflict strategy at a specific point in time, see Policy Advocacy Challenge 11.4.

Selecting Power Resources and Framing Strategy

Decisions must be made about who will use which power resources in which situations. If several people are involved in a project, they may divide the responsibilities for talking with specific people, making presentations, doing research, compiling lists of supporters, and performing other functions. For example, people seeking policy changes in an agency may decide the following: Joe will propose a place on the next staff meeting agenda to discuss modifying the intake procedure; Mary will comment on the inadequacies of the existing procedure at the staff meeting; Tom will make some comments that support Joe and Mary; Elise will suggest forming a task force to devise a new policy.

EPA 2.1.10f

Moreover, this group might decide to approach some staff members before the meeting to get support for the policy change. Similarly, a coalition of groups seeking a change in legislative policy might assign specific research to one group, ask another group to approach important legislators, and ask still another to compile a mailing list that can be used later in a letter-writing campaign.

Decisions need to be made, as well, about whether and how to use the Internet to mobilize support for a specific campaign or issue, and how to use it to influence decision makers.

Implementing Strategy

Having devised a strategy, policy advocates must implement it skillfully. They must use the full range of policy practice skills (interactional, political, and analytic) to carry out their strategy over an extended period. Skillful advocates sometimes have to deviate from their planned strategy when circumstances require improvisation.

Revising the Strategy

Policy advocates who hold rigidly to a strategy often imperil their success. They may have made miscalculations in devising their strategy, such as underestimating the strength of the opposition or the opponents' counter strategy. Unanticipated events also shape deliberations and may require a modification of strategy. President Barack Obama and his top aides had hoped, for example, to get some moderate Republicans to support the national health insurance proposal in summer 2009, but adopted a more partisan approach when they were unable to get any.

A Policy Advocacy Challenge: How to Block Ill-Advised Policy Proposals in the Policy-Enacting Task

The *blocking* of policies can be as important as initiating them, as the presidencies of Ronald Reagan, Bill Clinton, George W. Bush, and Barack Obama suggest. The Republican leadership in Congress attempted to block many proposals put forward by President Barack Obama, including his stimulus package, elements of national health insurance, and his banking regulations, and various tax and budget proposals. Because of the deep recession, as well as strong Democratic majorities in both houses of Congress in the first two years of Obama's presidency, the Republicans often failed in their efforts. They blocked many of his policy proposals in the second two years of his presidency, however, because they gained control of the House of Representatives in the Congressional election of 2010.

For an example of a blocking campaign, see Policy Advocacy Challenge 11.5 authored by Professor Robert Schneider.

It is the *combination* of blocking and initiating strategies by policy advocates that have made the United States, its states, and its communities more humane places.

We have provided, thus far, an overview of strategy no matter what the setting. Let us now discuss how policy advocates can do the following in specific settings.

Strategy in Legislative Settings

Policy advocates sometimes work to get a specific piece of legislation enacted—an ambitious undertaking in light of the sheer number of measures that legislators

Policy Advocacy Challenge 11.5

Blocking the Governor's Abolition of the Department of Aging

Robert Schneider, DSW, Professor EMERITUS, School of Social Work, Virginia Commonwealth University

In 1994, the conservative governor of Virginia, George Allen, was implementing with a vengeance his promise to taxpayers to reduce the size of state government. One particular target was the Virginia Department for the Aging (VDA), which was a freestanding agency with its own commissioner and board of advisors. The governor and his secretary of Health and Human Services (HHS), Kay Cole James, announced in September that by the end of the year, they would transfer this department into another department, the Department of Medical Assistance Services (Medicaid), all in the name of efficiency and eliminating duplication, of course. The VDA would lose its freestanding status, its commissioner would be reduced to an assistant director, the advisory board would be gone, control of the budget would shift to the Medicaid commissioner, and decision making on behalf of the aging would be buried deeper in the state bureaucracy.

As a 10-year member of VDA's board and its chairperson from 1985 to 1987, I read this announcement with grim uneasiness. Governors have every prerogative to make administrative shifts to improve state service delivery, and political pressure can be largely ignored. But this action was going to reverse years of effort to improve the status of the VDA. Several of us had worked perseveringly to upgrade this unit from an office on aging in another department to an independent department with its own budget, decision making, commissioner, and board. It would disappear, for the most part, with this plan. But what could I do? How could we stop this highly popular governor? The odds seemed slim to zero.

After a day or two of pondering and stewing, I got on the phone and called four other former chairpersons of the VDA's Governor's Advisory Board. Saying that there must "surely be something we can do," I suggested a meeting in Richmond the next week. When we met, we all agreed that we had to take action to at least delay this decision. A certain spirit of shared concern and determination evolved, and from then on, we became known as the Gang of Five.

Remember now, that this meeting was in early September, and a final recommendation from the governor was going to be made in November. How should we proceed? Here is what we did. First, we called on two very experienced veterans of state politics and human services administration to ask for advice. We met with them the following week, and from this meeting, we decided to delay the decision by insisting that some public comment period be allowed for citizen input. Public feedback is a very crucial process in Virginia, but this governor ignored it whenever possible. But the chances he would stop his decision were still unlikely, so we devised a backup plan. This strategy would go to the heart of the issue; that is, it would kill the decision in November by influencing the panel of decision makers, the Virginia Joint Commission on Health Care (JCHC), a legislative committee of the General Assembly of Virginia that made recommendations on all matters pertaining to health. The governor's proposal would first have to pass this group, and we believed that if we had any chance at all, this was the place not only to delay, but also to kill the proposal.

While writing to the governor and his secretary to delay the proposal for public comment, we began other tactics. Those of the Gang of Five who knew members of the JCHC were asked to contact them and explain the consequences of the governor's proposals. One of us was an extremely close friend of the commission's senior Democrat. The gang called on me to write our concerns into a statement that we could circulate far and wide. After consulting with the other four members, I drafted a two-page document outlining the issues, the potential effects of the new proposal, and some action steps that individuals or groups could take. I also began organizing a communication system so that we could write or phone all of the members of the JCHC, the key leaders of the Aging Network (a loosely organized group of policy advocates), the area agencies on aging, and the media.

We quickly discovered that there was little enthusiasm for the governor's proposal among the members of the JCHC. The Secretary of HHS also found out, and asked us to meet with the commissioner of the Medicaid department. In mid-October, the Gang of Five walked into the commissioner's office armed with the written analysis and other research, particularly around budget issues, and met with him and his well-prepared staff for two hours. They offered us some minor changes, such as retaining *aging* in the name of the agency, and promised us that the new assistant director would have full access to all decision making. We insisted that they show us how their proposal would improve the services for the older people of Virginia. Our argument was based on an opposite view, that, at no cost savings for taxpayers, much of the progress and the improvement of services for the aging would suffer significantly. At that meeting, we sensed that they were afraid of us and what we might be able to do, because there was already a rumor (not unfounded) that we were organizing a mass rally of older Virginians for the November JCHC meeting. We declined their offers and left our documents with them to study.

By this time, our confidence was rising, and support from the Aging Network was in evidence, even though much of it was quiet and almost secretive because many feared retribution. We wrote letters to the JCHC members and outlined the dangers of the shift. We called and met with them. Several regional agencies organized vans and buses of their clients to come to Richmond in November. However, we discovered that at the JCHC meeting, there would be time for comments only from commission members, not from others in attendance.

Through contacts with friends of the commission's chair, the night before the meeting I asked for the opportunity to speak to the commission. The next morning, in a room filled with older Virginians, the discussion opened with the Secretary of HHS outlining the reasons for the governor's proposal. The chairman of the commission, asking for clarification, caught my eye and asked if I would be kind enough to explain the point. This gave me the chance to make my speech and outline our Gang of Five's contentions. Interestingly, I was the only speaker from the gallery that morning. The commission wanted other points clarified and delayed its decision until its December 27, 1994, meeting.

While we had at least won a delay, we were not overconfident. We would be prepared for the December 27 meeting and also decided to go on with planning a mass rally in mid-January, just after the opening of the annual session of the General Assembly. The lieutenant governor, unlike the governor, agreed to speak at noon at our rally on the capitol grounds. Our efforts turned to mobilizing hundreds of seniors to come to Richmond in the winter. We decided to piggyback on an already scheduled Senior Day planned by the VDA to begin at 10 a.m. We sent invitations to agencies, individuals, associations, groups, legislators, and others to meet with us at noon *after* their earlier session in a nearby church, St. Paul's. We designed bright orange, three-inch stickers saying "SOS" (Support Our Seniors) and distributed about 4,000 of them. We also planned for many to come to the December 27 meeting.

However, the JCHC canceled its meeting on December 27 and rescheduled it for a week before our planned rally in January. Consequently, we had to alert all of our contacts of this change and hope that they would make the difficult adjustments in transportation and preparation. In early January, the JCHC met, and facing a sea of bright orange dots in the gallery, changed the agenda to deal first with the governor's proposal. Saying, "I see many of you are here for the obvious—let's get this item finished first," the chairman asked the commission members for comment. A few minor questions later, a nearly unanimous vote rejected the proposal. The secretary then spoke and acknowledged the vote, saying that she disagreed with it but would respect the decision. The chairman then suggested to the audience that those who wished to leave could do so. Orange dots began disappearing through the doors.

We followed up a few days later with our mass rally. It was great fun to see another sea of orange dots come out of St. Paul's church and the VDA's morning meeting, where

(continued)

the secretary again spoke and acknowledged the defeat of the governor's proposal. They all headed across the street to the Bell Tower, where the Gang of Five held its rally with 500 to 600 older Virginians. The lieutenant governor spoke eloquently about services to the aging. We were thrilled and amazed at what had happened, remembering our bleak prospects only three months before.

Much has happened between 1994 and 2010 illustrating how fluid the context is. Virginia Governor George Allen became U.S. Senator George Allen only to be defeated in 2006 by Jim Webb. Virginia Secretary of HHS Kay Cole James became director of the Office of Personnel under President George W. Bush where she served from 2001 to 2005, and is now the president and founder of the Gloucester Institute, a leadership training center for young African Americans. The Governor's Advisory Board to the Department for the Aging became the Virginia Council on Aging with half the previous membership. The VDA has had several new commissioners, including Dr. Ann McGehee, Julie Christopher, and, currently, Linda Nablo. The department lost its responsibility for long-term care policy development and planning to the staff of the JCHC. The Gang of Five keeps an eye on the department and stands ready to act.

EXERCISE

After reading this case, discuss the following questions:

- What objectives did Robert Schneider and his allies establish early in their crusade?
- What group or coalition took the lead in fighting the governor?
- What initial strategy, as well as backup strategy, did the Gang of Five develop?
- How did Robert Schneider get the chance to speak at the commission meeting?
- Why was securing a delay important?
- How did the Gang of Five mobilize pressure from multiple sources?

consider during any given session.[19] Policy advocates can develop their own action system to get legislation enacted, or they can be part of a larger coalition or network. No matter who takes the lead, policy advocates must undertake the tasks enumerated in Box 11.2.

BOX **11.2** | **Specific Activities That Policy Advocates Can Undertake within Larger Projects**

- Testifying before a legislative committee
- Lobbying specific legislators in person
- Writing a letter to a legislator as part of a larger campaign
- Telephoning a legislator's office about a specific measure (or organizing a phone tree)
- Writing a letter to a newspaper about a specific measure
- Participating in a demonstration about a specific measure
- Alerting a legislator to a specific issue or problem in the human services
- Raising funds for a specific advocacy project

Organizing Legislative Advocacy Projects in the Policy-Enacting Task

Organizing a Team or Coalition

Policy advocates need an organized group that will spearhead the drive toward enactment of a legislative proposal. It may be an existing group, such as an advocacy group; a coalition of groups established to secure legislation; or the National Association of Social Workers (NASW). This group needs leadership, such as a strategy committee that will pull together research materials and devise a master strategy. If an advocacy group is leaderless, its members will probably march in different directions and give out conflicting messages, undermining the group's effectiveness.[20]

An organized group is needed especially in legislative settings because legislatures are complex organizations with participants who make their living by supporting *and* opposing legislative proposals. To succeed in this environment, an advocacy team must operate with considerable efficiency. The team has to create a unified and effective strategy to keep its proposal from being lost among the hundreds of measures on the legislative agenda. If the proposal is controversial, like many that would redistribute resources or services to oppressed populations, it is likely to encounter opposition that can be overcome only by effective strategy (see Policy Advocacy Challenge 11.6).

Policy Advocacy Challenge 11.6

Managing a Legislative Advocacy Network

Julie Steen, Ph.D., Assistant Professor, University of Central Florida

After I earned my MSW, I began work as a legislative advocate at a statewide child abuse prevention agency in Florida. I was responsible for creating and coordinating a network of advocates committed to the well-being of children. We began with a group of social workers from child abuse prevention and treatment agencies. A number of adult survivors of abuse also joined the network after hearing about the cause. This network consisted of approximately 100 members and was aptly named STAND UP AND SHOUT. In coordinating the network efforts, I met with child advocates from other fields, including child health, early education and care, and developmental disabilities. These child advocates came together to form a broad coalition that was named ONE VOICE FOR CHILDREN. The advocates brought their own networks and merged them into one entity, allowing us to reach many more people and consequently to increase the impact of our advocacy efforts.

As the coordinator of the STAND UP AND SHOUT network, I was responsible for informing advocates across the state about the child welfare issues that were subjects of legislative proposals. I tracked the status of every bill during the legislative session. I created legislative updates and mailed these to the network members every week. I guided the advocates through the legislative process and encouraged them to make calls to legislators, meet with their local legislative delegations, and write letters to the editors of local newspapers.

Policy analysis was central to this work. Advocates must be fully aware of the details of each bill they are supporting or opposing. I analyzed the bills on our legislative agenda with special attention to the impact of the bills on children's well-being. The results of my analyses and legislative committee analyses became the source of messages for advocacy efforts that were used by members of the network in their communications with legislators—whether to support or oppose specific pieces of legislation. For example, I recommended that members of STAND UP AND SHOUT oppose a bill that would have placed our state in violation of federal law and that would have therefore threatened our state's ability to draw down federal funds.

(continued)

**Policy
Advocacy
Challenge 11.6**
(continued)

I also recommended that network members oppose a bill called the Family Bill of Rights, which was designed by its authors to limit the power of child protection agencies to remove children from homes that they believed neglected or abused them. The bill required a court order *before* children could be removed from their homes—a delay that might have led to serious injury to, or even the death of, some abused children. We placed an enormous amount of time and energy into defeating this bill, flooding legislators' offices with calls urging opposition to the bill, and succeeded in defeating the provision mandating a court order.

I saw many important issues enacted by the legislature during my time as a legislative advocate in Florida. We helped enact children's health insurance, mental health parity, and school readiness programs.

I was one of few social workers practicing as a policy advocate—most others were lawyers, public health professionals, and political scientists. My hope is that social workers will join the field of legislative advocacy in increasing numbers so that we can become formidable participants in improving the lives of children by getting legislation enacted that improves their lives. Legislative advocacy requires expertise, skills, passion, and idealism—but it enables us to advance social justice.

Some questions to ponder:

- Does the Internet make even more feasible the development of networks of policy advocates who influence legislative enactments?
- Should the staff of many social agencies become part of networks like STAND UP AND SHOUT?

A stifling or overly centralized team will be counterproductive because the collaborators need the freedom to be innovative and to use their distinctive strengths. Yet many good projects founder because proponents fail to set up a central leadership that will identify the key tasks, allocate these tasks to team members, and monitor the expeditious completion of the tasks.

Early in the process, proponents need to identify their allies without ruling out possible allies too aggressively; strange bedfellows often rally to an issue. Advocates should have a big-tent philosophy, to the extent this is possible, while also recognizing likely foes from their past records and prior statements.[21] (Remember that persons and groups do not become *actual* foes until they have taken action against a specific proposal.) Some groups or persons may agree to participate, but only on terms that are unacceptable to the proponents, such as demanding unacceptable provisions in the proposal.

Early in the process, policy advocates also should compile a *resource book* that includes the existing law, legal memoranda from attorneys who have been consulted, likely opponents, likely allies, congressional contacts on key committees (both aides and legislators in both supporting and opposing camps), civil servants from administrative agencies that will be affected by the proposal, and a set of key issues.[22] The organization's team has to know who the key players are. Once proposed legislation is introduced, it is immediately referred to a committee, and based on tradition, advocates should be able to predict how their proposal is likely to be routed. Then they need to analyze which members of the committee are likely to support and which are likely to oppose the proposal.

Because it contains sensitive information, this resource book (actually, a spiral notebook divided into sections) should not be disseminated beyond the key leaders of the coalition. (If a list of likely foes is widely seen, for example, they may become real foes.)

Establishing Policy Goals in a Legislative Context

At the inception of their work, policy advocates must decide what kinds of policy changes they seek. Do they want to develop new legislation or amend an existing piece of legislation? Do they want to increase funding for a specific program, or do they want to change the administrative regulations that guide the implementation of an existing program? (We discuss implementing issues in more detail in Chapter Thirteen.) Do they seek relatively modest changes or more ambitious reforms? To what extent are they willing to compromise with likely opponents of their proposal to increase the likelihood of its enactment?

Writing a Policy Brief: Specifying a Proposal's Content and Getting Early Sponsors

The first rule of legislative lobbying is to do your homework. Advocates have to write a *policy brief*, which comprises an analysis of the existing law, their proposal, why they want to change the existing policy, and the likely objections to their proposal (with rebutting responses).[23] (This policy brief should also be kept in a spiral notebook, separated into sections.) Advocates must know their issue so that they can state concisely (1) what they are concerned about; (2) how their issue affects other areas, such as likely costs and effects on other programs or laws; (3) an array of possible remedies with their likely costs and implementation problems; (4) an initial proposal (not yet in the form of a legislative bill) that addresses the problem; and (5) the likely arguments of opponents. (For an example of a policy brief, see Policy Advocacy Challenge 11.7.)

Policy Advocacy Challenge 11.7

An Example of a Policy Brief

Elaine Sanchez, MPP

Below is a (fictional) example of a policy brief that advocates might draft as a way to inform an agency about a particular issue and lobby officials to adopt their recommendations.

> FROM: Jane Johnson, MSW
> TO: Charles Smith, Secretary, New York Department of Education
> DATE: March 1, 2012
> MEMORANDUM: Profile of New York City Fujianese Student Population

OBJECTIVE

As a consultant for the Society for the Welfare of Undocumented Children, a community-based organization based in New York, I led research focused on the city's Fujianese population. Largely residing in Manhattan's bustling Chinatown, they face unique challenges that serve as additional barriers to children's academic achievement. As a smaller enclave of the broader generally well-performing Chinese subgroup, the community remains largely hidden in terms of the dialogue surrounding education policy.

My research team met with 100 Fujianese students from various New York public high schools and asked them to share their personal experiences navigating a foreign educational system. Focus groups consisted of male and female students, ages 16 to 20, who had arrived to the United States within the last year and a half. The following profile is the culminating product of student conversations, background interviews, and general research.

(continued)

Policy Advocacy Challenge 11.7
(continued)

BACKGROUND

The U.S. State Department estimated in 1994 that 100,000 Fujianese lived in the country; it also expected 10,000 more Fujianese each year thereafter.[1] According to one school social worker, those figures are highly conservative. Counting those who have been granted asylum, as well as immigrants' U.S.-born children, the true number is much higher, she stated.

Fujianese typically pay between $50,000 and $60,000 for a smuggler, or "snakehead" as they are commonly known, to bring a family member into the country.[2] Immigrants have a small, one-year window of opportunity to request asylum. Yet, that is only the first hurdle. Even if they achieve asylum, they still must work off their debt to the smuggler. Typically, it takes a Fujianese family three to five years to be released of their financial bondage.[3] As one article reported, this huge financial burden offers parents "too little time to raise their children or learn English."[4]

As a result, family dynamics are oftentimes strained. Focus groups highlighted the tensions that existed between children and their fathers. Young men and women alike talked about the pressure to make money and the difficulty for restaurant workers and day laborers to do so. "Money is more important, and the son is maybe no important," one male student said. In the majority of cases, fathers left for the United States when the students were still young, and the children followed suit at a later time. In consequence, a social worker said, girls are generally closer to their mothers and grandmothers who remain in China, and they struggle to build a relationship with the fathers who they have just met.

FINDINGS

- **Students believe learning English is key to their success in America; however, female students are at a higher proficiency compared to males.**

    A social worker said—and focus groups confirmed—that girls tend to become more acculturated than their male classmates. For example, she has observed that girls are more likely to date outside their own race. Meanwhile, male students admitted that interaction with other ethnic groups is limited to the classroom. Furthermore, they were more likely to mention that their speaking skills needed improvement.

    Every day the students speak English in school, and they attribute their progress to the fact that English is their main means of communication with teachers and staff. They write essays, do presentations, and study body language, all in the hopes of improving their English skills. Furthermore, they do not mind solely speaking English. Rather, they embrace it. "I need to learn English," one girl said. "I don't need Chinese. We come here and want to practice English. We already know Chinese." Learning English, they all agreed, is the key to their success in America.

Recommendation: Teachers should continue their English—only policies in the classroom; however, schools can consider instituting a Big Brother/Big Sister–type program for those who are having a more difficult time with language acquisition. In such a program, English Language Learners (ELLs) can be matched with native-born speakers, who can help build their speaking skills as well as their knowledge of American culture.

- **School is not a top priority for most Fujianese parents, who are more concerned with the family's debt.**

    According to focus group discussions, parental involvement in school was essentially nonexistent. For the most part, they did not attend parent-teacher conferences

---

[1]Qinbo, Gao. "Chinese Illegal Immigrants and US Tourist Visa (B-2 Visa)." 2004. TED Case Studies, No. 734. Taken from http://www1.american.edu/TED/chinavisa.htm.
[2]Zhang, Sheldon, and Ko-Lin Chin. "Characteristics of Chinese Human Smugglers: A Cross-National Study, Final Report." Taken from http://www.ncjrs.gov/pdffiles1/nij/grants/200607.pdf.
[3]Ibid.
[4]Ibid.

and did not look at report cards or progress reports. The groups explained that college was seen as an expensive enterprise, one without much return on investment. "I don't talk to them about school or college," one student said. "They haven't been to school here, and they don't understand college here. They don't speak English."

Many students said their parents believed that they will end up working in a restaurant whether they attend college or not. "Working at a restaurant" is emphasized and pushed. Going to college was encouraged, but not at the expense of a restaurant position that could help pay off debt to a smuggler. "They feel like money becomes a priority over family relationships because without money they cannot live on," one student said. Interestingly, the social worker said students with more involved parents are the ones who perform better in school.

Recommendation: Activities that bring parents and students together may help foster and develop family relationships.

- **Students have aspirations for successful careers, yet they lack the requisite courses and training.**

    When asked about their career goals, none of the students mentioned minimum wage jobs. Instead, careers that were mentioned included architect, designer, doctor, translator, and military officer. Because parents expect them to pursue restaurant positions, students are in conflict between their old and new worlds. The majority of focus group participants said they did not talk to family about their professional aspirations. Although most of the students were within two years of graduation, they were not aware of the training or courses they needed to take in order to pursue a college major in their desired field. "I'm confused about what kind of skills I have," one student said.

Recommendation: Schools should offer specific, tailored workshops for immigrant students who are unfamiliar with American college and employment processes. Increasing the number of teachers and advisers may also help confused students receive the individualized attention they deserve.

ADDITIONAL RECOMMENDATIONS

1. **Recruitment and retention of qualified social workers**

    Just as the Fujianese population is a hidden community, social workers communicated that they "felt invisible." One indicated that she did not receive credit when it was due and did not receive regular check-ins from her agency. However, without her, the Chinese students at her school would feel lost and disconnected. Providing more support to social workers who work with disadvantaged immigrant populations is essential to the well-being of students. The Department of Education and other agencies must find ways to boost and maintain a high level of morale among these individuals, who are often overworked and underpaid. They should also strive to recruit additional qualified social workers so that their achievements and concerns can be better recognized and addressed.

2. **Cultural sensitivity training**

    Teachers oftentimes do not realize that the lack of eye contact or raising hand is a cultural behavior, and consequently, Fujianese students get scored down for it. Nevertheless, many demonstrate proficiency in their Regents examinations. It would be beneficial for classroom instructors to undergo cultural sensitivity training so that they can be more aware of these types of issues. School districts can also consider serving culturally appropriate meals. Many students said it was difficult for them to get used to American food, such as pizza, but parents were too busy to pack lunch from home.

(continued)

Policy Advocacy Challenge 11.7
(continued)

3.   **Translation of important documents and other information**

The social worker said schools' language access services are inadequate for immigrant students. They do not account for the different dialects within a country. For example, a Fujianese parent may not understand Mandarin and may therefore miss out on important information. Schools must ensure that ELLs and their families have access to an interpreter who speaks their specific dialect.

EXERCISE

As you read through this example, think about arguments that opponents might raise concerning the writer's recommendations. What are some strategies that an advocate might employ in order to address these anticipated criticisms? How might you include these counterarguments in the policy brief?

Try outlining a memo on another issue. If you want practice in writing succinct policy memos, also try making this memo even more concise, such as by reducing its length by one-half. Sometimes, even one- or two-page memos can be highly effective in generating interest in a policy issue.

EPA 2.1.3c

The policy brief states the policy advocate's recommendations and serves as an orienting tool for policy advocates. It often is not shared with other persons, although it may be shared with legislative allies to give them an overview of the advocate's position. As a project unfolds, advocates and their allies have to stand together behind clearly formulated positions—not wanting allies to use different arguments and data when the proposal reaches the legislative process. Of course, an advocate may choose to modify a position as the legislative process unfolds in the context of political realities.

We can distinguish between the policy brief that advocates have developed for their own internal use, and proposals they subsequently present to legislators and others, which are often one- or two-page documents that state very succinctly the purpose, rationale, and content of a proposal. Because legislators and others are very busy, it is essential that documents that reach them be brief.

Most legislators are lawyers, so advocates need to have expert legal opinions early in the advocacy process. Sometimes, they commission a legal memorandum from an experienced law firm (for a fee that is negotiated in advance) to outline the existing law as interpreted by the courts and to tell them how other laws would be affected by the implementation of their proposal.[24] Alternatively, as we discuss later, advocates can get expert advice from staff assistants to legislators, members of legislative committees, or civil servants. The extent they need legal consultation depends, of course, upon the nature of the issue that they address.

Advocates must make key contacts early in the policy process to secure commitments to the general thrust of their project, even though they have not yet drafted a specific piece of legislation. Later, they will try to get some legislators to sponsor their legislation by agreeing to put their names at the top of the legislative proposal.

Establishing a Style in the Policy-Enacting Task

Legislative advocates usually have an out-front, assertive style. They have to draw attention to their proposal by making contact with many legislators, including those who are on the committees that will consider their proposal.

Personal lobbying, letter writing, and press coverage are often more effective than demonstrations.[25] Protests sometimes incite the opponents of a measure or lead to incidents that make the change effort controversial. Yet demonstrations and protests are sometimes essential to educating the public and making legislators aware that many people want them to take action with respect to a specific policy—as was illustrated by the Civil Rights Movement in the 1950s and 1960s, as well as huge demonstrations in 2005 and 2006 for immigration reforms at the federal level. To be effective, demonstrations and protests must be supplemented by legislative lobbying in which policy advocates develop specific legislative proposals and seek support for them. While advocates of immigration reform failed to convince Congress to enact it during the Bush administration despite bipartisan support for it, they hoped to be more successful in the Obama administration because Democrats had strong majorities in both legislative chambers.

The Internet provides powerful tools for influencing public officials as we have discussed. A policy advocate who has access to email addresses of a broad audience—or who possesses a widely used website—can ask persons to take specific actions at specific times, such as emailing key legislators or other public officials. Emails and websites can be used, as well, to mobilize audiences at key points in time, such as getting persons to attend important legislative hearings.

Policy advocates must decide whether or not they want to assume a relatively nonconflictual style. If they seek only modest changes in existing policy that they believe will attract widespread support, they might seek a relatively nonconflictual political process and a narrow scope of conflict. By contrast, some policy advocates might decide that considerable conflict is necessary to secure the enactment of a controversial reform that pits conservative legislators against liberal ones. In such a situation, they might broaden the scope of the conflict by seeking media coverage and by encouraging many groups to pressure legislators.

Selecting Power Resources and Framing Strategy

Once advocates have finished their research and put together a resource book, they have to develop a *strategy book* that lays out their tactics for the entire campaign. Like the resource book, this material should be kept confidential.[26] It should specify the following:

1. *Press representation.* This task should be done by people who can effectively speak for the legislative proposal. Also to be decided are who will issue press releases and who will be the contact persons if the press need additional information.

2. *Legislators to be contacted,* particularly on the committees likely to hear the legislative proposal. Advocates should also list the key aides of legislators and their personal phone numbers, as well as legislators who are likely to be friendly to the legislative proposal even if they are not on the key committees. Advocates should do a complete analysis of the voting records of these legislators on similar pieces of legislation; this information is available from such lobbying organizations as Americans for Democratic Action and the AFL-CIO's Committee on Political Education. They also should do an analysis of their home districts, making a page for each legislator, which will later serve as briefing material for the advocates who lobby the legislators. For each legislator, advocates should note whether they or their allies have special links with them, whether they know people who live within their constituencies, and whether specific arguments are likely to be particularly persuasive with them. Advocates should decide how to use the Internet to elicit emails or other personal actions, such as attending key events that can be part of the advocacy project.

3. *A committee to spearhead a letter-writing or email campaign,* to decide when letters or emails will be sent, what their substantive content will be, and who will send

them. As with legislative testimony, the advocates need to put forth a consistent argument with legislators. Letter-writing and email campaigns must be carefully planned, because legislators can be "turned off" by communications that are mass produced rather than those written by individuals who say in their own words why they want a specific piece of legislation to be enacted (or blocked).

4. *An initial plan for a blitz of the legislature.* A large group will make appointments with an array of legislators and their staff to push the issue on specific prearranged days. The plan should discuss when this will occur, who will participate, and which key legislators should be targeted.

So far, the advocates have only identified a specific problem and a proposed remedy, but they haven't drafted a specific legislative proposal. Nor have they lined up legislative sponsors.

The Internet enables advocacy organizations to develop a reservoir of persons who can be called upon during advocacy projects to undertake some of the tasks enumerated in the resource book (see Policy Advocacy Challenge 11.8).

Policy Advocacy Challenge 11.8

Using the Internet to Develop an Action System Using Volunteers

Jeff Martin, American Diabetes Association

The American Diabetes Association (ADA) has been using Convio's© Advocacy tool since May 2003 to maintain a strong advocacy program that relies on our volunteers at both the state and national level. One focus has been to get different states to enact SAFE AT SCHOOL (SAS) legislation to fund staff and programs needed to keep diabetic children safe while they are at school. For example, each school should have programs in place to maintain diabetic children through programs that test blood sugar, allow children to keep and eat snacks if they have low blood sugar, and allow children to carry and administer insulin (if blood sugar is high). The school should have a nurse or other staff person who has the requisite knowledge to help children maintain their blood sugar at healthy levels. Given the current epidemic of diabetes among American youth, SAS legislation is vitally needed.

The Internet enables us to collect and use information that is key to our advocacy efforts. It allows us to have lists of ADA volunteers in each state with their email addresses. It allows us to conduct needed surveys in different states. For example, when we learn that advocates have been unable to educate and negotiate with some local school districts in a specific state so that they implement needed safety programs, we can survey ADA volunteers in that state to see if they agree to support the introduction of SAS legislation in their state. We can then share information regarding volunteers' interest in participating with their local ADA office—so that it can then call on their assistance in a campaign that they develop to get SAS legislation enacted in a specific state. For most organizations, but particularly for those in the not-for-profit arena, the importance of this "force multiplier" capability cannot be overstated.

When we develop a campaign for SAS legislation in a specific state, we can use the Internet to enlist volunteers and give them background information on legislation. We identify which legislators we are targeting and give the volunteers specific messages about our position on the legislation that we wish them to send to legislators—and the mechanism to send that message. We can do all of this centrally, removing the need for any extra work by volunteers to orchestrate this. (We have learned that we increase the likelihood of volunteers' participation if we remove the need for them to do extra work.)

By having information at both state and federal levels and by sharing it back and forth, the ADA has had remarkable success in getting SAS legislation enacted—at last count in 24 states.

Some questions to ponder:

- In the case of the ADA, how might it recruit volunteers from the huge number of families that have diabetic children?
- How might the ADA assign volunteers to specific tasks in a campaign to get SAS legislation in a specific legislature?
- How might information about ADA volunteers in many different states help the ADA get needed legislation in Washington, DC?

Implementing Strategy

Implementing a strategy skillfully requires adherence to the conventions or protocols of legislative politics regarding lobbying, testifying, using the mass media, and writing letters.

Approaching Legislative Staff   At numerous points during their work, policy advocates talk with legislative committee staff that number roughly 7,500 in the Congress alone.

Policy advocates must devote considerable time to discussions with legislative staff; indeed, they will probably spend more time with them than with the legislators themselves. Most legislators rely on their staff to make recommendations about key issues—and often scuttle measures when lobbyists have failed to brief their staff.[27] In light of the sheer number of bills submitted to legislatures (20,000 are submitted to the Congress each year), legislators must depend on their staff.

We have already discussed that the policy brief developed for internal use by advocates must be condensed into a brief format so that legislators and others can quickly understand its rationale and substance. For example, a two- to three-page document that also might contain appendix materials is useful.

Advocates should realize that each legislator's office is like a small agency. The legislator often has a personal secretary who makes appointments; an administrative assistant; legislative assistants who specialize in such areas as domestic policy, foreign policy (in the case of the Congress), and liaison to committees on which the legislator sits; a press aide; and so-called caseworkers who manage constituent relations.

Advocates usually approach the chief staff person first, sometimes known as an administrative assistant or a senior legislative assistant. These aides are gatekeepers for legislators and political strategists, and they are sometimes more interested in a proposal's political merits than in its substantive merits—although they often want to know, too, whether a proposal has support in existing research, or what we call "evidence-based policy" in Chapter Fourteen. Advocates must convince this aide that the legislator's support of their issue will bring him or her substantial political gain, through positive public relations, press releases welcoming the legislator's support, and well-publicized events in the legislator's district to show his or her support for the proposal and the support of key constituency groups. Advocates should be even-tempered but appropriately assertive in their discussions, and they should not oversell their proposal by making inflated claims. (Advocates should remember that, in most cases, they are talking with seasoned political professionals who are very well versed in legislative politics and have knowledge of research.) If the administrative assistant likes their proposal, a legislator's support is often likely, though details are often worked out with lower-level staff who have substantive expertise in the proposal area. These aides are called legislative assistants.

In discussions with legislative assistants, advocates can focus more on the substance of their proposal than on its political merits. In these discussions, advocates give information about the proposal and its merits, and ask for advice. If legislative assistants like the proposal, they can often convince the administrative assistants—and the legislators themselves—to support the proposal.

At some point, advocates will work with a legislator's press aides, such as by drafting a press release for them that announces the legislator's support for the proposal.

(Advocates usually schedule appointments with administrative assistants or press aides through the legislator's personal secretary.)

Working with Committee Staff Proposals are processed by legislative committees, which have their own staff, usually appointed by the senior members of the committee. (Nearly 7,500 committee staffers work in the federal legislature; they are powerful participants in the legislative process.) Some of these staff are appointed by members of the majority party and some by members of the minority party. Because the staff are technically versed in specific areas, advocates should focus with them on the actual provisions of a proposal.[28] Advocates should seek meetings, perhaps over lunch, with committee staff who are responsible for the topic of the proposal; they should brief them and ask them what further information they need, offering to get it for them promptly. Advocates will probably need to keep in touch with key committee staff on a weekly basis or more frequently. They should also consult with staff members from the opposing party. Legislators' personal staff often defer to committee staff members' expertise.

Thus far, advocates probably do not have an actual legislative proposal, but simply a general position or a rough draft of a legislative proposal. At this point, to get help with the proper wording of the proposed legislation, advocates should ask for expert advice from the legal counsel of the legislative committee, the committee staff, or a legislative assistant of a friendly legislator who has sufficient expertise to help them in the drafting effort.

Policy advocates need sponsorship and support if their bills are to be enacted. They must find legislators who will agree to place their names as sponsors (or introducers) at the top of the legislation. Advocates should seek numerous sponsors from both political parties and sponsors who are highly placed in the legislative chambers, such as the presiding officer, the majority whip, and the chairpersons of the committees that will examine the proposed legislation.[29] Of course, as we have already discussed, a legislator's agreement to sponsor a bill is not an agreement to invest considerable energy in its enactment, although advocates hope that their discussions with legislators and their aides will convince them to commit their personal resources to it.

Advocates also should seek formal support from the head of government—the governor, president, or mayor—and from the director of the department or agency that will implement the legislation. Of course, their support cannot always be obtained, as many liberal advocates have discovered when they confronted conservative administrations.

Lobbying Legislators Advocates *lobby* legislators by having personal discussions with them or their aides to elicit support for a bill. In this effort, advocates should use the background material on legislators in their resource book and their strategy book. (See Policy Advocacy Challenge 11.9, which discusses the legislative strategy of members of Amnesty International.)

Through the legislator's appointment secretary, an advocate makes an appointment at least a week in advance for no more than 15 minutes. Advocates should be certain that legislative assistants are also asked to be present, to avoid the appearance of going over

Policy Advocacy Challenge 11.9

How to Lobby Your Member of Congress

Adopted from Amnesty International USA[1]

Meeting with your representative is a very effective way to lobby. Even if you cannot visit Washington, you can still meet your members of Congress. Your member has a district office near you that he or she visits several times each month. Wherever or whomever you meet, always prepare thoroughly for your conversation.

PREPARING FOR YOUR MEETING

- Gauge your representative's interest and to make an effort to match your requests to his or her initial level of interest.
- Re-familiarize yourself with your legislative agenda. You may want to write down talking points to hit on core messages.
- Practice what you are going to say so you sound natural to the staff person and not like you are reading straight from a script. Practicing will build your confidence and add to your effectiveness. Your legislative coordinator can assist with practice or organize a complete training session for your group.
- Call your legislative coordinator, or if there is not one in your state, call the government action network staff in Washington, DC. By making this connection, you can find out what your members of Congress have done recently on your topic of concern, get more detailed background on your legislators, and get tips to maximize the outcome of your meeting.

AT THE MEETING

- Be accurate. To build a working relationship and get action, you need to be a credible source of information. If you do not know something, just say so. Tell them you will find out and get back to them.
- Be brief. Members of Congress and their staffs are incredibly busy and so are you. Most members of Congress represent over 600,000 people. They appreciate it when you get to the point and respect their time. Because your meeting or call might be interrupted, get to your request in the first few minutes.
- Be courteous. Always, always be courteous. A "How are you?" after the initial hello works wonders! On the other hand, being abrasive is almost always counterproductive, and it provides a good excuse to ignore your request.
- Be specific. Make a point to mention the bill by number, give reasons why you support the bill, and let them know that you are a constituent.
- Be persistent. If you find that the staff people you need to speak with are out of the office, leave a message for them with your name and number. If they do not return your call within two to three days, then call again. Keep track of your calls, but remember that they are very busy.

FOLLOWING UP

After meeting with a member of Congress or an aide from his or her office, it is important to continue to assert yourself and stay on top of the situation. Follow these tips to maintain contact:

- Thank your representatives for listening to your concerns, especially if they take action. Commend them publicly, including letters to the editor or items in newsletters. (Be sure to share them with their staff.)

---

[1]Amnesty International USA (2009). "How to Lobby Your Member of Congress." Retrieved from: www.amnestyusa.org/get-activist-toolkit/plan-events-and-activities/how-to-lobby-your-member-of-congress/page.do?id=1101320.

(continued)

- Get the name of the staff person you speak to and try to deal with the same person each time. Remember that if your representatives are helpful and you praise them publicly, next time they may help you even more. The ultimate goal is to build a positive, long-term relationship.
- Provide information as needed. Expect to fax or email a lot of information to your representative's office. Offer to fax or email information as many times as necessary, because they get many requests each day. If you do fax something, call immediately to make sure that they have received it.

their heads. The legislative assistant should be briefed before the meeting. (As we noted earlier, some legislators will dismiss a project if their legislative assistants have not been briefed—and they themselves usually expect to have been briefed by their legislative assistants before they meet with an advocate.[30]) If possible, advocates should include in their delegation someone from the legislator's home district.

On their arrival, advocates should first talk with the legislative assistant, introducing him or her to their delegation and bringing additional briefing materials. When advocates enter the legislator's office, they should cordially introduce their delegation, praising the help they have received from the legislative assistant even if they have received little assistance. (They may need the assistant's further help later.) They should give the legislator a one- or two-page summary of their issue and briefly go over its main points, stressing the political gains the legislator will receive in his or her constituency from his or her support. Appendix materials can accompany the summary or can be provided later on request. Advocates should never bully legislators or make outlandish claims; they should present their case succinctly and with appropriate assertiveness.[31] Advocates should specifically ask the legislator to support their proposal and should keep their comments short, not exceeding 15 minutes unless the legislator lengthens the session. Do not get sidetracked by extraneous issues, and keep the legislator on the topic if he or she tries to shift the subject. Each member of the delegation should leave a business card. If the legislator asks questions to which they do not know the answer, the advocates should offer to get the answers to him or her promptly.[32] Remember, your reputation for honesty is one of your most important power resources in legislative settings—even though many people think most legislators are double-dealers, and not to be trusted.

The follow-up to the meeting should include short thank-you notes to the legislator and to individual staff members, briefly restating the basic points made in the meeting.

Advocates should not be awed by legislators, even those with considerable reputations. Instead, they should view the meeting as a service because it gives the legislator a chance to enhance his or her reputation by supporting their issue, and provides the legislator with facts and arguments that can be used to support the issue.

Branching Out to Reach Allies Advocates need an array of allies to support their projects,[33] including government agencies and other interest groups. Most government agencies have their own lobbyists, so their support of an advocacy proposal often means added clout with the legislature. Advocates should ascertain which agencies are most likely to help them by gauging which agencies' budgets, responsibilities, or prestige will be enhanced by the proposal, and which agencies are currently working in the area of the proposal. In their discussions with civil servants or politically appointed agency staff, advocates should emphasize that their proposal is intended to help the agency do its job even better. At some point in the legislative process, some agencies may issue a formal position on the advocates' proposal; if this position is supportive, the advocates should work closely with the agency's legislative liaison office to enlist its aid.

Advocates establish some allies when they form their team or coalition. They should then approach other interest groups that share the objectives of their project. Careful ground rules must be established: Advocates want the support of other groups, but they do not want loose cannons that take positions, make arguments, and use tactics that are divergent from those of the original team. The team cannot excessively muzzle or restrain its allies, but establishing some clearance and review methods will coordinate the collaboration. While endorsement by myriad groups looks impressive, advocates most want as allies groups that will commit time, resources, and public support to their proposal. Endorsements should include permission to use allies' names publicly.

Advocates can sometimes persuade legislators to write letters to their colleagues supporting the advocates' position. These letters may be very effective, especially when they come from respected or powerful legislators. (Several letters can be written or a number of legislators can sign a single letter.)

The Blitz   Policy advocates often decide to invade the legislature with a concentrated all-out mobilization of resources. A blitz takes many weeks of planning. Appointments for three- or four-person delegations to crucial legislators must be made weeks in advance; a master schedule of the visits must be devised; and delegations must have fact sheets on the proposal as well as information on the legislators they will visit.[34] At the appointment, the delegation should present arguments for its proposal and ask the legislator about his or her questions or concerns. After the blitz, the legislator's questions must be answered promptly—and members of delegations must send personal thank-you notes to the legislator. The leadership team reviews the feedback received by the delegations to gauge which legislators are supportive, uncertain, or opposed.

Getting Legislation Introduced   A sponsoring legislator introduces the advocates' proposal into the legislative process, so it is referred to a legislative committee. The chairperson of that committee then refers it to a subcommittee that schedules hearings on the proposal. Whether these hearings are scheduled at all, as well as their timing, is critical. Hearings on a proposal that are delayed to the end of a legislative session receive the required committee report so late that action cannot be taken by the full legislature.[35] Roughly two-thirds of bills introduced in Congress receive no hearings at all. The chances that early hearings will be held on a bill increase when the committee chairperson cosponsors it or when it is actually introduced by the incumbent administration. So advocates need to approach the chairperson of the legislative committee immediately after their proposal has been introduced. They can also ask their other congressional supporters to request that the chairperson schedule early hearings. In a few cases, their congressional supporters will decide that their measure should be reassigned to another committee or should even be reported from the committee by means of unusual parliamentary tactics that will bypass committee members who oppose it.

Testifying   Once hearings are scheduled, advocates should make certain that representatives of their group or coalition are invited to testify by getting friendly committee staff or staff of legislators to recommend them. Advocates should make clear that they want to testify and that they will keep their testimony brief. Sometimes they ensure a chance at testifying by offering a well-known person, but they should be certain that celebrities are well briefed and use arguments that the advocates' team has assembled.

The protocol for legislative testimony is simple. Advocates submit a brief written statement several days before their testimony. In the first two pages or so, the rationale, focus, and substance of the proposal are presented so legislators can quickly understand them. (Appendix materials that provide further detail can be attached.) This statement must be carefully written so that it reads well and also contains detailed information and data, often in the appendix, that cannot easily be given in a speech. It gives a fuller exposition of the advocate's position and is intended to be read by legislators and their aides.

However, the statement cannot be read at legislative hearings, where testifiers are expected to speak only for about 10 minutes. Advocates should list their main points, making their testimony dramatic and spontaneous so that it captures the committee's attention, perhaps by using specific cases as illustrations. Friendly legislators may prompt some committee members to ask questions that will elicit the strong points of the proposal or that will undermine the arguments of opponents. Advocates should be prepared for friendly as well as hostile questions from legislators; ideology and political interests often shape legislators' responses. If asked hostile questions, advocates should stand their ground, stick to their key arguments and data, and not volunteer information that goes beyond the questions asked. Advocates want to be seen as principled people with a well-reasoned case.[36]

Candor and honesty are highly valued in legislative hearings. If advocates do not know the answer to a question, rather than bluffing, they should say they will find the answer and send it in writing to the committee.

Using the Mass Media　The mass media can often help policy advocates reach a broad audience that will, in turn, place pressure on politicians to take action. Advocates have several options.[37] A press conference that makes their case for a proposal may be scheduled on the same day as a blitz or the first legislative committee hearing.

Of course, advocates must first get the attention of the mass media, which are besieged by people who want coverage. Advocates must make their story appear dramatic and relevant to larger social issues. They should establish personal links with key reporters in the print media, radio, and television, giving them full information about their issue and why it is important.[38] (Some reporters will be less friendly than others, and some critical stories about their project may appear if their issue is controversial.) To get reporters to come to a news conference, send written materials announcing it to reporters with whom you have established contacts and to others. You can also target the mass media in pivotal politicians' districts. If, for example, the chair of a legislative committee has bottlenecked a proposal, allies from an advocacy group in his or her district might call a press conference to pressure him or her into supporting the legislation.

Policy advocates sometimes use demonstrations to pressure legislators and to get coverage from the mass media. This tactic may not be as effective as lobbying legislators directly, but it will dramatize an issue and make clear that a substantial group is interested in it. Like legislative blitzes, demonstrations must be organized with care to prevent unnecessary altercations with police and to achieve maximum effect.[39]

Another tactic is writing guest editorials to be sent to the editorial offices of newspapers, radio stations, and television stations. Such editorials should not exceed 800 words and are more likely to be published if well-known persons write them or if they convey a dramatic, well-written message. Advocates can also write letters to the editors of periodicals, stating their central points briefly and dramatically.

Orchestrating Telephone and Letter-Writing Campaigns and Email Campaigns　Campaigns to call or write the offices of legislators may use the membership lists of community or professional groups. Letter writers should be provided with suggested themes, but not with form letters: legislators consider individualized letters more credible than standardized letters[40] (see Policy Advocacy Challenge 11.10).

Policy Advocacy Challenge 11.10

Writing Effective "Letters to the Editor"

Ronald B. Dear, DSW, Associate Professor Emeritus, School of Social Work, University of Washington

These are the 10 tips I offer my students when I give them the assignment of writing a letter to the editor of a newspaper or other periodical. These tips can also prove useful when writing letters to legislators and other public officials.

1. *Start with your reason for writing.* Be specific about the issue to which you are responding; for example: "I agree with your editorial of October 15 on the necessity of family leave policy, but you seem to have concluded…." You do not need to state the name of the periodical or, if you are writing to a newspaper, the section in which the article or editorial appeared—the editor will know.

2. *Be timely.* Write immediately when you see something to which you wish to respond. You are most excited and concerned at that point. Also, people quickly forget editorials, columns, and letters. Do not respond to yesterday's news or issues. A fine letter, sent too late, will never get published.

3. *Brevity is important.* Your letter should be no longer than one page, 200 to 250 words. Longer letters do, of course, get published occasionally, but they are the exception rather than the rule. To make your letter more readable, divide it into several short paragraphs rather than one long one.

4. *Get to your point right away.* Do not ramble. This is no time for a mystery. You are responding to something. Why? Make it clear.

5. *Address only one issue or topic.* Too many issues and topics make the letter confusing and raise the question about what it is, exactly, you are writing about.

6. *Tone.* Make it terse. Punchy. Humorous, if possible. Be provocative, but always be civil. Give strong opinions. Use logical, lively writing. Editors look for challenge, especially of their views. They like differences of opinion to be well stated.

7. *Give reasons for your views.* Be very specific and, when appropriate, use factual information. However, when you cite dates and facts, make sure they are correct; for example: "Recent poverty data, as cited in the *New York Times* on October 2…" or "The U.S. Statistical Abstract 2008, p. 412, shows that most elderly are not poor."

8. If you have expertise on the subject, say that you do—for example, "I have been a CPS worker for the past 12 years and…."

9. If you have personal (as opposed to professional) experience that is relevant, state it—for example, "I am a mother with three children, all in Seattle public schools, and I was appalled by the recent article on the upcoming levy."

10. *Be constructive as to what you think should be done.* You have commented and perhaps criticized. What would you do?

Finally, make sure you include your work and home phone numbers. Editors will always verify a letter before they publish it.

Effective letters are short, rarely exceeding two pages, which quickly get to the point. They describe the issue and the advocate's organization or interest in it, discuss the current law and the proposed changes in it, urge positive action, and make clear that the legislator's position will be closely followed in their home district (see Policy Advocacy Challenge 11.11).

Email campaigns have emerged as an important advocacy tactic, with large numbers of emails going to key legislators at key points as advocates develop substantial email lists of persons who support their cause. (Refer back to Policy Advocacy Challenge 10.5, as well as Policy Advocacy Challenge 11.8, which discusses how advocates can develop and use lists of volunteers who can be brought into an advocacy campaign at strategic

Policy Advocacy Challenge 11.11

Example of a Letter to the Editor

Elaine Sanchez, MPP

The following letter, penned by Niobe Way, was published in response to a column featured in the *New York Times* on May 11, 2009. It can be accessed at www.nytimes.com/2009/05/12/opinion/l12brooks.html.

To the Editor:

Re "The Harlem Miracle" (column, May 8):

While I applaud David Brooks for drawing attention to an effective inner-city school, I disagree with his assessment of why such schools are so effective.

The success of schools like the Harlem Children's Zone's Promise Academy is not because of the inculcation of "middle-class values" (when do middle-class kids ever learn to look at the person who is talking?). It is because of the teachers' and principal's high expectations of the students.

Robert Rosenthal's classic experiment in the 1960s showed that when teachers had high expectations for a group of randomly selected students in the classroom, those students excelled significantly over the school year regardless of how well the students did at the beginning of the school year.

We have empirical research that has proved the dramatic effect of teacher expectations for more than 40 years. When are we going to begin to take that knowledge seriously and act on it?

Niobe Way

New York, May 8, 2009

The writer is co-director of the Center for Research on Culture, Education and Development at New York University and president-elect of the Society for Research on Adolescence.

EXERCISE

1. How does the brevity of this letter make it an effective, or perhaps ineffective, advocacy tool?
2. Does the author present a convincing argument? Why or why not?
3. Read *New York Times* columnist David Brooks' original article to which the author was responding (www.nytimes.com/2009/05/08/opinion/08brooks.html). Practice writing your own letter to the editor and discuss how it differs from the above letter.

points.) Of course, emails cannot be used as an exclusive tactic, but must be supplemented by personalized letters and other communications. They need to be one tactic in a larger campaign to be effective.

Revising the Strategy

Advocates must revise their initial strategy at various points during their campaign because a campaign for an issue is an evolving phenomenon shaped by changing events.

For example, other groups and politicians often advocate rival measures. In such cases, policy advocates must try to influence the rival measures when their own measures are stymied. Many other factors can also necessitate changes in strategy. For example, expected opposition or support might not materialize or might increase, external events (such as a budget shortfall) might intrude, or a parliamentary obstacle might emerge or be removed.

Strategy in Agency Settings in the Policy-Enacting Task

EPA 2.1.8b

The seven strategy steps listed in Box 11.1 also are relevant to organizational settings. Here, too, policy advocates must develop a strategy that will enhance the achievement of their policy objectives.

Organizing a Team or Coalition

Policy advocates often want to obtain changes in agencies' policies as they work within them or as they monitor them from a funding agency. As in legislative settings, policy advocates need to assemble a team or coalition, even if it is loosely constructed, from among people with similar values, people from specific units or programs, members of informal groups or associations, union leaders, or people from different levels in the agency's formal organization.

Establishing Policy Goals in the Organizational Context

Policy advocates are involved in an array of policy goals. One is the extent to which they will respond to policies that descend on them from external sources, such as legislatures, government agencies, insurance companies, and the courts. Their responses include deciding not to seek funds from certain sources (thus avoiding specific policies), seeking external funding from programs whose policies they enthusiastically support, and seeking external funding from programs whose policies they partially accept. When they do accept funds, agency staff have to decide whether to comply with the policies that accompany the funds. They may have various amounts of discretion. For example, a not-for-profit agency that accepts funds for services to teenage mothers who receive welfare may strictly enforce the coercive policies of the welfare authorities or may soften the edges of these policies by not reporting some information to the welfare authorities or by taking other evasive actions.

Shaping informal policies is an important activity in social agencies. (In Chapter One, we stated that the shared beliefs and norms of staff constitute one form of social policy.) When they believe that current informal policies are having a negative effect, staff members can modify them by trying to modify the organization's culture through educational techniques, the use of consultants, and direct interventions with colleagues. They can also shape informal policies by promoting the hiring of people whose policy preferences concur with their own.

Policy advocates may also try to influence who oversees specific programs, in which services are provided, what budget allocations specific programs receive, and what kinds of funds the agency seeks from external funders. In each of these cases, a policy advocate shapes the agency's policies by influencing their implementation and budget choices rather than by trying to change official agency policies.

Agency staff can try to shape official policy at the highest levels of the agency, such as its mission, formal policies, and budgets, or they can concentrate on policies in specific agency units or programs, even bypassing higher-level staff when they believe they will receive more favorable responses at the unit or program level. (Recall that the student intern in Policy Advocacy Challenge 10.2 decided with her preceptor not to bring her innovation to high-level staff until it had been implemented as a pilot program.)

Astute tacticians analyze an issue's political economy. When doing force field analysis, they ask whether a specific policy will deter clients or attract a steady stream of clients and resources to the organization. They also note how it will enhance the agency's reputation, flow of clients, support from funding sources, or support from accrediting agencies. Because executives often favor maintaining staff morale, reducing internal conflict, and providing quality services, tacticians can also emphasize these kinds of positive consequences of a specific policy proposal.[41] Recall how the student intern in Policy Advocacy Challenge 10.2 planned to argue that developing group services for the children of institutionalized parents would increase referrals to the clinic and its prestige in the community.

Skillful tacticians view an organization's *formal attributes*—meaning its hierarchy and division of labor—as both constraints and opportunities. As a constraint, hierarchy intimidates persons who believe that their superiors will oppose a policy change. In organizations that lack a team-building atmosphere, some persons understandably fear that they may lose a promotion, a pay increase, or even the job by supporting even relatively small changes that top officials do not favor. Where intimidation and fear exist, support for proposed policy changes may be significantly reduced. When social service organizations are unionized (many public and nongovernmental agencies have unions), lower-level staff may be emboldened to support policy changes, though many unions restrict themselves to bread-and-butter issues, such as employees' wages and working conditions.

Hierarchy also provides opportunities. Astute tacticians can defuse the formal organization's negative aspects by finding allies for a proposed change within the higher ranks of administration. (The student intern in Policy Advocacy Challenge 10.2 hoped to defuse opposition to her proposal by obtaining Mr. Jones's support because other staff deferred to him on issues relating to outpatient services.) In rarer instances, they can use top officials' opposition to a suggested change to rally lower-level staff against these top officials, a tactic trade unions often use. This tactic must be used with caution, however, because it may merely entrench higher-level officials' opposition to a proposal and may lead to recriminations.

The division of labor is a constraint when it fragments organizations into competing units, causing members of one unit to oppose policy reforms that may benefit other units. When this win–lose ethos prevails, a policy practitioner may find it difficult to establish broad-based support for a change in existing policies. Indeed, the student intern in Policy Advocacy Challenge 10.2 feared that the director of training, Ida Brown, would oppose the innovation because it had come from Mr. Jones, a person she viewed as a rival. Divisions into separate units also can provide rich opportunities for coalitions if policy advocates can devise proposals that appeal to persons with different perspectives and interests, perhaps framing a proposal so that various units will have part of the action. The staff members of the unit that initiates a proposal might agree to a concession to another unit in return for its support.

Because organizations tend to have scarce resources, policy reformers must usually place *budget implications* at the fore in their force field analyses. A policy proposal's prognosis is usually bleak if it will cost the organization considerable funds and has little long-term prospect of generating offsetting funds from fees or external funders. Because it was unclear whether the student intern's innovation in Policy Advocacy Challenge 10.2 would generate fees or resources from funders, she probably should have devoted more energy to examining its fiscal implications.

When examining a proposal's budgetary implications, policy advocates need to consider fee-generating possibilities: whether external funders may be interested in funding it, whether the start-up costs will be offset by revenues once the innovation is institutionalized, and whether an inexpensive pilot phase is possible.

Policy changes that advance the important central goals of the agency (i.e., the *agency mission*)—or at least goals that the top management values—probably have a better chance than changes that are seen as irrelevant to these goals.[42] The student intern's

EPA 2.1.8a

innovation appealed to Mr. Jones in Policy Advocacy Challenge 10.2 precisely because he viewed it as furthering his commitments to community mental health and to outpatient services. When considering an issue's relationship to the agency's mission, policy advocates should refer also to the agency's context: Perhaps a proposal is not congruent with an agency's current mission, but it represents an innovation that addresses emerging community needs or issues that specific funders have prioritized.

It is easy to forget that policy advocates can obtain support for some proposals simply by emphasizing their relevance to beneficence or clients' well-being. As we discussed in Chapter Two, the hallmark of professions is the advocates' expressed ethical interest in helping clients. When conducting force field analyses, then, a policy advocate should ask what kinds of evidence will show that a specific proposal advances clients' well-being. Expert opinions, feedback from clients, evaluators' findings, and social scientists' work can buttress the case that a proposal will help clients. (The student intern could have strengthened her case for her innovation by finding evaluative or theoretical literature showing that her innovation would significantly help children.)

Recall our discussion in Chapter Four of *boundary spanners*, who derive power from their ability to lead an agency to sources of funds and referrals, which will enhance its survival. Strategists strengthen support for a proposal when they can show that it will bring new funds and referrals or will enhance the agency's prestige in the wider community.

An advocate must gauge the *informal relationships* among organizational participants when assessing a proposal's potential support. When we conduct force field analyses to examine agency employees' separate opinions, we may ignore important relationships among agency staff members. People often take cues from others whom they respect, so convincing a single pivotal person often brings many other persons' support. Policy advocates need to be able to understand long-standing patterns of association and deference in their agency when they try to predict a proposal's outcome.[43]

Using *intermediaries,* which we discussed in Chapter Ten, is particularly important in the politics of organizations. A policy advocate who is a direct-service worker often seeks higher-level intermediaries' support for a proposal, so that other employees will follow their superiors' leads. It also is useful to seek the support of intermediaries in other units of the organization, because some people defer only to the superiors in their own units.

Policy advocates should not reach premature conclusions about the feasibility of a specific policy proposal; even when the outlook is bleak, support may be gained for a proposal if it is framed correctly and if process tactics (such as timing and the use of intermediaries) are chosen well.

Specifying a Proposal's Content

EPA 2.1.10a

Policy advocates have to frame a proposal that specifies what they want to change in light of their objectives and the political realities—and whether they want merely incremental or larger shifts in policy. They can work on many fronts when participating in their agency's politics—changing official or informal policy, policy on implementing and budget choices, policy at higher levels of an organization, or policy in specific units.

Establishing a Style

Legislators are used to open, protracted, and public conflict among the members of different parties and persons with different ideologies. Indeed, they use conflict over specific issues to prove that they represent their constituents' interests better than the members of opposing parties do. In contrast, organizations' staff members tend not to want ongoing, protracted conflict, partly because staff members have to work together every day to implement agency programs. (Some leaders of organizations actively quell conflict to preserve their own power and preferences, to emphasize win–win decision-making processes, or to enhance the implementation of agency programs.)

If the politics of organizations tend to be more muted than the politics of legislatures, they can still be highly conflictual. Burton Gummer speculates that organizations are most likely to be politicized when they have scarce resources; when there is considerable internal conflict over the priority of different programs; when staff members have different service approaches or philosophies, such as different treatment methods; and when there is conflict between units, programs, or departments. He also notes that most organizations have at least some of these features.[44]

Style must be tailored to the setting and the issue. A frontal attack that polarizes the agency should be chosen only after all other alternatives have been weighed. Of course, conflict is usually unavoidable when major changes are sought that will infringe on the values and interests of key members of the organization.

Consensus-building efforts such as retreats, the use of external consultants who devise collaborative strategies, or group exercises that encourage full discussion of specific issues frequently meet with considerable success. These devices are also used, however, to promote the views of a specific faction, as when executives use external consultants as "hired guns."

Selecting Power Resources and Framing Strategy

An array of strategy options exists in organizations:

- *Option 1.* A direct-service worker decides to implement (or not to implement) a policy without consulting anyone. (We discussed issues of autonomy in Chapter Ten.)
- *Option 2.* A social worker decides, much like the student intern in Policy Advocacy Challenge 10.2, to begin a pilot program with the support of her supervisor before seeking high-level policy clearance.
- *Option 3.* A social worker decides to organize a broad-based coalition within his organization to seek a specific policy change. He decides to use a confrontive, polarizing style of politics, even though he realizes that the outcome is uncertain and that he risks alienating high-level officials.
- *Option 4.* A social worker decides to develop a program innovation, but only after consulting extensively and striking deals with several people that result in extensive modifications of her original proposal.
- *Option 5.* A social worker decides to change staff members' informal norms because she decides that they harm certain kinds of clients by giving them misdirected services. She persuades a high-level official to bring in an external consultant to give the staff technical training in new approaches to service delivery.
- *Option 6.* A social worker sets up a task force to seek a collaborative win–win solution to a problem in an agency. She believes that a collaborative planning project will produce a better solution than a conflictual approach.
- *Option 7.* Convinced that a proposal will be accepted only if it has the executive director's support, a social worker uses her supervisor as an intermediary to seek the executive director's approval for her proposal.
- *Option 8.* Despairing of any other approach, a social worker settles on whistleblowing, taking an issue directly to the mass media in hopes that external pressure on the agency will make its officials remedy some of its staff members' unethical behavior.
- *Option 9.* A policy advocate does not take an active role in developing a proposal but waits until a strategic moment to place pressure on people to modify the proposal. She uses her negotiating and mediating skills to develop a compromise proposal.

Revising the Strategy

As in legislative settings, strategists must often change their strategy as events unfold, investing greater political resources when they encounter more opposition than they had predicted, revising a proposal in response to a budget shortfall, or taking advantage of the fact that the expected opposition has not materialized.

Developing Strategy in Community Settings in the Policy-Enacting Task

Policy advocates in community settings also engage in the seven steps in formulating and implementing policy that we discussed in Box 11.1 as we now discuss.

Establishing Policy Goals in the Community Context

As in legislative settings, policy advocates must decide whether they will settle for incremental policy changes or whether they want major changes. This choice is, in turn, linked to estimates of likely support or opposition to the policy change. In some cases, an entire community will rally together for or against specific policies—and encounter scant opposition from the institutions they are challenging. In other cases, the community is polarized into competing groups. In still other cases, community groups encounter powerful entrenched interests that will not easily yield.

Specifying a Proposal's Content

Policy advocates can address an array of community issues: They may want a school to help dropouts or provide condoms to students; a zoning board to approve a halfway house for mental patients in a specific neighborhood; the city to fund an innovative program; an agency to establish a new program to serve a population that is underserved; or the community to help in an agency's operations, as through adding community residents to the agency's board.

Community-based policy advocates may create community forums or community planning projects to solicit ideas from residents about community improvements. In one instance, a social worker helped a community group obtain volunteer architects who, after many community meetings, developed a housing plan for the neighborhood. As this community group met with city officials, it persuaded them to allocate substantial funds to a housing-development project in liaison with federal officials.

Establishing a Style

Changes in community policies can sometimes be achieved without extensive conflict, such as when city officials concur with a recommendation by a community group. On less contentious issues, a policy advocate might develop a collaborative win–win process. To assuage community residents, for example, he or she might initiate certain safeguards to gain their support for a proposed halfway house. The policy advocate might convene a meeting of the community residents to develop these safeguards, such as establishing a 10 p.m. curfew for the residents of the halfway house.

Controversies arise when the interests of institutions or powerful officials are threatened, or when a community is divided into competing factions. When a coalition supported the placement of a welfare office in its neighborhood, for instance, it was countered by a powerful

Policy Advocacy Challenge 11.12

Challenges in Surmounting NIMBY

Bob Erlenbusch, Ph.D., Member of the Board of the National Coalition for the Homeless
Go to
www.cengage.com
to watch this video clip.

When policy advocates seek to place a residential or halfway facility in a community, such as a shelter for homeless persons, they sometimes encounter virulent opposition from local residents. This opposition is often called Not In My Back Yard or NIMBY. Assume that you encountered such opposition in a community. What strategies might you consider to surmount it? Watch the video clip of Bob Erlenbusch as he discusses strategies for averting opposition to shelters in specific communities.

group that opposed the office on the grounds that it would lower property values and bring criminal elements into the community. When a community is polarized or when advocates encounter entrenched interests, advocates need skill in mobilizing community groups, developing coalitions, and working with the mass media.

Selecting Power Resources and Framing Strategy

As in legislative settings, policy advocates in communities have to create a campaign to achieve their policy goals (see Policy Advocacy Challenge 11.12). Their strategy may include delegations to community leaders and administrators, petitions, letter-writing campaigns to local officials, demonstrations, stories in the mass media, community forums, and litigation. As it takes these actions, the campaign's leadership must try to sustain and build community support for its position.

Revising the Strategy

Relatively minor and noncontroversial policy changes can sometimes be achieved with modest effort. When a community campaign runs into significant and unexpected opposition, the leadership team has to review its options and perhaps embark on a more extended and ambitious effort.

Using Task Groups in the Policy-Enacting Task

No matter whether a policy advocacy project takes place in legislative, agency, or community arenas, policy advocates need skills in working with *task groups*, which focus on producing or influencing something external to the group itself. *Political strategy can only be effectively implemented in virtually any setting if effective task groups are established and maintained, so policy advocates must be familiar with them and skilled in working with them.* In contrast to groups for treatment, therapy, and education, task groups do not emphasize members' personal growth or learning.[45] Among the remarkable range of policy-related task groups[46] are those that concentrate on making and enacting policies, including the boards of agencies, legislative committees, and legislatures.[47] These groups often rely on policy recommendations from feeder groups, such as deliberative committees, subcommittees, study groups, or commissions that develop recommendations and forward them to decision-making entities.[48] Some of these groups are ongoing, such as an agency's program committee or the Select Standing Committee on Children and Youth in Congress. Executives and political leaders also establish ad hoc groups to study specific problems and make recommendations.

EPA 2.1.8b

Other task groups specialize in implementing policies.[49] Assume, for example, that a county mental health and substance abuse agency develops a new program for students in the school district and establishes an ongoing oversight committee to suggest policy changes when the new program is not realizing its objectives. Ongoing coordinating committees are created as well to promote the communication and policy development of various agencies.

Additional groups are set up for a variety of purposes. Many committees that staff can and should join exist in agencies to examine specific issues. Unions have become a potent power source in the human services system by mobilizing vast numbers of employees in public and nonprofit agencies.[50] Community organizations, like those modeled on the theories of Saul Alinsky, represent specific neighborhoods.[51] Many groups with varying amounts of power and resources serve as advocates for specific populations and institutions. Social movements spawn many groups with an overarching purpose, usually to advance the needs of a specific segment of the population, including advocacy groups for people who are homeless or people with AIDS.[52] Many national social movements have local affiliates, such as chapters of NOW or civil rights organizations. As we discuss later, coalitions merge the resources and power of member groups.[53]

Why Develop Task Groups?   Task groups are more effective than individuals who try to shape policy on their own.[54] For example, individuals who pool their ideas are apt to reach more well-considered solutions. Pooled resources, effective leadership, and pooled policy practice skills also result in more effective efforts to mobilize pressure for reform.[55] Highly placed officials often form task groups to avoid accusations of excluding various interests from their deliberations. (Sometimes, they control the membership of such a task group to be sure it approves only their preferred options.) Some executives also try to increase political support for specific measures by appointing blue-ribbon committees; such groups can give legitimacy to a policy because their members are influential persons.

Policy Advocates' Roles in Task Groups

Advocates participate in task groups as leaders, staff, or members. A *leader* is comparable to an orchestra's conductor or a football team's coach. The leader facilitates the group's work by helping to define its mission and acquire resources like funds and staff. He or she expedites the group's ongoing work by developing agendas and presiding at meetings, and helps shape the group's structure and membership by setting up subcommittees and a nominating process and by intervening at specific points to promote members' participation and decision making. As facilitators, leaders prevent or diminish excessive internal conflict and dysfunctional processes, such as scapegoating specific members. Besides the president or chair of a group, other leaders, such as treasurers and secretaries, perform important logistical tasks.

Staff expedite the work of the group. As expediters, they collect information, assemble materials, perform secretarial functions, and attend to logistical details to allow others to concentrate on developing ideas and taking specific actions. Between meetings, they often help the group's leaders plan upcoming sessions and accomplish specific tasks.[56]

The staff's role, however, places limits on their interventions within a group. Because they are background facilitators and expediters, rather than members or leaders, they must exercise considerable circumspection and restraint. They are apt to refrain from speaking when they disagree with the group's decisions, preferring to influence decisions more discreetly.[57]

Members of task groups provide ideas, perform specific tasks, give the group power by linking it to other interests, lead subgroups, provide resources, and sometimes assume leadership after a period of apprenticeship. While leadership is crucial, few task groups are successful without motivated and active members.[58]

What Successful Task Groups Need

Many task groups are highly successful in establishing and realizing their objectives through their deliberations and activities. Other groups flounder, split, procrastinate, or dwindle to nothingness, as many of us know from experience.

Theorists and researchers have identified several factors that contribute to a task group's success: the group's mission, leadership, developmental needs, procedures, structure, deliberative and interactional processes, and staff and resources.

The Task Group's Mission

Successful groups develop a mission that defines their objectives or goals. Although the mission often changes later on, the members should decide what they want to accomplish during the early stages of the group's existence. Several dangers exist. A group may establish unrealistic expectations, such as hoping to enact a major piece of legislation quickly. When it cannot accomplish this objective, the members' morale and the leaders' reputation may suffer. Another danger is that the group may fail to reach a consensus about its objectives, resulting in different factions and members having different expectations. In some cases, overt expectations clash with hidden ones, as when leaders possess personal agendas that they do not share with members.

The mission also includes agreements about procedural matters, such as the frequency of meetings, the way leaders are selected, and the group's size and its relationship to external bodies. Groups that do not agree on these matters and their major goals encounter controversies and misunderstandings.

The Task Group's Leadership

Skilled group leaders walk a tightrope. They should be directive and assertive, but should not dominate; they should encourage dissenting perspectives, yet prevent excessive or destructive conflict; they should perform tasks well, but be able to delegate; they should represent the group to the external world, yet not seek excessive personal credit; and they should emphasize the group's objectives, but not neglect the group members' social and emotional needs. Unskilled leaders may be domineering, passive, confrontational, dictatorial, or self-promoting.

A skilled leader understands the group's developmental, structural, and process needs and develops strategies to address them. At one point, a leader might encourage the group to engage in relatively unstructured brainstorming and, at another, to reach closure on a topic.

Effective leaders value democracy. They give members a considerable role in shaping the group's decisions, and they keep the group from engaging in the scapegoating of members who legitimately dissent.

The Task Group's Developmental Needs

Groups evolve through time as they strengthen their mission, engage in deliberations, and accomplish tasks. In early phases, they must agree on their mission, leadership, and procedures and form realistic expectations. During the middle phase, they should update their mission, develop and implement procedures, experience successes that give them a sense of momentum, and set up a division of labor that involves the members fully in the group's activities. In later phases, some groups should disband when they are no longer needed, whereas others should regenerate by revising their mission and seeking new members. Some groups do not progress through these stages of development. For example, not having established a mission, some groups keep returning to the question: Why do we exist? Other groups fail to change their mission as events unfold. Some groups continue to exist after accomplishing their original mission.

The Task Group's Procedures

Some people falsely equate leadership and group effectiveness with agendas, minutes, and bylaws, which are merely procedures. Procedures do serve a useful purpose.[59] Agendas allow anticipation of and planning for the future. Minutes provide a history that the group can review to ascertain how it has evolved and what new tasks it might undertake. Bylaws provide mechanisms for selecting leaders, replenishing membership, dividing tasks among officers and subcommittees, and handling funds.

The Task Group's Structure

Task groups must organize internally, establishing subcommittees or ad hoc groups to facilitate a division of labor. They have to decide how large they should be to accomplish their mission and to increase their political clout. They have to examine their relationships with other groups: Do they wish to merge with them, participate in coalitions, or maintain independence?

These kinds of structural issues pose significant challenges. A group that splinters into numerous committees, for example, may lack direction, but a group that is too centralized may fail to delegate responsibilities to its members. A group may lose its identity if it merges with other groups or joins coalitions, but it may lack clout if it remains isolated.[60]

The Task Group's Deliberative and Interactional Processes

To be productive, groups need modes of interaction that allow their members to examine options, to assess the group's strengths and weaknesses, and to make informed choices and develop strategies to implement them. Positive interaction occurs in an open atmosphere in which members believe that they are free to contribute ideas, that dissent is permissible, and that their ideas will be taken seriously, and in which brainstorming precedes final decisions.[61] Moreover, group members need to respect each other and the deliberative process and to honor the group's decisions.

Deliberations are stifled or abbreviated when leadership and group processes do not favor dissent, brainstorming, and democratic procedures. Social psychologist Irving Janis suggests that groups succumb to "groupthink" when they move too rapidly to unanimous positions, scapegoat dissenters, and do not fully consider the strengths and weaknesses of their positions.[62] Intolerant leaders, membership that fails to represent a variety of perspectives, and truncated deliberations contribute to groupthink.

Janis, Robert Bales, and other researchers suggest that a group should progress through a series of stages when considering issues: (1) brainstorming options in a risk-taking and tolerant atmosphere,[63] (2) carefully and gradually reducing these options to a revised list, and (3) formulating a final position only after extensive consideration of the options' strengths and weaknesses. This movement from large numbers of options to final choices occurs only when group members feel free to take risks and when the group tolerates internal dissent.

The Task Group's Staff and Resources

Groups that engage in complex work need staff and resources to accomplish logistical tasks, provide technical assistance, and facilitate the group's work. Staff may come from institutions, such as agencies, or may be volunteers. Resources may come from institutions, the membership, special events, private donors, or corporations or foundations.

Just like low-budget lobbyists, groups that lack resources or staff are at a marked disadvantage compared with richer groups. Of course, resources and staff do not guarantee success, and groups with few resources may accomplish a great deal.

Forming Coalitions in the Policy-Enacting Task

EPA 2.1.10a

Coalitions are temporary associations created to consolidate power in support of a specific issue, such as a piece of legislation. (We discuss ongoing associations, called *networks,* in the next section.)

Why are coalitions needed by policy practitioners seeking policy reforms for oppressed populations? Those who represent the poor, the powerless, or the stigmatized have an uphill battle; powerful interests and public apathy or opposition often impede social reforms. Moreover, powerful groups have coalitions of their own, such as coalitions of trade associations, agricultural interests, and tax-cutting groups.

Coalitions are different from many task groups, bringing together representatives of separate organizations to seek common action. The representatives agree to share the costs and labor of their common endeavor in a form of division of labor. When seeking the enactment of a piece of legislation, for example, one member group of a coalition may handle mailings, another the lobbying effort, and another the organization of a phone bank to telephone legislators at critical intervals.[64]

The success of a coalition depends on some of the same elements discussed under "What successful task groups need." As Milan Dluhy suggests, successful coalitions need the leadership of a small executive council that meets frequently and invests considerable energy in planning and overseeing the activities of the coalition. A single person can spearhead a coalition, but a coalition obtains power through the combined efforts of its member organizations. Coalitions must share the credit for their work, or the members will resent the publicity that a single person or an organization receives.[65]

The members of a coalition must define its goals and mission at the outset. Do they seek the enactment of a single piece of legislation, continuing pressure on legislators (or agencies), the education of the public about a social problem or the needs of a population, the development of innovative programs, or some combination of these and other goals? They have to decide as well when to disband the coalition or whether to transform it into an ongoing association (see the following discussion of networks).

Having developed a mission, the coalition's leadership needs to divide the labor. The leading group should establish subcommittees to focus on tasks such as research, lobbying, developing a phone bank, obtaining funds, and doing public relations (including creating a newsletter and reporting events to the mass media). The central leadership group could perform the coalition's real work, but establishing committees encourages broader participation. (The chairpersons of the committees often sit on the central leadership council.) With a division of labor established, the leadership council should meet regularly to monitor the committees' work and to coordinate a strategy for accomplishing the coalition's work.[66]

The leaders of coalitions have to decide what groups to enlist. It is easier to form coalitions of like-minded persons and groups because they are more apt to agree on policy and strategy. An advocate who wants to get more funding for child welfare in a local jurisdiction, for example, can form a relatively homogeneous coalition of children's advocates, social work leaders, and children's institutions. Coalitions that represent more heterogeneous perspectives are more challenging to form and maintain because such coalitions find it more difficult to arrive at a consensus on goals and strategy, but they sometimes have more clout because their members can appeal to different kinds of legislators, agencies, and citizens. For example, if the local chamber of commerce joins the child welfare coalition, although its leaders may not share some of the assumptions of children's advocates, they may be able to convince some moderate or conservative politicians to support the funding increases sought.

Establishing Networks in the Policy-Enacting Task

While coalitions are usually temporary alliances that end when they have accomplished their purpose, policy practitioners also establish ongoing networks of persons and organizations. These networks regularly inform their members of pertinent legislation, increase their members' political awareness, and foster the members' participation in the political process.[67] As a matter of fact, Rand Martin's organization, the AIDS-oriented Lobby for Individual Freedom and Equality, is a network, an ongoing organization with a governing council (see Policy Advocacy Challenge 10.7).

Assume that persons interested in state child welfare reform want a mechanism for sharing information about legislation, hearing about program innovations in different counties, and keeping abreast of national legislation. Envisioning their network as an ongoing organization with agency affiliates and individual members, they set up an executive council that establishes a division of labor, central offices, and a newsletter. This committee would schedule occasional meetings and workshops to supplement the newsletter. Like a coalition, this executive council also mobilizes the pooled efforts of its membership to support or oppose important pieces of legislation.[68]

Addressing Dysfunctional Group Processes

Some task groups are highly productive and others are less effective. Indeed, policy advocates sometimes have to use group process skills to improve a task group's functioning.

The degree to which advocates can intervene depends on the position they hold in the group, that is, whether they are staff members, leaders, or group members, whose different roles were described earlier.

Despite the constraints and opportunities that are provided by these different roles, all participants can diagnose or anticipate specific problems. When a task group or coalition loses momentum, the problem usually lies with a failure to develop a coherent mission, inadequate leadership, flawed internal processes, inadequate procedures, flawed structures, an inadequate process of deliberations, or insufficient resources. To diagnose which of these is the problem, we observe the group's operations from the vantage point of our role in the group. We often form our judgments from the complaints of other participants as well. We may also base a diagnosis on such developments as poor attendance and failure to achieve specific tasks.

Having diagnosed the problem, a participant in a task group, often along with others, needs to evolve a corrective strategy, such as having behind-the-scenes discussions, developing ideas during group deliberations, assuming some leadership functions, using power, mediating, directly assuming specific tasks, using humor, and seeking the advice of persons outside the group.

In meetings, members can promote more efficient deliberation in many ways, for example, by asking, "Don't we need to spend more time discussing this idea?" "Isn't it time to reach closure?" "Can we couple this idea with one that was suggested earlier?" or "Is there a different way to look at this problem?" They can also suggest procedures for considering ideas, such as breaking up into smaller groups to seek solutions to a problem.[69]

Even group members who are not leaders can sometimes assume leadership functions. For example, when a leader appears to be pressuring the group toward premature closure on an issue, a group member or a staff member can keep the discussion open by asking to hear more on the subject. Persons adept at parliamentary tactics sometimes use them to inject new perspectives and delay decisions. And between meetings, members may contact leaders directly to add issues to the agenda or to give their opinions on procedural, process, or structural matters. Of course, members and staff risk alienating leaders or erroneously usurping the leaders' functions if they do not use discretion.[70]

As in any collectivity, participants in groups have power resources, like expertise. When disagreements arise about specific issues or even about the group's leadership, processes, or structure, participants may use these power resources to shape decisions.[71] Group members also sometimes try to influence other members between meetings.

Group members need to use their power resources with discretion and without overriding the normal deliberative group processes. Excessive use of power resources can turn a group into a miniature legislative body whose members substitute threats, coercion, and parliamentary maneuvers for deliberation. At the same time, however, the use of power resources sometimes overcomes stalemates, stops destructive activities such as scapegoating, or makes beneficial changes in the group's leadership.

We discussed the use of mediation in Chapter Nine. Mediation may be the best solution when groups become polarized into competing factions.[72] Mediators can help group members identify their common values and can suggest structural or process strategies that will diminish conflict, such as bringing in a neutral facilitator. They also can identify compromises that will appease both parties to a conflict.

Effective persuaders often inject humor into their deliberations to ease tension, relax group members, and encourage the group not to take itself too seriously.[73] Humor can sometimes help in discussing specific group problems, as when a leader says, "At the rate we're proceeding, all the legislators we know will be dead before we come up with a bill."

Participants in groups or subcommittees sometimes take the bull by the horns and volunteer to do difficult or conflict-producing tasks that other members have shunned. When a subcommittee completes a task or develops a position on a difficult issue, for example, all its members have a sense of accomplishment and momentum.

An Advocacy Campaign in Sacramento, California

Policy Advocacy Challenge 11.13 provides an interesting model of policy advocacy because it spans communities and legislatures—in this case, Sacramento's city council. It also links the domestic economy with global issues, such as migration from developing nations as well as exporting of jobs abroad. As you read it, ask how its organizers resolved the seven steps that advocates confront when they develop policy advocacy campaigns.

Policy Advocacy Challenge 11.13

The Sacramento Living Wage Campaign

Emanuel Gale, Emeritus Professor of Social Work and Gerontology, California State University at Sacramento

The Sacramento campaign is part of a national movement addressing issues of low-wage workers who are struggling for economic survival at below federal poverty guidelines.

The dramatic changes during the past 25 years, including globalization, megamergers, deindustrialization, exporting of jobs, the increase in temporary jobs, the necessity of mothers to work, and the decline in incomes, have negatively affected the economic security of working families.

"Free trade" agreements, for example, North American Free Trade Agreement (NAFTA), World Trade Organization (WTO), and International Monetary Fund (IMF), are exploiting developing nations and enriching corporations and banks, at the expense of working families at home and abroad.

The widening gaps in incomes since 1975 have been documented by federal and state sources. The U.S. Bureau of Labor Statistics data, analyzing real wages in the United States, demonstrate that average hourly wages peaked in 1973. Despite economic expansion, wages in 1998 were 13 percent below 1973 wages.

A report of the Legislative Analyst's Office, "California's Changing Income Distribution" (August 2000), reviewed the average adjusted gross income by percentile of taxpayers between 1975 and 1998. The report documented that the bottom quintile lost 24.8 percent in purchasing power while the top quintile gained 66.3 percent.

LIVING WAGE CAMPAIGNS

The first living wage ordinance was enacted in Baltimore in 1994. Since then, 140 communities have adopted similar ordinances. In California, 27 municipalities have joined the movement, including Los Angeles, San Francisco, San Jose, Oakland, Santa Cruz, and Santa Monica.

The ordinances apply to entities receiving financial assistance, for example, service contracts, tax breaks, loans, grants, or land. Included generally are contracts over $25,000 per year, or city assistance over $100,000 per year.

The central provisions incorporate wages, benefits, worker retention, responsible bidders, temporary workers, and supersession by collective bargaining agreements.

While it is recognized that the ordinances cover a relatively small number of workers, campaigns are important to establish a community precedent regarding wages and benefits.

THE SACRAMENTO CAMPAIGN

1. *Planning:* Several key individuals, representing labor, community organizations, and key faculty from California State University, Sacramento, met early in 2000 to review issues in Sacramento. There was general agreement that there were serious economic problems for working families in Sacramento, the capital of the largest and wealthiest state in the nation. There was also agreement to explore the concept of a living wage campaign.

   The planning for the campaign included identification of key areas of work—research, mobilizing a broad coalition of organizations, planned community events, a draft ordinance, and contacts with elected city officials.

   A steering committee had met regularly to plan and coordinate the living wage campaign.

2. *Research:* Original research was not necessary because of extensive information that was already available. The essential task was to pull together information about Sacramento that presents an accurate picture of the city and California.

(continued)

This included data of household incomes, rentals, health insurance, child care, and transportation. Also available was the meaning of low wages, including federal poverty guidelines ($7.03/hr for a mother and her two children, $8.50/hr for a family of four) and the state's minimum wage. The California Budget Project, the Sacramento County Children's Report Card, and the Self-Sufficiency Standard documented the income necessary for a mother and two children to maintain a basic standard of living.

3. ***Organizing:*** People volunteered to target organizations in the community for support of the campaign. These organizations included labor, community groups, and the faith communities. Materials were developed describing the movement across the nation, the general concept of the living wage, and data about Sacramento.

During a six-month period in 2000–2001, more than 60 organizations had endorsed the campaign, including key representatives from the faith communities.

4. ***Community Events:*** The kickoff of the campaign was a forum on poverty in Sacramento in November 2000, attended by 325 people. The panel included three committed city council persons and many religious and community leaders. The program included presentation of data, testimonies from working people, and responses from the panel.

The next planned events were similar forums targeted in key city council districts.

The local council persons were invited to attend, and most did. The focus was to demonstrate that there was community support for the living wage campaign.

In May 2001, a major community rally was held in Cesar Chavez Plaza, across the street from the city hall. More than 500 people attended and called upon the city council to endorse the living wage.

In September 2001, a fundraising dinner attended by 300 people generated $7,000.

5. ***Draft Ordinance:*** A small group, including several volunteer attorneys, reviewed ordinances from around the country and California, and agreed upon the central principles to be included in the Sacramento ordinance. The central feature designated the living wage to be $10/hr including family health benefits or $12.84/hr without benefits.

The health proposal is unique to Sacramento because ordinances around the nation and California only included the worker. Data to determine the cost of health insurance was derived from the recent Henry J. Kaiser Family Foundation survey of California employers.

The attorneys have drafted the ordinance, which has been submitted to the city manager and his staff for review.

6. ***Political Process:*** Initial meetings were held with two city council persons who, it was believed, would support the Sacramento living wage campaign. They were receptive and agreed to provide leadership.

Meetings were also held with the city manager, who is a key player in the city. The mayor and city council members are all part-timers, which gives the city manager power on policy decisions.

The city manager also raised concerns about surrounding cities in the metropolitan area. With sales tax revenues an important revenue source, there is bitter competition among cities.

Materials were developed for the city council. Contacts were made with each of the other council persons to present the proposal. A meeting was scheduled with the mayor's chief of staff, preparatory to a meeting with the mayor.

By January 2003, more than 20 elected and appointed officials from throughout the Sacramento region endorsed the proposed Sacramento Living Wage Ordinance.

CONCLUSION

Unfortunately, despite widespread support, the Sacramento living wage campaign has not yet been successful in getting the Living Wage Ordinance passed. However, the effort has been significant because it has:

- Focused attention on addressing the struggles of working families.
- Been effective in organizing a broad coalition of more than 60 organizations supporting the campaign. It has also involved key faculty and students in a significant community campaign.
- Enabled the spotlight to focus on the problems in Sacramento, for example, wages, poverty, child care, affordable housing, and transportation.
- Focused attention on the political process and challenges in enacting a living wage ordinance.

There is an invalid assumption that research, data, and logic will determine social policy by themselves. What is needed is effective organizing so policy advocates can pressure policy makers to make humane policies!

EXERCISE

1. How does this case illustrate how policy advocates often need grassroots organizing skills?
2. What challenges did the policy advocates encounter when forming a coalition?
3. How did the organizers "co-opt" and involve public officials?
4. What interests do you think would likely oppose enactment of living wage legislation at the city or county level?
5. Is there a living wage campaign in your area? Perform an Internet search to find out. If so, how could you get involved? If not, what steps could you take to get one started?

What You Can Now Do

Chapter Summary

You are now equipped to engage in Task 6 of the policy practice and policy advocacy framework in Figure 3.1 by doing the following:

- Develop objectives and positions at the outset.
- Ground strategy in current realities by doing a force field analysis that includes persons' positions, contextual factors, situational realities, and likely future developments.
- Build alternative scenarios to select and revise strategy.
- Use seven steps in building strategy, including organizing a team or coalition or working through an existing advocacy group, establishing policy goals within a context, specifying a proposal's content and getting early sponsors, establishing a style, selecting power resources and framing strategy, implementing strategy, and revising the strategy.
- Use the seven steps in political strategy in legislative, agency, and community settings, including organizing a team or coalition, establishing policy goals, specifying a proposal's content, establishing a style, using selection power resources and framing strategy, implementing strategy, and revising strategy.

- Participate in advocacy to secure enactment of policy proposals, such as by helping to devise a resource book, policy brief, or strategy book; working with staff of legislators or legislative committees; getting sponsors; getting legislation introduced, testifying, and raising funds.
- Participate in advocacy to put external pressure on legislators, such as by helping to organize blitzes or demonstrations, using the mass media, organizing letter-writing campaigns, using the Internet to generate support and actions, and lobbying.
- Work with or organize advocacy projects in specific agencies to secure approval of specific policies.
- Work with or organize advocacy projects in communities to secure approval of specific policies.
- Work with or organize such task groups as coalitions, committees, task forces, and networks.

Having discussed how we implement political strategy in specific settings, in Chapter Twelve we turn to tactics to change the composition of government, because it is difficult for even the most skillful policy advocates to secure policy changes if they cannot find responsive legislators, heads of government, or civil service appointees. We shall note, as well, that some social workers also run for political office.

Competency Notes

EPA 2.1.3b   Analyze models of assessment, prevention, intervention, and evaluation (p. 366): Advocates must decide appropriate time frames to enact a policy.

EPA 2.1.3c   Demonstrate effective oral and written communication in working with individuals, families, groups, organizations, communities, and colleagues (p. 386): Policy briefs state the advocate's recommendations and serve as an orienting tool for advocates.

EPA 2.1.7a   Utilize conceptual frameworks to guide the process of assessment, intervention, and evaluation (pp. 366, 370): Strategy must be firmly linked to existing realities, including power distribution, past stances, vested interests and situational realities.

EPA 2.1.8a   Analyze, formulate, and advocate for policies that advance social well-being (p. 399): Advocates can obtain support for some proposals by emphasizing their relevance to clients' well-being.

EPA 2.1.8b   Collaborate with colleagues and clients for effective policy action (pp. 397, 403): Advocates must organize themselves into a coherent unit and develop a common strategy.

EPA 2.1.9a   Continuously discover, appraise, and attend to changing locales, populations, scientific and technological developments, and emerging societal trends to provide relevant services (p. 372): Advocates consider situational, institutional, and historical factors that offer clues as to how to get support for a specific policy.

EPA: 2.1.10a   Substantively and affectively prepare for action with individuals, families, groups, organizations, and communities (pp. 399, 406): Advocates can work on many fronts when participating in their agency's politics.

EPA 2.1.10f   Develop mutually agreed-on intervention goals and objectives (p. 377): Decisions need to be made about whether and how to mobilize support for specific issues.

Endnotes

1. Ron Dear and Rino Patti discuss the need for compromises in policy making in "Legislative Advocacy," *Encyclopedia of Social Work,* 18th ed., vol. 2 (Silver Spring, MD: National Association of Social Workers, 1987), p. 37.

2. George Brager and Stephen Holloway, *Changing Human Service Organizations* (New York: Free Press, 1978), pp. 107–128.

3. Kurt Lewin, *Field Theory in Social Science* (New York: Harper & Row, 1951).

4. William Coplin and Michael O'Leary, *Everyman's Prince* (North Scituate, MA: Duxbury, 1976), pp. 7–25.

5. Stephen Frantzich, *Computers in Congress* (Beverly Hills, CA: Sage, 1982), pp. 248–250.

6. Coplin and O'Leary, *Everyman's Prince,* pp. 20–25, 170–175.

7. Eric Schattschneider, *The Semisovereign People* (New York: Holt, Rinehart & Winston, 1960), pp. 1–19.

8. Allison Fine, *Momentum,* San Francisco, Jossey-Bass, 2006, p. 7.

9. See the discussion of organizations' traditions, objectives, and ideology in Brager and Holloway, *Changing Human Service Organizations,* pp. 57–66.

10. Brager and Holloway discuss the role of persons' tangible interests in shaping their position in *Changing Human Service Organizations,* pp. 85–92.

11. Julie Kosterlitz discusses feminist pressure in "Not Just Kid Stuff," *National Journal* 20 (November 19, 1988): 2934–2939.

12. See John Kingdon, *Agendas, Alternatives, and Public Choices* (Boston: Little, Brown, 1984), pp. 152–170.

13. See Perry Smith, *Taking Charge* (Washington, DC: National Defense University Press, 1986), pp. 17–26.

14. See Yeheskel Hasenfeld, *Human Service Organizations* (Englewood Cliffs, NJ: Prentice Hall, 1983), pp. 43–49.

15. Richard Fenno, *The Power of the Purse* (Boston: Little, Brown, 1966), pp. 193–195.

16. See Schelling, *The Strategy of Conflict.*

17. Eugene Bardach, *The Skill Factor in Politics* (Berkeley and Los Angeles: University of California Press, 1972), pp. 188–189.

18. Brager and Holloway, *Changing Human Service Organizations,* pp. 140–141.

19. My discussion of strategy in legislative settings relies heavily on Donald E. deKieffer, *The Citizen's Guide to Lobbying Congress* (Chicago: Chicago Review Press, 1997). While former Congresswoman Pat Schroeder praises the book in her preface, she adds a cautionary note that strategy prescriptions must be made with care because "members of Congress don't all react the same way."

20. deKieffer, *The Citizen's Guide,* p. 24.

21. Ibid., pp. 17–20.

22. Ibid., pp. 21–23.

23. I draw the term *policy brief* from Willard Richan, *Lobbying for Social Change* (New York: Haworth Press, 1996), pp. 155–182.

24. deKieffer, *The Citizen's Guide,* pp. 20–21.

25. Ibid., p. 31.

26. Ibid., pp. 27–35.

27. Ibid., pp. 89–103.

28. Ibid., pp. 105–113.

29. Ron Dear and Rino Patti, "Legislative Advocacy: Seven Effective Tactics," *Social Work* 26 (July 1981): 289–297.

30. deKieffer, *The Citizen's Guide,* pp. 105–113.

31. Marilyn Bagwell and Sallee Clements, *Political Handbook for Health Professionals* (Boston: Little, Brown, 1985), pp. 136–156.

32. Ibid., pp. 136–156.

33. deKieffer, *The Citizen's Guide,* pp. 115–121.

34. Ibid., pp. 147–155.

35. Ibid., p. 75.

36. Karen Haynes and James Mickelson, *Affecting Change: Social Workers in the Political Arena,* 2nd ed. (New York: Longman, 1986), pp. 76–78.

37. Bagwell and Clements, *Political Handbook,* pp. 216–234. Also deKieffer, *The Citizen's Guide,* pp. 37–49.

38. deKieffer, *The Citizen's Guide,* pp. 39–40.

39. Ibid., pp. 63–71.

40. Bagwell and Clements, *Political Handbook,* pp. 189–194.

41. D. J. Hickson et al., "A Strategic Contingencies Theory of Organizational Power," *Administrative Science Quarterly* 16 (June 1971): 216–229.

42. Ibid.

43. Rosabeth Kanter, *Men and Women of the Corporation* (New York: Basic Books, 1977), pp. 129–163.

44. Burton Gummer, *The Politics of Social Administration* (Englewood Cliffs, NJ: Prentice Hall, 1990), pp. 25–26.

45. Paul Ephross and Thomas Vassil, *Groups That Work* (New York: Columbia University Press, 1988), p. 1.

46. Tropman, Johnson, and Tropman, *Essentials of Committee Management,* pp. xiii–xiv.

47. Ibid., pp. 179–186.

48. Ephross and Vassil, *Groups That Work,* pp. 16–18, 22–24.

49. Tropman, Johnson, and Tropman, *Essentials of Committee Management,* pp. 196–203.

50. Dennis Chamot, "Professional Employees Turn to Unions," *Harvard Business Review* 54 (May 1976): 119–127.

51. Saul Alinsky, *Reveille for Radicals* (New York: Vintage Books, 1969).

52. Herbert Simons, *Persuasion,* 2nd ed. (New York: Random House, 1986), pp. 253–261.

53. Samuel Bacharach and Edward Lawler, *Power and Politics in Organizations* (San Francisco: Jossey-Bass, 1980), pp. 48–69; and George Brager, Harry Specht, and James Torczyner, *Community Organizing,* 2nd ed. (New York: Columbia University Press, 1987), pp. 193–200.

54. Robert Bales and Fred Strodtbeck, "Phases in Group Problem Solving," in Dorwin Cartwright and Alvin Zander, eds., *Group Dynamics: Research and Theory* (New York: Harper & Row, 1968), pp. 380–398. Also see David Sink, "Success and Failure in Voluntary Community Networks," *New England Journal of Human Services* 7 (1987): 25–30.

55. See Bacharach and Lawler, *Power and Politics in Organizations,* pp. 48–69; Brager, Specht, and Torczyner, *Community Organizing,* pp. 193–200; and Eugene Bardach, *The Skill Factor in Politics*

56. Tropman, Johnson, and Tropman, *Essentials of Committee Management,* pp. 5–23. For a compilation of literature on leadership, see Ralph Stogdill, ed., *Handbook of Leadership: A Survey of Theory and Research* (New York: Free Press, 1974).

57. Tropman, Johnson, and Tropman, *Essentials of Committee Management,* pp. 38–48.

58. Ibid., pp. 24–37.

59. Ibid., pp. 63–139.

60. Ephross and Vassil, *Groups That Work,* pp. 84–87, 166–183.

61. Irving Janis, *Victims of Groupthink* (Boston: Houghton Mifflin, 1972).

62. Ibid.

63. Bales and Strodtbeck, "Phases in Group Problem Solving," 47.

64. Milan Dluhy, *Building Coalitions in the Human Services* (Newbury Park, CA: Sage, 1990), pp. 53–57.

65. Ibid., pp. 59–63.

66. Ibid., p. 62.

67. Ibid., p. 52.

68. Marilyn Bagwell and Sallee Clements, *A Political Handbook for Health Professionals* (Boston: Little, Brown, 1985), pp. 189–194.

69. Ephross and Vassil, *Groups That Work,* p. 164.

70. Tropman, Johnson, and Tropman, *Essentials of Committee Management,* p. 45.

71. There is surprisingly little discussion of the positive uses of power in committees and task groups. Power is usually viewed as destructive of group processes.

72. Jay Folberg and Alison Taylor, *Mediation* (San Francisco: Jossey-Bass, 1984).

73. Ephross and Vassil, *Groups That Work,* pp. 158–159.

Suggested Readings

Gauging Political Feasibility

William Coplin and Michael O'Leary, *Everyman's Prince* (North Scituate, MA: Duxbury, 1976).

Understanding and Predicting Conflict

Morton Deutsch, *The Resolution of Conflict: Constructive and Destructive Processes* (New Haven, CT: Yale University Press, 1973), pp. 124–152.

Developing and Implementing Political Strategy

Eugene Bardach, *The Skill Factor in Politics* (Berkeley and Los Angeles, CA: University of California Press, 1972), pp. 183–240.

Ron Dear and Rino Patti, "Legislative Advocacy: Seven Effective Tactics," *Social Work* 26 (July 1981): 289–297.

Case Studies of Legislative Politics

Jeffrey Birnbaum and Alan Murray, *Showdown at Gucci Gulch* (New York: Random House, 1987).

Eric Redman, *The Dance of Legislation* (New York: Simon & Schuster, 1973).

Policy Practice in Legislative Settings

Donald deKieffer, *The Citizen's Guide to Lobbying Congress* (Chicago, IL: Chicago Review Press, 1997).

Willard Richan, *Lobbying for Social Change* (New York: Haworth Press, 1996).

Politics in Agency Settings

Burton Gummer, *The Politics of Social Administration: Managing Organizational Politics in Social Agencies* (Englewood Cliffs, NJ: Prentice Hall, 1990).

Politics in Community Settings

Kimberly Bobo, Jackie Kendall, and Steve Max, *Organizing for Social Change: A Manual for Activists in the 1990s* (Washington, DC: Seven Locks Press, 1991).

CHAPTER

12 Engaging in Ballot-Based Policy Advocacy

Policy Predicament

The makeup of local, state, and federal legislatures, as well as the mayors, governors, and presidents that are elected, greatly influences what kinds of social policies are enacted. No matter how skillful policy advocates may be, their challenges in securing policies that help vulnerable populations are more difficult if they confront relatively conservative elected officials. We discuss at this chapter's end how electoral politics shape the ability of the National Association of Social Workers (NASW) and its members to get its issues on the table and specific policies enacted (see Policy Advocacy Challenge 12.8 at the end of this chapter).

We have discussed the policy-enacting task (Task 6) in the policy practice and policy advocacy framework of Figure 3.1 in the preceding two chapters. We continue our discussion in this chapter when we discuss "ballot-based policy advocacy." Even highly skilled and dedicated policy practitioners will have scant success in obtaining policy reforms if some legislators and heads of government lack interest in them. The outcomes of presidential and congressional elections, such as the one in 2012, determine what social policies will be enacted and which ones will be abolished or poorly funded. If Republicans vow to rescind or impede implementation of the Affordable Care Act of 2010, for example, Democrats will retain and fully implement it. Hundreds of additional policies and programs will be similarly impacted by this election. Ballot-based policy advocacy seeks to change the composition of government so more public officials will want to advance social justice as mandated by the Code of Ethics of the NASW. Policy advocates also seek support for initiatives places on the ballot, such as specific propositions or other measures.

LEARNING OUTCOMES

We discuss the following in this chapter:

1. Why ballot-based policy advocacy is so important to policy advocates
2. How political campaigns are waged and the roles policy advocates can play
3. How some policy advocates can run for office themselves
4. How policy advocates can indirectly help progressive candidates
5. How policy advocates can influence outcomes of elections
6. How policy advocates can seek the enactment or the defeat of propositions

Why Ballot-Based Policy Advocacy Is Important

Persons who are interested in social justice must often turn for assistance to public policies enacted by municipal, county, state, and federal jurisdictions—and therefore must depend on the legislatures and heads of government (such as mayors, governors, and presidents) to enact enlightened ones. Public officials possess extraordinary resources and power compared with the private sector (see Policy Advocacy Challenge 12.1).

Federal and state authorities have enacted an enormous number of regulations in recent decades that protect vulnerable populations from discrimination, prohibit specific unsafe working conditions, redistribute monies from more affluent to less affluent groups such as through the Earned Income Tax Credit and the Supplemental Nutritional Assistance Program (SNAP, formerly food stamps), and finance the bulk of secondary education and a large part of postsecondary education. Countless other victories were

Policy Advocacy Challenge 12.1

Voting and Electoral Politics

Stephanie Davis, Research Librarian, University of California, Irvine

The outcome of elections often determines what kind of policies will even be placed on the agendas of public officials, not to mention which ones will be enacted. When Republicans won both branches of the Congress and the presidency in 2000, for example, the likelihood of the federal minimum wage being raised was greatly reduced during the next eight years. Democratic victories in the elections of 2006 and 2008 increased the likelihood that relatively liberal legislation would be enacted, such as when a Democratic-controlled Congress passed the Fair Labor Standards Act in 2007, which instituted a three-part increase, eventuating in federal minimum wage rising to $7.25 in July 2009. The chances for many other domestic reforms increased with the election of Barack Obama in 2008 as well as substantial Democratic majorities in both chambers of Congress.

EXERCISE

Using the sites given here, investigate how your state voted in the last two or three presidential elections or a past congressional election and answer the following questions:

- Which political party had the majority of votes in your state?
- What was the gender and age breakdown of votes?
- What kind of funding did the candidates receive?
- How does the winning candidate/political party impact an issue or topic of interest to you?

United States Electoral College
www.archives.gov/federal-register/electoral-college/

Project Vote-Smart
www.vote-smart.org

OpenSecrets.Org
www.opensecrets.org

Center for Voting and Democracy
www.fairvote.org

U.S. Census Bureau: Voting and Registration
www.census.gov/hhes/www/socdemo/voting/index.html

An excellent print source can be found in your library: *America Votes: A Handbook of Contemporary American Election Statistics* (CQ Press, published annually since 1956).

2.1.1a

achieved by advocates who pressured high-level public administrators, like the heads of human service agencies in state and federal governments, to issue administrative regulations that precluded discrimination against vulnerable populations in specific programs or that increased outreach to eligible persons not using important programs.

Policy advocates were able to achieve these policy victories only because they found key legislators, heads of government, and high-level public administrators sympathetic to their causes, or willing to be persuaded. Imagine working for social justice measures pertaining to African Americans, for example, in southern jurisdictions in eras preceding the enactment of federal civil rights legislation in the mid-1960s when few sympathetic legislators even existed, or working for legislation affirming the right of women to have access to birth control in the era preceding the heroic work of Margaret Sanger at the beginning of the 20th century when no female legislators existed because women did not even have the right to vote in federal elections. Sanger was jailed on numerous occasions merely for speaking publicly about birth control.

Yet even in the modern era, policy advocates have to battle to increase the number of persons in public office who really care about the plight of oppressed populations. The party that possesses a majority in specific chambers of Congress has extraordinary power. It selects the chairpersons of each of the congressional committees and its subcommittees. It prevails on many votes within committees. It prevails on many votes on the House and Senate floors. It can control the scheduling of votes by controlling the chairpersonship and the votes in the House Rules Committee.

If the *same* party controls *both* the Senate and the House *and* the presidency, it truly has extraordinary power. The president can often secure much of his policy agenda through a Congress that is generally acquiescent when his party controls both chambers.

The Republican Party had this extraordinary power from 2001 through 2006 because it controlled both Houses of Congress and the presidency during the presidency of George W. Bush, with the minor exception of a brief interlude from May 2001 through 2002 when the Democrats had a majority in the Senate when Senator Jim Jeffords from Vermont left the Republican Party to become an independent, but this interlude ended in the congressional election of 2002 when Republicans regained their Senate majority and widened their majority in the House and when they retained these majorities in the election of 2004 that re-elected President Bush. While Democrats took control of the House in 2006, it was not until President Obama was elected in 2008 that Democrats regained control of both chambers of Congress.

This extraordinary Republican power often meant that:

- Only Republicans could place items on the policy agenda in the Congress. If Democrats tried to initiate policy proposals in specific committees, they usually found that they were not scheduled for hearings or even discussed.
- Only Republicans could get legislation assigned to committees in the House, because the House Rules Committee acts as a scheduler.
- Republican committees in the House could send bills to the House floor under "closed rules" that allowed virtually no debate or discussion.
- Republicans could stop investigations of many congressional activities because they controlled the chairs and the membership of oversight committees. (Review Policy Advocacy Challenge 10.4 and the documentary "Capitol Crimes" by Bill Moyers.)
- The Republican president could mostly get his way with a Congress controlled by his own party.

Had the Democrats controlled even a single chamber *or* the presidency, as they did during the presidency of Bill Clinton and the first two years of Obama's presidency, they could at least have placed issues on the policy agendas of the committees of that chamber—or been able to use the presidential "bully pulpit" to get public support for some of their policies. Instead, Bush quickly translated his campaign promises into legislative proposals, such as getting a $1.35 trillion tax cut enacted, proposing significant increases in military spending, and seeking to privatize Social Security—not initiatives that many policy advocates favored.

Bush's appointees to high-level administrative posts, moreover, meant that policy advocates were less likely to obtain administrative regulations to their liking. Instead of the relatively liberal Donna Shalala (Clinton's secretary of Health and Human Services [HHS]), they now dealt with the relatively conservative Tommy Thompson, the former Republican governor of Wisconsin, who became Bush's secretary of HHS.

The election of Bush over Gore also had major consequences for the federal judiciary. By appointing scores of relatively conservative attorneys to judicial posts, Bush hoped to influence judicial rulings for decades to come on such issues as abortion rights, affirmative action, separation of church and state, gay rights, and devolution of federal powers to the states. Conservatives obtained a narrow majority on the U.S. Supreme Court and made a series of conservative rulings.

Imbued with a philosophy that emphasized individualism and decreasing the power and size of government, the conservatives downsized many programs. They opposed Democrats' efforts to increase the eligibility levels for federal funding of foster care, for example, so that most of its costs had to be borne by local and state governments—often leading to short funding that led to excessive caseloads for child welfare workers. They cut the Medicaid program and tried to disentitle it. They opposed increases in the minimum wage so that it remained at its lowest level in real dollars since 1969. They proposed replacing Medicare and Medicaid with medical savings accounts, but set at such low levels for these accounts that they would not cover the medical costs of many seniors and low-income persons. They made such huge cuts in taxes and increases in military spending that the nation developed huge deficits as opposed to the budget surpluses that existed at the end of Bill Clinton's presidency. Only a few remnant moderate Republicans, like Senator Olympia Snowe from Maine, demurred from these conservative policies.

It is true: The Democratic Party and its office holders had their own faults. They, too, could be guilty of corruption. They, too, could get the United States into ill-advised military actions abroad, as well as a bloated military budget. Yet clear differences existed between the two parties on social legislation—with the Democrats favoring governmental regulations and programs to a greater extent than Republicans.

Transformational Elections

As the congressional elections of 2006 loomed, it became clear that they could be a so-called transformational election in which one party's dominance might be challenged.[1] Transformational elections do not occur very often: The last one had been in 1994 when Republicans took control of both chambers of Congress, as well as many governorships and state legislatures.

Democrats would have to capture at least one chamber of Congress and reduce the size of the Republican majority in the other chamber. Even better for them, they would take control of both chambers. Were Democrats to regain control of the House, they would need to have a net gain of at least 15 seats in the 435 elections for House seats—and they would need a net gain of 6 seats to take control of the Senate in the 33 elections for Senate seats. (Only one-third of Senators come up for election during each congressional election because they serve staggered terms of six years as compared to two years for members of the House.)

Transformational elections are triggered by high voter turnout by one party, particularly among its base of loyal supporters. Republicans were able to turn out their conservative base in extraordinary numbers in 1994—centering upon evangelical and conservative persons in the South, Midwest, and mountain states. It was, to say the least, a political massacre; not a *single* incumbent Republican governor or legislator was defeated in 1994—and many incumbent Democrats were defeated—as Republicans gained solid majorities in both chambers of the Congress and in many state legislatures.

Many Republicans feared that the Democrats would return the favor in the congressional elections of 2006. Even in spring, President Bush's job approval rating had fallen to 31 percent. By August, public approval of Congress had fallen below 30 percent. Polls in October showed that Bush's ratings had only barely improved. Moreover, only 40 percent of voters believed the United States had "done the right thing" in taking military action against Iraq, and only 38 percent of the public believed the Republican Party "comes closer to sharing your moral values" as compared to 47 percent for Democrats. Remarkably, only 46 percent of persons approved of the way President Bush had handled the campaign against terrorism despite his efforts to publicize his counterterrorist initiatives—down from almost 90 percent soon after the destruction of Twin Towers in New York City in fall 2001. A solid majority of the public believed, moreover, that the Bush administration had lied to get the public to support the invasion of Iraq, such as alleging links between Saddam Hussein and al-Qaeda later found not to exist. A majority of the public believed that the Iraq war made the United States even more vulnerable to terrorist attacks by stimulating the growth of terrorists in the Middle East.[2]

The Republicans were bedeviled, as well, by corruption. Jack Abramoff, a high-powered lobbyist, was indicted on multiple counts for laundering money and offering illegal kickbacks to politicians in return for helping such clients as offshore corporations and Indian casinos. Abramoff, in turn, was linked to Tom DeLay, the House Majority leader—who resigned when he was indicted by Texas authorities for illegal donations of corporate money to Texas political campaigns. Bob Ney, a Republican Congressman from Ohio, resigned when he became a focus for influence-peddling. Even though some Democrats were likely, too, to be indicted, Abramoff had links with far more Republicans—even frequently meeting with Karl Rove, President Bush's chief political advisor.

Added to these discontents was a scandal involving Representative Mark Foley (R-Florida), which broke in September. Foley resigned from office when emails were discovered and made public that contained sexual advances to male House pages. As the public perceived a cover-up of this scandal by Republican House leaders—or at least a failure to take action when informed of the Congressman's behavior—public opinion turned against both the Republican Congress and the Republican leadership. This scandal was harmful to Republicans in yet another way: it soured many conservative voters on the GOP who strongly believed in family values and who disliked homosexuality. The Republicans' problems with public opinion and their conservative base energized many Democrats who saw the prospect of substantial gains in the 2006 elections after years of bad news at the polls. Republicans feared low voter turnout among the very group of evangelical and conservative voters that had powered them into control of Congress and the presidency during the prior decade.

As the nation moved from August to early October, experts raised the number of districts that were toss-ups or that leaned toward Democrats. Even between August and

October, the trend favored Democrats with as many as eight additional GOP House seats estimated by experts to be "at risk" of a Democratic victory. If 40 Republican seats had been "in play" in the House in August, as many as 48 districts were now estimated to be in play.[3]

Policy advocates' involvement in electoral contests was particularly essential in political races that experts viewed as up for grabs. Many of these races might be settled by a mere percentage point or less of the popular vote. Those candidates with the most volunteers, the most house-to-house contacts, the most effective campaign literature, the most resources, and the most sophisticated use of the Internet would prevail in close elections. Social workers' involvement in tight elections might even make the difference in some of them.

The 2006 congressional election indeed turned out to be a transformational one. The Democratic Party won a resounding victory—resulting in a Democratic takeover of the House (with a 233–202 advantage), and a tie in the Senate (with 49 for each side, and 2 Independents). It also ushered in an eras of "firsts"—with Nancy Pelosi elected as the first female speaker of the United States House of Representatives, putting her second in the line of presidential succession, and making her the highest-ranking female politician in U.S. history. It was also the first election in U.S. history in which the losses for one side (in this case, the Republicans) were so lopsided that the victorious party (the Democrats) did not lose a single incumbent or open seat in Congress or governor's mansion.

These gains were greatly magnified in 2008 when yet another transformational and historical election resulted in the election of Barack Obama, the first African American president, elected as president. An all-time record number of voters, 131.2 million, turned out to vote, making it the highest voter turnout rate in 40 years. Democrats won the Senate by a filibuster-proof 60 votes. They won the House with 21 additional seats, giving them a 257 to 178 advantage.

A number of factors contributed to the Democrats' landslide victory as well as Obama's win over Senator John McCain, the Republican presidential nominee. The situation in Iraq had continued to decline and appeared to be evolving into a civil war. President Bush's approval rating also continued to decline to the lowest final rating (22 percent) for an outgoing president ever recorded since Gallup began asking about presidential approval more than 70 years ago. The country's economy began a significant downturn beginning in 2007, leading many news sources to report that the economy was suffering its most serious downturn since the Great Depression. Republican nominee John McCain made a number of missteps such as declaring in September that "the fundamentals of our economy are strong." McCain selected Sarah Palin, Governor of Alaska, to be his running mate. She made many blunders, including misrepresenting her foreign policy experience, and failing to silence supporters who shouted, "Treason," "Terrorist," and "Kill him!" in reference to Obama during a campaign speech.

Obama's inspiring message of "hope" and "change" propelled him to victory in November. He reiterated his message of "a better day" and "yes we can" over and over again throughout the campaign season. So widespread was the message, that one could not avoid seeing the red, white, and blue posters, stickers, and t-shirts effectively depicting a confident, upward-looking Obama and the word HOPE.

Not only was Obama's election as the first African American president precedent shattering, but his campaign also broke numerous records. Obama raised an incredible amount of money—more than $500 million over the course of his campaign—far outspending his opponent, and far surpassing any amount ever raised by a presidential candidate. He used some of that money to do something no candidate in history had ever done; he purchased a half hour of prime-time air on all the major network television stations to run a campaign ad that was viewed by more than 33 million Americans. The Obama campaign also registered a record number of people, and especially young people, to vote. His "Vote for Change" voter registration campaign, which utilized effective campus recruitment, Internet, and door-to-door canvassing strategies, registered voters in all 50 states, including 200,000 new Democrats in Pennsylvania, 165,000 in North Carolina, and more than 150,000 in Indiana, for example. A record number of young people turned out to vote that November, and 66 percent of them voted for Obama. There was also a surge in the number of African Americans turning out to vote; 95 percent of them voted for Obama. A record 40 million people tuned in to their televisions and live Webcasting to watch Obama speak and accept his party's nomination for president that night at the 75,000-seat football stadium in Denver. Obama accepted his nomination and delivered a speech on the 45th anniversary of Martin Luther King's "I Have a Dream" speech, a coincidence that was not overlooked by the media who made numerous references to the historical nature of the event.

Obama won the election with 52.9 percent of the popular vote, and 365 electoral votes over McCain's 173. He carried 28 states, including the important swing states of Ohio, Florida, Indiana, and Pennsylvania, and the hotly contested states of Iowa and New Mexico. Two hundred and fifty thousand people gathered in Grant Park in Chicago, and countless more in living rooms and other gathering places all over the world, on election night, November 5, 2008, to watch Obama deliver his victory speech. The next day, newspaper headlines read "Historic," "Obama Wins," "Yes He Did," "A New Era," "In Our Lifetime," "Obama Victory Makes History," "Change Has Come," "American History," "Dream Realized," and, simply, "Obama!"

Bolstered by control of the House and the Senate, President Obama obtained social policy victories in 2009 and 2010 that rivaled those obtained by Presidents Franklin Roosevelt and Lyndon Johnson respectively in the New Deal and the Great Society. These included the American Recovery and Reinvestment Act of 2009, widely called the Stimulus Plan, that spent almost $1 trillion on infrastructure, schools, and many social programs to reinvigorate the economy; the Dodd–Frank Wall Street Reform and Consumer Protection Act that regulated banks and that established consumer protections; and the Patient Protection and Affordable Care Act that will insure roughly 32 million Americans by 2014. He secured the nomination of two women, Elena Kagan and Sonia Sotomayor, to the U.S. Supreme Court.

President Obama's power was greatly diminished, however, by the congressional elections of 2010. He had already suffered a blow when Democrats' hopes to retain 60 Democratic votes in the U.S. Senate were shattered when Republican Scott Brown succeeded Ted Kennedy, the late Democratic Senator from Massachusetts, in January 2010. With the rise of the Tea Party in 2009, Republicans vigorously contested seats in federal, state, and local governments by calling the Democrats' legislation "socialist." They alleged that Democrats had set back economic recovery through the spending programs of the Stimulus Plan, even though Democrats had inherited the Great Recession from the administration of President Bush. Saddled with unemployment that exceeded 12 percent and with millions of foreclosed homes that stemmed from speculative practices of big banks, Democrats proved unable to retain control of the House of Representatives, even though they narrowly maintained a majority in the Senate. The election of 2010 illustrates the importance of voter turn-out. If Republicans managed to turn out their base, many Democrats failed to vote, including young voters, blue-collar white voters, and female heads of households.

It is not surprising, then, that 2011 and 2012 were characterized by gridlock as Democrats and Republicans fought numerous battles over taxes, social spending, entitlements, and social policies. Both parties readied themselves for the presidential and congressional elections of 2012 that would determine the direction of the nation. If Republicans won the presidency and Congress in 2012, it was likely that the nation would extend tax cuts for affluent Americans, cut social spending, rescind some health reforms of the Obama administration, and possibly privatize Medicare. If Democrats won the presidency and Congress, reforms of the prior two years would be retained, as well as likely budget policies that would increase taxes on persons earning over $250,000, additional cuts in military spending, and relatively modest cuts in social programs. If the two major parties split control of the presidency and the Congress, gridlock would continue just as the nation had to make important decisions about national priorities as it encountered huge budget deficits and a massive federal debt.

The Limits of Electoral Politics and the Two-Party System

The two major parties differ significantly in the modern era in their positions on social reforms. At the federal level, for example, a majority of Democratic legislators are far more likely than a majority of Republican legislators to support an array of social reform issues. In 1992, for example, congressional Democrats supported packages of liberal issues 75 percent of the time, compared with only 18 percent of the time by congressional Republicans. This ideological schism between the two parties stems in part from their different constituencies. Democrats are more likely than Republicans to come from urban districts, the east and west coasts of the nation, eastern and middle-west northern industrial states, inner-city districts, and relatively liberal suburban districts, whereas Republicans are more likely to represent rural areas, some western states, southern states, and relatively conservative suburban districts. Republicans are more likely to represent relatively affluent voters.[4] So-called blue states, such as California and New York, are dominated by Democrats, whereas so-called red states, such as many rural and Southern states, are dominated by Republicans. Democrats receive a higher percentage of votes from female, African American, Latino, gay and lesbian, and disabled voters than Republicans. Although both parties contain liberal, moderate, and conservative legislators and voters, the Democratic Party has had larger liberal and moderate contingents than the Republican Party, particularly from the early 1980s onward. Moreover, while both parties get huge contributions from special interests, Democrats are far more likely to receive funds from trade unions, and Republicans get more from corporations. (Trade unions tend to favor more social reform measures than corporations.) It is accurate, then, to say that significant differences exist in parties' ideology, constituencies, sources of money, and positions on issues. For instance, persons who say they attend church once a week or more frequently are far more likely to vote Republican than Democratic.

We should not overstate the extent the Democratic Party is committed to social justice, even if Democrats as a group are more likely to support a policy advocacy agenda. The party has always had a big tent that included liberal, moderate, and conservative voters and public officials. Even in the heyday of the 1960s, when President Lyndon Johnson developed the Great Society with strong Democratic majorities in both chambers, many southern Democrats opposed civil rights measures and other reforms. Its base of support eroded somewhat in the three and one-half decades following 1968 as populations expanded in Sunbelt states and in the suburbs where voters tended to be more conservative than in the traditional liberal base of big-city enclaves and northern industrial states. A majority of U.S. voters resided in suburbs by the late 1990s. Wanting to contest Republicans for southern states and suburbs, Democratic leaders increasingly endorsed the argument that the party had to swing to the middle to be successful, with less emphasis on positions favored by trade unions and persons of color. This movement toward the center occurred dramatically during the two-term presidency of Bill Clinton, who favored co-opting many Republican issues such as fighting crime, "ending welfare as we know it," cutting federal deficits and debt, protecting military spending, and placing less emphasis on traditional liberal issues like affirmative action. Critics contend that this swing toward the middle, while sometimes enhancing Democrats' political fortunes, has also diminished their commitment to social justice on key issues.[5]

Critics of the two major parties, such as Ralph Nader, the Green Party's presidential candidate in 2000 and 2008, contend that both parties have been corrupted by the influence of monies contributed to them and their candidates by special interests. Members of both parties have been showered with contributions from corporations, Wall Street banks, pharmaceutical companies, health maintenance organizations, highway contractors, the National Rifle Association, military contractors, the mass media, and many other groups.[6] If some of these funds have gone directly to candidates, some of them—so-called soft money—have gone to the parties, who use them to support issue-based ads in particular races. These issue-based ads, in turn, are usually used by the two parties to support their candidates, such as by saying "support the candidate in this race who wants to raise the minimum wage" (a Democratic issue) or who "doesn't favor excessive gun control" (often a Republican issue).[7]

While neither of the two major parties assertively backed campaign finance reform to curtail soft-money contributions to political parties, its prospects suddenly improved in 2002 when Enron, the huge energy corporation, filed for bankruptcy after giving huge resources to politicians. Federal campaign finance legislation was finally enacted in March 2002, albeit with many loopholes. However, the Supreme Court's ruling in 2010, *Citizens United v. Federal Election Commission*, set back campaign finance reforms. Declaring the corporations and unions to be "persons," the Supreme Court allowed these entities to support specific candidates through so-called Super PACs that collected funds from donors and used them to finance massive advertising campaigns. The effects became clear during the Republican presidential primaries when a single donor and his relatives, magnate Sheldon Adelson who had formed Las Vegas Sands, singlehandedly financed Newt Gingrich's primary campaign in early 2010 with $11 million in contributions. President Obama, who had opposed the Supreme Court's decision, decided in February 2011 to establish his own Super PAC. A compelling case can be made that public officials will not be able to address many of the nation's serious economic and social problems unless it liberates its political system from big money from special interests.

Policy advocates sometimes support so-called third parties, such as the candidates endorsed by the Green Party in congressional and presidential elections of 2000, 2004, and 2008. Green Party candidates were considerably more radical than candidates from the major parties on domestic, environmental, and international fronts. By providing an alternative to the existing parties, third parties have the potential to push established parties to become more progressive. And some progressives hope that a third party might displace one of the major parties, providing voters with a truly progressive alternative.

Third parties also present a dilemma for policy advocates because the United States has a winner-take-all system rather than a system of proportional representation as in many European nations. In winner-take-all elections, only the party that gets the majority vote wins an election; in proportional representation, seats are allocated based on the percentage of votes that a party receives. So third parties in the United States get seats only when their candidate gets more votes than either of the candidates from the major parties—a daunting task because the third-party candidate has to convince huge numbers of Republicans and/or Democrats to shift parties. A Green Party in Italy would get 10 percent of the seats in a legislature if it got this share of the vote in parliamentary elections—rather than no seats, which would be the case in the United States if Green Party candidates received only 10 percent of the votes in local or national contests. Nor have third parties been successful in the United States, last succeeding at the presidential level in the late 1850s when the Republican Party, under the leadership of Abraham Lincoln, took the place of the Whig Party.

Developing Population Profiles

Astute candidates carefully analyze the voters in their districts long before ballots are cast.[8] Drawing upon data from previous elections, as well as polling data of their own, candidates estimate at the outset how close the election is likely to be. Some candidates realize they have little chance of winning, for example, when they encounter a popular incumbent or when they run in a district in which political opinion runs counter to their own beliefs and record. (A Democrat running in a strongly Republican district may realize he or she has an uphill battle at best.) In other cases, candidates may decide at the outset that they have a chance of winning, but that their races are likely to be closely fought. In still other cases, candidates may decide that they are favorites to win—or even that the election is theirs to lose. And in some cases, outcomes are exceedingly difficult to estimate.

Candidates' odds of winning increase in the following circumstances:

- They are incumbents rather than challengers because incumbents have many advantages, including name recognition, support from persons and groups who have benefited from policy actions they have taken in prior years, and an ability to raise money from those persons and groups who like to back a likely winner.[9]
- They have considerable name recognition in their electoral district, irrespective of whether they are incumbents.
- They run in a district where a strong majority of voters share their political and ideological preferences. Democrats who face Republicans in districts with strong Democratic tendencies are far more likely to prevail than Democrats in strong Republican or conservative districts.
- They can find early endorsers who have considerable standing in the district, whether influential people, newspapers, or other public officials.
- They can anticipate support from relatively large blocs of voters because of their ethnicity or race, their occupation (such as being an auto worker in a district with large numbers of blue-collar workers), their religion (such as being Catholic in a district with many Catholics), or their gender (such as being a female candidate who can strongly appeal to large numbers of female voters).
- They are able to raise significant resources compared with likely opponents, whether monetary resources or help from volunteers. The mass media, mailings, and campaign research, which cost money, are invaluable to candidates.[10]
- They are fairly certain they can turn out specific blocs of voters in a contest that will probably have a low turnout, such as an election for a school board seat. If a contestant in a school board election has the support of the teachers' union, and opposing contestants do not, his or her chances increase because the union will probably help turn out school personnel and contribute volunteers who will persuade other voters to turn out.

Of course, it is important that candidates not be excessively fatalistic even if they lack some of these advantages. Underdogs do win electoral contests. Favored candidates often make mistakes or take their reelection for granted. As many candidates have discovered, a defeat in a specific election is often followed by victories in subsequent contests for the same seat or for other seats as we illustrate later in this chapter with the victory of social work educator Victor Manalo.

Candidates often develop voter profiles of their districts, which identify blocs of voters who fall into at least four categories: probable strong supporters, probable strong opponents, probable swing voters whose support may be gained relatively easily, and probable swing voters who are tough prospects.[11]To these groups, we can add voters whose voting patterns are virtually impossible to predict. They also need to decide the likelihood that members of these various groups will actually vote, because it does no good to have strong support from voters who fail to turn out.

In developing voter profiles of their districts, candidates often make informed guesses based on party affiliations, demographics, and group affiliations. (See advice given to a political candidate by Professor Ramon Salcido in Policy Advocacy Challenge 12.5.)

African American or Latino candidates often can assume, for example, that voters with their ethnicity will favor them over other candidates, though they cannot assume complete support or that these voters will turn out to vote. Candidates of major political parties usually can assume that they will receive an edge from voters in their parties. Male and female voters may receive additional support from their gender groups. Other affiliations also can help some candidates, such as their religion, occupational group, and age.

Challengers can make informed estimates about incumbents by dissecting voting patterns from prior elections. Using census and voting data, they can discover in which precincts and with what demographic, racial, and political groups they ran strong or weak. Armed with this information, they can pinpoint their opponents' areas of strength and vulnerability.[12]

This population profile, which can be refined using poll and focus-group data, is vital to candidates. It enables them to estimate whether the election is likely to be closely contended, a landslide, or somewhere in between. If the election looks like it will be closely contended, candidates realize that they will have to invest great effort and resources in the election. The prospect of a landslide election is heartening to candidates who believe they will prevail, but disheartening to candidates who fear they will be on the losing end. In some cases, so many uncertainties exist in the population profile that candidates cannot make even tentative predictions—meaning they must gather more information as the race proceeds so they can devise intelligent strategies.

The population profile also is critical to candidates because it tells them where to channel their scarce resources. Candidates will not want to spend a lot of time speaking to voters who are certain to oppose them. Although they want to devote sufficient time and resources to encourage likely supporters to vote on Election Day, they do not want to allocate too many resources to them as compared with swing voters who might be converted through advertisements and personal outreach. (If they dissipate their scarce resources on certain supporters and opponents, they risk losing closely fought elections if opponents capture most of these swing voters.)[13]

Even if the prognosis is bleak or uncertain, candidates still may decide to run. Perhaps they want to gain name recognition for a future run for the same post or for another one. Maybe they want to educate voters about a specific issue. Or they may want community recognition to advance personal business or professional interests.

As candidates proceed with their analysis of likely voting behaviors of specific groups, they place this analysis over a precinct-by-precinct map of the electoral district. This enables them to decide where to target their mailings, precinct walking, advertisements, and telephone banks. If a candidate wants to reach Latino voters in specific communities, for example, he or she might seek endorsements from Hispanic leaders; run media spots on radio and television and in newspapers likely to be heard or read by Hispanic persons in these precincts; and recruit Hispanic volunteers to help with door-to-door visits and distribution of leaflets at local supermarkets. He or she also might try to get party officials to fund voter registration projects in these precincts.

Using Power Resources to Persuade Voters

Having identified the kinds of voters they want to prioritize, and even their geographic location, candidates need to convince voters to support them and to turn out on Election Day. They have numerous tools at their disposal (see Table 12.1). Indeed, astute candidates use all of these resources as part of their strategy.

TABLE 12.1   Power Resources for Influencing Voters' Views and Actions

1. Using One-on-One Retail Power Resources
   a. Personal door-to-door visits in precincts or at special events
   b. Visits by surrogate volunteers door to door or at special events
   c. Distribution of leaflets to voters at neighborhoods or other locations
   d. Working the crowd at local or other events
2. Using the Media
   a. Political advertisements in radio, television, and newspaper outlets
   b. Appearances on radio and television outlets
3. Interacting with Opposing Candidates
   a. Participation in organized debates
   b. Participation in organized forums for candidates
   c. Responses to opponents' positions in media advertisements
4. Developing Positions on Issues
   a. Articulation of a set of campaign promises that tells voters what policies a candidate will use in forthcoming elections
   b. Positions on specific issues
   c. Introduction of new issues
5. Demonstrating Positive Personal Characteristics
   a. Convincing voters through personal conduct and by citing one's past resume that a candidate possesses such desirable characteristics as integrity, diligence, fiscal discipline, and compassion
6. Conducting Negative Attacks on Opponents
   a. Attacking their positions on specific issues
   b. Attacking their personal qualities, such as by citing their prior activities
7. Getting Out the Vote
   a. Convincing supporters that they will suffer negative consequences if they fail to vote
   b. Election Day visits by campaign volunteers to voters to persuade them to vote (and even to provide them with transportation to the polls)
8. Securing Endorsements
   a. Getting endorsements from influential citizens, groups, and public officials from the electoral district
   b. Getting endorsements from influential citizens, groups, and public officials from outside the electoral district
   c. Getting endorsements from newspapers, radio stations, and television stations
9. Convincing Other Potential Candidates Not to Run
   a. Talking up one's campaign before it begins to convince other potential candidates not to run
10. Seeking Support from Party, Trade Unions, and Other Organizations

Using One-on-One Power Resources

Candidates need to make personal contact with many voters in a laborious one-on-one strategy. Through these contacts, candidates make voters believe that they have positive personal traits such as a concern for the voters' problems, high levels of energy, and an ability to listen. They can elicit suggestions or input about specific problems or policies. They can share their positions with voters to assure them that they care about their concerns. They can organize a sequence of local meetings in homes, churches, and community agencies, which allows them to present positions and solicit inputs from voters. When supplemented by campaign literature that highlights their accomplishments, positive personal traits, and campaign promises, candidates build grassroots momentum.

Using the Media

Name recognition is an extraordinarily valuable asset in political campaigns because many voters select names on ballots that are familiar to them—and they are more likely to listen to their messages. The media enhances the name recognition of candidates, whether through paid advertisements, personal appearances, coverage in news stories, or endorsements.[14]

Interacting with Opposing Candidates in Public Forums

Debates with opposing candidates are often important campaign events. They allow candidates to clarify their views and to distinguish them from opposing candidates; demonstrate they have a command of the issues; and place opponents on the defensive by questioning their positions or records.

Debate strategy needs to be carefully planned. Candidates need to anticipate likely positions and arguments of opponents, including how they might attack their own positions or records. They need, as well, to decide what issues to prioritize and what supporting arguments to use.[15]

Developing Positions on Issues and Demonstrating Positive Personal Qualities

Voters' decisions about whom to support are shaped by many factors. In a two-person race, voters make their decisions by evaluating both candidates in terms of perceived positive and negative attributes, making an overall ranking of each candidate, and then selecting the candidate with the highest ranking. Each voter does the following:

- Decides what attributes are worth considering for each candidate, both positive ones and negative ones.
- Decides what weight to give each attribute for each candidate.
- Ranks each candidate on each attribute.
- Decides, on balance, which candidate ranks the highest—and (if he or she votes) votes for that candidate.

To illustrate this process, assume a voter decides that the following attributes are important when comparing two candidates: honesty, correct positions on three pivotal issues (abortion rights, promoting good schools, and supporting patient rights), and a successful track record in public service. The voter goes through a mental process that we can simplify with a hypothetical example. Suppose a voter ranks each candidate, say

TABLE 12.2   A Voter's Perception of Two Candidates

ISSUES	CANDIDATE A RANK × WEIGHT	CANDIDATE B RANK × WEIGHT
Honesty (weight of 1)	$1 \times 1 = 1$	$-1 \times 1 = -1$
Pro Abortion Rights (weight 5)	$10 \times 5 = 50$	$8 \times 5 = 40$
Pro Schools (weight 2)	$5 \times 2 = 10$	$10 \times 2 = 20$
Pro Patient Rights (weight 1)	$-5 \times 1 = -5$	$8 \times 1 = 8$
Positive Track Record (weight 3)	$-5 \times 3 = -15$	$10 \times 3 = 30$
TOTAL	$+41$	$+97$

© Cengage Learning

from −10 to +10, on each of these attributes and then selects the candidate with the highest score after weighting the relative importance of each attribute. In our hypothetical example, our voter selects candidate B, with his positions on schools and, especially, his "positive track record" swinging the balance (see Table 12.2).

This example illustrates the tactical challenge faced by each candidate—assuming that large numbers of voters shared, roughly, the perspectives of this voter. Candidate A could try to enhance her positive scores on some attributes, paying particular attention to ones weighted heavily by the voter, such as a positive track record. Or she might try to increase negative scores of her opponent by challenging his record on issues in which he scores heavily with voters, such as abortion rights, schools, and a positive track record. She might say that he has shifted his stand on abortion rights, has not consistently supported schools, and has many blemishes in his previous track record of public service. Or she might try to add new issues to the list of issues on which she thinks she will score more positively than her opponent. Perhaps she decides to add environmental pollution or recreational space to her community. Or she might try to change voters' weighting of specific issues by contending that honesty (now weighted only 1) is the most important attribute voters should consider, perhaps adding some serious questions about her opponent's honesty.

A fluid situation often exists in campaigns.[16] At point 1, Candidate A selects specific issues for top priority but then adds issues or puts different emphasis on some existing ones as the campaign unfolds. Sometimes she makes these changes in response to her opponent, wanting to counter his charges, locate vulnerabilities in his positions, or change the topic when she believes he is scoring points against her on specific issues. Sometimes she makes these changes in response to polling data or focus groups that suggest that different issues or different emphases on existing issues will allow her to gain ground. Sometimes candidates discover that certain lines or arguments draw a sympathetic response from particular audiences, leading them to emphasize them. Or, conversely, they may drop or de-emphasize issues or arguments that draw a weak audience response.

Candidates need to develop a set of campaign promises early in the campaign,[17] which distinguishes them from opponents. These campaign promises give voters a sense that the candidate will deliver results during his or her term of office rather than being inactive or ineffective. These campaign promises need to be carefully considered because candidates can assume that opponents will attack them and may contend that they are not feasible (such as overly costly) or that they are ill-advised, too numerous, too vague, or too few. Sometimes opponents might say that a candidate's campaign promises are contradictory, such as when a candidate proposes a costly new program but at the same time promises to cut the budget or cut taxes.

Campaign promises are often linked, of course, to candidates' analysis of their electoral district. They want campaign promises that will mobilize likely supporters and appeal to some swing voters, and they want issues that will increase voter turnout.

Conducting Negative Attacks on Opponents

All candidates face a dilemma, whether to emphasize positive arguments or to make negative attacks on their opponents.[18] Take our example of Candidates A and B in Table 12.2. Believing that she trails her opponent, Candidate A could emphasize her accomplishments and positions regarding the various issues, as well as her own positive track record and honesty. Or she could attack her opponent's positions and, even more negatively, attack his character. Were she effective in doing this, some of Candidate B's positive numbers in Table 12.2 might diminish or even be converted to negative numbers. If she converted her opponent's position on having a positive track record from +30 to −50, for example, she would nearly catch up to him in the overall ratings.

However, negative attacks sometimes backfire. Candidate B might accuse Candidate A of running a negative campaign rather than discussing the real issues. Ethical issues exist as well (see Policy Advocacy Challenge 12.2).

Policy Advocacy Challenge 12.2

When to Be Negative and When to Be Positive

Bruce Jansson, Ph.D.

Most candidates face an ethical dilemma during their races. Knowing that voters are often less likely to vote for candidates with strong negatives on such personal traits as honesty, consistency, integrity, and diligence, they can often rapidly rise in polls by attacking opponents' personal traits. Sometimes they can find evidence of malfeasance, corruption, dishonesty, and lack of attention to citizens' needs (in the case of incumbents). When solid evidence is lacking, however, they can gain substantial advantage by making vague references, making allegations without credible evidence, or insinuating negative traits.

Why the temptation to go negative? Substantial polling data suggest that negative attacks can be efficient in lowering voters' opinions of opponents. Negative information is often effective in putting doubts into voters' minds about specific candidates. When used in television ads, negative messages are often particularly effective because they can be conveyed through vivid images, such as pictures of opponents in the company of unsavory people. Some candidates rationalize negative attacks by contending they merely want to beat their opponents to the punch.

What is lost in mudslinging campaigns is intelligent discussion of important issues that ought to be the basis for deciding who wins and who loses. Negative ads often feature untrue or simplistic allegations that are not buttressed by facts.

So what should Candidate A do in the following cases?

- She lags in the polls and believes her only hope is to attack her opponent's character.
- She wants to have a positive campaign, but finds her opponent has initiated a negative campaign against her.
- She believes her opponent lacks integrity and is dishonest, but lacks hard evidence to prove it.

---

[1]For a discussion of the pros and cons of negative ads, see Kim Kahn and Patrick Kenney, *The Spectacle of U.S. Senate Campaigns* (Princeton, NJ: Princeton University Press, 1999).

Getting Out the Vote

Nonvoters shape election results as powerfully as voters, as a simple example suggests. Assume that 100,000 voters support Candidate A, and 80,000 of them turn up at the polls. Assume that 125,000 voters support Candidate B, but only 75,000 of them actually vote. In this example, the least popular candidate wins the election only because Candidate B could not get more of his voters to actually vote.

This result is not unusual. As Frances Piven and the late Richard Cloward discuss, voters in lower economic strata are considerably less likely to vote than relatively affluent Americans, regardless of their ethnicity[19] (see Policy Advocacy Challenge 12.3). Because persons of color are disproportionately poorer than affluent Americans, they are considerably less likely to vote than Caucasians. So candidates with particular popularity among the less affluent members of our society and persons of color start electoral races with a significant disadvantage—unless they can entice their supporters to vote or can find offsetting support among more affluent persons. This is often not an easy task. While voter registration procedures have been greatly simplified across the nation to encourage registration, many poorer Americans still are not registered, and those who are registered vote in far fewer numbers than other voters. (Voters can now register when they obtain drivers' licenses and in many public agencies.)

Candidates can increase voter turnout by targeting populations and precincts having low turnouts with personal (or volunteer) contacts, leaflets, and advertisements. They can seek endorsements from leaders of low-turnout communities and populations. They can highlight the significance of the election to persons who would not normally vote and mount voter registration drives in areas where eligible voters are not registered. They can orchestrate Election Day activities, such as contacting voters by telephone and, in some cases, transporting them to the polls.

Policy Advocacy Challenge 12.3

Empowering Homeless Persons by Helping Them Vote

Bob Erlenbusch, Ph.D.

Go to **www.cengage.com** to watch this video clip.

When a social worker recently lobbied a state legislator in Sacramento, California, he asked her whether "the kinds of persons" she helped actually voted. Before she could answer, he said, "Of course they mostly do not—and I therefore give them little attention as compared to my constituents who *do* vote."

Listen to the online video as Bob Erlenbusch, member of the board of the National Coalition on Homelessness, discusses how he and other advocates were able to get large numbers of homeless persons to vote in Los Angeles County. After you hear this video, consider these questions:

- What effects did voting have on the politics of homelessness in Los Angeles County?
- Could similar projects be developed by social agencies that help other vulnerable populations?

Securing Endorsements

Endorsements often carry considerable weight in elections—assuming they come from persons and organizations that are respected by the candidates' natural supporters and swing voters.[20] Candidates often vie for endorsements from newspapers, party leaders, public officials, and community leaders—endorsements that candidates often feature on their campaign literature and in their personal appearances. They also compete for the support of Political Action Committees (PACs), which channel funds to candidates from trade unions, interest groups, and professional associations like the NASW.[21] (We discuss NASW's PAC later in the chapter.)

Endorsements can take the form of public statements by organizations and people. In addition, an endorsement can be an agreement to be listed on invitations and advertisements as sponsors of campaign functions, such as fund-raising events or important speeches.

Candidates obtain endorsements in several ways. They often emanate from prior friendships or working relationships, such as when a candidate has worked with specific public officials on previous occasions. Candidates often meet personally with potential endorsers and work hard to convince them that they will be effective public servants on issues that are important to the endorsers. Candidates often must convince endorsers that they have a good chance of being elected. They might provide them with electoral data that demonstrate that they have considerable support in their district and that likely opponents are vulnerable.

Convincing Other Potential Candidates Not to Run

Considerable jockeying for position occurs before each election as persons decide whether to run for specific offices.[22] It is to the advantage of a candidate not to encounter a crowded field in primary contests and not to encounter opponents in primary or final contests who possess widespread support and resources. Potential candidates cannot stop others from running, but they can try to discourage them by showing them that they will mount formidable campaigns. They can announce their intentions to run far in advance of the election to make clear that they will be serious contenders. They can talk to potential candidates in their own party to make clear their intention to run and to suggest that "if we beat up on each other in the primary, our likely opponent will have an easier time winning." They can approach campaign donors and seek early commitments as a way of showing potential candidates that they will have considerable resources. They can seek early endorsements from community leaders and public officials.

By starting early to build support and a campaign organization, candidates may also discourage some potential, and formidable, candidates from entering a race.

Gaining Support from Party, Trade Unions, and Other Groups

Candidates should assertively seek resources from organizations whose issues and perspectives are consonant with their own. Parties have resources to contribute to candidates, though they give priority to elections in which they believe they can pick up seats. Unions distribute funds through their PACs to candidates who support union and union-backed issues. The AARP not only contributes funds through its PAC, but also sometimes organizes elderly volunteers to work in specific campaigns. As we discuss later, issue-oriented groups sometimes run advertisements during campaigns that take positions on specific issues like gun control and offer support for candidates who agree with these positions. (Supports from external groups become more important as candidates seek higher-level seats in county, state, and federal jurisdictions.)

Finding Resources

Resources have become increasingly important to campaigns as the cost of advertising has risen dramatically, whether in newspapers, television, radio, or mailings.[23] The funds spent on campaigns for high-level offices in the United States have become truly remarkable and troublesome. Several points should be considered at the outset. The amount of resources required for a campaign escalates as candidates seek higher or more visible seats. A race for a school board slot or a host of local positions is relatively inexpensive, but the cost rises for some county seats, most state-level seats, and all federal seats. Indeed, social workers who want to enter the electoral process almost always begin with local races that require relatively few resources as compared with high-level races. As they build a track record in initial offices, they develop contacts and reputations that allow them to raise larger sums in subsequent races for higher-level posts.

While extremely important in many races, resources are not, by themselves, a guarantor of victory as billionaire Ross Perot discovered in 1992 when his massive resources yielded him a distant third-place finish in the presidential race. Some candidates succeed even when greatly outspent by opponents, such as Senator Ross Feingold (D-Wisconsin) who won the U.S. senatorial race in 2000 after rejecting many sizeable contributions from wealthy donors and PACs.[24] Yet considerable evidence demonstrates that large imbalances in resources usually favor the more affluent candidate.

Resources pose troubling ethical issues in the United States because some candidates, regardless of their merit, obtain much greater resources than competing candidates. For example, incumbents can raise resources much more easily than most challengers, and wealthy individuals can underwrite their own campaigns. Some special interests, such as corporate entities, can contribute much more than others, such as groups representing disadvantaged and oppressed populations. Federal, state, and local legislation limiting the so-called hard money that candidates can raise is often circumvented by soft money spent by political parties and special interests on media advertising for specific issues. Precluded from giving more than a certain amount of money to individual candidates, the National Rifle Association, for example, has released many advertisements to promote its interests. These ads help the candidates who oppose control of guns even when the candidates are not named in advertisements. Similarly, the major political parties can place issue-oriented ads in local races that favor their candidates, as can many other groups with deep pockets.[25] (Such tactics were partially limited by the enactment of federal campaign finance legislation in March 2002.)

The quest for resources has other troubling aspects. To the extent candidates devote more and more time to finding resources, they have less time to research and discuss issues. Even incumbents must devote considerable time to fund-raising while in office.

Yet resources are a fact of life in campaigns, and candidates for any office must devote considerable effort to raising funds so their opponents cannot buy their way into office.[26] Candidates need to estimate roughly what their opponents are likely to spend in a particular race so they can possess similar, if not greater, resources. Resources are needed to hire campaign staff, to hire political consultants, to advertise in the mass media, to produce campaign literature, and to make mailings. The cost of a 30-second ad in prime time on local television can range from $1,500 to $8,000 depending on the size of the market, though less expensive ads can be purchased on cable TV and radio and in newspapers. Imagine the prospect of seeing your opponent appear frequently in these media outlets in the weeks preceding an election when you could not afford any of them.

Other campaign costs also exist. Consultants who can provide important information about the local electorate and campaign strategy are costly. Campaigns sometimes use advertising firms to craft their ads—firms that use focus groups and sophisticated electronics to fashion ads that will be effective. Bumper stickers, yard signs, and billboard ads are costly to print, install, and dismantle. Direct mail is very expensive. Campaigns sometimes use professional polling firms to get baseline data at a campaign's outset and tracking data as the campaign proceeds. Even a sample of 400 people can cost more than $10,000 each time data are collected.

Still another reason exists for trying to find resources. Without them, candidates must perform some tasks that they might otherwise be able to turn over to staff. When candidates try to accomplish these tasks themselves, they have less time to devote to personal interactions with the electorate and to public appearances.

Every candidate gives priority to the recruitment of a resource that costs little but is worth its weight in gold: volunteers.[27] As they walk precincts, distribute leaflets at highly frequented places in the community, or operate phone banks, volunteers operate as surrogates for candidates. Many of them, after brief training, are highly effective in these roles—often making the difference between winning and losing a campaign. Volunteers are also ambassadors of goodwill in the broader campaign with their extended families and with acquaintances. Candidates sometimes have the good fortune to find volunteers with technical skills like the ability to use computer technology to identify specific precincts or groups of voters. Many successful candidates are even more likely to give postelection access to volunteers than to contributors because they realize the volunteers donated their personal time and energy to the campaign rather than merely signing a check.

Creating a Campaign Organization

Campaign organizations are unlike most organizations because they are time-limited and have a single purpose: to gather as many votes as possible for candidates in a matter of several months. Everything about them is dedicated to this urgent task.

Candidates exist at the top of the organizational chart, but they differ widely in the actual roles they assume during the campaign. Some candidates delegate very little—making the key decisions and overseeing their implementation. Other candidates place extraordinary reliance on their staff and consultants, basically following their advice with respect to strategy and implementation decisions. No single style is best because the capabilities of candidates, staff, and consultants vary widely. Experienced candidates who possess political instincts often can and should play a more central role than candidates who lack these attributes. Problems occur when candidates who lack political instincts and savvy make too many decisions—as Ed Rollins recalls when discussing George H. W. Bush's lackluster campaign in 1992 when Bush was bested by Bill Clinton.[28] Falsely assuming that his popularity from winning Operation Desert Storm would carry over into this election, Bush ignored domestic issues even when warned by Rollins and other advisers that this decision could cost him the election. When Clinton's staff adopted the motto, "It's the economy, stupid," they set the stage for a landslide victory over Bush.

The size and sophistication of a candidate's staff depend on the resources he or she can raise. In a campaign with extensive resources, staff could include a campaign manager, consultants, a director of research (polling and focus groups), a director of public policy, a media director, a recruiter and supervisor of volunteers, and a fund-raiser. In smaller campaigns for local seats, candidates may have virtually no staff, or may hire part-time consultants to help them with specific tasks. In some cases, candidates for local seats rely heavily on key volunteers with expertise in specific topics.

Because their work is so time-limited, effective campaign organizations are highly focused, work as a close team, and are highly motivated to succeed. While internal differences may emerge in the heat of the contest about strategy, effective campaign organizations quickly resolve them so they can develop a united strategy. Above all, effective campaign organizations believe in their candidates and put everything on the line to try to get them elected.

Developing Campaign Strategy: Strategy Options at the Outset of a Campaign

We have already discussed many elements of campaign strategy. Even before a primary contest begins, and before a final contest or a runoff contest occurs, candidates need to do the following:[29]

- Conduct an analysis of the electoral population in their districts to ascertain what groups and geographic areas are in play.
- Link this analysis to the development of an initial set of positions and campaign promises. They may decide what issues to select and what kinds of positions to take initially with respect to the issues. They may decide what issues to avoid because they believe them to be unimportant or because they work to the advantage of opponents. With respect to some issues, they may decide not to commit themselves to a position or to leave the position relatively vague.
- As they are doing this analysis, they need to examine strengths and weaknesses of likely opponents, both in terms of their electoral support and in terms of their likely or stated positions on issues. Campaigns are competitions, and candidates cannot compete if they fail to analyze opponents' positions.
- Raise funds, recruit volunteers, seek endorsements, and develop a campaign organization.
- Set priorities by deciding what expenditures of time and effort will yield the highest return in terms of issues, geographic portions and populations of the electoral district, campaign advertisements in the media, campaign appearances, and priorities in phone banking and distribution of leaflets. The selection of priorities lies at the heart of campaign strategy; resources must be targeted at activities that will yield results, rather than scattered over many low-yield undertakings.
- Develop a master calendar of events, activities, and expenditures that build toward the final vote—whether the primary or the final or runoff election. Candidates cannot expend most of their resources in the early phase of a campaign because they need to intensify their personal appearances, advertising, and outreach as the campaign nears its culmination—the final vote. Resources have to be rationed in the early and middle phases to allow an upsurge in the final phase. The early and

middle phases must not be neglected, however, because candidates want to build momentum as they go.

- Develop an aggressive absentee ballot campaign so that votes of absentee supporters are counted.

Strategy During the Mid-Phase of a Campaign

Little is set in concrete as the campaign unfolds. Polls and focus groups will show that some issues and positions are not resonating with citizens in the geographic areas or populations that the campaign targets. New issues may arise, as well, from unexpected developments in the community, region, or nation—such as a sharp economic downturn or a crisis in local schools.

Strategy must often be changed to counter tactics of opponents.[30] Campaigns are like chess matches because each side develops strategies to offset or counter its opposition. As campaigns progress, candidates need to do the following:

- Analyze their opponents' strategy. Try to understand how the opponent answered the same questions they addressed in the early phase of their campaigns (see the previous list).
- Ask whether they need to strengthen their outreach and advertising to specific geographic areas or populations in light of their opponents' activities; for example, they may discover through focus groups that opponents are making inroads on groups they had given high priority.
- Ask whether they should concentrate on new groups of voters who they had prematurely written off. Perhaps a focus group will suggest that certain kinds of swing voters are now up for grabs, whether because opponents have failed to try to reach them or have made serious errors in trying to reach them.
- Decide how to change the selection of issues and the positions on issues in response to opponents' selection and positions. Perhaps candidates need to offset or counter opponents' positions on specific issues if they seem to be gathering support from important parts of the electorate.
- Decide whether, when, and where to engage in public debates or forums with opponents. Candidates must decide how many public debates or forums to attend. If they are strong frontrunners and are not skilled debaters, they may want fewer of them—although excessive avoidance of debates or forums can work to the opponents' advantage. Persons who are long shots and good debaters will want more debates and forums to enhance their name recognition.
- Decide on an advertising strategy in the context of opponents' advertising strategy and how the campaign is progressing. There often is no need to advertise in areas that are already supportive of candidates, but advertising is very important if candidates lack name recognition (as compared with opponents), if opponents are aggressively advertising to specific populations that candidates had targeted, or if candidates are running behind in polls. If opponents are hoarding their advertising funds for a last-minute blitz, candidates may want to retain much of their advertising resources to counter that blitz.
- Decide to what extent positive versus negative messages should be included in advertisements and personal statements in the context of opponents' ads and statements. Many candidates suffer electoral damage if they do not quickly counter opponents' negative statements, but negative ads and statements sometimes can backfire.

End-Game Strategy Campaigns gather intensity as candidates approach the final vote. They ask two questions: What last minute strategies have the most potential for persuading key voters to change their minds, and what will make them turn out to vote? In some cases, of course, elections have already been decided by the last two weeks, but others still hang in the balance. Candidates need to do the following:

- Select final issues and positions that will change swing voters' minds.
- Make the case to supporters that they need to turn out.
- Place as many ads as the campaign budget allows in strategic places.
- Mount an assertive get-out-the-vote drive on Election Day.

Conducting Issue-Oriented Campaigns

During the Progressive Era at the start of the 20th century, reformers in the various states placed legislative proposals directly on the ballot, allowing citizens to bypass the state legislature. If supported by a majority of citizens, such propositions become law by referendum.

As policy advocates soon discovered, however, this option was a mixed blessing. If social reformers could get some of their ideas on the ballot, so could conservatives and special interests. When Proposition 13 was enacted in California in 1979, for example, it set off a wave of similar propositions in other states that slashed property taxes so markedly that many social programs had to be cut. Yet policy advocates have successfully supported the enactment of an array of measures of their own, such as ones dedicating revenues from marriage licenses to programs to stop child abuse and proposals to safeguard rights of gay men and lesbians.

Policy advocates must work on two fronts: They initiate propositions, and they battle those that others have initiated that they do not like. To initiate a proposition, they must draft it, campaign to secure enough signatures from registered voters to qualify it for the ballot, and raise funds for advertising and direct-mail efforts. If their proposition seeks to raise taxes, to establish major new programs, or to regulate powerful interests like gun dealers, they can expect considerable opposition from offended interests and conservatives.

Whether they support or oppose a specific proposition, policy advocates must use strategies similar to those used by candidates for office. They have to build a campaign organization that raises sufficient funds for a potent advertising campaign to be mounted. They need to recruit volunteers to distribute leaflets at shopping centers and other community sites, and they must enlist speakers who can make public appearances. They need strong liaison with editorial staff and reporters of newspapers so they get supportive coverage and endorsements of their positions. Because many propositions are on statewide ballots, candidates must decide which geographic areas in the state should be top priority.

Making Issue Campaigns and Electoral Politics Intersect

We noted earlier that electoral politics are sometimes influenced by issue campaigns. When propositions are on the ballot, candidates' positions on these propositions can shape elections' outcomes as well as the popularity of incumbents. When Republican Governor Pete Wilson endorsed Proposition 187 in 1994, which severely restricted the rights of undocumented immigrants, including their right to health care and use of public schools, his popularity plummeted among Latino voters with significant adverse electoral consequences for the Republican Party for more than a decade. Many Republican candidates subsequently lost key elections, allowing Democrats to gain the governorship and both chambers in California. Policy advocates can influence the outcomes of elections, then, by working on propositions—or on issue-oriented campaigns to secure specific legislation—in certain jurisdictions. They can assertively attempt to get politicians to state their positions on these issues in hopes that grassroots support for them will influence the outcome of key issues (see Policy Advocacy Challenge 12.4).

Policy Advocacy Challenge 12.4

Smoking Out the Positions of an Opponent

Gretchen Heidemann, MSW & Doctoral Candidate, School of Social Work, University of Southern California

Once he was selected as his party's nominee for president in 2008, John McCain selected Alaskan Governor Sarah Palin as his running mate. Palin was not, at that time, a well-known public figure. At a press conference announcing her as his choice for running mate, McCain said, "She's not from these parts, and she's not from Washington, but when you get to know her, you're going to be as impressed as I am." Republican supporters, swing voters, and indeed all persons interested in the outcome of the election wanted to find out more about who Sarah Palin was and what she stood for.

It did not take long for voters to learn about Ms. Palin. She presented herself quickly to the public as a self-described "hockey mom" and a "pitbull with lipstick." Within a few short weeks, just some of the things we learned about Sarah Palin were:

- She was a mother of five children, including an infant son who was born with Down syndrome and a 17-year-old unwed daughter who was pregnant.
- She opposed stem-cell research and abortion, but strongly supported the Second Amendment and the right to own a gun, and even promoted and engaged in aerial wolf hunting, a practice described by the Defenders of Wildlife Action as "brutal" and "savagery."
- She considered herself a political outsider and "whistleblower" despite allegations that she misused her power by pressuring public safety officials to fire her ex-brother-in-law.
- She had been a basketball player in high school with the nickname "Barracuda," and had also participated in various beauty pageants in her younger years.
- She spoke out against earmarks and pork-barrel projects, despite having supported, during her campaign for governor, the Gravina Island Bridge—or "Bridge to Nowhere"—a massive $233 million project supported by federal funds.

Most importantly, however, voters saw the selection of Palin for vice president as confusing and possibly hypocritical, given that McCain was lambasting Obama for his lack of experience. Palin had virtually no foreign policy experience, and had only been Alaska's governor for 20 months when he selected her as his running mate. Prior to that, she had served two terms as the mayor of Wasilla, Alaska, a town with a population of less than 10,000.

The public became very curious about Palin's foreign policy experience, especially when she began to tout that experience by making references to Alaska's close proximity to Russia. The media began questioning Palin about her stance on foreign policy, and exposed her lack of knowledge and experience, citing that her first-ever overseas trip was in 2007 to visit the Alaska National Guard Station in Kuwait. When Katie Couric, Chief Anchor of CBS evening news, interviewed Palin in September 2008, she exposed Palin's ignorance of foreign policy. When asked why Alaska's proximity to Russia provided her with foreign policy experience, Palin responded, "As Putin rears his head and comes into the air space of the United States of America, where do they go? It's Alaska.

It's just right over the border. It is from Alaska that we send those out to make sure that an eye is being kept on this very powerful nation, Russia, because they are right there, they are right next to our state." She was also unable to name a single national media publication that she reads.

Katie Couric later reported that she stopped the interview several times to ask Palin whether she realized the interview was being recorded because Palin seemed to be answering questions Couric hadn't even asked. According to Couric, "It didn't seem possible that she would intentionally answer the question that way, knowing people would see it." Couric also said that she gave the Alaskan governor numerous opportunities to come up with a media publication that she reads, and went out of her way to give Palin a "fair shake." The interview resulted in Katie Couric winning a Cronkite Award in the category "Special Achievement for National Impact on the 2008 Campaign."

EXERCISE

This case presents an interesting alternative to mudslinging: getting candidates to reveal their true beliefs by asking well-designed questions. We invite you to watch the interview and then discuss the following questions:

- Was Katie Couric's questioning of Palin fair? Was it effective in exposing the "true" Sarah Palin?
- When policy advocates attack the motivations or character of an opposing candidate, do they act ethically?
- What limits or boundaries should be placed on such negative attacks?
- Is it true that candidates who do not resort to such tactics are usually defeated?

In some cases, issue-oriented organizations, such as the AFL-CIO, gun control organizations, the AARP, the National Association for the Advancement of Colored Persons (NAACP), and the NASW, target key electoral districts several years before specific congressional and presidential contests.[31] Their goal is to build a cadre of members who care deeply about specific issues that are relevant to their groups, including, in the case of unions, raising the minimum wage, improving work-safety policies, and expanding medical insurance to uninsured workers. They develop leaders in their membership, who then hold meetings and forums for other members. In the case of the NAACP, the organization mounts aggressive voter registration projects among African Americans. When the elections near, it identifies the candidates who support its issues and work to help them by giving them resources, running issue-oriented ads, publicizing its endorsements, walking precincts, running phone banks, and distributing leaflets. Indeed, these examples tell us that campaigning begins long before many elections occur.

These tactics are not unique to relatively liberal groups. The Moral Majority, an umbrella term for conservative groups that include many fundamental Protestant churches, as well as other conservative groups, was instrumental in electing scores of conservative candidates from 1980 to the present, by using precisely these kinds of tactics. It relied heavily on clergy in fundamentalist churches to obtain names and addresses of their congregations—and used these lists to target political advertisements and door-to-door campaigning to fundamentalist voters. These tactics were highly effective in helping Republicans gain majorities in one or both houses of Congress and the presidency during much of the 1980s and early 1990s—and then from 2000 to 2006.

The nexus between electoral politics and issue-oriented organizations is unlikely to disappear as the Internet is increasingly used to link voters to larger movements and to political campaigns, as illustrated by two examples that converged in the presidential election of 2004. Howard Dean, a contender for the Democratic nomination for president, used the Internet site Meetup.com to develop supportive groups in hundreds of communities across the nation. These local groups could be part of Dean's larger presidential campaign, yet could shape strategies and issues locally as well. This was a marked departure from usual top-down political advertising that most campaigns had used before this point. Within one year, 190,000 persons joined these local groups.[32] In yet another Internet project, Wes Boyd and Joan Blades formed MoveOn.org in 1998 to use the Internet to prevent Congress from impeaching President Bill Clinton. It created a membership of more than three million persons over several years through "viral marketing," where individuals pass on emails to friends and families to create a larger and larger membership.[33] It became a major force in the 2004 presidential election in marshaling votes for the Democratic presidential contender, John Kerry. Barack Obama's presidential campaign made extensive use of the Internet in 2008 to mobilize voters in ways that supplanted the need for vast numbers of volunteers and paid organizers. His campaign took advantage of YouTube for free advertising through videos from friends or the campaign—with the campaign's YouTube videos watched for 14.5 million hours by viewers equivalent to $47 million in TV advertising.[34] Obama's speeches were widely viewed, such as his speech on race.

Participating in Electoral and Issue-Oriented Campaigns

Policy advocates can assume major roles in political campaigns as well as ballot propositions—and some run for office, as we discuss subsequently. As volunteers, policy advocates can do the following:

- Work inside the campaigns of specific candidates performing myriad tasks, such as organizing and working on phone banks, precinct walking, distributing leaflets, helping with focus groups and data gathering, and helping to prepare policy positions on important issues.
- Work on campaigns for or against specific propositions.
- Work with specific issue-oriented organizations as they build grassroots and membership support for specific issues and as they try to link such support to electoral campaigns.
- Work on voter registration, absentee ballot, developing forums, and get-out-the vote drives (see Policy Advocacy Challenge 12.5).

Policy advocates can also work with a PAC, such as NASW's PAC, which is called PACE. Because nonprofit organizations may lose their tax-exempt status if they engage in partisan politics, many of them have created these spin-off PACs. For example, the NASW formed PACE, its political action arm, in 1976. PACE solicits its funds from members of NASW, who make small annual contributions to PACE with their annual membership fee unless they choose not to or who make contributions any time of the year to national or chapter NASW PACE. One-half of membership fee contributions are used at the national level and one-half are given to state chapters. PACE keeps these funds in a separate account from the funds of NASW and has its own board of directors.

The national unit of NASW PACE endorses candidates for federal offices, and chapter units in each state endorse state and local candidates and collaborate with the national unit on federal elections. PACE currently has 46 chapter PACE committees. NASW PACE also trains and mobilizes NASW members to vote and volunteer for endorsed

Policy Advocacy Challenge 12.5

How Students Can Get Involved in Political Campaigns

Ramon M. Salcido, DSW, Associate Professor, School of Social Work, University of Southern California, and Jolene Swain, MSW, Field Coordinator, University of Southern California

BACKGROUND

The electoral project was conceived by the authors as a school of social work project to heighten awareness of the importance of voting and participating in the 1996 presidential election—but they have repeated the project in succeeding elections. The goal was to organize several activities that would result in students' participating in the election. The time frame for the project was four months. The activities included (1) voter registration, (2) an absentee ballots effort, (3) a forum rally, and (4) a get-out-the-vote drive.

The authors (a policy instructor and a field educator) initially took the lead in forming a planning committee because students did not yet have the experience in organizing for an electoral campaign. Moreover, both authors had worked closely during the summer with both the national and the state NASW PACs. The policy instructor also organized seven policy instructors and the field educator in the school to provide support to the students and to act as a link with the field agencies. A steering committee was organized, consisting of three student organization officers, four student volunteers, and the authors. The committee met once a week to do the planning and coordination.

Once the plan had been developed, the students took charge of implementation. Officers of the student organization, elected by students to represent them in the school's governance, met with the dean, presented the plan, and received approval.

ROLE OF STUDENT ORGANIZATION

The school's student organization became the key in implementing the electoral drive, contacting students and informing them of coming events. On September 10, 1996, the student organization sent a memo to every student, announcing the electoral campaign and giving key dates for voter registration training, the forum rally, and the availability of information kits. Similarly, a memo was sent to interested agencies to inform them of the voter registration drive, to encourage them to support students in the field to initiate voter registration activities, and to invite them to participate in the forum rally.

ACTIVITIES

VOTER REGISTRATION

Several tasks are involved in voter registration activities. The first step was to obtain large numbers of mail-in voter registration forms from the county office of the registrar (election office). The second was to train the members of the steering committee and other students about how to register voters and then to use this knowledge to register other students to vote. Eleven students were trained and promptly registered 32 other students to vote. Moreover, students registered 123 voters at seven field agencies.

ABSENTEE BALLOTS

The next activity was to have students participate in an absentee ballot effort. The faculty person contacted the county election office and obtained information on absentee ballot procedures, and two student members went to the county elections office to be trained on how to do absentee balloting. On September 30, 1996, the student organization sent another letter to each student, giving information on the steps in absentee voting, a request form for an absentee ballot, and a county number to call for information. A total of 420 information letters were sent to all students of the school.

(continued)

Student feedback informed us that the absentee ballot drive allowed many students to vote by mail during midterm. From an informal count by the policy instructors, it is estimated that about 30 percent (129) of the student body voted by absentee ballot.

ORGANIZING A FORUM

A forum was organized to provide information on all of the state ballot measures, including the so-called Civil Rights Initiative (a proposition that proposed to eliminate affirmative action in California), to inform participants of NASW's position and endorsed candidates, and to stress the importance of social workers' being part of the political process.

The forum was publicized in many ways. For example, the dean sent a memo to all students and faculty two weeks before the event. Policy instructors also emphasized the importance of the forum and encouraged students to participate as part of a class assignment. The student body president served as master of ceremonies. Forum speakers included a state Cal-PACE (the political action committee of the California chapter of NASW) person, who spoke about the state initiatives; a representative of a PAC concerned with persons with disabilities, who spoke about the impact of the so-called Civil Rights Initiative on clients; and a Los Angeles city council person (Laura Chick, MSW), who spoke about the importance of voting and getting others to vote. The state NASW Cal-PACE and National PACE provided the forum with a list of NASW-endorsed candidates and information on the ballot initiatives. An attempt was made to be educational and nonpartisan. After the presentations, political district maps were displayed, and students were asked to locate their geographic location and identify their political representatives. Sign-in sheets showed a total of 82 students, 3 clients, 6 faculty, and 9 field instructors.

GET-OUT-THE-VOTE DRIVE

One week before Election Day, the student organization sent letters to students reminding them to vote and asking them if they wanted to participate in any NASW-targeted races. A total of 120 students were personally contacted. About 62 students volunteered to work at NASW-targeted races, as well as in the effort to defeat the proposition that proposed to end affirmative action.

SUGGESTIONS

This kind of campaign project is only one of many possibilities for student participation in political campaigns. Other experiences could include participation in one NASW-targeted race as a school project, voter registration initiatives that include registering clients at field education sites, and students' organizing phone banks in a get-out-the-vote effort on Election Day. Our experience suggests the importance of (1) knowing the dates for voter registration completion and absentee ballots; (2) being familiar with the laws concerning electoral activities in the academy; (3) getting an endorsement from the dean; (4) realizing that students have time constraints; and (5) including in the planning field instructors representing social work training sites.

This case example of student involvement raises a number of interesting questions:

- Should schools of social work involve students in the electoral process?
- Should schools and fieldwork agencies engage in voter registration drives?
- Do policy courses motivate students to become involved in the electoral process?

candidates, funds field organizers in certain prioritized races, and lets members know how elected officials voted on issues tracked by NASW.

NASW PACE endorses candidates on the following criteria:

- Issues that candidates support or oppose
- Viability of the campaign in terms of money raised and name recognition
- Relationship to the social work community
- Leadership positions of candidates if they are incumbents
- Whether they come from an underrepresented group such as a racial minority group

NASW PACE staff interview candidates either in person or on the phone to obtain this information. PACE then determines the kind or kinds of support it will give, which can include a letter of endorsement, a financial contribution, publicity in NASW publications, volunteers, fund-raisers, and photo opportunities.

As we discussed in Chapter One, a recent survey by Shannon Lee and Nancy Humphreys found that 416 social workers have run for political office in recent decades at local, state, and federal levels—and eight persons with MSW degrees held office in the U.S. Congress in 2009.

NASW PACE has identified 150 social workers who hold elected offices at all levels of government, including six in federal positions that include Senators Barbara Mikulski (D-Maryland) and Debbie Stabenow (D-Michigan) and Representatives Susan Davis (D-California), Barbara Lee (D-California), Ciro Rodriguez (D-Texas), and Ed Towns (D-New York).

Deciding to Run for Office

Reasoning that they want to make policy decisions themselves, some policy advocates and social workers run for office (see Policy Advocacy Challenge 12.6).

Policy Advocacy Challenge 12.6

My City Council Campaigns, Past and Future

Victor Manalo, MSW, Ph.D., Associate Professor, School of Social Work, California State University, Los Angeles

It was the case that led me into politics. I had just started working for child protective services when I received Brenda's case. Brenda had just given birth to her sixth child, who had a positive toxicology screen for cocaine, and her five other children were in foster care. After a lot of hard work, Brenda had completed a drug treatment program and moved into a two-bedroom apartment with all six of her children.

Soon thereafter, I read that an initiative was going to be on the ballot that would sharply decrease welfare payments in the state. I knew that Brenda used a large part of her welfare check to pay her rent. I feared that any cuts in her welfare payment would force Brenda and her newly reunited and very fragile family back down the road of substance abuse and child neglect.

I became very angry and I knew that I had to act. I decided to work on the campaign to defeat that initiative. Thankfully, we defeated that initiative, but the political onslaught on our clients—the poor, the undocumented, the oppressed—continued.

After working on political issues since then, I became frustrated with elected officials who had no idea how to address the needs of our clients. In the policy classes that I taught, I tried to convince students that social workers should be proactive, instead of reactive; making the policies, instead of reacting to policies. Well, I finally convinced myself! I knew that, when the time was right, I would run for office.

I discussed my intentions with my wife, friends, and colleagues, all of whom were very supportive of my decision. I did not have much experience in electoral politics. So, I decided to get involved in my city.

(continued)

I started attending community events and city council meetings. I began writing letters to the editor to local newspapers. One editor liked my letters so much that she asked me to write a weekly column. As a result of my networking with city officials, I accepted an appointment to the city's planning commission, dealing with zoning and land use issues within the city.

In my two years on the commission, I have voted on issues ranging from affordable housing for seniors and granting permits to adult day health care centers to upgrading our city parks and improving our commercial district. When I found out that there were three city council seats up in the next election, I knew that I could make a difference.

I called the city clerk to find out how to file to run for city council. After collecting nominating signatures from 25 registered voters in the city and filing papers with the city and with the state's fair political practices commission, I became an official candidate for city council.

It was less than three months until Election Day and I had a lot of work to do. I began by asking for campaign contributions and volunteer time from family, friends, and colleagues by telephone, in person, and by email. I had social work students walking precincts and phone banking. Besides attending community events, talking to voters, and getting endorsements, I was putting up campaign signs late at night, designing and making copies of my campaign flyers, and preparing voter registration lists for volunteers.

I received endorsements from state and local elected officials, as well as from the California chapter of NASW, the California Democratic Party, and the Long Beach Press Telegram. The local Lions Club hosted a candidate forum where I used my public speaking skills to my advantage. We had sent out two strong mailers, and going into Election Day, I felt really positive about my campaign.

On Election Day, I was a nervous wreck. We went to the polling places to make sure my supporters voted; if not, we called to remind them to vote. That evening, my friends went to city hall to get the vote count because I was too stressed out. Unfortunately, when the precinct counts came in, my heart dropped—I knew that I would not have enough votes to win a city council seat.

Looking back upon the campaign, I realized I was not running for one of three open seats against five other candidates, but I was really running for one open seat against four candidates. Two of the seats were being sought by two incumbents (who nearly always get reelected), while the remaining four candidates fought for one seat. The eventual winner of that seat was a Portuguese man who was supported by a very organized and influential Portuguese community and whose family name was very well known. I came in fourth. I learned the importance of knowing your opponents.

Although I was very disappointed, I believe that my campaign was very successful. Losing a campaign the first time out is not unusual and many influential people from the community encouraged me to run again. As a result of my campaign, more people in the community now knew me and I had a strong base of supporters from which to build upon for the next election.

With the next election more than a year away, I began to make preparations. I attended city council meetings, community events, and local club meetings, telling people that I would be running in the next election. I learned more about the community and residents' concerns.

I put together a campaign committee that is responsible for running the campaign, so that I could focus on meeting voters. I raised campaign money early, so that I would have my signs, flyers, and mailers ready to go three months before Election Day. Also, I asked everyone that I know for campaign contributions. People are generous and they want to see you do well, but they will not give you money unless you ask!

Knowing what it takes to run a good campaign, I felt confident in my chances at winning a seat on the city council and using my social work knowledge and skills to bring people together to improve the city for everyone.

REASSESSING MY PRIORITIES

While I was much more prepared for the second election, I lost by a mere 21 votes! Of course, this was a very disappointing loss, especially since I had spent more than one year preparing for the election.

Not only did losing the election force me to reassess my priorities, but the birth of my third child two weeks before the election also gave me great pause. Do I really want to take more time away from my family and my work to prepare for another election, especially when there is no guarantee of success? As an assistant professor, do I want to jeopardize my quest towards getting tenure? The next election was two years later, and, in considering my priorities, I decided to sit it out. I wanted to spend more time with my family and focus on my work.

Nearly five years after my first campaign, and three years since my last campaign, I considered another run for city council, which was nine months away. One major difference for the third election is that there was an open seat. One of the incumbent city council members, who supported me in my last campaign, had just won the Democratic primary election for the state legislature. Were he to win in November, there would be an open seat, and I would have a powerful supporter.

I spent the next few months consulting with my family and my supporters to assess the viability of another campaign.

ON THE CAMPAIGN … AGAIN

In November 2006, my city councilman won his election to the state legislature, so I ran for the Artesia City Council yet a third time. Having experienced two losing campaigns, I knew I had to work hard! In March 2007, I defeated my opponent with 63 percent of the vote!

As a city councilmember, my priority is to serve my constituents. Over the past two years, I have addressed graffiti removal from buildings and trash removal from empty lots, as well as water main leaks and dangerous crosswalks. I collaborated with our local public schools on Walk to School Week, in which we encouraged families to walk to school to promote health and environmental awareness. In developing our downtown revitalization plans, I made sure that both local business owners and residents participated in the process. In addition, I supervised two social work interns to work directly with our youth and our seniors.

As a city councilmember, I am also a policy maker and fiscal manager. In January 2009, we found ourselves in the midst of an economic recession that drastically reduced our city's revenue. Facing a $1.3 million deficit, my colleagues and I have had to make difficult budget cuts and search for ways to increase our revenue. I have had to develop my budgeting and administrative skills and gain an understanding of the complexities of local government funding in California.

In November 2009, I faced re-election to a four-year term. While I am much more comfortable in front of my students in the classroom, I look forward to meeting the challenges that lay ahead and to continuing to serve the people of Artesia to the best of my abilities. I won this election by a one-sided vote and will do my best to create a better society. See photographs of Professor Victor Manalo in Artesia by going to his home page at www.victormanalo.com.

QUESTIONS TO PONDER ABOUT VICTOR MANALO'S ELECTORAL SUCCESS

- How does he illustrate the importance of persistence?
- What unique skills and perspectives does he, as a social worker, bring to the campaign process, as well as policy making once elected?
- How does he illustrate that candidates for office often gain experience first in local issues and memberships?

Selecting Other Public-Service Positions

Many social workers cannot or do not wish to run for office. Many other kinds of public-service trajectories are possible, however, including high-level administrative positions, civil service positions, and consultative positions (see Policy Advocacy Challenge 12.7).

While many social workers develop outstanding careers "in the trenches" in child welfare, mental health, health, and other organizations, some venture into public-service realms in which they interact with legislators, high-level civil servants, and other policy makers. Here are two examples of social workers who branched into public service.

BIO-SKETCH: CAROL TURNER, A.M., EDUCATION ADVOCATE, OFFICE OF THE MAYOR, PORTLAND, OR

You can be a good clinician and still decide to go into public service—as my career illustrates. I received training at the University of Chicago in psychiatric social work, graduating in 1965. My husband and I moved to Portland, Oregon, where I held clinical positions with nonprofit agencies over several decades, in addition to having a small private practice. I was not particularly "political," identifying myself professionally as a clinician.

I was very concerned about public education, however. The Portland School District, which my two children attended, was sorely in need of new leadership and ideas. Somebody asked me one day if I wanted to run for an opening on the school board—something I had not considered before. After making inquiries and deciding I might actually win, I entered a heated race in 1985—and, to my amazement, won the seat.

Since that point, my career has completely changed. I served on the Portland School Board for 12 years where I took part in scores of decisions that shaped policies of the district. For example, I dealt with significant school reform; curriculum development; policies related to prevention of alcohol and drug use by students and increasing student, family, and community assets; and the impact of gang violence and AIDS on a school district. As chair of the board for three terms, I was intimately involved with making major budget decisions and, the most important work of such boards, hiring a new superintendent. I also served as the president of the statewide association of school board members, in which I worked primarily on funding issues.

In 1997, I was offered a position with the Oregon Department of Human Services and worked in a consultative role with local agencies working on service integration and community development.

I was invited by the Portland mayor in 1998 to join her staff to give her advice on educational matters. My focus in my five years in this post was on developing ways that the city can help local school districts be successful in such arenas as stabilizing school funding, increasing volunteerism in schools, expanding after-school programs, and leading a community reading initiative and further developing early childhood programs.

I have found my public service career to be highly fulfilling. I have brought my social work experience and perspectives to the table on many occasions, helping to develop policies and programs that will help youth obtain an array of services that might otherwise not be available to them. Also, such clinical skills as listening carefully and understanding the complexities of human motivation have definitely come in handy in dealing with the pressures from various political constituencies.

So you do not have to be a macro student to get into public service or to run for office. You just have to have a willingness to take some chances and expand your horizons!

I am now an independent consultant to not-for-profit organizations, helping them to develop and implement strategic plans and programs, as well as consulting with schools.

BIO-SKETCH: MICHELLE M. WILSON, MSW, PROGRAM ANALYST, NATIONAL INSTITUTE FOR OCCUPATIONAL SAFETY AND HEALTH, CENTERS FOR DISEASE CONTROL AND PREVENTION

Since the beginning of my career in social work, I have always had a passion and respect for those in macro practice. Early on, I realized that social workers in macro practice play a vital role in the success and survival of any social policy or program. As macro practitioners, we are the advocates, evaluators, organizers, planners, researchers, and change agents for programs that affect people's everyday lives. We bring unique perspectives to the table. We look at things from a systems perspective, advocating and creating change at the macro, mezzo, and micro levels of society.

As I was finishing the second year of my MSW curriculum, I decided to apply for the Presidential Management Intern Program. It was an easy decision, but I had to compete with hundreds of other applicants for a few slots. But I knew that I brought to the interviews unique perspectives stemming from my social work education and internships. My second-year field placement was at the Los Angeles County Department of Mental Health, where I primarily focused on program planning and evaluation and policy research surrounding the issue of Institutes for Mental Disease. During my second year of graduate school, I also had the opportunity to work for the United Way of Greater Los Angeles. During this time, I conducted community-based research, looking at the overall development of children in Los Angeles under the age of six, which has now become a major social issue for Los Angeles County. My drive and passion for becoming a macro practitioner has also been inspired by past professors Rino Patti, Jacquelyn McCroskey, Vince Ornelas, and colleagues Marge Nichols and Jenny Gross, who in their own ways have opened my eyes to the need for macro practitioners and have encouraged me to become a "squeaky wheel" within the public sector.

When I learned that I was successful in receiving a presidential internship, I chose a two-year internship at the Centers for Disease Control and Prevention (CDC), where I could couple my passion for macro practice and public health. (I had received a B.S. in Applied Behavioral Science and Epidemiology at University of California, Davis.) A job with the CDC would give me, I decided, the means to become a change agent at the federal level, affecting social policies and programs from the top down. Within my job in the director's office at the National Institute for Occupational Safety and Health (NIOSH), I was involved in research analysis, project planning, strategic planning, performance measurement, policy formulation and analysis, and program evaluation. I then became a public health analyst in the office of the director of the CDC where I now work.

Why Social Policy Often Hinges on Elections

EPA 2.1.9a

All elections have import for social policy because they determine what kinds of people with what values will enact social policies relevant to vulnerable people. Held every two years, congressional elections are particularly important because the federal government has resources and powers far greater than state and local governments. These congressional elections shape social policy in the United States profoundly, even when they are "off-elections" not coupled with the once-per-four-years presidential elections (see Policy Advocacy Challenge 12.8).

Policy
Advocacy
Challenge 12.8

Social
Workers and
Policy Advo-
cacy in the
Obama Era

Gretchen
Heidemann,
MSW &
Doctoral
Candidate,
University of
Southern
California,
School of Social
Work

When Barack Obama was elected as the 44th president of the United States in November 2008, the NASW began to formulate a plan of action for how to engage the 600,000 professional social workers across the country in working with the president and Congress to "chart a new course of action for our nation." In December 2008, just a month before Obama's inauguration, NASW published a document "Turning Priorities into Action: How the Social Work Profession Will Help," which can be found at **www.socialworkers .org/advocacy/transition.asp**. The publication outlines NASW's platform in eight core areas: the economy, health care, education, Social Security, war, international peace building, community building, and equality for all. Specifically, the document offers up the services, knowledge, expertise, and effort of NASW's massive membership base to advance an agenda shared by the president. As the document states, "We wanted to provide this initial overview of critical areas where social workers can assist you with accomplishing your stated agenda" (p. 3). Thus, NASW delivered the document to the president in the hope of putting social workers at the forefront of national policy reforms.

Read NASW's "Turning Priorities Into Action" document and discuss the following questions:

- What are some of the ways in which social workers have been at the cutting edge of political and social reform in past eras?
- Since Obama took office in January 2009, can you think of any ways in which social workers have been directly involved in the president's or Congress' reform efforts in any of the eight core areas? If not, how can social workers get more involved?
- Drawing upon what have learned in previous chapters, what other steps should NASW, its chapters, and its members take to advance the agenda outlined in this document?
- Had Barack Obama lost the election, and John McCain instead won, how different do you think NASW's platform and this document would have been? Would it take on a less friendly tone? What strategies might NASW have used under such a circumstance?
- How does this document and the efforts of NASW to work with President Obama illustrate why ballot-based advocacy is so important?

Conduct an Internet search for NASW to find statements regarding NASW's support for President Obama's re-election campaign in 2012.

- What policy outcomes are likely under the following scenarios in the presidential and congressional elections of 2012: (1) Republicans win the presidency and take control of both chambers of Congress, (2) Democrats win the presidency and take control of both chambers of Congress, (3) one party wins the presidency and one chamber of Congress, while the other party wins the other chamber of Congress?

What You Can Now Do

Chapter Summary

We have completed our discussion of the policy-enacting task (Task 6) of the policy practice and policy advocacy framework in Figure 3.1. You are now equipped to do the following:

- Assess candidates' odds of winning seats by analyzing their districts, their name recognition, and other factors, while realizing that many electoral contests are highly unpredictable.
- Identify an array of power resources used by candidates to influence voters' views and actions.

- Understand the importance of resources for campaigns, while realizing that resources, alone do not guarantee victory.
- Be able to discuss an array of campaign strategies that arise at the outset, mid-phase, and end-games of campaigns.
- Work in issue-oriented campaigns, such as ones that seek passage of a proposition on the ballot.
- Understand how issue-oriented campaigns and electoral politics often intersect.
- Be able to participate in various roles as policy advocates during electoral campaigns and issue campaigns.
- Work with NASW's PACE.
- Consider whether to run for office at some future time.
- Understand different public-policy career trajectories.
- Identify close pending elections in which the involvement of policy advocates is particularly needed, in local, state, or federal jurisdictions.

We are now ready to examine in the next two chapters what happens after policies are enacted, when policy advocates participate in policy implementation and assessment.

Competency Notes

EPA 2.1.1a **Advocate for client access to the services of social work** (p. 418): Social workers pressure high-level staff to issue regulations that preclude discrimination against vulnerable populations.

EPA 2.1.9a **Continuously discover, appraise, and attend to changing locales, populations, scientific and technological developments, and emerging societal trends to provide relevant services** (p. 447): Social workers can refer to an NASW document on "Turning Priorities into Action," published before Obama's inauguration.

Endnotes

1. Bob Benenson, "Blue State Special," *Congressional Quarterly Weekly* (August 14, 2006): 2224–2241.
2. Ibid., p. 2226.
3. Adam Nagourney, "In House Races, More G.O.P. Seats Are Seen At Risk," *New York Times* (October 7, 2006): 1.
4. Robert E. DiClerico, *Political Parties, Campaigns, and Elections* (Englewood Cliffs, NJ: Prentice-Hall, 2000), pp. 191–250.
5. Bruce Jansson, *The Sixteen Trillion Dollar Mistake: How the U.S. Bungled Its National Priorities from the New Deal to the Present* (New York: Columbia University Press, 2001), pp. 295–299.
6. Darrell West and Burdett Loomis, *The Sound of Money: How Political Interests Get What They Want* (New York: W. W. Norton, 1998); and Jeffrey Birnbaum, *The Money Men* (New York: Crown, 2000), pp. 3–48. For discussion of campaign finance at the state level, see Joel Thompson and Gary Moncrief, *Campaign Finance in State Legislative Elections* (Washington, DC: Congressional Quarterly, Inc., 1998.)
7. Anne Bedlington, "The Realtors' Political Action Committee: Covering All Contingencies," In Biersack, Herrnson, and Wilcox, *After the Revolution*, pp. 170–183.
8. Gary Jacobson, *The Politics of Congressional Elections* (New York: Longman, 1997), pp. 1–51.
9. Jacobson, *The Politics of Congressional Elections*.
10. Thompson and Moncrief, *Campaign Finance*, pp. 99–114.
11. Beaudry and Schaeffer, *Local and State Elections*, pp. 18–37.

12. Jacobson, *The Politics of Congressional Elections*; Beaudry and Schaeffer, *Local and State Elections*, pp. 20–21.
13. Ibid., pp. 20–22.
14. Bruce Newman, *The Mass Marketing of Politics: Democracy in an Age of Manufactured Images* (Thousand Oaks, CA: Sage Publications, 1999), pp. 71–86; and Karen Johnson-Cartee and Gary Copeland, *Inside Political Campaigns* (Westport, CT: Praeger, 1997), pp. 149–184.
15. Public debates assume greater importance as candidates run for "higher" offices in mayoral, congressional, and presidential contests.
16. See Jacobson, *The Politics of Congressional Elections*.
17. Richard Scher, *The Modern Political Campaign* (Armonk, NY: M. E. Sharpe, 1997), pp. 88–111.
18. Kim Kahn and Patrick Kenney, "How Negative Campaigning Enhances Knowledge of Senate Elections," in James Thurber, Candice Nelson, and David Dulio, *Crowded Airwaves* (Washington, DC: Brookings Institution, 2000), pp. 65–95; and Kathleen Hall Jamieson, Paul Waldman, and Susan Sherr, "Eliminate the Negative? Categories of Analysis for Political Advertisement," in Thurber et. al., *Crowded Airwaves*, pp. 44–64.
19. Frances Fox Piven and Richard Cloward, *Why Americans Don't Vote and Why Politicians Want It That Way* (Boston, MA: Beacon Press, 2000).
20. Beaudry and Schaeffer, *Local and State Elections*, pp. 13, 102–103, 136–138, 169.
21. Biersack, Herrnson, and Wilcox, *After the Revolution*, pp. 1–17.
22. Kim Kahn and Patrick Kenney, *The Spectacle of U.S. Senate Elections* (Princeton, NJ: Princeton University Press, 1999), pp. 3–29.
23. Gary Moncrief, "Candidate Spending in State Legislative Races," in Thompson and Moncrief, *Campaign Finance,* pp. 37–58.
24. William Cassie and David Breaux, "Expenditures and Election Results," in Thompson and Moncrief, *Campaign Finance,* pp. 99–114.
25. Birnbaum, *The Money Men,* pp. 225–230.
26. David Breaux and Anthony Gierzynski, "Candidate Revenues and Expenditures in State Legislative Primaries," in Thompson and Moncrief, *Campaign Finance,* pp. 80–114.
27. Beaudry and Schaeffer, *Local and State Elections,* pp. 187–205.
28. Ed Rollins, *Bare Knuckles and Back Rooms* (New York: Broadway Books, 1996), pp. 216, 264.
29. Beaudry and Schaeffer, *Local and State Elections,* pp. 2–205.
30. Kahn and Kenney, *The Spectacle of U.S. Senate Elections*.
31. Robin Gerber, "Building to Win, Building to Last: AFL-CIO COPE Takes on the Republican Congress," in Biersack, Herrnson, and Wilcox, *After the Revolution,* pp. 77–93.
32. Allison H. Fine, *Momentum: Igniting Social Change in the Connected Age* (San Francisco, CA: Jossey-Bass, 2006), pp. 150–160.
33. Ibid, p. 46.
34. Clair Cain Miller, "How Obama's Internet Campaign Changed Politics," *New York Times* (November 7, 2008).

Suggested Readings

Campaigns

Karen S. Johnson-Cartee and Gary A. Copeland, *Inside Political Campaigns* (London: Praeger, 1997).

Richard A. Scher, *The Modern Political Campaign* (Armonk, NY: M. E. Sharpe, 1997).

Political Parties

Robert E. DiClerico, *Political Parties, Campaigns, and Elections* (Upper Saddle River, NJ: Prentice-Hall, 2000).

William J. O'Keefe, *Parties, Politics, and Public Policy in America, 7th ed.* (Washington, DC: Congressional Quarterly Press, 1994).

Political Consultants

James Thurber and Candice Nelson, eds., *Campaign Warriors: the Role of Consultants in Elections* (Washington, DC: Brookings Institution Press, 2000).

Campaign Finance

Joel A. Thompson and Gary F. Moncrief, *Campaign Finance in State Legislative Elections* (Washington, DC: Congressional Quarterly Inc., 1998).

Campaign Advertising

James Thurber, Candice Nelson, and David Dulio, eds., *Crowded Airways: Campaign Advertising in Elections* (Washington, DC: Brookings Institution, 2000).

Connections Between Issue and Electoral Politics

Hedrick Smith, *The Power Game: How Washington Works* (New York: Ballantine Books, 1996).

Megan Twohey, "Gunfights at the State Corrals," *National Journal* (2000), pp. 2376–2377.

Political Action Committees

Robert Biersack, Paul Herrnson, and Clyde Wilcox, *After the Revolution: PACs, Lobbies, and the Republican Congress* (Boston, MA: Allyn and Bacon, 1999).

Political Strategy

Gary Jacobson, *The Politics of Congressional Elections* (New York: Longman, 1997).

Kim Kahn and Patrick Kenney, *The Spectacle of U.S. Senate Campaigns* (Princeton, NJ: Princeton University Press, 1999).

Voting Behavior

Frances Fox Piven and Richard Cloward, *Why Americans Don't Vote and Why Politicians Want It That Way* (Boston, MA: Beacon Press, 2000).

Marketing in Politics

Bruce Newman, *The Mass Marketing of Politics* (London: Sage Publications, 1999).

PART 6

Troubleshooting and Assessing Policies

Having enacted policies, policy advocates must now turn to the implementation of enacted policies. This is a critically important part of policy advocacy because many meritorious policies are inadequately implemented. In **Chapter Thirteen**, we discuss policy advocacy strategies during implementation, which we call troubleshooting, Task 7 in the policy practice and policy advocacy framework. In **Chapter Fourteen**, we discuss policy assessment, because policy advocates must work to see if specific implemented policies are achieving successful outcomes—Task 8 in the policy practice and policy advocacy framework. Only as we assess policies as they are implemented can we find evidence-based ones that can be used to promote policy reforms.

Troubleshooting the Implementation of Policies in Task 7

Policy Predicament

Policies become effective *only* as they are implemented. In this chapter, we provide a case example of policy implementation. Policy Advocacy Challenge 13.7 focuses both on implementation *within* specific organizations and between organizations. It discusses how the Affordable Care Act (ACA) of 2010 will be implemented once it becomes mostly operative in 2014. This chapter discusses the policy-implementing task (Task 7) in the policy practice and policy advocacy framework in Figure 3.1. Someone who says that a policy exists only on paper suggests that the enacted policy has little effect on the implementers, for example, the direct-service staff of a social agency. When people say that direct-service staff members only halfheartedly implement a policy, they suggest that staff members honor it only marginally. As these examples suggest, implementation is vital to policymaking; without it, official policies are meaningless.

LEARNING OUTCOMES

This chapter provides a framework for understanding policy implementation, including alternative strategies that policy advocates can use to improve the implementation of policies. We discuss the following:

1. The importance of implementation to policy practice and policy advocacy
2. A systems approach to implementation
3. The importance of interorganizational processes to implementation
4. How implementation is often powerfully shaped by contextual factors
5. How some innovations are more difficult to implement or have a bleaker prognosis than others
6. How policy advocates can troubleshoot implementation to identify shortcomings
7. How policy advocates have many options for improving the implementation of innovations
8. How policy advocates sometimes sabotage specific policies
9. How policy advocates must draw on a range of skills to improve implementation

A Framework for Implementing Policy in Task 7

We can conceptualize policy implementation by means of a systems diagram that comprises (1) the context of implementation, (2) policy innovations, (3) oversight organizations and staff, (4) primary implementing organizations, (5) implementing processes within specific agencies, (6) interorganizational processes, (7) external pressures on implementers, and (8) the evaluation of policy outcomes (see Figure 13.1). This systems framework is useful because it enables policy advocates to track a policy's implementation from its enactment to its final outcome and to place it in its political, economic, and legal contexts throughout its implementation. It enables them to identify and analyze the action system that is set in operation once a policy innovation is enacted. It enables them to troubleshoot when the implementation process is flawed—and determine the kind of reforms required to secure more effective implementation.

EPA 2.1.7a

The implementing system in Figure 13.1 helps us analyze the implementation of specific innovations or policies in relatively simple situations wherein a single agency takes

FIGURE 13.1 Implementation Action System

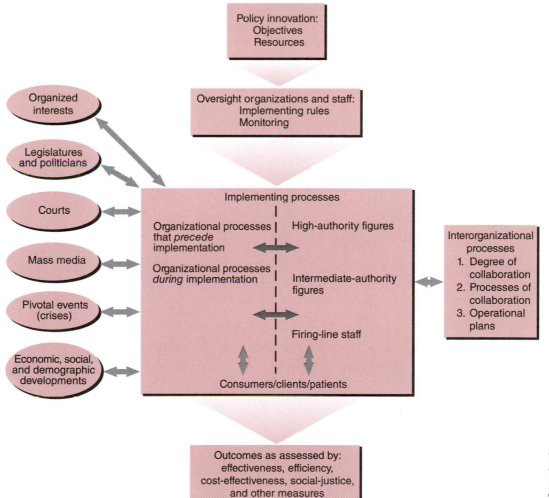

© Cengage Learning

the lead. In the case of child welfare policies or hospital-based health policies, specific child welfare agencies or hospitals become the lead or primary agency that implements specific innovations or policies. While they might collaborate with other agencies, as depicted in Figure 13.1, they are the lead agencies.

In situations involving more complex implementation, such as implementation of the ACA when it becomes mostly operative in 2014, multiple agencies may be lead agencies for portions of it, including federal, state, and local agencies. Contextual political, economic, and many other factors intrude—such as the president's ideology, partisan conflict, budget resources, and conflict between officials in different levels of government over who should take the prime responsibility for specific tasks at a given point in time. Some public officials and interest groups attempt to block implementation of specific pieces of legislation as illustrated by Republicans' pledge to prevent full implementation of the ACA.

We will use Figure 13.1 to orient our discussion through most of this chapter.

Considerable information can be obtained about the implementation of some social programs from the Web and from think tanks such as the Center on Budget and Policy Priorities (see Policy Advocacy Challenge 13.1).

The Context of Implementation

The context of implementation can powerfully shape how specific policies are implemented. (See the various factors on the left side of Figure 13.1.) Implementation never occurs in a vacuum.

The implementation of many policies is closely linked to ideology and partisan politics. Remember that heads of governmental agencies are political appointees who

Policy Advocacy Challenge 13.1 Using the Web to Learn about Troubleshooting: The Watchdogs—Investigative Agencies and Think Tanks Stephanie Davis, Research Librarian, University of Southern California, Irvine	Once a policy is implemented, the effect of the policy needs to be assessed. There are several websites where you can find evaluations, reports, studies, editorials, and other information on the impact of policies. Governmental agencies, community groups, think tanks, and nonprofit organizations all fulfill this purpose. **RESOURCES:** • Government Accountability Office (GAO): **www.gao.gov** • RAND Corporation: **www.rand.org** • Center on Budget and Policy Priorities: **www.cbpp.org** • National Institute for Research Advancement (NIRA): World Directory of Think Tanks: **www.nira.or.jp/past/ice/nwdtt/2005/index.html** **EXERCISE** Visit the GAO and RAND websites to become familiar with the mission and the political perspective of each organization. Next, visit the NIRA's World Directory of Think Tanks, and compare and contrast at least three other think tanks listed in the directory, including international think tanks.

usually reflect the viewpoints of the heads of government who appointed them. On such issues as substance abuse, family planning, health care, welfare, homelessness, juvenile delinquency, and Social Security, real differences exist between leaders of the two major parties—differences that are reflected in their appointments to agencies that administer policies in these areas. We have noted how many high officials in the administration of George W. Bush brought their free-market ideology into play as they implemented programs in New Orleans before, during, and after Hurricane Katrina. Republican Mitt Romney and President Barack Obama presented different views in the presidential contest of 2012 about the role of government with Romney minimizing its authority as compared to Obama.

We should not forget the role of courts, which frequently make rulings that influence the implementation of specific policies. Indeed, an entire field of administrative law exists that contains rulings on administrative procedures, rights of recipients, policies concerning commitments, and interpretation of statutes. Many Republican Attorney Generals in specific states sought to block implementation of the ACA by challenging the constitutionality of portions of the legislation in the U.S. Supreme Court, which delivered a ruling that was mostly favorable to the ACA in 2012.

When a policy innovation is enacted, powerful contextual factors assist—or impede—its implementation. Take, for example, the Adoption Assistance and Child Welfare Act of 1980, which proposed a major overhaul of the child welfare system. Before its enactment, many people were alarmed by the dramatic increase in the number of children placed in foster care because of their parents' alleged abusive behavior or neglect of basic needs. (The number of children in foster care had risen from 177,000 in 1961 to more than 500,000 in 1979.) The framers of the act wanted to dramatically reduce the number of children in foster care by inducing local child welfare departments either to reunite children with their natural parents or to place them with adoptive families.[1] To secure this change, they did the following:

- Required child welfare departments to provide additional funds to the child welfare system for hiring social service staff to give services to natural families
- Required each state to have a tracking system to monitor each child's progress so that no children became lost in the foster care or institutional system
- Required each state to have external reviewing bodies (either the courts or administrative bodies) assess each child's progress
- Mandated a case review after a child had been in foster care for 6 months and again at 12 months to make sure that caseworkers had planned permanent arrangements, either by reuniting children with natural families or by placing children with adoptive parents
- Mandated a formal review at 18 months to ensure that the permanency plan had been implemented, meaning that the child had been either returned to the natural parents or adopted
- Increased subsidies for adoptive parents, hoping that many African American and Latino parents would decide to adopt minority children, who, along with teenagers, had proved most difficult to place with adoptive parents

The act seemed an ingenious solution to a vexing problem. As child welfare authorities were soon to learn, however, this policy innovation (actually a set of innovations) would prove not to be a panacea. Indeed, by the late 1990s, foster care caseloads approached levels that had existed in 1980 before the legislation had been passed.

The problem resided partly in contextual factors that, singly and in tandem, frustrated the work of child welfare departments. *Negative factors* in the over three decades after the enactment of the 1980 legislation included the following:

- Top administrators of child welfare in state and county positions were so preoccupied with responding to child-abuse and child-neglect cases that they lacked time to give intensive services to children or natural families.
- Rigid hierarchies in social services precluded top officials' communication with low-level staff.
- In light of allegations that many children had been harmed when prematurely returned to their natural parents, many high-level administrators emphasized child removal, rather than efforts to improve the parenting skills of natural parents.
- The unions representing direct-service and clerical staff emphasized pay, fringe benefits, and workloads, rather than service-related issues.
- Many legislators did not believe that powerful constituents supported major improvements in child welfare programs.
- State legislatures and county boards of supervisors did not fund child welfare services sufficiently to allow caseloads to be reduced, because of local tax revolts and the absence of political or community constituencies concerned about child welfare.
- Institutions that received funds for children who stayed with them had economic incentives not to return children to their natural families or to place them with adoptive families.
- Because of declassification, in which many local and state governments removed professional training requirements from specific jobs, many supervisors and direct-service staff in child welfare departments lacked training in social work. Lacking treatment skills and concepts, they could not easily perform the complex tasks required by the new legislation.
- Many natural parents viewed the child welfare staff and juvenile court as adversaries that primarily wanted to take their children from them. Because direct-service staff were so burdened with child removal and investigation, they had scant interaction with natural parents. (An increasing number of natural parents obtained attorneys.)
- Many parents neglected their children because they lacked sufficient financial resources—a problem that worsened with the growing economic inequality in the United States in the 1980s and 1990s. Thus, many children were insufficiently fed and clothed. Moreover, poverty contributed to some abusive behavior by exacerbating intra-familial tension. Yet no system existed in child welfare agencies for providing job training or employment referral for parents.
- Innovative services, such as residential centers where troubled families can reside while receiving counseling, did not exist in most localities.
- Child welfare agencies often had few collaborative relations with schools, job-training agencies, or health services, so they could not develop innovative partnerships that might allow some natural families to surmount their economic difficulties.
- An epidemic of infants who were born drug-addicted occurred in the 1990s, leading to an infusion of hundreds of thousands of infants into the child welfare system. (Addicted newborns were often automatically placed in foster care soon after birth.)
- As child welfare agencies did reunite many children with their natural families, some of them were again abused or neglected, leading to widespread popular and political opposition to reunification. (Indeed, by the late 1990s, the pendulum had swung back to the extensive use of foster care!)

- While the welfare reforms enacted in 1996 were in their infancy in the late 1990s, some critics feared that they would exacerbate poverty among single-headed households as mothers were forced to take low-wage jobs, thus creating even more neglect and child abuse.
- Large numbers of adoptive parents for minority children, teenage children, and children with physical and mental problems did not emerge, even with adoption subsidies.

Of course, these negative contextual factors were somewhat offset by *positive ones*. Indeed, we can guess that, had the Adoption Assistance and Child Welfare Act of 1980 not been passed, far greater numbers of children would have entered and remained in foster care. *Positive factors* included the following:

- Because rapid increases in foster care became extraordinarily costly to local and state governments, they wanted to make the system more efficient.
- Subjected to litigation and adverse publicity stemming from scandals, such as ill-advised placement decisions and poor foster care, many officials and staff in child welfare departments wanted to reform their services.
- Finding it difficult to recruit foster care parents or adoptive parents, particularly for handicapped, ethnic, and adolescent children, many state and local officials were eager to cooperate with legislation to decrease the numbers of children in foster care and to promote adoptions.
- Many juvenile-court justices wanted to assume a more active role in reviewing cases and promoting permanent arrangements.
- Attorneys had increasingly publicized and defended natural families' rights to due process in court proceedings. This development made juvenile courts and child welfare staff less inclined to remove children quickly from their natural families.
- African American and Latino communities had developed considerable interest in same-race adoptions, rather than transracial adoptions, thus enlarging the pool of adoptive parents in ethnic communities.
- By the late 1990s, many local child welfare agencies had developed partnerships with an array of local agencies—and had even begun to subcontract with them to help natural families remain intact.

The Adoption Assistance and Child Welfare Act illustrates that major policy innovations are rarely panaceas for complicated problems like child abuse and child neglect. They must battle an array of contextual factors that exacerbate the problems they seek to solve. If positive contextual factors outweigh negative ones—and if negative ones do not gather momentum as time passes—the prognosis for implementation improves.

As shown in Figure 13.1, many kinds of contextual factors may affect implementation. In the case of public policies, legislatures and politicians watch implementers carefully, sometimes holding oversight hearings when they want to examine problems that have come to their attention. Litigation is sometimes initiated to question specific decisions by implementers or to question provisions in legislation. The mass media sometimes cover facets of implementation, either through positive stories that discuss successes or through negative stories that highlight failures. Crises and pivotal events sometimes shape the course of implementation, such as wrongdoing by implementers or incorrect decisions that adversely affect the lives of clients. (Numerous stories in the mass media about children being reunited with natural families only to be abused or neglected again powerfully undermined the basic premise of the Adoption Assistance and Child Welfare

Act that abused and neglected children should generally be returned to their natural families.) Economic, social, and demographic developments also influence implementation, as the problem of addicted babies mentioned earlier suggests with respect to the 1980 legislation.

As these factors pressure implementers, so also do organized interests, such as unions, professional associations, and interest groups. As the welfare reforms of 1996 were implemented, for example, governors and their directors of welfare as organized into the American Public Welfare Association assumed powerful roles. Organized interests will support or oppose specific changes in the federal legislation on the basis of their own experiences with its implementation. Leaders of professional groups such as the National Association of Social Workers (NASW) will seek to soften implementation so safeguards and exemptions are provided for women on welfare who cannot find work or who can find only such work that does not meet their family's survival needs (see Policy Advocacy Challenge 13.2).

EPA 2.1.9a

Policy Advocacy Challenge 13.2

How Has the Context Shaped the Rebuilding of New Orleans after Hurricane Katrina?

Bruce Jansson, Ph.D.

When Hurricane Katrina slammed New Orleans in August 2005, New Orleans and the state of Louisiana had many traditions in place that would both facilitate and hinder the rebuilding of the city. On the positive side of the ledger, many persons who lived in New Orleans loved their city with its culinary and jazz traditions, its longstanding family networks, its rich community life, and its national reputation that had attracted millions of visitors over many decades. On the negative side of the ledger, the city was among the most segregated in the United States, with extraordinary rates of poverty, disease, illiteracy, and crime. Its public systems of education and health were not only underfunded but also poorly rated by experts in these fields and in national rankings. Both the city and the state had traditions of political corruption, even if considerable progress had been made against them. New Orleans's city council was mostly a nonproductive group that followed the mayor's lead. Nor had Governor Blanco and the state legislature been proactive in addressing New Orleans's major social and economic problems. New Orleans also had a deteriorating economy—actually losing a significant part of its population during the several decades preceding Hurricane Katrina.

Nor were the citizens of New Orleans united. Some relatively affluent and Caucasian persons were happy that the hurricane had required huge numbers of low-income African Americans to leave the city—and some of them hoped they would not return. These persons were often not supportive of the development of low-income housing in their communities for low-income persons whose residences had been destroyed. The power base of the low-income African American community was greatly depleted by the forced evacuation of many of them to other cities and towns, making it more difficult for them to influence the plans that the residents of different parishes were developing in the fall of 2006.

The rebuilding of New Orleans would take place, as well, in a national context. On the positive side of the ledger, the enormity of the disaster—much like the terrorist attack on Twin Towers in 2001—triggered national sympathy for the citizens of New Orleans. This sympathy, in turn, generated great pressure on members of Congress and the president to enact scores of pieces of legislation to give assistance to New Orleans and other jurisdictions in the Gulf Coast region. The initial tepid response of the Bush administration to the disaster, moreover, created such outrage that the president knew that he would encounter political trouble if he did not become proactive and did not commit major resources to the relief and rebuilding efforts. On the negative side of the ledger, President Bush and his advisors were inclined to rely on private markets to solve the city's problems. The president opposed creation of a commission or authority that would oversee the city's rebuilding. He faced a huge budget deficit even before the hurricane devastated New Orleans—not to mention his commitments to wars in Iraq and Afghanistan.

The national context began to shift, however, when George Bush left office. In February 2008, when he was campaigning for president, Barack Obama spoke at Tulane University and addressed the issues of rebuilding the areas destroyed by Hurricane Katrina. For his remarks, go to **http://blog.nola.com/tpvideo/2008/02/barack_obama_speaks_at_tulane.html** (accessed July 31, 2009).

Undertaking to make the rebuilding of New Orleans "a priority of my presidency," he made the following promises in that speech:

1. To finish building a system of levees that can withstand a 100-year storm by 2011, with the goal of expanding that protection to defend against a Category 5 storm.
2. To restore the natural barriers—the wetlands, marshes, and barrier islands, which can take the first blows and protect the people of the Gulf Coast.
3. To guarantee that the director of FEMA (Federal Emergency Management Agency) will report directly to the president, and will have the highest qualifications in emergency management; and that he or she will be insulated from politics by giving the office a fixed term, as for the director of the Federal Reserve.
4. To order the FEMA director to work with emergency management officials in all 50 states to create a National Response Plan.
5. To make sure that rebuilding efforts benefit the local economy by providing tax incentives to businesses that choose to set up shop in the areas hit hardest.
6. To ensure that every displaced resident can return to a home by working with Louisiana to make the Road Home program more efficient, approving every application for Road Home assistance within two months, and increasing rental property, so that cost of renting a home could be brought down.
7. To provide incentives like loan forgiveness to bring more doctors and nurses to New Orleans, and to build new hospitals, including a new medical center downtown and a state-of-the art veteran's hospital.
8. To rebuild the criminal justice system by starting a new COPS for Katrina program to put more resources into community policing, and launching a regional effort that brings together federal, state, and local resources to combat crime and drug gangs across the Gulf Coast.
9. To create a first-class school system by speeding up payment of the $58 million that Congress recently appropriated for school repairs, allocating $250 million more to bring quality teachers back to the Gulf region, putting forward a loan forgiveness program to make it easier for students to come back to colleges and universities across the Gulf region, and giving students an annual $4,000 tax credit if they are willing to serve their community.

Some of those promises were upheld when President Obama, only one month into his term, issued an executive order extending the Office of the Federal Coordinator for Gulf Coast Rebuilding. The Gulf Coast additionally benefited when the president signed the American Recovery and Reinvestment Act of 2009 (ARRA, also known as the Stimulus Plan, in which $9.9 million was awarded for maintenance dredging of the Mississippi River's Southwest Pass, $200 million went to expand AmeriCorps, and Louisiana's Third Congressional District received $211,168 to expand services and provide quality health care to more Louisianians. The Democratic-controlled Congress recently appropriated $5.8 billion for levees and coastal restoration, $73 million for public housing in New Orleans, and $3 billion for the Road Home program; and they increased small business disaster loan assistance and funding for higher education. The Obama administration

(continued)

**Policy
Advocacy
Challenge 13.2**
(continued)

selected New Orleans for a "Strong Cities, Strong Communities" initiative. Yet, as of this writing, there is still much work to be done to if the president wishes to fulfill his campaign promises and rebuild New Orleans and the Gulf Coast.

Some questions to ponder:

- What additional contextual factors—positive or negative—do you think will influence the effort to rebuild New Orleans?
- To what extent does the context *change* through time—becoming *either* more *or* less supportive of a specific innovation or project? For example, do you think that national public opinion supportive of the rebuilding of New Orleans has become more muted, with passage of time and people's waning memory of New Orleans's plight? What new challenges do you think the residents of New Orleans face today, given that there are so many other issues on the national agenda?
- How did the election of Barack Obama as president and a Democratic-controlled Congress change the context for the rebuilding of New Orleans? Have the president and Congress done enough to channel resources toward the rebuilding effort?
- Were Republicans to win the White House and the Congress in 2012, how do you think rebuilding of New Orleans might change?

Policy Innovations or Major New Initiatives

A specific policy innovation (i.e., newly enacted legislation or a proposal for new programs in agencies, at the top of the diagram in Figure 13.1) is the starting point for implementation. Or a major social problem or issue can provide the impetus to implementation, such as the lack of health insurance by roughly 45 million persons in 2010. Many kinds of policy innovations and social problems or issues exist. Some are simple, such as a new policy that modifies an agency's intake services in a minor way. Others are highly complex, such as the ACA that sought to promote health prevention, regulate private health insurance companies, insure 32 million Americans, promote evidence-based medicine, and greatly expand the Medicaid programs. Some policy innovations or social problems require the collaboration of many people and agencies; others can be implemented by relatively few persons and one agency. Some policy innovations or social problems involve only a single task, such as changing intake procedures; others involve a sequence of tasks—or, in the case of New Orleans—a sequence of housing and economic issues, levee repairs, cleanups of toxic waste, debris removal, repairing of infrastructure, and many other developments. Some policy innovations or social problems require vast amounts of resources, but others need few resources. Some are mandated by higher authorities and are highly detailed; others are vaguely defined. Some policies are relatively noncontroversial, and others are opposed by powerful interests. Some innovations require implementers to make only modest changes in their traditional practices; others demand sweeping changes.[2]

Some social policy innovations or social problems, we should remember, are not programs like Head Start or Temporary Assistance for Needy Families, but *regulations*. Regulations include rules governing work safety, requirements that cigarette companies not market their products to teenagers, laws protecting confidentiality of patients and clients, laws prohibiting child labor, the federal minimum wage law, laws requiring states to provide abortions in the first trimester, regulations regarding public loitering (that apply to homeless persons), regulations regarding the licensing and training of social workers and other professionals, regulations governing affirmative action, and regulations giving patients certain rights when using health maintenance organizations. These regulations are often controversial, such as those regarding abortion and affirmative action. Some regulations are rigidly enforced; others are not. So regulations become a critical part of policy advocacy as advocates take positions on them, try to influence whether they are enforced, and (in some cases) try to amend or end them.

Even this cursory discussion suggests that some policy innovations and some efforts to address social problems are simpler to implement than others. A straightforward change in an agency's intake procedure that requires few resources and that the executive director has defined precisely can usually be implemented without much difficulty. Contrast this simple change with the ACA. Many Republicans vowed in 2012 to cut funding of key provisions of the ACA if they controlled the presidency in 2013 and beyond to sabotage its effective implementation.

Policy innovations and efforts to address social problems also become more problematic when they contain *internal contradictions* and *flawed strategies*.[3] Assume, for - example, that a policy innovation seeks ambitious changes in existing programs but allocates only minimal resources. This internal contradiction is illustrated by the Family Support Act of 1988 and the Personal Responsibility and Work Opportunities Act of 1996. In each case, the policy innovations sought sweeping changes, such as the elimination of welfare as we know it and the employment of large numbers of welfare recipients, but the resources allotted to these sweeping goals were modest. Similarly, New Orleans can be rebuilt only if massive resources are available over an extended period of time—not just allocated, as in the Bush administration, but actually spent.

It is easy to overlook the actual substance of policy innovations when predicting their fate. A policy is likely to be unsuccessful if it proposes ill-conceived strategies. Proposals to help low-income persons improve their economic standing are unlikely to be successful if they do not improve their education or job skills—but rely largely on policies that deter them from obtaining economic assistance by tightening eligibility to such programs as the Earned Income Tax Credit or the Supplemental Nutritional Assistance Program (SNAP) as urged by some conservatives. Even before a policy innovation has been implemented or a major problem addressed, we can estimate the likelihood that it will be actualized during the implementation process (see Table 13.1).[4] Of course, many worthy projects have an uncertain prognosis, so we should not abandon estimates but redouble our efforts to make them work effectively.

Once the implementation of policy innovations or efforts to address social problems begins, a battle over priorities often ensues. Different people give priority to some of the provisions and place less emphasis on others. Success for different persons or groups means the achievement of different objectives. Indeed, as the 1996 reform legislation moved toward full implementation in the summer of 1997, the protagonists had already staked out positions. People like Newt Gingrich emphasized reducing the welfare rolls and curtailing federal expenditures on welfare. More liberal politicians did not want to reduce the rolls at the expense of placing women in jobs (public or private) that consigned them to unacceptable poverty or unsafe working conditions.[5] (Because the legislation gave a degree of power to the federal government but gave the states wide latitude, the battles over the implementation of welfare reform occurred at both the federal and the state levels.) At the federal level, President Clinton's administration made key rulings instructing the states to require the minimum wage in public service jobs—a ruling strongly protested by some conservatives who believed it coddled former recipients.[6]

TABLE 13.1   The Prognosis for the Implementation of Specific Policies

CHARACTERISTICS OF THE POLICY INNOVATION	POSITIVE PROGNOSIS	LESS POSITIVE PROGNOSIS
1. Extent to which collaboration is needed	Relatively little	Extensive
2. Extent to which a lengthy sequence of tasks is needed	Short	Long
3. Amount of resources needed	Fewer	Considerable
4. Extent to which policies are clear	Clear	Vague
5. Extent to which large change from the status quo is needed	Not much	Major
6. Extent to which innovation is controversial	Noncontroversial	Controversial
7. Extent to which internal contradictions exist in the innovation	Few	Many
8. Extent to which the theory and assumptions behind a policy innovation is flawed	Not flawed	Flawed

© Cengage Learning

Policy innovations carry not only objectives or goals with them but also usually resources. As discussed in Chapter Four, public policies are funded by the authorization and appropriation processes of federal, state, and local governments. Authorizations put a maximum on the resources that can be allocated to specific policy innovations, and appropriations determine the actual amounts, which are often far lower than the authorization level. Policy advocates need to prioritize the appropriations process if they want the resources to match the intentions or goals of many policy innovations or efforts to address social problems.

EPA 2.1.10c

Oversight Organizations and Staff

In the case of publicly funded programs, oversight agencies are public funding agencies, such as the federal Department of Health and Human Services (DHHS), specific state agencies, county-level agencies, and municipal agencies. In the case of privately funded programs, oversight agencies include foundations, the United Way, the Jewish Federation, and other private entities that provide funds to nongovernmental organizations (NGOs).

In the case of the rebuilding of New Orleans, it is unclear who the oversight organization is. Because no commission or authority was developed to oversee its rebuilding, authority is dispersed among a vast number of city, state, and federal agencies—each with its own programs and resources. While President Bush had appointed a "coordinator" of New Orleans's rebuilding, he reported directly to the president rather than to a commission or authority located in the city or in the Gulf Coast region. Private entrepreneurs operate on their own to purchase land and build structures on it—but their actions are not linked to broader plans for the city. In this welter of agencies, levels of government, and the private sector, the rebuilding of New Orleans is haphazard and uneven. In relatively affluent areas, such as the Garden District, market forces *do* work because the district suffered much less damage than many low-income areas such as the Ninth Ward and because many businesses and relatively affluent persons chose to remain in, or to move to it, sustaining markets for its businesses. Low-income areas are far less fortunate than affluent ones because they usually suffered far greater loss of their homes and businesses due to their location below sea level.

Oversight agencies are critically important to the implementation of policy. They have clout over agencies because they provide them with resources, which they can withdraw if they believe the agencies are not performing adequately. They often monitor programs that they fund, though the degree of monitoring varies widely. Monitoring may include periodic visits, analysis of program statistics, and audits of budgets. They may provide constructive technical assistance to help agencies better accomplish specific tasks.

With respect to programs established by legislation, public oversight agencies often establish *administrative regulations,* that is, rules governing the implementing process that were not defined in the original legislation. (Recall from Chapter Ten that legislation is often vague regarding many facets of programs, partly because legislators do not anticipate details that emerge later or because they wish to avoid conflict by simply leaving them out of the legislation.) These administrative regulations, which define many intake, service, budget, and other details of publicly funded programs, have the force of law. Not only are executives and staff required to know about them but they also can suffer legal penalties if they violate them (see Policy Advocacy Challenge 13.3).

Policy advocates not only need to know about administrative regulations but also they need to try to influence their content. They are aided in this undertaking by the fact that oversight agencies are required to publicize proposed regulations before they are enacted, to hold public hearings about them, to invite written comments, and to take public sentiment into account before they issue the final versions. In other words, policy advocates can make certain that the oversight agencies receive input from citizens and agencies before they finalize or change administrative regulations.

In the case of policies that are initiated within agencies and funded from an agency's own resources, the executives and the agency board assume responsibility for oversight.

Policy Advocacy Challenge 13.3

Finding and Reading Administrative Regulations

Stephanie Davis, Research Librarian, University of California at Irvine

To find federal administrative regulations online that are contained in the *Federal Register* from 1994 to the present, go to **www.gpoaccess.gov/fr/**. You can search by keywords, enabling law, and issuing agency.

They decide the content of intake, service, and other policies—and decide what funds to allocate to specific programs.

Oversight organizations often use purchase-of-service contracts when giving funds to specific agencies. These contracts are often awarded in the course of a bidding contest where agencies are asked to say what they would charge for a specified amount of services. Oversight organizations sometimes select a specific agency to provide services, rather than using a bidding contest, when they establish that only that agency has the competency to provide a specific service.

These contracts are a critical part of the implementing process because they define the amount of services to be provided, such as 2,000 hours of counseling services or after-school services to 250 children. The contracts often establish minimum standards, like the qualifications of staff and the parameters of service. (The after-school services might specify tutoring and recreational components.) An evaluation component is often attached to contracts, where providers must develop an evaluative mechanism to gauge client satisfaction and outcomes. Contracts impose specific auditing and budget provisions.

These contracts have burgeoned from the 1980s to the present as governmental agencies have turned increasingly to NGOs to implement an array of services. For-profit agencies have become dominant players in many jurisdictions, even running the bulk of welfare reform services. Indeed, many NGOs receive the bulk of their funding from these kinds of contracts.

Contracts therefore have become a central part of the implementing process. Because often they define standards and content of services, as well as fund them, they should be viewed as policy documents. Sometimes, they contain provisions that detract from quality services, such as contracts that specify unrealistic goals in light of the funding they provide for specific projects. And sometimes bidders are awarded contracts primarily because they gave low bids and not because they possessed the competence to provide quality services.

Many contracts were issued by governmental agencies to private businesses in New Orleans in the wake of Hurricane Katrina. In the rush to clear some of the debris and to undertake other projects, however, some of them were no-bid contracts that were given to businesses that had links to specific public officials. It is estimated that more than \$1 billion was lost through fraud. Because no bids were sought, some of these contracts paid excessive amounts to the businesses that received them. Other contracts were poorly monitored, leading to nonperformance of contract objectives.

Primary Implementing Organizations

EPA 2.1.10a

Once a policy is launched, its fate hinges on the beliefs and actions of various people and groups. We emphasize *evolving* beliefs and actions of decision makers, executives, staff, and clients when we discuss implementing processes because these beliefs may shift as implementation takes shape.

The beliefs, interpretation, and mind-sets of those directly involved in the implementation shape its evolution. Direct participants include high- and intermediate-authority figures, firing-line staff, and consumers.[7] *High-authority figures* can choose to fully support a policy with verbal, financial, and time resources, or they can ignore a policy, neglect to address it, or actively oppose it. When analyzing the success or failure of a policy's implementation, we often examine the sort of leadership that is exerted on its behalf. Leaders' values, commitments, and priorities often influence whether they will lend their prestige, authority, time, and resources to a policy's implementation. When executives believe that a policy is unwise or intrusive, they are more likely not to enforce some of its goals or provisions. By contrast, when executives like an innovation, they may monitor its implementation, invest their own political capital to ensure its success, allocate resources to it, and ask staff members to go the extra mile.

Intermediate-authority figures, such as supervisors and administrative staff, are critical participants in implementation because theirs is a mid-level position between executives and line staff. When they favor a policy, they will report to higher-level executives any problems or issues they see in its implementation, and they will carefully monitor line staff to be certain that they implement the policy. Because of their proximity to line staff, they can be troubleshooters who help overcome barriers to implementation, whether in logistics or in the skills or orientations of line staff. If they dislike an innovation, they can sabotage it by opposing it or by failing to address implementation barriers.

We discussed in Chapter Ten under "Power in Organizations" the considerable autonomy of *firing-line staff.*[8] When staff members have considerable discretion, their perspectives must be examined. How do staff members understand a policy? How committed are they to its implementation? Do they have enough technical training to understand and implement it? Is the agency's informal culture supportive of the policy? If the staff is unionized, do the union leaders support the policy, or do they attempt to hinder its implementation?

The political scientist Michael Lipsky coined the term *street-level bureaucrats* to describe firing-line staff who are critical of the implementation of any policy. Direct-service workers can both implement and sabotage policies. If they fully understand and support a policy and are given technical supports in implementing it, if the agency's informal cultural is consonant with it, and if supervisors skillfully assist them in implementing it, the prognosis for its implementation rises considerably. The converse is true, as well. As Lipsky suggests, the power of firing-line staff is often augmented by their relative autonomy. What they do with specific clients, patients, or consumers, for example, is largely beyond the earshot of agency supervisors and directors, not to mention external monitors. So they have considerable latitude, which they can use to implement or to ignore a specific policy directive. Their personal views are often reinforced, or even shaped, by the informal policies and norms of other staff.

We should not overstate the autonomy of firing-line staff, however. Some of their activities can be closely monitored, such as what eligibility standards are used during intake, how many persons they serve, and what kinds of referrals they make.

Although usually ignored in the burgeoning literature on implementation, *consumers* profoundly shape the course of implementation. For example, high-level officials, wanting to get homeless people off the streets, may fund a project in which outreach workers attempt to persuade homeless people to enter shelters. Even if the workers implement this policy diligently, they will fail if large numbers of homeless people refuse to enter shelters, either because they see the outreach workers as unwelcome authority figures or because they believe the life in shelters is inferior to life on the streets. Indeed, social marketing theory, discussed in Chapter Seven, suggests that consumers will reject programs whose benefits do not seem to offset the costs and risks associated with them. If consumers perceive the time and effort involved in using services as greater than the actual benefits received, they are likely to refrain from using a program. If they do use a program, they decide how much effort to invest in it and what kinds of advice or directive to heed or not to heed. Even in the case of involuntary use of programs, such as when a person is required by a court to attend a counseling program, consumers can decide whether merely to make perfunctory appearances or whether to invest themselves in it.

We have discussed each layer of staff as though it was independent of the others. In fact, interactions between different layers of staff powerfully influence the course of implementation. In organizations where lower-level staff like their leaders, for example, an innovation is likely to be taken seriously if the organization's leaders support it. But the converse is likely in organizations where the leaders are not highly regarded. Consumers also pick up cues from firing-line staff. If they sense that the staff does not favor an innovation, they may be less likely to participate in it. Organizational processes that precede an innovation often provide valuable clues to whether and how prime organizations, and their collaborators, will implement a policy innovation.

Before implementing a specific policy innovation, organizations have *standard operating procedures* that their staff members have evolved, such as techniques for reaching their clientele, organizing waiting lists, addressing their clients' needs, and making referrals. These standard operating procedures may prove to be well suited to a particular innovation, but they also may frustrate implementers by being contrary to the procedures needed to implement a new policy.[9]

EPA 2.1.10h

As discussed in Chapter Four, organizations also have missions, that is, goals and their priorities that define their approach to specific problems. When a policy innovation is congruent with its mission, staff and leaders are more likely to implement it. The reverse is also possible, if it is not. Take the case of a school district that is asked by higher authorities to cut the dropout rates of its students by engaging in aggressive outreach programs and intensive counseling. If the staff in some schools view students' attrition as outside their central mission of providing educational services to students who do attend classes, they may not invest energy in this new policy.

Organizations' patterns of resource allocation may profoundly shape a new policy's fate. If an agency has had to make numerous budget cuts before initiating a costly policy, its officials and staff members may not support its implementation. If they have given higher priority to other kinds of activities in their budget, they may be unwilling to shift resources to a new policy.

Interorganizational Processes

As implementation unfolds, prime implementing organizations are often joined by *collaborating organizations*, which perform tasks, provide services, and otherwise interact with the prime implementers (see Policy Advocacy Challenge 13.4). Sometimes, these collaborations are planned, or are even mandated in the policy innovation itself, such as when policies require case management services, referral systems, or the merging of several different agencies to provide a specific service. In other cases, collaborations emerge accidentally or serendipitously as the prime implementers undertake their work. Perhaps a child welfare agency develops links with local schools, even though the legislation does not require these links.

Whether interorganizational linkages develop among organizations charged with helping specific clients or consumers is a fascinating issue in implementation. Everyone realizes that clients, patients, and consumers often need assistance from many kinds of agencies and programs—such as children nearing age 18 who are about to be released from foster care. They often need job training, educational counseling, specialized counseling or substance-abuse services, housing, a supportive network of friends, and resources. Yet getting interorganizational collaboration is often no easy matter. As Catherine Alter[10] discusses, it can be associated with such costs or difficulties (for a specific agency) as delays in solutions due to problems with communication, loss of autonomy, conflict over goals and methods, and loss of resources and time. On the other hand, interorganizational collaboration can result in better services for clients, sharing costs, learning new technologies, finding innovative solutions, and gaining resources.

Policy Advocacy Challenge 13.4

Crossing Organizational Boundaries

Patsy Lane, MSW, Director, Department of Human Services, City of Pasadena

As city child-care coordinator, my primary job was to implement the city child-care policy adopted by the mayor and the city council. The goal of this policy is to expand the supply, quality, affordability, and accessibility of child care throughout Los Angeles by working with city staff in various departments, elected officials, consumers, employers, providers, developers, and others who affect child care in Los Angeles.

Because the policy did not approve any mandates for child care, one focus of this work involved trying to find incentives to get planners, land developers, and builders to include child care as they designed and built workplaces and residential communities. In order to find opportunities for such incentives, I had to first become familiar with the permit and approval process for property development in Los Angeles. After meeting with city staff in several departments that issue such permits and approvals and learning how the process works, we sought input from people from the development community about problem areas in the process and possible opportunities for improvements or changes that might offer incentives. There were lots of suggestions that were not "do-able" because of financial, regulatory, or political constraints, for example, to eliminate or greatly reduce city fees or eliminate steps in the review process. However, one area (among several) that seemed possible involved long delays in securing sewer permits. We found that the city sewer system was very close to capacity, so new building projects had to wait until sewer capacity became available (generally because of the demolition or elimination of an old property) before getting the sewer permit—often a delay of several months. On further investigation with the department responsible for issuing sewer permits, we learned that the city's elected officials had approved a set-aside of a small percentage of the available sewer for "priority" projects to add developments that include space dedicated to licensed child care for at least a minimum number of children. Thus, developments such as new office buildings, condominium or apartment buildings, and business parks could save up to several months of waiting (which to date had cost both time and money) by including dedicated space for licensed child care.

OUTCOME

Within the first three months of implementation, there were some four project applications under the new child care set aside for sewer permits—as opposed to only four major commercial or residential developments proposing to include child care in the prior year.

LESSONS LEARNED

Among the many lessons learned on this project, the primary ones include the following:

- Sometimes, to accomplish a social policy goal, one must step out of one's "comfort zone" (i.e., the social service world) and understand that field's process, players, practices, and so on to find opportunities for implementing the original goal.
- Looking for such opportunities requires learning more than one perspective. In this case, we reviewed both the official city permit process (from start to finish) and the customer's experience with that process. Without those perspectives, we might have created an incentive that would have been opposed by staff and/or elected officials, or one that had no value to the customer and therefore would not increase licensed child-care space in Los Angeles.
- Sometimes, you have to look and learn in many unexpected areas. As a social worker, I never envisioned having to learn all about how sewer permits are issued—but I'm very glad I did!

Interorganizational collaborations include a spectrum from relatively incidental, for example, occasional interactions of two agencies in providing services to specific clients, to integration, where two or more agencies actually merge. Clearly, the incidental collaborations are simpler to put in place, such as joint referral systems and collaboration on modest projects. Even with these simple collaborations, staff from the two (or more) agencies must establish communication, develop common approaches, and trust one another. As collaboration becomes more ambitious, such as when agencies develop major programs jointly, it is more difficult to orchestrate. Such collaborations require extensive negotiations to decide who does what and how resources are shared. They can excite considerable fears by staff in all agencies involved, such as whether one agency will take undue resources or credit or will contribute equal effort. In more ambitious projects, some kind of joint governance is needed to allow decisions to be made as joint projects evolve.

The most ambitious interorganizational collaborations are called service integration, where an actual merger occurs, whether programmatically or budgetarily. In such cases, clients or consumers are not aware that separate agencies even existed. Such ambitious collaborations are relatively rare in the human services—not because they are not needed, but because of turf and funding realities. Executives of specific agencies are often reluctant to give up their autonomy and resources to interorganizational projects or mergers—even when they might provide consumers with a broader package of services. In fairness, however, collaborations and mergers can consume considerable time on the part of executives because of their logistical challenges. In some cases, moreover, specific agencies can lose visibility and resources in merged agencies as compared to other parts of the merged organization.

Interorganizational collaborations are often frustrated by fragmentation in funding from high-level sources. Look at our example of foster children nearing emancipation at age 18.[11] Because child welfare, education, health, and counseling agencies receive their resources from different oversight agencies or from different legislation, no mechanism often exists for pooling their funds to serve specific populations, such as children in foster care.

Case management is not a panacea for spanning organizational boundaries even if it is often highly useful—precisely because it is usually not a joint program but a one-way referral system from one agency to other agencies. Case managers often lack resources to purchase services from other agencies, which makes them vulnerable to rejections of their referrals by them. When cases are referred to other agencies by a case manager absent resources, they often are given less priority than are cases in which funders provide resources.

Interorganizational collaborations still remain, then, at the frontier of human services. They often arise from the determined efforts of staff at the grassroots level rather than from high-level edicts. While little data exists, we can surmise that some interorganizational collaborations improve the well-being of clients when compared with single-agency services, because they provide a fuller set of services that address various needs in tandem.

At a minimum, executives in agencies with services germane to a specific population, like foster children about to "graduate" from foster care at age 18, should not only meet together but also gather data and plan services that will meet their clients' needs. We know, for example, that a high percentage of emancipated foster children become homeless and unemployed, and become substance abusers. Without pooled services that address all these needs in tandem, their plight will remain unmitigated by human services. The same observation holds for other populations, such as persons with AIDS, homeless persons, substance abusers, school dropouts, and persons released from correctional institutions (see Policy Advocacy Challenge 13.5).

EPA 2.1.10d

Policy Advocacy Challenge 13.5

Needed Collaboration to Address the Root Causes of Homelessness

Gretchen Heidemann, MSW and Doctoral Candidate, School of Social Work, University of Southern California

Meeting the needs of the homeless in any community requires remarkable levels of coordination between disparate agencies. Refer to Figure 2.3 in Policy Advocacy Challenge 2.9, which shows the complex and interlocking causes of homelessness. If we truly want to end homelessness and prevent future individuals and families from becoming homeless, we need to coordinate the efforts of not-for-profit, faith-based, and governmental agencies that provide:

- Emergency shelter and food
- Transitional, supportive, and affordable housing
- Job training, preparation, and placement
- Welfare and other safety net supports
- Substance-abuse treatment and recovery services
- Mental health care and counseling
- Medical care and health care coverage
- Domestic violence services
- Services for veterans
- Services for emancipated foster youth
- Services for people being released from jails and prisons
- Services for victims of natural disasters

If we do not make these links, we have no hope of ever addressing the root causes of and ending homelessness. Policy advocates should work to enhance collaborations when they have good reason to believe that they can enhance the well-being of specific populations.

EXERCISE

Imagine you are a policy advocate in your community wanting to coordinate the efforts of various social service and governmental agencies to address the problems of homelessness. Choose just one target subpopulation of homeless individuals, such as the chronically mentally ill or veterans, and make a list of the agencies and organizations that would need to collaborate to address the needs of this population. What types of systems would need to be in place to enable these entities to communicate with one another? How would you assist them in collaborating to gather data and plan services? What would you do to make sure that appropriate referrals were being made between agencies? How would you address issues of autonomy, conflict, and resource allocation? What innovative policy solutions might emerge when, for example, a soup kitchen partners with a culinary training program to provide clients with marketable job skills? Can you think of any drawbacks to interorganizational collaboration with regard to your homeless subpopulation?

Another collaborative approach utilizes persons from different professions *within* a single organization. Persons with diabetes should receive assistance not only from physicians but also from dieticians, physical therapists, and social workers in hospitals—as should persons with other chronic diseases such as cancer and heart disease.

EPA 2.1.8b

Diagnosing Implementing Processes

Once a policy innovation is in place or a major social problem has been addressed, we would want to analyze critically the organizational processes that follow its initial implementation to find errors or problems. The following questions can determine whether internal implementing processes have been initiated that will support the innovation or the effort to address a major issue or problem:[12]

- Is the policy innovation clearly communicated and explained to implementing staff so they are familiar with its goals and provisions?
- Did the implementers have timely and good information and data to help guide implementation, such as demographic and other data about communities, clients, or persons they serve? They also need information about factors that could make the problems that they address even more formidable. For example, a program serving homeless persons would want to know if economic or other factors might markedly increase the number of homeless persons in a specific jurisdiction in the near future.
- Do high-level officials understand the innovation they wish to implement as well as existing policies that are germane to the implementing process? For example, do they understand federal and state legislation as well as other guidelines?
- Have clear goals been established at the outset of an innovation or a project? Are implementing processes monitored to see if the guidelines have been met—and, if not, are corrective actions planned?
- Are clear timelines established that are realistic, and are they met?
- Have appropriate logistical tasks been accomplished? If a project serves homeless persons, for example, have outreach staff and shelters been positioned so that they are truly accessible to them? Have sufficient numbers of staff been hired to implement key tasks?
- Does role clarity exist so that implementing staff know who has responsibility for what?
- Is someone charged with overseeing the implementation of the policy innovation at its outset and in ensuing time periods? And does she or he have the authority and expertise to engage in troubleshooting when snafus develop?
- Is in-service training provided to staff that lack skills needed to implement the innovation?
- Is implementation of the policy innovation built into staff promotion and performance review?
- Do staff receive bonuses or other rewards for additional work on the innovation?
- Are new staff hired to perform key tasks in the innovation?
- Do executives in the primary organizations demonstrate real leadership, carefully monitoring the innovation and troubleshooting its implementation?
- Does the prime organization allocate new resources to the policy innovation when they are needed or seek them from external sources?
- To the extent that belief systems of implementers impede or interfere with the implementation of an innovation, have efforts been made to change them? If, for example, persons working with homeless persons *do* view them primarily in criminal terms (i.e., illegally occupying public spaces), their views would need to be addressed and changed if the project meant to provide homeless persons with caring and nonjudgmental services.

EPA 2.1.9b

When few of these internal actions and processes accompany the implementation of a policy innovation, the prognosis for effective implementation declines.

We also want to analyze implementation processes that are (or are not) initiated across organizational boundaries, particularly when a policy innovation's objectives require collaborations with other agencies and the community:[13]

- Are collaborative relationships with external organizations fashioned in a timely manner?
- Are contracts with outside agencies established with clear performance and cost standards—and are they monitored regularly? Is corrective action taken if they are not appropriately implemented?

- In the case of public or governmental agencies, do they interface sufficiently with the private sector and the NGOs, as well as community institutions such as churches, synagogues, and temples, and advocacy groups and community groups?
- Are outreach and community education initiated to the extent that a policy innovation's objectives require these activities?

Policy innovations sometimes specify collaboration among primary organizations and other organizations. An educational establishment, for example, may be required to involve health agencies providing family-counseling information to teenagers. Increasingly, federal and foundation grants favor projects that propose collaborations. Whether and how these collaborations actually develop will have important ramifications for a policy innovation.

Accidental or serendipitous collaborations may also emerge. As an agency implements a policy innovation, it may have to depend on other organizations for certain tasks or services that are essential to the policy innovation. Interactions between primary organizations and oversight agencies also figure prominently in implementation processes.[14]

While many collaborations among social agencies *did* arise in the wake of Hurricane Katrina, the rebuilding process was hindered by the relative absence of planned and mandated coordination of agencies and programs on the large scale needed in a city that was so devastated. In the absence of such coordination that meshed the economic, social, housing, transportation, education, and medical systems, many of the city's residents did not find their needs adequately addressed in the months and years following Hurricane Katrina.

Implementation of policies is a dynamic process. Policies in action are different from written policies because they are shaped by this dynamic process. All social workers are part of this process, whether they are firing-line staff, supervisors, or administrators—or whether they work in governmental or nongovernmental agencies.

Actual Outputs: Assessment of Implemented Policies

The framers of policy innovations want the policies to achieve specific goals, such as social justice, fairness, effectiveness, and cost-effectiveness, but it is not always easy to evaluate outcomes objectively. We often rely on reports and statistics from those who actually implement a policy to ascertain whether it has been implemented satisfactorily. However, agencies and providers may slant these data in order not to jeopardize continued funding from higher officials. Program evaluations that assess policies' implementation require considerable time and resources to complete, as well as the cooperation of the agencies that implement specific policies.

Perceptions of program outcomes, whether based on empirical studies, secondhand reports, or informal observations, often become an important part of a policy's context. When some legislators believe that implementing staff have not complied with existing policy, they may cut the funding of a program or try to modify the original legislation to make the official policy more precise. For example, at many points in the last three decades, conservative politicians have sought to tighten welfare programs because they believed that agency staff were not enforcing the work requirement provisions.

It is particularly a challenge to evaluate complex and multifaceted projects such as the rebuilding of New Orleans. It is difficult to define what constitutes success or failure—or to obtain data that tells evaluators to what extent indicators of success have been achieved. For example, should evaluations focus on the rate of rebuilding of structures in the city and the extent jobs have returned to the city? Should evaluations focus upon rates of school dropouts, crime, mental illness, or other social indicators? Or should evaluations focus on some combination of these factors?

Even when evaluators agree on the outcomes that they wish to measure, they often discover mixed results when they look at their data. The welfare reforms enacted in 1996, for example, did markedly reduce the size of welfare rolls in the succeeding decade and did lead to some recipients receiving relatively high-paying jobs. Yet many women who left the rolls remained under or near official poverty levels. Researchers sometimes face the conundrum of determining whether their evaluation suggests that the glass is half full or half empty.

The topic of assessing implemented policy will be addressed further in Chapter Fourteen, wherein we discuss evidence-based policy.

Reforming the Implementation Process in Task 7

While some policy innovations are poorly implemented in their initial phase, implementation may improve markedly as leaders and staff take corrective action, either because they favor the innovation or because they are pressured by external authorities. Innovations ultimately succeed or fail not because of abstract forces but because of the actions or inactions of implementing staff. (See Box 13.1.)

Policy advocates have several options when they want to improve implementation. They can target one or more of the facets of implementing action systems that we portrayed in Figure 13.1.

Amending the Policy Innovation   Policy advocates can amend the original policy innovation. In the case of legislation, they can offer amendments or even seek to annul it. Legislation is not written in stone. In subsequent legislative sessions, policy advocates can convince legislators that they made some mistakes in the original version. Advocates often find it difficult to reopen the original legislation for amendments in the years following its enactment because legislators, having developed the legislation through elaborate compromises, are reluctant to reopen what is usually a Pandora's box. Moreover, some legislators may argue that a specific problem must be addressed by changes in the administrative regulations or implementation processes, not in the legislation itself. However, if they can make a good case that the legislation was fundamentally flawed, advocates can get changes in the original

---

BOX 13.1   **Reform Options for Policy Advocates during Implementation**

1. Changing the policy innovation itself: its content, its objectives, or its funding
2. Changing the activities or nature of oversight organizations: their administrative regulations or their monitoring
3. Naming different agencies or adding new agencies to be primary implementing agencies, or requiring new collaborations by these agencies
4. Changing the internal and external implementing processes of primary implementing organizations
5. Modifying the context
6. Influencing the assessments (evaluations) of policy outcomes
7. Obtaining additional resources
8. Placing pressure on implementing agencies through whistleblowing or other forms of pressure

EPA 2.1.8a

legislation by following the strategy guidelines discussed in Chapter Eleven. As one example, the Adoption Assistance and Child Welfare Act of 1980 was modified several years after its initial passage to allow adopted children to retain their eligibility for Medicaid. Advocates hoped that this amendment would encourage people to adopt children with disabilities or children with other health problems. The welfare reform legislation of 1996 can be reformed to place greater emphasis on helping low-income mothers with children receive job training and education, such as community college degrees.

Modifying Policies of Oversight Agencies   Policy advocates can try to change the administrative regulations that guide implementation, as when the Clinton administration required that minimum wages be paid to welfare recipients placed in public workfare programs. Advocates can also seek greater or improved monitoring of implemented programs. They can try to alter the content and nature of specific purchase-of-service contracts so they have better goals, policies, and funding.

Modifying the Choice of Primary Implementing Organizations   Policy advocates can modify the choice of agencies charged with implementing a policy innovation, for example, by adding new agencies, withdrawing contracts or funds from some agencies, or promoting new partnerships.

Intervening in Implementing Processes   Policy advocates can intervene in implementing processes in various ways, such as by insisting that the policy innovation be communicated more forcefully to staff, that in-service training be provided, and that staff be rewarded as they implement the program—or punished if they do not.

Intervening in Interorganizational Processes   Policy advocates can try to enhance interorganizational collaboration to foster more effective services. They might seek specific negotiated agreements between organizations that promote specific kinds of collaboration, or they might agree to share resources to create a joint project. They might decide also to institute exchanges of technical knowledge.

Modifying the Context   Policy advocates can try to modify the context by offsetting negative factors and strengthening positive ones. If they publicize problems or faults in the implementation of a policy, for example, they can build pressure on implementers from the outside, such as activating an advocacy group that demands corrective action. They also might draw the attention of the media to flawed implementation or develop task forces that try to solve specific implementation problems in a collaborative fashion, such as an interorganizational task force.

Influencing the Evaluation of a Policy's Outcomes   Policy advocates should seek evaluations of a policy's implementation. When the genuine accomplishments of a policy's implementation are not understood, policy advocates can publicize its achievements to the mass media, to legislators, and to citizens. When evaluation suggests negative outcomes, advocates should ascertain whether they stem from defects in implementation or in the policy itself.

Working for Enhanced Funding   Some meritorious policies fail to be implemented because insufficient resources are allocated to them. In this case, policy advocates can pressure not the implementers, but the funders, such as county or state legislators or public officials, or federal legislators.

Whistleblowing   When fraudulent or illegal activities occur during implementation—or when the well-being of clients, patients, or consumers is violated—policy advocates should engage in whistleblowing if other remedies do not work.

Do Policy Advocates Ever Sabotage Policies?

EPA 2.1.10k

We have assumed, so far, that policy advocates usually want to enhance the implementation of policy innovations. But what if policy advocates dislike a policy innovation, such as all or portions of the ACA? Congressional Republicans discussed strategies they might use in 2013 and 2014 to block its implementation, such as not providing appropriations for some of its provisions, opposing expansion of Medicaid programs in many states as required by the legislation, appointing high federal officials opposed to its implementation, and bring further suits against the legislation in federal courts.

This situation is both similar to and different from whistleblowing, which we discussed in Chapter Ten. Distressed by wrongdoing in organizations, such as fraud or other illegal activities, whistleblowers divulge information to outsiders. In the sabotaging of policies, however, policy advocates themselves take actions to subvert an existing policy. They can openly defy it, try to subvert it surreptitiously (perhaps by not implementing it in certain cases), or logjam it by creating logistical snafus that render it difficult to administer. Consider the case of the Medicare policy requiring older patients to be discharged rapidly after surgery. Assume that a social worker believes that this policy sometimes harms older patients who have experienced considerable physical or mental trauma in the wake of surgery. An inventive social worker could contend that a shortage of beds exists in convalescent homes (when no such shortage exists), "obtain" a physician's statement that medical complications preclude discharge (when, in fact, patients with similar medical assessments frequently are discharged), "lose" the required paperwork to delay discharge, or coach the patients to demand that they be retained, hoping this insistence will deter medical officials from discharging them. (See Policy Advocacy Challenge 13.6.)

EPA 2.1.2b

Policy Advocacy Challenge 13.6

Ethical Dilemmas in Policy Implementation

Gretchen Heidemann, MSW and Doctoral Candidate, School of Social Work, University of Southern California

The Code of Ethics of the NASW outlines the ethical principles—ideals to which all social workers should aspire—and the ethical standards that are relevant to the professional activities of all social workers. Yet, despite these clearly articulated guidelines, ethical dilemmas frequently arise in practice. When it comes to implementing policy at the organizational, community, and even higher levels, social workers might face dilemmas in honoring client self-determination, and honoring privacy and confidentiality. Let us consider a couple examples.

1. Imagine you are a medical social worker at a private hospital. The hospital hires a new chief executive officer (CEO) who, for religious reasons, opposes abortions and institutes a hospital policy against performing abortions, providing abortion counseling, or even referring patients out to family planning clinics. Regardless of your own personal beliefs about abortion, as a social worker you are committed to honoring your patients' self-determination. A young woman who has been raped comes to see you seeking a referral to get an abortion.

2. Imagine you work at a homeless shelter. The well-intentioned director, who is not a social worker, implements a new policy barring any staff from reporting clients to children's services without first consulting with her. She does this because she believes these families need to be protected against society's stereotype of them as bad parents. One evening at the shelter, you witness a husband degrading and physically assaulting his wife in front of their two young children. The next day, you tell the director about the incident, and remind her that you are mandated (i.e., required by state law) to report abuse. She thanks you for bringing the attention to her concern, but the only action she takes is to have a conversation with the couple and ask

them to keep their personal matters private. Over the next few days, you continue to witness abuse.

Consider your options in both of these situations. What would you do? If you quietly make an exception for the patient in the first example, will you continue to do so—and risk getting dismissed—if you are confronted by other clients in similar circumstances? Would you resign? Would you form a team to confront the CEO and try to get the policy overturned? In the second example, knowing that the mandatory reporting laws are very clear and you could risk losing your license, do you report the family despite the agency policy? Do you try again to talk to the director and change her mind? Do you take the issue to the media and expose her, risking your own job? How far would you go to sabotage a policy you felt was unjust?

EPA 2.1.2c

Is such sabotage by policy advocates ethical? Outright and continuing sabotage of official policy involves substantial risks and ethical dilemmas for social workers in specific settings. If a social worker is hired to implement the welfare reform of a specific state and cannot in good conscience enforce its provisions, she or he could be dismissed or even prosecuted for knowingly violating the law. In such cases, social workers may have to resign and work against the policy as policy advocates on the outside. Yet bending the rules for specific individuals is often ethically permissible. In such cases, social workers pit beneficence against compliance, deciding in egregious cases to help clients escape specific provisions that threaten their well-being. Who is to doubt that some older patients do need a delay in discharge after surgery, when immediate discharge threatens their well-being? To those who say that social workers play God in such cases, policy advocates can reply, "But doesn't professional training and experience equip us to determine when clients' well-being is endangered?" Moreover, in some cases, policy advocates do not violate existing policy but take advantage of ambiguities in it that do allow for exceptions.

Case Study of Implementation

A case study of the of the implementation of the ACA is presented in Policy Advocacy Challenge 13.7. We discuss some implementation issues at organizational and intergovernmental levels.

Policy Advocacy Challenge 13.7

A Case Example of Implementation: The Affordable Care Act (ACA) of 2010

After protracted conflict in the Congress between Republicans and Democrats, legislators and the president approved the ACA in 2010. It may be the most far-reaching social legislation ever enacted. Rather than establishing a separate health financing and delivery system like so-called single payer or government models in most European nations and Canada, the legislation relied on existing insurance companies and health providers to provide new and augmented services and insurance. The legislation has three prongs: (A) improving health coverage, (B) improving health preventive services, and (C) improving the quality and efficiency of health services.

A. Some of the provisions were geared toward providing *health coverage* to roughly 32 million persons who were uninsured when the legislation was enacted, including
  • Requiring states to organize Health Insurance Exchanges and Small Business Health Options Program Exchanges to allow individuals and small businesses with up to 100 employees to purchase coverage by 2014—and allowing small

(continued)

businesses with less than 25 employees to qualify for tax credits to cover part of their costs of insuring their employees even beginning in 2010.

- Ending punitive policies of private health insurance companies in 2010, including denying insurance to persons with preexisting conditions, allowing coverage of dependents living with their parents until they are 26, and ending lifetime limits on benefits.

- Greatly expanding Medicaid by establishing nationwide eligibility for persons earning less than 133 percent of the Federal Poverty Level (FPL) for any person, including single and married persons in 2014. Requiring states to expand their Medicaid programs to meet this standards.

- Placing limits on out-of-pocket costs of consumers by 2014 with federal subsidies to low- and moderate-income consumers for the cost of their premiums as they move from the FPL to 400 percent of the FPL by 2014—and placing limits on out-of-pocket costs for all other consumers as well.

- Establishing an "individual mandate" that requires persons eligible for private insurance to obtain it—and levies fines on them if they remain uninsured. (This provision was upheld by the U.S Supreme Court in a ruling in 2012 when its constitutionality was questioned in a specific law suit.)

B. Some of the provisions were geared toward providing *new services*, including

- Requiring health insurance plans to augment their coverage, including providing an essential health benefits package that includes a comprehensive set of services by 2014—with certain exceptions for plans that have made only minimal changes to their health benefits since health reform was enacted.

- Requiring insurance companies to cover the full cost of preventive services for adults, including annual checkups, flu shots, cancer screenings (including mammograms and colonoscopies) with no consumer fees like co-pays and co-insurance from 2010 onward—including any preventive services assigned a rating of A or B on a scale from A to D by the U.S. Preventive Services Task Force that advises the federal government (see www.Healthcare.gov for a full list).

- Requiring many preventive services for women and children beginning in 2012 including wellness exams, reproductive services, and examination of their eyesight and hearing (see www.Healthcare.gov for a full list).

- Increasing funding of preventive services offered by Medicare and Medicaid, including giving Medicare patients personalized prevention plans and free annual wellness exams by 2011.

- Increasing services of community-based clinics in underserved areas by providing $15 billion to them beginning in 2010 from a Prevention and Public Health fund that also funds augmented health services of schools and at places of work.

C. Some of the provisions advance the *quality and efficiency of medical care* such as

- Requiring every patient to have a "medical home," i.e., a provider that is required to give them comprehensive inpatient and outpatient services.

- Creating an Innovation Center in the Centers for Medicare and Medicaid services that will create systems and strategies for improving the cost and efficiency of care in 2011.

- Creating financial incentives for hospitals and physicians to improve the outcomes of their services in 2012 and 2015 respectively—and reimbursing ones whose patients have excellent outcomes at higher rates.

- Initiating pilot projects to provide "bundled payments" for patients for their combined inpatient, outpatient, and physicians services. Providers would

receive funding for these bundled services rather than for separate services as under current arrangements.
- Moving toward standardized billing procedures.
- Requiring use of electronic medical records.

Assume that you work in a hospital or clinic that is subject to incentives and mandates to accomplish A, B, and C. You discover that many patients do not know that they can receive these benefits and services as illustrated by a patient in early 2012 who wrote that "I went for a physical and was asked for a co-pay. I thought preventive care didn't require a co-pay under the new health law. The woman behind the desk at my doctor's office didn't seem like she knew. What's the answer? Co-pay or no co-pay?" Columnist Lisa Zamosky responded that "It's not surprising that the woman you spoke with at your doctor's office wasn't familiar with details of the Affordable Care Act … A December public opinion poll conducted by Kaiser Family Foundation … reported that 42% of Americans are unsure of how health reform will affect them and their families".[1] You discover that many physicians do not provide them.

You now confront implementation issues in your hospital or clinic that you need to help solve as an ethical social worker who is committed to advancing patients' well-being. Review Box 13.1 that identified some options for reforming the implementation process. You want patients to have better information—and you want providers to give them benefits and services at allowable fees under the ACA. Brainstorm some alternative strategies that you might consider from your vantage point in a specific clinic or hospital.

1. How might you alert your U.S. Senator or Representative that specific services or benefits are not provided—or at excessive fees? Or how might you ask NASW to contact federal officials to inform them of your findings?
2. How might you persuade the federal DHHS or the specific agency within DHHS that implements the legislation to devote greater resources to monitoring it?
3. Might you want to ask your state's health department or agency to assume a greater role in monitoring the implementation of the ACA's implementation in your local area?
4. Might you want to join with other social workers, nurses, medical residents, and physicians in your clinic or hospital to ask top administrators in your clinic or hospital to:
   - Develop and disseminate information sheets to all incoming patients that detail benefits and services to which they are entitled—and the fees that providers can and cannot levy for them.
   - Conduct an evaluation of patients to ascertain if they received those services and benefits to which they are entitled and at allowable fees.
   - Develop highly visible computer sites where patients can go to discover the services, benefits, and fees to which they are entitled under the ACA at www. HealthCare.gov.
   - Develop a cadre of trained "patient advocates" who are mandated by the clinic or hospital to conduct outreach to its patients to ask them if they have received services or benefits to which they are entitled and at appropriate fees, and to partner with them to obtain remedial action if necessary.
   - Develop community-based education and advocacy programs to educate persons about the services, benefits, and fees mandated by the ACA and to ascertain if they have received them at allowable fees.

---

[1]Lisa Zamosky, "Health 411: Preventive Care Could be 100% Covered," *Los Angeles Times* (February 13, 2012) E1.

(continued)

5. Work to change the context in your clinic or hospital if it proves resistant to helping patients receive those services to which they are entitled—and at allowable fees. Regrettably, some administrators and professionals may wish to charge excessive fees for specific services—or not provide them at all if they regard them as reducing their current revenues from fees not allowed under the legislation. Many clinics and hospitals have hierarchical structures that give physicians and top administrators pre-eminent status—and these institutions may be resistant to allowing social workers, nurses, and medical residents to be advocates for patients. How might you work to promote advocacy for patients in these settings? Would you work with others to create a more collaborative environment?

6. Influence the assessments (evaluations) of policy outcomes.
   - Ask patients if they know their rights under the ACA.
   - Do exit interviews with a sample of patients to ascertain if they received benefits and services at acceptable fees as mandated by the ACA.

7. Obtain additional resources for advocacy services.
   - Seek additional resources from clinic or hospital administrators to fund assessments, to hire more advocates, and to disseminate information to patients.

8. Place pressure on a clinic or hospital.
   - Contact federal or state authorities if responsible efforts to bring them in compliance with the ACA are not effective.
   - Participate in community-based advocacy projects. For example, the Medicare Advocacy Project in Los Angeles conducted research on whether area hospitals were providing patients with advance-directive forms to convey their wishes for end-of-life care as required by federal legislation. By disseminating data to the mass media, this project pressured local, state, and federal officials to improve Patient Self-Determination Act's implementation.

Policy advocates will need to engage some intergovernmental issues during the implementation of the ACA, as well. The ACA legislation required states to expand the eligibility of their Medicaid programs markedly in 2014 to provide coverage to persons earning less than 133 percent of the FPL—a policy that would vastly increase the size of Medicaid programs of every state. It promised that the federal government would cover the added costs of these Medicaid programs for a significant period of time. Many Republican governors balked at this requirement and found comfort in a portion of the ruling of the U.S. Supreme Court that upheld the constitutionality of the individual mandate in 2012. This portion of the ruling appeared to argue that the federal government lacked the constitutional power to require states to expand their Medicaid programs—a possibility that might only be decided in future rulings of federal courts. Some policy advocates should lobby their state governments to expand their Medicaid programs because millions of persons will otherwise remain without health coverage in 2014 and succeeding years. The ACA also required Medicaid programs to raise fees paid to physicians for primary care to higher levels of the Medicare programs. Some policy advocates should lobby their state governments to implement this provision because, without it, many physicians would likely refuse to serve Medicaid recipients.

Considerable discussion of an impending shortage of primary care physicians received considerable coverage in the press in 2012 (see, for example, Annie Lowrey and Robert Pear, "Doctor Shortage Likely to Worsen with Health Law," *New York Times*, July 29, 2012, pp. 1, 20.) Far less attention has been devoted to the likely shortage of social workers to work in clinics and hospitals funded by provisions and requirements of the ACA. How might NASW address this problem nationally?

What You Can Now Do

Chapter Summary

You are now equipped to do the following when undertaking the policy-implementing task (Task 7) in the policy practice and policy advocacy framework:

- Analyze whether specific policy innovations are being implemented.
- Diagnose why specific policies are not implemented by using a systems framework.
- Analyze implementation both within and across organizational boundaries.
- Initiate strategy to improve implementation.

Competency Notes

EPA 2.1.2b   Make ethical decisions by applying standards of the NASW's Code of Ethics and, as applicable, of the International Federation of Social Workers/ International Association of Schools of Social Work Ethics in Social Work, Statement of Principles (p. 476): Social workers face ethical dilemmas in practice.

EPA 2.1.2c   Tolerate ambiguity in resolving ethical conflicts (p. 477): Advocates can take advantage of ambiguities that do allow for exceptions.

EPA 2.1.7a   Utilize conceptual frameworks to guide the process of assessment, intervention, and evaluation (p. 455): Advocates can use a systems framework to track a policy's implementation from its enactment to its final outcome.

EPA 2.1.8a   Analyze, formulate, and advocate for policies that advance social well-being (p. 475): Advocates can amend the original policy innovation, change the administrative regulations, or modify the choices of agencies.

EPA 2.1.8b   Collaborate with colleagues and clients for effective policy action (p. 471): Persons from different professions within a single organization can collaborate.

EPA 2.1.9a   Continuously discover, appraise, and attend to changing locales, populations, scientific and technological developments, and emerging societal trends to provide relevant services (p. 460): Social workers responded to the context that shaped the rebuilding of New Orleans after Katrina.

EPA 2.1.9b   Provide leadership in promoting sustainable changes in service delivery and practice to improve the quality of social services (p. 472): Once a policy is in place, social workers should analyze critically the organizational processes that follow to find errors or problems.

EPA 2.1.10a   Substantively and affectively prepare for action with individuals, families, groups, organizations, and communities (p. 466): A policy's fate hinges on the beliefs and actions of various people and groups.

EPA 2.1.10c   Develop a mutually agreed-on focus of work and desired outcomes (p. 464): Policy advocates need to prioritize the appropriations process if they want the resources to match the intentions or goals of policy innovations.

EPA 2.1.10d   Collect, organize, and interpret client data (p. 470): Agency executives should gather data and plan services that will meet their clients' needs.

> **EPA 2.1.10h   Initiate actions to achieve organizational goals** (p. 468): Organizations' missions, staff, and leaders should be congruent with the policy innovation in order for a successful implementation.
>
> **EPA 2.1.10k   Negotiate, mediate, and advocate for clients** (p. 476): Policy advocates may dislike a policy and take actions to subvert an existing policy.

Endnotes

1. For an overview of the strategy, see Congress, House, Ways and Means Committee, Subcommittee on Public Assistance, *Hearings on Amendments to Social Services, Foster Care, and Child Welfare,* 96th Cong., 1st Sess., March 1979, pp. 22–157.

2. Robert Montjoy and Laurence O'Toole, "Toward a Theory of Policy Implementation," *Public Administration Review* 39 (September–October 1979): 465–476.

3. Jeffrey Pressman and Aaron Wildavsky, *Implementation* (Berkeley and Los Angeles: University of California Press, 1974).

4. Laurence O'Toole and Robert Montjoy, "Toward a Theory of Policy Implementation," *Public Administration Review* 44 (November–December 1984): 491–503.

5. Richard Berk, "Gingrich Promises to Fight Clinton on Welfare Law," *New York Times* (August 23, 1997): 1, 9.

6. Jason DeParle, "White House Calls for Minimum Wage in Workfare Plans," *New York Times* (May 16, 1997): 1.

7. Mary Ann Scheirer, *Program Implementation: The Organizational Context* (Beverly Hills, CA: Sage, 1981).

8. Michael Lipsky, *Street Level Bureaucracy* (New York: Russell Sage Foundation, 1980).

9. Yeheskel Hasenfeld, "Implementation of Social Policy Revisited," *Administration and Society* (February 1991).

10. Catherine Alter, "Interorganizational Collaboration in the Task Environment," in Rino Patti, ed., *The Handbook of Social Welfare Management* (Thousand Oaks, CA: Sage Publications, 2000), pp. 283–302.

11. Jane Waldfogel, "The New Wave of Service Integration," *Social Service Review* (September 1997): 463–484.

12. Scheirer, *Program Implementation.*

13. John O'Looney, "Beyond Privatization and Service Integration," *Social Service Review* (December 1993): 40–54.

14. Bruce Jansson, "The Political Economy of Monitoring: A Contingency Perspective," in Harold Demone and Margaret Gibelman, eds., *Services for Sale* (New Brunswick, NJ: Rutgers University Press, 1989), pp. 343–359.

Suggested Readings

Theoretical Perspectives on Implementation

Erwin Hargrove, *The Missing Link: The Study of the Implementation of Social Policy* (Washington, DC: Urban Institute Press, 1975).

Yeheskel Hasenfeld, "Implementation of Social Policy Revisited," *Administration and Society* 22 (February 1991): 451–479.

Robert Montjoy and Laurence O'Toole, "Toward a Theory of Policy Implementation," *Public Administration Review* 39 (September–October 1979): 465–476.

Carl Van Horn and Donald Van Meter, "The Implementation of Intergovernmental Policy," in Charles Jones and Robert Thomas, eds., *Public Policy Making in the Federal System* (Beverly Hills, CA: Sage, 1976).

Models of Interorganization Collaboration

John Fleischman et al., "Organizing AIDS Service Consortia: Lead Agency Identity and Consortium Cohesion," *Social Service Review* (December 1992): 501–534.

John O'Looney, "Beyond Privatization and Service Integration," *Social Service Review* (December 1993): 40–54.

Privatization and Links to Informal Systems

Charles Hoch and George Hemmens, "Linking Informal and Formal Help: Conflict along the Continuum of Care," *Social Service Review* (September 1987): 434–447.

Julie Kosterlitz, "Unmanaged Care?," *National Journal* (December 10, 1994): 2903–2907.

Lester Salamon, "The Marketization of Welfare: Changing Nonprofit and For-Profit Roles in the American Welfare State," *Social Service Review* (March 1993): 16–39.

Structural–Political Perspectives on Implementation

Jeffrey Pressman and Aaron Wildavsky, *Implementation* (Berkeley and Los Angeles: University of California Press, 1974).

Political–Economy Perspectives on Implementation

Eugene Bardach, *The Implementation Game* (Cambridge, MA: MIT Press, 1977).

Micro or Agency Perspectives on Implementation

Yeheskel Hasenfeld, "The Implementation of Change in Human Service Organizations," *Social Service Review* 54 (December 1980): 508–520.

Mary Ann Scheirer, *Program Implementation: The Organizational Context* (Beverly Hills, CA: Sage, 1981).

Staff Perspectives on Implementation

Michael Lipsky, *Street-Level Bureaucracy* (New York: Russell Sage Foundation, 1980).

Ethical Issues in Policy Implementation

Sissela Bok, "Blowing the Whistle," in Joel Fleishman, Lance Liebman, and Mark Moore, eds., *Public Duties: The Moral Obligations of Government Officials* (Cambridge: Harvard University Press, 1981), pp. 204–220.

Robert Goodin, *Reasons for Welfare: The Political Theory of the Welfare State* (Princeton, NJ: Princeton University Press, 1988), pp. 184–223.

Donald Warwick, "The Ethics of Administrative Discretion," in Fleishman, Liebman, and Moore, eds., *Public Duties*, pp. 93–127.

Assessing Policy: Toward Evidence-Based Policy During Task 8

Policy Predicament

While we think our *proposed* policies will be effective, we do not know if they are effective until we have evaluated *actual* or *implemented* policies in Task 8 of our policy framework. We discuss how a significant body of evidence suggests that the policy of diverting juvenile offenders from incarceration to community diversion projects enhances their well-being and saves society considerable resources in Policy Advocacy Challenge 14.5 at the end of this chapter.

LEARNING OUTCOMES

We discuss the following in this chapter:

1. How "rationalists" want a greater role for research in policy making
2. How to define evidence-based policies
3. Why evidence-based practice requires support policies
4. Why policy assessment is a form of argumentation
5. Some technical tools
6. The importance of countering policy innuendos that lack a basis in research
7. Some barriers to evidence-based policies

The Rationalists' Hope

This chapter discusses the policy assessment task (Task 8) of the policy practice and policy advocacy framework (see Figure 3.1). Imagine a world without red states or blue states, without well-endowed special interests, and without ideologically driven politics. Imagine a world in which the policies that are developed and enacted to address social problems are driven by a single notion: *what works*. Imagine that society invests considerable resources in evaluating policies after they are enacted and implemented.

Rationalists' hopes are often dashed, however, when they observe that many policies and programs that *are* formally evaluated are not enacted as illustrated in Policy Advocacy Challenge 14.1.

Policy Advocacy Challenge 14.1

How Ideology and Politics Sometimes Overrides Evidence-Based Policy

Bruce S. Jansson, Ph.D

Donna Shalala, Secretary of the Department of Health and Human Services in the late 1990s, approached a microphone to announce a new departure in the prevention of HIV/AIDS: providing sterilized needles to drug addicts so that they would not exchange contaminated ones that often transmitted HIV/AIDS to unsuspecting drug addicts. Considerable research had demonstrated that distribution of sterilized needles sharply cut the transmission of HIV/AIDS such as the Centers for Disease Control's finding that roughly one-fifth of new HIV infections and the vast majority of hepatitis C cases were caused by needles that were exchanged with other drug users (http://en.wikipedia .org/wiki/Needle-exchange_programme). Researchers also refuted the argument of many conservatives who argued that access to these needles would increase the use of illegal drugs by addicts.

At the last minute, however, the secretary was called to take a phone call from a top aide of President Bill Clinton—and informed that the president had decided to cancel the new policy. A disappointed Donna Shalala abruptly canceled her presentation. The president and his aides had decided that the new policy would provide political fodder for conservatives in a forthcoming election, who would argue that distribution of sterilized needles would promote substance abuse.

EXERCISE

1. What other policy issues in contemporary society are strongly linked to ideology so that findings of researchers and scientists are dismissed by significant segments of society?
2. Can persons with progressive views support policies like the distribution of sterilized needles with arguments that might appeal to some conservatives, such as cost savings from averted cases of HIV/AIDS?
3. Can persons who favor needle exchange programs focus their efforts on states or local units of government? (NOTE: Forty-eight states had needle-exchange programs by 2006 as well as programs to allow persons to purchase needles at pharmacies without a prescription.)
4. Does the policy pendulum often swing with changes in the balance of power in Congress between conservatives and liberals? For example, the Congressional ban on needle-exchange programs that was put in place in 1988 was lifted in 2009 in the wake of the Democratic landslide victories in the presidential and congressional elections of 2008—but was imposed again in December 2011 as conservatives regained control over the House of Representatives and increased their numbers in the Senate in the congressional elections of 2010.
5. Just because a positive evaluation of a policy fails to convince others to adopt it, such as with respect to needle-exchange programs in the Clinton administration, does that mean it will not *subsequently* influence policies. (NOTE: Many states enacted needle-exchange programs, and they were approved by the Obama administration until near the end of his first four years in office.)

EPA 2.1.3a

Defining Evidence-Based Policies

Evidence-based policies are ones that achieve positive outcomes where they are evaluated with research. As we shall see, use of research methodology to evaluate policies does not guarantee that they *are* effective because many factors, singly and in tandem, can lead different persons to question the findings or to offer alternative ones.

The policy-assessing task represents both the ending and the beginning of social policy practice. People often regard policy assessment as the final step in the policy-making process; having had a policy proposal enacted, they wish to determine whether it has been a success. However, assessment is also the beginning of policy practice when policy advocates' negative assessments of existing policies suggest that they are flawed, motivating them to develop, enact, and implement new policies.

Policy practitioners often want to know whether an existing policy is flawed or meritorious because the answers have important implications for a number of people and institutions. A policy can harm (or at least fail to help) its intended beneficiaries. A policy that helps consumers but absorbs "unacceptable" amounts of resources is likely to be criticized by those who wish to use the resources more efficiently. A policy that helps some people but discriminates against others—that helps the male victims of a social problem, for example, while providing little help to its female victims—would be widely regarded as an unfair or inequitable.

Policy assessment forces us to ask how, if at all, the world is different because a specific policy exists, and what, if any, difference it would make if we removed or modified the policy. Each of the different kinds of policies that we discussed in Chapter One can be evaluated. Researchers can evaluate specific *regulations* to see if they bring their intended result: do minimum required staff-to-child ratios in child care settings bring better outcomes for children? Do *needs-meeting policies*, such as food stamps, allow low-income persons to sustain their physical well-being? Do *opportunity-enhancing policies,* such as charter schools, improve students' achievement and graduate rates as compared with public schools? Do specific *social service policies*, such as child welfare services in a specific jurisdiction, increase family reunification while also decreasing the extent to which these children are neglected or abused when they are returned to their families? Do *referral and linkage policies* lead more consumers to enroll in such programs as Medicaid or the Earned Income Tax Credit? Do specific *civil rights policies*, such as ones protecting LGBT children and youth from discrimination and bullying in educational institutions, have their intended outcomes? Do *human rights policies*, such as specific ones developed by the United Nations and India, decrease the number of childhood marriages in Africa and India? Have *equality-enhancing polices*, such as systems of taxation in the United States, reduced inequality or increased it? Have *asset accumulation* policies, such as tax incentives to low- and moderate-income persons to start individual saving accounts, brought significant improvements to their economic well-being? Have *infrastructure development policies*, as well as *economic development policies*, such as road improvements and small-business loans, significantly increased the economic development of specific areas? Would tax incentives given to persons to vote increase their *political participation*? Have *budget policies* of specific states, such as cuts in funding of secondary education during and after the Great Recession, significantly harmed educational outcomes of students?

Policy research can be located at many Internet sites as illustrated in Policy Advocacy Challenge 14.2.

Why Supportive Policies Are Needed for Evidence-Based Practices

To better understand how evidence-based practice requires supportive policies, assume that you work in a school district and want to implement services for parents of children with attention deficit hyperactivity disorder (ADHD). Even at this direct-practice level, however, you would face important obstacles. You would have to persuade the school district's administrators to allow you and your fellow professionals to implement this intervention. They

Policy Advocacy Challenge 14.2

Evidence-Based Policy at Home and Abroad

Although new to the field of social work, the idea of evidence-based policy has already been conceived and is being applied broadly in the fields of medicine and public health. For example, the World Health Organization's Global Burden of Disease Study, which began in 1990, is a comprehensive regional and global assessment of mortality and disability that utilizes evidence-based input to inform public health policy.[1]

Evidence-based policy is also being used widely in the UK, Australia, and New Zealand, where numerous organizations dedicated to its advancement exist:

The Economic and Social Research Council is the UK's leading agency for research funding and training in economic and social sciences.
    www.esrc.ac.uk

The Evidence Network is an information resource provided by the Centre for Evidence and Policy at King's College in London. The Evidence Network provides access to a wide range of information resources in social and public policy, and hosts a peer-reviewed journal, *Evidence & Policy: A Journal of Research, Debate and Practice.*
    www.kcl.ac.uk/schools/sspp/interdisciplinary/evidence

Evidence for Policy and Practice Information and Coordinating Centre is part of the Social Science Research Unit at the Institute of Education, University of London. The EPPI Centre is at the forefront of carrying out systematic reviews, developing review methods in social science and public policy, and making reliable research findings accessible.
    http://eppi.ioe.ac.uk/cms

The Social Policy Research Centre at the University of New South Wales in Australia conducts research and fosters discussion on all aspects of social policy in Australia.
    www.sprc.unsw.edu.au

The Campbell Collaboration provides a searchable list of reviews of social research principally in the United States and Europe.
    www.campbellcollabation.org

---

[1]Murray and Lopez, "Evidence-Based Health Policy: Lessons from the Global Burden of Disease Study," *Science* 274 (1996): 740–743.

EPA 2.1.6b

would have to agree to let you prioritize it, including planning and implementing it. They would have to give you resources needed to implement it, including ones needed to develop training sessions, hire (if necessary) additional staff, and recruit parents to the participate in the intervention. They would have to find resources to hire staff to undertake tasks in which the implementers of the parent-training project could *not* engage because they would lack the time. Even though you identified research that had shown that this project would be effective, your school administrators would likely need to fund an evaluation of parent-training in *this* setting and with *these* children.

This scenario suggests that it is futile to discuss evidence-based practice in specific settings without linking it to policies except in those rare instances when a single professional can implement evidence-base practice without policy support in her or his practice setting. Recall that we defined social policies to be "collective strategy that prevents and addresses social problems." If parent training of children with ADHD is to become a "collective strategy" in this setting, it needs to be accompanied by policies that provide or mandate:

- Necessary resources, including resources from the school district's budget or from grant proposals developed to obtain resources from external sources, such as state or federal governments, private foundations, or private donors

- Necessary approvals of the project from high-level administrators
- Allocation of sufficient staff to the intervention by the school district or by specific schools within the district
- Interagency agreements with mental health and other agencies that are asked to assume a role in diagnosing children or providing the intervention
- Decisions about whether to continue the parent-training program from its initial implementation into future years

Evidence-based practices cannot take place in many settings, then, unless and until they are supported by social policies. These social policies can be regarded as integral to the evidence-based practices themselves because they will not become a reality without them.

Policy Assessment as Argumentation

EPA 2.1.8a

A noted researcher, the late Donald Campbell, provocatively suggested that program evaluation should be regarded as a form of "argument," and that the program evaluator should make a good case that others may contest.[1] In this context, policy evaluators become debaters, who must defend their arguments.

Consider, for example, the research of a woman hired to assess a new program that provides special services to the natural parents of children who have been removed from their homes and placed in foster care due to neglect or abuse.[2]

She develops the policy assessment matrix in Table 14.1 to guide her work. She wants to compare families that do and do not receive special services to see if the services lead to positive outcomes. Across the top of the table she places three criteria: rates of reunification, cost per case during the first 18 months, and children's developmental well-being.

Why did the policy practitioner select three measures of outcome, rather than only one? She knew that many legislators and government officials were particularly concerned about the relative costs of the new policy experiment. They wondered whether the costs of providing special services would partially or completely be offset by the reduction in the numbers of children in foster care placements or in subsidized adoptions. Some legislators had originally resisted the policy because they doubted that it would save funds, such as a conservative legislator who called it "another scheme by do-gooder social workers to get more money to fund their pet projects."

TABLE 14.1   Policy Assessment Matrix

POLICY ALTERNATIVES	EVALUATIVE CRITERIA		
	RATES OF REUNIFICATION	COST PER CASE DURING THE FIRST 18 MONTHS	CHILDREN'S DEVELOPMENTAL WELL-BEING
Special services to natural parents (experimental group)			
The existing situation: the provision of relatively few services (control group)			

© Cengage Learning

The practitioner also wants to check the rates of reunification of families that received and did not receive the special services. Many people want families to be reunified because they believe that long-term or permanent removal of children from their natural families detracts from their well-being. Surely, the practitioner reasons, we should obtain information about whether special services increase the likelihood of family reunification.

She realizes, however, that an analysis of costs, as well as of rates of reunification, may yield an incomplete and even misleading evaluation of the new policy. In a phenomenon known as *goal displacement*, implementers mistake secondary goals or objectives for the most important ones. Unlike some legislators, many social workers are concerned about the ultimate effects of policies on their clients' well-being—in this case, the healthy development of the children who had been placed in foster care. She decides, then, to measure the children's developmental well-being in both the experimental and control groups.

The researcher chooses three measures of outcomes then, to obtain a clearer picture of the new policy. She realizes, of course, that she may discover mixed outcomes; the new policy may save the taxpayers money, for example, but may not have advantages over the existing policy in serving children's developmental needs.

Assume that three years have passed so that the evaluator has enough data to assess the outcome of the policy innovation. She discovers that the special services had reduced child welfare costs by a small but significant amount, i.e., from an average of $9,500 per child in the regular program to an average of $7,000 on each child in the special services program.[3] The special services program increases reunification somewhat: if only 19 percent of children had been reunified with parents in the regular program, 27 percent of children had been reunified with their parents in special services program.[4] After three years, however, the children in the special services program had not achieved higher scores on several measures of child development than the children in the regular program.

Although these findings are fictitious, they nicely illustrate some dilemmas that program evaluators often encounter in the real world. When subjected to rigorous, quantitative evaluations, many policies reflect relatively modest gains on some outcomes and no gains or only modest gains on others.[5] Of course, the relatively modest changes sometimes occur in a negative direction; in this case, for example, the children in the special services program *could* have scored somewhat lower than other children on developmental measures.

We can conjecture why some policy innovations do not produce the marked changes that their framers intended. Because many factors shape people's behavior and development, such as their prior experiences, their economic condition, and the persons with whom they associate, programs in the human services often cannot be expected to transform the lives of clients, patients, and consumers dramatically and quickly.[6] The instruments that researchers use may also fail to capture some important dimensions of human behavior.

This researcher has established, then, an *argument* in favor of special service by obtaining data that confirms her hypothesis that special services to natural parents cut child welfare costs and increase reunification, even if they did not improve child development.

Researchers often confront others who develop *counterarguments* when examining their research. The researcher concluded her work by saying, "On balance, my findings suggest that the special services program should be enlarged so that it covers all children whom the courts remove from their natural home because of their parents' abusive or neglectful behavior." Let us also assume that some conservative legislators strongly contested this proposal, doubting that "hiring a lot more social workers to provide intensive services to the natural parents will really cut our costs."

The ensuing debate between the policy evaluator and the conservative politicians could involve several dimensions, or axes.[7] First, the evaluator and conservative politicians could debate whether the glass is half full or half empty. Are the cost reductions and increased rates of reunification *sufficiently large* to justify continuing and enlarging the special services program? No scientific method exists for resolving this dispute because people derive their positions from their values, not even statistics. Public officials may *still* believe the findings do not reach a sufficient threshold. Conservatives who opposed the special services program at the outset and who are suspicious of social workers may insist on a higher standard of evidence than persons who favored the program at the outset.

Conservatives might also question the time frame of the research, by asking, in our example, whether 18 months is enough to reveal whether the special services program is truly effective. "How do we know," one of them asks, "whether some or many of the children who have been reunified with their parents will not have to be placed again in foster homes in the near future?" (Recall that the researcher followed the cases of the children over only 18 months.) The evaluator responds that "18 months is long enough to allow reasonable inferences." However, this dispute cannot be easily resolved because values often shape one's position; a skeptic is likely to want a stricter standard of proof, such as a study that follows a policy's beneficiaries for a longer period.

People could also question the practitioner's weighting of her criteria. Someone might say, for example, "The special services program may save some funds and may somewhat increase the rate of reunification, but I think that the children's well-being ought to be the prime consideration."

As the policy practitioner presents her findings, she may encounter some questions about the accuracy of her data. "How do we know," someone may ask, "whether your findings are truly accurate? Maybe the children and families you chose for the special services program did not have problems as severe as those of other children and families." Another may ask, "How do we know that you did not select particularly talented and motivated social workers to staff the special services program? Maybe the program's success stemmed from their skills, rather than from the special services program itself." Someone else may ask whether the child development instruments used to measure the children's well-being provided accurate information about their development.

We have emphasized technical arguments that opponents can use to make a counter-argument against a researcher's argument. In other cases, they choose to ignore the research as was illustrated by the opposition of many conservatives to needle-exchange programs. They opposed these programs on moral or ideological grounds by contending they legitimized and even encouraged drug addiction even if data showed that the programs did not increase drug usage.

Some Technical Tools

EPA 2.1.6b

Evaluators encounter five challenges when assessing specific policies. We introduce them, but suggest that you consult research texts for further elaboration of them.

First, they must find *comparison groups* that are or are not exposed to a specific policy. They can randomly assign persons to the policy to develop experimental and control populations that are, and are not, exposed to the policy. In the case of needle-exchange programs, they might want to offer needle exchanges for some addicts but not for others—assuming they can surmount the ethical objection that addicts who do *not* receive sterilized needles are more likely to develop HIV and hepatitis C. They can use the criteria that they developed in the first step of their research to compare outcomes of the two groups, such as whether the policy achieves better results for the experimental group on one or more of the criterion than with the control group.

It is often not possible to assign persons randomly to experimental and control groups because of the difficulty of developing (in this case) lists of addicts in advance and assigning them randomly to these groups. In quasi-experimental designs, members of comparison groups often occur naturally, such as addicts in different jurisdictions where needle-exchange programs are, or are not, introduced. Researchers might, for example, examine public health records in different jurisdictions to ascertain whether rates of HIV and hepatitis C are lower in those jurisdictions where needle-exchange programs have been introduced. Or they might identify a group of addicts in a specific area and compare their rates of HIV and hepatitis C before and after their participation in needle-exchange programs.

They can identify comparison groups, as well, through naturally occurring experiments. They might compare the health of persons or populations before and after the implementation of a needle-exchange policy. They might conclude, for example, that needle exchanges *do* decrease transmission of HIV and hepatitis C when comparing the incidence of these diseases before and after the introduction of needle exchanges.

It is beyond the scope of this discussion to examine the many design, instrumentation, and sampling techniques in forward-looking studies. The research literature explores alternative designs, such as experimental and quasi-experimental designs; several sampling techniques, such as random sampling and stratified sampling; and a host of instrumentation or testing options, including questionnaires and observational techniques.[8]

Second, researchers gather data to examine outcomes of a specific policy with respect to specific criteria and with reference to specific comparison groups. Data may come from subjects themselves, such as through interviews or physical examinations, from public health or other public records, from family members, or from other sources. They must gather data in ways that make it as accurate as possible. If they use questionnaires, for example, they will test them before using them to assess their validity (the extent to which they measure phenomenon that researchers intend) and reliability (the extent to which they measure phenomenon accurately through time).

Third, researchers develop a sampling strategy that ranges in rigor from convenience ones to random samples. Samples sometimes come from available sources of data.

Fourth, researchers use statistical analysis to determine the probability that differences between comparison groups could have occurred by chance as compared to effects of the policy that is being evaluated. They also use it to identify the relative power and interactions of many variables.

Fifth, researchers have to interpret and present their findings to stakeholders in ways that make them likely to retain the policy if the researchers believe that it meets one or more of the criterion that they established at the outset of their research.

Some researchers use qualitative methodology to measure the merit of specific policies.

Policy Advocacy Challenge 14.3 Using Mixed Methods Bruce Jansson, Ph.D.	Quantitative and qualitative research are often combined in a "mixed methods approach." Assume you are evaluating the effectiveness of a needle exchange policy in your jurisdiction. Assume that police often raid shooting galleries where addicts convene and share needles. Also assume that local police are reluctant to abandon their law-enforcement approach to drug addiction. Assume, as well, that advocates of needle exchanges do not know how addicts will perceive this new policy—or the people who implement it. 1. What criteria and outcomes might a quantitative researcher select, and what evidence or data might this evaluator use? 2. What research questions might a qualitative researcher ask, and what evidence or data might this evaluator use? 3. How might these two research methods be linked or combined to obtain a fuller understanding of the effects of a needle-exchange program?

Countering Innuendos That Lack a Basis in Research

2.1.7b

One should realize that opposition to constructive social policies, such as Supplemental Nutritional Assistance Program (SNAP, formerly food stamps) often takes the form *not* of formal research, but innuendos that *imply* that these programs are ineffective. Take the example of statement by Mitt Romney, the Republican nominee for president in 2012. Romney alleged that most federal low-income spending goes for "overhead" and "bureaucrats," such as SNAP, Medicaid, and housing vouchers. He said, "What unfortunately happens is with all the multiplicity of federal programs, you have massive overhead, with government bureaucrats in Washington administering all these programs, very little of the money that's actually needed by those that really need help... actually reaches them." In fact, budget data for a range of federal safety-net programs reveal that federal administration costs range from 1 percent to 8 percent of total federal program spending.[9]

Newt Gingrich, another contender for the Republican nomination, insisted that spending on SNAP was runaway in nature. He linked the program to President Barack Obama by calling him "the food stamps president"—a statement that implied the size of the program stemmed from advocacy from Democrats. He implied that it was a disincentive to work, luring many Americans into welfare rather than seeking employment. In fact, increased usage of SNAP largely stemmed from unemployment and low wages associated with the Great Recession and its aftermath as the program's cost increased from about 0.275 percent of GDP in 2005 to over 0.5 percent of GDP in 2009 through 2012. *Almost half of SNAP recipients are working people whose wages do not lift them from low income and poverty.* Enrollments in SNAP are expected to recede in coming years as the economy improves.[10] Policy advocates need to consult research experts to analyze the accuracy of many assertions such as:

- Few users of safety-net programs work
- Low-income African American children rarely have heads of households who are employed
- Medical savings accounts would render Medicaid unnecessary as a federal-state program for low-income persons
- Increases in welfare or Medicaid benefits in a specific state will lure low-income people to it from other states in large numbers
- Bilingual programs harm the education performance of Latinos
- Tax increases for millionaires will cut the nation's economic growth
- Welfare reforms in 1996 at the federal and state levels, which made access to welfare considerably more difficult for single heads of households, have greatly increased the incomes of low-income minority women by forcing them into the workplace

Some Barriers to Evidence-Based Policies

Many policy proposals emanate from the agenda-building process that we discussed in Chapter Six, such as from ideas or developments in the political, problem, and solution streams in a specific agency or legislature *rather than from specific technical or research findings.* Public officials often develop specific policy proposals that they think will get them votes in elections, so they want policy proposals that are appealing to their constituencies. Some public officials distrust researchers in general, viewing them as liberals or as elitists even when they provide overwhelming evidence of the merits of specific policies like needle exchange programs or climate-control policies to stem the emergence of global warming. Still others dispute data that inequality is increasing in the United States even when this data comes from the respected U.S. Bureau of the Census. Others question budget estimates of the bipartisan Congressional Budget Office, even seeking its termination when its findings conflict with their ideology.

Some barriers come from researchers themselves. They sometimes cannot communicate their research to public officials who are unschooled in statistics and research methodology. Researchers often disagree with one another *even when* they propose policies based upon research findings. They may disagree about the criteria used to judge the relative merits of a specific policy—or their relative weight or importance. Even when discussing the same empirical findings, researchers may differ about their interpretation or meaning. Some of them may attribute specific outcomes to a policy, for example, while others may believe other contextual factors caused them. The inability of specific job development programs to locate employment for their graduates may stem, for example, not from defective training strategies, but from the Great Recession that led to mass unemployment even for many highly trained persons.

Definitive research does not exist with respect to how to prevent or address many social problems. We do not know how to prevent divorce. We do not know how to cure many physiological problems as attested by high death rates from many kinds of cancer. We do not know how to redevelop many low-income areas that remain plagued by poverty. We do not know how to prevent the formation of gangs in many urban areas.

We often do not know why specific social phenomena exist. Take the case of the marked reduction in crime in the United States during the Great Recession and beyond. Rates of crime usually increase during recessions, but they markedly decreased during the Great Recession for unknown reasons.

The Campbell Collaborative, a respected Internet site for social science research, documents the lack of definitive research with respect to a host of issues, including:

- Whether cognitive-behavioral therapy helps children and young people who have been sexually abused—or helps foster care parents better manage children with behavioral problems—or reduces violent behaviors of men who engage in violent behaviors with their partners—or reduces criminal behavior of adolescents after they have been released from residential settings—or improves the well-being of sexually abused children—or decreases negative thoughts, feelings, and beliefs of gang members—or decreases antisocial behavior of youth in residential treatment[11]
- Whether exercise has positive short-term effects on the self-esteem of children and young people[12]
- Whether additional monies given to socially or economically disadvantaged families affect their health, well-being, and educational attainment[13]
- Whether parenting training for parents with infants and toddlers reduces the development of emotional and behavioral problems of their children[14]
- Whether parent training programs improve the general behavior of children with ADHD or help their children to make friends[15].

Policy research faces another barrier: findings with respect to one population may not apply to other ones. Treatments for diseases that are successful with men may not help women. Mental health interventions that are successful with Caucasians may not be effective with Latinos. Persons in rural areas may be less responsive to specific initiatives than persons in urban areas.

**Policy
Advocacy
Challenge 14.4**

Making Policy
Choices in a
Turbulent
Environment

Bruce S.
Jansson, Ph.D

Assume that you are the mayor of a city in your geographic area. Assume that your city runs a deficit of $80 million per year on an annual budget of $500 million as your tax revenues decline during the Great Recession. Assume that policy advocates variously want the following policy enactments: (1) a gang prevention program, (2) enhanced garbage-collection and street-cleaning programs, (3) an economic development program for a specific low-income area, and (4) construction of shelters and subsidized housing for homeless persons.

Also assume that each of these policy advocates buttresses their requests with policy research. You are a relatively liberal public official who faces a tough election where you will be opposed by an opponent who will attempt to portray you as a "big spender who is bankrupting our city." You need votes of blue-collar voters, who are swing voters, to win the election. Which of the advocates' policy recommendations might you support and why?

Many policies that seek to advance prevention, such as reduction in gang violence, clinical depression, or school dropouts obtain only modest improvements as we discussed in Chapter Seven, partly because it is difficult to target interventions on true positives as compared to false positives or false negatives. School officials are reluctant to invest resources in programs to reduce school dropout rates if they do not obtain dramatic results at a time when school budgets have been slashed in many jurisdictions during and after the Great Recession of 2007 to 2009 and beyond.

Policy reformers often find it difficult to obtain effective implementation of new policies in organizations. Many persons are resistive to innovations. Staff may lack requisite skills. Chief executives may be reluctant to provide leadership. New policies may require the expenditure of major resources that are not available.

Returning to Values

Persons can support or oppose policies on purely moral grounds. Some programs can be defended on moral grounds when there is no empirical evidence of their effectiveness. For example, social workers can support hospice programs for those who are terminally ill because they provide caring, humanistic services to those who are suffering. An empirical finding that hospices save the government money by reducing the time people spend in hospitals would provide an *additional* justification, but social workers can defend the hospice program exclusively on moral grounds. Glenn Tinder argues,

> Consequences do not count, at least not decisively (when defending social programs). If someone restores a lost wallet to the owner, we do not ask how the money it contained will be spent in order to determine whether this was an appropriate act. If someone helps save a friend from unemployment and poverty and the friend later dies of drink, we do not conclude that the original assistance was unwise. Indeed, a strict sense of justice is apt to be severely indifferent to consequences.[16]

EPA 2.1.2a

Research and values complement one another with respect to many social issues.

Evidence-based policy and policy evaluation need not be reserved for technical experts. All of us can make important contributions, and we can use many kinds of arguments to support or oppose policies. Indeed, assessing policies is the starting point for creating a world in which evidence and ethical values of social work function hand in hand to produce effective social welfare policies for vulnerable populations.

Policy Advocacy Challenge 14.5

Should We Incarcerate Juvenile Offenders or Divert Them to Community Programs?[1]

Juvenile offenders, disproportionately from Latino and African American populations, are processed each year by juvenile-justice authorities. The Campbell Collaboration did a so-called meta-analysis in 2010 of juvenile research to determine whether juvenile offenders fared better if they were incarcerated, such as in juvenile camps or juvenile institutions, or "diverted" from the juvenile-justice system, through supervision in the community. (They defined the former option as "formal system processing" as compared with "diversion.")

The meta-analysis included 7,304 youth, ages 17 and younger, who were in 29 randomized experiments over a 35-year period. Participants in research studies analyzed in this project included so-called low-level offenders who were guilty of offenses of low or moderate severity, including small property crimes and disorderly person violations. They also included youth who commit serious felony offenses.

The researchers wanted to know if youth who were diverted to communities were less likely to re-engage in delinquency than youth who were incarcerated, whether low-level offenders or serious felony offenders.

This project produced important findings:

- Juveniles with low-level offenses who were placed in institutions were more likely to report they had engaged in offending than youth who were diverted to communities by a small but statistically significant amount
- Youth who stayed in institutions for long periods from 3 to 13 months were *not* less likely to commit juvenile offenses than youth who stayed in them for shorter periods
- Community-based supervision of youth is as effective as incarceration for youth with serious offenses in decreasing rates of antisocial activity

EXERCISE

1. Who would like, and who would dislike, these research findings by ideology, political party, and by other factors that you might identify?
   - For low-level offenders
   - For serious offenders
2. Assume you are a policy advocate who works with a community-based organization in a specific jurisdiction that wants "more humane treatment" of juvenile offenders. What policy advocacy tasks might you undertake to get local juvenile-justice and other public officials to reform juvenile-justice to include more diversion of low-level and serious offenders?
3. What "counter-arguments" can you anticipate that opponents of greater community diversion might make?

---

[1] Anthony Petrosino, Carolyn Turpin-Petrosino, and Sarah Guckenburg, "Formal System Processing of Juveniles: Effects on Delinquency," *Campbell Systematic Reviews*, (2010):1. Retrieved at http://cambellcollaboration.org on 2/17/2012.

What You Can Now Do

Chapter Summary

We have discussed Task 8 of the policy practice and policy advocacy framework. You are now equipped to do the following:

- Discuss why "Rationalists'" desire greater reliance on research in policy making
- Identify the nature of evidence-based policies

- Identify supportive policies that are needed for evidence-based practices
- Analyze why policy assessment is a form of argumentation
- Identify some technical tools used to assess policies
- Counter policy innuendos that lack a basis in research
- Identify barriers to evidence-based policies
- Link values and research

Competency Notes

EPA 2.1.2a   Recognize and manage personal values in a way that allows professional values to guide practice (p. 494): Persons can support or oppose policies on purely moral grounds.

EPA 2.1.3a   Distinguish, appraise, and integrate multiple sources of knowledge, including research-based knowledge and practice wisdom (p. 485): Use of research methodology to evaluate policies achieves positive outcomes.

EPA 2.1.6b   Use research evidence to inform practice (pp. 487, 490): It is futile to discuss evidence-based practice without linking it to policies.

EPA 2.1.7b   Critique and apply knowledge to understand person and environment (p. 492): One should realize that opposition to constructive social policies often takes the form of innuendos that imply these programs are not effective.

EPA 2.1.8a   Analyze, formulate, and advocate for policies that advance social well-being (p. 488): Program evaluation should be regarded as a form of argument, and the evaluator should make a good case that others may contest.

Endnotes

1. Donald Campbell, "Experiments as Arguments," *Knowledge* 3 (1982): 327–337.
2. Michael Wald suggested this example in his article, "Family Preservation: Are We Moving Too Fast?" *Public Welfare* 46 (Summer 1988): 33–38.
3. These are hypothetical numbers.
4. These are hypothetical numbers.
5. Richard Berk and his colleagues make this point in "Social Policy Experimentation: A Position Paper," *Evaluation Review* 9 (August 1985): 387–431.
6. See Scarvia Anderson and Samuel Ball, *The Profession and Practice of Program Evaluation* (San Francisco: Jossey-Bass, 1978), pp. 6, 110–125.
7. For a discussion of the value-laden choices that arise in program evaluation, see Martin Rein, "Value-Critical Policy Analysis," in Daniel Callahan and Bruce Jennings, eds., *Ethics, the Social Sciences, and Policy Analysis* (New York: Plenum Press, 1983), pp. 83–111.

8. An extended overview of program evaluation appears in Anderson and Ball, *The Profession and Practice*; and Peter Rossi and Howard Freeman, *Evaluation: A Systematic Approach,* 5th ed. (Newbury Park, CA: Sage, 1993). For a brief overview, see Carl Patton and David Sawicki, *Methods of Policy Analysis and Planning* (Englewood Cliffs, NJ: Prentice Hall, 1986), pp. 300–328.
9. Robert Greenstein and CBPP staff, "Romney's Charge that Most Federal Low-Income Spending Goes for 'Overhead" and 'Bureaucrats' is False," *Center on Budget and Policy Priorities* (January 23, 2012). Retrieved on February 27, 2012 at www.cbp.org.
10. Stacy Dean, "Five Things You Probably Don't Know About Food Stamps," *Center on Budget and Policy Priorities* (January 20, 2012). Retrieved on February 27, 2012 at www.cbp.org.

11. http://campbellcollaboration.org/lib, accessed on February 27, 2012; see projects 8, 19, 27, 31, and 39.
12. Ibid., project 8.
13. Ibid., project 41.

14. Ibid., project 6.
15. Ibid., project 143; http://campbellcolloration.org/lib, accessed on February 27, 2012.
16. Glenn Tinder, "Defending the Welfare State," *New Republic* 180 (March 1979): 21–22.

Suggested Readings

Overviews of Assessment of Policies

Frank Fischer, Gerald Miller, and Mara Sidney, eds., *Handbook of Public Policy Analysis: Theory, Politics, and Methods* (New York: CRC Press, 2007).

Joseph Wholey, Harry Hatry, and Kathryn Newcomer, eds., *Handbook of Practical Program Evaluation* (San Francisco: Jossey-Bass, 2010).

General Discussions of Evidence-Based Policy and Policy Evaluation

Scarvia Anderson and Samuel Ball, *The Profession and Practice of Program Evaluation* (San Francisco: Jossey-Bass, 1978).

Richard Berk et al., "Social Policy Experimentation: A Position Paper," *Evaluation Review* 9 (August 1985): 387–431.

Carl Patton and David Sawicki, *Basic Methods of Policy Analysis and Planning,* 2nd ed. (Englewood Cliffs, NJ: Prentice Hall, 1993), pp. 362–297.

Michael Patton, *Utilization-Focused Evaluation,* 3rd ed. (Thousand Oaks, CA: Sage, 1997).

Peter Rossi and Howard Freeman, *Evaluation: A Systematic Approach,* 6th ed. (Newbury Park, CA: Sage, 1999).

Ian Sanderson, "Evaluation, Policy Learning and Evidence-Based Policy Making," *Public Administration* 80.1 (2002): 1–22.

William Solesbury, "Evidence-Based Policy: Whence It Came and Where It's Going," ESRC UK Centre for Evidence Based Policy and Practice, Working Paper 1: (October, 2001).

Policy Evaluation in Its Political and Economic Context

Richard Nathan, *Social Science in Government: Uses and Misuses* (New York: Basic Books, 1988).

Carol Weiss, "Where Politics and Evaluation Meet," *Evaluation* 1 (1973): 37–46.

Carol Weiss, "Ideology, Interests and Information: The Basis of Policy Positions," in Daniel Callahan and Bruce Jennings, eds., *Ethics, the Social Sciences, and Policy Analysis* (New York: Plenum, 1983), pp. 213–248.

Ethical or Value Issues in Policy Evaluation

Bruce Jansson, "Blending Social Change and Technology in Macro-Practice: Developing Structural Dialogue in Technical Deliberations," *Administration in Social Work* 14 (1990): 13–28.

Martin Rein, "Value-Critical Policy Analysis," in Callahan and Jennings, eds., *Ethics, the Social Sciences, and Policy Analysis,* pp. 83–111.

Case Studies of Policy Evaluation

Emil Posavac and Raymond Carey, *Program Evaluation: Methods and Case Studies* (Englewood Cliffs, NJ: Prentice Hall, 1980).

Carol Weiss, ed., *Evaluation Action Programs* (Boston: Allyn & Bacon, 1972).

Qualitative Forms of Evaluation

Michael Patton, *Qualitative Evaluation and Research Methods* (Newbury Park, CA: Sage, 1990).

Name Index

Subject Index